THE LANDS
OF
MISSION
SAN MIGUEL

by
Wallace V. Ohles

Illustrations by

Helly Blythe
Virginia Cassara
Colleen Connor Cobb
Steve Kalar
Ernie Morris
John Partridge
Keith Tarwater
Donalee Thomason

To Frank & AJ Book:
Best wishes —
Wally Ohler
Thank you for your
work on Mission
San Miguel.
Love &
respect —
Wally
1-24-0

Published by

Word Dancer Press
950 N. Van Ness
Fresno, CA 93728

In Association with The Friends of the Adobes, Inc.
P. O. Box 326, San Miguel, CA 93451

Printed in the United States of America
Typesetting and design by Donna Parker Mettee

ISBN 1-884995-13-6

Library of Congress Catalog Number: 97-21252

Ohles, Wallace V., 1938-
        The lands of Mission San Miguel / by Wallace V. Ohles : illustrations by
Helly Blythe . . . [et al .] .
            p.   cm.
        Includes bibliographical references and index.
        ISBN 1-884995-13-6
        1. San Luis Obispo County (Calif.) --History, Local.   2. San Luis
Obispo County (Calif.) --Biography.   3. Mission San Miguel Arcangel
(San Miguel, Calif.) --History--19th century.   4. San Miguel
(Calif.) --History.   I. Title.
F868 . S18035   1997
979.4'78--dc21   97-21252
                                                                      CIP

CONTENTS

Mission San José
Founded June 11, 1797

Mission San Juan Bautista
Founded June 24, 1797

Mission San Fernando
Founded September 8, 1797

Dedication

The Lands of Mission San Miguel
was written to honor the bicentennial
of the founding of
Mission San Miguel, Arcangel on July 25, 1797.

This book is dedicated to my friend,

ELLA M. ADAMS

"The History Lady of San Miguel"

Wallace V. Ohles

Acknowledgements

I would first like to thank the artists who generously contributed their beautiful drawings: Helly Blythe, Virginia Cassara, Steve Kalar, Ernie Morris, John Partridge, Keith Tarwater and Donalee Thomason.

Half of this book would not have been possible without Dorothy Kleck graciously loaning her original copies of *The Inland Messenger*, the *San Miguel Messenger* and the *San Miguel Sentinel*.

Bonnie Nelson and Kim Oeck were open and generous in loaning their treasured photographs. Bill Dellard loaned photographs and Barbara Dellard read and made helpful suggestions on how part of the manuscript could be improved.

Virginia Culbert and Art Robinson spent years doing research on the Rios-Caledonia Adobe, and much of their work appears in the pages of this book. Barbara Robinson was subjected to listening to the progress of this volume, from beginning to end.

Audrey McFaddin was kind enough to provide information about the O. P. McFaddin family; Charlie and Rick Montgomery contributed information about the Montgomery families of Indian Valley and the photographs of the Indian Valley School. Art and Florence Von Dollen provided information about the Von Dollen families. I am indebted to these friends for their contributions.

Rose Rios Jones generally assisted by loaning material and providing oral traditions about the Rios and the Gil families. Myra Manfrina graciously provided information concerning the Jose Camilo Rios family.

Alan Gil provided genealogical information on the Gil families, and James E. Green provided information on the Avila families. Patrick Orozco, of Watsonville, provided new information concerning the Gil and Rios families. I am grateful to each of these gentlemen.

Eleanor Garrissere did much of the genealogical research on the Rios and Avila families, and she is thanked for sharing all this information.

Ron Kiel, of the Foreign Language Department at Paso Robles High School, translated the letter of Petronilo Rios to Thomas O. Larkin; I thank him for this service.

Gratitude is hereby expressed to Al Davis and Rolande Amundson for information concerning Camp Roberts and the Nacimiento Ranch, and to Shirley Tharaldsen, who loaned family materials, photographs and provided information about the Nacimiento Ranch. Lynn Camsuzou is thanked for providing information concerning Vineyard Canyon homesteads.

To Hy Blythe, I owe thanks for interesting conversations about the Nacimiento Ranch, and attempts to sort out the Robert G. Flint families. Thanks go to Bruce McVey, who provided the history of the Douglas family.

Rosemary Netto graciously loaned material from the Stanley family and material on the early years of San Miguel. Marj. Mackey contributed information about Atascadero, and photos of the Pedro Estrada adobe. Carla Willhoit allowed us to use some of her precious pictures of early Templeton. I am very grateful to each of these ladies.

Norma Moye loaned photographs of early Paso Robles, and Ben Holsted obtained, for our use, the sketches of Missions San Antonio and San Miguel by Colleen Connor Cobb.

Don Rader, of the Paso Robles City Library has gone out of his way to be helpful, as has the staff at the San Luis Obispo City/County Library. The staff at Mission Santa Barbara Archive-Library and the staff at the Bancroft Library could not have been more helpful.

I would like to thank Phil Dirkx; he was the person who informed me, in 1969, where El Paso de Robles Adobe had been located. Myrtle Boatman is thanked for loaning a copy of Annie Morrison's *History of San Luis Obispo County and Environs*.

"Thank you," to Cecelia Swetland and her Mom for their assistance in printing out the final draft.

Ella Adams has been a fantastic resource for photographs and written and verbal material; I am indebted to her for her original writings, her advice and her friendship. Thank you, to "the History Lady of San Miguel."

The officers and board members of "The Friends of the Adobes, Inc." are thanked for the encouragement given all along the way.

I would like to pay tribute to the "giants" upon whose shoulders today's compilers of local history stand.

Mazie Adams
Myron Angel
Louisiana Clayton Dart
Panza Farley
Eva Carpenter Iversen

Chris Jespersen
Othor MacLean
Don McMillan
Annie L. Morrison
Lura Rawson
Leo Leonidas Stanley
Al Willhoit

In the Patron Section of this book are listed people who kindly donated funds which made the printing of this volume possible.

Finally, Steve Mettee of Word Dancer Press has been a great person to work with, as a publisher; he could not have been more helpful.

Introduction

That there was available a history of the northern part of San Luis Obispo County, in one volume, has been a wish of this writer since the late 1960s. That one did exist has not been the case. Most people looking for such a history would need to collect "Pioneer Day Editions" of *The Daily Press*, *The Country News*, and various editions of the *Atascadero News* and *The Telegram-Tribune* in order to glean items concerning North County history. We are happy that these four newspapers provided various articles on local historical items; much use has been made of these newspaper articles in writing this book.

This writer wanted to compile a history of the area, and present it in honor of the celebration of the bicentennial of the founding of Mission San Miguel, Arcangel in 1797.

This work is not an attempt to be an exhaustive history; its purpose is to provide a fairly concise, one-volume history for the general reader. It is hoped that this work would be useful to elementary and high school students who are given exposure to local history.

This book had its beginning in a study of the building which we know today as the Rios-Caledonia Adobe in San Miguel, and of the people who owned it through the years. The person who supervised the construction of the adobe building later owned it; he also was the owner of El Paso de Robles Rancho, and was part-owner of the San Miguel Mission. Thus, Petronilo Rios (1806-1870) and the story of his life would have a prominent place in this narrative.

The purpose of the building which came to be called the Rios-Caledonia Adobe was to serve as the administrative center for the San Miguel Mission and property, as the lands were being given away and sold by the Mexican government. By the time the adobe administration building was completed, about 1836, the various structures of the Mission were in the process of falling into ruins.

As were the rest of the old Spanish missions of California, Mission San Miguel was somewhat like the great medieval estates of Western Europe. This mission had been the hub of the socio-economic unit located north of the Cuesta.

Then the time came when the missions were subjected to the process of "secularization." By 1841, there was no priest stationed at Mission San Miguel, and by 1842, only thirty Indians remained at the mission. From about 1842 to 1846, we know very little about what was going on at either the mission or at the adobe. The church part of the mission was respected, except by the action of termites and the elements.

After the work on this book was begun, Dorothy Kleck, of Paso Robles, was kind enough to loan to "The Friends of the Adobes, Inc.," her original copies of San Miguel's pioneer newspaper, *The Inland Messenger*, which later became the *San Miguel Messenger*.

Since the material to be found in these newspapers is not readily available to the general reader, this writer decided that information from newspaper articles which chronicles San Miguel and neighboring areas, for the years 1886 and 1887, would be included in this book.

The scope of the book must be narrowed, in order to make the work possible. Our main emphasis was to look at much of the lands which were removed from the control of Mission San Miguel, and to see what happened to these lands between approximately 1845 and 1900.

However, this book is not intended to be a history of the entire "North County," nor is it a history of Mission San Miguel itself. Most of this history has already been written. *San Miguel, Arcangel - The Mission on the Highway*, by Father Zephyrin Engelhardt, O.F.M, is the definitive history of the Mission, at the present time.

Some of the former lands of Mission San Miguel have been more than adequately treated by other authors. Geneva Hamilton has written about Ranchos San Simeon, Santa Rosa and Piedra Blanca; thus, the area of Cambria, Cayucos and the coastal region have been studied. Fraser MacGillivray has published a comprehensive history of Adelaida and the San Marcos area. Donalee Thomason, in her book *Cholama - The Beautiful One*, has written about Parkfield and Cholame. The Creston Women's Club has published books on the history of Creston, so we will not duplicate their efforts.

Most of the area around Atascadero has little recorded history, until the time of Edward G. Lewis, after the turn of the century. This history falls outside the time-period studied in this book.

Virginia Peterson is writing a history of the Paso Robles area, so we will only examine Paso Robles up to about the time that the City of El Paso de Robles was incorporated. Most of the history of the Paso Robles area will be covered in her book. Since the Santa

Margarita Rancho was land which belonged to Mission San Luis Obispo, it falls outside the scope of this book.

What is left for this book to cover?

A biography of Petronilo Rios has never been published, so this book will devote several chapters to the examination of the details of his life, in as much depth as is possible.

The history of San Miguel, as a town, will be studied by examining the Rios-Caledonia Adobe and its owners through the years. We have some written records of the adobe, where we do not have them for the early town of San Miguel. We will then look at the history of the surrounding region, as it is related to the arrival of the railroad. Extensive use of *The Inland Messenger* and the *San Miguel Messenger* will allow us to study the town of San Miguel before and after the railroad arrived, as well as the areas near San Miguel where people settled and homesteaded.

Most of the history of the settlement on the Estrella Plains will be reserved for a future book, which will include the history of the Estrella Adobe Church. However, we will examine the Ranchos El Paso de Robles, Santa Ysabel, Huer Huero, Asuncion and Atascadero. We will take a look at El Nacimiento Rancho, and the early beginnings of communities at Parkfield, Templeton and Shandon.

One chapter is the story of the Nygrens- - -the last family to occupy the Rios-Caledonia as a home. Charles F. Dorries, who twice preserved the building from destruction, will be the subject of a chapter in this narrative.

Ella Adams, "The History Lady of San Miguel," wrote the following words to introduce a newspaper article about the Caledonia Adobe. We will use her introduction to put us in the frame of mind to examine the various topics of this book, which concern the lands of Mission San Miguel.

In the years since their building from native earth, the old walls have echoed many changes. The slow creak of ox-cart, the drum of hooves as dispatch riders or *vaquero* rode by, the rattle of horse-drawn stages, the soft strum of guitar and whisper of silk as couples turned in dignified dance, the clink of glasses and click of poker chips, the first train whistle in 1886, the happy voices of school children in 1887, construction sounds in building the first 101 . . . the hurrying rush of traffic on new 101 and the roar of jets overhead.

All of these were a part of the echo.

MISSION SAN MIGUEL
PROPERTY AND PADRES

Mission San Miguel, Arcangel had been founded on July 25, 1797, by Father Fermin Francisco de Lasuen, who was a successor of Father Junipero Serra as *Presidente* of the missions. Almost two years earlier, the site selection was being made for the mission which was to be named for the "Most Glorious Prince of the Celestial Militia, Archangel Saint Michael."

Father Buenaventura Sitjar, of Mission San Antonio de Padua, along with Sgt. Macario Castro, Corporal Ygnacio Vallejo and a few soldiers surveyed the region, from the Rio Nacimiento to the Arroyo de Santa Ysabel, and for three leagues on either side. (A league was equal to 2.63 English miles.) They were looking for springs, good land and timber. The group which was surveying the region reported that water was available from Arroyo de Santa Ysabel, Arroyo de San Marcos, springs nearby and water pools among the willows along the Salinas River.

Under the date of August 27, 1795, Father Buenaventura Sitjar reported the following to his superior.

> **Stone for filling in the foundations of the walls are sufficient in the hillsides of the mesa itself and nearby. On the other side of the willow run, in the hills about a quarter of a league, are large rocks, some of which are lime stone, but the Arroyo de San Marcos is the place where are many lime stones like those they burn at San Antonio.**
>
> **There are so many of such large water pools on the tracts of land they occupy that, even if there were no spring whatever, with only the water which enters them from the Arroyo de Paso de Robles, and the water from the rain, there would be water enough to supply the Mission and its fields.**

Father Lasuen, Mission San Miguel's founder, had been born in Spain on June 7, 1736. He volunteered for the American missions at the age of 23. He landed at Vera Cruz, Mexico, and entered the San Fernando College in Mexico City. Under Junipero Serra as *Presidente*, Lasuen joined Father Francisco Palou on his trek as far as Mission San Gabriel, where Lasuen remained until 1775.

After Serra's death, on August 28, 1784, Palou remained in California as interim president of the missions. Lasuen was appointed *Presidente* on February 6, 1785. He arrived in Monterey by January 12, 1786, and for the remainder of his life, Mission San Carlos Borromeo was his official headquarters.

During 1797, Father Lasuen founded four missions: San Jose de Guadalupe on June 11th; San Juan Bautista on June 24th; San Miguel, Arcangel on July 25th; and San Fernando Rey Espana on September 8th. Lasuen died at Mission San Carlos Borromeo at Carmel, on June 26, 1803.

San Miguel, Arcangel was the sixteenth of twenty-three missions established in Alta California- - -twenty-two of them by the Spanish government, and one under the leadership of Mexico.

William Zimmerman, in his 1890 work entitled *A Short and Complete History of the San Miguel Mission*, states that "Statistics of 1815 inform us that San Miguel, in subscribing for subsistence for troops in 1815, furnished wine and wool, and that home-grown cotton was woven in San Luis Obispo."

The subject of weaving brings up an interesting story which is related in Robert Archibald's book, *The Economic Aspects of the California Missions*. He states that Father Luis Martinez, of Mission San Luis Obispo, wrote to Governor Sola on March 22, 1816, and requested the services of an Irish weaver named Henry who was being held in Monterey. In another letter, of March 31, 1816, Father Martinez wrote to the governor concerning his disappointment that the weaver had been sent to Mission San Miguel, instead of to Mission San Luis Obispo. How long this Irish weaver remained at San Miguel is not known at this time.

We have the names of some important people from 200 years ago- - -the first guards stationed at Mission San Miguel: Corporal Jose Antonio Rodriguez, Manuel Montero, Jose Maria Guadalupe and Juan Maria Pinto.

These men made up the *escolta*, the escort, or mission guard.

The year 1806 saw the construction of 27 huts as living quarters for the Indians. A granary (65 feet long), a storage and carpenter room (42 ½ feet long) and a sacristy (23 ½ feet long) were constructed in 1808. In 1810, a house (61 ½ feet square) was constructed at Rancho La Playa at San Simeon.

During the year 1810, under the guidance of Padre Juan Cabot, thousands of adobe bricks were made and stored for use in the construction of the present-day church structure at San Miguel. [When the mission was restored in the 1930s, some bricks were discovered containing the bodies of birds inside, instead of the usual straw. During what period of time these unusual adobe bricks were made is not known.]

Father Juan Cabot was generally known as "el marinero," the mariner, in contrast with his older, dignified brother, Father Pedro Cabot, of Mission San Antonio, who was called "el caballero," the gentleman.

A house was constructed at Rancho Asuncion in 1812, and the next year a building (56 ½ feet long) was erected on Rancho El Paso de Robles, six miles south of the hot springs.

The year 1814 saw some building done at San Miguel. In 1816, the stone foundations of the present church building were laid at its site, which is three-quarters of a mile west of the Salinas River.

A house was constructed at Rancho del Aguage, in 1815, near the Vineyard Spring; the rancho contained an area of twenty-two acres. The vineyard, situated at the distance of about three miles from the Mission, was known as "La Mayor." The name Vineyard Canyon comes from the location of this site. An adobe house, with two rooms and a small parlor, was built there in 1815 to house the vineyardist; his job was to care for the Mission's vineyard, orchard and garden. Built of adobe, and roofed with tiles, it was protected from winter rain and summer sun by a tile-roofed corridor. The floors were of earth. The location acquired the name of Rancho del Aguage, or "Ranch of the Wells."

Slips of thorny brush, known as dahlia, were carried in from the Nacimiento area, and were planted in a circle below the spring. This planting formed a living corral for the sheep; it was too thick for the sheep to escape through, and no maintenance was required.

The mission's church building was completed about 1818. The corridor of the mission is said to have sixteen arches because this was the sixteenth mission to be established. In fact, there are only twelve actual arches; the four openings on the north end of the corridor are formed by square support pillars. Other construction which was accomplished resulted in homes for the neophytes, or Christianized Indians. Eventually, the dwelling houses of the neophytes would cover an area of more than forty acres.

In 1825, weaving rooms were constructed at the Mission, and in 1830, the house (85 by 31 feet) was constructed at San Simeon. Hubert Howe Bancroft mentions that in 1829-1830, an Irish carpenter by the name of John Bones [or John Burns], was living at Mission San Miguel. This man had arrived in California in 1821, probably a deserter from one of the vessels which had sailed into Monterey. He was 23 years of age when he arrived in California. William Trevethan, who came to California in 1826, was a *mayordomo* at Mission San Miguel in 1829-1830. [The year 1840 found William Trevethan in Monterey; he petitioned for a lot on which to build a house. The lot was fifty *varas* by fifty *varas*, "situate in the rear of Sr Tomas O. Larkin, and in a straight line with the Fort and Gualterio Duckworth's house." His petition was granted, "with the condition that he must run the line towards the pine woods (*Pinal*), leaving a street of 24 *varas* between the said lot and the house built by Sr Beltran." This is according to Book of Spanish Translations, Volume 2, page 339, in the County Recorder's office in Salinas.]

By 1832, construction, under the guidance of the Franciscan Fathers of Mission San Miguel, ended. The construction of the two-story building, 45 ½ by 30 feet, which has come to be known as the Rios-Caledonia adobe, was done under the auspices of the Mexican government, beginning about 1835. [Credit is given to Ella Adams for providing the dimensions of various mission buildings. The research had been done by Ed Wolf, a brother of Dorothy Kleck.]

Area of Mission spring in Vineyard Canyon.

From Mission San Miguel's church building, the mission property extended 18 miles north as far as the southern portion of Mission San Antonio's land, and 18 miles south as far as the northern portion of Mission San Luis Obispo's land. The northernmost portion of San Miguel's property was Rancho San Bartolome, or Pleyto, a distance of seven leagues.

The southernmost property of Mission San Miguel was Rancho La Asuncion, a distance of seven leagues. Mission San Miguel was said to be bounded on the east "by the Tulares" - - - 66 miles distant, and on the west by the seashore - - - 35 miles away.

So, Mission San Miguel's lands extended 14 leagues, about 37 miles, from north to south; the lands extended 36 leagues, about 95 miles, from east to west.

We will take a look at the early missionaries who were responsible for the land and the Indians of Mission San Miguel.

Padre Marcelino Cipres (1769-1810) was first assigned to Mission San Antonio; in December of 1800, while on a visit to San Miguel, he suffered severe stomach pains, along with Fathers Juan Martin and Baltasar Carnicer. Everyone believed that the illness was the result of poisoning by the Indians.

Three Indians were accused by Father Cipres. A small military force from Monterey, under the charge of Gabriel Morego, was sent to investigate. The accused Indians were arrested. At Soledad, the Indians were able to escape, due to a sentinel being drunk on duty. The Indians were re-arrested; in 1802, the priest in charge asked that the Indians be released, after being flogged in the presence of their families. The priest believed that the Indians should be punished for "their boast of having poisoned the padres."

Father Cipres died at Mission San Miguel on January 31, 1810 and was buried in the sanctuary of the Church. Those who assisted at the time of his death were Fathers Juan Cabot, Pedro Cabot and Juan Martin.

On April 14, 1797, Padre Francisco Pujol (1762-1801) had arrived in San Francisco. He served at Mission San Carlos from 1797 until 1800; from December 27, 1800 until January 17, 1801, he assisted at Mission San Antonio. On January 17, 1801, he arrived at Mission San Miguel, and found that several missionaries there, as well as at San Antonio, had fallen ill. Padre Pujol also became ill and was taken back to San Antonio on February 27th. His companion, Padre Pedro Martinez, also fell sick but recovered. Padre Pujol died on March 15, 1801, and was buried in the church with full military honors. On June 14, 1813, Pujol's body was transferred, with that of Padre Sitjar, to a grave in the new church at Mission San Antonio.

The Concepcion had brought Padre Baltasar Carnicer (1770-?) to San Francisco, along with Padre Pujol. Padre Carnicer served at Mission San Miguel from July 9, 1797 until August 26, 1798. After serving for a time at Mission San Carlos, he was re-appointed to San Miguel. While there, in December of 1800, he, along with Padre Juan Martin, and the visiting friar, Marcelino Cipres, was attacked by the violent stomach pains. The three recovered; Carnicer became fearful of remaining at San Miguel, and was re-assigned to Mission San Carlos, where he arrived on March 29, 1801.

Padre Juan Martin (1770-1824) was first assigned to Mission San Gabriel, where he served from March 1794 until August 7, 1796. His next assignment was to Mission La Purisima between September of 1796 and August 6, 1797.

He had a long term of service at Mission San Miguel from December 3, 1797 until August 17, 1824. Padre Martin was responsible for building most of Mission San Miguel, including the church, which was begun in 1816. He was unsuccessful in convincing Governor Jose Joaquin Arrillaga of the need to found a mission in the San Joaquin Valley. Padre Martin died on August 29, 1824; on August 30th, Padre Luis Antonio Martinez gave ecclesiastical burial to the body of Padre Juan Francisco Martin.

The truth of the poisonings came to light with the publication, in 1965, of Father Fermin Lasuen's collected writings. According to Lasuen, the poisoning was caused from drinking mescal (a Mexican liquor) which had been stored in a copper container lined with tin, and not by any misdeeds of the Indians. This information is contained in a letter written to Padre Jose Gasol by Padre Fermin Lasuen, dated November 25, 1801.

[On November 13, 1912, two large marble slabs were placed over the graves of Fathers Martin and Cipres, within the sanctuary of the church. The mission bells tolled 41 strokes, in memory of the years of service of Father Cipres, missionary of San Luis Obispo who died at San Miguel, and 54 strokes in memory of San Miguel's great builder, Father Juan Martin.]

The poisonings were not the first major problems suffered by the Padres at Mission San Miguel. Padre Antonio de la Concepcion Horra (1767-?) became a problem almost from the very beginning. President of the missions, Padre Fermin Francisco de Lasuen, assigned Padre Horra to work with the experienced missionary, Padre Buenaventura Sitjar, for the founding of Mission San Miguel. Less than a month after the July 25, 1797 founding, Padre Horra began showing signs of insanity. The soldiers of the guard, and the Indians, were horrified and frightened, because the padre shouted and acted like a madman. The padre had fancied himself a great ruler; he compelled the Indians to discharge their arrows, and the soldiers to fire rounds of cartridges. It is said that Padre Horra wanted to kill ants which bothered him.

Father Sitjar conferred with Father Lasuen, and the President sent Jose de Miguel to the mission; he was to attempt, by gentle means, to persuade Padre Horra to accompany him to Monterey. Two surgeons at Monterey examined Horra and declared him insane; the governor made it official, and Horra was returned to Mexico. From there, Padre Horra was returned to Spain on July 8, 1804.

Padre Juan Vicente Cabot (1781-1856) arrived at Monterey on August 31, 1805. La Purisima mission was his first assignment. He ministered at San Miguel from October 1, 1807 until March 12, 1819; after serving at San Francisco and Soledad, he returned to San Miguel and served from November 7, 1824 until November 25, 1834. During his first term at San Miguel, he was assistant to Padre Juan Martin; during his second term, he was in charge of the mission.

He sent a military expedition from San Miguel into the San Joaquin Valley on October 2, 1814. The expedition went as far as present-day Visalia; on the way, several Indians were baptized. From November 4 through 15, in 1815, Father Cabot accompanied a second expedition, this one led by Juan de Ortega. A third exploration of the Tulare country was made in 1818. Although no mission was ever formed in the San Joaquin Valley, a significant number of Tularenos were baptized at Mission San Miguel.

In his report to Governor Jose M. Echeandia, in November of 1827, Father Juan Cabot informed him that "Between the east & north, this Mission owns a small spring of warm water & a vineyard distant two leagues." Other locations listed in this 1827 report were those situated to the south of the Mission. They included Rancho de Santa Ysabel (Saint Elizabeth), where there was a small vineyard, and Rancho San Antonio (Saint Anthony), where barley was planted.

The other listing included Rancho de la Asuncion (The Assumption), which had a spring with sufficient water for a garden, and Rancho del Paso de Robles (The Pass of the Oaks), where wheat was sown. At the last two named locations, there were adobe buildings, roofed with tile, for keeping seed grain.

It is this writer's belief that it is possible that two portions of Mission San Miguel's land acquired the popular name of Santa Ysabel; at the moment, this is simply speculation. The Santa Ysabel most familiar to us is the 17,775-acre grant known as Rancho Santa Ysabel, located on the east side of the Salinas River, and south of the present-day City of Paso Robles. A possible location for another Santa Ysabel would be on the west side of the Salinas River at the location of some springs. Could either Mustard Springs or Mustang Springs, in the vicinity of the area northwest of Paso Robles be the location? What about the Indian Springs region, which extends to the Oak Flat area northwest of Paso Robles?

Eight miles of canals were said to have been built to carry water to Mission San Miguel. The springs at Santa Ysabel did produce an immense volume of water; however, Rancho Santa Ysabel was located 3 leagues from the mission, or about 7 ¾ miles. This is a subject of fascination that deserves much further research. This topic will be addressed further in the chapter on Rancho Santa Ysabel.

As we consider mission lands and what became of them, we need to consider an important distinction in our vocabulary. When we hear the word "rancho," what usually comes to mind is a land grant from the Mexican era of California history. The word "rancho" makes us think of a ranch, which would necessarily involve cattle or sheep; a rancho, however, could simply be a plot of farmland. It should be noted that not all ranchos became land grants. Some local examples are Rancho San Marcos (Saint Mark) and Rancho San Antonio (Saint Anthony).

Rancho San Marcos extended throughout the area known today as Adelaida. Rancho San Antonio comprised the flat farmland which is on the east side of the Salinas River, and extends from the Estrella River south to the gulch at today's Wellsona Road. Local residents refer to the gulch as "Shirt-tail Creek."

In the year 1818, the Tulare Indians seem to have taken the offensive against the missions in the Salinas Valley- - -San Miguel and Soledad- - -and also Mission San Antonio. In May of that year, an expedition under Sergeant Ygnacio Vallejo was sent against the Tularenos. According to Zimmerman, in his work *A Short & Complete History of the San Miguel Mission*, "There were two hard fights, one at Pleito on the Nacimiento river, the other to raise the siege of San

Miguel in both of which the Indians were terribly punished and driven back to their territory."

Communication between Mission San Miguel and its property on the coast was made by way of a cart trail. This cart trail had its beginnings with the aboriginal Indians at the coast creating regular trails over the Santa Lucia Mountains. These trails were used for centuries as trade routes of the Indians of the Salinas River valley and even further east.

Fraser MacGillivray, in his book about Adelaida, states that "The survey maps of that time do show a 'trail from the coast to San Miguel' which crosses the Peachy Canyon area and for several miles follows the approximate alignment of Adelaida Road along the east boundary of the present Chimney Rock Ranch in a northerly direction, then easterly past the Santa Helena Ranch, and northerly again to San Miguel. This could have been a segment of the trail to Rancho Santa Rosa which, for a time, was also operated by Mission San Miguel."

MacGillivray goes on to state that "A consensus among the old timers seems to indicate that the mission trail to the coast entered the Santa Lucias in the vicinity of Lime Mountain and followed the general course of San Simeon Creek to the ocean."

Chimney Rock is the most prominent rock outcrop

View of Chimney Rock from the south.

along the Mission Cart Road connecting San Miguel to the coast.

The Indians from Mission San Miguel were used to clear and construct the cart trail which would be adequate to haul logs from the headwaters of Santa Rosa Creek. This crude cart trail was extended to the ocean and to the Bay of San Simeon, most likely making use of the trade routes previously established by the Indians.

The sandy beaches near San Simeon were perfect for landing and embarking cargo. The bay had been used as early as 1800 for the purpose of dealing with unauthorized trading vessels. Ships were required, by the Mexican government, to pay duties at Monterey; this payment authorized a ship to trade anywhere in California until it had filled its hold with hides and tallow. If a ship's captain had not paid the duties, he was considered to be a smuggler.

Coves along the coast near Rancho Santa Rosa were used as "drops" for hides to be picked up by schooners taking part in the illegal trade along that part of the coast. The seamen used the term "drop" because hides were hauled to the edge of the cliff above the landing cove, and were dropped to the sandy beach below. On Rancho Santa Rosa, the drop amounted to between 75 and 100 feet.

In 1851, William Casey Jones' report to the Secretary of the Interior in Washington, D. C., said that Mission San Miguel's land extended to the seacoast, across the Santa Lucia Range to Rancho del Playa, a distance of between 12 and 14 leagues. This rancho was located at present-day San Simeon. This was the site of the first outbuildings which were constructed by workers from Mission San Miguel; the project began in 1810. An adobe house of two rooms was constructed there in 1814. In 1830, an adobe, measuring 85 feet by 31 feet, was built.

Chimney Rock.
Drawn by Helly Blythe

Monterey District, 1830.

Jones' report states that to the south of Mission San Miguel was Rancho Santa Ysabel, three leagues off with a vineyard; San Antonio, where barley was raised, was at three leagues distance. Paso de Robles, at 5 ½ leagues, was where wheat was raised, and Asuncion was 6 leagues distant. The Spanish league was equal to 2.6 English miles.

The wording of the Jones report makes it sound like San Antonio and Santa Ysabel were both three leagues distant, or about half the distance to El Paso de Robles, which was about 8 ¾ miles from the mission. A map found in one of Bancroft's volumes shows a Santa Ysabel on the west side of the Salinas River. (It is worth noting that in this instance, Rancho Santa Ysabel and Rancho San Antonio were the same distance from Mission San Miguel; this could reinforce the theory that there was a Santa Ysabel farther north than the Santa Ysabel area southeast of the present City of Paso Robles. We know that Rancho San Anto-

nio was not as far south as the Santa Ysabel that we associate with the area southeast of present-day Paso Robles.)

During the years of 1840 to 1846, three governors of Mexican California made grants of land from property which had belonged to Mission San Miguel. Governor Juan B. Alvarado made five grants, Governor Manuel Micheltorena made six grants, and Governor Pio Pico made three grants. In later chapters, we will look at the names of initial grantees, realizing that in many cases, other people ended up receiving the title to the property.

Governor Alvarado began the bestowing of land, which had belonged to Mission San Miguel, with the 48,805.59 acres of Rancho Piedra Blanca on January 18, 1840. Exactly one year later, on January 18, 1841, Julian Estrada received the 13,183.62-acre Rancho Santa Rosa.

Smaller acreage, of 4,348.23 acres, was awarded to Trifon Garcia in the Rancho Atascadero, by Governor Alvarado, on May 6, 1842. Three days later, on May 9, 1842, Alvarado granted Rancho Huer Huero to Mariano Bonilla.

The Rancho Huer Huero grant was of one square league, or 4,439 acres. Governor Alvarado's last grant from San Miguel land was that of Rancho San Simeon. Jose Ramon Estrada received 4,468.81 acres on October 1, 1842.

The grants made by Governor Micheltorena, from Mission San Miguel land, were all made in the year 1844. The first one was the Rancho Cholame, of 26,621.82 acres, to Mauricio Gonzales on February 7th. Mauricio was the son of Rafael Gonzales- - -a person with whom we come into contact in other chapters.

The next two grants were made on the same date: May 12, 1844. Francisco Arce received the Rancho Santa Ysabel, of 17,774.12 acres; Pedro Narvaez received the 25,993.18-acre El Paso de Robles Rancho.

According to Blomquist, in his 1943 Master's thesis, two men, in addition to Francisco Arce, had petitioned for Rancho Santa Ysabel: Pedro Narvaez and Ezecuel Soberanes. Since Soberanes was in possession of other land, his request was not considered.

To decide which of the other two should have the Santa Ysabel, Governor Micheltorena held a conference at his residence on March 16, 1844. At the conference, it was agreed that Arce should have the Santa Ysabel, and Narvaez would be given the neighboring Rancho El Paso de Robles. Each man agreed to pay a fair price for the buildings and other improvements on their new possessions.

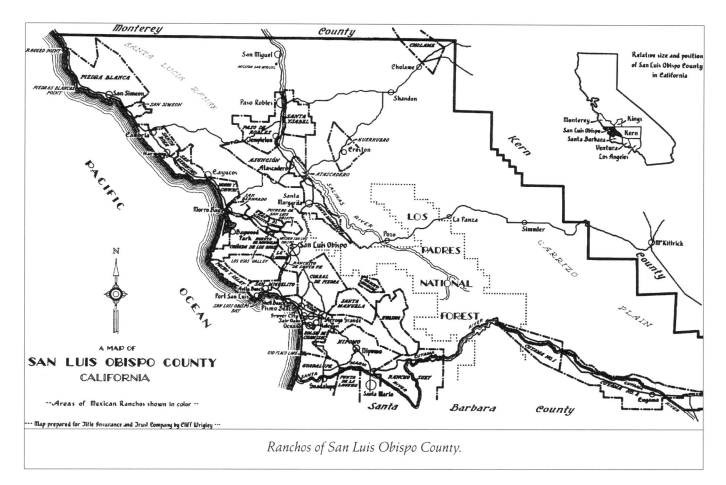

Ranchos of San Luis Obispo County.

On July 16, 1844, Governor Micheltorena awarded to the Christian Indians of San Miguel three grants of land; they were of uncertain size and unclear location. The grants were named El Nacimiento, Las Gallinas and La Estrella. The United States Land Commission later rejected the claims to these three pieces of property because the lands had not been occupied and cultivated as required by regulations.

An appraisal was made of the abandoned Mission San Miguel on July 31, 1844. The empty buildings and nine leagues of land were evaluated at $5,875. The survey was made by Andres Pico and Juan Manso, according to Pico's *Papeles varios Originales.* Some of the buildings were described as being in a bad state of disrepair, a few without windows or doors, and one without a roof.

Governor Pio Pico actually made three grants from land belonging to Mission San Miguel. On June 19,

1845 Pedro Estrada received San Miguel's southernmost holding, Rancho Asuncion of 39,224.81 acres. Pio Pico removed another part of Mission San Miguel's land by adding three additional leagues to Mariano Bonilla's Rancho Huer Huero. After this addition, on March 28, 1846, that rancho totaled 15,684.95 acres.

The final land grant made of the Mission San Miguel region was for ten square leagues of frontier land lying south of the Huer Huero, and east of the Santa Margarita ranchos. The land grant was known as San Juan Capistrano y el Camate. Two men, Trineo Herrera and Geronimo Quintana, were the grantees. In 1847, they built two houses near the center of the tract; they also planted wheat, barley and some fruit trees. At one time, they had 400 head of cattle on the place. Their title was later declared invalid, because it was dated July 11, 1846- - -four days after the conquest of Monterey by the American Forces.

Secularization of the Missions

When the missions were founded, their lands were intended to extend from one mission to another. It is easy to understand this concept if we picture in our minds the various counties in our state; their lands extend from boundary to boundary, with the county seat the administrative center of each county. The mission would correspond to the county seat as the administrative center for all of that mission's lands.

The missions controlled large tracts of land, from their very founding, but the missionaries themselves owned none of the land. There are two important reasons for making this statement. One is that the rules of the Franciscan order forbade the acquiring of property by the missionaries. The second reason is that the missionaries held *usufructuary title* to the land. This term refers to the concept of using and enjoying all the advantages and profits of the property of another person without the owner losing the title to the property. Thus, the missionaries were allowed to enjoy "the fruits" of the land without owning the property.

In theory, every mission was temporary. According to Walton E. Bean, Professor of History at the University of California, Berkeley, "If the plan had worked as the Spanish government hoped, each mission would have been secularized ten years after its founding. That is, the pueblo would receive a grant of four square leagues of land; the fields, town lots, and other property would be parceled out among the Indians. . ." The governing of each mission community would pass to native officials who had been trained for the purpose. The mission church would be turned over to parish priests, known as 'secular' clergy. The missionaries were then supposed to begin their work all over again farther on, in a continuous process of expanding the frontier.

The 'secular' clergy were distinct from the missionaries, who were called 'regular' clergy because they lived under the regulations and vows of a particular religious order. In the case of the California missions, the clergy were members of the Order of Friars Minor, generally known as Franciscans. They are called this after the founder of the Order, Saint Francis of Assisi. The Order of Friars Minor had been founded in 1209, in Assisi, Italy.

Under the process of "secularization," the missions were to be removed from the control of the Franciscan missionaries who had founded them, and be placed under "civilian" control. In practice, this process of secularization did not work as the Spanish government had hoped. For one thing, Mexico threw off the control of Spain in 1822.

Jose Maria Echeandia, Mexican governor of California, published at San Diego (the town he considered to be the governmental capital) on December 11, 1828, a plan for the secularization of the missions. After Echeandia's plan was adopted in July of 1830, he issued a proclamation for carrying it into effect. However, a new governor, Manuel Victoria, came into power shortly afterward, and Victoria revoked the decree.

The late historian, Othor MacLean (1909-1995) has written on this subject. "Back at the time of 'secularization,' there had been much pompous rhetoric from the newly liberated liberals of Mexico over 'liberating' the Indian 'slaves' held in 'bondage' by the Franciscan friars up in Alta California.

"In their taking over the mission property, these benign *politicos* were but assuming guardianship of the mission property for the benefit of the primitive natives- - -so they insisted. And maybe they were sincere in their good intentions; but most certainly they lacked good judgment.

"Back during the mission years, the mission farms were the mainstay of the whole provincial economy, furnishing food not only for the Indian neophytes of the missions themselves, but for the army posts and the civilian population as well. Unfortunately, with the disintegration of the mission system, the whole provincial economy went down the drain."

MacLean went on to write that "Bankrupt and with debts owed by the provincial government mounting, the governors began selling off mission property to keep the provincial government from disintegrating completely."

Francis J. Weber, in his book concerning the Catholic Church in Southern California, takes a little different view. "Secularization, or the achievement of total autonomy, always was and is the goal of every missionary endeavor. It was only the extremely slow assimilation of the California natives into the overall civilization program, that accounted for elongating the timetable in California."

According to W. H. Hutchinson, "Secularization of the missions- - -that is, stripping them of all functions save that of parish church- - -was the most significant internal development during the Mexican period." He wrote that statement in his book, *California: The Golden Shore by the Sundown Sea*. This Mexican period lasted for 24 years- - -1822 to 1846.

A large push for mission secularization, in the 1830s, came from an unexpected source. In Mexico City, Jose Maria Padres, an influential liberal politician, organized a colonization project for California, involving Jose Maria Hijar. Padres and Hijar were to be the directors of the Cosmopolitan Mercantile Company. A wealthy Mexican land-owner, Hijar put up the money, and Juan Bandini lent his influence as California's deputy in the Mexican congress.

Padres got Mexico's acting president, Diego Farias, to name Hijar not only chief of colonization, but governor of California as well. Jose Maria Padres had formerly been a young lieutenant, under Jose Maria Echeandia, in the Corps of Engineers.

At the behest of Padres and Hijar, the Mexican congress, in 1833, adopted the Secularization Act, which provided for the immediate breakup of the missions and transfer of mission lands to settlers and Indians. By the act of November 20, 1833, the Mexican government caused the lands to revert to the public domain and were thus subject to being distributed as grants.

On November 20, 1833, the Mexican congress directed the general secularization of the missions. Some of the provisions were:

Article 1   The Government shall proceed to secularize the missions of Upper and Lower California.

Article 2   In each of said missions a parish shall be established under the charge of a parish priest of the secular clergy, with a sal-

ary from $2,000 to $2,500 per annum, at the direction of the Government.

Article 4   The Churches. . .and sacred vessels and ornaments. . .shall be assigned to the uses of the parish.

Article 7   Of the buildings belonging to each mission the most appropriate shall be designated for the habitation of the curate, with the addition of a lot of ground, not exceeding two hundred *varas* square, and the remaining edifices shall be specially adjudicated for a court-house, preparatory schools, public establishments, and workshops.

On receiving word in California of the 1833 Act, Governor Figueroa, with the help of the *diputacion* drafted a plan for secularizing 10 of the 21 missions, to be administered by commissioners appointed from among the *Californios*. (The *diputacion* was the local legislature, created under the Mexican constitution. The members were elected, but they served more as advisors to the governor than as independent legislators.)

Padres and Hijar were planning to obtain the missions, and were bringing from Mexico administrators for the secularized missions. Padres and Hijar recruited 204 colonists for California- - -99 men, 55 women and 50 children. They sailed from San Blas on August 1, 1834. Most of the males were skilled workers: farmers, butchers, blacksmiths, shoemakers, tailors and school-teachers; this was a far cry from California's usual importation from Mexico of soldiers and convicts.

When Figueroa had arrived in California as governor, he brought with him ten Mexican priests, known as Zacatecans (from the name of their college, Our Lady of Guadalupe, in Zacatecas, Mexico.) These priests were placed in charge of the northern missions. Since they had taken the required loyalty oath, which some of the older Spanish priests had refused, these Zacatecan priests were to replace the earlier missionaries, the so-called Fernandinos. The latter were Spaniards from San Fernando College in Mexico City, and did not wish to take the loyalty oath to Mexico.

The neophytes (Christianized Indians) were dismayed, because most of them were devoted to their former priests. A situation developed in which the

Fernandinos were looked upon by some citizens as less than patriotic.

In the autumn of 1834, shortly before the arrival of the Padres-Hijar colony, Governor Figueroa received from President Santa Anna, who had just assumed power, orders which countermanded the new appointments. Santa Anna had sent a special courier in a record-breaking overland trip to tell Figueroa to remain in office.

In the end, Padres and Hijar were deported by the governor, and the colonists were allowed to either return to Mexico or to stay in California, whichever they desired. Two colonists who remained, and who were to become important in the history of San Miguel Mission, were Jose Mariano Bonilla and Ygnacio Coronel.

Less than half of the colonists from the Padres-Hijar expedition wanted to remain in California; most of the colonists who did remain settled in the Sonoma Valley. Governor Figueroa ordered the new colonists to settle on Alta California's northern frontier- - - today's Napa and Sonoma counties, because he had hoped that the settlers would serve as a buffer against intrusion by Russians and the British.

Most of the people who came to California with the Padres-Hijar Colony were returned to Mexico, because Governor Figueroa was concerned that the colonists might plot a revolution. The governor had the colonists put aboard the *Rosa*, and he specifically ordered Mariano G. Vallejo to place two other men aboard the ship; those men were Rafael Padres and Ygnacio Coronel.

In a March 21, 1835 message, Figueroa added, "If in addition to these you know of others who may have decided in favor of revolutionary ideas, have them put on the ship too, so that only those who have conducted themselves with prudence and good sense remain in the Territory."

On March 27th, Vallejo wrote to the governor that all of the men were on board the *Rosa* except Ygnacio Coronel, who had started off for Monterey by land. We know that Ygnacio Coronel remained in California, because he became the administrator of Mission San Miguel on July 14, 1836.

Conservatives in Mexico rallied around Santa Anna and, in the fall of 1835, abolished the 1824 federal constitution. It so happened that on September 29, 1835, Governor Figueroa died of an apoplectic stroke while at San Juan Bautista. Hubert Howe Bancroft considered Figueroa to be "the best Mexican governor ever sent to rule California." The guns at Monterey blazed forth with a tribute every thirty minutes for a period of six days; he was buried beneath the sanctuary of the church of Mission Santa Barbara on October 29, 1835, one month after his death. However, the passing of Governor Jose Figueroa plunged California into a struggle for control of the governorship.

Under the setup in 1836, Mexico was ruled by the military dictatorship of Santa Anna. Juan B. Alvarado became provisional governor of California. He had the *diputacion* proclaim California "a free and sovereign state," on November 7, 1836, until Mexico would restore the federal constitution of 1824. The capital was restored to Monterey from San Diego; it had been moved to that town by Governor Echeandia.

Edward Staniford, Professor of History at Chabot College, has written that "California's political structure took a peculiar turn from the national pattern in these years. The territory experienced a round of political-military maneuvering between rival contenders for the governorship."

Staniford went on to state that "In the game of

General M. G. Vallejo
from daughter Lulu Vallejo Emparan

musical chairs that took place between members of the *diputacion* (Alvarado and Castro) and Mexican-appointed officials (Mariano Chico and Nicolas Gutierrez), the governorship within one year passed from Castro to Gutierrez to Chico, back to Gutierrez, and then settled on Alvarado."

This hectic year was 1836. Nicolas Gutierrez served for four months, Mariano Chico served for three months, Nicolas Gutierrez served for another three-month term, and then Juan Bautista Alvarado became the governor.

It was during this period of political upheaval that the two-story adobe at San Miguel was being completed. With this background in mind we look, in the next chapter, at how Mission San Miguel was affected by the forces of secularization.

THE SECULARIZATION OF MISSION SAN MIGUEL

In 1831, Governor Jose M. Echeandia named Jose Castro as San Miguel commissioner, his duties being to distribute the mission's land and properties to the Indians. The office of commissioner, or administrator, of the mission existed until abolished by secularization.

According to the historian John Walton Caughey, "No one asserted that the California Indians were ready for secularization. But pressure was brought to bear on the authorities because of a desire on the part of certain individuals for the mission lands, admittedly the best in the province." Caughey was speaking of the missions in general, and not specifically about Mission San Miguel.

It is possible to look back and learn what the area along the Salinas River, in what would later become northern San Luis Obispo County, was like 160 years ago. Alfred Robinson, in his book *Life in California, During a Residence of Several Years in That Territory* gives us a first-hand account of this region, prior to the fall of 1834. We are able to approximate the date, because Robinson mentions Father Juan Cabot, who served at Mission San Miguel until November 25, 1834.

Our horses were excellent, and we galloped briskly over a smooth and level road for several leagues, without checking their speed, except to ford a small river, or ascend a few hills in the vicinity of the Mission of St. Miguel. From the tops of these we saw spread out before us a charming valley, through which our course lay.

It was mid-day when we descended the last hill, and rode up to the house. Father Juan Cabot, its director, was absent, having gone to pass a few days with the *padre* of St. Luis Obispo.

So I repaired to the *mayordomo*, presented my letter, and requested immediate dispatch. As it was necessary to send some distance for his horses, the delay of a couple of hours, ere they were procured, gave me ample time to look about the Mission.

Like that of St. Antonio, it possessed few resources, owing to its distance from the sea-coast, and the moderate extent of its domains. It was founded in the year 1797; and is built near the extremity of a small pass through the hill, where the sun casts its burning heat in a degree almost insufferable.

They say there, in proof of the warmth of the Mission, that the fleas cannot endure the summer months, and during the heat of the day may be seen gasping upon the brick pavements!

Having already ridden fourteen leagues, I felt little inclined to extend my journey farther, for my whole frame seemed as if it had undergone a severe pummeling, but ambitious to achieve my morning's undertaking, I again set off, following close at the heels of my guide.

Shortly after our departure we reached a place where a sulphurous hot spring boiled up from the ground, and formed a little rivulet which crossed the road. Father Juan had erected a small house over the spot for the purpose of shelter, and convenience for bathing, and it was resorted to by many persons, suffering with rheumatic disorders, who generally obtained immediate relief.

We afterwards stopped at the sheep farm belonging to the Mission of St. Miguel, where were two large houses and a number of straw huts. Gardens were attached to them, in which a variety of vegetables were cultivated by the Indians, who were there as keepers of eight or ten thousand sheep. Some distance off, on the other side of the valley, was a vineyard of excellent grapes, and from which were annually made considerable quantities of wine and brandy. Further on, some three or four leagues, we reached *el rancho de Santa Margarita....*

On January 6, 1831, commissioner Jose Castro (who later became military commandant of California, headquartered in Monterey) had the Indians assemble in front of the Mission San Miguel church before three witnesses: Juan Bautista Alvarado, Jose Maria Villavicencio and Jose Avila. Through an interpreter named Francisco, those assembled were informed of the governor's decree of secularization. The proclamation had to be repeated the next day, since many of the Indians had been absent.

"Through the medium of the interpreter, Castro was told that while the Indians respected the decisions of the government, they were poor, had no good land, nor the means to cultivate it, and that most of them had not been well-trained to work. For these reasons they said they wished to continue under the existing system." This quote is from Leonard Blomquist's thesis; his information came from *Departmental State Papers*, III, 3-5.

Juan Bautista Alvarado, a future governor of Mexican California, tells of climbing up on a cart in the mission courtyard and vividly describing to the Indians the advantages of "freedom." He requested that those who wished to remain with the padre to stand to the left; those who preferred "freedom" were to stand to the right. Nearly all went to the left. "As Alvarado later recalled, he was much chagrined that only thirty or forty Indians went to his right, then seeing themselves outnumbered, joined the hundreds who had gone to the left. The larger group meanwhile were shouting, 'We want to remain with the Padre. He is very good to us and we like him.'" Leonard Blomquist included this quote in his thesis, and it comes from Juan Bautista Alvarado's *Historia de California*, III, 6-7.

At that time, not everything was running smoothly for Mission San Miguel. Father Juan Cabot had written the following to Governor Figueroa on February 4, 1833: "Since the New Mexicans have come into this province with the commerce of wool and the purchase of horses, the mission has suffered a great loss of horses and 108 mules." Father Cabot suspected that the animals had been taken to New Mexico. The padre continued, "At the close of 1832 several of them passed by the Rancho of Asuncion and four colts and a mule were taken from a herd. After a few days others passed and took with them a mule with a forged brand."

Actual enforcement of the Secularization Act was begun, as we have seen, by Governor Jose Figueroa in 1834; he ordered ten missions secularized. This process was extended to six other missions in 1835, and to the remaining five in 1836. The process was completed by Governor Manuel Micheltorena in 1844. What this meant for Mission San Miguel, immediately, was that a residence for the civilian mission administrator was needed.

Petronilo Rios was a sergeant in the Mexican army, and is believed to have been in charge, at this time, of the *escolta*, a guard of five soldiers assigned to protect the population of Mission San Miguel. Under the supervision of Rios, an adobe building one-half mile south of the church was constructed by Indian labor during the period of 1835 to 1836. It is probable that adobe bricks for the building were taken from the ruined walls which had surrounded the Mission.

[Margaret Work was a founder of "The Friends of the Adobes." Writing in 1971, she informs us that west of the two-story main building were five adobe structures; they included a barn, a granary, a chicken house, a brick-lined oven and, no doubt, a cluster of Indian dwellings. The whole area was enclosed by an adobe wall, in the usual manner of a *rancheria*, or Indian village. There would be a large supply of adobe bricks to be used in construction. Dr. Hartwell B. Stanley, writing in 1897 as the official historian of the centennial celebration of the founding of the mission, stated that "Over two miles of adobe walls, fifteen feet high and five feet thick, formerly surrounded the court, corrals and yards." John P. Courter, Jr., writing in 1905, stated that "It is estimated that at one time twenty-two miles of wall surrounded the Church and other buildings, but not little of it remains. The wall averages eight feet high and two and one-half feet thick, and is built of large, flat adobe bricks."]

Mission San Miguel was confiscated by decree on August 9, 1834. The missionary was discharged and a salaried administrator was placed in control of the property as well as the Indians. On July 14, 1836, the mission was delivered to Ygnacio Coronel (1796-1862), who had been appointed administrator. The amount of time between August of 1834 and July of 1836 causes this writer to wonder if it were difficult for the government to find someone to accept the position of administrator at Mission San Miguel. His salary was $600 per year. Is it possible that such an imposing and attractive building was constructed in order to help attract an administrator?

The area may have been sparsely populated, but San Miguel was located on El Camino Real, and everything that went between Monterey and the southland went past the mission and the adobe.

Since Ygnacio Coronel occupies an important position in our cast of characters, we will pause for a closer look into the life of this person.

Ygnacio Coronel had been a soldier in the Spanish army, beginning in 1810; he was made a corporal of cavalry in 1814. In 1823, he retired from the army with the rank of *alferez*, or ensign. Ygnacio, his wife Francisca Romero, and five children came to California as colonists with the Padres-Hijar expedition. Between his retirement from the Spanish army and his arrival in California in 1834, Ygnacio Coronel had become a teacher. In 1836, the former school master was 41 years old, and was occupying Rancho Corralitos near Monterey. We saw, in an earlier chapter, that Governor Figueroa wanted Coronel sent back to Mexico; however, the governor died in September of 1835.

Ignacio Coronel, ca. 1855.

Ignacio Coronel
(1796-1862)

When Ygnacio Coronel arrived in San Miguel, as administrator, he most likely brought his family, composed of his wife and their sons and daughters: Josefa, age 20; Antonio Franco, age 18; Micaela, age 15; Soledad, age 10 and Manuel, age 4. All of these young people had been born in Mexico. This family of seven would fit nicely into the newly-constructed two-story adobe building. He most likely lived in, and worked out of, the two-story adobe building until the spring of 1837.

Some of the record-keeping which probably took place in the adobe residence of the new administrator resulted in the inventory of Mission San Miguel for 1837. Since Ygnacio Coronel was not replaced by Ynocente Garcia until March 30, 1837, it can be assumed that Coronel did much of the inventory work.

The inventory placed the value of the mission property at $82,806. The buildings of the mission proper, which formed a quadrangle (measuring roughly 230 by 305 feet) were valued at $37,000; the *rancheria*, consisting of 74 neophyte dwellings, amounted to $3,000. The value of $5,243 was placed on goods in the warehouse, implements, furniture and manufacturing outfit. The garden, 166 vines and the fence were valued at $584.

The amount of $10,162 was placed as the value of ranchos San Simeon, Santa Rosa, Paso de Robles and Asuncion, including the buildings. There were 5,500 grape-vines at the vineyards of Aguage and Santa Ysabel combined; their value was placed at $22,162. The value of Aguage alone was $16,162, according to the figures Blomquist obtained from *State Papers Missions* VIII, 24-26.

Livestock, which included the wild cattle at La Estrella, was valued at $20,782. Crops which were growing were valued at $387. The mission also had credits of $906, while the debts amounted to $231. The inventory demonstrates that at San Miguel proper, there were shops for iron work, hats, shoes, woodworking and weaving. There were also a soap house, or soap-making vats, and a tannery, which was in a separate adobe structure.

Coronel was accused of being brutal to the Indians and most of them ran away. Hubert Howe Bancroft states that the Indians "were somewhat unmanageable at times, on account of their intimate relations with the Tulareno gentiles."

In spite of having been provided with a new adobe building to live in and work out of, Ygnacio Coronel considered San Miguel to be a bad assignment, and resigned his post. He moved to Southern California, and founded the first school of consequence in Los Angeles, about 1838. He taught from 1844 until about 1856; he died in Los Angeles in 1862.

With this background on Ygnacio Coronel and his family, we return to San Miguel to see what transpired after their departure.

Ynocente Garcia, who called himself Jose Antonio Inocencio Garcia, took Ygnacio Coronel's place on March 30, 1837. It is not certain when the Coronel family moved out of the adobe.

Garcia had been born at Los Angeles on December 28, 1791. His parents were Felipe Santiago Garcia and Petra Lugo; both had been born in La Villa de Sinaloa, Mexico. Felipe Garcia, with his wife, was enroute to Monterey, as a member of Captain Don Fernando de Rivera's expedition when their first-born child was born.

Juan Jose Garcia was born on the plains south of San Luis Obispo, at the place known as "Oso Flaco." The baby was baptized at Mission San Luis Obispo on November 11, 1774. This date allows Juan Jose Garcia to join the list of persons who have the claim of being the first "white" child to be born in California. The expedition arrived in Monterey late in November of 1774. Ynocente Garcia had eight brothers and eleven sisters.

On April 18, 1807, Ynocente Garcia enlisted as a soldier in the army of Spain; he was assigned to the *escolta*, or mission guard, at Mission San Miguel. He served there for four years. Joaquin de la Torre, a brother-in-law, was Corporal of the Guard at Mission San Miguel at the time. (In 1840, Joaquin de la Torre would be granted Rancho Arroyo Seco, of four leagues, west of present-day Greenfield, in Monterey County. His claim for 16,523 acres would be patented on June 30, 1859.)

Also at San Miguel was a brother-in-law, Miguel Archuelta and Garcia's sister, Maria Antnonia Archuelta. It was through the instruction of Miguel Archuelta that such figures, important in California history, as Mariano Vallejo, Juan B. Alvarado, Jose de Jesus Pico and Jose Castro, learned to read.

After his four years in the mission guard at San Miguel, Ynocente Garcia was transferred to Mission Soledad, and soon afterwards to Monterey. Ynocente Garcia would be married twice; by Maria del Carmen Ramirez, he was the father of sixteen children, and after marrying Bruna Cole, they became the parents of three children.

On his way to take over as administrator at Mission San Miguel, Garcia discovered young Jose Mariano Bonilla when he found him confined by revolutionaries at Mission San Antonio de Padua. Bonilla's crime had been the carrying of a weapon- - -he had been quail-hunting. Garcia secured Bonilla's release, and asked the young man to serve as his secretary at San Miguel. Ynocente offered him "60 *pesos* a month from my own pocket to take charge of my accounts at San Miguel, telling him to come with me, for I was sure that Senor Alvarado would not disapprove. He accepted gladly, and together we set out for San Miguel."

Concerning Mission San Miguel, Garcia said: "I did not approve by any means of the way the neophytes

were behaving; for they would go out on the roads to rob travellers, and steal horses, even the very horses from the mission, which they ate. . . ."

When they arrived at Mission San Miguel, Ynocente Garcia stated that:

> **The padre turned over everything by inventory, Bonilla being the notary. I returned to the padre, the church with all it contained and made no change in his living quarters. I set myself forthwith to place the Indians in order and to prevent abuse and robbery of any kind. I planted great quantities of grains; at the end of two or three years I was able to harvest 800 *fanegas* of corn, 300 or 400 *fanegas* of horse beans, 300 *fanegas* of peas and 96 *fanegas* of beans. I also set out many fruit trees, tobacco, lettuce and other vegetables. But since there was no market for anything, I opened wide the granaries so that the Indians could eat at their discretion; even then a large part of the corn was wasted, then I saw the futility of planting so much.**

A *fanega* was a Spanish measure of grain and seed which was equal to 1.58 U. S. bushels, or the equivalent of 100 dried pounds. The *fanega* was also a Mexican land measure, equal to 8.81 acres. Garcia was probably talking about harvesting crops, rather than about the amount of land on which the crops had been planted. He continues with his impression of the task he faced.

> **When I saw so much disorder and pilfering, I lost all interest in further developing the mission; in fact, it was no longer possible; for it had no longer any good lands on which to plant; the best Indians had been taken away from the mission by Senor Hartnell for the petty officers of Monterey, and those he left me were of no use to me. For they devoted themselves to thievery. Once, four of them stole four horses, four women and four copes from the church with which to make sweatbands for their horses, and took everything to the sierra beyond the Tulares. With a single man and aided by the pagans, I was able to capture the thieves and what they had stolen, including the women. I sent them with their indictments and in irons to Senor Alvarado, to whom I sent a letter telling him to dispose of the mission for nothing could be done for it.**

(The "copes" to which Garcia referred above are

large, cape-like vestments which priests wear during certain religious ceremonies.)

> **I wrote to Alvarado to tell me just what to do with the Mission, because I was bored with it all. He replied that I should turn it upside down and do whatever I wanted with it; adding that I should devote myself only in keeping order so that the Indians wouldn't kill anyone, and that the government would pay me 300 *pesos* a year for it. I knew very well that this business of paying me money was so much talk. But I staid on keeping order for the good of my family and some others, but I never received any of the promised money.**

Garcia relates that while he was serving as administrator of Mission San Miguel, during the year 1837, Isaac Graham and a party of men forced the doors to the *monjerio*, and abused the occupants. The *monjerio*, which had been built in 1798, was an apartment for young, marriageable Indian girls; the girls were locked up during the night, under the care of a female chaperone. During the day, the girls were taught sewing, deportment and the domestic arts. This was the traditional way girls were guarded and trained in Spain. Garcia abolished the *monjerio*, leaving each family to care for its women.

Isaac Graham (1800-1863), a mountain man from Kentucky, arrived in California in 1834. He had established a distillery at Natividad, near Monterey. He and his followers had aided the attempt of Juan B. Alvarado to establish California as "a free and sovereign state" in 1836. Then he tried to overthrow Governor Alvarado in 1840; Alvarado exiled him to Baja California. In later years, on his Santa Cruz rancho, Graham ran a sawmill and did leather-tanning. Hubert Howe Bancroft called him "a loud-mouthed, unprincipled, profligate and reckless man."

Late in 1834, Father Juan Cabot, after serving at San Miguel for twenty-one years, retired to Spain. His brother, Father Pedro Cabot of Mission San Antonio de Padua, took his place in November 1834, and served until September 1835, when he was sent to Mission San Fernando. Father Juan Moreno, in October of 1835, succeeded Father Pedro Cabot until October 24, 1840.

In 1838, Father Moreno had complained bitterly that there was no food or clothing for himself and his Indians at Mission San Miguel. Father Moreno had been born on January 27, 1799, in Old Castile, Spain.

Moreno and the two Jimeno brothers were the last recruits the California missions received from San Fernando College in Mexico City. According to Blomquist's writing, concerning Father Moreno, "In 1838 he wrote to Jose de la Guerra, *sindico* of the missions, asking at different times, for various articles. In July he requested that De la Guerra pay six dollars for one and a half dozen knives which had been greatly needed for the *matanza* and which Moreno had bought in spite of having no money. Later he remarks that he lacks many things and that the warehouses of the mission have nothing left but the poles." (A *sindico* served as an attorney; the *matanza* was the slaughtering of cattle.)

Father Moreno complained about more than simply the poverty of the church. Blomquist informs us that "Garcia had turned over to him an unspecified number of cattle in lieu of salary. These were pastured on the San Simeon Rancho at a place called the "Pinalito." In 1839, the inventory refers to San Simeon as the rancho "where Father Juan Moreno has his herd of cattle." (The 1874 map of the County shows a small creek about four miles south of the community of San Simeon; the creek is called the "Arroyo del Padre Juan." Hubert Howe Bancroft, in a footnote, says that Father Moreno was very skillful in throwing the *reata* and very proud of his success in lassoing bears.)

Father Moreno had been given permission, in 1839, to cultivate the garden at La Asuncion. He remained at San Miguel until October of 1840, then he retired to the little garden at La Asuncion, northeast of present-day Atascadero. After two years there, he was forced to retire to Mission Santa Ynez, where he died on December 27, 1845.

In a belated attempt to prevent abuse of the Christianized Indians while the process of secularization was taking place, Governor Alvarado had appointed as Visitor-General of missions, William Edward Petty Hartnell; he served in this capacity from 1839-1840. During 1839, Ynocente Garcia was still the administrator of Mission San Miguel in name, but Bonilla was the acting administrator during June and July of that year. Hartnell, the newly-appointed inspector of the missions, arrived at San Miguel in the afternoon of July 31, 1839. He ordered that the house and garden of Rancho de la Asuncion be put at the disposal of Father Moreno and that the padre be allowed to take one of the looms from the mission to use wherever he thought it convenient.

The following is an entry in Hartnell's diary for July 31, 1839.

In El Paso de Robles . . . the Indians complained a great deal that they had understood that several places that they need very much were going to be taken away from them, namely: Santa Rosa, where the mission has all its cattle and horses; La Assuncion, where there is a good house and orchard; El Paso de Robles, where there is a large granary and *siembras* planted to wheat and barley; and San Simeon, where there is a house, granaries, and a chapel, sheep, and most of the Mission *siembras*. . . . They ask to be rid of the administrator; they want to be alone with the padre. They complain especially about Manuel Ortega, Majordomo of San Simeon, saying that he treats them very roughly, that he does not give them enough to eat, that he has been a scoundrel with women, beating and imprisoning those that did not want to yield to his desires. Everybody, both men and women have great aversion to him.

(The word *siembras* refers to sown land.)

Hartnell could do little more than make a partial record of the mission system's disintegration. However, he did dismiss Ortega. Ortega had come from Mexico to Santa Barbara in 1832; while there, he married Andrea Cota.

At Mission San Miguel, in 1839, we have seen that Hartnell listened to the Indians' fears that lands would be taken away from them. Father Engelhardt, historian of the missions, states that the Indians were willing to cede La Estrella, Cholam, Guerguero and Canamo. Edith Buckland Webb, in her *Indian Life at the Old Missions*, informs us that one of San Miguel's ranchos was named Canamo or hemp-field. We do not know the location of this rancho. Some of the clothing for the Indians was made from this material.

In early August, Hartnell listened to a dispute at San Miguel concerning some blankets which the Indians claimed had not been distributed. A more serious matter faced Hartnell in August of 1839- - -a *mayordomo* had been poisoned by two Indians who were arrested for the murder. (A *mayordomo* was a foreman of a rancho.)

On August 24, 1839, Ynocente Garcia reported to the government's secretary, Manuel Jimeno, that Garcia had investigated the violent death; he found that the *mayordomo* had been poisoned by the neo-

phyte named Canuto. Canuto and his accomplice were captured and were at the disposition of the judge. (A "neophyte" was a Christianized Indian.)

Let's take a moment for a little information on the person who was performing the duties of Visitor-General of the missions in 1839-1840. William E. P. Hartnell had been born in England in 1798 and arrived in South America in 1819, where he lived for a few years. After arriving in California, he was baptized a Catholic at Mission San Carlos, at Carmel, in 1824. The next year he married Maria Teresa de la Guerra.

During the ten weeks it took to sail across the Atlantic Ocean, Hartnell had taught himself the Spanish language. In 1827, partially due to his fluency in Spanish, Hartnell was appointed British Vice Consul in Monterey. In order to obtain a rancho, in 1830 Hartnell swore allegiance to Mexico and became a citizen of California. In 1834, he was granted the Alisal, or Patrocino Rancho of ¾ of a league; it was located about five miles north of the present-day town of Chualar, in Monterey County. There he established California's first public college. Maria Teresa de la Guerra de Hartnell later claimed 2,971 acres, and this grant was patented on February 12, 1882.

Meanwhile, in November of 1839, there were complaints from the administrator that the Indians were running away, and complaints from the padres that Ynocente Garcia was flogging the Indians excessively, and otherwise interfering with the padre's prerogatives. During 1839, the number of Indians Mission San Miguel had charge of was 360.

The last Franciscan padre at Mission San Miguel was Father Ramon Abella. He had been born in the archdiocese of Zaragosa, Spain, on May 28, 1764. With twenty-two companions, Abella sailed from Cadiz and disembarked at Vera Cruz, Mexico, on June 26, 1795. As a volunteer for the California missions, Abella was assigned to Mission San Luis Obispo in July of 1834, where he remained until November of 1841; he also took charge of Mission San Miguel from December 1840 until July of 1841.

Father Ramon Abella, the last of the padres of the San Miguel Mission period, was found lying on a rawhide bed, in one of the rooms of Mission San Luis Obispo. Although emaciated by starvation, he was still dividing his small store of *carne seca*, or jerked beef, with the neophytes.

In 1841, the French diplomat Eugene Duflot de Mofras wrote about Father Ramon Abella that "the poor friar was bedded down on an ox-hide, and used the horn of an ox as a drinking cup, and for nourishment had only some strips of meat dried in the sun. The venerable Father distributes the little that is sent him among the Indian children, who with their parents occupy the tumble-down houses that surround the Mission. . ."

When Father Ramon Abella died at Mission Santa Ynez on May 24, 1842, he had spent forty-four years in California- - -the longest record of service of any missionary in the province. By 1842, Mission San Miguel was almost completely deserted; only 30 Indians remained.

In May of 1842, Father Narciso Duran ceded both San Luis Obispo and San Miguel to Bishop Diego. The Bishop in July, 1842, placed the Reverend Miguel Gomez in charge of San Luis Obispo with jurisdiction over San Miguel. These two missions, therefore, became the first ones transformed into parishes in Up-

Perfecta Encinales was 115 years old in 1906 when photo was taken on September 9th. She was the last of the Salinan mission Indians; lived at San Antonio.

per California under the direct jurisdiction of the Bishop of the diocese.

The California State Archives has on file "Unclassified *Expediente* Number 278:

The Presbyter Miguel Gomez. La Estrella, at Mission San Miguel.

The Presbyter Jose Miguel Gomes, . . . Parish priest of the pueblo of San Luis Obispo in the year 1844 there was granted by . . . Micheltorena in favor of this settlement, the ex-Mission of San Miguel with the lands that surround the same (the title whereof I have in my possession, the record of which must be on file. . .) from among which lands at that time I solicited as my private property the one known as La Estrella, and although the same was offered to me, and some steps and reports were made, asked of Don Mariano Bonilla and others, I did not get the respective title on account of the only circumstance of not having been able to present the map, but now that I do so annexing it in due form, I pray your Excellency to be pleased to grant me the same declaring the ownership thereof in my favor adding thereto the portion named San Juan Capistrano, which is contiguous to the aforesaid place and lies on the side of the Tulares, from which fact it has never belonged, nor does now belong to any of the occupied or established points. . .

San Luis Obispo June 6, 1846

(As we will see in another chapter, Francisco Arce tried to obtain La Estrella during the summer of 1842.)

Father Duran, in obedience to a request from the government of Mexico, prepared a report on the state of each of the missions. Under the date of March 18, 1844, he had the following to say about San Miguel: "Mission San Miguel, Arcangel, is today without livestock, and the neophytes are demoralized and dispersed for want of a priest to care for them."

While the situation was deteriorating at Mission San Miguel, Ynocente Garcia turned over the church to the rector, and all the property to the Indians. Ynocente Garcia was succeeded, in 1841, by Jose de Jesus Pico. No baptisms took place at Mission San Miguel after April 17, 1842 until August 16, 1851.

Walter Colton (1797-1851), who was named *alcalde* of Monterey by Commodore Stockton, wrote the following, in 1849, about Mission San Miguel.

This inland mission is situated sixteen leagues southeast of San Antonio, on a barren elevation; but the lands attached to it sweep a circuit of sixty leagues, and embrace some of the finest tracts for agriculture. Of these the Estrella Tract is one; its fertility is

enough to make a New England plow jump out of its rocks, and a hundred emigrants will yet squat in its green bosom, and set the wild Indians and their warwhoop at defiance. In 1822, this mission owned 91,000 head of cattle, 1,100 tame horses, 3,000 mares, 2,000 mules, 170 yoke of working oxen, and 47,000 sheep. The mules were used in bringing back dry goods, groceries, and the implements of husbandry. But now the Indian neophytes are gone, the padres have departed, and the old Church only remains to interpret the past.

Historian Robert Glass Cleland, Professor of History at Occidental College, has an apt description of the effect of secularization—"It led to the rapid disintegration of the mission-controlled communities, scattered the partly civilized neophytes like sheep without a shepherd..."

Jose Antonio Inocencio Garcia also known as Inocente Garcia.

LAND GRANTS: RECEIVED AND LOST

In order to be considered as a possible grantee of land in California, it was required that the person be a citizen of Mexico, by birth or naturalization, and proclaim belief in the Roman Catholic faith. If the person were a naturalized citizen, he would need to be connected by marriage with a Mexican family.

The process of obtaining a grant began with the preparation of a petition, accompanied by a *diseno*, a crude, hand-drawn map; these were presented to the governor. After an investigation, if no objections were received from any source, and if the governor were satisfied with the petitioner's qualifications, the governor would write on the margin of the petition, "Let the title issue." The results of the investigation were contained in a report called the *informe*.

If the governor agreed to the grant, and he issued the *concedo*, the grant papers would be made ready. Once issued, the *concedo* gave the petitioner the legal right to develop his land, even though he still lacked the title.

A grant was then written, signed by the governor and delivered to the person who was now the grantee.

The size of the grant was indicated in so many leagues, and almost always contained the words *mas o menos* - - -"more or less." Because of the plentiful supply of land, there was no need to be precise. As soon as provisional title had been granted, the land was "surveyed." The survey started from a *mojonera*, a pile of stones or earth with a cross on it, as a landmark. The survey was done from horseback by two riders with a rawhide *reata*, or lariat rope, fifty *varas* in length, or 137 ½ feet.

Long stakes were tied to each end of the rope. The mounted cowboys stretched out the rope between them; one rider thrust his stake in the ground, and the other rider galloped ahead and planted his stake. As this process was repeated, the riders would guide themselves haphazardly along what they thought was the boundary line of the property. From this informal survey came the rough estimate of the grant's dimensions.

Most grants were five leagues or less in size. The Spanish league was equal to approximately 4,439 acres.

A *borrador*, or blotter copy of the grant, was retained in the governor's office. During the years 1844 and 1845, a summary of the transaction was entered in a record book called the *toma de razon*. (The term *razon*, when used as *gente de razon*, literally means "people of reason." According to Rose H. Avina, this phrase is not correctly translated as "white people," but rather "civilized beings," who were Spanish, mestizo or Indian.)

The petition, *diseno* and *borrador* were then assembled in a file called an *expediente*, and placed in the provincial archives. All of these matters now officially complied with, the *alcalde* led the grantee, by the hand, over his land. During this procedure, the grantee picked up earth and pulled out bunches of grass and scattered it to the four quadrants while shouting, "*!Viva el presidente y la Nacion Mexicana!*" By this action, the grantee was demonstrating that he had the right to dominate the land.

The above procedure was known as the Act of Possession, and took place in the presence of witnesses---the owners of adjoining lands.

(Details of the Act of Possession are taken from Rodolfo Larios' work entitled *Alta California, Estados Unidos Mexicanos: A Cultural Interpretive History and Geography*.)

The petitioner's papers were then submitted by the governor to the territorial legislature, or assembly, for final approval. If the assembly denied the grant, the petitioner could appeal to the central government. This final step in obtaining the title was the duty of the governor's office; all information concerning the grant was forwarded to the *Territorial Diputacion*. Approval by the government body was seldom refused.

Land grants had to be occupied within one year; this requirement could be met by building a house and corrals, introducing livestock, or planting an orchard. Once the grantee had received full title to the land, he had the right to sell the land, if he wished to do so.

By 1846, 790 grants had been made in California to 725 individuals; only fourteen of these grants were made during the period of Spanish government. Naturalized citizens received 122 of these grants, 56 went to former citizens of the United States, 40 went to former British subjects and the rest to other Latin Americans or Europeans. Sixty-six women were among the grantees, as were 92 Indians.

There were 43 grants made in San Luis Obispo County. Ten of these grants were from land that had belonged to Mission San Miguel. San Luis Obispo County consists of 3,334 square miles, or 12,133,760 acres. Approximately 196,105 acres of county land was granted from the former domain of Mission San Miguel. The ten grants do not include the three grants given to the Christianized Indians- - -Las Gallinas, El Nacimiento and La Estrella- - -which were not confirmed by the United States Land Commission. The number does include San Juan Capistrano y el Camate, which also was not confirmed. The remainder of the grants in San Luis Obispo County were from lands which had belonged to Mission San Luis Obispo.

The Treaty of Guadalupe Hidalgo, ending the Mexican-American War, specifically promised that private property rights would be safeguarded. The accepted usage among civilized nations required that the new sovereign be responsible for protecting the individual person in possession of his property, regardless of the change in government.

Despite the provision to protect property rights, the United States passed legislation, in 1851, which created the United States Land Commission. Its purpose was to review the validity of land claims which were based on Spanish and Mexican grants.

The worst feature of the law that the United States passed, concerning California land titles, was that claimants were considered guilty until they had proved their innocence- - -their claims were considered to be faulty or fraudulent until positive proof to the contrary was presented.

The Land Commission held its hearings from January 1852 to March 1856. All its sessions were held in San Francisco, except for one brief term at Los Angeles.

The single Los Angeles session was brought about because on February 28, 1852, forty-one ranchers met at the home of Ygnacio Coronel, in Los Angeles; these ranchers expressed disapproval of the requirement of transporting witnesses and documents, as well as lawyers, to San Francisco where the hearings were held. (This is the same Ygnacio Coronel who was the administrator of Mission San Miguel from July 14, 1836 to March 30, 1837.) It was contended that one-third of the land of Los Angeles County could be forfeited, if its owners were forced to validate their titles in San Francisco.

Henry Dalton, Antonio F. Coronel, Abel Stearns and Antonio Cot were appointed as a committee to forward a petition of protest. As a result of these efforts, the Land Commission agreed to hold a brief session in Los Angeles in the fall of 1852, but thereafter the commission met only in San Francisco.

Of the 813 cases presented to it, totaling over 12 million acres- - -the combined area of Massachusetts, New Hampshire and Maine- - -all but a few cases were appealed to the District Court; 99 eventually went to the United States Supreme Court.

According to Walton E. Bean, Professor of History at the University of California, Berkeley, "Ultimately 604 claims, involving about four million acres, were rejected. Some of the cases dragged on in the courts for several decades, and the average length of time required to secure evidence of ownership was 17 years from the time of submitting a claim to the board."

Among the General Instructions from the U. S. Surveyor General for California, a survey was to be connected with the adjoining lines of the U. S. Survey, so as to indicate the precise location of the tract. The judicial league was to be considered equal to 5,000 lineal Spanish *varas*, or 4,635 English yards, and consequently the *vara* equal to 33.372 English inches and the Sitio Mayor, or square league, as containing 4,438.683 acres.

With seventeen years the average length of time between submitting the claim and receiving a patent, or certificate of title, it is no wonder that many *Californios* lost their lands during the process. The claim of Petronilo Rios for El Paso de Robles took fourteen years! Rios had filed his claim on May 25, 1852, and finally received the title on July 20, 1866.

Petronilo Rios received the patent, or clear title, to Rancho El Paso de Robles after he had sold it. The change of ownership of this rancho took the following form.

Petronilo Rios   **Dated Aug. 1, 1857**
    to   **Recorded Sept. 21, 1857**
         Patented July 20, 1866
Daniel D. Blackburn
James H. Blackburn
Lazare Godchaux

Petronilo Rios of the County of San Luis Obispo, State of California, the party of the first part for and in consideration of $8,000.00 lawful money of the United States of America, grants, bargains, sells, releases, revises, and

conveys unto Daniel D. Blackburn, James H. Blackburn, and Lazare Godchaux of the County of Santa Cruz, the parties of the second part and to their heirs & assigns, all the certain tract of land lying and being situated in the said County of San Luis Obispo and being bounded on the south by the Rancho "de la Ascunsion" on the east by the River San Miguel and on the west by the place called "Lagirejo," said tract of land being all of the Rancho "Paso de Robles" containing six leagues more or less and being that was granted on the 12th day of May 1844 by Manuel Micheltorena, then Governor of California to Pedro Narvaez and afterwards conveyed by the said Narvaez to the said Rios. But the said Rios is not to be responsible for the costs of obtaining a patent for said land.

Presence of:
Arnold Thuthauer   (s) Petronilo Rios
James White   (s) Catarina A. de Rios

The word "Lagirejo" used above is spelled "higuejo" in another document. The area referred to is called Legueje Valley on the official map of the El Paso de Robles grant. This area was located to the northwest of the junction of Willow Creek Road and Dover Canyon Road. In this area had been a large concentration of Indians at a site which was called Lhuegue- - -another variant spelling.

On August 8, 1859, the San Luis Obispo County Board of Supervisors divided the ranchos of the county into four classes, according to the quality of the soil and the accessibility of their location. Tax assessments were made accordingly.

    1st Class: $1.25 per acre
    2nd Class: $1.00 per acre
    3rd Class: $0.75 per acre
    4th Class: $0.50 per acre

Former Mission San Miguel property did not rate at the top of this scale. Not one of San Miguel's former ranchos was rated first-class. Second-class properties included Ranchos Atascadero, Santa Rosa, San Simeon and Jose de Jesus Pico's portion of Piedra Blanca.

Third-class properties were Ranchos Cholame, Paso de Robles, Huer Huero, Santa Ysabel and John Wilson's portion of Piedra Blanca.

Rancho Asuncion was rated a rancho of the fourth-class.

Edward Staniford, Professor of History at Chabot College, has written: "Conniving lawyers and swindlers divested rancheros and settlers of their lands by legal trickery and exorbitant fees. . . ." Staniford listed, as reputable lawyers, such names as Halleck, Larkin and Hayes and said that they took only token fees from rancheros who were attempting to preserve their property.

Many claimants did not have the money required to pay for the lawsuits. The claimants were forced into the position of borrowing the money at 2 or 3 per-cent *per month*. To meet expenses of proving his title, the ranchero had to borrow money at ruinous rates of interest, sometimes as much as five percent per month. If the interest was not paid each month, the unpaid sum would be added to the principal, and it began drawing interest at the ruinous rates mentioned.

The *Californios* were not used to this system. Under the laws of Spain and Mexico, only what was produced on the land was subject to being taxed- - -not the land itself. But when California became a state, the burden of taxation fell on real property- - -the land. This had been the basis of the American tax system since the beginning of the Republic.

In the final analysis, it was the interest rates which nibbled away at the patrimony of the *Californios*.

PETRONILO RIOS —THE BEGINNING

Petronilo Rios was born in Mexico, most likely in 1806. His parents were Gregorio and Marciana Zayas Rios. They were both born in Mexico about the time of our Revolutionary War- - - or in California history, during the time of the founding of the first missions. When Petronilo was 18 or 19 years old, he became an artilleryman in the Mexican army. The premier historian of California, Hubert Howe Bancroft takes notice of him as of 1824 or 1825, shortly after Mexico became independent from Spain.

Petronilo Rios (1806-1870)

As an artilleryman, Petronilo Rios was first stationed at El Castillo de San Joaquin, the permanent naval artillery fortification, which had been located at the entrance to San Francisco Bay. This strategic spot was where the southern footing of the Golden Gate Bridge is situated today. The fortification had been built by the Spanish in 1794.

Petronilo Rios' years of military service are given, by Bancroft, as 1827 through 1840, and Bancroft's notation makes it appear that Petronilo Rios spent these years in the San Francisco military district. We will learn that this is not the case. Most of his service was spent in the Monterey military district, and some of it in San Miguel.

We know that Petronilo Rios was stationed at San Francisco in 1827, because on January 1, 1827, a popular election took place for the choice of twelve municipal electors in San Francisco. One of those elected was Petronilo Rios.

Sometime between 1827 and 1829, Rios must have been transferred to Monterey, because in that year he was a participant in a bloodless revolt against Governor Jose Maria Echeandia. This man was the first Mexican appointee for governor. He arbitrarily moved the capital to San Diego so that his fragile health would not be endangered by the Monterey fogs.

A preliminary revolt had taken place in October of 1828. On the 8th of October, a large part of the cavalry soldiers at Monterey refused to serve any longer unless they received their pay. These soldiers were joined by the *escoltas*, or mission guards of the missions from San Luis Obispo to San Juan Bautista; this would include the *escolta* at Mission San Miguel.

The soldiers marched out of the Presidio with their weapons. Lieutenant Romualdo Pacheco, acting commander at Monterey during 1827-1828, persuaded the rebels to return to their duties; several of the soldiers were placed in prison for their actions, to await a decision by the supreme government concerning their fate.

Concerning the 1828 revolt, Jose de Jesus Pico gives us some first-hand information. Jose de Jesus Pico (1807-1892) was the original owner of the Piedra Blanca grant. Under the authority of Mexico, Pico would eventually be the civil administrator of several missions: San Antonio (1838-1841), San Miguel (1841-1843) and San Luis Obispo (1845-1846).

The parents of Jose de Jesus Pico were Jose Dolores Pico and his wife, Maria Isabel Cota de Pico; they came to California with Juan Bautista de Anza in 1775-1776. Don Jose Dolores Pico was buried at Mission San Miguel on June 1, 1827 (Book of Burials, Mission San Miguel, entry 1558).

From 1827-1831, Jose de Jesus Pico was a soldier in the Monterey Company. Concerning the 1828 revolt Pico tells us the following.

We were about eighty men and we roamed about for a month without obeying anyone. About 30 or 40 appeared in court and were pardoned. But about forty of us (among whom the ringleaders were Felipe Arceo, Raimundo and Gabriel de la Torre, Pablo Bejar, Jose de Jesus Pico and Francisco Soto), stayed longer, refusing to return to the infantry; but finally persuaded by our families, we returned to Monterey and appeared in the court of justice. They put the forty of us in jail. . .they kept us prisoners for about a year, awaiting the decision of the government of Mexico.

The politics of Alta California during the Mexican period of 1822 to 1846 are very complicated. We will ignore as much of the political disputes as possible. However, we will take an in-depth look at the 1829 Solis revolt, because Petronilo Rios was involved in that incident.

Jose Maria Echeandia had been a lieutenant-colonel of engineers in Mexico before he became the first governor of California to be appointed under the 1824 republican constitution of Mexico. Joaquin Solis and others had been banished to California for offenses committed in Mexico. Solis was to be banished for a period of 10 years, and was living on a rancho near Mission San Juan Bautista, not far from the Presidio of Monterey.

The soldiers at Monterey were willing to join Joaquin Solis as a protest because they had not received their pay for a long time; they also complained that they had been forced to cut up their blankets to make clothing to replace worn-out garments.

The following is more first-hand information from Jose de Jesus Pico, speaking about being in jail at Monterey, after roaming about with eighty other soldiers in 1829:

When they told us that the order was coming, or had come, they would punish one out of five or ten (I don't remember which), it was then we formed the plan of revolution and we called upon Joaquin Solis to command us,

believing him to be competent for that purpose, but we were disappointed.

One night the forty of us escaped from the jail, we took by surprise the quarters of the cavalry, infantry and artillery and we took possession of them; then we imprisoned the officers that there were in Monterey. . . .

Hubert Howe Bancroft states that the ringleaders of this revolt were Mariano Peguero, Andreas de Leon, Pablo Vejar and the two brothers Raimundo and Gabriel de la Torre. Brothers Raimundo and Gabriel de la Torre were in command of the *escolta*, or mission guard, of San Miguel and San Luis Obispo, respectively; they came to Monterey with their men and those of San Antonio and Soledad, arriving on the night of the revolt.

Joaquin Solis along with a group of partisans, seized the principal officials in charge of the Presidio of Monterey. The officials who were seized included Mariano Guadalupe Vallejo, acting commander of the company, Juan Jose Rocha, Manuel Jimeno Casarin and Andres Cervantes; these officials were roused from their slumber and were locked up in the jail before dawn. There had been no resistance beyond verbal protest, except that the doors of Vallejo and Rocha had to be kicked down by Estaban Espinosa. Vallejo had been called at 2:00 a.m., on the pretext that an important message had just arrived; suspecting something, he did not open the door.

Mariano Guadalupe Vallejo had been born in Monterey on July 7, 1808; he was the 8th in a series of 13 children. He entered the military service in 1823 as a cadet of the Monterey company; in 1827, at the age of 20, he was promoted to *alferez* of the San Francisco company. *Alferez* (ensign) is a rank which is intermediate between a non-commissioned officer and a commissioned officer.

Juan Jose Rocha had arrived in California with Echeandia in 1825, as a Mexican brevet *alferez*, under sentence of banishment for two years. For a period, Rocha commanded the Monterey detachment of the San Blas military company. In later years, his name appeared frequently in official records, partly due to his activities as acting commander of the southern forces in the sectional hostilities of 1837.

Manuel Jimeno Casarin came to California in 1828, and was a brother of the friars Jimeno; he was *subcomisario* of the Monterey custom house from 1828-1830. In 1835, Manuel Jimeno Casarin would be a member of the *diputacion* (the local legislative body), and the *comisionado* (commissioner) for the secular-ization of Mission San Luis Obispo, and would serve as acting governor during the illness of Governor Juan B. Alvarado in 1841. Andres Cervantes was a Mexican artillery sergeant at Monterey from 1829 to 1836.

The first overt act of the rebellion took place at Monterey on the night of November 12, 1829; this happened to be at a time when Governor Echeandia was in the southern part of the territory. Pablo Vejar would later state that Echeandia would have been shot, had he been in Monterey at the time, since the soldiers considered him responsible for all of their troubles.

A leader was needed and none of the conspirators had a rank higher than corporal, nor did any of them feel competent to take command. On November 13, 1829, Raimundo de la Torre was dispatched with a summons to Joaquin Solis. This summons was signed by Mariano Peguero, Andres de Leon, Gabriel de la Torre and Petronilo Rios.

Solis came in from his rancho on the 14th, and assumed the position of *comandante-general* of the California troops. Soon after his arrival, Solis had the imprisoned officers transferred from the jail to a warehouse. The next morning, Solis went to see Jose Maria Herrera, a financial agent of the government. He asked Herrera to draw up a manifesto or *pronunciamento*. In a day or two, Herrera produced one, which was read first to Solis and afterwards to his confederates- - -according to Solis' telling of the incident.

The *pronunciamento* was read aloud to a group of foreigners, including W. E. Hartnell, David Spence and others. They more or less approved the document "from motives of courtesy," as David Spence would later testify. It was read to the soldiers and approved by them the same night. Later, many claimed that they were not pleased because it was a plan of revolution, rather than a petition for redress of grievances. Bancroft says that these claims were an afterthought, in most cases.

Herrera afterwards claimed that he informed Solis, upon his request for a manifesto, that the officials who had been imprisoned should be released, and that Herrera only consented to compose the document upon the supposition that their release depended upon his doing so. Dated at Monterey November 15, 1829, the manifesto was signed by the same people who had signed the summons: Mariano Peguero, Andres de Leon, Gabriel de la Torre and Petronilo Rios. This time, the signature of Joaquin Solis was added.

Petronilo Rios' part in the revolt consisted of his writing the summons and writing the list of grievances against Governor Echeandia, as they were dictated by Jose Maria Herrera at his home.

The manifesto said that the well-being of the entire Mexican nation was the desire of the supreme government, but this desire had been scandalously thwarted in California by the governor. Education had been neglected, public finances had been allowed to fall into disorder; the administration of justice, both civil and criminal, had become detestable; the discipline of the troops had relaxed; public affairs in general were reduced to such a degree of evil that patience had ceased to be a virtue.

Under these circumstances, the troops of Monterey had decided upon various reforms and had freely chosen Joaquin Solis as their leader. Their objectives were: to convoke a new territorial *diputacion* (legislature); to remove Echeandia from office; to choose a different person to administer the treasury; to have a different *comandante-general* in control of the troops.

The paper closed with a promise that those who had taken up arms would not lay them aside until their objectives had been accomplished. As soon as the manifesto was decided, it became important to raise money. The rebels released Manuel Jimeno Casarin and the other officials in order to get possession of $3,000 due the treasury from customs. This money had come from about nine thousand pesos in duties that had been paid from the English brigantine *Danube*, which was anchored in Monterey.

Meliton Soto, a citizen, was sent south with letters which were designed to advance the cause of the rebels. Raimundo de la Torre read the plan to the soldiers of

Custom House, Monterey.

every *escolta* from Mission Soledad to Mission San Luis Obispo.

Herrera and Solis then had a consultation concerning the next steps to take. The question was whether to proceed first to revolutionize San Francisco or Santa Barbara. The decision was in favor of the former, and Solis set off with 20 men. After accepting the surrender of the Presidio of San Francisco, and dismissing Ygnacio Martinez from command, Solis returned to Monterey.

The next move was toward Santa Barbara. It had been arranged that an uprising in favor of Solis was to take place there on the night of December 2nd. Romualdo Pacheco, the *comandante*, and Roderigo del Pliego had been seized and thrown into prison. The outbreak took place just after the arrival of Meliton Soto with dispatches from the north. Pacheco and Pliego were later released.

Roderigo del Pliego was a Mexican *alferez* who had arrived in California in 1825, and was attached to the Monterey company; in 1827, he was transferred to the Santa Barbara company. Bancroft states that he was "a bad fellow" who left California in 1831 with Governor Victoria.

Romualdo Pacheco had come to California in 1826; he was a sub-lieutenant of engineers who served two years as Governor Echeandia's aide-de-camp. According to Bancroft, "Pacheco was a brave and skillful officer, intelligent, courteous, popular, and of unblemished character; a man against whom nothing was ever said, except that some California officers complained of his too rapid promotion as a newcomer." [His son, also named Romualdo, was born about a month before his father's death at Cahuenga Pass in 1831. This younger Romualdo became the 12th governor of California (February 27 to December 9, 1875). Pacheco, as lieutenant governor, became Governor when Newton Booth gave up the office to become a United States Senator. Romualdo Pacheco was the first native son to hold the office; he was the only one of Spanish descent to be a California state governor.]

In the meantime, Joaquin Solis was marching southward toward Santa Barbara. Governor Echeandia, upon being informed of the rebellion, was on his march northward from San Diego, the town he had named capital of California. On December 28th, Solis, then at San Miguel, wrote that the governor had arrived in Santa Barbara with 150 men. Solis asked Padre Juan Cabot, of Mission San Miguel, to request of Padre Luis Martinez of Mission San Luis Obispo to arouse the Indians to revolt. Cabot warned Padre

Martinez of the scheme, and urged him not to become embroiled in the affair.

Echeandia issued a proclamation, dated Santa Barbara January 7, 1830, addressed to the soldiers of Solis. He told them that he had been placed in his office by the supreme government and could not yield it without a struggle. He told them that he had a military force that was vastly superior in number. He felt no hostility to them; if they would submit, he would work to obtain their pardon and even their leaders would be safe "in life and limb."

On the next day, Echeandia wrote Solis a long and dispassionate letter saying that if he and his soldiers had complaints to make, it should not be done with guns in their hands. Solis paid no attention but marched with his soldiers toward Santa Barbara. On January 20, 1830, Solis and about 100 followers occupied Mission San Miguel on his way south in order to surprise Santa Barbara.

The armies met at Santa Ynez, and when within cannon range, Solis opened fire, expecting to see his adversaries flee at the first shot. But they stood firm, and prepared to return fire. Before they could do so, however, Solis and his soldiers abandoned the field, leaving everything behind them. It was a complete rout, but without loss of life.

Romualdo Pacheco and a party of soldiers pursued Solis as far as Monterey, and near that town arrested Solis, Herrera and the other chief conspirators, which included Maximo Guerra, Raimundo de la Torre and Meliton Soto; these people were thrown into prison.

Governor Echeandia, after the rout, returned to Santa Barbara and, among other things, on February 30, 1830, ordered the arrest of Father Luis Antonio Martinez, the missionary of Mission San Luis Obispo, on the charge of complicity in the rebellion.

Echeandia had held a grudge against Father Martinez since the Mexican congress had decreed, in October of 1824, that all Californians must sign an oath of allegiance to Mexico. Father Martinez, at Mission San Luis Obispo, was an outspoken critic of this requirement. Born in Spain on January 17, 1771, Father Luis Antonio Martinez arrived at Santa Barbara on May 8, 1798, and was soon sent to Mission San Luis Obispo, where he spent his entire missionary life- - - June 16, 1798 to February 2, 1830. He died two years after his exile.

Father Luis Antonio Martinez was the most famous of the fathers who served at Mission San Luis Obispo. He began his long term there in 1798; speaking the native idiom, he was able to keep the Indians in order. He is the hero of the story in Helen Hunt

Jackson's book, *Ramona*. There, the priest is described as beloved by Spaniards and Indians.

In the story, the padre tells how he entertained his guests- - -a general and his bride. He "caused to be driven past the corridors, for their inspection, all the poultry belonging to the Mission. In orderly ranks, they marched; first the turkeys, then the roosters, then the white hens, the black, the yellow, next the ducks and lastly the geese." Before it was done with, the general and his wife nearly died with laughter.

Father Martinez, in a written defense, objected to his arrest, and stated that Solis and his forces had been fed and housed in the tradition of mission hospitality when they stopped at Mission San Luis Obispo on their way back and forth. Stating that he was 70 years of age, had been in the country for 34 years, and although he was a Spaniard, from the beginning of the revolution against Spain, he had stated that California ought to follow whatever path Mexico decided. All he asked now was his passport and to be allowed to leave the limits of the republic.

Echeandia called a council of military officers and they decided that the priest would be sent out of the country. Father Martinez was put aboard the brig, *Thomas Nolan*, which happened to be in port. Captain Stephen Anderson had to give his bond that he would take the exiled priest directly to Callao, Peru, and put him on the first boat to Europe. They sailed on March 20, 1830.

From Santa Barbara, Echeandia marched to Monterey, where a military tribunal was created. On April 1, 1830, Solis, Herrera and the other conspirators imprisoned there were put on trial. All were convicted, and fifteen of them were sentenced to be placed on board the American bark, *Volunteer*, with John Coffin Jones, Jr. the master. They sailed for San Blas, Mexico, on May 9, 1830.

Herrera was confined to a room, constructed for the purpose, on deck; Solis and the other thirteen prisoners were in irons. Gabriel de la Torre later said that his brother, Raimundo, was tried by court-martial and acquitted, whereupon the rest were discharged without trial. Those who had belonged to the Monterey cavalry company were dropped from the company rolls in 1836.

Two of the people who had signed the summons sent to Solis, and who also signed the manifesto were among those deported to Mexico; the two signers who were not among the prisoners were Gabriel de la Torre and Petronilo Rios. [In 1839, Gabriel de la Torre was granted the Rancho Zanjones, of 1 ½ leagues, two miles southeast of the town of Chualar; the 6,714-acre rancho was later owned by David Jacks.]

California's first revolution was over.

Later in the same year, Governor Echeandia submitted his resignation. Father Martinez's case was reopened under Governor Victoria, and the priest was vindicated; however, by that time, the padre was gone.

We notice that Petronilo Rios' part in the revolt simply consisted of his writing the summons to Joaquin Solis and writing the list of grievances against Governor Echeandia as they were dictated by Herrera. However, Petronilo Rios' participation to this extent was a significant contribution to this important event in California history, and it has allowed us to examine some activities in the history of our state that we might otherwise overlook.

It is important to stop and use our imagination concerning Mission San Miguel and the old adobe. Located on El Camino Real, all the activity which took place between the capital at Monterey and all points to the south passed right in front of their doorsteps! El Camino Real was "the royal road." C. M. Gidney, in his two-volume, 1917 *History of Santa Barbara, San Luis Obispo and Ventura Counties of California* states that "The high-sounding name related rather to the King's couriers and messengers by whom it was chiefly used than to its regal perfection as a road."

After passing Mission San Miguel, El Camino Real turned west and headed out what is today's 10th Street, toward the Nacimiento River. (Various writers state that the road went behind the mission.) El Camino Real then proceeded in a northwesterly direction into the San Antonio Valley. The road crossed the river in the vicinity of Pleyto- - -the present site of San Antonio Dam. El Camino Real then headed westerly to Mission San Antonio de Padua, the third of California's missions. It was founded by Father Junipero Serra on July 14, 1771.

Since the 1940s, it has not been possible to follow this route of El Camino Real, because the road crosses military property- - -Camp Roberts. The name of the road, on Camp Roberts, is Bee Rock Road. Part of the original road has been obliterated by San Antonio Lake and the dam which forms it. Still, much of the parade of California history has passed by Mission San Miguel, and has gone by in front of the Rios-Caledonia adobe since about 1835.

PETRONILO RIOS AND CATARINA AVILA

From 1831-1832, an artillery detachment of eight men, in the San Francisco Military District, was under successive command of Petronilo Rios, Lazaro Pina and Antonio Mendez. Lazaro Pina was a Mexican artillery corporal at Monterey in 1829 and at San Rafael in 1832. He was back in Monterey in 1836, and was killed at the battle of Cerro Gordo, Texas, in 1846. Antonio Mendez served as Mexican commander of artillery at San Francisco from 1831-1832; he was back in Mexico in 1836.

In 1835, the San Francisco company was transferred to Sonoma, where its force was reduced in 1837, but raised to nearly 50 in 1839-1840. The population of Monterey, during the decade of 1831-1840, was approximately 700 persons. Census figures for 1836 show that the town had 255 men, 146 women and 293 children. Of these, 30 were Indians and 42 were considered foreigners.

The military company at the Presidio of Monterey varied from 20 to 50 men, including *invalidos*. (An *invalido* was a retired military man.) There was generally an artillery force of 5 men, under Sergeant Jose M. Medrano in 1831-1832, and Petronilo Rios in 1839-1840. We notice that the years between 1832 and 1839 are not mentioned.

Regarding the lack of records, Hubert Howe Bancroft had this to say about the Presidio of Monterey, during the years 1831-1840: "The military organization was still kept up, but the records are even more fragmentary and confusing than in the past decade, so much so indeed. . .that it is not worth while to attempt the presentment of details either in notes or text." With the lack of records for us to examine, it is not possible to state for certain where Petronilo Rios was located each year. It is believed that he was stationed at Mission San Miguel during some of the period between 1832 and his discharge in 1840- - -just the period of time that Bancroft tells us we do not have documentation.

We know that Petronilo Rios was in San Miguel in 1833, because his first child was born there. Toward the end of his career, we know that some time was spent on duty at Monterey.

While stationed at Mission San Miguel, Petronilo Rios held the rank of Corporal, and was in charge of the *escolta*, or mission guard, made up of five soldiers. We know the names of the members of the first *escolta* to be assigned to guard the population of Mission San Miguel in 1797, but we do not have any information about the *escolta* that Petronilo Rios was in charge of in the 1830s.

When he was 26 years old, Petronilo Rios married Catarina Avila, age 20; she had been born in California in 1812, most likely in Monterey, because she was baptized there on March 16, 1812. Petronilo and Catarina were married in Monterey, "Alta California," on May 2, 1832. They would go on to have twelve children, three of whom would die before reaching the age of one year. Their fifth child, Jose Maria Alejo, was born prematurely at age seven months in 1838, and lived until sometime in 1839.

Catarina Avila Rios

Catarina Avila Rios came from hardy stock and a famous family. We will pause to appreciate the background of Catarina Avila Rios. Her grandparents were members of the group which has been called *Los Fundadores*. This group was made up of those persons who came from Mexico to California in the first fifteen years of its settlement.

Ygnacio Antonio Linares (1745-1805), Catarina's grandfather, had been born at San Miguel Orcasitas, Sonora, Mexico; his parents were Gregorio Linares and Manuela Gonzales. About 1767, at San Miguel Orcasitas, Ygnacio married Maria Gertrudis Rivas (1752-1813); his bride had also been born at San Miguel Orcasitas.

On May 1, 1771, Ygnacio Linares enlisted in the army at Guaymas; he gave his age as 26. He was recruited from the Presidio de Tubac by Juan Bautista de Anza; Ygnacio would be a soldier at the San Francisco Presidio from its founding.

Ygnacio Antonio Linares brought his wife, Maria Gertrudis Rivas, and their family to California as part of the second De Anza Expedition, first settling in San Francisco. Ygnacio and Maria eventually were the parents of 12 children.

In 1774-1775, De Anza had blazed an overland trail from Sonora to Mission San Gabriel in Alta California. He then used the trail in 1775-1776 to lead livestock and 240 colonists, of whom 166 were women and children, to California.

The Linares family had three children when the expedition started, on September 29, 1775. The names of the children and the approximate years of birth were: Maria Gertrudis Linares (about 1768), Juan Jose Ramon (about 1770), and Maria Juliana (about 1771). Maria Gertrudis and Juan Jose Ramon had been born at San Miguel Orcasitas, Sonora, Mexico. Maria Juliana Linares was born at Tubac Presidio, Mexico.

Maria Gertrudis gave birth to their fourth child on the trail, with Captain Juan Bautista de Anza performing the duties of doctor and midwife. Father Pedro Font, a Franciscan missionary, served as chaplain and cartographer for this expedition. Here are pertinent parts of his diary:

Friday, November 24. - I said Mass. A pregnant woman was ill this morning, and so we remained here today. She got better after the commander aided her with a delicacy which he had, namely a plate of food...

Sunday, December 24. - I said Mass. We set out...at half past nine in the morning, and halted about two in the afternoon in the same canyon...having traveled some four short leagues to the west-northwest.....In the afternoon they called me to confess the wife of a soldier who since yesterday had been suffering childbirth pains, the one of the delicacy which I mentioned on November 24. She was very fearful of dying, but having consoled her and encouraged her as best I could I returned to my tent, and at half past eleven at night she very happily and quickly gave birth to a boy.

Monday, December 25. - Because a little before midnight on this holy night of the Nativity, the wife of a soldier, the one whom I mentioned yesterday, happily gave birth to a boy, and because the day was very raw and foggy, it was decided that we should remain here today. I therefore had an opportunity to say three Masses, and after them I solemnly baptized the boy, naming him Salvador Ygnacio.

Tuesday, December 26. - A little before we entered the narrow part of the canyon a fine sleet began to fall, and lasted until after we had halted. The day and the night continued very wet and cold, but the mother recently delivered had the spirit to continue the journey...

Thursday, December 28. - I said Mass. Perhaps because of the severe cold of last night and the shaking caused by the journey, the woman recently delivered was somewhat ill, and for this reason we remained here today...

One of the first "white" children born in California, Salvador Ygnacio Linares, arrived on Christmas Eve, 1775, while the expedition was encamped near the upper end of Coyote Canyon, at Upper Willows (or Fig Tree Spring), in today's Riverside County. Salvador Ygnacio Linares was the third and last child born since the expedition left Tubac.

Ygnacio and Maria Gertrudis Linares were to have eight more children; some were baptized at Mission Dolores in San Francisco, and the others, at Mission Santa Clara. Ygnacio Linares settled at San Jose in 1784.

Maria Antonia Linares, the tenth child of Ygnacio

and Maria Gertrudis, was born on March 15, 1786 at the Pueblo of San Jose. On September 17, 1805, she married Jose Guadalupe Avila at Mission Santa Clara. This couple would become the parents of Catarina Avila- - -future wife of Petronilo Rios. They had a total of ten children. Those older than Catarina were Guebio Antonio (born 1806), Ana Maria (born 1807), and Rosalina (born 1810); the children younger than Catarina were Vicente (born 1817), Francisco (born 1819), Marcella Vallejo (born 1828), Jose Ygnacio (born 1830), Maria Antonia (born 1831) and Adelaida (born 1833).

Petronilo and Catarina Rios were living in San Miguel by 1833, because their first child, Jose Camilo Guadalupe, was born there on July 19th. His godparents were Don Fimoico Maafe and Rosa Avila. The size of the Rios family was increased by the birth of Maria Luisa on September 23, 1834, in Monterey.

Maria Luisa's godparents were Jose Maria Castanares and his wife, Ana Maria Gonzales; she was the daughter of Rafael Gonzales- - -a person whose life was intertwined with that of Petronilo Rios. Later we will see that Maria Luisa's godfather would play an important part in the early history of Alta California.

Rafael Gonzales came to California with Figueroa in 1833, and served as the first Mexican administrator of customs at Monterey. He was the *alcalde* (judge-mayor) at Monterey for a time after l835, the year Governor Figueroa died. Rafael had served as Figueroa's secretary; from 1839 through 1843, Gonzales was a member of the *junta* in Monterey.

In 1836, Rafael Gonzales had been granted the San Justo Rancho in today's San Benito County. The San Justo Rancho consisted of 34,615.65 acres, and extended from the crest of the Gabilan Mountains to the present town of Hollister. Gonzales abandoned this grant by giving up his claim to the land. Jose Castro obtained the grant on April 15, 1839. [Rafael Gonzales died at Monterey in 1868, at the age of 82.]

Early in 1835, we find Petronilo Rios again in Monterey. From the Book of Spanish Translation, Book 1, page 13 (in the Monterey County Recorder's Office in Salinas) we find the following:

The Ayuntamiento in Session of March the fourteenth granted to Petronilo Rios the lot he petitioned for whereon to build a house (said lot) having a frontage of twenty-five *varas*, and as many more (*varas*) in depth,

situated (towards the) north of Mr. Julas lot and in direct line with the house of Mr. Llin; he agreeing to pay the charge fixed by the Hon. Territorial Deputation.
Witness my hand in Monterey,
March 14, 1835.
Dave Spence, Sec.
Fco del Castillo Negrete

(On the margin of this document has been written: "Monterey, Oct. 2, 1844. This house changed hands by legal sale (thereof) made by Mr. Rios to Don Salvador Munras this day. Escobar")

[The *vara* is equal to about 33.385 inches or 2.781 feet. The *ayuntamiento* was the town council. The "honorable territorial deputation" is usually called the *diputacion*. This body was the local legislature created under the Mexican constitution in force at that time; the members were elected, but acted more as the governor's advisors than as independent law-makers.]

Let us take a look at the people mentioned in the above document.

David Spence was a native of Scotland who came to California, by way of Peru, in 1824; in 1829 he married Adelaida Estrada. He was *alcalde* of Monterey in 1835, and the holder of many offices under both the Mexican and United States governments. In 1834 and 1839, he was granted the Rancho Encinal y Buena Esperanza, of 13,391 acres; it was about two miles north of the present-day Chualar, and was adjacent to the Rancho Buena Vista, owned by his father-in-law, Jose Mariano Estrada. Spence's grant was patented on May 23, 1862.

Salvador Munras was a brother of Estaban Munras. Estaban was a Spaniard from Catalonia who came to California about 1818. Estaban Munras has been born in Barcelona, Spain, in 1798. In 1820, he was a trader at Monterey, and was acting as a diplomatic observer. Because of his friendship with Padre Juan Cabot of Mission San Miguel, Estaban Munras agreed to supervise the Indians in their work of frescoing and painting the interior walls of Mission San Miguel, beginning in 1821. It is said that the project took approximately three years. On February 12, 1822, Estaban Munras married Catalina Manzaneli.

On November 9, 1835, Catalina Manzaneli de Munras was granted the Rancho San Francisquito, of two leagues, six miles southwest of Carmel. Catalina had been born at San Blas, Mexico, on April 13, 1798. Her father was a native of Genoa, Italy; her mother, Maria Casilda Ponce de Leon, was a descendant of the famous explorer and navigator. Her stepfather was Manuel Quixano, a native of Spain stationed in Monterey as physician to the Spanish troops in California.

In 1835, Estaban Munras was granted the Rancho San Vicente, of two leagues, which was across the Salinas River from the lands of Mission Soledad. Estaban Munras died at Monterey on September 3, 1850. Concepcion Munras, and others, were claimants for 19,979 acres, which were patented on June 29, 1865.

Francisco Castillo Negrete was a Mexican judge who came to California, and arrived in Monterey, in September of 1834 with the Padres-Hijar company; he had an appointment as a district judge of California. Negrete also acted as legal advisor to Governor Gutierrez. In 1835, he served as secretary to the *ayuntamiento* for half the year; he also became a partner to Jose Maria Herrera. Hubert Howe Bancroft rated Negrete as "a very able lawyer, and a brilliant, accomplished gentleman."

During the 1830s, Mission San Miguel must have been experiencing a period of great decline, because Mrs. Angustia de la Guerra Ord stated that "When I returned there in 1835, I found not even a glass in which to drink water and had to drink from a cup I had brought myself. All of the assets of the Mission, herds, etc., had disappeared."

On October 28, 1835, Jose Simon was born, to Petronilo and Catarina Rios. We do not know where, but Rafael Gonzales and his wife, Carmen Sierra, were his godparents. Jose Simon died before becoming one year old. The friendship between Petronilo Rios and Rafael Gonzales is indicated by the fact that Rafael and his wife were chosen to be the godparents of three of the Rios children.

Petronilo Rios, in 1836, was listed in the census of Monterey as a landowner, 30 years of age; hence, his year of birth is assumed to be 1806. Three more children were born to Petronilo and Catarina while Petronilo was serving in the army. Juana Josefa Ysabel was born on May 22, 1837, at Monterey; her godparents were Juan Julien and his wife, Concepcion Avila. [Juana Josefa Ysabel Rios would marry Atenogenes Gil at Mission San Antonio de Padua on February 20, 1858. They would be the parents of a son, Juan Antonio Primitivo Gil; he was born in San Miguel, and Petronilo and Catarina Rios served as god-parents.

The date of birth is given as January 24, 1856. Juana Josefa Ysabel Rios Gil would pass away on June 30, 1860.]

Jose Maria Alejo was born on July 17, 1838; this premature child was born in seven months, and lived some months into the year 1839. His godparents were Rafael Gonzales and his wife, Carmen Sierra. Estaban was born on December 26, 1839; his godparents, too, were Rafael Gonzales and his wife, Carmen Sierra. The place of birth for these three children was most likely in Monterey.

It was during the period of years 1835 to 1836 that Petronilo Rios was believed to be supervising the construction of the two-story adobe, one-half mile south of Mission San Miguel, which later came to be called the Rios-Caledonia. There is no documentation for this period of Petronilo Rios' life, that we have been able to find.

The services of Petronilo Rios must have been highly valued, because in 1839, he was the Commander of Artillery at the Presidio of Monterey. During this period of time, Rios was promoted to the rank of Sergeant. Soon after his promotion, Sergeant Rios lodged complaints with his commander that he was having trouble getting funds and supplies for the artillery from the *sub-comisario*.

On March 22, 1839, he signed an "account of the pieces of artillery, tools to service them and other arms which exist at the plaza today." On April 22, 1839, he signed an "account of the tools and other things necessary to serve the Battery at this place, as well as to repair the Guardhouse of the Fort."

From the Book of Spanish Translations, Book 1, page 39, we learn the following about Petronilo Rios' activity in Monterey.

RIOS

David Spence Justice of the Peace of Monterey, vested with the powers of the Ayuntamiento by virtue of the law of March 20, 1837, has this day granted to the citizen Pretonilo [sic] Rios, an increase of eight *varas* frontage, its depth being limited by that of the lot (already) granted to him.

Monterey, Sept.5ᵗʰ 1839.

Manuel Castro,
Sec.

In the left margin of the above document is written the following:

Monterey, April 10, 1849. At this date there was granted to Don Salvador Munras, the actual owner of this lot, an increase of fourteen *varas*, from East to West, and thirty-three *varas* from North to South - in front of the house in which he lives, and is his own property.

Florencio Serrano, Alcalde

Salvador Munras, as we will see later, bought this property from Rios. The reason for the notation in the margin was to keep the line of ownership correct.

Petronilo Rios made a large investment, in the summer of 1840. It is not known whether this was before or after he had ended his career with the artillery. The transaction is found in the Book of Spanish Translation, Book 2, pages 97-99 at the Monterey County Recorder's Office in Salinas.

MARCUS WEST TO PETRONILO RIOS TRANSFER OF A HOUSE

In the Port of Monterey, July 12, 1840, before David Spence, constitutional Justice of the Peace, personally appeared (the foreigner) Marcus West, a resident of the municipality, sold to Petronilo Rios, a house, in the Capital, containing six rooms and a kitchen, with shingle roof, and built on a lot of 90 *varas* frontage by 60 *varas* in depth. The lot is between the house of Jorge Kinlock and the house of the native (Indian) Gregorio, for the sum of $2,000.

Assisting witnesses: Don Antonio Maria Osio, Don Estaban Munraz and Don Benito Diaz, all present and residents of this place.
Signed   David Spence, Marcus West
Asst.   Manuel Castro
Asst.   Jorge Allen

The "foreigner" Marcus West was a native of England. Jorge Kinlock had arrived in Monterey in 1829; he was a cabinet-maker.

It is admitted that we lack proof of what years Petronilo Rios spent at San Miguel. The time that he and his family did spend in San Miguel has endeared them to most county residents who are aware of them. We admit a prejudice in his favor.

Is it possible that Petronilo Rios could remain in charge of the five soldiers at San Miguel, but that the job did not require him to be present there every day? Most of the Indians were dispersed by this time; the services of an army Sergeant, to be in charge of the *escolta*, would not have been needed on a daily basis. For this reason, it is reasonable to assume (to wish?) that Petronilo Rios could be "in charge" of the detachment at San Miguel, and still be able to be Commander of Artillery at the Presidio of Monterey.

It is believed that Petronilo Rios' career in the Mexican army came to its end in 1840. Mission San Miguel was almost abandoned by that time. Eugene Duflot de Mofras, French writer and traveler in California, wrote that he had found less than thirty Indians at Mission San Miguel in 1841.

We have seen that Rafael Gonzales and his wife were the godparents for three children of Petronilo and Catarina Rios. The Rios-Gonzales connection is also to be seen in the fact that Rancho San Bernabe, near present-day King City, consisting of 13,296.98 acres, had been granted by Governor Alvarado to Rafael Gonzales in 1836. In 1839, Jose Castro was involved.

We have already seen that Gonzales and Castro were both owners of the Rancho San Justo- - -granted to Gonzales in 1836 and taken over by Castro in 1839. In 1841, Petronilo Rios obtained a portion of the Rancho San Bernabe grant. The year 1841 suggests that his is where the Rios family moved upon Petronilo Rios being released from the army.

That summer, Thomas O. Larkin has two entries in his "account books" concerning Rios. On June 7, 1841 it reads: "P. Rios bought 1 *Bible*." The entry for June 8-9, 1841 states: "sold other books to P. Rios." Perhaps Petronilo had spare time to devote to reading, now that he was retired from the army.

The purchase of the *Bible* brings to mind a remark made by a great-granddaughter of Petronilo and Catarina Rios, Mrs. Rose Gil Rios Jones of Atascadero; she is the daughter of James (Santiago Ramon) Rios and Marcella Gil Rios. Mrs. Jones stated that the Rios side of the family was "very religious," but that the Gil side was hardly religious at all.

In the fall of 1841, Petronilo Rios did some shopping that was of a more serious nature. The Book of Spanish Translation, Book 1, page 52 has the following:

On the tenth day of September 1841, there

was granted to the citizen Petronilo Rios, a lot of twenty-five *varas* frontage (situate) on line with, and the North of, the one which stands the building of the citizen Don Joaquin Gomez.

As witness my hand in Monterey the day and year above written.
Manuel Castro, Sec.

On the twentieth day of November (in the year) eighteen hundred and forty-one, there was granted to Petronilo Rios, a citizen, a lot of twenty-four *varas* frontage (being) an addition to the one (formerly) granted to him (situate) on line with, and to the north of Don Joaquin Gomez; and of same depth as that previously granted to him.

Witness my hand in Monterey, the twenty-second day of December 1841.   Manuel Castro, Sec.

This second entry can be found in the Book of Spanish Translation, Book 1, page 35, at the Monterey County Recorder's Office in Salinas.

It is thanks to the investigative work of a descendant of Petronilo and Catarina Rios that we have learned a large amount of Petronilo Rios' history. Much information was not discovered by "The Friends of the Adobes, Inc.'" until it was collected and shared by Alpheus E. and Eleanor Garrissere. The Garrisseres began their communication with Virginia Culbert in the early 1980s.

Eleanor Garrissere's husband is a descendant of Petronilo and Catarina's daughter, Maria Antonia Gregoria (1842-1890), who married Jean Falque in 1859. Maxima Falque (1864-1945) married Jean Garrissere (1842-1918) in 1887.

In 1919, Alphonse Garrissere (1890-1955) married Marie Revallier (1893-1978). Alpheus Garrissere married Eleanor Azevedo in 1947. We have the Garrisseres to thank for much of the research that has been done on the families and descendants of Petronilo and Catarina Avila Rios.

A member of the Board of Directors of "The Friends of the Adobes, Inc.," is John Craspay of Bradley. John went to school with Alpheus Garrissere. There is a Garrissere Gulch west of the town of San Ardo; a cattle brand was registered which belonged to A. J. Garrissere.

A J. M. Garrissere adobe had been built in Paris Valley, west of San Ardo. Paris Valley received its name because of the many French and Basque people who settled in that region.

Alpheus and Eleanor Garrissere are residents of the City of San Jose, where Ygnacio Linares, the ancestor of Catarina Avila Rios, had settled in 1784.

PETRONILO RIOS: AFTER HIS ARMY CAREER

Petronilo Rios ended his career with the Mexican army sometime in 1840. On January 7, 1842, while a resident of Monterey, he bought the San Bernabe Rancho from Jesus Molina for $12,000. One square league had been granted to Jesus Molina on March 10, 1841, and two square leagues to Petronilo Rios on January 8, 1842. The San Bernabe Rancho was located to the northwest of present-day King City. The King City-Jolon road passes through this rancho, consisting of 13,296.98 acres, which had originally been granted to Rafael Gonzales in 1836 by Governor Alvarado. Rafael Gonzales was the godfather for three of Petronilo and Catarina's children, as has been noted earlier.

It is interesting to learn how Jesus Molina acquired the San Bernabe Rancho. The details are found in The Book of Spanish Translations, Book 1, pages 326-327, at the Monterey County Recorder's Office in Salinas.

Jesus Molina - Petition
(To Prefect 1st Dist. For Grant of tract called "San Bernabe")

To Prefect of 1st Dist.:

I, Jesus Molina, a citizen and resident in this place, come before your Honor according to law and say:

That having married (in this County) a Neophyte of San Antonio Mission, two children being the fruit of this union, all being with me, as also my wife's fathers and two of her brothers. This large family depends on my personal labor for its support, and at same time I being anxious to secure a place - even if it be small, where I can farm and grow some live stock; and there being vacant, and unclaimed by any one (unoccupied) a tract (of land) called San Bernabe, distant six miles from San Antonio; and being of the extent of a "site" for "grown cattle" at most, as shown in the plat duly attached hereto, I request your Honor to grant it to me.

Wherefore, I pray that on attending my petition you may —passing all the customary procedure — grant to me the above-mentioned place (called) San Bernabe, which I shall consider a favor &c.

Monterey, May 6th 1839

On behalf of petitioner, because he does not know how to write.

Jose Abrego
San Antonio Mission, May 8, 1839

The place called San Bernabe solicited by the citizen Jesus Molina (in the opinion of the administration) can be granted to him, since it is not occupied nor is it needed now by the Ex-Mission of San Antonio, notwithstanding that it has a small house erected thereon. But even this can be granted too, considering that the wife of the petitioner is a Neophyte of said place. - All of which the subscriber begs to report in compliance with the foregoing decree, submitting it to the Prefecture as provided.

Jose de Jesus Pico

Monterey, May 6, 1839

Referred to the administrator of the Ex-Mission San Antonio, that he may report what in his opinion may seem Just and let him return through the proper channel the espediente[sic] to this Prefecture.

Castro

The Book of Spanish Translations, Book 1, pages 343-346, has the following:

JESUS MOLINA
TO PETRONILO RIOS
DEED CONVEYING
SAN BERNABE RANCHO

In the Port of Monterey. . .on the 7th day of January, 1842, before me Jose Zenon Fernandez, Judge of first instance of this Dis-

trict, and before the assisting witnesses. . .
personally came

Jesus Molina, a citizen and resident of this
place of legal age (twenty-five years old) . .
.sells, conveys. . .unto Petronilo Rios, a citizen (also of legal age - twenty-five years old -
a resident of this place, and to me personally
known) a Rancho called "San Bernabe"
which is his own property, by concession to
him made by the Government of this Department, and which original title he presents and
is annexed hereto; and said Rancho is
bounded by the Ranchos known as Las Posas,
San Benito and San Lorenzo.

Together with a house - located on a lot 50
varas square - said house being twenty-five
varas long - from East to West, and seven
varas wide from North to South - containing
three good rooms with brick flooring, heavy
dobe [sic] walls, wooden upper story, but containing two small rooms without any flooring and walls without garret.

Said five rooms have five doors and two
windows, with wooden gratings and wooden
blinds. The said house is roofed with tiles and
all are in good state of preservation. And
grantor hereby declares that the. . .property. .
.is free and clear of all encumbrances; and as
such he now sells it for the price of twelve
hundred dollars. . . .

In witness whereof grantor has hereunto
set his hand with myself before the subscrib-
ing witnesses. . .the instrumental ones being
Don Teodoro Gonzales, Don Gumecindo
Flores, and Florencio Serrano, all of whom
were present, are residents of this place, and
are to me personally known.
(The grantor did not sign, because he can
not write.)
Petronilo Rios
Jose Z. Fernandez
Franco. Jose Ribero, Asst.
Manuel Castro, Asst.

The idea that Petronilo Rios was 25 years of age in
1842 does not square with other records. In that year,
he was about 36 years of age.
Teodoro Gonzales, a Mexican who lived at

Monterey from the time of his arrival, came to California in 1825, as an otter hunter. He remained in California after it was conquered by the United States;
he died in the early 1880s.

Early in 1842, Petronilo Rios petitioned for an addition to Rancho San Bernabe.

To the Hon. The Prefect of the 1st District,
Petronilo Rios, a Mexican by birth, resident
of this Department, and married to a native
of the same, to Your Honor in due form of law,
and proper respect do represent, that. . .to the
support of my family, which is a large one,
depending on me, that I should increase the
extent of the tract of land known by the name
of San Bernabe, within the limits of the Establishment of San Antonio, which I possess
by purchase I made of the same; and as it does
not comprise more than one square league,
according to the title thereof, I desire to have
it increased without prejudice to my
coterminous neighbors, and occupy the vacant
lands that may result, up to the hills on the
East, whereof there is no claimant. I ask Your
Honor to be pleased to grant me the increase
I pray for, after the result of the measurement
that may be made by the Judge, who shall give
the possession. . .that it shall not be more than
four leagues, and in the event that it should
not contain that quantity, then to concede to
me the only amount that may be vacant.
Wherefore I pray Your Honor to admit this
petition with the corresponding map, which.
. .I promise to perfect it, while you are pleased
to forward my petition to the Superior Departmental Government in order that it may grant
my petition. I swear I do not proceed in malice and make the other usual oaths.
Petronilo Rios

Monterey February 18, 1842

Let the agent of the Establishment of San
Antonio report every thing he may deem
proper in reference to the subject.
Estrada.

To the Hon. the Prefect of the 1st District,
Your Honor can accede to the petition of
Don Petronilo Rios for the land of the Rancho
which belonged to Ynes Molina, in consider-

ation of the fact that now she had no longer any stock, or even means of occupying the land, which appertains to this Establishment, no prejudice resulting therefrom.

This is all I can state to Your Honor in reference to the matter.
Mission San Antonio   March 5, 1842
Jose de Jesus Pico

The San Bernabe adobe was located about two miles from the junction of present-day Highway 101 and Jolon Road. The grant extended on both sides of the Salinas River, with San Lorenzo Creek as the northern border on the east side, and Pine Canyon as the northern border on the west side. The southern border of the rancho was the mouth of Quinado Canyon. The rancho took its name from Canada de San Bernabe, whose name goes back to at least March 8, 1776, when it was mentioned by Pedro Font in his diary. [The name honors Saint Barnabas, a native of Cyprus and one of the seventy-two disciples of Christ.]

From the western-most point of Rancho San Bernabe, a trail led up Pine Canyon and through the forest, down to Rancho Milpitas. The King City-Jolon Road passed through this rancho. Petronilo Rios, and his family, probably lived at the San Bernabe until they moved to San Miguel. They first lived at La Estrella; then, in 1851, they moved into the Caledonia adobe, in San Miguel, one-half mile south of the mission.

During the drought of 1863, Francisco Garcia, along with Pancho Narvaez, came into possession of the San Bernabe. In 1846, Henry Cocks, an English marine of a U. S. man-of-war, deserted at Monterey, and had married a daughter of Francisco Garcia. He became a naturalized citizen in Monterey on September 1, 1851.

Cocks moved to the San Bernabe in 1853. Claim was filed on February 9, 1853, and was confirmed on March 20, 1855; an appeal was dismissed on June 8, 1857. Cocks received the patent for the land in 1873. Cocks became a famous justice of the peace for Monterey County. During this time, the adobe was known as Cocks' Station. In 1882, Nicolas Verdugo and his wife, Catarina Espinosa, had a stage stop, hotel and restaurant there. On September 15, 1888, the roof of the adobe was struck by lightning and the shingle roof burned off. The roof was never repaired and the adobe was abandoned to squatters. In 1971, what was left of the walls was knocked down.

July 13, 1843 found Petronilo Rios in a court dispute in Monterey. The following is from the Book of Spanish Translation, Book 1, page 275.

P. RIOS vs J. ANZAR
(For possession of Tract of Land)

On the 13th day of July 1843 personally came before me the citizen Petronilo Rios, representing Da Anta Linares with a referee in the person of citizen Jose Abrego, and the citizen Juan Anzar with the citizen Florencio Serrano as his referee. The Formen claims a right he acquired from the Department of Gov't in (and to) a tract of land upon which he built a house, and sale of same was prevented by the latter at the time of obtaining possession, to which the latter replied that the tract in question is his own and proves the possession he acquired of same the year 1835 by competent judge.

After several arguments by both parties and concessions by the referees, they were (finally) convinced that, to avoid a costly judgment and perhaps complicated cause Anzar should give to Rios two hundred and fifty dollars in silver coin for the house and land above mentioned. This was agreed to and conditioned that the payment should be made within a month, this tribunal issuing the document of sale at the expense of said Anzar. In witness whereof I have hereunto set my hand with the subscribing referees.

Jose Z. Fernandez   Petronilo Rios
Juan M. Anzar
Florencio Serrano   Jose Abrego

The "Da Anta Linares" most likely refers to Dona Antonia Linares, with "Da" being an abbreviation for "Dona," and "Anta" being an abbreviation for "Antonia." She was godmother for Petronilo and Catarina's son, Jose Juan Franquilino, who had been born on July 6, 1843.

Jose Abrego had arrived in California with the Padres-Hijar Company in 1834. He amassed a sizable fortune in Monterey, as a merchant dealing in hats and soap. From 1839-1846, Abrego was treasurer, in charge of the territorial finances. During the Alvarado-Castro revolt, it was Jose Abrego who located the only cannonball in Monterey. This famous shot brought about the surrender of Governor Gutierrez. Bancroft states that he was young, intelligent and of good repute.

An interesting point about Jose Abrego is that he was proud to have imported, at the cost of $600, one of the first three pianos in all of California. The piano, a spinet, had been manufactured in London in 1830; it was brought to California by a sea captain named Stephen Smith.

Governor Alvarado awarded to Jose Abrego the contract for the construction of the two-story government building called *El Cuartel*. This building, in-

Cuartel House, Monterey, California, 1875.

tended to house the soldiers of the Monterey company, was constructed in 1840; it was built of adobe and redwood at the cost of $11,000. This building, during the years of American occupation (1846-1849), served as headquarters of the military governor and his staff. An upper room at one end became the office of Walter Colton and Robert Semple's newspaper, *The Californian*, the first newspaper in California.

Abrego had constructed for his wife, Maria Josefa Estrada, their home: *Casa Abrego*. This house was enlarged and expanded until it covered almost a square block. The timbers used in the ballroom were an unusual feature; they came from the shipwrecked smugglers' ship, the *Natalie*, on which Napoleon was said to have escaped from the island of Elba. Jose Abrego remained a highly respected member of the community of Monterey until his death in 1878, at the age of sixty-five.

On May 28, 1845, Governor Pio Pico, without consulting the Supreme Government of Mexico, had his four assemblymen, Botello, Figueroa, Carlos Carrillo and Ygnacio del Valle pass the decree for the "Renting of Some and For the Converting of other Missions into Pueblos." Article 1 provided that "There will be sold at this capital, to the highest bidder, the Missions

of San Rafael, Dolores, Soledad, San Miguel and La Purisima, which are abandoned by their neophytes."

Article 4 stated: "The public sales of the Missions of San Luis Obispo and San Juan Capistrano shall take place on the first four days of the month of December next, notices inviting bidders being posted up in the towns of the Department. . . .In the same manner, will be sold what belongs to San Rafael, Dolores, San Juan Bautista, Carmelo and San Miguel on the 2d, 3d and 4th of January next."

Within this proclamation was the requirement that if the neophytes (Christianized Indians) did not return to Mission San Miguel within a month, the mission would be declared without owners and subject to sale.

On October 28, 1846, Governor Pio Pico issued a proclamation, ordering the sale of Mission San Miguel. This sale would usher in another chapter in the life of Petronilo Rios and his family. By this time, there had been three additions to the Rios family; again, we do not know where the children were born. Maria Antonia Gregoria was born on May 12, 1842; her godparents were Mariano Silva and his wife, Maria de la Fosse. Mariano Silva arrived in California as Captain of the Artillery at Monterey, and served from 1840 to 1846. He surrendered the city to Sloat in July of 1846; he went to Mazatlan in 1847 or 1848.

Jose Juan Franquilino, also called Jose Francisco, was born on July 6, 1843; the godparents of this child were Vicente Avila and Maria Antonia Linares. Jose Ygnacio had been born on July 31, 1845, but died at birth. The last names of Jose Juan Franquilino's godparents indicate that they could be relatives on the maternal side of the family. It is of interest to note that Rafael Gonzales and his wife were not used as godparents for the last three children. Would this indicate that the Rios family was not living in Monterey at the time?

[We will see that the name of William Reed, the partner of Petronilo Rios, is variously spelled in the records; sometimes it is spelled "Reid" and at other times it is spelled "Read." One would note that the name has two different spellings in the same document.]

The steps to acquire Mission San Miguel, the church building and the mission's property, began with a request to Governor Pio Pico. The following is contained in what is named "Unclassified *Expediente* No. 294."

Guillermo Reid *et als*
Lands of Ex-Mission San Miguel

Jose Juan Franquilino Rios (1843-1883).

To His Exc the Governor

Guillermo Read, a native of London, and a resident of the Mexican Republic since about fourteen years ago, married with a native woman and having a family. Also Petronilo Rios and Jose Miguel Garcia, Mexicans by birth. We three, to the gratitude of Your Excellency in due form of law do represent: that in view of the fact that the Establishment of the Ex-Mission of San Miguel is vacant, containing some habitable rooms, where families can lodge, and comprising a tract of land sufficient to raise cattle and yield crops, as shown by the map, a duplicate of which is duly annexed, to the extent of twelve square leagues, a little more or less, making as boundaries in the direction of the South, on one side (from the river named San Miguel) Las Gallinas and from the other side Santa Ysabel; on the North by Chumal & Cholame, on the East by El Valle, and on the West by the Sierra de las Tablas and the [gap] porteruela del Nacimiento.

Wherefore we pray Your Excellency to be pleased in the exercise of the authority you are worthily vested with, to grant us the ownership of said Establishment of San Miguel, with its tenements and land to the extent of twelve square leagues as comprised according to the map and now vacant. A favor and grace for which we will ever be thankful swearing it is not done in malice & making the necessary Oaths etc.
Petronilo Rios
Guillermo Read Miguel Garcia X

Postscript - Common paper is used in the absence of the proper stamp.

Angeles June 13, 1846

Let the present petition be returned to the interested parties, as the Government is on its way to the North, where the petitioners will make application, and the proper decision will be rendered thereon.
Pico

Pio Pico, Constitutional Governor of the Department of the Californias,
Whereas the residents of this Department, Guillermo Reid, Petronilo Rios and Miguel Garcia, have made application for their personal benefit and that of their families, for the lands which are vacant at the Mission of San Miguel, now entirely abandoned, and for the tenements existing at said Mission; having previously made the investigations in the matter in accordance with the laws and regulations of the 18 August 1824 and of the 21st November 1828; in the exercise of the authority in me invested, in the name of the Mexican Nation, and previously authorized by Excellent the Departmental Assembly for the alienation of such Missions as may be proper, I have by a decree of this date, thought proper to grant them the vacant lands that may be left from such previous concessions as may have been made, and also the existing tenements in San Miguel, subject to the approval of the Excellent the Departmental Assembly and under the following conditions:
1st They may fence the lands they have asked at San Miguel now vacant, and not belonging to the property of private persons, without detriment to the roads & servitudes.

They will enjoy them freely and exclusively making of them such use. . .as may best suit them, but they cannot sell nor alienate them to anyone, but if they should be under the necessity of doing so, after complying with the requirements of the regulations of the year 1828 on the subject, they will advise the Government for the proper decision.

2nd They will pay to the Departmental Gov't as an indemnity for the existent tenements in San Miguel the sum of six hundred dollars.

3rd They will request the proper judge to give the judicial possession in virtue of this title by which the boundaries shall be marked and the necessary land marks set.

4th The lands of which donation is made to them are stricktly those which may result to be vacant outside the limits of the contiguous property of others. The judge who may give this possession will have them measured according to the ordinance taking care that it be done correctly, and will inform the Government of the number of leagues they may obtain.

5th They will not prevent the native Indians at that place from settling there if they wish to do so, for which purpose there can be marked out such lands as may be useful to them in proportion to the means of each of them. Consequently I order that holding the present as a firm and valid title, the same be recorded in the respective book and delivered to the interested parties for their security & further ends.

Given in Santa Barbara on common paper in the absence of that of the proper stamp, this 4th of July 1846.

Mission San Miguel bears the distinction of having been the last mission sold - - - on July 4, 1846. Three days after the sale of Mission San Miguel, Commodore John D. Sloat, on his flagship *Savannah*, arrived at Monterey with 250 marines and sailors. That day, July 7th, the American flag was unfurled at Monterey. Governor Pio Pico fled to Mexico on the night of August 10, 1846.

Daniel E. Krieger, in his book *San Luis Obispo: Looking Backward into the Middle Kingdom* tells us that Rios and Reed ". . .planned to raise sheep, and harvest the timber near Cambria, which was on mis-

Drawing made in 1864.

sion lands." Visitors to the Rios-Caledonia today will be able to see some of the original timbers which were brought from the forests near Cambria and made into 14-foot rafters for the construction of the adobe.

The adobe's construction had begun about 1835 as a residence for the civilian administrator who was on his way to become the administrator of Mission San Miguel. Petronilo Rios supervised the construction of the adobe.

The following is an interesting document from the fall of 1846. It appears that Miguel Garcia wanted to distance himself from Petronilo Rios.

I, Miguel Garcia say: That by my free will, and with no other desire than to please myself. . . I obligate myself to separate myself from the companionship of my *padrino* the Senor Petronilo Rios, remenising in the favor [?] of time that my said *Padrino* has given me

La Casa de Senor Rios.

on the Establishment of San Miguel, renouncing forever all right that I might by law have to the same, and I am resolved to take the [?] of living with my [?] which is mine agreeable to me; this and I have said being the only case for my doing so, because I can certify truthfully, for I have received no bad treatment from my said *Padrino,* but on the contrary have received many favors, I witness thereof I ask that this. . .may be made out & signed by two witnesses. I not knowing how to write.

Monday, September 11th, 1846
Asst. Escobar
Asst. M. Rafael Gonzales

State of California, County of Santa Clara
    Be it recorded that on this 16th day of April A.D. 1852, before me the undersigned Notary Public in and for the County and State aforesaid, duly commissioned and sworn personally appeared I, Rafael Gonzales to be well known to be one of the subscribing witnesses to the foregoing instrument in writing and he having been by me only, sworn, on both deposed and said that he was present when Miguel Garcia signed the said instrument in writing, and that said Garcia signed the same freely & voluntarily and declared that he executed the same for the uses and purposes in the said writing specified.
    In testimony whereof, I have hereunto set my hand and affixed my seal of office at the City of San Jose County & State aforesaid, the day & year last aforesaid.
    I, Alexander Yvebl
    Notary Public

With this, Miguel Garcia drops out of the story.

William Reed was an English sailor who came to California in 1837. (The fourteen years mentioned in the document above would have put him in California as early as 1832.) He worked as a lumberman in the Monterey district in 1837-1839; he was also named as pilot and mate of the schooner, *California,* during the period of 1837-1839. Later, because of his occupation as a ship pilot, Reed was called "Piloto" by the Indians and his Mexican friends.

Reed's experience in lumbering allowed him to work as a sawyer for Ynocente Garcia, the second administrator of Mission San Miguel. Ynocente Garcia has written that "Pilot Reed (who years later was murdered with all of his family and others at San Miguel), I placed in charge of the sawmill. Everything was peaceful then."

William Reed married Maria Antonia Vallejo, who was said to be a niece of Petronilo Rios' wife, and an illegitimate daughter of Mariano Guadalupe Vallejo.

William Reed and his family had been living in buildings at Mission San Miguel since 1845.

Edwin Bryant, traveling with John C. Fremont, has this to relate on December 10, 1846:

We passed the Mission of San Miguel about 3 o'clock, and encamped in a grove of large oak timber trees three or four miles south of it. . . . All the buildings, except the church and the principal range of houses contiguous, have fallen into ruins, and an Englishman, his wife and one small child, with two or three Indian servants, are the sole inhabitants.

Bryant later adds, "The Englishman professes to have purchased the mission and all the lands belonging to it for $300!"

The following letter to Don Jose Mariano Bonilla, *Alcalde* of San Luis Obispo, gives an idea of the status of the mission property, during the period of American occupation and prior to statehood. (Again, we note a variant spelling of William Reed's last name.)

View of Mission ruins, looking toward northeast.

STATE DEPARTMENT OF THE TERRITORY OF CAL.,
MONTEREY, SEPTEMBER 15th, 1847

Sir: In reply to so much of your letter of the 4th inst. as relates to the mission of San Miguel, the Governor directs me to say that the question of title to the lands of said mission cannot now be decided; and that until the subject can be further investigated, the present occupant, Mr. Read, will be left in possession.

As a difficulty seems to occur in determining what rooms in the mission properly belong to the parish priest, the Governor directs that you select three rooms in said mission for the use of the priest, and put him in possession of such rooms; you will, however, in this selection choose such rooms as will give the least inconvenience to the family of Mr. Read.

Let both the priest and Mr. Read fully understand that their possession is in no way to affect the validity of existing titles. With respect to the possession of the buildings, etc., at San Luis Obispo, as directed in my letter of the 24th of August, I have now to remark that that order was not intended in any way to affect the validity of existing claims to said property. It was only temporary in its character, and cannot affect any title or claim which Mr. Wilson and others may have to the mission or mission lands.

You will therefore proceed to put the parish priest in possession of such lands and tenements as in your opinion properly belonged to the priest, on the 7th of July, 1846.

You must, however, let the priest and other claimants perfectly understand that this possession gives them no title whatever, but is merely a temporary arrangement for the mutual convenience of the parties concerned, the question of title being left for future decision.

Very respectfully,
Your obedient servant,
H. W. Halleck, Lieut. of Engineers and
Sec. of State for Ter. of Cal.

William Reed seems to have had some concern that his ownership of the property might not be secure. He wrote his questions to Governor Richard B. Mason. The reply he received was from Henry W. Halleck, Secretary of State.

Monterey, September 18, 1847

Sir: I am directed by the Governor to acknowledge the receipt of your letter of blank date, and say to you that the existing government has no intention of interfering with your title to the Mission of San Miguel; but as the title is incomplete, and as there are other claimants to the property, it has been deemed best to make a temporary arrangement between yourself and the priests, until the subject could be satisfactorily examined by the proper authorities.

Another letter, to Jose Mariano Bonilla, *Alcalde* of San Luis Obispo, throws some light on the matter.

Monterey, November 30, 1847.

Sir: Your letter of the 22nd instant is before me. The Indians you speak of as belonging to the Mission, can be put in possession of the land that was granted to them by Micheltorena in 1844.

I am etc., R. B. Mason, Governor of California

On October 10, 1848, Dr. Rob Murray at Monterey wrote a letter to Dr. John S. Griffin in Los Angeles. From this letter, we learn a little more about William Reed and his activities.

I found that Mr. Reed had left San Miguel for the Placer taking with him the two horses which you left there. I wrote him by Warner to sell both horses for the largest price in gold and turn the money over to Warner for you. I took the liberty to alter your orders, because I thought that riding them to the Placer had repaid Reed for the keeping of them.

We are reminded that Rios, Reed and Garcia had purchased Mission San Miguel, and its property, on July 4th, 1846. Petronilo Rios, along with his family, had moved into a large, one-story adobe house which was located on the Estrella River, approximately six miles east of the mission. The location of the adobe was perhaps ¾ of a mile east of the spot where today's Airport Road crosses the Estrella River.

While the Rios family lived at La Estrella, a man by the last name of Colgate was said to have been the caretaker back at the Caledonia adobe and the mission. This item of information comes from Eva C. Iversen's book, *Mission San Miguel Arcangel*.

The Great Register of San Luis Obispo County for 1867 and also for 1871 both list a "Louis Gonzaga Colgate," as an inn-keeper in Hot Springs district. The

La Estrella Adobe.

Drawn by Steve Kalar

Dolly Bader and Virginia Peterson in 1954 at ruins of La Estrella Adobe.

La Estrella Adobe, 1962.

man's first name most likely would be "Luis," because Luis Gonzaga is an historical person; it is entirely possible that this is the Colgate that Eva C. Iversen had mentioned. Mr. Colgate was a naturalized citizen; the Great Register shows that his date of registration was April 6, 1867.

Our tentative identification of Mr. Colgate, and his role in connection with the Mission San Miguel property, is confirmed by an item in the September 2, 1887 edition of the *San Miguel Messenger*: "Louis Colgate, sometimes called Don Luis, a party well-known in this county, was found dead in his bed at the Lick House, San Jose, last Friday. It is said that he was, for a number of years, in charge of the Mission property at this place."

According to Helen S. Giffen, in her book, *Casas & Courtyards: Historic Adobe Houses in California*, Petronilo Rios' first residence was the adobe on Estrella River. He did not move into the Caledonia adobe until he found that he would not be able to secure the title to the land on the Estrella River from the United States Land Commission.

Part of the problem with proving legal title to the property, was that circumstantial evidence later showed that the transaction of selling Mission San Miguel, and its properties, took place about July 11th, rather than July 4th. By July 11th, the United States had control of California.

La Estrella adobe had been constructed during earlier mission days as a residence for the *mayordomo* of the rancho. The *mayordomo* was a ranchero's resident manager and overseer of rancho employees. The rancho system was highly dependent on Indian labor and a typical rancho might have around a hundred of such Indian workers serving as domestic servants, *vaqueros* and field laborers. What the Indians received in return for the hard work of the rancho was food, clothing and shelter. At that time, La Estrella was mainly used for raising sheep.

The name La Estrella (meaning "the star") is explained by Lt. George H. Derby, who was ordered to make a topographic report to the headquarters of the Tenth Military District in Monterey in April of 1850, while California was still a Territory of the United States. According to Lt. Derby:

La Estrella Adobe site looking west, 1997.

La Estrella Adobe site looking north, 1997.

Four valleys diverge from this point, through the south-west one of which leads the road from San Luis Obispo, entering from the main coast road near the rancho of Paso de Robles.

The peculiarity of the divergence of these four valleys, and their corresponding ridges from this point resembling the rays of a star, has given it its very appropriate name- - - Estrella.

This report was written at Monterey, July 10, 1850, to Major Edward R. S. Canby. George Horatio Derby was a Massachusetts-born army officer who established a reputation for being a practical joker while at West Point.

Following his service during the Mexican War, he was assigned to California, during the 1850s, as a lieutenant charged with making explorations and reports on the region. Edward R. S. Canby would go on to become a General, and then be killed by Modoc Indians on April 11, 1873; this took place during peace negotiations during the Modoc Indian War of 1872-73, in northern California.

On July 16, 1844, Governor Manuel Micheltorena had granted to the Christian Indians of San Miguel three pieces of property: Las Gallinas ("the hens"), El Nacimiento (on present-day Camp Roberts) and La Estrella. Neither the size nor the location of these grants was specified; they were not given to individuals, but the land was to be held in trust, by the church, for all Indians of Mission San Miguel.

Ynocente Garcia, Mission San Miguel administrator from 1836 to 1841, also mentions "Los Duraznos" and "La Vina" as other ranchos where the Indians were to receive possession of the land. The locations of these two ranchos are not known at this date. Garcia said that the Indians did not want the above-mentioned lands, but were hoping to be given El Paso de Robles, La Asuncion, or some other mission lands which were considered to be better than the ones being offered.

The Indians were also willing to part with Cholame, Huer Huero and Canamo ("hemp field"). In any case, the United States Land Commission later rejected these claims; the reason for the rejection is that the neophytes had not occupied and cultivated the lands as individual property, as required.

Since Petronilo Rios, William Reed and Miguel Garcia had purchased Mission San Miguel on July 4, 1846, La Estrella and these other properties would have been considered part of the purchase. Also considered part of the purchase would have been the Caledonia adobe.

During this period, the final three children were added to the Rios family. Victoria was born on December 23, 1846, Maria Ygnacia Victoria was born on January 31, 1847 and Jose Ygnacio was born on December 24, 1849. He was given the name of the male child who had been born in 1845, but had died at birth.

It is interesting to note that Jose Ygnacio's ancestor on his mother's side, Salvador Ygnacio Linares, had been born on Christmas Eve in 1775.

Governor Mariano Chico, Jose Maria Castanares and Children of Petronilo Rios

Jose Maria Castanares, and his wife Ana Maria Gonzales, were the god-parents for the second child of Petronilo and Catarina Rios. This child, Maria Luisa, was born on September 23, 1834. What makes this of interest to people over 160 years later is the fact that the god-parents were involved in one of the most attention-catching incidents in early California history.

A Mexican from Puebla, Jose Maria Castanares came to California in 1833. He served as clerk for the administrator of customs, Rafael Gonzales. Rafael Gonzales was a Mexican who had been appointed as administrator of customs at Monterey in 1829; he did not arrive in California until he came with Governor Figueroa in 1833. Gonzales had been a lieutenant in the Mexican war of independence from Spain; Hubert Howe Bancroft stated that Rafael Gonzales was "an ignorant man of good character." In 1833, Alfred Robinson, who had come to California from Massachusetts in 1829, was in the employ of Bryant & Sturgis Company, following the hide & tallow trade. In his book, *Life in California Before the Conquest*, Robinson had this to say about Rafael Gonzales: "A new administrator of the customs had also arrived. . .His name was Don Rafael Gonzales, alias, 'El Pintito'- - -as well calculated to discharge his duties as he was to navigate a steamboat through the Straits of Magellan."

In 1835, Rafael Gonzales was *alcalde* (judge-mayor) of Monterey, and was the Governor's secretary. In 1836, Gonzales was granted Rancho San Justo el Viejo y San Bernabe; this land was located near present-day Hollister, in San Benito County. Rafael Gonzales and his wife would later be the god-parents of three of the Rios children.

It was a daughter of Rafael and Carmen Gonzales, Ana Maria Gonzales, who married Jose Maria Castanares. He was 29 years old in 1836; his amours with Ildefonsa Herrera, wife of *sub-comisario* Jose Maria Herrera of Solis Revolt fame, were the basis of a *cause celebre* at Monterey. Ildefonsa was the daughter of Captain Miguel Gonzales.

Captain Miguel Gonzales came to California from Mexico as a captain of artillery in 1825. (This is the same time period that Petronilo Rios came from Mexico, and both men were in the artillery.) Captain Gonzalez was *comandante de armas* at Monterey from 1826-1828.

Jose de Jesus Pico, in his *Acontecimientos en California*, has written the following about Captain Miguel Gonzalez.

> **That same year of 1826 the majordomo of San Juan, Inocente Garcia, was beaten brutally by order of the Commander of Monterey and Captain of Artillery, Miguel Gonzalez, "the Monkey." It was said that it was because he treated with utmost contempt a sister-in-law who was having illicit relations with an artilleryman; but I believe that it was because Garcia, who was a very strong and agile man, beat the artilleryman and a captain in the same manner.**

> **That Gonzalez was a very despotic man, a real devil and very ugly- - -small of body and dark- - -he scarcely knew how to read or write and continually had the soldiers beaten. He was a man whom we did not like, but we went to his home many times, because he had two daughters, one of them pretty, called Alfonza, the same who later became the wife of the Sub-commander Don Jose Maria Herrera, and who caused so much scandal in Monterey in 1836, when Don Mariano Chico was the Governor of the Province.**

Hubert Howe Bancroft has written that Gonzalez was often in trouble and was finally sent away in 1830.

Jose Maria Herrera had been expelled from California in 1830 because of complicity in the Solis Revolt; he returned to Monterey in 1834 with the Padres-Hijar company to resume his former position as manager of territorial finances. This time, Herrera did not become involved in territorial controversies, but he acquired disagreeable prominence because of his wife. She had an illicit relationship with Jose Maria Castanares.

At the time we are examining, Mariano Chico (1796-1850) was the governor. Chico was the 10th Mexican governor of California, and had been appointed departmental governor on December 16, 1835; he arrived in California at the end of April of 1836.

On June 23, 1836, from Los Angeles, Governor Chico notified the territorial assembly, at Monterey, that he had determined to put Missions Santa Ynez and San Buenaventura into secular hands. He stated that he would do likewise with Mission San Miguel, except that he was having difficulty finding a suitable person to take over San Miguel. The governor gave as the reason for his decision to remove the two missions from church control was the fact that Father Duran had refused to offer High Mass on the occasion of Chico's swearing to the new constitution while at Santa Barbara.

As will be seen in another chapter, Ygnacio Coronel was later deemed a fit person for the position at San Miguel, and Chico appointed him as *comisionado* of San Miguel on July 14, 1836.

It is interesting to see what Pio Pico, who would later be the final Mexican governor of California, had to say about Mariano Chico.

I knew nothing of his character, only that it was said that he was a crude man, very extravagant, with pretensions of being a poet, physician, etc.

The description of Governor Chico, by Jose de Jesus Pico, was a little more specific. In his *Acontecimientos en California*, Jose de Jesus Pico wrote:

Senor Chico was tall, slender, blond, good-looking and of good manners, about fifty to sixty years old- - -toothless- - -and he wore green glasses- - -he was a man of very bad temper and he arrived like one who comes to conquer a lawless country. Chico brought with him a young woman of twenty-five to twenty-eight years, very beautiful and of graceful build, whom he presented to society as his niece- - -but the news that she was not a niece but his concubine did not take long to arrive from Mexico.

This naturally produced a disagreeable effect among the upright families of Monterey, and although the latter continued to show marks of respect to Senor Chico because he was Governor and Commander General, they avoided all contact with the young woman whose name was Cruz.

Chico made himself very unpopular- - -he had serious disagreements with the body of magistrates and with other persons, most particularly with *Alcalde* Don Jose Ramon Estrada because of certain scandals between the wife of Commissary Jose Maria Herrera and Don Jose Maria Castanares, of which I give no details because I know that the particulars are recorded in the public archives, from which they can be obtained.

Mariano Chico quickly alienated most Californians by his insistence on centralized government; he wanted the province to be dependent on Mexico in all matters. He also offended people by his personal behavior, and made himself the most hated ruler the province ever had.

The above-mentioned amours were more or less notorious in Monterey for some time before the persons more directly interested chose to make trouble.

Dona Ana Maria Gonzales began to agitate the matter in February 1836, and was prosecuted by Herrera for slander. The case lasted from April to June, and was then dismissed by Herrera, who in May had begun another prosecution against Castanares and Ildefonsa Herrera for adultery.

On May 28th, the two allegedly-guilty people were arrested for adultery by the *alcalde*, Jose Ramon Estrada. [Estrada would later be the grantee of Rancho San Simeon.] Castanares was locked up in jail, and Ildefonsa was deposited, as was the custom, in the house of a respectable citizen, Francisco Pacheco; Ildefonsa was a friend of Governor Chico's niece, Dona Cruz, who was known to be the Governor's mistress

While Castanares was in prison, and his paramour was in enforced seclusion, a company of *maromeros*, or rope-dancers, who were acrobats who performed their stunts while swinging from ropes around a large pole, gave a performance in one of the buildings of the Presidio, at which everyone in the town of Monterey was present. When Governor Mariano Chico entered, he was accompanied not only by his mistress, Dona Cruz, (whom he introduced as his niece), but also by her friend Dona Ildefonsa Herrera, who had been liberated from house-arrest, for the occasion, at the request of Dona Cruz.

There was so much indignation and excitement at the appearance of this notorious pair in the Governor's place of honor, that some ladies left the room in disgust. *Alcalde* Jose Ramon Estrada felt that his authority as a judge had been insulted by Ildefonsa's release from house-arrest, and her presence at this event. *Alcalde* Estrada released Castanares from jail and gave him a prominent seat at the show, across from where the Governor was seated. From that location, Castanares is said to have ostentatiously saluted his paramour at the Governor's side. Governor Chico was beside himself with rage.

Angered by the boldness of the *alcalde*, the next day Governor Chico marched with a military escort to the hall of the *ayuntamiento* (town council), and placed Estrada under arrest. The military force at Monterey was small, and most of the soldiers were in sympathy with Chico's enemies.

Returning to the writings of Jose de Jesus Pico, we learn:

> **Chico stripped Estrada of the verge of justice and placed him under house arrest. But Estrada did not remain arrested. About fifty of us were called to arms, among whom I remember Don Santiago Estrada, Don Francisco Soto, Trinidad Espinosa, me, etc. Almost all had been soldiers- - -we presented ourselves armed to Don Jose Ramon Estrada in his house to offer him our services. Of this Senor Chico had knowledge but he did not dare to take measures against us- - -in truth we had a very small force in Monterey and that which he had sent for in the South did not come to him- - -besides, all the troops were of our people and friends of Don Jose Ramon Estrada. At the first skirmish that would have occurred, Senor Chico would probably have lost his life.**

The arrest of *Alcalde* Ramon Estrada was probably on June 27th. Teodoro Gonzales, the *regidor* (councilman) took the position of *alcalde* and seems to have incited the citizens to resist Chico's encroachment on the rights of the municipal authorities. The governor feared that not only his authority, but his life, was in danger. This critical state of affairs lasted for several days. Then, on July 15th, orders were sent by the governor for troops to come to Monterey.

However, Indian troubles at San Diego and also on the Sonoma frontier gave the military officers at each place a convenient excuse for not promptly obeying the order of their chief for assistance.

On July 29, 1836, the Governor sent a communication to the *diputacion* (local legislature), stating that since there was great popular excitement because of his suspension of the *alcalde*, and since he had no moral or physical support, he would be going to Mexico at once, "in quest of aid by which to restore order."

Herrera withdrew his suit, on July 30th, and consented to the freeing of the prisoners, on the condition that Castanares should leave the place, and not come within twelve leagues of the Custom House, as long as he remained in California.

Meanwhile, another bitter controversy had been raging between Dona Ana Maria Gonzales and Herrera, who hated each other much more heartily than they did their unfaithful spouses. Herrera had made some charges against the lady's character in his slander suit. Now Dona Ana Maria Gonzales brought suit to obtain certain documents needed for her own justification, but which her opponent declared she intended to use to his detriment to keep the scandal alive.

At the end of June, Herrera suspended prosecution of Castanares because "the public tranquillity had been disturbed by events growing out of the matter, and harmony lost between the authorities, so that very serious consequences were to be feared unless the cause of contention were removed."

Mariano Chico sailed from Monterey on the *Clementine* on July 31, 1836. When he arrived at Santa Barbara, the people of that town prevented him from landing there. Chico never came back to California. He would become governor of Agua Caliente in 1844, and *commandante-general* of Guanajato in 1846. In Chico's place, Lieutenant-Colonel Nicolas Gutierrez was left in charge. A very few days after Gutierrez took command, the inhabitants of Monterey rebelled against him. The leaders of this rebellion were Juan Bautista Alvarado and Jose Castro.

During Alvarado's term of office (1836-1842), his uncle Mariano Guadalupe Vallejo and Jose Castro were military *commandantes*, and were called "co-governors" by some historians.

Concerning this rebellion, Jose de Jesus Pico gives some details, in his *Acontecimientos en California*, about the hostilities.

> **Gutierrez already knew what to expect and he had made trenches everywhere, placing a cannon in each post and in the entrance to the church- - -it was well parapeted with an immense number of sacks and bags of sand. The troops were concentrated inside the Presidio . . . .Our troops were drawn up at the side of El Castillo.**
>
> **A ship was there that the American Captain Hinckley commanded. The latter was asked for powder and cannon balls because in El Castillo, which we found abandoned,**

there were no arms- - -all had been taken inside the Presidio. Some cannons had been left there because Captain Munoz, commander of Artillery, believed that even if we should have a plaza for cannons, we would not know how to manipulate them; but he was mistaken, because among us there were men who had been artillerymen. With the balls and powder that Hinckley sent us we made cartridges; for this I even gave my cotton ponchos- - -with which the small sacks of powder were made.

Meanwhile, Alvarado and Castro went with *Licenciado* Pena to El Castillo and they loaded a cannon which was placed in charge of my brother-in- law, Carlos Villa- - - they fired a cannon shot and the ball hit the ridge of the office of the Commanding General- - - another shot, fired at the steeple of the church, demolished a piece of stone. . . .We entered Monterey with a flag of truce and saw that there was no difficulty in conferring. . . .Finally, in a few days, Gutierrez, Munoz and Nicanor Estrada were embarked for Mexico.

On February 19, 1842, Ana Maria Gonzales Castanares sued her husband, Jose Maria Castanares, whose illicit love-life had scandalized Monterey in 1836. *Alcalde* Jose Fernandez sent Ana Maria home to her father, Rafael Gonzales, to think it over. Nearly a year passed before she withdrew her complaint and rejoined her husband on December 7th.

Jose Maria Castanares was claimant for Rancho Arroyo de los Calsoncillos, eleven square leagues, in present-day Santa Clara County. The grant was made on December 28, 1843, by Governor Manuel Micheltorena. The claim was filed on March 2, 1853, but was rejected by the land commission on April 24, 1855. The appeal was dismissed, on February 12, 1857, for failure of prosecution.

In 1845, Jose Maria Castanares was sent to Mexico by General Castro on a mission of which little is known; he never returned to California. In 1847, he was serving as a colonel in the Mexican army.

On July 24, 1841, Rafael Gonzales had been the grantee of Rancho San Miguelito de Trinidad, of five leagues; its location is in present-day Monterey County. His claim was filed on February 9, 1852 and confirmed by the land commission on March 1, 1853. The district court approved the grant on September 24, 1855, and the appeal was dismissed on February 17, 1857. The grant, which had been made by Governor Juan Bautista Alvarado, consisted of 22,135.89 acres.

For a time, Rafael Gonzales lived in San Juan Bautista. When he moved back to Monterey, he hired Jose Maria Gil (1821-1891) to operate the San Miguelito Rancho while he lived in Monterey.

Don Jose Maria Gil had been born in Madrid, Spain, on December 14, 1821; his father, Jose Leon Gil, was a native of Scotland who had married a Spanish lady by the name of Louisa Ollas. When Jose Maria Gil was about seven years old, he and his parents went to Mexico. At the age of twenty-one, Jose Maria Gil came to California; after spending some time as a successful gold-seeker, he located near Jolon. There, he purchased 260 acres of land and became a prosperous sheep and cattle rancher. In 1850, he married Juliana Gomez, who died seven years later, leaving him three sons; they were Mariano (born 1853), Jose Maria (born 1856) and Miguel Tai Maria (born 1856). In 1860, Mr. Gil married Maria Linares, who bore him nine sons and five daughters. Three of the sons, Albert, William and Augustine became bankers in Central America.

In Monterey, Rafael Gonzales was granted, in 1841, a large town lot behind the newly-constructed government building, *El Cuartel*. He built a two-story adobe house on that property. In January of 1856, Gonzales sold the house and surrounding property to Jose Abrego, who re-sold it one month later. [In 1856, a Frenchman, Juan Giradin and his wife Manuela Perez, purchased the adobe; they were Robert Louis Stevenson's landlords. Broke and in poor health, the twenty-nine year old Scotsman had arrived in Monterey in 1879. Stevenson resided in the building, then called the "French Hotel," for about one month. Since that time, it has been called the "Stevenson House." The people of California have two people to thank for the fact that we have the "Stevenson House" as an historical monument. Mrs. Celia Tobin Clark and Mrs. Edith Van Antwerp saved the building from destruction when they purchased it and gave it to the people of California.]

Rafael Gonzales and his wife, Carmen Sierra, were the god-parents for three children of Petronilo and Catarina Rios: Jose Simon in 1835, Jose Maria Alejo in 1838 and Estaban in 1839. (A son of Rafael and Carmen Gonzales was Mauricio Gonzales, who was granted Rancho Cholame in 1843. This rancho, consisting of six leagues, extended on both sides of what became the boundary between Monterey County and San Luis Obispo County.)

During the drought of 1863-1864, Rafael Gonzales lost five thousand head of cattle on Rancho San Miguelito; Jose Maria Gil left the San Miguelito in order to maintain his stock on his own property west of Jolon. One of the daughters of Jose Maria and Maria Linares Gil was named Marcella; she married James (Santiago) Ramon Rios. He was a grandson of Petronilo and Catarina Rios, and had been born in San Miguel on May 1, 1859. James and Marcella became the parents of seven children, one of whom is Mrs. Rose Gil Rios Jones of Atascadero. [Rose's brother, Frank William Rios, was born in the Caledonia adobe in April of 1901, and lived in the Santa Margarita area until he passed away in 1971.]

Another daughter of Jose Maria and Maria Linares Gil was named Mariah; she became the wife of Egobilo (E. H.) Rios, a brother of James (Santiago) Rios. Egobilo, or "Bill" and Mariah raised a family of five children. He had been born in San Miguel on October 12, 1863; he died in 1892.

Rafael Gonzales died at Monterey in 1868, at age 82.

In 1869, the San Miguelito was sold to Charles Polemas of New Jersey; this man brought the first race horses into Monterey County. He also bred vast numbers of turkeys, which he had herded, like droves of cattle, into the Salinas Valley. Two great-grandsons of Petronilo and Catarina Rios were involved in herding these flocks of turkeys.

Alexander Gil and Leon Gil took a two-horse wagon, and two extra horses, to haul water and food for themselves, the horses, two sheep dogs and for the turkeys. One of the two persons walked, while the other person drove the wagon. This trek took thirty days. Alexander Gil and Leon Gil were grandsons of Jose Maria Gil, mentioned above.

TWO DECEMBERS:
1846 AND 1848

Action during the American conquest of California directly touched the area of northern San Luis Obispo County in December of 1846. John Charles Fremont passed through this region, as he led his "California Battalion of Mounted Riflemen" from Monterey south to suppress the activities of the armed *Californios*.

John C. Fremont, military explorer, opened many western trails and was the officer to whom the Californians surrendered in 1847.

From a daguerroeotype by Brady

For some background, we need to be aware that John C. Fremont, while on one of the "scientific" surveys he was sent by the United States government, arrived in the Sacramento Valley earlier in the year of 1846. He went to Monterey to obtain a permit, from the Mexican government, to remain in the Sacramento Valley for the winter. Instead of heading back there, he camped on Hartnell's Alisal Rancho. Fremont was ordered to leave the territory, but instead, moved to

the top of Hawk's Peak and raised a United States flag. (The peak today is called Fremont's Peak.)

The Mexican commander, General Manuel Castro, gathered a force of several hundred men to force Fremont out of his position. Fremont retreated, "slowly and growlingly," toward Sacramento, and avoided conflict- - -as had been his instructions from the United States government.

Soon afterwards, war broke out between the United States and Mexico. Fremont enlisted volunteers from among the American settlers in California, and formed the "California Battalion of Mounted Riflemen." He went to Monterey, which was in American hands, and received the commission as lieutenant-colonel; he was given orders to secure men and horses for the war in Southern California. In pursuit of this objective, a band of Fremont's men was driving horses from San Juan Bautista to Monterey.

Captain Charles D. Burrass, in charge of originally bringing the 500 horses from Sacramento, had a miscellaneous group of 34 people, including ten Walla Walla Indians and two Delaware Indians. This group arrived at San Juan Bautista on the same day, November 15th, as another group led by Captain Bluford K. Thompson. Thompson's group of 35 men was made up of American rancheros, runaway sailors, Englishmen, Germans and Negroes. The two groups joined forces, although neither company had been trained together and there was no unity of command.

On November 16, 1846, at Rancho La Natividad, northeast of present-day Salinas, this group was attacked by a force led by Manuel Castro. This "Battle of Natividad" was the only military engagement of the Mexican War, in this state, that was fought outside of Southern California. The *Californios*, who numbered about 150, inflicted serious injuries upon their opponents; four or five were killed, and an equal number wounded. Castro's forces suffered somewhat more severely, and retired from the field.

Fremont and his expedition of 430 people entered San Luis Obispo County, just after they had made a thirteen-day journey from Mission San Juan Bautista, experiencing many difficulties along the way. The grass in the region had been too sparse to sustain their horses. When the Battalion left San Juan Bautista, they had a herd of 100 cattle, which was intended to supply them with meat along the way. The cattle were slaughtered at the rate of 13 or 14 per day.

At Rancho Los Coches ("the pigs"), between Soledad and today's King City, Fremont and his men camped. They also helped themselves to four oxen, four horses and fifty bullocks, valued at $580. At the time, Los Coches belonged to Maria Josefa, a daughter of Feliciano Soberanes; she had married William Brenner Richardson, a tailor who had come from Baltimore, Maryland, in 1839. He built Los Coches adobe in 1843. The property was in her name because her husband never became a Mexican citizen. A granddaughter, Mrs. Adelina Richardson, has a copy of the unpaid bill in her possession.

Because their food supply was rapidly being exhausted, foragers for Fremonts forces were happy to discover the large number of sheep that were being raised in the vicinity of Mission San Miguel.

Some interesting information, concerning Fremont's capture of Mission San Miguel, can be found in the writings of Dr. Hartwell B. Stanley, official historian for the 1897 Centennial Celebration of the founding of Mission San Miguel. We need to take a digression for a short time, because Dr. Hartwell B. Stanley had a section of his writings called "Treasure Trove," which was not included in the printed centennial pamphlet. Ella Adams provided a copy of this information; it had been given to her by Dr. Leo L. Stanley, son of Dr. Hartwell B. Stanley.

Every ancient structure or ruins in the world has its legends of hidden treasure. San Miguel Mission is no exception to the general rule. There are numerous stories of fabulous amounts of bullion, coins and jewels being hidden in and around the walls of the ancient structure.

An old Mexican, whose name need not be mentioned here, died in abject poverty near the mines of a once prosperous mining camp. A few days before his death, he told me that he was in San Miguel Mission when Fremont summoned it to surrender.

When the news reached the Mission that the invaders were approaching, he and five other men were ordered to bury the treasure. According to this account, the valuables were placed into a large rawhide bag and securely sewed up with leather thongs. When

so prepared for burial, there was as much gold and silver, principally gold, as all six of them could handle.

They took it to a small house at one corner of the Mission grounds which was then occupied as a sentinel post or guard-house. They dug a deep hole, deposited their charge in it, and after having laid a tier of tiling over it, refilled the excavation.

At the time he related this to me, he said he was confident the burial treasure had never been discovered, for all who took part in the burial, except himself, were long since dead. Several times he had returned with the intention of disinterring the treasure, but was always so closely spied upon that he could never accomplish his object....

I gave but little credence to the story; but authenticated history seems to verify some parts of the narrative.

When Fremont, the Path-Finder, approached the Mission, it seems as though his guide had not told him of its existence. Coming to the top of the hill, opposite the Mission, he was surprised to see what appeared to be a large Fort, over which floated the Mexican flag. Calling his guide's attention to it, he was told that it was the Mission San Miguel. Fremont remarked that it made no difference to him what it was; the Mexican flag must be replaced by the Stars and Stripes.

Hill where Fremont camped, December, 1846 (looking northwest).

Calling an aide and an interpreter, and giving them a flag of truce as well as a small body-guard, he directed them to go to the fort (as he supposed it to be), and demand of the commandant to run the Mexican flag down and surrender to the authorities of the United States.

After a long parley, they sent word back to Fremont that they were fully garrisoned and did not propose to surrender, as long as a man remained alive within.

Fremont trained a small field piece on the wall and opened fire. At the first shot, which took away one corner of the enclosure wall, the Mexican flag was lowered. The American forces marched in, acknowledged the surrender, and raised the Stars and Stripes. To their great surprise, they found not more than twenty armed men within the walls.

Thirty years afterward, General Fremont told me in an interview, which I had with him, that to this day it puzzled him to know why the commander did not surrender the Mission when first summoned. No doubt, it was to gain time in which to bury the treasure.

There is another legend that there are several thousand dollars in gold and silver coin hidden in a clay or pottery jar near a little ditch or ravine near the Mission. This money was obtained from the sale of a ship-load of hides, horns and tallow sold to a Boston Skipper near the year 1839. This story is perhaps true.

The only authentic account I have been enabled to ascertain of any buried treasure, in or around the Mission, was of a man who, in 1868, while tearing down one of the old adobe walls, found a piece of parchment or paper neatly folded, and on being opened, contained the sum of twenty-eight dollars and fifty cents.

Today, just north of Mission San Miguel, the following inscription is found on a monument:

Lt. Col. John C. Fremont
and his 430 American volunteers
camped on this hill
Dec. 10-11, 1846
and took the Mission San Miguel
Fremont's march from
San Juan Bautista to San Fernando
brought about the

Cahuenga capitulation
Jan. 13, 1847
ending the Mexican War in California

Fremont Monument.

Attached to the top of the monument is an iron arrow, pointing to the hill on which Fremont's men camped during this engagement.

Fremont's army "took" Mission San Miguel, in spite of the cannon, which can be seen at the Mission today. The cannon, dated 1697, had been cast in Spain. Mexican soldiers left the cannon at the Mission, and it was found in the debris, years after the Mission was abandoned.

Captain Francis L. Mennet, a surveyor and Civil War Veteran, refurbished the cannon and fired it as a national salute for the 4th of July in 1896. He also fired it each day at dawn, during the three-day centennial celebration at the Mission in 1897. The *Souvenir History of San Miguel*, by Dr. Hartwell B. Stanley in 1897, shows a picture of the cannon on a carriage. [The cannon was stolen the night of August 28, 1965 and was later found in a barn in Salinas; it was returned to the Mission on July 21, 1966.]

To return to Fremont, in 1846, his expedition reached Mission San Miguel on December 10, 1846. A

Cannon cast in Spain in 1697.

"spy" had been captured just north of San Miguel; this person was an Indian servant of Don Jose de Jesus "Totoi" Pico.

We will take the time to learn the background of Jose de Jesus Pico. He had been born in Monterey on March 27, 1807. Pico was educated at the school at Monterey for the priesthood, but he never became a priest. He was a grandson of Santiago de la Cruz Pico, who came to California from Mexico in 1776 with the second De Anza expedition.

The owner of the 49,000-acre Rancho Piedra Blanca, "Totoi" Pico was a first cousin of Pio Pico, the last governor of Mexican California (1845-1846). "Totoi" Pico had made the mistake of entrusting incriminating papers to William Reed at Mission San Miguel. Reed gave the documents to Petronilo Rios, who was to deliver them to Pico's brother-in-law, Rafael Villavicencio, who occupied land southeast of San Luis Obispo- - -the Rancho Corral de Piedra. Rios was captured, and then was released upon handing to Fremont the papers in question.

Jose de Jesus Pico later related:

> **I had been employed for the transmission of official dispatches and documents to Monterey from Pilot Reed, owner of the mission of San Miguel, who was English and not adherent to the Americans.**

> **Reed entrusted them to retired Sergeant Petronilo Rios to carry them to their destination, delivering them to my brother-in-law Captain Villavicencio, but they seized him on the way and handed all the papers to Fremont.**

Fremont and his group then advanced toward San Luis Obispo. The captured lookout, an Indian named Santa Maria, was executed by firing squad at the Santa Margarita Rancho on December 13, 1846.

Edwin Bryant was traveling as a member of Fremont's group; he gives this eye-witness account in his book, *What I Saw in California.*

> **The Indian captured at the rancho yesterday was condemned to die. He was brought from his place of confinement and tied to a tree. Here he stood some fifteen or twenty minutes, until the Indians from a neighboring *rancheria* could be brought to witness the execution. A file of soldiers were then ordered to fire upon him. He fell upon his knees, and remained in that position several minutes**

> **without uttering a groan, and then sank upon the earth. No human being could have met his fate with more composure, or with stronger manifestations of courage. It was a scene such as I desire never to witness again.**

On December 14th, "Totoi" Pico was arrested; he was tried by courts martial, and sentenced to be executed at dawn on December 17, 1846. However, Fremont pardoned Pico in San Luis Obispo, sparing him from being executed, and took him to Los Angeles as a prisoner. Pico's pardon by Fremont was said to have been the result of pleading by Dona Ramona Carrillo Pacheco Wilson, along with some residents of San Luis Obispo who had been assisted by Pico in the past.

After John C. Fremont and his battalion passed through the area in December of 1846, things were fairly quiet for the isolated region along El Camino Real.

Things changed drastically, two years later- - -on December 4, 1848.

On the afternoon of December 4, 1848, five "white" men and one Indian arrived at Mission San Miguel, where Reed and his family were living. Petronilo and his partner, William Reed, had obtained the Mission on July 4, 1846. Reed had recently returned from delivering sheep to his father-in-law, General Mariano G. Vallejo, for re-sale to the gold-miners of northern California.

The group which arrived on December 4th consisted of the following: Pete Raymond, a desperado who had killed a man by the name of J. R. Pfister at Murphy's Camp, but had escaped from jail; Joseph Peter Lynch, who had deserted from General Kearney's command at Fort Leavenworth; Peter Remer, who had belonged to the New York Volunteers in 1847, and Peter Quin, an Irishman who had just come to California.

These last two people were deserters from the warship *Warren*; the final member of the group was Sam Bernard (or Barnberry), accompanied by John, an Indian from Soledad. Lynch and Raymond had murdered two companions while on the way from the gold fields to Soledad.

At the mission, these men sold 30 ounces of gold to Reed for $30 per ounce; they stayed there that night, and left the next morning. They went as far as San Marcos Creek, and then returned to the Mission and spent the rest of the day and part of the evening. (Some accounts have it that the group went as far south as Rancho Santa Margarita, before returning to San Miguel.)

During the evening of December 5th, they murdered everyone at the Mission. The victims included: William Reed; his wife, Maria Antonia Vallejo, who was expecting a baby; their 4-year old son; a brother-in-law, Jose Ramon Vallejo; the mid-wife, Josefa Olivera; the 15-year old daughter and the grandson of Martin Olivera; a Negro cook; an Indian sheepherder and his grandchild. Eleven were killed in all, counting the unborn child.

The group had been warming themselves near the cooking fire, which was slowly dying. Sam Bernard (or Barnberry) offered to go outside to get some firewood. He returned with an axe hidden in the armload of wood, and struck Reed several blows with the axe; the Indian stabbed Reed with a knife. Reed was wearing his hat at the time he was killed; he had several gashes on his nose. The women must not have gotten ready for bed, because when they were found, they were still wearing day-time clothing.

Ralph J. Leonard, a retired Lieutenant-Colonel of the U.S. Army, has done an in-depth study of the murder of the Reed family. In his work entitled *The San Miguel Mission Murders*, he gives the details of the incident from the record of the interrogations of Joseph Lynch, Peter Quin and of Peter Remer. Lynch and Quin signed their confessions; Peter Remer used a witnessed mark for his signature.

According to Lynch, Sam Bernard (or Barnberry) and the others went to Reed's rooms and killed the women and children, and then took the bodies to the carpenter's shop. After the killings, they went to Reed's room and drank some wine; then, using an axe, opened all the chests and rifled them of their contents, taking the money and valuables. About half an hour after the murders, they left the Mission that evening, and slept the rest of the night near the house at Rancho El Paso de Robles, which was located approximately one mile south of the present-day town of Templeton.

Leon Gil, a grandson of Petronilo Rios, later stated that the night after the murders, the killers "camped at my grandfather's place at Templeton, with the intention of killing him also, if necessary, in order to secure the gold which they had expected to get at Mr. Reed's. But on account of there being so many Indians about, they were afraid to attempt it. One of the Indians went over, as Indians are apt to do, to the men's camp after they left, and there picked up an earring, which he brought to Don Petronilo. He recognized it as one that he had often seen Mrs. Reed wearing."

[This statement must have been given no earlier than 1887, because the town of Templeton did not exist prior to that time, nor was that name used prior to the arrival of the railroad.]

Catarina Avila Rios, in 1877, related that it was known that the murderers ate breakfast at Rancho El Paso de Robles, because of some cups that were found there by some Indian servants; they also found a new knife and a small box that contained some gold articles that belonged to the late Maria Antonia Reed.

The murderers spent the next night near a creek about two leagues south of Mission San Luis Obispo. [The Spanish league equaled 2.63 English miles.] At that point, the Indian left the group. It is possible that this location was the Corral de Piedra Rancho. (Leon Gil has said that years after the murders, Mariano Soberanes, of the Los Ojitos Rancho, visited at the Rios house in San Miguel. He chanced to see an old Indian who was working for Leon's grandfather, Petronilo Rios. Soberanes recognized the Indian as the one who was with the group who murdered the Reed family.)

The group then went to Rancho Los Alamos, and obtained four horses. Near Las Cruces, they spent the night; the next night was spent at Los Dos Pueblos. They passed Santa Barbara during the late evening of the next day, and camped about a mile from town. The following day, at about eleven o'clock in the morning, they stopped at Rancho Ortega, about five or six miles below Santa Barbara, and bought something to eat. They left about one o'clock and had gone no more than a mile when they were met by the posse.

Miss Ella Villa (Villavicencio) related a story to Chris Jespersen, which he included in his county history book. Ella Villa, the grand-daughter of Captain Jose Maria Villavicencio, grantee of Corral de Piedra, related the story that Senora Villavicencio said that the desperados had stopped at their rancho. The Senora thought it strange that one of the men should be wearing "the conspicuous, blue, brass-buttoned coat of 'the pilot,' as Reed was called by his friends."

Meanwhile, on the evening of December 5th, James P. Beckwourth was carrying the mail from Captain William Dana's Rancho at Nipomo to Monterey. He discovered the bodies, and rode with the news to the nearest ranch, that of Petronilo Rios, southeast of San Miguel, and probably five or six miles away. Beckwourth then continued his ride to Monterey.

James P. Beckwourth (died 1866).

There, he would deliver the mail and also inform the military governor, Colonel Richard B. Mason, of the murders.

It should be noted that at the time of the murders, Petronilo Rios must not have been living at the Caledonia adobe, which is located one-half mile south of the Mission; he was living at La Estrella. One reason for making this deduction is that the distance of five or six miles is not far enough to refer to the Rancho El Paso de Robles, located south of Templeton, and owned by Rios. This site is approximately fourteen miles from Mission San Miguel. Petronilo Rios and his family must have been living at the adobe on the Estrella River, southeast of San Miguel, and a distance of approximately six miles.

On December 6th, John M. Price, *alcalde* of San Luis Obispo, also discovered the bodies at Mission San Miguel. (An *alcalde* was an office which was a combination of mayor and justice of the peace.) On the 7th of December, Price signed a document as *Jusgado* of San Luis Obispo, and designated Trifon Garcia as his representative to take all measures necessary to apprehend the murderers. Trifon Garcia was a son of Ynocente Garcia, and the owner of Rancho Atascadero.

Petronilo Rios helped bury his partner, and the other victims of the crime, in the cemetery of Mission San Miguel. According to Eva C. Iversen, "Just outside the rear door of the sacristy, a little to the south-west and near the old first church wall, the bodies of the slain were all buried in one grave."

According to Catarina Avila Rios, her husband "returned to bury the family; consequently he ordered two tombs opened in which they were all buried gathering all of the remains that had been left." Thomas Savage provides this quote from the *Recuerdos* of Mrs. Rios, which were furnished to Vicente P. Gomez on June 20, 1877, in Santa Clara.

The action taken by citizens of Santa Barbara commenced on December 10, 1848, when Cesario Latillade requested the formation of a posse. This became a 37-member semi-vigilante group which caught up with the murderers on the crown of Ortega Hill, overlooking the present town of Summerland. Cesario Latillade was the vice-consul of Spain at Monterey since 1847, and was allowed to reside at Santa Barbara. He accidentally shot and killed himself at Santa Barbara in 1849.

Sam Bernard (or Barnberry) was mortally wounded by Ramon Rodriguez, who was, in turn, killed by a bullet from that bandit's gun. Pete Raymond jumped into the surf, in an attempt to escape, and was drowned. Peter Quin was wounded and captured; Joseph Lynch and Peter Remer were also captured, and later gave their confessions.

A temporary court sentenced the murderers to be hanged. From the time of the Mexican surrender in January of 1847 until statehood in September of 1850, California was a military territory of the United States. Mexican Santa Barbara had some question about the authority of the temporary court, so its findings were presented to Colonel Mason in Monterey. His response was to send Lieutenant Edward O. C. Ord, of the Third Artillery, and nine soldiers to Santa Barbara as a firing squad.

Joseph Lynch, Peter Remer and Peter Quin were executed by firing squad, in Santa Barbara, on December 28, 1848, near the corner of De la Guerra and

Reed burial site, San Miguel Mission Cemetery.

Chapala Streets. They were buried in the cemetery of Mission Santa Barbara.

The Santa Barbara historian, Walker A. Tompkins, in a November 28, 1963 letter to the *San Miguel Banner*, states that "The executed men received the last rites of the Church and were buried in the *campo santo* at Santa Barbara Mission." (Hubert Howe Bancroft believed that Peter Remer and Peter Raymond were the same person.)

An inventory of gold dust and silver seized from the prisoners lists the following: a stocking containing 80 *pesos* in silver; another stocking with 82 *pesos* in silver; a kerchief containing 100 *pesos* 2 *reales* in silver and one ounce of gold; another kerchief containing one gram of gold and a paper with 7 *pesos* 5 *reales* in silver.

Petronilo Rios, William Reed's partner, sent word to Pablo de la Guerra that all recovered money should be given to the widow of the man in the posse who was killed by the murderers. This item of information came from the interview, already mentioned, that was given by Catarina Avila Rios, in 1877. This interview was by Vincent P. Gomez, who was collecting historical information for Hubert Howe Bancroft.

Pedro Narvaez, Petronilo Rios and El Paso de Robles Rancho

Beginning in the year 1840, Mission San Miguel started losing land under the process called secularization- - -removing land from church control. In addition, the government of Mexico found it expedient to pay military personnel with land, rather than with sometimes non-existent cash money.

We now focus our attention on what was happening to El Paso de Robles, one of the important ranchos of Mission San Miguel, which was located a few miles south of the mission. El Paso de Robles was one of the wheat ranches of Mission San Miguel; it was also used for grazing sheep. The adobe on this rancho, built as a residence for the *mayordomo*, and also a granary, was located on El Camino Real, about one mile south of present-day Templeton. It had been constructed in 1813; this rancho was the property of Petronilo Rios between the years 1845 and 1857.

The State Archives in Sacramento has the following document on file:

Pedro Narvaes petitioning for the place known by the name of Paso de Robles

I, Pedro Narvaes, First Lieutenant in the National Army, and Captain of this port, needing land for a little sheep that I own and the place of Santa Ysabel being vacant, including the house of Paso de Robles, which place pertains to the lands of the Mission of San Miguel. I pray Your Excellency to be pleased to grant me the same; the boundaries of which are on the north the place called Las Gallinas; on the south the Rancho of Ascuncion; on the east the Tulares, and on the west the place of Legaejo. . . eight square leagues.
November 26, 1843

(First, a word about spelling. Most of the time,

El Paso de Robles Adobe, later "Blackburn Adobe."

Drawn by Ernie Morris

Pedro's last name is spelled with a "z" on the end. In the above document, his last name ends with an "s." The name of the place which is used as the western boundary of El Paso de Robles has at least three different spellings. "Legaejo," in this document, is the only place this spelling has been found.)

The petition from Pedro Narvaez was forwarded to Jose Mariano Bonilla, "In as much as Don Mariano Bonilla is in this place and is acquainted with the petitioner." According to Bonilla, "the land is vacant and the house is abandoned and is in a ruinous condition and the only value exists in the tiles with which it is covered, three rooms and the (eating place) of one room only existing."

"In consideration of the merits of Senor Narvaes," Governor Manuel Micheltorena gave the order, "Let title issue," dated May 12, 1844. El Paso de Robles grant was six square leagues, or over 25,000 acres.

Pedro Narvaez was a Mexican naval lieutenant, and had served as Captain of the Port of Monterey from 1839 to 1846. He married Rita, a sister of Josefa Estrada, the widow of Rafael Gomez, who was remarried to Jose Abrego. Bancroft states that Narvaez was Captain of the Port until 1844; however, Thomas O. Larkin, United States Consul in Monterey, was writing to Narvaez in his capacity of Captain of the Port, as late as January 20, 1846.

Leonard Blomquist, in his Master's thesis, written in 1943, provides some additional information; he obtained the details from *Land Case No. 351, S.D.* "Because of his official duties as Captain of the Port of Monterey, Narvaez was prevented from going upon the rancho and operated it through a *mayordomo*. He stocked it, built a new house to be used as a kitchen, and repaired the old one. However, continued Indian raids caused him to sell the rancho to someone who could stay on it. Such a person was Rios, who may have been working for Narvaez at the time. Rios, who later became a partner of William Reed in the purchase of the mission buildings, moved onto the Paso de Robles in April, 1845."

In 1839, Petronilo Rios had served as Commander of Artillery at the Presidio of Monterey, so it can be assumed that Narvaez and Rios were well acquainted with each other. In the thesis, *History of the Upper Salinas*, Dale Rae Eddy states, concerning Narvaez, "Ranching was evidently not to his liking, for the year following the date of the grant found him the military commander at Monterey. The rancho passed into the hands of Petronilo Rios sometime between 1844 and 1845."

The California State Archives contains a document with the following brief notation, which explains the "sometime between" in the previous statement: "Don Petronilo Rios may possess and enjoy" the Rancho El Paso de Robles. "I sign this on the eighth of April 1845. Pedro Narvaes."

A little more light is shed on this transaction by the words of Ynocente Garcia, who had been the civil administrator of Mission San Miguel between 1836 and 1841. Garcia states that Pedro Narvaez sold the rancho "for 300 *pesos* to a certain Rios in order to gamble it;

Thomas Oliver Larkin, about 1849.
Walter Colton

this sum did not cover the value of the tiles left on the rancho; at the time of the transfer there were at that rancho 1,000 *fanegas* of wheat which the worms got." (A *fanega* was a Spanish measure of grain & seed equal to 1.58 bushels, or the equivalent of 100 dried pounds. A *fanega* was also a Mexican land measure equal to 8.81 acres.) Most likely, Garcia was using the Spanish meaning of the word *fanega*, referring to the amount of harvested and stored grain. If he were using the Mexican meaning (amount of acres planted), he would have been talking about over 8,000 acres; this would have been approximately one-third of the entire El Paso de Robles Rancho. In addition, it is easier to imagine that worms ate grain that had been stored, rather than grain that was growing.

Meanwhile, financial and real estate transactions

began to come under the purview of Thomas O. Larkin. He served as the U. S. Consul in Monterey from 1844-1849. According to David J. Langrum in his book, *Law and Community on the Mexican Frontier*, Larkin "also capitalized on his position at the seat of government by operating as a clearinghouse for many of the commercial obligations of the expatriate community. In a country without financial institutions, he operated much as a bank."

Thomas O. Larkin was probably the most important American in Monterey; he had been born in 1802, and arrived in Monterey in 1833 to join his step-brother in commercial activity. Larkin's step-brother was Captain John Cooper; Cooper's wife, the former Encarnacion Vallejo, was a sister of General Mariano G. Vallejo. John Rogers Cooper was a half-brother of Thomas O. Larkin by his mother's second marriage. Cooper settled in Monterey in 1826, became a Roman Catholic and a Mexican citizen, then married General Vallejo's sister.

On July 22, 1841, Thomas O. Larkin received the following letter from John H. Everett at Santa Barbara.

> **Please call on Capt Silva or Sargento Rios and see that they or whoever holds my obligation to them endorses on it the amt of ninety dollars in cash paid here to order of Rios for the Artilleria. He ought to have informed me I had to pay here & I would have deducted it from the amount of the note.**
>
> **Business is very dull, no hides have been yet received on board. We shall probably leave this Sunday for Sn Pedro & shall not stop long in San Diego as we shall not at present put up our house so you may expect us back in Monterey before long. *Muchas saludes a su esposa y lo demas amigos mios en* Monterey and I remain Yrs truly**
>
> **J. H. Everett**

It is most likely that Petronilo Rios had ended his army career in 1840. Perhaps this is why Mr. Everett was having a problem with some money concerning Sergeant Rios and the artillery. Everett was not able to reach Rios, by way of the military, because Rios had already been released from duty.

The John H. Everett who wrote to Larkin concerning this monetary problem with Petronilo Rios was the supercargo of the 286-ton bark, the *Tasso*. The "supercargo" was an officer on a merchant ship who had charge of the cargo; he represented the shipowner, and was the owner's commercial agent on the California coast. In this case, the ship was owned by Joseph B. Eaton and was working for the company called Curtis, Stevenson and Price out of Boston. A "bark" was a sailing vessel with its two forward masts square-rigged and its rear mast rigged fore-and-aft.

Bancroft informs us that John H. Everett had come to California in 1836, probably as clerk on the *Alert*. Between 1841 and 1844, Everett worked as supercargo of the *Tasso*. Bancroft remarked that John H. Everett was said to have been much less popular with the Californians than other traders of the period. During the winter of 1841-1842, the *Tasso*, under Captain Samuel J. Hastings, departed California with 35,000 hides.

William Heath Davis makes an observation about John H. Everett, in Davis' book about recollections and remarks by one who visited California in 1831 and again in 1833; he then resided here from 1839 until his death in 1909. The book, *Seventy-five Years in California*, was originally published in 1889. The following is from this book.

> **As an exception to the uniformity of friendship and good feelings which prevailed on the coast in early days between the foreigners and Californians, and, in fact, between all classes in all their relations, I wish to mention that Everett, who has been spoken of as coming here on the *Alert*, was a disagreeable man. He arrived again in the bark *Tasso* as supercargo, with Captain Hastings, in 1840. Mean, selfish, and repulsive in his appearance and manners, his unhappy disposition was shown by his continually quarreling with Captain Hastings, who was a gentleman.**

Bark "Tasso"

Solid-wheeled carreta.

Drawn by Ernie Morris

However, notwithstanding his unpopularity and the general disfavor with which he was regarded, he succeeded in filling his vessel, for the reason that the people were in want of the goods which he had brought, and therefore they took them in exchange for hides and tallow. Everett, contrary to the usual custom of the merchants, never made presents to the people or showed them any friendly courtesies. They themselves were always generous to strangers, making them welcome to whatever they had. They would have disdained an offer of compensation for such kindness. But the merchants, having been so well treated by them, and having shared more or less in their hospitality, naturally reciprocated the good feelings and showed their appreciation and friendship by making presents from time to time, thereby cultivating a kindly spirit.

The entire province of California was dependent upon the outside world for all manufactured articles. During the years when the missions were in power, trading was done through them. Rancheros bartered their hides and tallow at the missions, and then mission personnel did the bartering with the trading vessels. Hides were brought to the coast by the thousands; to get them there, giant two-wheeled *carretas* were used. During the peak year of 1836, upwards of 200,000 hides were shipped to Boston alone.

When the missions went into decline, after 1834, trade in hide and tallow declined accordingly until the missions ceased to function in 1845-1846. Rancheros had to do their bartering with the American merchants through the officer called the supercargo.

In the spring of 1844, the year Narvaez acquired the Paso de Robles Rancho, Petronilo Rios must have been staying on his San Bernabe Rancho near present-day King City, because he wrote a letter from there to Thomas Oliver Larkin in Monterey.

S. Bernabe

Mr. Tomas O. Larkin June 25, 1844
Dear Sir,
I have received two letters from Mr. Everett in which he reminds me to pay the bill I have with the ship "Tasso," which he runs. By next August I will definitely be able to satisfy said bill; I have not been able to do so until now, because I have been waiting for the Judge of Monterey to order my debtors to pay me, so that I can pay my debts. It would not be necessary to live subject to this were it not for the misfortune that this past year, and the year before, were so dry that we had no harvest, and the cattle has not been, and still is not, ready to be slaughtered.

However, I am determined to make any sacrifice; and as such I beg you to be so kind as to represent me, so as not to delay Mr. Everett's pay, lest he lose his business through no fault of mine, and to offer for sale the house you know I have in Monterey which, due to

the problems in which I find myself, may be sold for two thousand silver *pesos* (2,000) or its equivalent in *esquilmos*. You understand how difficult it is to set up a factory, and because of this, you will see that I really spare no effort.

Please be so kind as to make all this known to the aforementioned Mr. Everett, to whom I offer my utmost consideration and appreciation.

At your order, yours devoted who kisses your hand.

[Signed] Petronilo Rios

(*Esquilmos* are crops or farm produce.)

As we have seen, Rios wrote his letter in the summer of 1844 from Rancho San Bernabe. This was where he made his home, following his retirement from the army. Rancho San Bernabe was located in what is now Monterey County; from the banks of the Salinas River, the lands of the rancho extended back to the hills on both sides of the river. Two older grants, made by Governor Alvarado, were consolidated into this one rancho. The first grant had been made to Jose Molina on March 10, 1841; the second one was made to Petronilo Rios on April 6, 1842.

John H. Everett wrote to Larkin, on July 13, 1844, concerning money owed to him by Petronilo Rios and Jacob Dye. Everett's letter was written from Yerba Buena.

. . . With regard to Rios he writes me, he is using all his means to pay me up this year. I wish therefore you would say to him to have in Monterey by first of Sept. all he can possibly raise & at same time take a document legalized by the Alcalde mortgaging his house &c for the amount. Should he wish to pay over anything now he can do it, to Mr. Howard Mellus of McKinlay, taking a recpt as on my a/c. My wish is, to close up myself, the business this year before I leave & could he not get some one to advance him cash on his house & I will make a discount of 12 ½ to 20% for the cash. Mr. Dye has also written me and pleads distress &c but he must find some means or other to pay. I have waited patiently enough on both Dye and Rios & they ought to pay me now even if they make some sacrifices. With this letter I send a letter for Dye and for one Rios, please see them delivered.

If worst comes, at the least secure Dyes debt by a mortgage on his house &c on interest- - -but I have no doubt myself if he is willing to make some sacrifice he can pay his a/c now. . . .Sunday 14th 6 pm. *Guipuscuana* not yet arrived- - -no other news. Screw up Rios & Dye as hard as they will bear.

Yrs Truly   John H. Everett

On Friday, July 26, 1844, from the "Pueblo de Sn Jose," Everett wrote another letter to Thomas O. Larkin.

. . . I requested you to follow up Rios & Dye & if no more could be got from them, to get some legal document with their houses in pledge for their amts. Since Rios has paid those $400 I would wish you to get from him on my a/c what hides he may have on hand & turn them over to Watson & at same time take a document legalised by Jusgado for what may remain, to pay next year with interest at 2%.

He ought not to expect that I shall allow him for the cash at rate of 12*rs* the hide, as I myself have sold hides at 14*rs* & when the barque was abt leaving paid as high as two dollars- - -in fact considering how long I have waited, he should be contented to pay the cash without any premium. Do the best you can with him & at least get what hides he has if no more than 50 or 60 . . . ."

Wealth was counted in cattle, at that time; a bullock produced on an average of 25 pounds of tallow. However, a ranchero's ability to dispose of hides and tallow was determined by the size of a very limited market. The ranchero had no objection to anyone killing one of his animals for food; the hide, however, would have to be left where the owner could easily retrieve it. According to Robert G. Cowan, "The hides were generally worth about two dollars, and together with the tallow, the entire animal was worth in the neighborhood of four dollars after processing."

In the fall of 1844, Petronilo Rios completed the following real estate transaction; it is recorded in the Book of Spanish Translations, Book 2, pages 7-9, in the Recorder's Office for Monterey County in Salinas. (Please note that there are two spellings of the last name of Munras in the same document.)

**PETRONILO RIOS
TO SALVADOR MUNRAS**

In the capital of Monterey October 2, 1844 before Marcelino Escobar 1st constitutional Alcalde & Judge of the First Instance came citizen Petronilo Rios, a resident of this district, sells & gives at public sale unto Don Salvador Munraz, a resident merchant of this Capital, a house in this port and located between the house of Don Antonio Mendez and Don Francisco Day, upon a lot 33 *varas* of front line and 25 in depth, together with the building, which consists of six rooms on ground floor with dobe [sic] walls, back yard of dobe and stone-shingle roof, all in good state of preservation, sells for the price and sum of $1,500 in coin, which amount he has already received.

Don Jose Abrego
Don Jose Maria Castanerez
Don Jose de la Rosa
Attest:
Marcelino Escobar
Petronilo Rios   Salvador Munraz

Attached to the above document is the following statement.

For the greater security and formality of this sale, I concluded to give (grantee) Judicial possession of the house referred to in the foregoing document, for which purpose I went personally with my assistants and the said Munras to the said house, where I found the grantor, and, in full view with the knowledge and permission of several witnesses, and after reading again the foregoing document, delivered to the purchaser (grantee) quiet and peaceable possession of said house, room after room, in each of which the said Munras sitted himself, touched the walls, doors and floors; opened and closed the doors, scattered handsful of dirt on all sides in the back yard, and made other demonstrations in proof of (his) having taken the (legal and) Judicial possession, without the least opposition from any of the parties. - he remaining as owner in control of the said property.

And for the effectualness of this act I interposed and do (now) interpose my judicial authority that this proceeding (act) may have the required solemnity.

In witness whereof, the parties (hereto) set their hands with myself in this (said) Capital, the day and date above written.

Marcelino Escobar
Petronilo Rios

Salvador Munras

One can not help but wonder if Petronilo Rios sold this house in order to satisfy his debt with John H. Everett, supercargo of the *Tasso*. John H. Everett can claim a footnote in California history. During the revolt against Governor Manuel Micheltorena in 1845, Everett left California on the *Guipuzcoana* on December 2, 1845. He carried the news to Mexico that Alvarado, Castro and Vallejo had pronounced their opposition to the governor, while they were at Rancho Alisal on November 14th. Everett reported that they had 300 armed *paisanos*.

Pedro Narvaez has his name in the annals of California history for actions in addition to being the grantee of El Paso de Robles Rancho. It so happened that Narvaez was Captain of the Port of Monterey when Commodore Thomas Ap Catesby Jones, in command of the U. S. Pacific Squadron, received a false report that the United States and Mexico were at war. Jones went ashore at Monterey and demanded surrender.

On October 19, 1842, just before midnight, Captain Pedro Narvaez, representing the military authority and Jose Abrego, representing the civil authority, were sent on board to arrange the terms of surrender. Thomas O. Larkin served as interpreter. After two hours of discussion, the terms were settled, to be signed at 9 a.m. The articles of capitulation were signed by Captain James Armstrong, Jose Abrego and Pedro Narvaez; these articles subsequently received the approval of Commodore Jones, Juan B. Alvarado and Captain Mariano Silva.

The territory which was surrendered was the district of Monterey, which extended from San Luis Obispo to San Juan Bautista. It was specified that Alvarado signed the articles of capitulation "from motives of humanity; the small force at his disposal affording no hope of successful resistance against the powerful force brought against him." Later, Commodore Jones learned of his error, concerning war with Mexico, so he lowered the stars and stripes on October 21st, and sailed to Los Angeles to apologize to Governor Micheltorena.

Before we leave Pedro Narvaez, we should see what Thomas O. Larkin has to say about the man, as

Monterey Bay

Drawn by Virginia Cassara

American control of California was being completed. On July 10, 1846, Larkin wrote the following letter to Commodore John Drake Sloat, who served as military governor of California from July 7th through July 29th of 1846.

> **Don Pedro Narvaez, Captain of the Port, Captain Mariano Silva, the military commander, and two or three others have returned to their families, leaving Castro at a distance this morning of fourteen leagues, going south, over 50 men leaving him this morning. Narvaez and Silva, through a friend, have tonight informed me they shall present themselves to you tomorrow. I have sent assurances of safety. They say some of Castro's paid soldiers will come in tomorrow, having run from him.**

Pedro Narvaez must have returned to Monterey. He had the distinction of being on the first jury to be impaneled in California. This jury was summoned, on September 4, 1846, by Walter Colton, who had been named *alcalde* (judge-mayor) by Commodore Stockton. The jury was composed of one-third Mexicans, one-third Californians and one-third Americans. In addition to Pedro Narvaez, the jury was composed of Juan Malarin, W. E. P. Hartnell, Manuel Diaz, Jose Abrego, Rafael Sanchez, Charles Chase, George Minor, Milton Little, Robert H. Thomas, Florencio Serrano and Talbot H. Green.

The jury was to hear the case of Isaac Graham vs Charles Roussillon, "involving property on one side and integrity of character on the other." The verdict acquitted the Frenchman of fraudulent intent, and

found a balance due plaintiff of $65. Graham was satisfied, and retracted in writing the charges he had made.

We have met Isaac Graham in an earlier chapter. Charles Roussillon was a French trader who probably got to California in 1843, or possibly earlier. He was living in Santa Cruz in 1846. At that place, he constructed a schooner, *Santa Cruz*.

Additional information concerning Pedro Narvaez includes the fact that on September 17, 1846, Florencio Serrano made a list of some 26 different families with boys in the Monterey Public School. Pedro Narvaez is listed as having one boy, of the 37 who were enrolled, in the school. Narvaez is also noted to have drawn the oldest preserved map of the city of Monterey, dated 1849.

Pedro Narvaez must have enjoyed living in Monterey. The first indication that we have, concerning his owning property there, can be found in a document in the Book of Spanish Translations, Book 1, page 369.

"Deed of Conveyance of a house."

In the Capital of Monterey, July 28th 1843, before Teodoro Gonzales, Justice of the Peace, came Don Eduardo Watson. He sells unto Don Pedro Narvaez a house in this Port, situate about 21 *varas* distant from the house of Don Juan B. Bonifacio. The lot of 50 *varas* front by 50 in depth, including the building, which consists of two rooms below, of dobe [sic] and stone walls, covered with tile roof in good state of preservation.

This property had been purchased in November 1835 from "foreigner" Juan Rainsford. Pedro Narvaez bought it for $500 in coin.

Thus, it seems that Narvaez would rather live in Monterey than make use of El Paso de Robles Rancho which he had been granted on May 12, 1844. For the next five years, we find nothing recorded concerning Pedro Narvaez.

Then we find the following in the Book of Spanish Translations, Book 1, page 95, found in the Recorder's Office for Monterey County.

PEDRO NARVAEZ

On a petition of Don Pedro Narvaez, is a decree with verbatim reads as follows;

Monterey, December 4th, 1849-

The Illustrious Ayuntamiento of this Port in conformity with the report of the commission on Solares, contained in his petition dated Oct. 9th of this year, has deemed it proper to grant to Don Pedro Narvaez, of a lot of twenty-five *varas* front on the East, and thirty-two *varas* deep extending to and adjoining the fence of the Government house.

Let entry hereof be made in the book of *Solares*, and return this (document) to the grantee, that it may serve as his title.

Thus I, Ygnacio Esquer, First Constitutional Alcalde did order and sign. Ygnacio Esquer

Ambrosio Gomez
   Sec.
This concession duly entered on page 275 of the Book of *Solares*. Kept in the Archives - in my charge.
   (Date, same as above.)   Ambrosio Gomez
                                        Sec.
[*Solares* were building lots.]

With this transaction, Don Pedro Narvaez passes out of the scene.

EL PASO DE ROBLES GRANT

We have seen that Pedro Narvaez was granted El Paso de Robles Rancho in 1844, and that he had transferred it to Petronilo Rios on April 8, 1845. Dale Rae Eddy's *History of the Upper Salinas* gives us some of the details concerning ownership of this rancho. When California became United States territory, and later a state, the problem of land claims had to be settled.

Petronilo Rios filed his claim on May 25, 1852. We know that he and his family were living at the Caledonia in San Miguel, at that time, because he had obtained a license, from the County of San Luis Obispo, to vend liquor and merchandise from his adobe home.

The Board of Land Commissioners, sitting in session in San Francisco, rendered a decree of confirmation in favor of Rios on July 3, 1855. [Note that Rios' name is spelled 'Petronillo' in this document.]

Paso de Robles Rancho

The United States of America, To all to whom these presents shall come, Greeting: Whereas it appears from a duly authenticated transcript filed in the General Land office of the United States, that pursuant to the provisions of the Act of Congress approved the third day of May, One thousand eight hundred and fifty two, entitled "An Act to Ascertain and Settle the Private Land Claims in the State of California," Petronillo Rios as claimant, filed his petition on the 25th day of May 1852, with the Commissioners, to ascertain and settle the private land claims in the State of California, sitting as a Board in the City of San Francisco, in which petition, he claimed the confirmation of his title to a tract of land called "Paso de Robles," containing about six square leagues, situated in San Luis Obispo County and state aforesaid, said claim being founded on a Mexican grant to Pedro Narvaez made on the 12th day of May 1844 by Manuel Micheltorena then governor of California; and Whereas the Board of Land Com-

missioners aforesaid on the 3d day of July 1855 rendered a decree of Confirmation in favor of the claimant as follows:

**Petronillo Rios
vs
The United States**

In this case on hearing the proofs and allegations, it is adjudged by the Commissioners that the claim of the said petitioner is valid, and it is therefore decreed that his application for a confirmation be allowed; the land of which confirmation is hereby given is situated in the County of San Luis Obispo and is known by the name of "Paso de Robles" containing six square leagues to be located within the boundaries to wit:

On the north by the land called Las Galinas, on the south by the Rancho Asuncion, on the east by the River San Miguel and on the west by the land called higuejo reference being had to the grant and map accompanying the expediente on file in this case; which decree or decision having been taken by appeal to the District Court of the United States for the Southern District of California, the said Court as appears from a duly certified transcript on file in the General Land Office on the 21st day of February 1857 ordered that the appeal be and is hereby dismissed and that the claimant have leave to proceed under the decree of the Commissioners heretofore ordered as a final decree.

And Whereas under the 13th section of said Act of 3d of March 1851, there have been presented to the Commissioners of the General Land Office a plat and certificate of the survey of the tract of land confirmed as aforesaid authenticated on the 4th day of January 1862 by the signature of the Surveyor General of the public lands in California, which plat

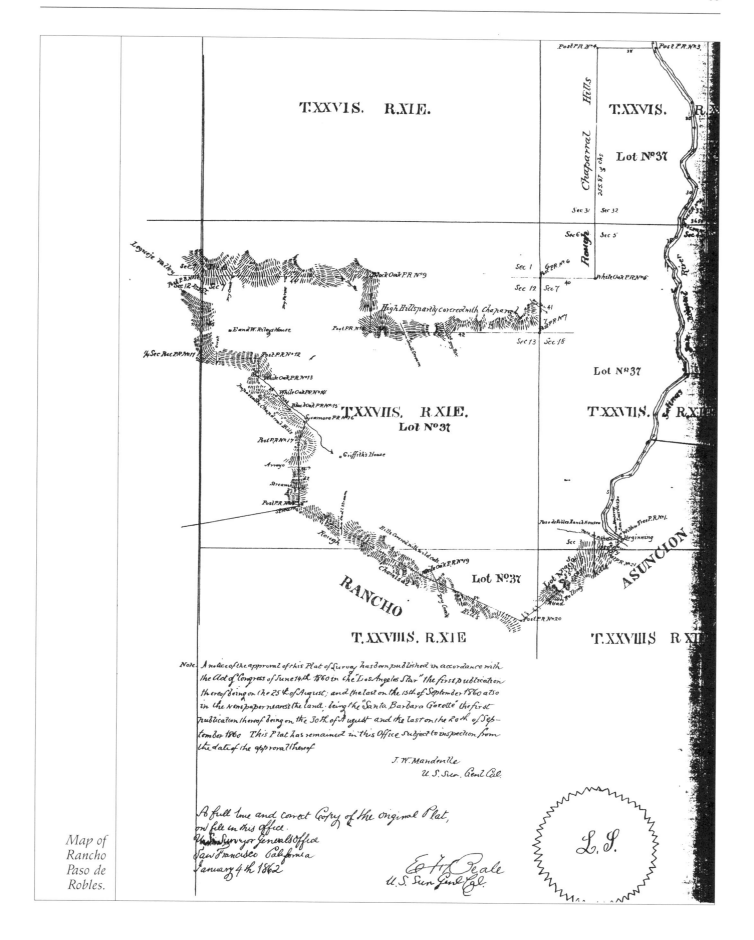

and certificate are in the words and figures following, to wit:

U. S. Surveyor Generals office, San Francisco, California

Under and by virtue of the provisions of the 13th section of the Act of Congress of the 3d of March 1851 entitled "An Act to Ascertain and Settle Private Land Claims in the State of California" and of the 12th section of the Act of Congress approved on the 31st of August 1852, entitled "An Act Making Appropriations for the Civil and Diplomatic Expenses of the Government for the year ending the thirteenth of June eighteen hundred and fifty two, and For Other Purposes." And in consequence of a certificate of the United States District Court for the Southern District of California, of which a copy is annexed, having been filed in this office whereby it appears that the Attorney General of the United States having given notice that it was not the intention of the United States to prosecute the appeal from the decision of the U. S. Board of Land Commissioners appointed under said Act of March 3d 1851 to ascertain and settle private land claims in the State of California said decision having confirmed the title and claim of Petronilo Rios to the tract of land designated as "Paso de Robles" the said appeal has been vacated and thereby the decision of the said U. S. Board of Land Commissioners heretofore rendered in favor of the said Petronillo Rios has been final. The said tract has been surveyed in conformity with the grant thereof and the said decision.

And I do hereby certify the annexed map to be a true and accurate plat of the said tract of land as appears in the field notes of the survey thereof made by 'Brice M. Henry' Deputy Surveyor in the month of August 1859, under the directions of this office which having been examined and approved are now on file therein.

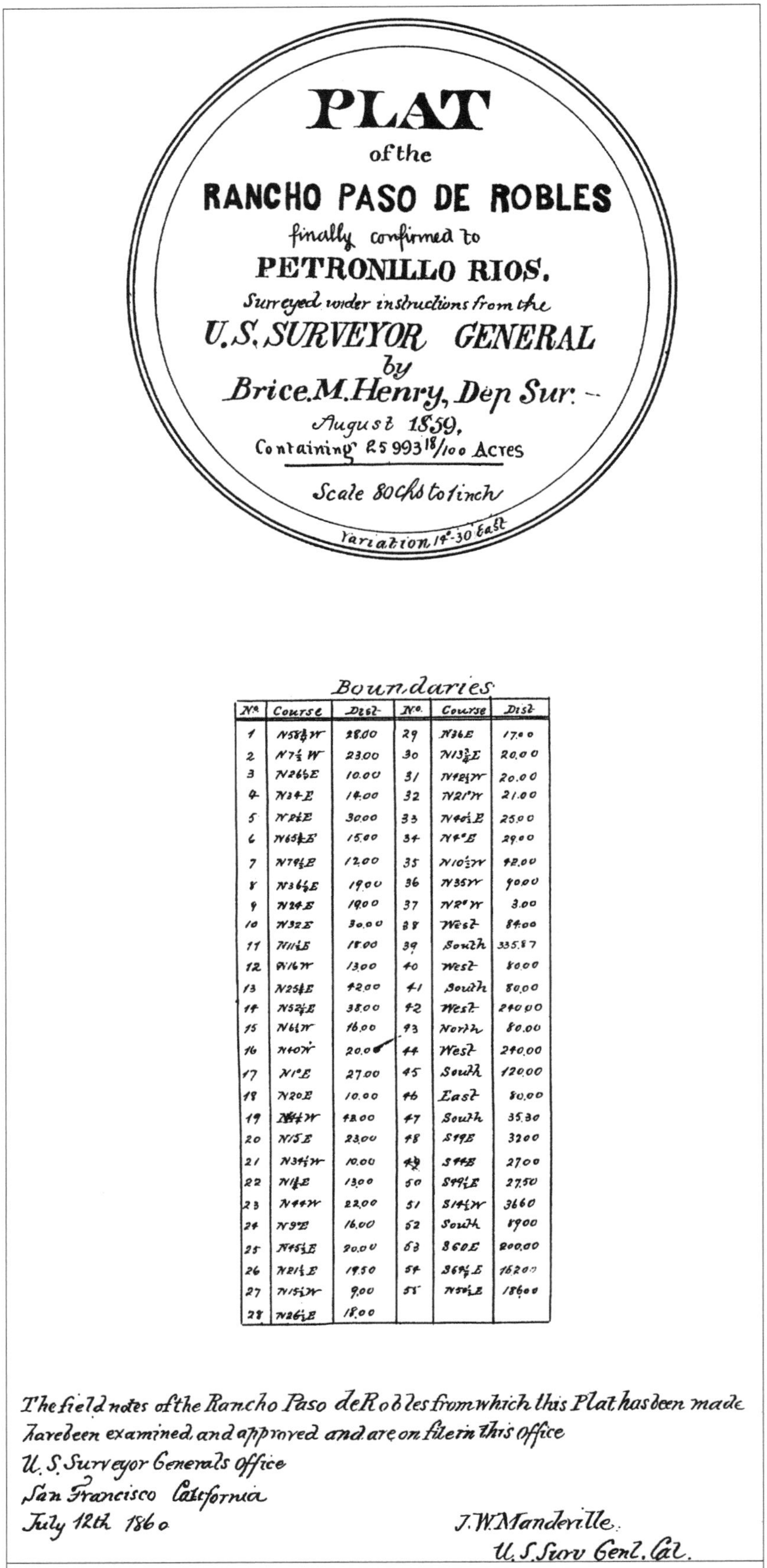
PLAT
of the
RANCHO PASO DE ROBLES
finally confirmed to
PETRONILLO RIOS.
Surveyed under instructions from the
U.S. SURVEYOR GENERAL
by
Brice.M.Henry, Dep Sur.
August 1859.
Containing 25993 18/100 Acres
Scale 80 Chs to 1 inch
Variation 14°-30 East

Boundaries

No	Course	Dist	No.	Course	Dist
1	N58¾W	28.00	29	N36E	17.00
2	N7½W	23.00	30	N13¾E	20.00
3	N26½E	10.00	31	N42½W	20.00
4	N34E	14.00	32	N21°W	21.00
5	N2½E	30.00	33	N40½E	25.00
6	N65¼E	15.00	34	N4°E	29.00
7	N79½E	12.00	35	N10½W	42.00
8	N36½E	19.00	36	N35W	40.00
9	N24E	19.00	37	N2°W	3.00
10	N32E	30.00	38	West	84.00
11	N11½E	18.00	39	South	335.87
12	N16W	13.00	40	West	80.00
13	N25¼E	42.00	41	South	80.00
14	N52¼E	38.00	42	West	240.00
15	N6¼W	16.00	43	North	80.00
16	N40W	20.00	44	West	240.00
17	N1°E	27.00	45	South	120.00
18	N20E	10.00	46	East	80.00
19	N4¼W	42.00	47	South	35.30
20	N15E	23.00	48	S49E	3200
21	N34½W	10.00	49	S44E	2700
22	N1½E	13.00	50	S49½E	27.50
23	N44W	22.00	51	S14½W	3660
24	N9°E	16.00	52	South	8900
25	N45½E	20.00	53	S60E	200.00
26	N21½E	19.50	54	S69¼E	162.00
27	N15½W	9.00	55	N50½E	186.00
28	N26½E	18.00			

The field notes of the Rancho Paso de Robles from which this Plat has been made have been examined and approved and are on file in this office
U. S. Surveyor Generals Office
San Francisco California
July 12th 1860
J. W. Manderville
U. S. Surv Genl. Cal.

Plat of the Rancho.

And I do further certify that in accordance with the provisions of the Act of Congress approved on the 14ᵗʰ day of June 1860, entitled "An Act to define and regulate the jurisdiction of the District Courts of the United States in California, in regard to the survey and locations of confirmed private land claims," I have caused to be published once a week for four weeks successively in two newspapers to wit:

The Santa Barbara Gazette a newspaper published in the County of Santa Barbara being the newspaper published nearest to where the said claim is located, the first publication being on the 30ᵗʰ day of August 1860, and the last on the 20ᵗʰ day of September 1860. Also in the *Los Angeles Star*, a newspaper published in the City and County of Los Angeles, the first publication being on the 25ᵗʰ day of August 1860 and the last on the 15ᵗʰ day of September 1860, a notice that the said claim had been surveyed and a plat made thereof and approved by me and I do further certify that the said approved plat of survey was retained in this office during all of the said four weeks, and until the expiration thereof subject to inspection, And I do further certify that under and by virtue of the said confirmation survey decree and publication the said Petronillo Rios is entitled to a patent from the United States upon the presentation hereof to the General Land Office for the said tract of land, the same being bounded and described as follows. . ."

The survey of the rancho takes four and one-half pages of paper, 8 ½ by 15 inches, and written from one edge of the page to the other edge. The survey notes start with: "Beginning at a willow sapling four inches in diameter marked 'P. R. No. 1' on an island in the center of the Salinas or San Miguel River opposite a ditch which river divides this Rancho from the Rancho 'Asuncion,'. . ." P. R. No. 3 is "one and three fourths miles south of the place known as Las Gallinas." P. R. No. 9 is "a black oak forty inches in diameter, from which a white oak thirty inches in diameter bears west distant forty links. . ."

An interesting geographic feature is mentioned in conjunction with P. R. No. 10: "a post on a hill side north of Legueje Valley at the intersection of Range ten and eleven East, Township twenty-seven south at corner to sections one, six, seven, twelve. . . ." This region is north of Dover Canyon, toward Adelaida.

Two dwellings are mentioned in the survey: Riley's house and Griffith's house. It is interesting to look at their locations on the map, and to try to imagine where they were located. Also on the map, and mentioned in the survey, is the Paso de Robles Ranch House. It is probable that the 'Legueje' mentioned above would refer to a concentration of Indians at a site called Lhuegue.

The patent was finally issued by President Andrew Johnson on July 20, 1866. However, before the patent was issued, Petronilo Rios had sold the rancho. On August 1, 1857, Rios sold El Paso de Robles rancho to James H. Blackburn, Daniel D. Blackburn and Lazare Godchaux for $8,000. The amount of acreage purchased was 25,993.18 acres. According to the agreement, Petronilo Rios was not to be held responsible for the cost of obtaining a patent for the rancho, which had been applied for but had not been issued.

This fact could substantiate a tradition in the Rios family that Petronilo believed that he was merely granting a lease to the Americans for the use of the land, rather than actually selling it. Petronilo Rios must have known that he did not yet have clear title, since the patent had not been issued in 1857. This makes the leasing scenario easy to believe, since the United States patent, or title, was not received until 1866.

According to Myron Angel, a steam saw-mill was "one of the conveniences of the rancho." The saw-mill was used in making lumber for fences, bridges and other purposes, with the forests of oak furnishing the material. Angel said that the mill was capable of cutting 6,000 feet of oak lumber a day. Old-timers of the

View at Lhuegue.

area could recall the mill, where oak wood was split into pickets.

Daniel Drew Blackburn moved upon their new purchase almost immediately. James Hanson Blackburn and Lazare Godchaux continued in the business they owned in Watsonville until 1859; they then sold out and James H. Blackburn moved to San Luis Obispo County.

In 1860, the rancho was divided; Daniel took one league, the one which included the springs. On August 8, 1866, he sold to Mr. Thomas McGreel, for $10,000 "one undivided half part of Rancho Paso de Robles." This person, in turn, sold a portion to Drury Woodson James, for $11,000. In 1873, McGreel sold a fourth-interest to James H. Blackburn. The rest of the rancho land remained in the hands of James H. Blackburn and Lazare Godchaux. In 1865, Lazare Godchaux had moved to San Francisco.

Drury Woodson James had been born in Logan County, Kentucky, on November 14, 1826. He was the eighth child of John James and his wife. Drury's mother died when the child was three months of age; his father died within the following year. Mary, the first-born of the James children, took the responsibility of caring for the three youngest boys: William, Robert and Drury James.

On May 19, 1846, Drury Woodson James enlisted as a private in Captain Triplett's Company of the First Regiment, Kentucky Infantry, for twelve months. He later joined a group of men planning to go to the gold fields of California. This group left the Missouri River on April 1, 1849; they arrived at Hangtown (today's Placerville) in August of that year.

Drury James lived in the area of La Panza from 1860 until 1869. In 1860, Drury James and John G. Thompson had purchased 10,000 acres of government land along the San Juan River, for $1.25 per acre; they stocked it with 2,500 head of cattle. This became the nucleus of the La Panza-Carrisa Ranch, which in time covered over 50,000 acres. During the drought years of 1862, 1863 and 1864, James and Thompson drove their cattle to the Tulare and Buena Vista Lakes, in order to keep them alive. The two men also owned the Camatti Ranch, in addition to the Carrisa and La Panza.

In 1860, the assessed value of their land was $18,500. The tax records for 1864 show that Thompson and James paid taxes on 300 acres of land at La Panza, valued at $1,500; other listings include: improvements $500, furniture $50, two wagons and two sets of harness $100, 40 tame horses, 4 tame mares, 2 tame mules, 1000 head of Spanish cattle. Total value was $4,850, and the tax was $157.63, and was marked "paid."

Drury James was visited by his nephews, Frank and Jesse. Alexander Frank James (born January 10, 1843) and Jesse Woodson James (born September 5, 1847) were the sons of Robert James and Zeralda Cole James. Robert James was a Baptist minister who left Missouri for California in 1848. The length of the James boys' stay in California is not known, but there is a period of several months which are unaccounted for during the period of 1868-1869. This period is between the Russellville, Kentucky, hold-up on March 20, 1868 and the bank robbery in Gallatin, Missouri, on December 7, 1869. It is generally assumed that much of this time was spent in California. According to Angus MacLean: "In interviews, after they had returned to Missouri, Frank and Jesse each spoke of having been on Uncle Drury's 'Lapansu Ranch,' but they stretched the dates of their arrival and departure to furnish alibis for some of their shenanigans in the Midwest."

Drury James and John Thompson, in 1869, sold La Panza to Jim Jones and Jacob Schoenfeld; Thompson then returned to Kentucky. On the eve of his departure, Thompson gave Drury's wife a check for $10,000 as a "token of good-will." James then purchased one-half interest in the Paso de Robles Hot Springs and the one league of land surrounding it. His first visit to the springs had been when he was on his way to the south on a cattle-buying trip in 1851. That year, he camped at the springs.

Returning to the Petronilo Rios part of our story, Chris N. Jespersen, in his 1939 *History of San Luis Obispo County*, tells about the Rios family tradition that Petronilo lost the title to his land through a misunderstanding. Part of the land had been sown to wheat, barley and oats, but the rancho was chiefly devoted to grazing sheep and cattle. It is believable that he was under the impression that he was being paid for a grazing lease of some kind.

It is not known what years, if any, the Petronilo Rios family may have lived in the adobe of El Paso de Robles Rancho. Leonard R. Blomquist, in his master's thesis, *A Regional Study of the Changes in Life & Institutions in the San Luis Obispo District 1830-1850*, has stated that "Rios moved onto the Paso de Robles in April, 1845." The expression "moved onto" does not necessarily mean that the Rios family moved into the El Paso de Robles ranch house. The expression could have the meaning of simply taking possession. If the family lived there at all, it most probably would have been sometime prior to 1852, because we know that in 1852 and 1853, Petronilo Rios was living in the Caledonia in San Miguel; he had purchased a license to sell goods from that building.

The adobe house on El Paso de Robles Rancho had been built in 1813, by workers under the supervision of the padres from Mission San Miguel. According to Annie L. Morrison's history of San Luis Obispo County, there were iron bars on the doors and windows. Whether these iron bars had been installed originally is not known at this time. However, the windows of most early buildings were protected by iron bars; the Custom House in Monterey is an example.

Here is an interesting aside, concerning the location of El Paso de Robles adobe. In 1976, a man and his wife had an adobe home built southwest of Templeton, in the area of Santa Rita Creek. They learned that their land contained alluvial soil that was perfect for the formation of adobe bricks. This particular soil ran twenty-two feet deep. According to the Fresno company which consulted them concerning their soil, the nearest location which had a large amount of this type of soil was located in northern California, near Santa Rosa. Was the site which was chosen for El Paso de Robles adobe structure somehow connected with the close proximity of "perfect" adobe-making soil? It might be worthwhile to remind readers that the missionaries who came from Spain to Alta California brought with them adobe construction techniques which had hundreds of years of use in Spain and North Africa.

The artist Edward Vischer, visiting the missions along El Camino Real in 1872 gave this description: "...'Casa Paso de Robles' crumbling to pieces on one end, while the other is alive with traffic; quaint old ruin with its well-established name for genial hospitality and the ample wherewithal in stock in the field, and in a well provided larder to do honor to its not infrequent guests from the neighboring Paso de Robles Springs."

James H. Blackburn had taken up residence at the old adobe ranch house, and occupied it between 1857 and 1872, in which year he constructed a new home about 200 yards north of the adobe. The lumber for this house was brought by team from Port Harford, now Port San Luis. The new home was surrounded by lawns and an orchard.

After Blackburn vacated the old adobe, it was used for store-rooms and laborer's quarters. The roof tiles from the "Blackburn Adobe" were sold to help provide a tile roof for the railroad depot at Burlingame, according to local historian, Annie L. Morrison. According to Louisiana Clayton Dart, the late curator of the San Luis Obispo County Historical Museum, tile taken from the roof of the old adobe was used to build a wall fence around the Daniel Blackburn home. Perhaps there was enough tile on the old adobe to be used in both places: the Blackburn home and the Burlingame railroad depot.

Annie L. Morrison said that in 1917, only a few yards of crumbling wall remained to mark the place where once stood a landmark which was about a century old. All traces of the adobe building were removed when Highway 101 was constructed along that part of El Camino Real.

James H. Blackburn never married. Later, when he died, he left most of his estate to Daniel & Cecelia Blackburn and their children. It is interesting to note that when James H. Blackburn died on January 27, 1888, a reporter writing for the *San Luis Obispo Morning Tribune* described the monument which had been constructed at his gravesite. The reporter stated that the whole granite work probably cost in the neighborhood of $8,000. Ironically, that was the amount which Petronilo Rios was paid for the entire El Paso de Robles Rancho 31 years before.

At the time of his death, James H. Blackburn owned an undivided fourth interest in the townsite property. Under the provisions of his will, he gave one-half of the property to Cecelia Blackburn in trust for her ten children; thus, each received one-eightieth part of the townsite property.

Daniel D. Blackburn and Drury W. James had married sisters, in a double wedding ceremony in San Luis Obispo, performed by Father Sastre on September 15, 1866. The brides were Cecelia and Louisa Dunn, daughters of Patrick and Mary Ann Dunn; Mary Ann Dunn's ancestors had come from Australia about 1850. P. H. Dunn, brother of Louisa James and Cecelia Blackburn, operated the general store, which also included the post office, telegraph office and Wells, Fargo & Co. office, as well as fourteen upstairs bedrooms to accommodate travelers.

Following their marriage, Drury James took his bride to live in the adobe on the La Panza Ranch; Louisa remained there for two years. Frank and Jesse James spent several months, in 1868-1869, at Drury James' adobe on La Panza Ranch. Frank James had been going through various mining districts of the state, trying to locate the grave of his father, Robert James, who came to California in 1850. [Robert James was buried at Marysville.]

Louisa James' fear of a raid by "wild Indians" caused the couple to move into town; they arrived in their new home on the day before the birth of their daughter, Nellie. Drury and Louisa James eventually became the parents of seven children.

The James House, 1939 (above, south side)

In 1869, Drury W. James had built a two-story home at 925 Spring Street, where the Melody Ranch Motel now stands. The house had six outside doors to as many porches, and four fireplaces. The ten rooms included a kitchen, which was separated from the main house by an open walkway. A staircase of imported Spanish cedar was a particularly beautiful feature of the front hall entrance.

The R. C. Heaton purchased the Drury W. James home directly from the James family, when that family moved to San Francisco in 1894. Two of the Heaton's four children, Lenore, and Wayne, were born there.

Rollin Clyde Heaton had been born on June 13, 1864 in Dowagiac, Michigan. He arrived in San Luis Obispo County at the age of 21. He worked for a time as a teacher in the Encinal district, and then homesteaded a quarter section of land in the area of the Gillis Ranch, near Willow Creek. There he chopped wood for a living; finally, with a brother, he started a nursery in what was to become Paso Robles.

R. C. Heaton fell from a wagon near the home of David & Susan Pate; because of this incident, R. C. met their daughter, Grace Ellen Pate, who was also a school teacher. Grace E. Pate taught at Avenal School, near Pozo, at Summit School and at Bethel School, on the York Mountain Road.

Grace Ellen Pate had been born in a log cabin on Jack Creek, eleven miles west of Paso Robles, on February 1, 1872.

The marriage of R. C. Heaton and Grace Ellen Pate took place on December 14, 1893, in Templeton. Following his marriage, Mr. Heaton launched his furniture and mercantile business; the R. C. Heaton Corporation had been founded in 1886.

Heaton's furniture and mercantile business was originally located on Pine Street between 12th and 13th Streets; later, it was moved to 13th and Park, where it prospered until the business was closed on August 31, 1983. R. C. Heaton found time to be founder and president of the First National Bank of Paso Robles.

D. W. James House, built 1869.

Drury James Home lower left corner.

In 1908, Heaton had a well drilled on the former Drury James property; the water was used for irrigation, even though it contained sulphur and had a temperature of nearly 108 degrees F. In 1915, R. C. Heaton had eight bath houses built on the property for the exclusive use by tenants renting on the property.

It is interesting that in 1934, R. C. Heaton sold the Italian Cypress tree from the property to William R. Hearst for $125. The tree, and a seven-foot by seven-foot ball of earth, were moved to the Castle.

After the Heatons left the James house, it was used for a short time as a tea room, then it was converted into apartments. Heaton sold the land to Mr. and Mrs. James Van Stelten; they had a motel constructed on part of the land.

In June of 1966, two hundred sacks of cement were used to cap the well, so that the sulphur would not cause deterioration of the city's sewer lines.

R. C. Heaton died on August 16, 1958. Grace Heaton died on October 16, 1963, at age 90.

The September 3, 1886 issue of *The Inland Messenger* ran this ad:

West Coast Land Company
San Luis Obispo, Cal.
Incorporated March 27, 1886 Capital
$500,000
Directors: Geo. C. Perkins, John L.
Howard, Isaac Goldtree,
E. Jack, C. H. Phillips
Officers: John L. Howard, President,
Isaac Goldtree, Vice-Pres.
R. E. Jack Treasurer. C. H. Phillips
Secretary and Manager

The Paso Robles, Santa Ysabel
and Eureka
RANCHES
Recently purchased by the West Coast Land Co., are now offered for sale in the subdivisions. This immense body of land, including 12,000 acres unsold of the Huer Huero ranch, belonging to C. H. Phillips, comprises 64,000 acres of rich virgin soil. It lies in a compact body, in the center of San Luis Obispo county, and is within from nine to twenty miles of the sea-coast. It is covered with white and live oak timber, is one of the most picturesque bodies of land in the state, and requires
NO IRRIGATION
It has an abundance of living water, and where not sufficient for domestic use, good water can be had at a depth of from ten to forty feet.

It has an average annual rainfall of twenty-one inches, exceeding by six inches that of Santa Clara county, one of the most prosperous counties in the State.

The extension of the Southern Pacific Railroad from Soledad southward traverses these lands for fifteen miles, throughout their entire length, placing the property within eight hours of San Francisco.

These lands are offered at from $10 to $30 an acre, and are all susceptible of the highest cultivation. In salubrity of climate, productiveness of soil, and location as to market, they are equal to lands in Los Angeles and other counties, which readily bring from $100 to $200 and upwards; and as to price and terms, offer the best inducements to those seeking homes of any part of the Pacific Coast.

The subdivision of the famous
PASO ROBLES RANCH
Has been completed. The maps and catalogues are now being prepared, and will be sent free on application.

This ranch, containing 20,400 acres, has been subdivided into 230 lots. It is twelve miles from the sea-coast, and is twenty miles north and west from San Luis Obispo city.

This ranch was one of the earliest granted by the Mexican Government, and having been held by the same party for thirty years, has never before been offered for sale. It consists exclusively of lands of the choicest character, and is second to none in the State for the production of wheat, wine, fruits, raisins and olives.

TERMS OF SALE

One-third cash; balance in four equal payments, at two, three, four and five years; interest six per cent, per annum. The mortgage-tax paid by the mortgagee makes the interest about four per cent net to the purchaser. A deposit of $25 will be required in all cases to cover expenses of sale.

H. Phillips, Manager
West Coast Land Company, San Luis
Obispo, Cal.
Send for free catalog and map.

There is an interesting semi-connection with the James H. Blackburn residence and the charcoal industry that used to be wide-spread in our area of concern. Much of the information comes from an article that Louis Bergman wrote for the "Pioneer Edition" of *The Daily Press*, on October 8, 1978.

Many people are aware that local citizens of Italian descent, at the beginning of this century, made charcoal on a commercial basis. In 1908-1909, the Dupont Powder Company brought 40 to 50 men, along with horses and equipment, on the train. Among these workers were Italians, Japanese and Hindus from India. About the time of World War I, the Japanese in the area were cutting wood, but at first, they did not make charcoal.

The Japanese began their charcoal-making about 1919, and revolutionized the charcoal-making process; they did this by building burning-ovens in the side of a hill. They did not use the method previously used by Italian charcoal-makers, which was to build a huge pyramid of oak wood, then cover it with earth to form a type of oven. [Jack Normowsky invented the charcoal briquette; he mixed finely-ground charcoal and corn meal. He had a factory just on the edge of Paso Robles.]

The former James H. Blackburn residence was used as a gathering place for the Japanese workers. As we have already seen, the house stood near old Highway 101, near the river, and about a mile south of present-day Templeton.

The first manager of the Japanese charcoal-making operation was Frank Otomoki; later, Henry Kunihiro was the manager. Other names related to this business included: Kujiwata, Fijino, Kato and Nakamitzi. Charlie Hayashi cut wood and burned charcoal in Dover Canyon (the approximate western boundary of El Paso de Robles Rancho), until all Japanese were required to go to assembly centers at the beginning of World War II.

Louis Bergman, in an oral-history tape recording, said that Charlie Hayashi hid out in Dover Canyon, and Louis would bring him food and other necessities. When Charlie finally went to the relocation center, he gave his money to Louis to place in his own bank account, so that it would be available when

Stock Ranch and Residence of J. H. Blackburn (view looking south).

Charlie Hayashi returned. After World War II, Charlie Hayashi did come back, and he cut wood in Dover Canyon for about six months.

At first glance, the above information may seem to be unrelated to our topic; however, these Japanese workers were following in the footsteps- - -almost literally- - -of the local Indians who would assemble at that location, beginning around 1813. There, the Indians would receive their work assignments, whether it was planting, reaping or herding.

PETRONILO RIOS: THE CONCLUSION

We have seen that Petronilo Rios and his family, in the 1840s, were living in the adobe ranch house on Rancho San Bernabe, northwest of present-day King City. By August 4, 1851, Petronilo Rios was back in San Luis Obispo County.

That he was back in San Luis Obispo County is demonstrated by the fact that he served a one-year term as *Juez de Campo*, or Judge of the Plain. The office of *Juez de Campo* has an official ancestry that goes deep into the Spanish-American period; it was established in 1823 under Spanish Law. This law gave the Judge of the Plain the authority to appoint the members to, and define the duties of, the *ayuntamiento*, or town council. Between the years 1846 to 1849, the judges were appointed by the *Alcalde*, or judge-mayor; after 1849, they were appointed by the *ayuntamiento*.

The Judge of the Plain was an important office for some years after California became United States territory, because stock-raising was the chief, if not the only, occupation of the *Californios*. The officer was in charge of the rodeos. The purpose of the annual rodeo was to separate and brand the cattle belonging to individual owners- - -an operation decidedly necessary when pastures were unfenced. The *Juez de Campo* presided over the rodeo, settling controversies and generally helping to maintain order during the round-up.

The importance of this office caused the State legislature to retain it alone, when all other Spanish-Mexican offices were abolished. The first Judge of the Plain, for San Luis Obispo County, was appointed in August of 1850. In 1851, two Judges were appointed for the township of San Luis Obispo, one Judge for Nipomo township, and two Judges for the township of the third precinct. The two judges for the third precinct were Petronilo Rios and Jose Vasquez. A Judge of the Plain had to attend every rodeo; there were 30-some rodeos every year in different parts of the county, thus the need for having several officers to hold this position.

Compensation for this office came from fees for services provided. For any fire on the plains, compensation was $3 per day, payable out of the county trea-sury. For attending any rodeo, $2 per day was paid by the person calling for the rodeo. Upon any question of ownership, each judgment made was done at the rate of $1, paid by the party against whom the judgment was given. For arresting a person and taking him before a magistrate for examination, the payment was the same as would be made in criminal cases. Disputes over land questions involved an authority higher than that of the Judge of the Plain.

The office of Judge of the Plain became obsolete in 1852, and the police functions were assumed by the sheriff and constables; the judicial functions were assumed by the justices of the peace.

The Assessment Roll of Real Estate and Personal Property in the County of San Luis Obispo for the year 1851 provides much information concerning Petronilo Rios. (In 1851, there were only 72 property owners in all of San Luis Obispo County.)

In 1851, Petronilo Rios had 53,280 acres, valued at $29,900 and personal property amounting to $6,600. In that year, he owned lots #1, #2, #4 and #5 in Block 24 in the town of San Luis Obispo. Block 24 is bounded by Santa Rosa, Osos, Monterey and Palm Streets; this is the block on which the present Government Center is located.

The County Courthouse which preceded the present building served from 1873 to 1940. After this building was dedicated in 1873, the *Tribune* editor was rankled because the surroundings had not been cleaned up. It seems that "a mean adobe shanty" stood close to the building, and "a prickly pear hedge" denied people quick access from the nearby Andrews Hotel. These items would have been remainders from twenty years earlier- - -during the time Petronilo Rios owned part of the property. According to Myrtle Reese Bridge, in her work called *Early History of San Luis Obispo County*, John Pinkney Andrews and Ernest Cerf gave the land for the court house. It can be assumed that Andrews, Cerf and Rios all owned portions of Block 24 at one time. We have not found out how Block 24, of which Petronilo Rios owned four lots, was used between 1857 and 1873.

A San Luis Obispo real estate transaction, on the part of Petronilo Rios, took place in 1852.

> This Indenture made this 3rd day of May One Thousand eight hundred and fifty two, between Petronilo Rios of the first part and Mariano Lazcano of the second part both of the County of San Luis Obispo, State of California, witnesseth that the said party of the first part for and in consideration of the sum of Eighty Dollars to him in hand paid by the said party of the second part, the receipt whereof is hereby acknowledged both bargained and sold and by these presents doth bargain and sell unto the said party of the second part and to his heirs and assigns for ever.
>
> All that certain portion, tract or lot of land, lying and situate in the town of San Luis Obispo, State of California aforesaid bounded and described as follows to wit:
>
> On the North by the land of Guillermo G. Dana, on the South by a lot of Luis Quintana, on the East by the principal street leading to and from Monterey, and on the west by a lot of the said Marino [sic] Lascano, said described Lot fronting the store of Messers Sparks & Pollard and being twenty three yards in front, by twenty seven in depth. Together with all and singular the hereditaments and appurtenances thereunto belonging or in any wise appertaining to have and to hold to the said party of the second part, his heirs and assigns in the sole, use and benefit of the said party of the second part, his heirs and assigns forever.
>
> In witness whereof I have hereunto set my hand and seal the day and year first above written.
>
> Sealed Signed and
> delivered in presence of (s) Petronilo Rios
>   Como Testigo
>   Jesus Salas

Attached to the above document, recorded in the Book of Deeds "A" in the office of the County Recorder in San Luis Obispo, is the following document.

> Know all men by these presents that I Esteban F. Quintana of the Town and County of San Luis Obispo, State of California, for and in consideration of the sum of Three Hundred Dollars ($300) paid to me by Petronillo Rios of said County and State the receipt whereof is hereby acknowledged, have bargained, sold, quit claimed and conveyed, and by these presents do bargain, sell, quit claim and convey unto the said Petronillo Rios all my right, title and interest of in and to all that certain piece or parcel of land called the Rancho de la Augua [sic] Caliente composed of two (2 leagues of land *Ganado Mayor*) it being the same tract of land which said Petronillo Rios sold to me in the year A.D. 1840.
>
> To have and to hold the above granted premises to him the said Rios his heirs and assigns forever, which said Rancho I have never sold or conveyed in any manner whatever to any person or persons.
>
> In witness whereof I have hereunto set my hand and seal this 3rd day of October A.D. 1852.
>   (s) Esteban Quintana

[*Sitio de Ganado Mayor* was a square that measured 5,000 *varas* on each side, which equalled 4,438.68 acres. The *Sitio de Ganado Mayor* was divided into the following units:

Criadero de Ganado Mayor - one quarter, or 1,109.67 acres.

Sitio de Ganado Menor - two-thirds, or 2,959.12 acres.

Criadero de Ganado Menor - one-third, or 1,479.56 acres.]

Esteban Quintana was a prominent citizen of San Luis Obispo; he served as an *alcalde* in 1845 and 1849. The assessment roll of real estate and personal property for 1851 lists lots and improvements in San Luis Obispo at $275, and personal property at $2,836. During the 1850s, the San Luis Obispo post office was moved from a small adobe building on the corner of Monterey and Chorro Streets to the Murray adobe opposite the Mission. In 1860, it was moved into an adobe, owned by Quintana, on the northwest side of Monterey Street above Chorro. By 1860, Esteban Quintana had under his control the "San Bernardo Rancho, etc.," assessed at $23,553.50. In 1876, Quintana owned a store, in San Luis Obispo, which adjoined the Goldtree Block.

At the present time, research has not discovered the details of the sale of the property by Petronilo Rios in 1840.

Records show that during the years 1852 and 1853,

Petronilo and his family resided at the adobe in San Miguel, and was authorized by the sheriff to vend merchandise, at this home, for a fee of $5 per month. He was authorized to vend liquor by paying an additional license tax of $5 per month.

During the year 1852, county records indicate that Petronilo Rios owned Paso Robles property of 26,640 acres, plus the 26,640 acres that he owned in the area of San Miguel, in addition to the lots he owned in San Luis Obispo. The assessment on this property was listed as $11,000.

In 1853, the records show property at Paso Robles and San Miguel; the number of 48,840 acres is given, with $11,000 in value. On February 24, 1853, Petronilo Rios filed a claim with the U. S. Land Commission for title to Mission San Miguel, which had been purchased on July 4, 1846. The land commission rejected the claim on May 15, 1855. The appeal was dismissed on December 17, 1856, for failure of prosecution. [On September 24, 1861, Petronilo Rios and Estaban Rios transferred Mission San Miguel to the Catholic church authorities for the sum of "one dollar lawful money."]

Adelaida Avila was the youngest child of Jose Guadalupe Avila and Maria Antonia Linares. She was born in 1833, and was the sister of Catarina Avila, the wife of Petronilo Rios. During the year 1853, when Adelaida was 20 years of age, there was an interesting real estate transaction.

This Indenture made this fourteenth day of May in the year one thousand eight hundred and fifty three, Between Adelaida Avila of the Mission of San Antonio in the County of Monterey and State of California of the first part, and Petronilo Rios of the Hacienda and ex-Mission of San Miguel in the County of San Luis Obispo and State aforesaid of the second part.

Witnesseth, That the said party of the first part, for and in consideration of the sum of Two thousand Dollars to her in hand paid, the receipt whereof is hereby acknowledged, hath sold, assigned and conveyed, and doth hereby sell, assign and convey to the said party of the second part, his heirs and assigns, the undivided third part of the ex-Mission of San Miguel in San Luis Obispo County, consisting of nine leagues of land of (25,000,000) square varas each in . . . more or less, which

was decreed to me as the heir at law of William Reed and his wife of said County deceased, by order and decree of the Probate Court of said County bearing date May 9, 1853.

(s) Adelaide Avila {seal}
(s) Doroteo Ambris

As of the end of December, 1996, the above-mentioned "order and decree of the Probate Court" has not been located in the archives of San Luis Obispo County.

Doroteo Ambris was the priest in charge of Mission San Antonio de Padua, from 1851 until his death in February of 1882. We will meet him later in an important transaction Petronilo Rios made, concerning that mission. William Reed's wife was said to be the niece of Catarina Avila Rios; Catarina and Adelaida had a sister, Marcella Vallejo, who had been born in 1828. Perhaps she was the mother of Maria Antonia Vallejo, the wife of William Reed.

The 1854 records show an interesting change: Paso Robles is listed, but the records show "2/3 San Miguel," in addition to the lots in San Luis Obispo. The value is given as $10,000 for land and $7,000 for personal property. Year 1855 indicates Paso Robles, 2/3 San Miguel and lots in San Luis Obispo.

Between 1852 and 1857, the tax rate was 50-cents on $100; the tax on real estate was 50-cents an acre or less. For taxable purposes, the assessment was about one-half of what was considered the full value of the property, whether real property or personal property. The tax rate was increased to $2.20 per hundred, in 1857.

In early 1857, the amount of land in San Luis Obispo County that was owned by Petronilo Rios amounted to 53,280 acres, in addition to the city lots in San Luis Obispo.

The years 1856 and 1857 are identical: 26,640 acres, Rancho Paso Robles and "houses in San Miguel." We know that on August 1, 1857, Petronilo Rios made his transaction with the Blackburns and Godchaux. In 1858, records simply show personal property, valued at $4,420.

Earlier, on August 1, 1857, Petronilo Rios had sold his 25,993-acre El Paso de Robles Rancho. On October 17, 1857, Petronilo returned to Monterey County to make a transaction, which can be found in Book A of Pre-emption Claims, page 317, in the Recorder's Office in Salinas.

Mission San Antonio de Padua today.

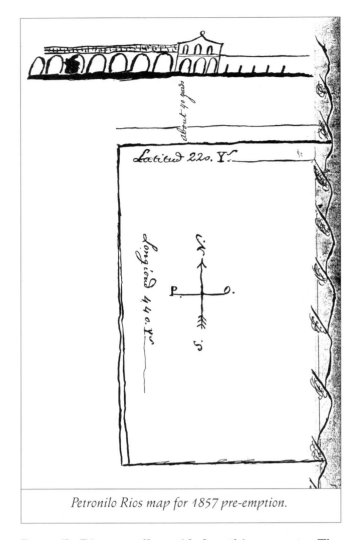

Petronilo Rios map for 1857 pre-emption.

Petronilo Rios
State of California   County of Monterey

On this 17 day of October A. D. 1857 before me personally came Petronilo Rios Who being by me duly Sworn says that he is a Citizen of the United States and of said State that he did on the 4th day of September 1857 take possession of & now actually occupies as a preemption claim the following described tract of land situate in the County of Monterey, Township of San Antonio and being immediately in front of the Mission Church distant from said Church about 40 yards more or less, being 220 yards East and West by 440 yards North and South as appears by a map or plat of said claim hereto attached that these lines do not embrace more than 160 acres of land that he (deponent) has taken no other claim under an act of the Legislature of said State passed April 20th 1853 before me entitled an act Prescribing the mode of maintaining & defending possessory actions on Public lands in this State & to the best of his knowledge & belief said land is not claimed under any existing title.

     Sworn to & subscribed before me
                Petronilo Rios
                Jas. H. Gleason
                County Recorder
                Monterey County
Received for Record Nov. 17, 1857 at 3 p.m.
Recorded at request of claimant.

There is no record, nor family tradition, that

Petronilo Rios actually resided on this property. The "actually occupies" phrase in the above document could probably be satisfied by "running cattle" on the property.

The year 1857 was a busy one for Petronilo Rios; not only did he dispose of El Paso de Robles Rancho, and pre-empt 160 acres in front of Mission San Antonio, but he also served as Superintendent of Schools for San Luis Obispo County. Eight persons passed this office around during 1857, due to "poor and irregular pay." The other people who served as Superintendent, during 1857, were: E. W. Howe, Valentine Gajiola, Fred Wickenden, Samuel Pollard, Ygnacio Sequer, J. J. Simmler and William G. Dana.

During the 1855-1856 term, John Wilson had served as superintendent; Wilson was one of San Luis Obispo County's wealthiest land owners. Following the school year of 1857, during which eight people held the office, P. A. Forrester assumed the position, and served the entire year.

Mission San Antonio de Padua

Drawn by Colleen Connor Cobb

During the 1850s, the two-story adobe in San Miguel provided rooms for a school, which it did on more than one occasion. In fact, the Caledonia is said to have provided some of the first school rooms in the county, outside of the actual mission buildings in San Luis Obispo and San Miguel.

It would appear that during the period of 1857-1858, Petronilo Rios disposed of the lots he owned in San Luis Obispo.

The tax records for 1859 give us a short lesson in the life of Petronilo Rios. The tax assessor's office found the following: 11 tame horses at $25 each; 26 *manada* animals [mares & colts] at $10 each; 350 stock cattle at $10 each; 7 oxen at $20 each; 1 wagon at $50; 1,000 sheep at $2 each. There are also listed 150 tame cattle, but a money amount is not given.

A continuing lesson is found for us in the year 1860. Rios was assessed $200 for "improvements on public land." It is possible that this item and figure are related to the fact that some property was returned to the Catholic Church in 1859. Also in 1860 were listed household and kitchen furniture $200; 450 stock cattle $3,600; 1,000 sheep $2,000; 10 tame horses $250; 25 mares & colts $250.

For the year 1860, Rios had two wagons; presumably they were together valued at $100. The property assessment in 1860 was $6,580. The year 1861 is the same as 1860. As we have seen, on September 24, 1861, Petronilo Rios and Estaban Rios were involved in a transaction with "Joseph S. Alemany, late Roman Catholic Bishop of the Diocese of Monterey." For "one dollar lawful money" the church was given San Miguel "Mission buildings, cemetery containing 10 acres & 95/100, orchard of said mission 4 & 18/100 of an acre; vineyard 18 acres & 84/100."

In 1862, property on which assessments were made included 350 stock cattle; 15 tame horses; 1 wagon and furniture. *Manada* animals numbered 25 again; the number of sheep appears to be 200, although it could be 2,000.

San Luis Obispo County tax records for 1863 seem to be missing. In 1862, 1863 and 1864, the valuation of property throughout the county had to be reduced, due to the drought. However, in 1864, the figures show improvements on public land $600; 350 Spanish cattle, 9 tame horses; 20 *manada* animals; 1,000 mixed sheep; 1 wagon & harness ($25); furniture ($30). The value was $2,570 and the tax was $83.53- - -and was marked

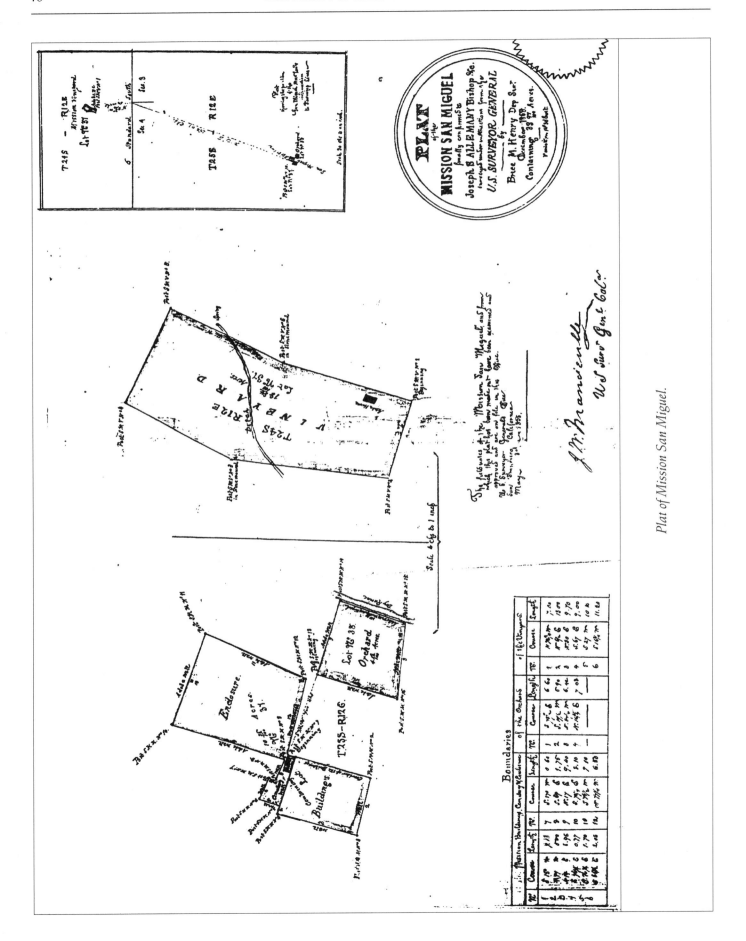

Plat of Mission San Miguel.

"paid." It is well to remember that a terrible drought was suffered by this region of the state during 1863 and 1864. Myrtle Reese Bridge, in her 1961 work entitled *Early History of San Luis Obispo County*, states that when her grandparents settled in 1866, skeletons of cattle which had died were still seen everywhere.

For the convenience in taking the census, San Luis Obispo County was divided into five townships; four of them were on the coast-side of the mountains, where most of the residents lived. All of the territory north and east of the Cuesta was lumped under one heading- - -Salinas Township. The post office department referred to much of this same area as "Hot Springs."

It appears that Petronilo Rios was still active in real estate in Monterey County. The Recorder's office in Salinas indicates, in Book E of Deeds, page 81, that Petronilo Rios was grantor to Alexander Cameron of the "Rancho called San Antonio de Potrerade la Milpitas" situated in the County of Monterey, State of California." This transaction is dated July 31, 1861.

> Know all men by these presents that the undersigned Petronilo Rios for and in consideration of the sum of four hundred dollars to me in hand paid by Alexander Cameron the receipt whereof is hereby acknowledged, has remised, released and quit claimed and by these presents do sell, remise, release and quit claim unto the said Cameron and his heirs and assigns forever, all my rights, titles, interest, estate, claim, property, possession or demand, of in and to the Rancho called San Antonio de Potrero de las Milpitas situated in the County of Monterey, State of California, together with all and singular the tenements hereditaments and appertenances thereunto belonging or in any wise appertaining with all the improvements including adobe houses, fences and corrals and all kinds of appertenances.
>
> In witness whereof I have hereunto set my hand and seal this 25th day of June 1861 day of A. D. one thousand eight hundred sixty-one, Petronilo Rios {L. S.}
>
> Signed, sealed and delivered in presence of Thomas Cameron Antenajerner Gil.
>
> This day personally appeared Atenojnoz Gil and made oath that the signature to the foregoing deed of conveyance is the signature and hand writing of Petronilo Rios and that he executed the foregoing conveyance freely and voluntarily for the purposes and uses therein set forth,
>
> Monterey June 28th A. D. 1861
> Atenojnoz Gil.
> Subscribed & Sworn to before me
> this 28th day of June A. D. 1861.
> Wm. H. Rumsey, County Judge
> Rec'd for record July 13th 1861 at 2 p.m.

[Antenajerner Gil and Atenojnoz Gil were most likely the same person. His name was Atenogenes Gil, the husband of Juana Josefa Ysabel Rios, the fourth child of Petronilo and Catarina Rios. Alexander Cameron sold this property to Hiram Rush and Juan M. Luco for $500, on July 6, 1861.]

The Book of Deeds "F," page 501, in the Recorder's office for Monterey County contains the following transaction:

> This Indenture made the twenty-fourth day of December One Thousand eight hundred and sixty six Between Petronilo Rios of the County of San Luis Obispo, State of California, party of the first part, and Doroteo Ambris of the County of Monterey, State of California, party of the second part.
>
> Witnesseth that the said party of the first part, for and in consideration of the sum of three hundred dollars, to him in hand paid by the said party of the second part, at or before the ensealing and delivery of these presents, the receipt whereof is hereby acknowledged Has remised, released and quit claimed, and by these presents does remise, release and quit claim unto the said party of the second part, and to his heirs and assigns forever, All his right, title and interest in and to that certain pre-emption claim situate in the County of Monterey, State of California and Township of San Antonio, described as follows to wit:
>
> Being immediately in front of the Mission Church of San Antonio and distant from said Church about 40 yards, more or less, being 220 yards East and West by 400 yards North and South. Embracing 160 acres of land together with house, fencing, corrals and all improvements thereon.

Said claim being recorded in Recorder's Office Monterey County page 317 of Book "A" Pre-emption Claims.

Together with all and singular the tenements, hereditaments and appurtenances thereunto belonging, or in anywise appertaining, and the reversion and reversions, remainder and remainders, rents, issues and profits thereof. And also all the estate right, title, interest, possessory rights, property, possession, claim and demand whatsoever, as well in law as in equity, of the said party of the first part, of, in or to the above described premises, and every part and parcel thereof, with the appurtenances, unto the said part of the second part, his heirs and assigns forever.

In Witness Whereof, the said party of the second part has hereunto set his hand and seal the day and year first above written.
Petronilo Rios {Seal} Signed, Sealed and Delivered in the presence of Francis Sylvester, Subscribing Witness.
State of California, County of Monterey ss. On the eleventh day of February A. D., One thousand eight hundred and sixty seven before me, William M. R. Parker, County Clerk, and ExOfficio Clerk of the County Court, in and for said County, personally appeared Francis Sylvester, personally known to me to be the same person whose name is subscribed to the annexed Instrument as a witness thereto, who being by me duly sworn, deposed and said, that he resides in the County and State aforesaid, that he was present and saw Petronilo Rios known to him to be the same person described in and who executed the annexed Instrument, as a party thereto, Sign, Seal, and Deliver the same; and that he, the deponent, thereupon signed his name as a subscribing witness thereto.

In Witness Whereof, I have hereunto set my hand, and affixed the Seal of said Court, the day and year in this Certificate first above written.
M. R. Parker Clerk {County Court Seal} Recorded at request of Mariano Gonzales February 11th A. D. 1867 at 5 min. past 4 o'c P. M.

The grantee was Doroteo Ambris, one of the first priests ordained in California (January 1, 1846). Father Ambris came to California with Bishop Francisco Garcia Diego, and was the first secular priest to be in charge of Mission San Antonio de Padua. When he died in 1882, the remains of Father Doroteo Ambris were buried in the sanctuary of the mission.

An interesting footnote is that it was Father Doroteo Ambris who recorded the marriage of Juan Falque and Maria Antonia Gregoria Rios, daughter of Petronilo and Catarina, on April 18, 1860.

The Book of Deeds "F," pages 502-503, contain the following transaction:

This Indenture made the Twenty fourth day of December in the year of our Lord, One thousand eight hundred and sixty six Between Petronilo Rios of the County of San Luis Obispo, State of California, party of the first part and John W. Miller of the same State, County of Monterey, party of the second part.
Witnesseth, That the said party of the first part, for and in consideration of the sum of two hundred and fifty (250) Dollars gold coin of the United States to him in hand paid, the receipt whereof is hereby acknowledged, Has granted, bargained, sold, remised, conveyed and quit claimed, and by these presents Does grant, bargain, sell, remise, convey and quit claim unto the said party of the second part, and to his heirs and assigns forever all the right, title, and interest of the party of the first part, in and to that certain piece, parcel or lot of land lying and being situate in the State of California, County of Monterey, and city of

Mission San Antonio de Padua, 1870s.

Monterey, commencing at the lot and house of Joaquin Gutierrez and running on the line of Main Street to the land of Jacob P. Leese and running back to Pacific Street being twenty four (24) *varas* more or less fronting on Main Street and running back thirty two (32) *varas* more or less to Pacific Street being a portion of a lot granted by an *Alcalde* of Monterey to Graciano Manjores and by him conveyed to A. S. Taylor, and by said Taylor conveyed to Ambris and by Ambris to said party of the first part.

Together with all and singular the tenements, hereditaments and appurtenances thereunto belonging and the rents, issues and profits thereof. To Have and to Hold all and singular the above mentioned and described premises, together with the appurtenances, unto the said party of the second part, his heirs and assigns forever.

In Witness Whereof, the said party of the first part has hereunto set his hand and seal the day and year first above written Petronilo Rios {Seal}

Signed, Sealed and Delivered in the presence of Francis Sylvester, Subscribing Witness, State of California, County of Monterey ss.

On this eleventh day of February A. D. One Thousand Eight Hundred and sixty seven before me William M. R. Parker, County Clerk, an ExOfficio Clerk of the County Court, in and for said County, personally appeared Francis Sylvester personally known to me to be the same person whose name is subscribed to the annexed Instrument as a witness thereto, who being by me duly sworn, deposed and said, that he resides in the County and State aforesaid, that he was present and saw Petronilo Rios known to him to be the same person described in and who executed the annexed Instrument, as a party thereto,

Sign, Seal and Deliver the same; And that the deponent, thereupon signed his name as a subscribing witness thereto.

In Witness Whereof, I have hereunto set my hand and affixed the Seal of said Court the day and year in the Certificate first written above.

M. R. Parker Clerk {County Court Seal}
Recorded at request of John W. Miller
Feb. 11th A. D. 1867 at

10 min. past 4 o'c P. M.

This Indenture, made the twenty-fourth day of December One thousand eight hundred and sixty six between Doroteo Ambris of the County of Monterey and State of California, party of the first part and Petronilo Rios of the County of San Luis Obispo, party of the second part.

Witnesseth, That the said party of the first part for, and in consideration of the sum of Three hundred Dollars to him in hand paid by the party of the second part, at or before the ensealing and delivery of these presents, the receipt whereof is hereby acknowledged, Has remised, released and quit claimed, and by these presents, Does remise, release and quit claim unto the said party of the second part, and to his heirs and assigns forever.

All the right, title and interest of the said party of the first part in and to that certain piece, parcel or lot of land, situate lying and being in the City of Monterey, County and State aforesaid. Commencing at the lot and house of Joaquin Gutierrez, now occupied by him, and running on the line of Main Street to the land of Jacob P. Leese and running back to Pacific Street and being twenty four (24) *varas* more or less fronting on Main Street and running back thirty two *varas* more or less to Pacific Street being portion of a lot granted to Graciano Manjores by the *Alcalde* of Monterey and purchased from him by A. S. Taylor and by Taylor conveyed to the party of the first part.

Together with all and singular the tenements, hereditament and appurtenances thereunto belonging or in issues and profits thereof. And also all the estate right, title, interest, property, possession claim and demand whatsoever, as well in law as in equity of the said party of the first part, of, in or to the above described premises, and every part and parcel thereof, with the appurtenances.

To Have and To Hold, all and singular the above mentioned and described premises, together with the appurtenances unto the said party of the second part has hereunto set his hand and seal the day and year first above written, Doroteo Ambris {Seal} Signed, Sealed and Delivered in the presence of *blank* , State of California, County of Monterey ss.

On this twenty fourth day of December A. D. One Thousand Eight Hundred and sixty six, before me William M. R. Parker, County Clerk, and ExOfficio Clerk of the County Court in and for Said County, personally appeared Doroteo Ambris personally known to me to be the individual described in and who executed the same freely and voluntarily and for the uses and purposes therein mentioned.

In Witness Whereof I have hereunto set my hand this Certificate first above written.

W. M. R. Parker, Clerk
{County Clerk Seal}
Recorded at request of Mariano Gonzales
Feb. 12th A. D. 1867 at
25 min. past 10 o'c A. M.

The year 1867 is the next to the last transaction date that we can connect with Petronilo Rios. Edith Buckland Webb, in her book *Indian Life at the Old Missions*, states that the last of Mission San Miguel's stock was taken to Lompoc by Petronilo Rios. (The final transaction will be addressed later in this chapter.)

Stephen Rios (1869-1950), grandson of Petronilo and Catarina Rios, worked on the historic 35,575-acre San Marcos Rancho, north of Santa Barbara. Stephen's older brother, Bonifacio Gusto or "Justo," born in 1861, was also a *vaquero* on the San Marcos Ranch in the upper Santa Ynez Valley, past where Lake Cachuma is now located.

James Ramon (Santiago) Rios, another grandson of Petronilo and Catarina Rios, left San Luis Obispo County to become cattle superintendent for William Dibblee on the San Julian Ranch in Santa Barbara County. He worked for Dibblee for forty years.

Augustine "Gus" Rios, a great-grandson of Petronilo and Catarina Rios, was born on May 27, 1899 in Jolon, and left home at the age of twelve. He worked for forty years as a *vaquero* on the San Julian Ranch. It is said that at times Gus rode a black horse, wore a black hat, black leather vest, black chaps and black *tapaderos*. He retired after twenty years as foreman of the Muscio Ranch near Santa Maria, where he died on August 3, 1973.

The Great Register for 1871 does not list Petronilo Rios. Camilo Rios does have his name appear in 1871; he is listed as 34 years old, a farmer at Hot Springs. Francisco Rios is listed as 24 years old, and a farmer at Hot Springs.

By 1874, the only Rios names from Petronilo's family listed on the tax assessment rolls are Francisco Rios, with 637 acres of land, in addition to being listed along with Stephen M. Rios in ownership of Section 36, Township 25, Range 12 - - -which is the area of land surrounding La Estrella Adobe.

Petronilo and Catarina's oldest son, Jose Camilo Rios, resided on the Caledonia property with his wife and family from 1857 to 1875. Camilo and his wife, Maria Antonia Castillo Rios, had eleven children, all born in San Miguel. It is said that this family had moved to Lompoc in 1875 when that community began as a temperance colony, although Camilo's name appears in the Great Register of San Luis Obispo County in 1880. However, the date of registration is given as August 21, 1875, so the family could have moved not long after that date.

In 1880, the Great Register for San Luis Obispo County has the Rios family represented by Camilo Rios, a laborer in San Miguel; Estevan Rios, a farmer in San Miguel; and Francisco Rios, a stock-raiser at Hot Springs. The Great Registers for the years 1882, 1890 and 1892 do not list any Rios names at all.

The 1880 Census for Lompoc lists the following family and their ages: Camilo Rios 50; Maria (his wife) 39; Canuto 23; James (Santiago Ramon) 21; Maria 19; Justo 18; Egobilo 15; Charles 13; Frank 12; Teresa 7; and Victoria 5. Children not listed would be Josefa, who would have been 22, and Steve, who would have been 11 years old. Josefa married Fermo Anthony Frazzi; she died on April 15, 1945 in Stockton, California.

A more accurate list of Camilo and Mary's children, with their years of birth, is as follows: Canuto 1857; Josefa 1858; James (Santiago Ramon) 1859; Justo 1862; Mary 1863; Egobilo 1863; Charles Osbando 1867; Frank 1868; Steve 1869; Teresa 1873 and Victoria 1875. It has always been said that all eleven children were born in San Miguel.

Camilo Rios died on December 7, 1916 in Santa Barbara. His wife, Maria Antonia, had died in Lompoc on June 17, 1913.

"The Friends of the Adobes, Inc." has a priceless booklet, much of it written in the beautiful penmanship of Petronilo Rios. In it are recorded his children's birthdates. He called this record "Memories." This booklet, which measures 3 ¼ inches by 5 inches, was donated by Mrs. (Maria Luisa Raimunda Rios) Louise Clinton. She was the great-granddaughter of Petronilo and Catarina Rios; her father was Canuto (1857-1920), who was the first child of Jose Camilo (1833-1916) and Mary Castillo Rios (1843-1913). She said that her nickname was "Cookie," but didn't know where she picked it up.

In another chapter, it had been remarked that the Petronilo Rios family was "religious." This idea is reinforced by the fact that in the "Memories" booklet, Petronilo Rios listed the names, birthdates and god-parents of each of his children. He also recorded the fact that each child had been baptized and confirmed. We only wish that he had listed each child's birthplace.

It is important to understand the attitude of most *Californios* concerning the position of god-parents. Antonio Coronel (1817-1895) wrote the following in his book, *Things Past: Remembrances of Sports, Dances, Diversions and Other Domestic and Social Customs of Old California.*

The god-sons and god-daughters were under obligation, whenever they happened to meet the god-father, to take off their hats and recite a short prayer, after which he gave them his blessing. The god-parents were required, in case the god-children lost their father or mother, to fill that place, and if the god-children lacked means to live and educate themselves the former were obliged to supply it, and also to give them counsel.

This co-parentage was a bond of affinity existing between the father and mother of a boy or girl on the one hand and god-parents on the other; this bond was so regarded by the church, but not by the civil law. Whenever an infant was baptized, the priest explained these bonds and called attention to the obligations that were contracted.

[Antonio Coronel, at age 18, lived for a year, with his family, in the Caledonia adobe; his father was administrator of Mission San Miguel from July 14, 1836 to March 30, 1837.]

This writer recently learned of what is most likely the final transaction made by Petronilo Rios. On pages 762 and 763 of Book "B" of Deeds in the San Luis Obispo County Recorder's office, can be found the following document.

Miguel Garcia
to
Petronilo Rios   **February 2, 1870**

Indenture between Miguel Garcia, party of the first part, of the County of Santa Clara and Petronilo Rios, part of the second part, for the sum of $1, that certain tract of land lying and being in the county of San Luis Obispo and known as the Mission of "San Miguel" granted by Governor Pio Pico in the year of One thousand eight hundred and forty six to Guillermo Reed, Petronilo Rios and Miguel Garcia (the party of the first part herein).

                    his
Miguel X Garcia   {Seal}
                    mark

Signed, sealed and delivered in the presence of W. B. Rankin.

State of California
County of Santa Clara

On this second day of February AD one thousand eight hundred and seventy before me W. B. Rankin a Notary Public in and for said County of Santa Clara duly commissioned and sworn and qualified, personally appeared the within named Miguel Garcia whose name is subscribed to the annexed instrument as a party thereto, personally known to me to be the individual described and who executed the said annexed instrument as a party thereto and who duly acknowledged to me that he executed the same freely and voluntarily and for the uses land purposes therein mentioned.

In witness whereof I have here unto set my hand and affixed my official seal the day and year in this certificate first above written.

W. B. Rankin

Recorded at request of Petronilo Rios February 10th A.D. 1870 at 30 minutes past 9 o'clock A.M.

Charles W. Dana,
County Recorder
by R. Pollard, Deputy

This transaction is of great interest to this writer for several reasons. The first is that almost immediately after Mission San Miguel was purchased by Reed,

Rios and Garcia in July of 1846, Miguel Garcia drops out of the picture. In a document dated September 11, 1846, he decided to "separate myself from the companionship of my *padrino*" - - - Petronilo Rios. A second interesting thought is that Mission San Miguel, proper, along with the cemetery, orchard and vineyard, were returned to the Catholic Church in 1859; Miguel Garcia would have no legal right to re-sell this mission. [Virginia Peterson states that the reason the interior of the church portion of Mission San Miguel was preserved throughout the years is that members of a Garcia family took care of the church. She was told that this family later moved to Pozo, which would lead one to believe that they were related to Ynocente Garcia, one-time administrator of Mission San Miguel.]

The third interesting part involved in this transaction is the fact that it was made about three months before the death of Petronilo Rios. Perhaps Petronilo was attempting to get his affairs in order, and believed that he needed to have paid Miguel Garcia for his third of the original purchase of Mission San Miguel.

At the present time, we do not know for certain where Petronilo Rios was living at the time of his death. Death records were not required to be kept, by the State of California, until 1905. A search of death records in the counties of San Luis Obispo, Santa Barbara, Monterey, Santa Cruz and Santa Clara has not yielded the information desired.

The federal census for 1870, lists every person in each dwelling, as of the first day of June. This year of Petronilo Rios' death, shows that Catarina Rios (age 59), Maria Rios (age 36) and Petronella Rios (age 18) were living together in Santa Clara Township, Post Office San Jose. It can be assumed that Petronilo Rios had also been living there until he passed away on the 11th of May at 11 o'clock in the morning in the year 1870.

A notation has been made in the "Memories" booklet: *D. P. Rios murio el 11 de Mayo a las 11 del dya Ano 1870.* Catarina Avila Rios passed away at 3 o'clock in the morning on the 20th of November in the year 1889. The "Memories" booklet contains this notation: *D. C. Avila de Rios murio el 20 de Noviembre a las 3 de la manana Ano 1889.*

Vaya con Dios, Petronilo and Catarina.

THE SETTLEMENT AT EL PASO DE ROBLES

The credit for having constructed a shelter house and a place for bathing at the sulphur springs of El Paso de Robles, is given to Father Juan Vicente Cabot. Bathing in the springs alleviated the pain and suffering caused by rheumatism and arthritis. Down through the years, Indians as well as missionaries came from great distances to make use of the springs.

Father Juan Cabot served two terms at Mission San Miguel. His first period of service was from October 1, 1807 until March 12, 1819; his second period was from November 7, 1824 until November 25, 1834. It was during Father Juan Cabot's first term of service that the adobe house was constructed on El Paso de Robles rancho. The year of its completion has been determined to be 1813. Perhaps it was during this period of time that Father Cabot had a shelter constructed at the hot sulphur springs.

Dan Krieger, Professor of History at California State Polytechnic University, in an article written for the *Telegram-Tribune*, in 1989, stated that "The warmth of the mud baths healed their aching bones. Rheumatoid arthritis was a common complaint among the peoples of the Salinas Valley during the 500-year epoch of cold, very moist climate which had begun during the mid 1300s." Luckily, Father Juan Cabot was an understanding person. In an article for the *Telegram-Tribune*, in 1992, Dan Krieger informs us that "Many of the other mission friars prohibited bathing, because of its association with the Indians' *temescal* ceremony, involving mystical instruction by a *shaman*. Cabot saw that the bathing was necessary to alleviate the suffering from arthritis and rheumatism."

In an article for the Pioneer Day Edition of *The Daily Press*, in 1987, Virginia Peterson wrote that Missions Santa Ynez, San Luis Obispo and San Antonio de Padua all brought their sick people to bathe in and to drink the thermal waters of the springs; the main spring was located at the northeast corner of present-day Spring and 10th Streets. Due to the presence of the springs, the Indians in this area were some of the most healthy in the state. William Zimmerman, in his 1890 book, *A Short & Complete History of the San Miguel Mission*, said that "Its death rate was less than that of any other establishment, except San Luis Rey. . . ."

In 1864, a correspondent to the San Francisco *Bulletin* described his arrival at the springs. He reported that the timber lining of the spring was in as good condition as when the padres put them in over eighty years previously. The reporter added that the flow of the water was more abundant that it had been previously, due to the collapsing of another underground spring, which was caused by the earthquake of 1856. This event, according to the reporter, had released an additional stream.

If the correspondent's estimate of time is correct, it would mean that some construction at the spring would have taken place prior to the founding of Mission San Miguel. Mission San Antonio de Padua had been founded in 1771, and Mission San Luis Obispo in 1772. It is entirely possible that people from either or both of these missions could have erected some sort of structure at the springs. In the case of Mission San Antonio, this would have been 26 years before Mission San Miguel was founded.

It would be of interest if we could be certain how El Paso de Robles received its name. Mrs. Virginia Peterson mentions the legend that the name "Paso de Robles" refers to a huge oak tree, hundreds of years old, which fell across Paso Robles Creek; the tree became a foot-bridge during the rainy season. The word *paso*, in Spanish, can have the meaning of "crossing" and "passage," as well as "pass."

The 1979 Pioneer Day Edition of *The Daily Press* mentions that Mrs. D. D. Blackburn had spoken to an old Indian, from whom she sought information concerning the early days. According to the Indian, a storm once arose that flooded Paso Robles Creek, so that to cross it was impossible. As luck would have it, a large up-rooted oak fell across the creek in such a fashion that it formed a natural foot-bridge. Hence, the passage over the oak.

J. Fraser MacGillivray, in his book, *The Story of*

Adelaida, informed his readers that a map, prepared by Manuel Agustin Mascaro and dated July 29, 1782, denotes a general area as "de los Robles." The area, west of the Salinas River, is in the general area of Adelaida.

These ideas are interesting, but not proof of how the name came to be used. Perhaps the meaning is simply "the Pass of the Oaks."

Some writers cite Padre Pedro Font's diary of the De Anza Expedition of 1775-1776 as the date when the name Paso de Robles was bestowed, as the expedition passed through the growth of live oaks at the site. However, Padre Font's diary gives a different view of the question.

March 4. - We set out from the mission of San Luis Obispo at nine in the morning, and, at a quarter to five in the afternoon, halted at a place called La Asuncion, on the banks of the Rio de Monterey (which the Rio de Santa Margarita has already joined), having traveled some ten leagues: about one to the northeast; four to the north; one to the north-north-west; two to the northwest; and two to the west-northwest.

March 5. - We set out from La Asuncion at a quarter to nine in the morning, and, at a quarter past four in the afternoon, halted beside the Rio de San Antonio, at a place called Primer Vado, having traveled some ten leagues; about three almost due north; five, northwest; and two, west-northwest.

March 6. - We set out from Primer Vado at a quarter to eight in the morning, and, at four in the afternoon, arrived at the mission of San Antonio de los Robles. . . .The mission of San Antonio is situated in the Sierra de Santa Lucia. . . in a canyon - not very narrow and some ten leagues long - that is entirely covered with great oaks; for this reason the mission is called San Antonio de la Canada de los Robles.

"Primer Vado" was the first ford of the San Antonio River.

It seems to this writer that it is not correct to cite Father Pedro Font, when trying to determine when and why Paso de Robles received its name. We do know that the Padres of Mission San Miguel mentioned the name, in 1828, as a rancho where wheat was sown.

In January of 1864, a San Jose doctor, T. D. Johnson, purchased one league of land from the Blackburns for $20,000. Johnson was responsible for the construction of the first El Paso de Robles Hotel, and for the first bath-house over the main spring at 10th and Spring Streets. Both buildings were completed by June of 1864. Fifty guests registered during the first week after opening.

Dr. Johnson's patients could make use of the sul-

JAMES H. BLACKBURN (left) and Daniel Blackburn were partners in founding of the City of Paso Robles. Until the past few years there was no change in the limits of the city which they helped incorporate back in 1889. (Blackburn collection.)

James H. Blackburn(left) and Daniel Blackburn were partners in founding of the City of Paso Robles. Until the past few years there was no change in the limits of the city which they helped incorporate back in 1889.

(Blackburn collection.)

phur baths, and be provided with room and board at a monthly fee of $9, with medical attention free. Perhaps this policy was partly responsible for the fact that by September of 1864, Dr. Johnson had returned to San Jose, and the Blackburns regained possession of the one league of land, which included the spring, and which property now included a hotel.

San Luis Obispo County tax records for 1864 show that Dr. Johnson had 4,438 acres of land at Hot Springs; he had 54 head of American cattle, 4 wagon horses, 1 yoke of American oxen, 100 hogs, 1 wagon & harness, and household furniture. The total assessed value was $12,445 and the tax due was $404.47.

A sign that a substantial community was beginning to form is that three years later, the "Hot Springs" post office was established on June 14, 1867, with Edward McCarthy as postmaster. The "Hot Springs" post office also served the areas of Santa Margarita, Eaglet, Cashin's Station, Eagle Rancho, Estrella and Morehouse settlement.

Prior to the establishment of the "Hot Springs" post office, mail brought by stage could be picked up at the hotel, where it was left on the mantle of the fireplace to be shuffled through by the addressees.

Three years later, on May 2, 1870, when Charles Knowlton was postmaster, the name of the post office was changed to "Paso Robles."

On May 12, 1867, a newspaper article described four of the springs of El Paso de Robles.

THE MUD SPRING - In a northerly direction from the hotel, on immediate bank of the Salinas River, and close to the stage road approaching Paso Robles from the north. The mouth of the spring proper is about two feet in diameter. Four or five feet below is the mud pool, over which is a rude board structure six feet square, roofed with boughs. Into this mud pool runs the water from the spring, and into the mud the most obstinate of the rheumatic cases are "stuck."

Such is the warmth of this mud, the very grittiest of patients insist on being pulled out at the end of 15 minutes immersion. To the taste and smell, the water of the Mud Spring is not so highly impregnated with sulphur as the water of the Hot Spring, but a slightly saline flavor is perceptible.

The treatment here is: Immerse the affected part of the body in the mud and keep it there until it is "done through." The mud is as black as ink and a patient rising therefrom must look like the imp of darkness. Although more disagreeable than the water baths, the

mud baths act with much greater force and the cure is much quicker.

The spring is quite invaluable to a large class of patients, and could be much pleasanter and a source of more profit to the owners if a small outlay was made to improve the surroundings.

THE COLD SPRING - Two miles in a northwesterly direction from the hotel is the Cold Sulphur Spring, which is situated at the bottom of a small ravine, the sides of which are picturesquely dotted with oaks and manzanitas.

The spring is uncovered except for a green roof of Nature's providing: a cottonwood tree, one of a group of three, and the only trees of the kind to be found within many miles overshadowing it. The water is of as cold a temperature as is the water of the generality of springs in California, and is but slightly impregnated with sulphur.

THE TEPID SPRING - Half a mile southeast from the hotel, and a quarter of a mile from the west bank of the Salinas River, is the Tepid Sulphur Spring, surrounded by a rank growth of rushes and a course grass, and is covered by a brush house. The basin is about two feet deep and the water tastes highly sulphurous. The temperature is lukewarm and it is visited more from curiosity than of use.

THE HOT SPRING - To the unaccustomed palate, the first taste of the water of this spring is extremely nauseous, but as the draught is repeated, the nauseous effect is lost. Those who partake of the water for any length of time acquire a fondness for it and imbibe it by the glassful with as much relish as an old toper manifests when absorbing a toddy.

I found the temperature of the water as hot as was endurable. One jot hotter would have brought me speedily out under fear of being parboiled. The feeling passed into one of blissfulness, as perspiration began to pour from head and face. Ten minutes satisfied me for a beginning.

In a "Scrap" of 1868, the correspondent for a San Francisco newspaper reported that the plunge, though still lined with the rude timbers of the Padres, was in a separate house. The pool was four or five feet deep, two feet long, and eight feet wide. The mud baths, whose medical virtues were said to be even superior to the water baths, were located about one mile north of the City of Paso Robles. There were also the Iron Spring and the Sand Spring.

In 1875, E. Malcolm Morse, a leading physician of Washington, D. C., wrote *A Treatise on the Hot Sulphur Springs of El Paso de Robles.* Part of what he had to say is the following:

Midway between the Mission of San Miguel Arcangel and La Casa del Paso de Robles are the hot and cold springs of the Paso de Robles Rancho. . .far back in the misty times of tradition, the Aborigines told each other of the medicine water, welling hot from the earth, in the valley of the Salt River.

The Main Spring - the reservoir is 8 feet square; flow is 4,500 gallons per hour.

Mud Spring - ½ miles north of Hot Springs Hotel. Bath house, which covers the Mud Spring, is divided down the center, by a raised platform. On one side is a plunge bath of tepid gas, and sulphur-impregnated water; on the other is the famous bath. The mud is taken from the hot bog, dried and screened, and then thrown into the two vats which box the two hot springs. These vats are each 3 feet deep and 8 feet square. From the bottom of these vats springs the water, in one, with a mean temperature of 122 degrees F.; in the other, 140 degrees F.

Twelve hours after the mud is changed (which is done every few days) it is permeated by the gas and water and is ready to use.

An easy carriage runs to the "Mud Spring" every three hours, commencing at 6 o'clock a.m., and making the last trip at 3 o'clock p.m. Later than 5 p.m. or earlier than 6 a.m. the bath is open to gentlemen, on payment of a small fee; otherwise this bath is free.

100 feet distant from "The Mud" is the "Sand Bath," with a mean temperature of 140 degrees F.

Soda and White Sulphur Springs flank the Mud Spring, one being north and the other south, and both about 200 yards distant from it. Neither is housed. The water from both is very cold.

The Iron or Chalybeate Spring - The "Iron Spring" is 600 yards east of the Main Spring, and near the bank of the Salinas. It has a moderate flow of cold water; it is boxed though not covered.

Passengers to El Paso de Robles from San Francisco leave by Southern Pacific Railroad 6:30 a.m., stops for dinner at Gilroy; runs through Soledad, the terminus, where it arrives at 4:25 p.m.

Concord coaches are waiting at Soledad; they take passengers across the Salinas River to Thomas' Hotel. Take an early supper and prepare for the stage ride. Leave Thomas' at 5:30 p.m., arrive at Lowe's 9 p.m.; and stop over until next morning, thereby avoiding all night travel.

The stage arrives at El Paso de Robles at 12 midnight. The whole journey from San Francisco being made in 28 hours. Through fare $16, round tickets at reduced prices.

In 1882, a stone basin was built around the main spring; the flow was about 40 gallons per hour. There were then two plunges, one exclusively for the ladies.

In the early 1880s, the prospect that the railroad would pass through El Paso de Robles gave encouragement to Drury James and the Blackburn brothers, who believed that a town around the hot springs might prosper. They engaged F. P. McCray, of Hollister, to lay out a town site with the resort as the nucleus.

According to San Miguel's newspaper, *The Inland Messenger*, on May 7, 1886, "C. F. Sharp, late of the Andrews Hotel, has taken charge of the office of the Paso Robles Hotel." The July 9th edition of that paper informed its readers that "The surveys on the Paso Robles Ranch have been completed." On July 16, 1886, *The Inland Messenger* reported that "The Paso Robles resort is being well patronized, and as the facilities for travel are improved the number of guests will increase. It is probable that the capacity of the institution will have to be enlarged in the near future."

One week later, the newspaper from San Miguel stated that "The railroad surveying party moved camp last Tuesday to Paso Robles, in the region of which they are to run several preliminary lines."

On September 10, 1886, *The Inland Messenger* informed everyone that "The proprietors of the Paso Robles Springs are laying off a town in the vicinity. It is a central point and a beautiful town-site." According to the same newspaper, on October 8, 1886, "It is announced that the proprietors of Paso Robles will have 300 lots ready to sell at auction when the railroad reaches that point."

A chaparral picket fence, over two miles long, ran through this area from north to south, to mark the

Paso Robles Depot.

Robles, which commenced last Wednesday, should be mentioned as an eminent success. There were three or four hundred persons present, and a lively competition was developed among bidders. The prices realized were generally good, ranging from $100 to $1,000. The sale was conducted by a gentleman from San Jose. The lots have a frontage of fifty feet, being twice the size of lots in San Miguel, which forms an important consideration in fixing the price. The sales made the first day are said to aggregate $25,000, and the business is still progressing on up to our time of going to press."

Readers of the San Miguel newspaper, on November 19th, learned that "The hotel facilities at Paso Robles are found too limited for the demands of the public, and additions are soon to be made." According to the December 3, 1886 edition of the same newspaper, "T. H. Reddington, formerly of Los Gatos, has charge of the garden and orchards at Paso Robles."

On January 14, 1887, *The Inland Messenger* carried a story which had appeared in the *Paso Robles Leader*. "The Articles of Incorporation of the First M. E. Church of Paso Robles are about to be filed. As soon as completed, the work of constructing a church edifice will be commenced. The following are the trustees elected for the first year: S. W. Fergusson, H. G. Wright, Richard M. Shackelford, W. L. Hatch, Levi Exline, J. W. Smith, Irving Gordenier."

R. M. Shackelford had been born in Washington County, near Mackville, Kentucky on January 17, 1836; he was the son of James S. and Sarah A. Shackelford, both also born in Kentucky. He was one in a family of nine daughters and two sons.

When eight years of age, R. M. and his family moved to Missouri. At the age of 16, he started to drive a bull team across the plains. This memorable journey began on March 14, 1852 and ended in Sacramento on September 23, 1852.

The year 1857 found him working in a milling enterprise in Marysville; in 1866, he located in Los Gatos, where he maintained a lumber yard and also operated a general merchandise store. He moved to Salinas in

western boundary of a vast wheat field, which lay next to the Salinas River. This fence later became the eastern boundary of Spring Street, and its direction determined the bearings of all the streets.

The work of laying out the site started in 1886, but was not finished until 1887, when G. F. Spurrier and Van R. Elliott completed the survey begun by Mr. McCray. El Paso de Robles Rancho was divided in 1887 and sold to the eager buyers; they were numerous, due to the railroad having been completed as far as present-day Templeton.

A sign that the town of Paso Robles was continuing to form is an article from the November 12, 1886 edition of the San Miguel newspaper. "A. R. Booth, the popular druggist of San Luis Obispo, has purchased the Paso Robles Drug Store and will immediately put in a complete stock of drugs and be prepared to fill all orders with which he may be favored."

Readers of the November 19, 1886 issue of *The Inland Messenger* could learn that "A new paper, bearing the euphonious title of *El Paso de Robles Leader*, arrived in the mail . . .last Monday. It is a neat-appearing seven-column folio, and contains a large amount of reading matter of special interest to prospective investors in Paso Robles property. Its publisher is the El Paso de Robles Leader Publishing Co., of which H. G. Wright is announced as manager." [Mr. Wright's daughter, Mabelle, was the first child to be born in the new town.]

On the same date as above, the same newspaper informed readers that "The auction sale of lots in Paso

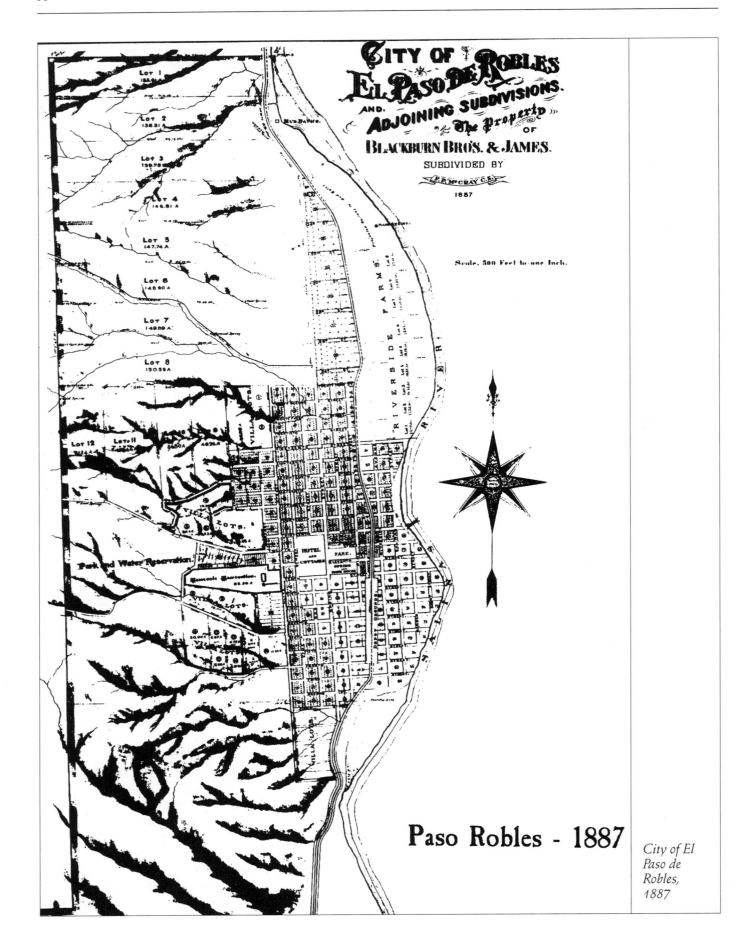

Paso Robles - 1887

City of El Paso de Robles, 1887

1869; that year, he and a partner bought the San Lorenzo Ranch, of 2,200 acres, on the Salinas River.

He disposed of the ranch in 1873, and moved to Hollister, where he engaged in milling. He arrived in Paso Robles in 1886, and two weeks after settling there, was appointed a school trustee; he served continuously for nearly thirty years.

Mrs. Shackelford, the former Mary L. McQuestin, was a native of Galena, Illinois. The Shackelford were the parents of four children.

The San Miguel newspaper was renamed on April 29, 1887; on May 20th, the *San Miguel Messenger* informed its readers that "The raffle for a piano, mentioned some months since in the columns, will take place at P. H. Dunn's store in Paso Robles, next Saturday, the 21st instant. (Editor: N. Bennett won.)."

The *San Miguel Messenger*, on June 10, 1887, carried the following:

**Special Masonic Notice
Laying the Corner Stone at Paso Robles**

All Free & Accepted Masons and their families are hereby extended a cordial invitation to attend the ceremonies on the laying of the Corner Stone of the Masonic Temple at Paso Robles on Friday, June 24th, at 2 p.m. Arrangements will be made for special passenger rates along the railroad and stage lines for intending guests.

**M. Bennett
H. Victors
N. S. Giberson
Committee**

The June 17, 1887 edition of that paper stated that "S. P. Sitton has been appointed Justice of the Peace and J. W. Bane Constable for Paso Robles Township." The same issue also informed people that "Grant & Woster have taken the contract to put up the Masonic building at Paso Robles for $8,624."

One week later, the same paper carried the news that "Mr. P. H. Dunn, of Paso Robles, whose health is very much impaired, went north Wednesday. He will go to a hospital for treatment."

On June 24, 1887, the *San Miguel Messenger* printed an article entitled, "The Masonic Ceremonies," which had been taken from the *Paso Robles Leader*.

The following is the official program of

the ceremonies to be observed at the laying of the corner stone of the Masonic Temple at Paso Robles on Friday, June 24th:

The procession will form at the Lodge room on Twelfth street, and march thence to the building of the Masonic Hall Association, where ceremonies will be performed by the Grand Lodge of the State of California. The procession will then re-form and, preceded by a band of music, will march over the new bridge to the picnic grounds on the other side of the Salinas, where the oration will be delivered by the Grand Orator. Everybody will then be expected to assist at the barbecue. In the evening the spacious dining room of the hotel will be thrown open for a grand ball, which will be led by the San Luis Cornet band. To all of which the public is cordially invited.

The June 24, 1887 issue of the paper printed another article taken from the *Paso Robles Leader*. It was entitled, "The Paso Robles Bridge."

Work on the bridge is progressing most satisfactorily. The first bent is entirely completed, all the planking having been laid and is now in readiness for the passage of teams. The second bent is in place and is nearly completed. The piers for the third section are all finished and early in the week the timbers will be put up. By the latter part of the coming week the structure will be ready for use.

A change has been made in the plans, and instead of having three spans, it will be made of four, which will bring it to the edge of the second bench on the opposite side of the river, and take it entirely across the first bench. This obviates any danger whatever from the effect of high water.

The bridge over the Salinas River at Paso Robles was paid for by the Blackburn Brothers and Drury James. James H. Blackburn directed that three of his fattest cattle be selected and slaughtered to provide food for the celebration of the occasion.

The Masonic Temple which was constructed on 12th Street was said to be the first building of its kind between Los Angeles and San Francisco.

Readers of the *San Miguel Messenger*, on July 8, 1887, learned that "The iron work for the planing mill, of the Southern Pacific Milling Company at Paso Robles, also the front for the new Masonic building at the same place, went south by rail a few days ago."

On July 29, 1887, the paper printed an article that had been run in the Templeton *Times.*

An Immediate Public Duty

The West Coast Land Company and Blackburn Brothers & James have done what ought to have been assumed as a public expense. Their keen, business instincts taught them that to make the tens of thousands of fertile acres East of the Salinas a source of profit to Templeton and Paso Robles ample traveling facilities must be provided, and disparing of public aid they went down into their private pockets and built two bridges and several excellent roads leading to them . . .

According to the September 16, 1887 edition of that newspaper, "W. J. Sherman has been appointed a Justice of the Peace for Hot Springs Township, Paso Robles; vice Woodward resigned." One week later, on September 23rd, the same newspaper printed some school information. "It is surprising what can be sometimes accomplished in a climate like that of Paso Robles, by the judicious expenditure of a comparatively small amount of money. They have lately built a school house at that place, costing about $3,000, which an exchange says is the handsomest building of the kind in the State. Our school trustees will give satisfaction to their constituents if they approximate so great a result with $8,000."

The *San Miguel Messenger,* on September 23, 1887, informed its readers that "Mr. George F. Weeks, who has filled the editorial chair of the *Paso Robles Leader* for some months past, has resigned that position and gone south seeking opportunities for investment. Mr. Wright resumes the editorial duties, and will make a good paper."

According to the San Miguel newspaper, on October 21, 1887, "The Masonic building at Paso Robles is completed. The first floor front will be used by Eppinger & Moore as a store. The second floor, in addition to Masonic rooms, will include two or three offices."

The paper, on October 28, 1887, informed readers that "Geo. F. Weeks, formerly of the Paso Robles *Leader,* has again gone south on business. He goes to San Bernardino."

The November 18, 1887 edition of the *San Miguel*

Messenger stated that "On the 1st of December, the Bank of Paso Robles will open business. J. H. Blackburn is President, D. Speyer, Vice President and cashier, and R. E. Jack, Manager. The capital stock is $100,000."

An ad in the same newspaper, on December 23, 1887:

**J. H. Blackburn, President
I. Goldtree, Vice-President
D. Speyer, Cashier
R. E. Jack, Manager**

**Bank
of
Paso Robles
Transacts
a General Banking Business**

**Interest
Will be paid on Time Deposits
Loans
Made on Good Personal Security
Buy and sell exchange on
San Francisco, New York, London and
all other points desired.
Agents:
San Francisco, Anglo California Bank
New York, J & W Seligman & Co.
London, Anglo California Bank, limited
Dublin, Royal Bank of England**

According to the November 25, 1887 edition of the *San Miguel Messenger*: "Paso Robles is to have another paper called *The Moon.* At first we were disposed to think the report all "moonshine," but later information confirms it as a fact." *The Moon*, edited by A. D. King, joined the *El Paso de Robles Leader*, and the *Independent*, owned and edited by Charles H. Arnold, as weekly newspapers.

The same newspaper, on the same date, informed readers that "The people of Paso Robles celebrated the anniversary of the first sale of town lots last week by a dance."

"An election was held at Paso Robles last week," according to the December 9, 1887 *San Miguel Messenger*, "on the question of issuing bonds to the amount of $5,000 for the construction of another schoolhouse, and the proposition was carried unanimously." The newspaper on the same date informed readers that "Dr. D. L. Deal, formerly of Modesto, is expected to locate at Paso Robles soon. He is highly recommended by some of the leading citizens of that place."

The *San Miguel Messenger*, on December 9th, published the following comment. "The *Moon*, a five column paper printed at Paso Robles, has made its appearance. It announces that it has 'come to fill a long felt want;' that it has 'come to stay,' that it 'will be made so far as possible, humorous and readable, and in proportion to its opportunities it will aim to be second to no paper on the coast.' The paper has the appearance of being fairly patronized by the business men, and is doubtless on the highway to success. It has the best wishes of the *Messenger*."

According to the *San Miguel Messenger*, on December 23, 1887, "Our neighbor of Paso Robles, the *Leader*, appears to imagine that there is some one, or a greater number of people, living in San Miguel who are 'jealous of the prosperity of Paso Robles.' We think our contemporary is indulging the imagination a good deal in that idea. For, whatever may be the facts, the people of San Miguel are not aware that Paso Robles has anything of which a resident of San Miguel would be warranted in being jealous."

The *Paso Robles Leader*, on February 4, 1888 printed the following headline: "At Rest, J. H. Blackburn. His Demise Occurs at 9:45 p.m. Friday, January 27, 1888."

BLACKBURN - In Templeton on Friday, January 27th, 1888, James Hanson Blackburn aged 67 years.

The above announcement which came like a shock, was not at all unexpected. For several weeks previous he had been suffering from pneumonia, the effects of a cold taken, on a cold raw day while out surveying. Every thing that could be done or physicians suggest was done but with no avail. He continued to sink lower and lower, until he finally sank into a calm repose about 9:45 o'clock on the Friday night above mentioned, from which the body knows no awakening.

Mr. Blackburn was in San Luis about the first of the month; then appearing in the best of health and spirits, a splendid specimen of manhood, looking younger by twenty years than his actual age, cheerful and social, with every faculty of mind and body apparently unimpaired by age or infirmity, looking forward to a bright future of prominence in the public esteem and enjoyment in life of an honorably earned and grand fortune. Returning to his ranch he exposed himself in one of

the cold storms of the early part of the month, taking a severe cold resulting in pneumonia, attacking his heart and brain and causing death. The stalwart pioneer cannot always expose himself recklessly to the elements, as even to him comes weakness and infirmities. In the preparation for organizing a company for constructing a railroad to the San Joaquin valley Mr. Blackburn was made chairman of the committee, and much was expected of him. In the progress and building of Paso Robles much depended on him, and in every part of the county his loss will be felt.

On Monday, February 25, 1889, a special election was held to decide whether Paso Robles should incorporate as a city. After the election returns were canvassed by the Board of Supervisors, it was declared that 91 votes were cast for incorporation, and 53 votes were cast against it. The following officers were declared elected: Trustees - J. H. Glass, D. W. James, G. R. Adams, W. E. Grant and J. A. Van Wormer. City Clerk - W. J. Sherman; Marshall - F. Misenheimer; Treasurer - Fred Jack.

On March 11, 1889, Paso de Robles was duly organized, formed and incorporated under the laws of the State of California. By petition of the Board of Trustees, the name was changed from "Paso de Robles" to "El Paso de Robles," on November 29, 1889.

The City of El Paso de Robles was incorporated with Drury James as president of the Board of Trustees. At that time, it was reported that 800 persons resided within the city limits. The total acreage encompassed within the original city was 1,485.65 acres.

The Paso Robles newspaper, *The Moon*, published this article May 21, 1892.

Gathered To His Fathers
Another Old Pioneer of San Luis Obispo
County Passes Away

Patrick Dunn, an old resident of this county, died at the residence of his son, Frank J. Dunn, near Cayucos on Thursday. Mr. Dunn was the father of Mrs. D. W. James and Mrs. D. D. Blackburn, now residents of this city, and of Patsy Dunn, formerly of this place, who died in the City of Mexico about one year ago, as well as of Mr. F. J. Dunn, at whose residence he has made his home for sometime past.

Mr. Dunn was established in business in the City of San Luis Obispo when there were

but few English-speaking people in the place. He was proprietor of the Eagle Hotel, then the leading hotel of the town. He prospered in his business and was a familiar figure and a popular man there for many years, but with the advent of the English population and the changed methods of doing business, he met with reverses and finally disposed of his property there and went to other parts.

He was a genial, whole-souled and intelligent man, the soul of politeness and generosity, the latter trait being the main factor in preventing the accumulation of the fortune that his talents were other wise capable of gaining for him. He was nearly eighty years of age and had not been in robust health for some time.

Early hotel on left, Hotel El Paso de Robles under construction.

On August 17, 1895, the *Paso Robles Record* would inform readers of the following.

> **The remains of P. H. Dunn which were temporarily buried in the Catholic cemetery, were removed yesterday to San Luis Obispo for permanent interment.**

The new Hotel El Paso de Robles was designed by the famous architect, Stanford White; he had established his reputation, prior to 1878, when he designed and then supervised the erection of the Trinity Church in Boston. In California, White designed the Hotel del Coronado in San Diego. On Sunday, October 11, 1891, meals were served in the spacious dining room of the Hotel El Paso de Robles. The hotel opened its doors for business the next day.

The following description of the new hotel is taken from a brochure entitled, "The Celebrated El Paso de Robles Hot Sulphur Springs and World Renowned Mud Baths." The brochure was written about 1892.

The New Hotel
This magnificent hotel has been thrown open for the occupancy of guests, and embodies, in the way of modern improvements and comfort-giving accessories, everything that can be found in the most pretentious of metropolitan hotels.

Architecturally, the hotel is one of the most attractive in appearance in the country. It is in the composit style, embracing the best elements of the *renaissance*, combined with the symmetry and strength of the Queen Anne periods.

The hotel is three stories high, and has a frontage of 285 feet, with an extreme depth of 240 feet. Semi-circular towers ornament the north and south wings.

A striking addition to the external beauty of the structure is the Solarium - - - a large tower rising directly over the center of the building, and from which eyrie-like elevation the guests can view the beauties of the surrounding country.

A veranda sixteen feet wide runs the whole front of the first floor, including both wings. This forms a spacious open air promenade, and has become a favorite resort with guests.

Passing the portal of the main entrance leads the guest into the office, a handsome apartment, 58 x 72 feet. Large, roomy halls lead to the dining room and to the wings.

Waiting room of the Hotel.

location. Every new and modern convenience has been utilized for the comfort of guests: each room contains a fire-place and electric bells. The hotel uses the incandescent electric light.

The hotel is furnished in the most elegant and attractive manner. All parts of the hotel show every convenience that modern ingenuity can invent, and it goes without saying that the most carping critic of luxurious living, the widely traveled tourist, the invalid, or the business man, will be satisfied with the accommodations and appointments of the EL PASO DE ROBLES HOTEL.

The building is built of masonry, embellished with beautiful sandstone arches, and is absolutely fire-proof. Two large balconies, parallel to the second and third stories and directly above the main entrance, add to the interior comforts of the hotel, as well as to its exterior beauty. Each room facing the front and wings of the hotel has a separate balcony.

The north wing of this floor is devoted to the gentlemen's Billiard Room, forty feet square. Adjoining is the Reading Room, a large and well lighted apartment. Its dimension is 50 x 25 feet. Off the Billiard Room are three Club Rooms. In this portion of the building will also be found a model barber shop.

The south wing contains the Parlors and Reception Rooms, respectively 50 x 25 feet. In proximity to these apartments, is a Billiard Room for the exclusive use of the ladies. The main Dining Hall, capable of comfortably seating three hundred guests, has been made a feature of the hotel---its size is 50 x 80 feet. It is richly decorated, and is used as a Ball Room, at stated times, for the entertainment of guests. Two private Dining rooms, 15 x 20 feet, adjoin the main Dining Room.

A large staircase leads to the upper floors, which is divided into suites, reception rooms and single apartments, according to

Dining Room of the Hotel.

El Paso de Robles Hotel c. 1908.

Frank W. Sawyer, M. D., medical director of the Paso Robles Hot Springs Hotel had a brochure published entitled "Paso Robles Hot Springs." His pamphlet provides some information that is not given in other brochures.

The lithia, iron and natural mineral waters from the springs are at the fountain in the hotel lobby, being brought there directly from the springs. The sulphur water, at natural heat, can be secured at the fountain on the South Lawn, close at hand.

The entrance to the bath-house, reached from the hotel's main south corridor, is built of marble, mosaic, novus glass, and highly polished white cedar. It has an elaborate ven-

Daniel Blackburn Home about 1916.

tilating system by which air throughout can be changed every twenty minutes.

This big bath-house is built directly over the main hot spring, which has a daily flow of more than two million gallons. By this arrangement, one gets the water in the bath direct from Nature's great reservoirs, thousands of feet below the surface. The swimming plunge bath pool is also fed direct from the spring, with the sulphur water flowing in and out all the time.

The pool is eighty by forty feet, and has its own suites of dressing rooms, shower baths and entrance.

Daniel and Cecelia Blackburn were the parents of ten children. In 1889-1890, Daniel Blackburn had a new residence built in Paso Robles, on Spring Street between 8th and 9th Streets, on the east side of the street. The Bank of Santa Maria now occupies part of that property. The residence was a three-story home with fireplaces in the bedrooms, a billiard room, and it was surrounded by lawns. This mansion was later used as a music conservatory- - -the Paso Robles School of Music, with John J. Jackson as the director. Later, Dr. Glass had a sanitarium in the building. The mansion was the home of the Rollin C. Heaton family from 1914 to 1920. The top story was removed, following a fire in 1920; the mansion was destroyed by fire in 1923.

The balustrade of this mansion was saved from the fire, and it can be viewed today in the two-story house which contains the office of Paso Robles Insurance, at 500 12th Street, in Paso Robles. The owners of the insurance company purchased the home in 1973. This large Colonial Revival building had been constructed by the Blackburns in 1872, within the El Paso de Rob-

Blackburn Home about 1920, top story removed after fire.

les Hot Springs Hotel complex. Initially, it was used as an exhibition hall for traveling salesmen, and later by a Chinese family who worked at the hotel. It was used, for a period, as a meeting hall for the "Townsend Club" of Paso Robles. It was purchased by the Henry Clemons family, in 1939, and moved to its present location.

On June 17, 1891, El Paso de Robles Hotel Company, who owned the hotel and springs, sold the property to Mr. & Mrs. D. W. James, E. F. Burns, R. M. Shackelford, W. M. Coward and B. D. Murphy. These people formed the corporation known as El Paso de Robles Spring Company. On May 26, 1889, Mr. E. F. Burns was given the position of manager of the hotel and springs.

In 1892, the Blackburns sold their half to R. M. Shackelford and William M. Coward. Originally from Kentucky, Coward had been a resident of Woodland, California, for the previous twelve years. These men made one payment of $25,000. They were unable to make another payment, so Drury W. James returned their $25,000 and assumed the debt. After two dry years and a depression, Drury W. James transferred the El Paso de Robles Ranch and Hotel to the bank.

The first person to build in Paso Robles was J. B. Testerman, and his cottage was constructed on Pine Street. Lots 1 and 2 brought the highest price- - - $1,125; on this lot, the Adams Block was erected in 1887, to be occupied by A. R. Booth, and the Paso Robles Bank, with David Speyer of San Miguel as cashier.

The Masonic block was built next to Adams. Mr. Daniel D. Blackburn, a member of the lodge, during the same year, bought all of the stock, thus becoming sole owner of the building. The next important structure was the Alexander Hotel, built by E. A. Stowell in 1889 on the corner of 12th and Park Street.

The Blackburn Block, on the northeast corner of

12th and Park, was built in 1892, and is surmounted by the town clock, which was a present from the owner, Daniel D. Blackburn. The acorn-shape of the clock was suggested by Mrs. Daniel Blackburn. The *Paso Robles Leader*, on March 22, 1893 printed the following article.

Paso Robles is fast putting on city airs. The clock now erected in the Blackburn building is another evidence of it. This clock has four faces, which will show the time day and night. It also has a magnificent sounding bell on which the hours and half hours will be sounded.

The clock is manufactured by the Seth Thomas Company which insures it being a good one. A gentleman came down from San Francisco and has been at work since Monday setting up the above mentioned clock. It is such a spirit of enterprise that has been displayed by the citizens of Paso Robles from time to time that has made this place so much of a city in so short a time. Paso Robles is a good place to live in.

The above clock is arranged so that the faces will show the time at night if lights are kept in the tower during the night. Mr. Blackburn thinks that he has spent enough in the clock, and if the city thinks it will be any benefit to have the clock show at night, that they can pay for the lighting. As a matter of enterprise the *Leader* thinks the city can well afford to pay for the electric lights in the clock tower, so that the time of night can be told as well as the day.

The work of erecting the big clock has been under the care and management of Mr. McConnell, a gentleman who has the manage-

No one knew that an unreinforced brick building could not stand an earthquake, or weather the seasons, or pounding of traffic on an adjacent street, when the Nyberg buildings were built. So the buildings stand at 12th and Park streets today.

Present-day view of the Blackburn Building.

ment of the Chronicle clock and the Ferry clocks of San Francisco.

Paso Robles' first library had its beginning on the second floor of the Blackburn building, when a reading room was opened. [The building was sold in 1920, to Auguste, Alida and Karl Nyberg, for $35,000. In 1946, the clock stopped working but the acorn tower was left alone because of its distinctiveness. In 1973, its present owners, Armand and Mary Mastagni, purchased the building. The clock works, at the present time.]

The Testerman family has been in the Paso Robles area since 1870, when brothers John and Charles Games Testerman arrived. As seen above, John Testerman bought a lot on Pine Street in 1886, and built the first house in the new town. Later, rooms in this building were used for John's boot-making shop and wife Mary's dress-making shop. John and Mary Thomas Testerman raised three daughters: Pearl Hurley, Melvina Testerman and Evaline Claybrook.

Charles Testerman worked on many of Paso Robles' first buildings, as well as at the Stone Canyon Mine. In later years, he built a home for his family on South River Road, and used some of the lumber from the old Stone Canyon Mine.

Charles and his wife, Victoria, became the parents of seven children: Theodore, Agnes, Leonard, Charity, Lenora, Amelia and Charles Guy. Charles Guy Testerman married Ella Starnes in 1912 and were the parents of Leonard, Eleanor, Gladys, Marvin and Adella. Eleanor married Bud Schlegel; Gladys married Darwin Fox; Marvin married Elizabeth Thomas, and Adella married Lester Dauth.

The El Paso de Robles Hotel was the grandest hotel ever constructed in San Luis Obispo County;

more than 1 million bricks were used. It had cost $160,000 to build. The *Tribune* stated that the hotel "is absolutely fireproof."

On Saturday, January 19, 1895, Paso Robles' newspaper, *The Moon*, had printed the following article.

"THE MOON" CHANGES

With this issue, *The Moon* passes out of my hands as proprietor, Mr. G. Webster, of San Miguel, having purchased the entire plant.

It has been my aim to give the people of San Luis Obispo county, and of Paso Robles particularly, a good, readable paper. *The Moon* has always battled for the interests of the people, without fear or favor, and its success has been phenomenal.

It pains me to part with *The Moon*, but man was not placed on earth to live always, and as I am in feeble health, it is better that a younger and more experienced person should guide its destiny.

During the five years that I have managed *The Moon*, my experience has been that the merchants have recognized the paper as a valuable advertising medium, and for the support accorded me in my endeavor to publish one of the best papers in the county I return my heartfelt thanks.

For the new proprietor, I can say that he understands the newspaper business thoroughly, and will give the people a paper to be proud of. I bespeak for the new proprietor of *The Moon* a constant increase of circulation and advertisements.

To my friends and patrons, I extend my well wishes for the future.   A. D. King

1888 Hot Sulphur Springs Bath House.

1906 Bath House from south-east.

The *Paso Robles Leader*, on January 29, 1908, informed its readers that "A large Bath house of thirty-seven rooms and a plunge had been built over the Hot Springs in 1888. After the new hotel was occupied, the bathing facilities were not suitable for the class of hotel patronage and another bath house, one of the finest and most costly in the United States was erected in 1906, back of and connected with the hotel."

[The above quotation refers to two of the three bath-houses which were located in "downtown" Paso Robles. The 1888 bath-house was located on the northeast corner of 10th and Spring Streets. The 1906 bathhouse was located across Spring Street, on the northwest corner of this intersection. At the present time, it is a parking area for the Paso Robles Inn.]

W. H. Weeks was appointed, by the City Trustees, to draw plans and specifications and act as supervising architect of the Paso Robles Hot Springs Bath House. For his services, Mr. Weeks was to receive 5% of the cost of the building. Weeks began working in March of 1904. The $60,000 structure was opened in January of 1906. It featured a new sulphur well, yielding a million gallons of 106-degree sulphur water a day.

A group of twelve business men in Paso Robles noted that the curative power of the sulphur springs

1906 Bath House from north-east.

was limited to the use of residents of the hotel. They petitioned and won the right to drill for sulphur springs adjacent to the City Park. According to the *Paso Robles Leader*, on May 10, 1905, "The city bath house bonds have been sold to S. F. Kean & Co., of Chicago, for $25,025."

The Municipal Bath Springs, at today's Fairbairn Building, obtained their supply from an artesian well 392 feet deep, with a 6-inch casing. The temperature was 108.6 degrees F. The main springs, on the grounds of El Paso de Robles Hotel, flowed at 2,000,000 gallons per day; the temperature was 107.6 degrees F.

Other important buildings in the infant City of El Paso de Robles included the Paso Robles High School, constructed in 1893, in the block that is located between Vine and Oak Street, and 17th and 18th streets. The high school faced to the east toward Oak Street. It was the first high school in the county; the first class graduated in 1896. A favorite prank at the three-story school was a flag race. A flag was placed on the steep roof of the building, then the contestants risked

Municipal Bath House.

"life and limb" to retrieve the banner. The other main prank took place in the assembly hall. Students would shuffle and stamp their feet until the whole top story swayed to and fro. Eventually, the top story was condemned and removed. During this time, students had classes in the Legion Hall. [The graduation ceremonies for the class of 1924 took place at the T & D Theater, because the auditorium on the third floor of the school was no longer available.]

The Carnegie Library, in the City Park, was started in 1907, and the cornerstone was laid on January 19, 1908. William H. Weeks, of Watsonville, was the architect and R. A. Summers, of San Jose, was the contractor.

We earlier saw that W. H. Weeks was involved with

First High School in San Luis Obispo County at Paso Robles, constructed 1893.

Laying of cornerstone, Carnegie Library.

the Paso Robles Hot Springs Bath House. He had been born in Canada in 1864, on Prince Edward Island; he came to Watsonville, by way of Denver, in 1892. His first architecture office was opened in Watsonville in 1894. He had so much business that he had to open a branch office in Salinas.

Other buildings in this county for which Weeks was the architect include the first permanent classroom structure at Cal Poly, Stover's Sanitarium (later called French Hospital) on Marsh Street, and the Old San Luis Obispo Senior High School.

School Building, after third story was removed (facing Oak Street).

The *Paso Robles Record*, on June 8, 1901 reported the "Death of D. D. Blackburn. The Pioneer Founder of Paso Robles. Passes Away Sunday at 1 o'clock at His Home in this City."

The flags were raised at half-mast early Sunday afternoon, announcing the death of Daniel D. Blackburn, one of San Luis Obispo county's best known citizens and one of the founders of Paso Robles.

For days the aged gentleman had been watched over tenderly by the immediate members of his family and a few intimate friends for his death had been hourly expected since the previous Thursday. He had been an invalid for several years and confined to his home for many months before the final demise.

Nearly all of his immediate family were present during his final illness. The immediate cause of death was old age, the deceased being past 85 years of age. Several times during the past few months it was thought that Mr. Blackburn was nearing his death but the skill of the attending physician and a strong constitution kept life in the body grown frail with many years. He was a stalwart man in his prime, being above the average in stature but time had left him but a shadow of his former self.

The body was conveyed from the residence to Masonic hall where the funeral service was held according to Masonic rites. The pall bearers were made up of members of Masonic lodge of which the deceased was a devoted member. They were R. M. Shackelford, A. R. Booth, D. Speyer, and H. Eppinger of Paso Robles; Judge Spencer and P. B. Prefumo of San Luis and Jas. Cass and A. M. Hardie of

Cayucos; Mr. J. E. Steinbeck, Past Master and Chas. Trussler, Master of Paso Robles Lodge performed the beautiful ceremony of the order and Rev. Hege, Chaplain of the lodge delivered an address and read the prayers of the ceremony.

A choir composed of Mrs. Earll, Mrs. Ladd, Mrs. Sweeny and Dr. McLennan rendered several appropriate hymns.

A long concourse of carriages followed the hearse to the Odd Fellows cemetery where after the concluding ceremonies of the order the interment was made.

The flower pieces contributed were many and beautiful.

Mr. Blackburn was married in this county in 1866 and his wife and ten children survive him. The sons and daughters of the deceased are Mrs. Margaret Frost, Frank, James, Fred, The Misses Aimie, Susie, Harriet and Josephine all of this city and Dr. D. D. Blackburn of San Francisco and Harry H. Blackburn now in the east.

For a period of about eighteen years, El Paso de Robles had a street car line, which went from the railroad depot to the mud baths at the north end of town.

W. C. Little, an engineer brought in to survey the original town site, had surveyed the right-of-way for the street car track in 1886.

The *Paso Robles Leader*, on February 4, 1891 printed the following article, entitled "The Street Railway."

Mr. G. R. Adams returned home from Los Angeles on Monday having gone down overland and returned by steamer via Port Harford. He reports to the *Leader* that he has purchased 67 tons of new English steel rails, and 1500 set of fish plates and bolts for the street rail road from the depot to the Mud Baths. The rails weigh 16 pounds to the yard. He also purchased a two-wheeled road scraper.

The rails left Los Angeles Monday and will probably be here this week. Mr. Adams proposes to push this road as fast as possible.

On April 8, 1891, the *Paso Robles Leader* reported the following:

The improvements along Spring Street in the Adams addition still continue. The grading is now nearly done and the track laying will soon commence. Mr. Adams leaves for

Horse-drawn Street Car.

San Francisco in a few days to purchase the cars and materials necessary for the completion of the road.

Three small street cars were brought to Paso Robles, but only one or two were ever seen on the tracks. The cars were said to have started out as part of San Francisco's Mission Street Line. Around the turn of the century, Thaddeus Sherman acquired the street car system from the Southern Pacific Company.

Usually there was one car and one horse; sometimes there were two horses hitched in tandem. Each car had an old straw broom fastened to two opposite corners of the cars in such a way that the broom swept the rails clean as the car went down the tracks.

The street car line began at the Southern Pacific depot, and ran down Pine Street to 12th Street; it then went west two blocks to Spring Street. The line then went north about 35 blocks to the Mud Baths, a distance of about 2 ½ miles. At the end of the runs at the depot and at the north end of town, the single-trees or double-trees were disconnected and the team brought to the opposite end of the car for the return run.

The street car barns were situated about where the Avalon Motel is located today, at 3231 Spring Street. The line did not cross the railroad tracks at the north end of town, so people had to walk to the Mud Bath House.

The tracks for the line ran down the center of the street, and the horse and wagon traffic went on each side of the tracks. Since the streets were all dirt, the horses' hooves tore up the streets, and the dust was blown around by the wind. This situation eventually left deep ruts on each side of the track. Eventually, the City Council wanted to repair the section of the line that went down Pine Street from the depot and up 12th to Spring Street. This particular part of the

Old Horse Car Barn

line was not being used daily, because a tally-ho carriage met the trains and carried the guests to the hotel.

On April 24, 1909, the *Paso Robles Record* printed Ordinance No. 118.

An Ordinance to declare the track and rails of the Paso Robles Street Car Company, on Spring Street, a nuisance.

The Board of Trustees of the City of El Paso de Robles do obtain as follows:

Section 1. The track and rails of the street railway, on Spring Street, in the City of El Paso de Robles, California, being in places so far above and in other places so far below the level or surface of said Spring Street as to be a menace to life and property and a nuisance.

Section 2. The City Attorney is hereby authorized and directed to begin such action as he may deem best to abate said nuisance.

Section 3. This ordinance shall take effect immediately after publication.

The foregoing ordinance was introduced at a regular meeting of the Board of Trustees of the City of El Paso de Robles held on March 15, 1909, by the following vote:

Ayes: Trustees Ladner, Brooks, Taylor, Bennett

Noes: None. Absent: Glass

Approved this 19th day of April, 1909.
E. Ladner, present pro tem
President of said Board

Attest: Edw. Brendlin, City Clerk

According to the *Paso Robles Record* for May 8, 1909, the Board of Trustees had met "on Thursday, May 6th, in extra session with all trustees present, to finish the business of the regular meeting of May 3rd. The city clerk being absent, trustee Bennett was appointed to act as clerk *pro tem*.

"The object of the meeting was to bring Mr. Sherman, the local representative of Street railway, which is operated on Spring street, before the board, in order that he might state some proposition whereby he and the board might come to a harmonic settlement, in regard to the removal of said railway. After some discussion, Mr. Sherman requested the board to give him time to get the power of attorney. Board adjourned."

At a City Council meeting on August 29, 1909, it was decided that the line must be improved or the tracks would be disposed of. Mr. Sherman thought this idea was unfair, and turned it down.

Hiram Taylor, a city councilman, learned that a three-quarter interest in the railway was owned by a party in Los Angeles. He went south and purchased a majority of the stock, for the sum of $500. When he returned, he announced his possession of the stock, and declared that he would refuse to operate the railway.

Paso Robles' street car line came to an end on September 1, 1909. At midnight, Hi Taylor had a group of men remove one rail for a distance of five blocks; the rails were hauled to a vacant lot. It was Hiram Taylor, originally a stockman from Slack's Canyon, who later built Hotel Taylor on the northeast corner of 13th and Spring Streets.

The *Paso Robles Record*, for October 2, 1909, printed an item entitled "Spring Street Railway Cleaned Up." It stated that "C. S. Smith bought two street cars that belonged to Taylor-Sherman Railroad Company and will put them in his back yard."

The home of Clark and Olive Smith, was located on the west side of the 1800-block of Spring Street. Today, Hometown Nursery is situated on the property.

Monument to City Founders.
Photo by Bill Dellard

The cars were used as a play-house by daughters Isabel, Maude and Meredith and son, Clark, Jr. The street cars finally went to pieces and were hauled to the dump.

A fire started in the El Paso de Robles Hotel at 9:05 p.m. on December 12, 1940, in the wastebasket of one of the third-floor service closets. The blaze spread through a laundry chute to the huge open attic, and soon engulfed the entire building. The fire was discovered by the night clerk, J. E. Emsley; the man, 55 years of age, dropped dead after he ran down the stairs and sounded the alarm. E. W. Santelman, hotel manager, was able to route the 200 guests safely out of the building. Concerning the firefighters, Elsa Orcutt Hewitt stated that "The fire was so hot it melted the front of their rubberized jackets, while it was so cold outside, the backs of their jackets were stiff. Thank goodness, it was cold and the cinders rose straight up; otherwise, the whole town could have burned down."

As we close this chapter, we see that what had started as a "settlement" had evolved into a small "city" with a very bright future.

MISSION SAN MIGUEL LANDS

RANCHO SANTA YSABEL

During the years of 1840 to 1846, three governors of California made grants of land from property which had belonged to Mission San Miguel. Governor Juan B. Alvarado made five grants, Governor Manuel Micheltorena made six grants and Governor Pio Pico made three grants. We will look at the names of the initial or original grantees, realizing that in most cases, other people ended up receiving title to the property.

Two grants were made on the same date: May 12, 1844. Pedro Narvaez received the 25,993.18-acre El Paso de Robles Rancho; Francisco Arce received the Rancho Santa Ysabel, of 17,774.12 acres.

Mission San Miguel had used the Santa Ysabel rancho chiefly for raising sheep; there was also a large vineyard at this location. An interesting item of infor-

mation comes from William E. P. Hartnell, who had served as Visitor General of the Missions in 1839. In his diary, he stated that "The Indians apparently did not consider the possibility of the Rancho de Santa Ysabel being taken from them. It was here they raised crops for their own use."

According to Helen Mabry Ballard's 1923 work entitled *San Luis Obispo County in Spanish and Mexican Times*, "...on the present Santa Ysabel Ranch still exist the fields and orchards of the mission."

Originally, the site had been selected, due to a spring which had a flow of several thousand gallons per day. Two large houses had been built on the property, one in 1814 and the other in 1816. One of the adobes was of two stories, and was used as a school for the local Indians. The adobes were located approxi-

Adobe buildings at Santa Ysabel and vicinity.

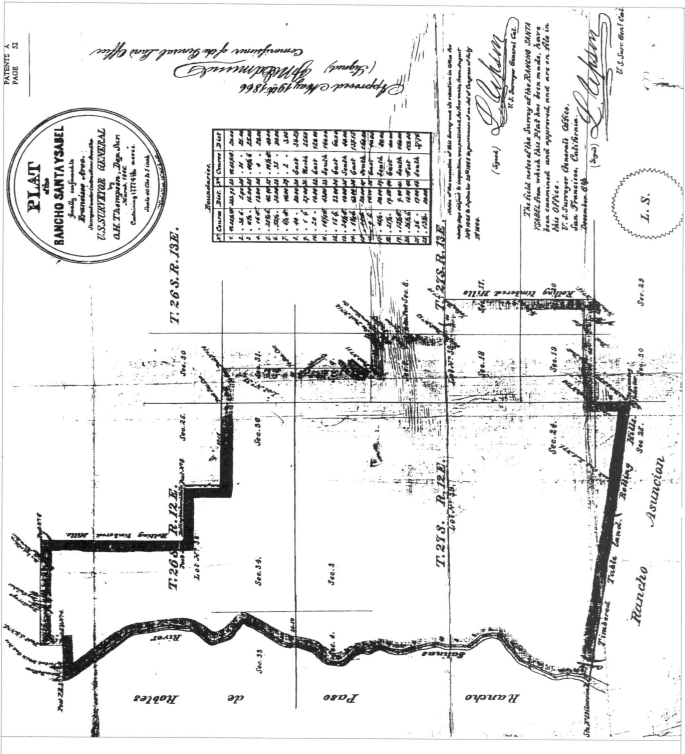

Map of Rancho
Santa Ysabel.

mately one mile south of the present-day intersection of South River Road and Santa Ysabel Road.

It has frequently been stated that water from the Santa Ysabel springs was carried, by canals, to Mission San Miguel. In Dr. Hartwell B. Stanley's *A Souvenir History of the Mission of San Miguel*, published in 1897, he states that "In order to obtain sufficient water they built a ditch eight miles long, taking the water from the Salinas River just below where the flourishing city of Paso Robles now stands."

In an unpublished work by Edith Buckland Webb, the author of *Indian Life at the Old Missions*, she states that there are two traditions concerning the old mission irrigation system. The first tradition is that water from the springs was carried across the Salinas River in flumes, and thence by canals to the mission. The other tradition is that the water was used to irrigate the fields to the east of the Salinas River, while the fields on the west side were watered by a canal coming from the river somewhere near a lake or lagoon.

Edith Webb states that William L. Morehouse, a pioneer of 1865, who at one time owned a tract of land along the west side of the Salinas River, a little to the south of Paso Robles, said that at the time he lived on that place there was, about two miles north of Lake Ysabel, a large lagoon which filled up every year by the overflow of the river.

Because of broken tiles and the banked-up appearance of the side of the lagoon next to the river, Mr. Morehouse believed that the lagoon was the remains of an old reservoir. He said that the old canal, which was easily traceable all the way to the mission, began at that lagoon. Edith Webb stated, "This seems to be excellent information from an eye-witness who viewed the old canal not longer than 25 years after the abandonment of the mission by the Franciscan Fathers."

Let us move forward in time, for a moment, and consider a "Letter to the Editor" of the *Paso Robles Record*, dated December 24, 1895.

Editor Record:- One of the poorest, well traveled roads in this part of the country is that short section of road running toward the river just south of the San Miguel Mission. There is no other piece of road in this part of the country over which there is more general travel or over which more grain is hauled. Part of this road is good, but from the railroad track to the river it is in very poor condition, as outside of the narrow beaten road it is so rough that a person would be in danger of being upset were he to drive there, and in the grain hauling season the dust in this track gets so deep, and the holes so bad, that the large grain laden teams, after pulling through the soft river sands, are unable to pull their wagons over this short piece of road. Mission irrigation canal also extends into the road here at one point and makes a dangerous spot.

As this is the only really bad piece of road in this neighborhood, and can be so readily fixed with plow and scraper, it is strange that it has been allowed to remain in this condition so long, and it is hoped that our roadmaster will give it his attention this fall. Tax-payer.

It is of interest to this writer that as late as 1895, someone could refer to the Mission irrigation canal. Whether or not it came all the way from Paso Robles is another question.

Mrs. Webb also said that there were two legends as to how water was carried across the creeks and canyons. One was that tiles, like those used in roofing, only much larger, were made; these large tiles were used in some way in the construction of flumes. She mentions that the water-pipes, used in Mission San Antonio's irrigation system, were about twelve inches long, five inches in diameter at the larger end, and four inches at the smaller end. The other legend was that large pine trees, brought from the mountains near Cambria, were split in two, hollowed into great troughs, and used for carrying the water across places where the natural slope of the land and the pressure of the water were not sufficient to carry the stream where it was needed.

Shirley Harriet Hannah wrote a Master's thesis in 1934, at the University of California, Los Angeles; it was entitled, *The Early Development of the Salinas Valley*. She included, among several photographs, a photo of a hand-hewn log on the ground in front of Mission San Miguel. The log is 57 feet long. She does not mention whether or not the log had been hollowed-out.

Having considered these items of interest, we return to the beginning of Rancho Santa Ysabel. As was mentioned earlier, Rancho Santa Ysabel, of 17,774 acres, was granted to Francisco Arce on May 12, 1844. Francisco Arce has an interesting footnote in California history, due to being involved in the first action of the Bear Flag revolt in 1846.

People who live in the Spanish Camp area of rural Paso Robles, or who live in the part of the City of Paso Robles which is situated on the east side of the Salinas River might be interested in knowing something about the person who formerly owned the land on which they now live.

Francisco Arce had been born in 1819 in Baja California, and came to Monterey as a young man in 1833; from 1839 to 1845, he was employed most of the time as a secretary.

In the Book of Spanish Translations, Book 1, page 41, in the Recorder's Office in Salinas can be found the following document.

ARCE

David Spence, constitutional Justice of the Peace, vested with the powers of the Ayuntamiento by virtue of the law of March 20th 1837, granted to the citizen Franco Arce a lot of forty *varas* frontage and fifty (*varas*) in depth, (situated) in a straight line - due North - from the house of the foreigner Eduardo, leaving twenty-four *varas* - for a street - next to the lot of the latter (Eo); and for the purposes that may demand it, I hereunto set my hand in Monterey, on the 5th of February 1840.

David Spence   Manuel Castro, Sec.

In 1842, Francisco Arce sent a request to Governor Alvarado.

Wishing to dedicate myself to the growing pursuits of agriculture and the raising of cattle, which now a days is the most important business in the Department, I solicit the favor that Your Excellency be pleased to grant me in fee a tract of land which is now vacant appertaining to the Ex-Mission of San Miguel named La Estrella distant from said Establishment about three leagues . . .

June 10, 1842
Francisco Arce

An answer to this request was sent one month later from the governor.

Monday, July 10, 1842

Let the agent in charge of the Establishment of San Miguel report if the land petitioned for is in a condition to be granted to any private person.

Alvarado

For whatever reason, Arce was not granted La Estrella. In 1843, he was serving as secretary to Governor Manuel Micheltorena. While in Monterey, he became active in military and civil affairs.

The California State Archives contains a small document in which Francisco Arce petitions the Mexican government for Rancho Santa Ysabel. He said that the land he requested was "bounded on the north by San Miguel, on the south by La Asuncion, bounded on the east by a place known as Estrella; on the west by the hills. . . ." The size of the land requested was "four square leagues, more or less." The document was signed on January 4, 1843.

On May 12, 1844, Francisco Arce was the grantee of Santa Ysabel Rancho, and on May 20th was employed to collect debts owed to some of the missions. Padre Mercado of Mission San Jose and Padre Muro of Santa Clara gave Arce power of attorney to recover mission livestock which had been lent out to different individuals; the largest item of this loaned stock was 6,000 sheep.

Mariano G. Vallejo denied having any sheep belonging to the missions, but stated that the correct number was 4,000 and that the sheep had been legally taken by him as an aid to the government.

Arce declined to take part in the revolt against Micheltorena, and after Micheltorena's departure in 1845, he became secretary to General Castro and was also *alferez* of auxiliaries.

By 1846, an open rupture had developed between Governor Pio Pico and Jose Castro, commander of the army at Monterey. Pico attempted to move the capital to Los Angeles, from its ancient seat at Monterey; this town had been California's capital since February 3, 1770.

Early in April, Governor Pio Pico declared it his purpose to subdue General Castro by arms, and was actively engaged in raising an army in the south in order to capture Monterey and occupy the northern country.

Jose Castro sent agents to Mariano G. Vallejo at Sonoma to buy horses for his cavalry; about 200 were purchased from Vallejo and his neighbors. At the time, Francisco Arce was serving as a lieutenant under Mariano G. Vallejo. Along with Lieutenant Jose Maria Alviso, and an escort consisting of Jose Noriega, Blas Alviso, Blas Pina and three others, Lieutenant Francisco Arce was driving the horses from Sonoma to re-inforce Castro's militia in Monterey.

Arce and his men stayed the night of June 8, 1846 at Sutter's Fort, and the next night at Martin Murphy's rancho on the south bank of the Cosumnes River. On the morning of June 10, 1846, they were surprised by a group of 12 to 15 people, led by an American, Ezekiel Merritt; members of this group included William B. Ide, Robert Semple, Granville P. Swift and H. L. Ford. This group captured the horses.

In his *Memorias*, Francisco Arce says that it was at first the intention of the Americans to kill him and his companions, and that they were saved only by the intercession of Martin Murphy and his wife. According to Bancroft, the Americans had no intention of kill-ing them, but Merritt was a rough man who may have tried to make them think they were going to be killed.

According to Thomas O. Larkin, U.S. Consul in Monterey, when Arce protested that they had been taken unawares, Merritt offered to return the horses, let Arce's men give a signal when they were ready, and Merritt and his men would "try them again."

Francisco Arce and the rest of the Californios were released to carry the news that the Americans intended to seize Vallejo's stronghold at Sonoma and Sutter's New Helvetia. A horse was allowed for each man, and also released were a few horses which were claimed as private property by Jose Maria Alviso. Bancroft made the observation that most writers have taken pride in representing the number of Merritt's men as twelve, and of Arce's party as larger. Thomas O. Larkin's letters demonstrate that the forces probably had twelve members on each side.

Merritt and his people drove the rest of the horses back to John C. Fremont's camp at the junction of the Sacramento and American Rivers. Four days later, Merritt's group occupied the town of Sonoma, and made prisoners of its leading citizens, including Mariano G. Vallejo.

This incident with the horses was the first action of the Bear Flag Revolt. It took place at a major ford on the Cosumnes River at what is today the intersec-tion of Highway 99 and Grant Line Road near the present-day city of Elk Grove.

Francisco Arce served throughout the war be-tween the United States and Mexico as a lieutenant and finally as a brevet captain. [To be breveted meant receiving a rank higher than that for which pay was received.] At one time, according to Bancroft, Arce was a member of the San Patricio legion of Irish desert-ers; he was taken prisoner, and narrowly escaped death "on account of his Irish physique" - - - whatever that might have meant.

Arce, as Jose Castro's secretary, at the end of the war fled to Mexico with his commander. In 1848 he served in Lower California in some capacity. The year 1849 saw Francisco Arce returning to Monterey, with-out leave, and serving again as secretary of the pre-fecture. [A prefecture was an administrative district, in use after 1836; the office was both administrative and judicial.]

On September 27, 1849, Francisco Arce found him-self in a legal dispute with Thomas O. Larkin in Monterey; the subject of the dispute was for posses-sion of a house. Book 1, of Translation of Spanish Records, page 277, in the Monterey County Recorder's Office provides the details.

F. Arce vs T. O. Larkin
(for possession of a house)

Port of Monterey CA Sept. 27, 1849

Before me Jose Abrego, 3rd Magistrate of the Ayuntamiento and in charge of the 2nd tri-bunal of this jurisdiction personally came Francisco Arce and Thomas O. Larkin.

The former suing the latter for the pos-session of a house that he purchased from him in the year 1846, agreeing to pay (it) in install-ments out of the commissary, as he actually did.

To this Mr. Larkin answers that he does not owe any house, and if it is money that he owes, the matter shall be tried.

To which Arce replied that if Larkin would give him five thousand dollars he would with-draw the suit, leaving the house in Larkin's favor.

Said Larkin failed to agree to this; the money Arce had left in his possession was about $300, left on deposit and not on account of payment of a house.

Sr. Arce answered that he could prove by several certificates that he was in possession of the house, formerly known as the Pacomio house.

The documents were examined and Abrego and the referees proposed a settlement: according to a document given by Thomas O. Larkin, dated March 24, 1846, he sold to Francisco Arce a house for the sum of $400. He received $80 on account; Larkin also received $300 in merchandise from Arce, but did not know to what account this amount was to be applied. It was determined that Larkin must fulfill his contract. Arce stated that he was satisfied.

Previously, Francisco Arce had petitioned for a parcel of land, 50 by 60 *varas*, in Santa Clara County. This was granted to him by Governor Pio Pico on June 13, 1846. Arce's claim was filed on March 1, 1853, and confirmed by the Land Commission on June 12, 1855; the District Court confirmed the grant on March 9, 1857.

In the fall of 1850, Francisco Arce was in Monterey to conclude some legal matters. In the Book of Translations, Book 2, pages 181-182, in the Monterey County Recorder's Office is found the following.

Francisco Arce to E. Brown
September 27, 1850

I transfer this document in favor of Mr. Elisha Brown as a legal sale that I made to him of the land referred to in this title, less ten *varas* of front, with the corresponding depth - if it is of 30 *varas* front by 50 deep, more or less.
Francisco Arce
Witness: Jacinto Rodriguez
Witness: A. G. Toomes
Rec'd for record Oct. 2d 1850 at 11 a.m.

In the Port of Monterey, Upper California, Sept. 27ᵗʰ, 1850, it was agreed between Don Franco Arce and Mr. Elisha Brown that the former (first party) sells & transfers really and truly forever, unto the latter (second party) the lot that the former owns and belongs to him (lawfully) since the year 1840. - of the extent of 30 *varas* front by 50 in depth, a little more or less, and (said lot) or land being situate back of the house of Don Santiago Watson, forming a street and bounded on the North by the house and lot of Don Alberto Toomes and on the south by the house of Santiago McKinlay.
Said land grantor sells unto said Don Elisha Brown, for the sum of one thousand dollars current silver coin, which I received to my entire satisfaction; and I renounce all rights that I have or may have in and to said mentioned lot, and I transfer to (said) Don

Elisha Brown the title whereby I have been accredited as the only owner of said mentioned land.
In testimony whereof, the contracting parties hereto have signed these presents before two witnesses.
Witness: Wm S. Hughson
Witness: Albert G. Toomes   Franco Arce
Rec'd for record Oct. 2d, 1850 at 11 a.m.

On September 22, 1852, Francisco Arce filed the claim for Rancho Santa Ysabel; the claim was rejected by the U. S. Land Commission on December 13, 1853. However, the grant was confirmed by the District Court on January 12, 1857. (The patent, or title, was finally received on May 21, 1866.)

San Luis Obispo County taxes for Francisco Arce in 1850 amounted to $66.00. By way of comparison, this same year, Petronilo Rios paid $153.80 in county taxes.

In 1851, Arce's assessed value of real estate and personal property amounted to $8,880. In 1851, Mauricio Gonzales paid $99.00 for the assessed value of Rancho Cholame, which was $7,992 for 26,640 acres. Ynocente Garcia had an assessed value of $4,440 on 8,880 acres of the San Jose.

The year 1852 found Francisco Arce back in Lower California, asking for an antedated leave of absence, Mexican naturalization, and land; he got married in 1853. Subsequently he came north again.

On December 31, 1853, he sold to Jeremiah Clark, for the sum of $3.00, one undivided eighth part of Rancho Santa Ysabel, containing 4 square leagues. In 1854, Arce paid taxes on 17,760 acres of the Santa Ysabel, valued at $8,880. The taxes amounted to $133.30, and there was a notation on the tax records: "ranch rejected."

San Luis Obispo County Book of Deeds A, page 106, shows that on October 12, 1855, Francisco Arce, of the County of Monterey, sold to Manuel Castro, of the County of San Francisco, 4 square leagues of land, known as the Ranch of Santa Ysabel. The price was $4,000. The document stated that a more particular description could be found in the original grant map contained in the *expediente* filed in case number 356 before the U. S. Land Commission.

Book of Deeds A, page 189 shows that on April 26, 1859, Francisco Arce and Gertrudis Bernal de Arce, his wife, were residents of the County of Monterey. They sold, for $3,000, to Teodoro Gonzales, four square leagues, more or less, of Santa Ysabel.

Canyon above Hot Springs.

Ysabel Hot Sulphur—Rustic Bath House, Paso Robles.

San Luis Obispo County Book of Deeds F, page 444 shows a transaction between Francisco Arce and his wife, Gertrudes Bernal de Arce, and Maurice Dore. For $5.00 in gold coin, Dore received the Rancho Santa Ysabel, consisting of 17,774 12/100 acres. This transaction is dated October 31, 1874.

It is incomprehensible to this writer how this property could be sold this many times without Arce having to buy it back between sales. He did not receive the patent on it until May of 1866.

In 1877, Arce was living on the Alisal rancho near Salinas. He later made a claim of $5,000 against the State of California, and in addition, claimed to have a grant of San Jose Mission land; he was also a claimant of Rancho Santa Margarita.

According to Ynocente Garcia, who had served as the administrator of Mission San Miguel, Arce sold the Rancho Santa Ysabel to Francisco Rico. However, there has not been found a record of Rico owning his property. It is not known if Arce ever resided on the Santa Ysabel rancho. Early in the year 1878, Francisco Arce died "leaving a family in straitened circumstances," according to Bancroft.

The Dore family, on Rancho Santa Ysabel, ran as many as 30,000 head of sheep on the property. The county tax assessment records for 1864 indicate the following: 17,752 acres of the Santa Ysabel ranch at 80-cents per acre, $5,325; improvements $250; six tame horses, two spring wagons three sets of harness $150; 20 tons of hay at $10; 3,293 mixed sheep at $1.50; 74 bucks at $5; furniture $25. Total value was $11,410; the tax was $370.83, and was marked "paid."

The R. R. Harris Map of September 1874 shows "Ranch House M. Dore" on the Rancho Santa Ysabel. This would refer to Maurice Dore. At some point, ownership again changed hands. About 1886, the Hun-

tington family made plans to build a hotel and a city around the spring; they had a concrete basin poured around it. At that time, it was speculated that the railroad would follow a course on the east side of the Salinas River.

We learn from the August 19, 1887 edition of the *San Miguel Messenger* that "The Templeton *Times* says W. V. Huntington has gone to the Eastern States on business. He has subdivided his property on the Santa Ysabel into three farms of about a thousand acres each, fenced the land, built houses and barns and sunk wells and leased to good tenants."

"It is announced that R. M. Shackelford intends to set out 10,000 rooted olive-cuttings on the Ysabel ranch the coming winter." This was according to the *San Miguel Messenger* of September 9, 1887.

Two weeks later, on September 23, 1887, the *San Miguel Messenger* carried a story entitled "New Health Resort on the Santa Ysabel."

The announcement is made that a San Francisco syndicate have purchased the mineral springs on the Santa Ysabel Ranch, some

Lake Ysabel, Paso Robles.

four miles from Templeton, together with some 800 acres of land, paying $40,000 therefor, and will fit up a health resort that will surpass anything of the kind in the State. The flow of mineral water there is said to be very abundant, and the water has been demonstrated to be possessed of medical qualities of the first order. We hope all that is mentioned may be realized.

"The Santa Ysabel Hot Springs" was the title of an article in the October 21, 1887 *San Miguel Messenger*. The San Miguel newspaper had obtained the article from the *Templeton Times*.

We mentioned lately the sale of the property about the Santa Ysabel Hot Springs, to a syndicate, the composition of which was unknown, but of which General Dimond, who was so warmly supported for the gubernatorial nomination at the Los Angeles convention, was the representative.

There seems to be little doubt that the owners, whoever they may be, have both the ability and the intention to thoroughly develop and utilize their acquisition.

Certainly there is every opportunity to make this one of the most beautiful and attractive resorts in the State. We are informed, however, that speedily all things here are to be radically changed.

There is to be a fine hotel and beautiful grounds, rides and drives are to be laid out, there are to be elegant bath houses, and every possible appointment of a great health resort, and in the vicinity there will be beautiful villas erected. Wealth and fashion are to deport themselves here and health and pleasure sought, pursued and found.

An article from the Paso Robles *Leader* was carried in the October 21, 1887 edition of the *San Miguel Messenger*. "It is reported that N. Elliott has sold 100,000 bricks to the Southern California Land & Immigration Company, to be used in the erection of the hotel at the Santa Ysabel Spring."

The hotel was never built. Around the turn of the century, many school picnics and barbecues were held next to the spring. Several bath-houses and wooden tubs surrounded the spring, and a person should still be able to see, next to the spring, a concrete slab in the earth from one of the houses. There were two

springs at the bath house; the larger one flowed about 200,000 gallons per day, and the temperature was 94 degrees F. These springs were used for bathing, but the principal use was for irrigating the land.

The Paso Robles newspaper, *The Moon*, printed an article on July 30, 1892.

The Santa Ysabel

One of the neatest properties in the vicinity of El Paso de Robles is that of the Santa Ysabel Land and Water Company. This company owns the famous Santa Ysabel springs and fifteen hundred acres of the fine land surrounding them. The company is not selling land or speculating in any way. The men composing the company, of which Mr. D. W. Hersburgh is president, have associated themselves together with the object of improving the property systematically and expect to be repaid for their investment when the country hereabouts is more fully settled and developed.

They have worked quietly, without any attempt at or desire for notoriety. Few people, even in the vicinity of Paso Robles, are aware of the amount of work that has been done or of the great expense that they have endured in improving the property.

Twenty-eight acres have been prepared and planted with a variety of fruits this last spring, and as much more land is occupied with nursery and vegetable gardens. Many rare ornamental trees and shrubs are being cultivated with a view to the ornamentation of the landscape in the vicinity of the lake and springs. Large fields of corn, alfalfa and other forage plants are grown for the cows belonging to the dairy. From this dairy the company supplies an extensive list of customers in this city with fresh milk.

The vegetable garden also supplies large quantities of vegetables for the town market. Two or three hundred acres have also been planted to grain and hay. These industries, of course, will bring in some return for the owners, but it is not expected that the property will be self-sustaining until the orchards come into bearing and the roughest of the clearing and opening up of the land has been completed.

The main Santa Ysabel spring is one of the

grandest natural fountains in the State. This spring is located in the canyon one mile back from the river. The water gushes out in a stream five or six feet wide and as many inches in depth. The temperature is in the neighborhood of 109 degrees Fahrenheit, and analyses which have been made show that the water is strong in all those mineral ingredients peculiar to other medicinal waters in this vicinity.

A few hundred yards below this spring is an artificial lake of considerable extent upon the surface of which ride three elegant pleasure boats. A raft is anchored in the center of the lake and a group of bath houses are located along the shore.

To the west of the spring and lake, the hill rises abruptly at an angle of forty-five degrees and is clothed with a thick jungle of live oaks, while to the east the hills are low and rolling, being covered with wild oats, bunch grass and scatterings of white oaks.

The landscape is picturesque and it does not require the eye of an artist to see that it is capable of being developed into a magnificent health and pleasure resort. . . .

The drives are properly surveyed and graded, and all the appointments are kept in a neat and orderly condition by the attendants. The lake and springs are already a favorite resort, and one visited daily by numbers of people from Paso Robles and the country surrounding.

The Santa Ysabel grant is one of the oldest in the country, and in its day was one of the richest and was always a great favorite with the native people.

Between the springs and the present lake there remains the ruins of a great dam which was thrown across the canyon to retain the water of the spring many years ago. So long ago, indeed, that large trees have grown up since the water made a break in the dam and destroyed the reservoir.

Many traditions cluster about the place, and there is enough of its early history known to make it interesting to visitors, but much that is now known will soon pass away and be lost if steps are not taken to preserve them. The company would do well to collect these old reminiscences and traditions. The time will soon come when they will be valued.

View from summit of hill back of ranch house.

Remains of prehistoric dam with cross-section.

Donald MacDonald wrote an article entitled "Among the Oaks at Paso Robles Hot Springs" for the *Sunset Magazine* in 1902. His description: ". . .the beautiful Santa Ysabel rancho with a lake of hot mineral water boiling forth from the largest hot springs in the state. Santa Ysabel with its oak-lined drives, its hot springs and its hills, its dairy farm and orchard is an endless source of pleasure to those who know it."

In 1904, W. C. Morrow published a work called *Roads Round Paso Robles*. In this work, we find the following.

> **The Santa Ysabel is now a fine modern dairy ranch, with Holstein cows. The hot sulphur spring pours out 600,000 gallons a day farther up the wooded canyon. Shortly beyond the point where the main east-side valley road opens for us into the Santa Ysabel, the waters of the great hot spring has been dammed, and there is a swimming lake of mineral water. A mile farther on is the great spring itself, with concrete plunge baths.**

A dam, 250 feet long, had been built and by 1889, a lake had formed which was 14 feet deep and covered two and one-half acres. The lake was a popular location for baptisms to take place. The larger of the "Santa Ysabel Hot Springs" flowed about 200,000 gallons per day, with a temperature of 94 degrees F.

The Paso Robles newspaper, *The Moon*, published the following article on July 22, 1893.

Hot Springs Stream, near mouth of canyon.

LAKE YSABEL
**A San Miguelite Siege of Twilight
Nights of Summer**

In the heart of the hills, approached by a narrow, winding road, fringed by tall forest trees, lies Lake Ysabel. Last week a party of pilgrims from San Miguel came to worship at this shrine of nature, to leave behind them for a little while the heat and dust of July days, and among green leaves and running streams to wander into dreamland. With that lovely expanse of blue and those dense woods filled with the soft murmur of a little brook, it was hard to realize they were only three miles from Paso Robles. The glamour of the forest was upon them.

Yonder town, with its noisy bustle and petty cares, was that the true type of life; or was man made to dwell with nature, to lie under a tree and dream away his days? To these gentle pilgrims the fluttering leaves seemed to whisper "Yes."

I call them "gentle," for they were ladies, sober matrons, and they returned from dreamland in time to spread a cold dinner on the ground. Soon a poet joined the group, and he sang of sweet clover fields, of flowers wet with dew, silvery streams, the solemn, never changing pines and the twilight nights of summer. They felt the magic of the North, the land of sinew and of brains. With his closing words, "It might have been," they came back reluctantly to the land of heat and dust. At San Miguel that afternoon the thermometer stood at 90 degrees, but here it was what the poet sings: "Sweet day, so cool, so calm, so bright; The bridal of the earth and sky."

All too soon the time came to leave those blue waters, those leafy arches, that delicious coolness, and the pilgrims started for home, envying Paso Robles, not for her park, her big hotel, her mud baths, but for that forest gem, Lake Ysabel.

During the 1940s, the waters were said to be 96.3 degrees F. Today, the spring flows at only about one-fourth of its original volume. The springs on Santa Ysabel are located about ¾ of a mile east of the Salinas River, and about 3 miles south of the City of Paso Robles. They are on private property, and permission of the land owners would need to be obtained, prior to any inspection of the location.

The reservoir was destroyed by flood waters, during the heavy rains of 1968.

RANCHO HUER HUERO

On May 2, 1842, Governor Juan B. Alvarado granted to Mariano Bonilla the Rancho Huer Huero of one square league, or 4,439 acres. Mariano Bonilla later asked for an augmentation of three leagues, because the scarcity of water had caused his cattle to spread out so widely into the surrounding vacant land.

As a result of his request, the boundaries were extended so that they reached Rancho Santa Margarita on the west, and to Estrella Valley to the northeast; this made the Huer Huero a much greater area than the three leagues requested. According to the *diseno*, the hand-drawn map which described the grant, the land was largely *lomas montuosas* - - -hills covered with trees and brush.

Speaking of Rancho Huer Huero gives us the opportunity to say something about this unusual name. Concerning "huero," some say that its means "blonde," although the word for blondishness would probably be spelled "guero," with two dots over the letter "u." Others say that the word means "putrid" or "rotten," especially referring to rotten eggs; here it could refer to the odor of sulphur water. One writer says that the word means "Babbling Stream," another says that the word means "Bubbling Spring," and still another says that it means "Whirling Stream in Winter."

What seems most probable to this writer is that the name "Huer Huero" was the result of an Hispanic attempt to pronounce the Salinan word, "Huohual," which was the name of a *rancheria* (native village or settlement) in the area which supplied Indians for Mission San Miguel.

Jose Mariano Bonilla, the grantee of Rancho Huer Huero, had been born in Mexico City in 1807; he later became a prominent lawyer in that city. Bonilla had arrived in California, with his two brothers Vicente and Luis, in 1834 as a colonist with the Padres-Hijar expedition. Mariano and Luis had signed on with the colony as teachers. This information is according to Mariano's great-grandson, Isaac Antonio Bonilla, in a letter of August 18, 1972.

In 1837, Jose Mariano Bonilla married Dolores Garcia, a daughter of Ynocente Garcia. Bonilla served as secretary to his father-in-law. It was Ynocente who suggested that his son-in-law petition the government for a grant of the Huer Huero Rancho. This land is located southeast of Rancho Santa Ysabel and east of Rancho La Asuncion.

Ynocente Garcia has written that Governor Alvarado "made me a concession of all of the vacant lands between the missions of San Miguel and San Luis Obispo. [This must have been a misunderstanding on the part of Garcia. Don Ynocente supposed that he had a grant for the whole of the land embraced within the San Jose Valley, near Pozo, to the extent of 5 or 6 leagues. Early in 1854, the old gentleman and his sons treated the place as government land, and recorded possessory claims upon the more favored portions of the tract. It turned out that he had only made application to the Mexican government for a grant to the premises, but no further action had ever been taken on the petition.]

By his first wife, Carmen Sanchez, Ynocente Garcia was the father of sixteen children. He had three children by his second wife, Bruna Cole. Ynocente Garcia died, November 26, 1878, at the age of 87- - - the oldest inhabitant of San Luis Obispo at the time.

Mariano Bonilla occupied the Huer Huero in 1839, and built a house and corral on it the next year. [An adobe building that had belonged to Bonilla would later serve as the first school-house for the town of Creston. It was located approximately one mile north of that town.]

Ynocente has written that he "ordered Victor Arroyo and my sons to move all the cattle that I had at San Simeon to the Huer Huero for Bonilla." In the *Garcia Papers*, Ynocente spells the word "GueGuero," with two dots over each letter "u." The grantee also acquired about 500 sheep and 100 horses; a *mayordomo* or foreman was left in charge of the rancho. In 1844, Tulare Indians attacked; three *vaqueros* were killed, the house was burned, and the corrals were destroyed.

The next year, Bonilla had a new house and corrals built, and he brought in more cattle. The Indians attacked again and stole the cattle. This time, they killed Mariano's brother, Patricio.

Sometime after November of 1847, Bonilla turned over his rancho holdings to Francis Ziba Branch, a person who had been a trapper from the Santa Fe party; he came to Los Angeles with the William Wolfskill expedition in 1832. It is said that Mariano Bonilla exchanged the rancho to Branch for one dollar and 253 head of cattle.

Francis Ziba Branch had been born at Scipio, Cayuga County, New York on July 24, 1802. In 1835, he married Manuela Carlon, a daughter of Seferino Carlon, who was a soldier at Santa Barbara.

On April 6, 1837, Governor Juan B. Alvarado granted the 16,955-acre Rancho Santa Manuela to Branch; this rancho was located near present-day Arroyo Grande. On November 6, 1847, Francis Z. Branch purchased Rancho Huer Huero from Mariano Bonilla. Branch built a house, erected a corral and stocked the place with cattle, hogs and horses necessary for herding the stock.

Branch seems to have taken no part in the hostilities involved in the American occupation of California, but he lost some of his best horses as a result of the struggle. In 1846, John C. Fremont was badly in need of mounts; he sent scouting parties out to round up horses from the surrounding ranchos. Some Indians led the foragers to Branch's herds, and 65 of his best horses were taken.

Francisco Ziba Branch was appointed *Juez de Campo* (Judge of the Plain) for Nipomo township, in 1851. This was the same year that Petronilo Rios also served as *Juez de Campo*. There were five such officers in the county at one time, due to there being at least 30 rodeos a year. One of the major duties of the Judge of the Plain was to supervise the rodeo, where cattle of the various owners were separated.

Branch was the first Assessor for San Luis Obispo County, and served from 1850 to 1852. The terrible drought during the years 1863 and 1864 caused much damage to Francis Branch. At the beginning of 1863, his herds numbered 20,000; at the close of 1864, only 800 animals were left.

The year 1856 saw David P. Mallagh in control of the Huer Huero. Three years later, in 1859, Flint, Bixby & Co., purchased Rancho Huer Huero, on which to run sheep and cattle. The company consisted of two brothers, Thomas and Benjamin Flint, and their friend, Llewellyn Bixby.

Benjamin had come to California in 1849, to try to find gold; his brother and his friend followed two years later. Finding that meat was bringing a high price in California, the young men decided that they could make more money supplying the demand for meat than by digging for gold.

They returned to Indiana and came back to California with 3,000 head of sheep and 125 head of cattle, which they bought in Utah. During this journey, they averaged 12 miles per day.

[In 1855, the Flint, Bixby & Company, in partnership with Col. William W. Hollister, had bought the San Justo Ranch, in present-day San Benito County, from Francisco Perez Pacheco for the sum of $25,000. Pacheco had acquired the rancho from General Jose Castro for $1,400; it had been previously granted to Rafael Gonzales in 1836, who abandoned it.]

When they sold the Huer Huero rancho in 1884, Benjamin Flint retained an interest in the land. The purchasers were Thomas Ambrose, Amos Adams, Jonathan V. Webster and Calvin J. Cressey. The land was surveyed, and the town of Huer Huero was neatly laid out in nine 300-foot-square blocks. The year 1886 saw Chauncey H. Phillips assuming the title to Rancho Huer Huero.

Francis Z. Branch died at his home on Rancho Santa Manuela on May 8, 1874.

Mariano Bonilla subsequently served as *sub-prefect*, then *alcalde* of San Luis Obispo. (A prefecture was an administrative unit, in use after 1836.) After the adoption of the state constitution, Bonilla became the first county judge in 1850. Later he served as district attorney, and was elected as a county supervisor, in which office, he served until 1866, when he retired to private life.

After selling Rancho Huer Huero, Mariano Bonilla applied for a grant to the Cuesta Ranch, where he is said to have owned one of the first two flouring mills in San Luis Obispo County. He made use of a water-power grist mill which had been built in 1798, and was the second to be built in Alta California. It was of the type commonly used in Mexico and Spain, in which the water wheel rotated horizontally on a vertical shaft.

Some farmers brought their grain from a distance of forty miles, in order to make use of this mill. The Cuesta or Bonilla mill had the capacity of 25 barrels of flour per day, as indicated by a report to the county assessor in 1874. [In 1891, A. F. Hubbard moved the water-powered flour mill to Carrisa Plains, and converted it to steam power. Nels Beck bought the Hubbard property in 1938.]

There is some dispute as to whether his residence was at the adobe situated at what came to be called "Estrada Gardens," or at an area slightly to the south and across Reservoir Canyon Road. Harold Miossi has written that Bonilla lived south of the mill site.

Jose Mariano Bonilla died in San Luis Obispo on March 19, 1879.

An article in the *San Luis Obispo Tribune*, dated April 12, 1902, provides information about the Bonilla family.

Mrs. Dolores Bonilla Laid to Rest at Arroyo Grande Yesterday. She Was Born March 10, 1822. Was Wedded in 1837 to Jose Mariano Bonilla and Came Here.

The late Mrs. Dolores Bonilla was laid to rest yesterday afternoon at Arroyo Grande. The funeral was conducted by Rev. Father Lynch and was largely attended. The pall bearers were Jose Villa, Joaquin Estrada, John Price, Theo. Valuenzuela, Alexander Newsome and Jose I. Feliz.

Mrs. Dolores Bonilla was born March 10, 1822 at San Jose. She was wedded in 1837 to Jose Mariano Bonilla. Don Inocente Garcia, then the administrator of the Mission of San Miguel was the father of the bride. After the wedding Mr. Bonilla acted as secretary to his father-in-law. He was afterwards appointed by Governor Alvarado as administrator of the Mission of San Luis Obispo, at which place he made his home. Mr. Bonilla died March 19, 1879 at the age of 71 years and Mrs. Bonilla has since lived with relatives in this county.

This pioneer woman is survived by the following children: B. Bonilla of San Francisco, F. Bonilla of Santa Barbara, Mariano Bonilla of Santa Margarita, Mrs. A. Torres of Santa Margarita, Mrs. R. F. Branch, Mrs. A. Estrada and Mrs. Fred Branch of Arroyo Grande.

Antonio Garcia, a brother and Mrs. R. Lopez of Bakersfield and Mrs. E. G. Correa of San Luis Obispo are sisters of the deceased.

Unidentified people sitting in front of the Linne Hotel.

Deceased was the mother of 15 children, 8 of whom are dead. She has 43 grand children.

The "Estrada Gardens' takes it name from Joaquin Estrada, who moved his family to the ranch at the foot of the Cuesta, after he was forced to give up the Santa Margarita Rancho. The adobe at Estrada Gardens had been built in 1841, the same year that Joaquin Estrada had received the 17,734-acre grant. This land had belonged to Mission San Luis Obispo. Martin

Murphy took over the Santa Margarita Rancho on May 1, 1861. Joaquin Estrada died on May 2, 1893 at the age of 78.

In this century, Mrs. Annie Lowe had owned the adobe and 300 acres surrounding it since 1934. In 1974, the adobe had been condemned by the County, and was to be razed. Mrs. Loraine Zuiderweg, daughter of Annie Lowe, donated the adobe's hand-made red tile roof to the County of San Luis Obispo, for use in restoring the Rios-Caledonia Adobe in San Miguel. Thanks to these two ladies, some original roof tiles from "Estrada Gardens" have been preserved in the North County. The tiles may be seen today at the Rios-Caledonia Adobe, where they adorn the Maintenance Building, and sit atop the roof over the Wishing Well.

In the years 1887 and 1888, a colony was being formed to the northwest of the Huer Huero Grant; the settlement was called Linne. About seven miles southeast of Paso Robles, Linne was named in honor of Karl von Linne, the Swedish naturalist and botanist. People who are familiar with the Dresser Ranch, near the intersection of Linne Road and Sandy Creek Way, know the site of the former village of Linne. The hotel was on the south side of the Huer Huero River.

Around 1885, Andrew Anderson, the person who formed the colony on the Huer Huero River, had advertised the following: "Acres of bountiful land for sale, bordering the gushing, trout-filled Huer Huero River in Linne, California." Mr. Anderson had moved to San Luis Obispo County from Stromburg, Nebraska. Anderson purchased land from Dr. Dresser; the down payment to Dr. Dresser was said to have been a gold watch.

Many families from the mid-west left their homes and farms to move to the area of Linne. Buyers, eagerly awaiting the roaring Huer Huero River, in 1887, encountered nothing but a "big sand patch" when they arrived. They later learned that the river was dry nine months of the year, and was sometimes dry all year long.

The October 14, 1887 edition of the *San Miguel Messenger* ran an article entitled, "Important Land Sale."

It is reported that a sale of a tract of nearly 5,000 acres of land belonging to the Huer Huero grant lying about fourteen miles southeast of this place has been made to a Swedish Company for colonization.

It is claimed that there are forty families now waiting for the opportunity to go on the land. The Swedes are frugal, peaceable and industrious people and they will doubtless build up a happy and prosperous community on this purchase.

The post office at Linne was established on January 22, 1889, with Andrew Anderson the first postmaster. On May 21, 1891, it was moved 1 ½ miles to the southeast.

An early prominent settler was Anders Olaf Malmberg, who had been born in northern Sweden in 1835; his wife, Elizabeth, had been born in 1836. He left the land of his birth in the spring of 1868, and settled in Cherokee County, Iowa, where he homesteaded. He and his family were among the first settlers to arrive in the Linne area in 1887.

After purchasing land from Dr. Ralph Dresser, the Rev. Anders O. Malmberg built a barn, that was first used as the family home, as well as for the Swedish Baptist Church. After the Linne school was built, in 1887, church services were held in the school-house.

Malmberg was appointed postmaster, May 21, 1891, by John Wanamaker, Postmaster General; Malmberg ran the post office in his home until it was discontinued on November 14, 1925 and moved to Paso Robles. Anders O. Malmberg passed away in Linne in 1934, one month short of 99 years of age.

Bill Erickson, a grandson of Anders O. Malmberg, had been born in the Swedish settlement of Linne in 1909. Erickson's uncle, Edward Malmberg, used to drive a horse-drawn carriage they called the hearse. Bill remembered there being a graveyard up on the hill, which had wooden grave-markers that have since disappeared.

The Linne Hotel, built around 1890, by a man named Samuelson, contained 14 rooms. To construct the 6-chimney structure, river-bed mud was used to make the bricks; they were never fired, and as a result were crumbly. Decorations on the walls of the second floor consisted of scenes which had been painted by an amateur.

Philip Samuelson, son-in-law of the land promoter, Andrew Anderson, came to San Luis Obispo County in 1888; the had been born in Dalehusby, Dalene, Sweden on January 21, 1864, the son of Rev. Adreas Samuelson. At Linne, Philip Samuelson was married to Miss Alma Anderson, who had been born in Westmanland, Sweden. Her father was Andrew Anderson, a watchmaker and jeweler; he had come to San Luis Obispo County in 1887, and bought 5,000 acres from the Dunning and Dresser Land Company.

Mr. Samuelson in front of the Linne Hotel.

Bill Erickson has stated that a single fence-line that bordered their property was the dividing line between Linne and the German settlement of Geneseo. The settlement of Geneseo was situated on land that was in proximity of Rancho Huer Huero, and was about twelve miles east of Paso Robles.

By 1884, there were three families in the Geneseo District: those of Charles Pepmiller, the Herts and the Gruenhagens. Mr. Pepmiller sent an advertisement to the *Geneseo Republic*, the newspaper in the community of Geneseo, Illinois. The ad stated that 3,000 acres of land were available near the Huer Huero River. Following the publication of that ad, families were attracted from Kansas, Illinois, Wisconsin and even from Denmark. Among the newcomers were the Martin, William and John Ernst families. The name Geneseo comes from Geneseo, Illinois, their former home.

There were two grammar schools in the area, one in Linne and the other in Geneseo. Before the Linne School was built, classes were held in a clump of trees where an apple orchard was later located on Creston Road, near the present-day Sunny Brook Angus Ranch. When the population and attendance dwindled, the schools were combined at the Geneseo schoolhouse, located on the corner of Creston Road and Geneseo Road.

[Both the Linne and Geneseo school-houses have since been moved to the Chandler's Webster ranch in Creston. The Linne school district merged with the Geneseo district in 1924; this combined school district merged with that of Paso Robles in 1962.]

The "Dresser Ranch" is named for William O. Dresser. He had been born on May 11, 1847 at Beloit, Wisconsin, and attended school near Rockford, Illinois.

At the age of 13, he crossed the plains with his family. After spending time in Stanislaus and Merced Counties, he came to San Luis Obispo County in 1882.

He bought 8,000 acres of the Eureka Ranch, on the Huer Huero River, four miles from Paso Robles. The purchase price was about 10-cents per acre. The brick house he built there became the first Linne Post Office; on one of his properties, he had the first flowing well.

On September 21, 1875 William O. Dresser married Mary M. Rickey, a native of Ohio. Seven children were born of this union: Dr. Ralph O. Dresser, a graduate of the University of California, who practiced medicine in Paso Robles; Miss Bertha Dresser was a trained nurse at a hospital in San Francisco; Nellie became Mrs. Clarence Brewster, a graduate nurse, and resided in Portland, Oregon; William Rollo Dresser assisted on the Paso Robles ranch; Ruby became Mrs. Frank Cummings, of Paso Robles; Sadie became Mrs. Roy Warden, of Paso Robles. A brother, Irvin, was accidentally killed on a hunting trip at the age of 19.

In 1893, the William O. Dresser family moved to the land which became the "Dresser Ranch." One year later, their last child, Wanda, was born. Between 1896 and 1906, William O. Dresser was a member of the Board of Education and also Clerk of the Board, in Paso Robles. During the same years, he was a City Trustee. Mr. Dresser died on October 29, 1916.

William Rollo Dresser married Birdie Luttrell Dresser; she taught school in Paso Robles, San Miguel and Morro Bay. Birdie Dresser served as the principal of the San Miguel Elementary School during the years of the Korean War. She also served on the Paso Robles Library board for twenty-one years.

The children of William Rollo Dresser and Birdie Luttrell Dresser are William Ralph Dresser, of Paso Robles, and Donna Dresser Helt, of San Diego.

Donna Dresser Helt has provided the following information from a letter, dated August 28, 1996.

One of the highlights of growing up and living on the ranch was when our parents had as their guest, in September of 1936, Clark Gable. He arrived one afternoon for an afternoon dove hunt and another one the next morning. He stayed overnight with us and our mother cooked him a dove dinner with all the trimmings.

Our mother was reading *Gone With the Wind*, and Mr. Gable mentioned he was reading it for the second time. Mother then told him if the time would come when it was made

into a moving picture, he would be perfect for the part of Rhett Butler. His reply was, "I have already thought of that." It became a reality.

Ralph Dresser has stated that Andrew Anderson had persuaded his grandfather to approve the building of the Linne Hotel. The two-story Linne Hotel was the property of the Dresser family for more than 80 years. It once served as a hotel stop on the stagecoach route from the San Joaquin Valley to the Pacific coast. The stage stopped overnight so that the driver and passengers could stay at the hotel. An old adobe building, used as a post office, used to stand nearby, but it dissolved in the 1930s. [The hotel burned down, one evening in 1962; the fire had been set by vandals. Portions of the brick walls were left standing, and people have taken away the bricks a few at a time. Today, there is nothing to mark the site.]

The Inland Messenger, of October 1, 1886, printed an article under the title, "Substantial Improvement."

Mr. J. F. Webster of Oakland, who purchased a 1,400-acre tract from the Huer Huero ranch near Creston, is at work in a manner that demonstrates his faith in the country. He has put up a large amount of expensive fence, and otherwise planned his improvements with reference to taste as well as permanence. A correspondent of the *Mirror* says: "He has 7,000 vines of fine variety, of a year's growth, which give excellent promise, and his orchard containing some 1,700 fruit trees of different kinds. Mr. Webster intends building a substantial residence upon his ranch, and when this work is accomplished he calculates to bring his family here from Oakland. He believes that he has obtained one of the best pieces of land to be found anywhere in the country.

The same newspaper, on November 12, 1886, under a section called "Local Brevities," informed its readers that "The *Tribune* reports a peach tree of 10 feet growth in one year from the bud. It was raised near Creston on the Huer Huero."

The January 21, 1887 edition of *The Inland Messenger* has the following comment: "The Templeton *Times* says that over fifty families are settled in and adjacent to the Iron Spring district, on the Huer Huero ranch."

According to the *San Miguel Messenger*, on July 22, 1887, "The *Tribune* says quite an extensive fire swept through the Huer Huero country, spreading over an area of some twenty miles, destroying much grass, the dwelling of Henry Tuley, a Mr. Shively, and other property."

The same paper, on August 5, 1887, stated that "We understand that Mr. Thomas Ambrose, of Creston, lately sold a tract of 300 acres to a party from Los Angeles, at the rate of $50 per acre. It is also stated that W. W. Hickey, of the same place, has been offered $75 per acre for his place near Creston. From these prices one would suppose that the boom has struck the Huer Huero country."

Readers of the *San Miguel Messenger*, on December 16, 1887, learned that "J. M. Gore, surveyor, is now subdividing the Dunning and Dresser tract, embracing something over 4800 acres lying between the Huer Huero and Santa Ysabel ranches. The tract is owned by a Mr. Anderson and is being laid off in 40-acre tracts. The work is well underway, and when completed the lands will be offered for sale."

RANCHO LA ASUNCION

At La Asuncion, an adobe was constructed in 1812 and a granary, 82 feet in length, was built in 1813. The location for the adobe was originally selected, due to the presence of a spring. La Asuncion was one of Mission San Miguel's wheat farms, and was the southernmost rancho of the mission. The adobe house was originally constructed as two stories, with a chapel at one end of the building. Between 1841 and 1860, the adobe had been occupied by neophytes, or Christianized Indians. To the north was a vineyard. ["La Asuncion" is Spanish for 'the Assumption.' This refers to the belief that after her death, the body of the Virgin Mary was assumed into heaven. It was mentioned as a place name March 4-5, 1776, by Father Pedro Font.]

The Rancho Asuncion, of 39,225 acres, was granted to Pedro Estrada on June 19, 1845. He had petitioned for the land on August 26, 1843. Since he was an officer in the military at Monterey, he could not operate the rancho himself; a brother (whose name is not mentioned), managed the rancho for him. [Leonard Blomquist obtained this item of information from Land Case No. 76, S.D.] The legal proceeding for acquiring the grant follows.

ASUNCION

The United States of America   To All To Whom these Presents shall Come Greeting:

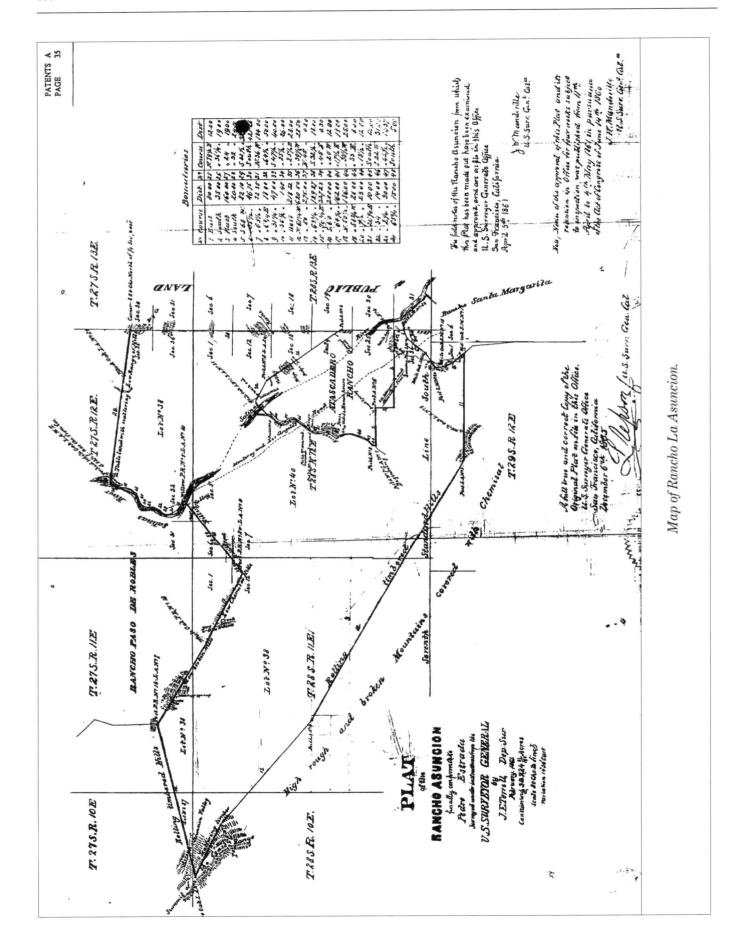

Map of Rancho La Asuncion.

Adobe at La Asuncion.

Whereas it appears from a duly authenticated transcript filed in the General Land Office of the United States, that pursuant to the provisions of the Act of Congress, approved the third day of March One Thousand Eight Hundred and Fifty-one, entitled "An Act to ascertain & settle private land claims in the State of California," Pedro Estrada as claimant filed his petition on the 13th day of February 1853, with the commission to ascertain & settle the Private Land Claims in the State of

California, sitting as a Board in the City of San Francisco, in which petition he claimed the confirmation of his title to a tract of land called "La Assuncion" situated in the County of San Luis Obispo and State aforesaid, said claim being founded on a Mexican Grant to the Petitioner, made on the 19th day of June 1845 by Pio Pico then Governor *ad interim* of the Department of the Californias, and approved by the Departmental Assembly on the 11th day of July 1845.

And whereas the Board of Land Claims aforesaid on the 24th Day of January 1854 rendered a decree of confirmation, in favor of the claimant, which decree or decision as appears from a duly authenticated transcript, on file in the General Land Office, having been taken by appeal to the District Court, of the United States for the Southern District of California, the said Court by a decision filed February 2d, 1856 in the cause entitled "Pedro Estrada appellee, *ads* The United States appellant" ordered, adjudged and decreed, that the said decision of the said Board, he and the same is hereby affirmed; and it is further adjudged and decreed that the claim of the above named appellee is good and valid, and the same is hereby confirmed, to him to the extent of eleven square leagues of land, within the boundaries described in the Grant, and the map to which the Grant refers, to wit-

The lands of Paso de Robles on the north, the ranch of Don Triffon Garcia on the south (called "Atascadero") and the hills on the East and West. Provided that if there should be less quantity than eleven square leagues of land within said boundaries, the confirmation is hereby made of such less quantity and the Attorney General of the United States, having given notice, that it was not the intention of the

Estrada Adobe excerpted from picture taken about 1915-16.

Estrada Adobe in 1967. Located on Traffic Way from 1812 to 1977.

United States to prosecute the appeal in this cause, the aforesaid District Court on the 24th day of February 1857, ordered and decreed that the order of appeal therefore granted in this cause, be, and the same is hereby vacated, and the appellee have leave to proceed under the decree of this court heretofore rendered in his favor as a final decree.

And whereas it further appears that this cause having been brought before the aforesaid District Court, in the matter of Survey the following proceedings were had, in said Court at the December term 1863.

The patent, or title, was received by Pedro Estrada on March 22, 1866. The adobe house was located on what is today's Traffic Way, 2 ½ miles northeast of the City of Atascadero. This section of the road was at one time part of the original El Camino Real. Across the road from the site can be found evidence of the pure-water spring that came to be called "Estrada Springs." Steve Buelna called them, "Sapo Springs," for some reason. The presence of the springs made the place a necessary stage-stop in the days of horses and wagons. In 1964, there were still some tules growing in the sheltered thickets which marked the spot. [In 1996, water from the spring trickles across the road.]

Pedro Estrada moved into the Rancho Asuncion adobe in 1860; by that time, the structure was in a state of disrepair. The roof and the upper part of the walls were in a sad state of dilapidation. Estrada had the Indians remove what was left of the roof, and take down the top part of the crumbling walls. The roof

was then replaced on the strengthened lower walls. After this work, what became known as the Estrada Adobe consisted of five rooms.

The roof tiles and adobe bricks, which had been used in the construction of the house and nearby granary, were made from the earth taken from a spot slightly to the northeast of the house, under the direction of the padre from Mission San Miguel. The depression, caused by the removal of the earth, was enlarged into a reservoir. Years later, when the railroad tracks were laid, a fill across the old reservoir depression was necessary.

Fred Shoemaker, of Paso Robles, who at one time lived neighboring the Estrada Adobe, remembered that the W. L. Morris family was living in the adobe during the years of 1921 and 1922. There were cement floors in the structure, and a tiled roof that kept the adobe bricks intact. By 1936, three rooms and a tiled shed were still standing.

According to Mr. Shoemaker, Pedro Estrada, while drunk, gambled away most of his ranch. When he became sober, Estrada was supposed to have threatened to kill the man who had taken his ranch on a gambling debt. The winner of the property, whose name Shoemaker did not know, gave Estrada 200 of the 39,255 acres of the rancho.

We do not know how valid the "gambled-away-the-ranch" story is. Martin Murphy had obtained the deed to some of the property on May 11, 1868. Later, Pedro Estrada sold much of his property to Jason H. Henry. Edward G. Lewis purchased the property from Henry on April 8, 1913. Lewis divided the Henry Ranch into many different tracts; one was named the Estrada Tract.

The 200-acre portion of the property, which Estrada had retained after the supposed gambling loss, was purchased, in 1917, by Delia Holden; she bought the Estrada Tract from Edward G. Lewis, and held the land until the early 1940s. James McCloskey, of Santa Barbara, purchased the property from Holden; McCloskey then leased the land to Walter Goodell, who started a dairy on the property.

Pedro Estrada had remained on his portion of the land until his death on January 30, 1897; he died in the adobe a poor man, and was supposed to have been buried, on February 1, 1897, in the Templeton Cemetery. However, cemetery records have not shown this to be a fact. Some people said that Estrada had been buried on the ranch in the Indian cemetery; this site had been destroyed in 1918, when work crews built a water reservoir for the newly-established town of Atascadero.

James R. "Bud" Davis, and his wife Bea, purchased

the McCloskey property in 1947, and set up house-keeping. Around 1970, Bud and Bea Davis had a home constructed near the spring site on the property. The 176-acre ranch was home to the Davis family for over thirty years.

The Estrada Adobe had remained in fair condition until 1916; however, removal of its roof tiles, between 1947 and 1951, left the adobe structure vulnerable to erosion. The last vestige of its remains was bull-dozed in May of 1978. A lone pear tree, which had been planted by the padres of San Miguel, remained, along with some grape-vines, to mark the site.

RANCHO ATASCADERO

In 1839, Jose Mariano Bonilla and Trifon Garcia petitioned the Mexican government for the grant of a tract of land called "Rancho de las Asuncion y Atascadero." Bonilla withdrew from this transaction, leaving Garcia to be awarded Rancho Atascadero. This rancho, comprising one square league, was composed of *lomas con pinos* and *lomas con pinos y chamisal* - -hills with pine trees and underbrush. The word "Atascadero" is understood to mean "miry place."

To the northeast of Rancho Atascadero was situated Rancho Huer Huero, and to the south was Rancho Santa Margarita, the northernmost rancho of Mission San Luis Obispo.

On May 6, 1842, Trifon Garcia was granted the 4,348.23 acres of Rancho Atascadero by Governor Juan B. Alvarado. Garcia had a difficult time developing this rancho, due to the constant raids by Tulareno Indians from the east; they rustled Garcia's cattle and burned the buildings of his rancho.

Maria Antonio Ortega, on February 24, 1843, filed a claim for Rancho Atascadero. However, the land com-

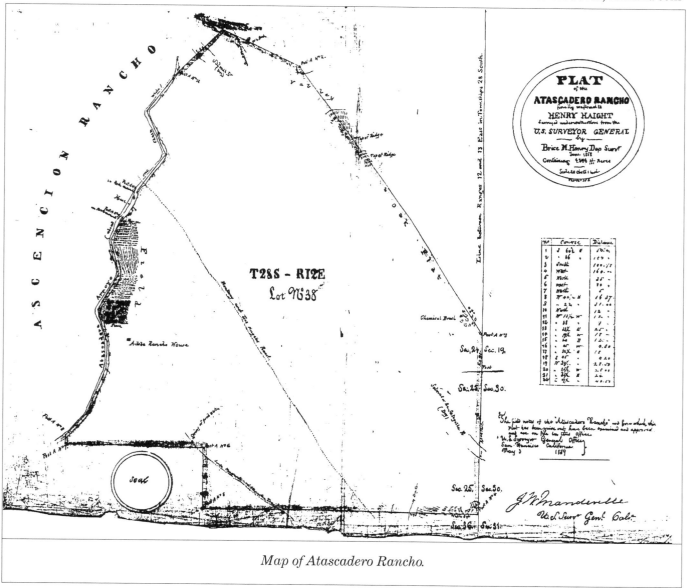

Map of Atascadero Rancho.

mission later rejected this claim on January 2, 1855, and the appeal was dismissed on February 1, 1867, due to failure of prosecution.

On March 9, 1846, Trifon Garcia had sold Rancho Atascadero, for 500 pesos, to William Breck. On December 29, 1847, Rancho Atascadero passed into the hands of Samuel W. Haight. Samuel and his brother, Henry, were uncles of Henry H. Haight, the tenth state governor of California, who served from December 5, 1867 to December 8, 1871.

Henry Haight came to California in 1850; his brother, Samuel, had come to California with Stevenson's Regiment in 1847. During 1856, Atascadero was owned by a Fletcher M. Haight and Edward W. McShane.

The Haights kept control of Rancho Atascadero until 1857, when it was bought by Joaquin Estrada. The claim of Henry Haight was patented on June 18, 1860.

Estrada took up residence at Atascadero in 1861, after he had sold his estate at Rancho Santa Margarita. In August of 1864, Joaquin Estrada needed money, so he mortgaged the rancho to Nathan Goldtree and Morris Cohen for $4,750. A year later, Goldtree and Cohen foreclosed and sold the property to Martin Murphy, Jr.

The Eagle Ranch, which was located to the southwest of the present-day City of Atascadero, began as an unimproved area used by a Mexican family named Siqueiro. Little is known about this family, except that in 1876, Mrs. Maria Siqueiro sold 160 acres to Albert F. Benton for $275,000.

Albert Frederick Benton, had been born in Germany in 1848. His parents brought him to the United States in 1854. After working with his brother in the wholesale grocery business, he came to San Francisco, then to San Luis Obispo County in 1869. Benton first settled in the Estrella region. That same year, he married Hannah Murton and he became a naturalized citizen.

At his newly-acquired property, he farmed and raised hogs, but lost many animals to grizzly bears.

The Prussian, J. Henry Baron Von Schroeder was a veteran of the Franco-Prussian War of 1870-1871. He retired from the army in 1880; in 1882, he received the Iron Cross decoration for his twelve years of distinguished service and gallant action in the field of combat. The Baron, the eldest son of Charles Freiherr Von Schroeder, arrived in San Francisco in January of 1881. There, he met and fell in love with Mary Ellen

Donahue, daughter of industrialist Peter Donahue. Mary Ellen's father insisted that before there could be any thought of marriage, Von Schroeder would have to become a land-owner and a "good American." He joined a party of men bound for a hunting trip in Central California. While staying at Paso Robles Hot Springs, he learned about Benton's Ranch, which he visited in order to hunt grizzlies, deer and other game. After being there for six months, he arranged to buy it from Benton, and retained him as his superintendent. The Baron gave the place the name Eagle Ranch. The wedding did take place on November 29, 1883, at the home of Cardinal McClosky in New York City.

Meanwhile, Benton was back at Eagle Ranch following the plans which were left with him by the Baron; he was supervising a huge building and landscaping program. The house consisted of ten rooms on the ground floor. A wide veranda encircled the front of the building, and decorative towers graced the roof line.

A granary, two barns, a bunkhouse, blacksmith and carpentry shop were constructed. Elaborate gardens were planned, with water to be supplied from one of the nearby peaks and brought in by means of a tunnel.

Von Schroeder remained at the ranch until the outbreak of World War I. The United States Govern-

Baron John Henry Von Schroeder, purchaser of the Eagle Ranch.

Courtesy of the County Museum Collection

ment confiscated the 2,000-acre ranch as belonging to an enemy alien. In 1919, the land was sold to Frederick Forrest Peabody. Today, some of the ranch property is occupied by Chalk Mountain Golf Course and Atascadero State Hospital.

The headquarters for the Jason H. Henry Ranch stood where the Safeway Market and Thrifty Drug Store are today situated in Atascadero. The old Henry ranch house on Ramona Road, near the Monterey Road School, is the only remaining building of the old Atascadero Rancho; it is said to have been built about 1896, but it may have existed on the site as early as 1876.

There was a town which existed within the boundaries of Rancho Atascadero before J. H. Henry sold out to Edward Garner Lewis, in 1913. Two small grave stones remain at the outer border of the city limits of Atascadero. The town was called Dove. It was on a corner of the Eagle Ranch, about 350 yards from the Southern Pacific Railroad tracks on the north side of La Paloma Creek; it was just south of the property occupied by Atascadero State Hospital. Its location was 16 miles north of San Luis Obispo, and 8 miles south of Templeton.

The main building at that site housed a general store, post office and living quarters for the Tim Araujo family. Other buildings served as blacksmith shop and storage building. Dove had a small water tank on the opposite side of the creek and on a hill; water was pumped from a well near the creek.

Mail was brought in by rail once a day to Eaglet Station at Dove. It was not far from a stage stop known as Cashin's Station, which was between Dove and Santa Margarita. On July 30, 1886, San Miguel's newspaper, *The Inland Messenger*, informed its readers that "At the Von Schroeder place, in the mountains west of

Atascadero Lake from the east.

Cashin's, the mercury stood at 116 degrees in the shade last week." The same newspaper on the same date stated that "Father Mut, often celebrating Mass at Cashin's Station, next Sunday, will proceed to San Jose Valley and organize a committee to supervise the erection of a church in that vicinity."

The San Miguel newspaper, on September 3, 1886, stated that "Baron Von Schroeder who has, without regard to expense, been fitting up a place in the mountains some four miles west of Cashin's Station, has now 26,000 French prune trees a year old past. He has also a variety of other choice fruits, all enclosed with a rabbit-proof fence which is four miles long. . . . Mr. A. F. Benton is superintendent of the ranch."

Some additional information concerning the name Cashin can be gleaned from an October 7, 1887 article in the *San Miguel Messenger*. "Thomas Cashin's interest in the Cashin place, on the Santa Margarita, has been purchased by Daniel Sheerin, of San Francisco, who will improve the premises, add another building, establish a grocery store in conjunction with the house and place the whole in charge of his son Thomas Sheerin."

The Dove post office was established on June 17, 1889. The first postmaster was Thomas J. Sheerin; other Dove postmasters were James P. Sherwin, 1891; William Mankins 1892 and Enoch S. Arvine 1895. After the turn of the century, postmasters included Eryene D. Arvine, Timothy Araujo and Sarah Araujo. The Dove post office was discontinued on September 15, 1915, and moved to Atascadero.

The cemetery for Dove once contained about 20 graves, most with wooden crosses and some with rock or concrete headstones, with names still readable. Two which lasted through the years bear the names of "Maria R. Deltames, born 1867, died 1872," and "The memory of our Jennie, who died Jan. 27, aged 12 years, 8 mos. And 14 days." The oldest date recorded is 1872, and the newest grave is dated 1903.

When the Araujo family moved away, the town just sort of dried up and ceased to exist. Some residents of the area remember a tiny school at Dove. Nothing remains of the old Araujo adobe.

On July 4, 1913, Jason H. Henry signed over his 23,000-acre "Atascadero Ranch" to E. G. Lewis. Lewis reportedly paid approximately $850,000 for the ranch, at an average of about $37.50 per acre.

Edward Garner Lewis was born on March 4, 1868 and died on August 10, 1950. The first of the civic center buildings to be completed was the Printery, in 1916. The first issue of the *Atascadero News*, edited by L. D. Beckwith, and published by E. G. Lewis, came out

January 22, 1916; in September it was followed by the *Illustrated Review*, a rotogravure picture magazine. In 1924, the rotogravure presses were moved to Los Angeles, where they were used by the *Chronicle* and *The Los Angeles Times*.

EL NACIMIENTO

The name "Nacimiento," as given to the river, apparently arose through a misunderstanding, according to Erwin G. Gudde, in *California Place Names*. On September 21, 1769, the Portola expedition camped on the river, while on its way north in search of Monterey Bay. Padre Juan Crespi referred to the river as "a very large arroyo, whose source (*nacimiento*), so they said, was not far off."

In 1774, the De Anza expedition came to the same river; De Anza must have assumed that the previous expedition had named it Nacimiento. This would associate the word with "the Nativity," which is another meaning of the word, and not with "source of the river."

On April 16 and April 24, 1774, De Anza mentioned the name of the stream. On August 27, 1795, a padre speaks of *el nacimiento* between San Antonio and San Luis Obispo. The lack of capitalization on the word *nacimiento* would seem to indicate that the meaning of "source" was intended. Later documents mention *rio del Nacimiento*.

The California State Archives in Sacramento contain a petition, instituted in 1839, by Juan Antonio Espinosa "for the land known by the name of Nacimiento."

I have acquired a small amount of stock, which may minister to the support of my family, which is composed of four children, the only son being in the military service, property is vacant, and although it is said to pertain to the Ex-Mission of San Miguel, it is not cultivated by the same nor occupied by any stock ...

On June 28, 1839, the petition was passed to the administrator of the Mission for his approval on the matter. Part of the response is as follows:

Although the administrator of this establishment is absent and it is his duty to report in such cases, that the matter may not be delayed, I in place of the administrator report:
That the land may be granted to the petitioner, as asked for, excepting the part marked

as plain, between the Arroyo of la Nacimiento and this Ex-Mission, since this part is very necessary to the same Establishment.
San Miguel   July 9, 1839
As Majordomo
J. Mariano Bonilla

Rancho Nacimiento was granted, along with Las Gallinas and La Estrella, to the Christianized Indians of Mission San Miguel, on July 16, 1844. These grants were later rejected by the U. S. Land Commission.

The Nacimiento River is mentioned as forming a part of the original northern boundary of San Luis Obispo County in the Statutes of 1850:

Beginning three English miles west of the coast, at a point due west of the source of the Nacimiento River, and running due east to the source of said river; thence down the middle of said river to its confluence with Monterey river. . .

A number of changes were made to the northern boundary of the county before a satisfactory location was reached. In 1851, the boundary was defined as:

Beginning at the junction of the Monterey, or Salinas and Nacisniento [sic] river; thence up the Nacisniento ten miles, following the meanderings of said river . . .

For ten years, the boundary remained as described; in 1861, an attempt was made to locate it with reference to the United States survey lines.

On December 1, 1857, two Basque cattle dealers, M. Graciano and Pedro Obiesa, were murdered on the Nacimiento River. The area near the mouth of this river, and for miles on each side, was called "The Dark and Bloody Ground" of this section of the country by Walter Murray, the newspaper writer who arrived in San Luis Obispo in the fall of 1853.

The name of Robert G. Flint has a strong connection with the Nacimiento Ranch. According to J. M. Guinn, whose history book was published in 1903, Robert G. Flint had been born on February 27, 1862, in London, Ontario, Canada. His father, Pirney, was a native of England and a stone mason; Pirney was married to Ann Elson, a native of Canada, and they were the parents of two sons and six daughters.

A Flint had been referred to as "Old Man Flint," and Pirney is probably a likely candidate for this title.

It is possible that he went by the name of Robert G. Flint, because a person of that name took part in early real estate transactions.

By September of 1868, Robert G. Flint was established on the Nacimiento River. The Salinas and San Antonio Rivers formed part of the boundary of the Nacimiento Rancho, and the Nacimiento River ran through it. At that time, three Americans passed through on their way south from Watsonville. Soon after they reached San Luis Obispo, it was learned that the men had stolen horses in Watsonville, and had committed larceny at the house of Ferdinand Frankenheim and Robert G. Flint.

Warrants for the arrest of James Southerland, Benjamin Harris and Charles Rolette were issued. The warrants were placed in the hands of Deputy Sheriff Juan V. Avila; he summoned Bonifacio Manchego, and some others, to assist in making the arrest. The thieves were followed to the Arroyo Grande; Harris surrendered, but Rolette and Southerland fled.

During the pursuit, Southerland shot Manchego through the stomach and he died the next day. Southerland was soon captured, and brought to San Luis Obispo. There were threats of lynching among some people in that town; however, the Grand Jury was in session and the prospect of a speedy trial caused people to wait for legal action to take place.

The prisoners were immediately indicted for grand larceny, to which they plead guilty, and were each sentenced to four years in state prison, all within a week of the arrest. Southerland was also indicted for murder and tried in District Court; he was found guilty of murder in the second degree and sentenced to sixteen years in state prison.

A person by the name of Robert G. Flint had paid $3,375 in gold coin to William Pinkerton on October 10, 1871. This was payment for land in San Luis Obispo County, at Section 30, Township 24 South, Range 11 East; it was on present-day Camp Roberts, and formerly Nacimiento Ranch.

On January 4, 1879, a Robert G. Flint paid $1 to Drury W. James for land in San Luis Obispo County at Section 26, Township 28, Range 16 East and also Section 2, Township 29, Range 16 East. These parcels are south of French Camp and east of Camate Ranch headquarters.

These two transactions indicate that Robert G. Flint was becoming established on both the Nacimiento Ranch and the San Juan Ranch.

We have seen that a Robert G. Flint had been born in 1862. The years 1871 and 1879 indicate that this Robert G. Flint could not have been the person born in 1862; perhaps he was "Old Man Flint."

J. M. Guinn says that Robert G. Flint, at the age of 21 (1883), located on the Nacimiento Ranch; he remained on the ranch for thirteen years. Three years after going to work on the Nacimiento Ranch, he became a naturalized citizen of the United States (1886). At one time, he owned 660 acres on the Nacimiento River. According to Guinn, in 1895 Robert G. Flint engaged in the butcher business. About that time, Robert G. Flint married Anna Davis.

Anna Davis was from an old-time family of the San Miguel area. Her mother, Mrs. Elisa May Davis (nee Sumner) had been born in Mississippi on February 25, 1830. On July 7, 1843, at Sutter's Fort, with General John Bidwell serving as one of the witnesses, Elisa and George were married by Captain Sutter. George and Elisa May Davis are said to have been the first "American" couple to have been married in California.

In 1860, Mr. and Mrs. Davis "took up" land on the San Antonio River in Monterey County; after 1868, they lived in San Luis Obispo County near San Miguel.

Mr. and Mrs. George Davis were the parents of seven children. Their four sons were Charles, Buchanan, David and Joseph B. The October 15, 1895 issue of the *Paso Robles Record* would report that "The Davis Brothers have rented about 800 acres of land on the Nacimiento ranch, lying near the mouth of the Nacimiento on the north side. They are already hauling lumber for a house and barn."

The three daughters of Mr. and Mrs. George Davis were Eliza Davis (who married Newton Azbell in 1868), Mrs. R. B. Still of San Miguel and the above-mentioned Anna Davis, who married Robert G. Flint.

Robert and Anna Flint were the parents of one child, a daughter they named Anna Ethel Flint, who had been born around 1895. She later married Everett

Charles and Dave Davis, family came to area in 1854. Father George Davis ran sheep, and helped build the first school. Charles was constable.

John Hoy of Indian Valley. Everett and Anna Ethel Hoy were the parents of Florence Elizabeth Hoy, who later married Donald E. Butler. When Anna Davis Flint's husband died, he was buried in San Luis Obispo.

According to the writings of Don McMillan, a Robert G. Flint was a cousin of the Robert G. Flint of the Nacimiento Ranch. This second Flint family consisted of two sons and two daughters. Charlotte H. Flint, who never married, had been born in Canada about 1865; she had a brother, Peter Flint, also born in Canada, about 1872. A sister Fannie was the youngest child; she married and moved to Oroville. According to Leo Stanley, Peter was a bachelor who was a "Beau Brummel." [The 1918 voter registration index lists a Peter Flint, restaurant keeper; in 1934, Peter Flint is listed as "retired."] The fourth child was "Bob," who was said to be a great horse fancier. The father of these four people is given as George Flint.

The puzzle of the various Flints intensifies. On November 1, 1885, a Robert G. Flint died, leaving five children; a wife is not mentioned in legal documents which have been examined. According to the terms of the February 21, 1887 estate deed, the children were three daughters and two sons. The daughters were named Hannah Mary Flint (age 17), Elizabeth Flint (age 11) and Eliza Flint (age 9); Samuel Gibson was their guardian. To each of these daughters, their father bequeathed $20,000.

Robert G. Flint's two sons were Robert Flint (age 15), born in 1870, and George B. Flint (age 13), born in 1872. [These children had cousins named Peter Flint (born in 1872) in Canada, and the Robert G. Flint, who married Anna Davis.]

Under the terms of the 1887 estate deed, Robert was bequeathed the San Juan Rancho, the cattle and personal property, plus $6,965. George was bequeathed the Nacimiento Ranch, its 2,750 head of cattle, plus $3,401. The amounts of $6,965 and $3,401 were the net profits of the two ranches during the administration of the estate.

To each child was bequeathed one undivided fifth part of "all other property not now known or discovered which may belong to said estate." The amount of $24,337.72 left in the estate allowed Robert, George and Hannah to realize $4,867.54, while Elizabeth and Eliza Elson received $4,867.55.

The 1870 United States Census shows a Robert G. Flint, a stock-raiser, 53 years of age; he is listed as having been born in England. Age 53 would have him be born about 1817. In his household were Elisa, age 29 (a native of Canada), Elizabeth Elson, age 29 (a native of Canada) and listed as "housekeeper." There is also a 39-year-old Henry F. Robinson listed with the household; he was the cook, and had been born in England. A Hannah M. Flint is listed as being 7 ½ years old, and had been born in California. The names are those found in the 1887 estate deed, but the ages do not match. To this writer, it is reasonable to believe that a Superior Court document of 1887 would have more accurate information than a census document of 1870.

We have seen that George B. Flint had inherited the Nacimiento Ranch in 1887. *The Inland Messenger*, on May 17, 1886, stated that "The stage road northerly from this place, has been changed into a lane enclosed with fences on the Flint ranch, giving it a more direct course than the old track. The new road is on similar ground to the old, and with a reasonable amount of labor can be made a good one."

On June 25, 1886, the same newspaper reported that "J. L. Woodmansee, who has proved up and paid for his pre-emption claim, about a mile northwest of here on the stage road, has purchased the possessory claim of Miss Lottie Gould, adjoining, and has moved upon it as a homestead."

In 1887, the Southern Pacific Rail Road Company was the plaintiff, in San Luis Obispo Superior Court, against Hannah Mary Flint, Robert Flint, George B. Flint, Elizabeth Flint and Eliza E. Flint and C. D. P Jones and R. W. Bliven as Executor of the last will of Robert G. Flint, deceased, defendants. There was a Decree of Condemnation, and the case came to trial on March 25, 1887. A result was that "the sum of $500 is a full, fair and just compensation and value of the right-of-way taken over the lands. . . ." Also provided for was "$4,500 for damages sustained or which will accrue to the larger parcel of which the property condemned."

By May 6, 1887, the newspaper in San Miguel had changed its name to the *San Miguel Messenger*; on that date, it reported that "Charles Cooper will, in a few days, move to the Nacimiento to take care of a large stock ranch belonging to Mr. Burnett."

On August 5, 1887, the newspaper in San Miguel reported that "We are informed that the contested land case between F. and Wm Zimmerman and Mrs. Elicy Davis a homestead claimant, involving the right of way northwest of town, has been decided in the San Francisco office in favor of the Zimmermans."

On December 23, 1887, the newspaper in San

Miguel reported that "Mr. L. H. Ward, of the Bee Rock ranch, beyond the Nacimiento, has been appointed postmaster of a new office called Nacimiento. It is on the old stage road eight miles from Pleyto, and about the same distance from Bradley."

On January 20, 1895, a Paso Robles newspaper mentioned that "Geo. B. Flint and his cousin, P. Flint left San Miguel last week for London, Canada."

"Farming the Nacimiento" was the title for an article in the same issue of *The Paso Robles Record*.

> The Nacimiento ranch, lying near San Miguel, owned by G. B. Flint, is being subdivided and leased for grain farming. Among those who have leased tracts of this ranch are Frank Smith, Davis Brothers, A. B. Fancher, Z. A. Edrington, R. Kirk and D. B. Shaw. The last named is a larger farmer from near Shandon, and he expects to sow about two thousand acres. This move on the part of the young proprietor of that ranch shows business shrewdness, as it has been demonstrated that the stubble after the removal of a good crop of grain will afford more feed for stock then the natural growth of the soil without cultivation. The farming of this large tract will add much to the business of San Miguel.

The same newspaper, on March 2, 1895, printed the following article.

> It will be seen from notices appearing in another column that G. B. Flint the young proprietor of the Nacimiento ranch, has discharged Robert B. Flint from his employ and gives notice that he is no longer authorized to act as his agent in any respect. An action has also been commenced in the Superior Court by Geo. B. Flint against Robert B. Flint for $5,000, money received by the latter and not paid over or satisfactorily accounted for, and an attachment has been issued and levied upon 500 acres or more of land near the Nacimiento river, which was, some months since, conveyed by the former to the latter. This action is a surprise from the fact that the relations of these parties have been of the most friendly and confidential character.

One week later, the newspaper noted that "Pete Flint returned to San Miguel from Canada last Thursday." Two weeks later, on March 23, 1895, readers of the newspaper learned that "Young Geo. B. Flint of the Nacimiento ranch was recently married in San Francisco to Miss Olive Holmes of that city."

"B. F. Rucker, the well-known butcher of San Miguel, has sold his shop to Robert and Pete Flint. Chas. Forbes will remain in the shop. Mr. Rucker will give his attention to buying and shipping stock." This item was printed on April 6, 1895 in *The Paso Robles Record*.

"Large Transfer of Property" was the headline on a May 25, 1895 article in the same newspaper.

> The ownership of a large tract of land in any community is always a matter of public interest. The Nacimiento ranch, consisting of from 30,000 to 40,000 acres of land near San Miguel, falls under the rule and the recent changes and peculiarities in its management have been the object of the attention and comment of both the press and the public.
>
> It is now announced on apparently the best of authority that the entire estate has been transferred by young Flint. The real and personal property has been transferred to his wife and the cash assigned to Dr. Steiner, of Paso Robles. As Flint has neglected to settle some bills, the settlement of which has been more or less urged upon him, this transfer is being criticised, and may lead to litigation.
>
> The career of this young man in the brief period that has elapsed since his guardian was discharged, in connection with others who have figured in his affairs, will furnish a chapter of interesting reading covering nearly ev-

San Miguel Meat Market c.1910, owned by Charles R. Forbes. (Charles Forbes behind the counter and Stewart Clemons in front).

erything from romance to robbery, the details of which the *Record* hopes to be able to lay before its readers in some future issue.

In a court action on May 23, 1895, the plaintiff George B. Flint admitted that the employed Robert Flint on September 1, 1894 for the term of one year to superintend and manage the Nacimiento Rancho, and other property, and to act as his agent and bookkeeper, at a salary of $1,000 per year. On June 29, 1895, the case of Geo. B. Flint vs Robert G. Flint was dropped from the Superior Court calendar. The case was dismissed on August 20, 1896.

Readers of the June 8, 1895 issue of the *Paso Robles Record* learned that "The matter of the Nacimiento road has been laid over by the board of supervisors until the July term. The citizens of that section are unable to see why it should take three or four months to remove obstructions from a road that has been traveled ever since the Mission Fathers first passed through this valley."

One week later, the same newspaper stated that "The cases of People vs Lynch, Allen and others, for tearing down fences erected across the road on the Nacimiento ranch, pending at San Miguel, were dismissed Monday for want of prosecution. The defendants were put to considerable trouble and expense in these cases, though they never had a color of merit."

The newspaper, on June 29, 1895, informed its readers that "The case of Geo. B. Flint vs Robert G. Flint, has been dropped from the Superior court calendar. Geo. B. Flint, of the Nacimiento ranch, has a carload of lumber at San Miguel, and we understand he will fit up a dairy and hog ranch at Mustang springs on the San Marcos creek. The location and natural facilities are well adapted to that purpose, and the move is an eminently wise one."

There was some news about the other Flints, Peter and Robert, in the July 20, 1895 issue of the *Paso Robles Record*. "Flint & Flint have moved their meat market into the Spencer building which has lately been fitted up for that purpose, and Chas. Theriet has moved his jewelry store into a room in the same building." The same paper informed readers, on October 5, 1895, that "R. G. Flint has purchased his brother's interest in the meat market, while Pete has purchased the Withrow blacksmith shop."

"The San Miguel Pleyto Road," was the headline on an October 19, 1895 article in the *Paso Robles Record*.

In pursuance to action taken by the Board

of Supervisors at their last session, Supervisor Waite has given Geo. B. and Olive Flint, owners of the Nacimiento Ranch, notice to remove all obstructions in the road running west from San Miguel, across said ranch, within ten days. The obstructions referred to are gates that have been put up across said road within six or eight years past.

We have been informed by an attorney, who is acting for the Flints, that the notice will be disregarded, and that a legal fight to the finish confronts the county authorities in their attempt to enforce the opening of the road.

The same newspaper, on November 2, 1895, stated that "It will be noticed from the proceedings in the Superior Court this week, that Geo. B. Flint & Olive Flint, his wife, have sued San Luis Obispo County, to enjoin its officials from removing the obstructions (gates) from the road from San Miguel to Pleyto, across the Nacimiento ranch. William Shipsey and W. R. Cooley appear as attorneys for the plaintiffs. A temporary injunction was issued on a $500 bond. This will bring the question of the existence of a public road on that route to an authoritative decision."

Several references have been made that Robert G. Flint died, about 1895, when he was driving a wagonload of lumber, and it shifted forward and crushed him to death. Whether this was the brother of George B. Flint or his cousin, is not known.

On December 21, 1895, the newspaper stated that "A large amount of new land is being broken and sown to wheat on the Nacimiento ranch immediately south of the Nacimiento river, and west of the railroad." From the February 29, 1896 issue of the paper, it was learned that "John Journey moved his family to the old ranch house on the Nacimiento Ranch, Sunday. C. B. Watts, manager of the Flint ranch, has had the fence taken down above the Indian Valley crossing to allow the public to pass through that way until the crossing can be fixed."

"The San Miguel and Nacimiento Road Settled," was the headline on the March 7, 1896 article in the *Paso Robles Record*.

The matter of the location of the road from San Miguel to the Nacimiento river, across the Flint ranch, which has for nearly a year past been the subject of much personal controversy and some litigation, has at last reached a settlement. The right of way is granted to the

county nearly straight across the ranch from Woodmansee's line, substantially on the route designated by Mr. Flint, senior, before his death. The crossing of the Nacimiento, however, will be carried a little further down stream in order to reach a point with a substantial gravel bottom. This road will require some grading and a number of small bridges, but it ought to develop into a good road.

The same newspaper, on January 18, 1896 reported that "A correspondent from Lynch says that ice has formed on some of the sheltered parts of the Nacimiento river of sufficient thickness to sustain the weight of a man and horse—something that has never been known in the memory of the oldest inhabitants."

Flint sold the Nacimiento Ranch to an Australian rancher, A. F. Benton, who also owned considerable property near Atascadero, as well as other parts of the north county. The January 18, 1896 edition of the *Paso Robles Record* stated that "A. F. Benton, of the Eagle ranch, is making numerous improvements there preparatory to the arrival of Baron Von Schroeder, who is expected about May." Benton sold the Nacimiento Ranch to Baron von Schroeder.

John Heinrich Baron von Schroeder's property in San Luis Obispo County included the 36,500-acre Rancho Nacimiento, the Eaglet Ranch southwest of Atascadero, acreage east of San Simeon and town lots in Paso Robles and Morro. He had been born in Hamburg, Prussia, on April 25, 1852. The Baron had married Mary Ellen Donahue, from a wealthy San Fran-

Nacimiento River

cisco family; the wedding took place on November 29, 1883 in New York City..

By the fall of 1899, financial reversals depleted an estate that at one time amounted to $3 million. All that remained of his San Luis Obispo holdings, by June of 1914, were the Eagle and the Eaglet Ranches. He left for Germany, despite his advanced age of 62, and earned another Iron Cross during the war. He never returned to the United States, and died on May 9, 1927.

The *San Miguel Messenger* printed the following notice.

To Whom it May Concern: We hereby notify the public that no one will be permitted to hunt, camp or otherwise trespass upon the Nacimiento Ranch without written permission of the owners. All trespassers will be prosecuted to the full extent of the law.

A. F. Benton & Co.   March 10, 1899

Before returning to Germany in 1910, Baron von Schroeder sold the Nacimiento Ranch to Isais (I. W.) Hellman, a San Francisco financier, for $350,000.

The *Paso Robles Record*, in January 1, 1910, printed the following article.

It is understood that the Nacimiento ranch consisting of more than 37,000 acres in the northern end of this county, owned by J. H. von Schroeder and A. F. Benton has been sold to a syndicate headed by J. R. Gasson, of San Diego. A deposit of $100,000 has already been made, which practically assures the completion of the transaction.

The purchase price is $10 per acre or $370,000. It is the intention of the purchasers to subdivide this immense tract into small

Pictured at Nacimiento Ranch are Mrs. Clement Belardoz, Kathern, Honer, and an unidentified girl.

farms that will be placed on the market at reasonable prices.

It is predicted that these small farms will be eagerly sought after, and in a few short years, will be the homes of more than 75 prosperous families. It is hoped that this is the forerunner for the breaking up of these large holdings, which have undoubtedly done much toward the retarding of growth and development of San Luis Obispo County.

Hellman had been born in Reckendorf, Bavaria, on October 3, 1842; he came to Los Angeles in 1859 with his brother, Herman. Isais became a shopkeeper, and by 1865 had started his own dry goods, clothing and shoe store, which opened on April 15, 1865. He also started real estate and banking interests in Los Angeles, and was involved with the Bixbys. He moved to San Francisco in 1890.

Under the ownership of Hellman, with general managers Fred H. Bixby and Steve Wilson, from 1910 to 1920, then Eli Wright from 1920, the ranch profitably produced cattle, mules, horses, hogs, wheat, barley and alfalfa. By 1910, there were three large barns, blacksmith shop, as well as an implement shed and stallion-barn, with stalls, located at the ranch headquarters.

The *San Miguel Sentinel* reprinted an article from *The Rustler*, King City's newspaper. The 1910 article was entitled "The Nacimiento Rancho. An Authoritative Statement of Some of the Projects of the New Ranch Company."

Fred H. Bixby of Long Beach, the superintendent of the new Nacimiento Ranch Company, was in San Miguel the first of the week. *The Rustler* enjoyed a pleasant talk with Mr. Bixby, who was exceedingly frank and courteous in his statements as to the future conduct of the affairs of the vast holdings.

"The land will be leased to experienced farmers, with families, who will live on and cultivate the land for a term of years. They will be assisted in every way by the Nacimiento ranch company to successful and profitable farming, stock raising and fruit cultivation. Practically all the land from the stone house, three miles from San Miguel, to Bradley, has already been leased to families, principally from Southern California, who have taken advantage of liberal terms offered

by the company, and who will almost immediately take up their abode on the land."

In answer to a question concerning the names of the families, Mr. Bixby named D. Gardner, J. A. Valenzuela, A. W. Orrick, D. D. Williams, W. J. Gibbons, J. H. Newell, and others, "each with energetic families; and besides, Mrs. W. B. Cruess and her son, C. A. Hollaburton [sic] and C. J. Metzler, already on the land..."

Mr. Bixby added, "The new comers will be a gain to your community and a loss to Southern California of considerable importance. I know them and know their thrift and capabilities." [The name should be Haliburton. Eli Wright had a cousin, Eli Hart, who married Maud Haliburton.]

"The company is prepared to spend vast sums of money to accomplish results. The development of water will receive prompt attention, and live stock— horses, mares mules and bulls will be, in fact are being shipped in. The first carload of horses and mares have already arrived and been unloaded here in San Miguel and taken to the ranch, another shipment will follow."

He added, "A new pumping plant will be built at once in close proximity to the main ranch house, capable of irrigating 1,000 acres of alfalfa, the cultivation of which will begin very soon. There is no trouble about water, and the company will develop and use it in plenty."

The newspaper went on to report that "Mr. Bixby will only be at the ranch at stated intervals, once or twice every month, but V. E. Wilson, also of Long Beach, the new foreman, will reside there and transact much of the business of the company. . . ." (Vestal E. Wilson was known as "Steve.")

On November 11, 1900, the United States Army had published Special Order No. 261, which stated the intent of Congress to survey lands suitable for four new army camps; one camp was to be situated in California. The contenders for selection in this state were: the Conejo Ranch in Santa Barbara County, the J. H. Henry Ranch (future site of the City of Atascadero), Santa Margarita Ranch, and Rancho Nacimiento.

During the administration of President Theodore Roosevelt, a board was appointed under an act of Congress on February 3, 1901. The board determined that "the Nacimiento" was suitable for "a camp for one regiment of cavalry." Favorable aspects of "the Nacimiento" were: a fine stand of timber, a compactness of the land and the abundance of water, which was provided by three fine streams.

The Nacimiento Rancho had long been considered a potential site for an army-training facility; the Baron offered to sell it in 1902, but the government was unable to come to a decision about the site.

On March 1, 1902, the Chief Engineer ordered a further survey, and the land of Nacimiento Rancho was assessed at $5.76 per acre. The Chief Engineer recommended the site to Secretary of War Elihu Root.

San Francisco newspapers reported, in January of 1904, that General Arthur MacArthur, father of Douglas MacArthur, had appointed medical officers to a board which studied the issue; that medical board favored the J. H. Henry Ranch. This conflict helped cause the House Committee on Military Affairs to decide that the proposed facility would not be located in California. Consequently, for the next several decades the Nacimiento remained a ranch, rather than a military installation.

The *San Miguel Sentinel,* on April 28, 1917, reported that "The Nacimiento Ranch have been holding its big spring rodeo this week, Monday and Tuesday they worked at the San Antonio, Wednesday and Thursday at the Mustang Springs, and Friday and Saturday at the home ranch."

The same newspaper, on September 1, 1917, carried an article entitled "To Plant Sugar Beets Here If Soil Proves OK. Large Tract of Nacimiento Ranch to be Leased to Union Sugar Co."

Mr. E. R. Lilienthal & Mr. L. Harris of the Union Sugar Co. of San Francisco were here a few days ago looking over that portion of the Nacimiento Ranch lying on each side of the Highway from the Stevenson Ranch to Nacimiento switch, and also the land on the banks of the Nacimiento River, about 2,000 acres in all.

They took samples of the soil to be analyzed and if it proves satisfactory the land will be leased and planted to sugar beets. Large pumping plants will be installed as the beets will require irrigation.

The men seemed to think the land was very good beet land, and if it proves so, they will start immediately with operations. If started, other ranches in this vicinity, which can be irrigated will follow suit, and owing to the large profit in beet raising it will be a great inducement for them to do so.

I. W. Hellman died on April 9, 1920 and I. W. Hellman, Jr., died on May 10, 1920. The Nacimiento Ranch was part of an estate for the next twenty years. Eventually, Edward Hellman Heller, a cousin of War-

ren Hellman, took control; he sold the ranch to the government, and handled the transition period. A Mr. Hooper served as manager and an efficiency expert, at this period of time.

From 1920 to 1940, Eli Wright was foreman of the Nacimiento Ranch. Much of that time, Fred H. Bixby was a manager, and Warren Hellman was a bookkeeper. During this time, Eli Wright maintained a pack of 19 greyhounds to keep the ranch clear of coyotes.

Eli Joseph Wright had been born on March 28, 1881, on Wyss Creek, in the Adelaida area, southwest of the Nacimiento Rancho. Eli's parents were Joseph Wright, born September 20, 1847 in Iowa and Minerva J. Burden Wright, born February 18, 1858 at Sebastopol, California. Maude Viola "Babe" was the youngest sister of Eli Wright. They had two older sisters: Nancy Allen, born May 8, 1876 and Marian, born September 20, 1877.

When Eli Wright was about fifteen years old, he worked for George Flint. His family was then living on the "White Tract," a short distance southwest of the ranch headquarters. After Mr. Joseph Wright left

Eli Wright

the ranch, Eli and family moved into the house that had been built by Mr. Flint. In 1928, the old house was torn down and replaced by the present ranch house, located about seven miles northwest of San Miguel on the banks of the Nacimiento River.

On October 20, 1907, Eli Wright married Ida Hortense Kingery, who had been born on Dry Creek, in the Estrella area, on December 30, 1889. Her parents were Augustus Kingery and Addie May Bailey Kingery. "Gus" Kingery was a stage-coach driver in the San Miguel area, primarily driving the Parkfield stage. Augustus Kingery had been born in Oregon on July 8, 1859; his wife, Addie May Bailey, had been born on Santa Rosa Creek, in San Luis Obispo County, on February 1, 1871.

The children of Eli and Ida Hortense Wright were Katherine Alma (born April 3, 1908) and Doris Adelaide (born July 21, 1914). Hortense, with the help of one girl, did the cooking for the men of the ranch. These two people also did the chores for the main house and the "Club House." The latter was for the use of

Katheryn Wright Stanley, 15 and Doris Wright Uchytil, 9.

guests from San Francisco, who were usually the young Hellmans, Hellers and Ehrmans- - -grandchildren of I. W. Hellman.

One time the county game warden stopped by the ranch house around suppertime, and the hospitable Wrights invited him to stay for dinner; on the menu was fresh salmon from the Nacimiento River. After everyone enjoyed the dinner, and the game warden had left, it was realized that the main course, the salmon, had been illegally "gigged." Whether or not the game warden was aware of the source of the evening meal is not known.

Eli Wright passed away on January 20, 1973 and Ida Hortense Wright lived until January 22, 1976.

In the 1940s, the Nacimiento Ranch and the Porter-Sesnon Ranch comprised the largest portion of land of what would become Camp Nacimiento Replacement

An older Eli Wright.

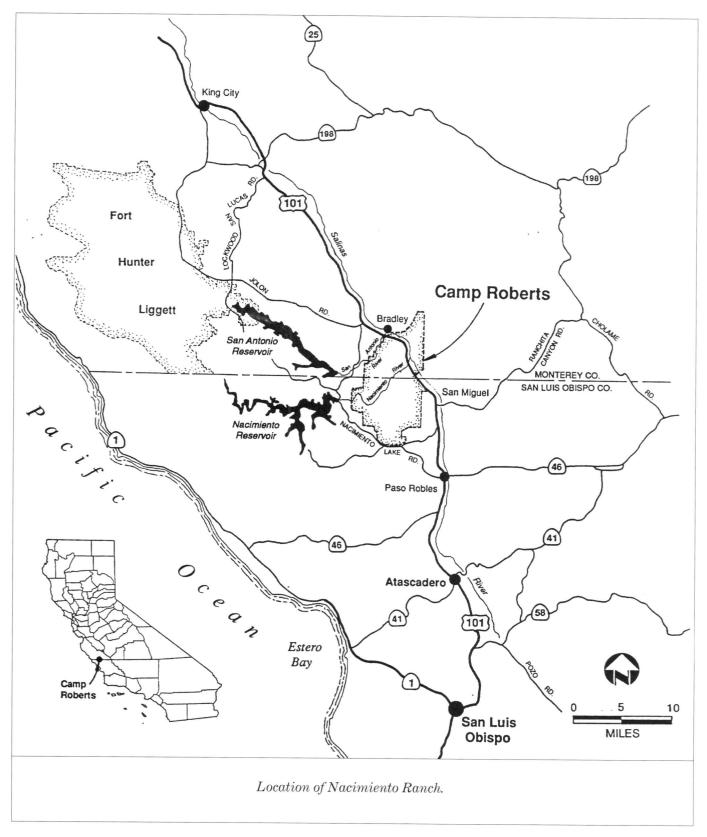

Location of Nacimiento Ranch.

Training Center. What is now Camp Roberts, of 42,540 acres, was acquired by leasing seven adjoining ranches in 1940, with the finalization of purchase taking place in 1943. A display at the Camp Roberts Museum shows the following information.

Original Owner	Acres	Total Cost	Per Acre
Wells, Fargo Bank	35,790.87	$442,000	$12.00
B. F. Porter Estate	6,300.00	82,000	13.01
So. Pacific Milling Company	984.35	15,000	15.00
F. H. Newlove	560.00	23,100	41.25
Ed & Emil Kruse	320.40	3,800	11.86
Emil Rothe	320.00	3,800	11.86
G. Thornburg & Irene V. Carpenter	160.00	800	50.00
	44,435.62	$570,500	

When the United States government signed the lease in 1940, the Hellman estate retained the ranching rights on 450 acres of the ranch. Camp Roberts officially began its mission as a Training Center in March of 1941.

Margarito Cisneros, long-time employee on the Nacimiento Ranch, was the last person to leave the ranch. He remained behind to help load ranch equipment which had been sold. He moved his family into a two-story house on L Street in San Miguel.

The camp was being constructed, under the name of Camp Nacimiento Replacement Training Center, when the name was changed in order to honor Corporal Harold W. Roberts. Corporal Roberts had given his life while assisting his comrades in combat during the First World War. While assigned to the 344th Tank Battalion, Corporal Roberts was driving his tank to the aid of another during heavy fighting in the Montrebeau Forest in France. His vehicle slid into a water-filled shell crater. As his tank was filling with water, he told his gunner, "There's only time for one of

The Margarito Cisneros home in San Miguel.

us," and he shoved the gunner out of the tank; Roberts died, trapped in the tank. He was posthumously awarded the Medal of Honor. Corporal Roberts, from San Francisco, was nineteen years of age when he laid down his life for his friend.

STAGES OF THE
SAN MIGUEL AREA

From the *California Star*, published at San Francisco, March 13, 1847, we learn the following:

Regular mail-order readers will be pleased to learn, that Governor Kearney has established a semi-monthly mail, to run regularly between San Francisco and San Diego. This mail is to be carried on horseback by a party consisting of two soldiers, and is to commence on the 9th inst. Starting every other Monday from San Diego and San Francisco, the parties to meet at Captain Dana's ranch the next Sunday, to exchange mails; start back on their respective routes the next morning, and arrive at San Diego and San Francisco on the Sunday following, and so continuing. The mail will thus be carried once a fortnight from San Diego to San Francisco, and from San Francisco to San Diego.

Coast Line Stage on the Cuesta, 1876.

It is of interest to remember that on December 5, 1848, when the Reeds had been murdered at Mission San Miguel, one of the discoverers of the murdered family was a mail-rider, James P. Beckwourth.

When the post office was established at San Luis Obispo in 1855, Walter Murray was given the mail contract. A two-horse wagon traversed the Cuesta pass in making the trip to Monterey once a week, carrying mail and passengers. The roads were little better than the trails; if needed, "passengers not only paid a good round sum for the ride, but had to get out and push uphill or help pry the wagon out, if it bogged down." These are the words of Annie Morrison, in her history of San Luis Obispo County. Morrison continues, "The mail from San Luis Obispo to Santa Barbara was carried on horseback by a man Murray hired for the job. Passengers going north, stage and team, stayed overnight at San Miguel. The next lap was to Jolon, and the third day all hands reached Monterey, if things went well. . . ."

Writers of local history have stated that there are records at Stanford University Library which indicate that there was a stage stop at the Exline Ranch, approximately three miles north of Paso Robles Hot Springs. In fact, it has been stated that the Exline's was the only stage stop between San Luis Obispo and Monterey, during the early years.

[Bernard Exline came to San Luis Obispo county in 1868, and homesteaded 160 acres three miles north of the Hot Springs; he purchased land until he owned an entire section in one body, all of which he used for growing grain or raising livestock. He married Elizabeth Huey. In 1875, Levi Exline came to the Paso Robles area and pitched at tent near the Salinas river; two years later, he located his Oak Flat homestead, three miles west of Paso Robles, where he lived with is wife, Emma Stone Exline. The Levi Exline place was near the former Bader ranch house west of Paso Robles, and north of "Resthaven."]

In March of 1861, the Overland Mail Company obtained the government contract for transportation of mail three trips a week over the "coast route" between Monterey and Los Angeles, via San Antonio, San Luis Obispo, and Santa Barbara. The Overland Mail Company, however, operated over the coast route for only a few months. In September 1861, the mail contracts were transferred to Owen Tuller and Charles McLaughlin. E. S. Alvord, in 1862, got the contract, a tri-weekly one which he expanded to seven times a week.

In August 1866, the United States authorized a daily mail contract between Los Angeles and San Francisco; Adams & Lovett, successful bidders for the contract, announced the mail stage would also carry passengers beginning in September. U. S. mail contracts were necessary in order for a stage line to survive, financially.

By May of 1867, the "Overland Mail Line," operated by W. E. Lovett & Co., with William Buckley as superintendent, ran through San Buenaventura, Santa Barbara, San Luis Obispo, and Paso Robles Hot Springs. North of San Juan Bautista, it was designated the "Coast Line of Stages;" to the south, it was called "The San Juan-Los Angeles Stage Company."

In 1868, Lovett sold the line to Flint, Bixby & Co.; Bixby was Lovett's brother-in-law. Lovett called his stage line "The Coast Line, San Juan & L. A. Stage Company."

By March of 1868, the railroad had been constructed at both ends of the line and the stages ran between these rail-ends. From Santa Barbara, the stage traveled north through Guadalupe, San Luis Obispo and Paso Robles, connecting with a short railroad at Soledad.

The stagecoach era flourished in Southern California, because the Southern Pacific Railroad did not reach Los Angeles until 1876. The Coast Line of Stages, from Los Angeles to San Francisco, once known as the "Overland Stage," advertised in the Los Angeles *Star* a service as far as San Jose where rail connections could be made for San Francisco.

Earlier, we saw that overland mail service began as a two-horse stage wagon that went between San Luis Obispo and Monterey. Walter Murray, who founded the San Luis Obispo *Tribune* in 1869, had the contract for this route, plus the mail service to Santa Barbara. The southbound service consisted of a single horseman riding one time per week to and from Santa Barbara.

The first day's journey north from San Luis Obispo would take passengers as far as the Caledonia Inn, south of San Miguel. Passengers would rent a bed for the night, and then proceed to Jolon in the San Antonio Valley. Monterey would be reached late in the afternoon of day three. Passengers continuing on to San Francisco were left at Hill's Ferry on the banks of the Salinas River, near the Los Coches Inn, south of the town of Soledad.

Not until November of 1886 did the Board of Supervisors of Monterey County decide to establish a ferry across the Salinas River at Hilltown; the contract for the service was let to G. A. Bromley.

Stage stop at Caledonia Inn, San Miguel.
Drawn by Ernie Morris

Roderic Hill, writing in the 1930s, in a newspaper article entitled "The Old Stage Road," stated that "The stages were old Concords which were hung on leather straps in the place of springs. . . ." The stages had wheels six feet high, and were drawn by four horses.

According to Roderic Hill, "There were no bridges and the stages had to ford all the streams they came to. If the stage got stuck in the middle of a stream, as it frequently did, the men passengers had to get out and push. Also, when the stage came to a steep grade, the men passengers had to get out and walk so the horses would be able to pull the stage up the grade."

The details of the following information comes from an article, written by W. Turrine Jackson, for the Fall 1974 *Historical Society of Southern California Quarterly.*

So frequent were the stagecoach robberies, during the summer of 1870, that it became apparent that there was an organized gang at work. The first incident occurred on June 4th; the stage, on its way from Los Angeles to San Juan Bautista, was stopped near the Pleyto stage station.

The driver was forced to "throw down the box," before being allowed to proceed. The box was taken to a nearby creek, broken open, and approximately $100 removed.

On July 1st, the Wells, Fargo & Co. treasure box was taken from the stage about thirty miles north of Paso Robles. At approximately the same time, the stage was stopped again, not far from the Pleyto stage station. Two men on horseback obtained the express box. These two incidents prompted the company to offer a $500 reward for the capture of the culprits.

Wells, Fargo & Co. sent its Detective Noyes from San Francisco, on July 7th, to investigate. Near San Luis Obispo, he got on the track of the robbers, and followed them to Cambria; there he learned that the citizens had formed a vigilance committee for protection against the gang.

At Natividad, a small town near Salinas, information concerning the gang's activities was obtained from a young boy who had lived with the desperadoes. About the same time, the stage was again robbed, this time the holdup took place approximately forty miles nearer San Juan Bautista.

The stage-driver followed the trail of the escaping highwaymen, as they went south; two of them were arrested by the vigilantes at Natividad. That evening, a man appeared in town and claimed to have been robbed on the stage; he insisted that the men being held were not those who had committed the crime. This man had almost secured the culprits' release from authorities before he was recognized by other stage passengers as a member of the gang.

In the United States District Court in San Francisco, warrants were sworn out for the arrest of the three men and their transfer to that city for trial in the federal court on the charge of disrupting the mails.

Wells, Fargo & Co. detectives and police officials immediately headed south to make the arrests; however, before they arrived, one of the men had been released by local authorities in Monterey. Another pursuit of one hundred miles south to Pleyto was necessary before the man was recaptured.

The press reported that, "The detectives state that the country for some distance around when the robberies occurred, is infested with gangs of desperate men, who invade farms and carry off cattle, and commit all kinds of atrocities, making the organization of a Vigilance Committee necessary, for the protection of life and property."

The Los Angeles *Star* of June 13, 1871 reported that a passenger named Joe asked the stage driver to stop near Paso Robles. Rather than simply "near Paso Robles," the location of this incident would have been between Pleyto and San Miguel. The passenger calmly stepped to the ground, drew a revolver- - -and blasted out his brains. An act such as this probably means that the passenger was psychotic, whether or not he might have found the trip dangerous or boring. Ella Adams informs us that this man was buried by his neighbors near where the present-day San Antonio Dam is situated. They marked his grave with a square pillar of native rock. One of the people who helped to bury the man was Henry Kahl, who lived in the area near Bee Rock Hall.

In 1871, a stagecoach ran daily from San Miguel to San Luis Obispo, a 5 ½ hour trip. Another ran to Soledad in Monterey County, according to William Norin in his book about the McDonald Clan and Estrella.

A danger to passengers during stagecoaching times was that the top-heavy vehicle could capsize, if the horses were permitted to go "all out." Just such an incident took place in July of 1871. The driver of the southbound stage out of Pleyto had somehow been thrown from his seat and run over. This was unnoticed by the lone passenger, a young woman.

The uncontrolled team ran for about two miles until the stagecoach struck a stump and capsized. Yet the horses continued, dragging the overturned stagecoach at a much reduced speed. The young lady broke out the glass windows, using only her bare hands, and managed to crawl out of the stagecoach.

Once free from the overturned vehicle, she ran and caught up with the leading horses and brought them to a halt. Then she unhitched the horses and tied them to the stage's wheels. The young lady then concentrated on finding the driver; she did not know whether he was back on the road or under the wreck.

After she determined that the driver was not under the wreckage, she backtracked in the darkness, looking for the driver's body. After going for approximately three miles, she came upon the unconscious man; he had a broken leg and was suffering from severe internal injuries, due to having been run over by the wheels of the stagecoach.

The young lady straightened the driver's broken leg and bound it with strips of cloth she took from her clothing. She was able to see a light in the distance, so she walked the two miles for help. After obtaining a jug of water, she returned to the injured man and remained with him for the rest of the night, and part of the next day, until help arrived.

The Los Angles *Star*, on July 9, 1871, reprinted the following article from the San Luis Obispo *Standard*:

Miss Plunkett is from Oakland, and was on her way to take charge of the public school at San Miguel. . .She is about eighteen years old, handsome, smart, and able, has a good disposition and deserves the commendations and kindly assistance of the people wherever she may go. We are in favor of such young ladies always to be in charge of our public schools.

The Santa Barbara *Press* stated that it felt that the girl was entitled to a more handsome reward than teaching school in San Miguel. If this story of the incident is true, the school in which Miss Plunkett would be employed would be a little adobe school which had been erected near where the San Miguel Flouring Mill is located today. This site is near where River Road crosses the railroad tracks in San Miguel. [In a 1996 visit to the San Luis Obispo County Office of Education, in an attempt to confirm Miss Plunkett's employment, it was learned that their records of teachers in this county only go back to 1895.]

By 1872, as many as six stages a day stopped in San Miguel, at the Caledonia, on their way between San Francisco and Los Angeles. The next year, 1873, the Southern Pacific Railroad had built a line as far south as Salinas. Flint, Bixby & Co. operated the service from the Salinas railhead to San Luis Obispo. The railroad reached Soledad on August 12, 1873.

The first known office of Wells, Fargo & Co. in San Miguel was shown on an 1874 map of San Luis Obispo County; the office site was in Goldtree's store, which was situated on the mesa where the cemetery is located today.

The Los Angeles *Star* and the Ventura *Signal* both reprinted, from the San Luis Obispo *Tribune*, a check list of stage stations and distances, together with the fares from Salinas south, in 1873.

> **From Salinas to:**
> **Alizal, 9 miles, fare $2.00**
> **Deep Wells, 6 miles, fare $2.00**
> **Soledad, 14 miles, fare $4.00**
> **Last Chance, 18 miles, fare $7.00**
> **Lowe's, 9 miles, fare $8.50**
> **Jolon, 8 miles, fare $10.00**
> **Pleito, 18 miles, fare $11.00**
> **Nacimiento, 15 miles, fare $12.00**
> **San Miguel, 8 miles, fare $13.50**
> **Hot Springs (Paso Robles), 7 miles, fare $15.00**
> **Santa Margarita, 12 miles, fare $16.00**
> **San Luis Obispo, 9 miles, fare $16.00**

On July 15, 1875, the Coast Line of Stages was robbed about ten miles northwest of Mission San Miguel; the following June, it was robbed again at the same place. After the second stage robbery, the sheriff rode "shotgun" to protect gold shipments brought in by express. The sheriff of his respective county would meet at the county line.

Both Ella Adams and Alfred Edwin Reed, grandson of E. L. Reed (who ran the stage station at the

Caledonia for a period of time), have done research at the Wells, Fargo & Co. headquarters in San Francisco. They wanted to establish the dates that Wells, Fargo & Co. had an office in San Miguel. Listed are the results of this investigation.

WELLS FARGO AGENCY

1879 - Goldtree & Company	Permit	#4484
1880 - Goldtree & Company		#2132
1881 - Goldtree & Company		#6169
1882 - Goldtree & Company		#2154
1/1/1887	E. S. Barry	#2139
9/1/1888	E. S. Barry	#2140
1/1/1889	E. S. Barry	#2141
1/1/1890	E. S. Barry	#2142
1/1/1892	E. S. Barry	#2143
1/1/1899	C. J. Whisman	#7232

There is no explanation for the lack of an agent for the years 1884, 1885 and 1886; nor for 1891. There is no agent listed for 1893, 1894, 1895, 1896, 1897 or 1898. There is no agent listed for the years 1900, 1901 or 1902. It is possible that these records were lost in the San Francisco fire of 1906. However, it might help to clear up the matter by noting the difference between a "stage line" and an "express company."

According to Waddell F. Smith, in *Stage Lines & Express Companies in California*, "The stage line. . .carried passengers. It may or may not have had a mail contract. . ." Further, "The stage line also carried express for many express companies who may have cared to put packages thereon. . . .It must be remembered that the express companies on one hand and the stage line operations on the other, were two completely different sets of business, each performing a different service for the public."

After the turn of the century, Wells, Fargo & Co. agents were:

1/1/1903	L. D. Murphy	Permit #2144
7/30/1904	L. D. Murphy	#3509
1/1/1906	L. D. Murphy	#2145
1/1/1907	L. D. Murphy	#2146
1/1/1908	L. D. Murphy	#2148
1/1/1909	L. D. Murphy	#2149
3/1/1910	L. D. Murphy	#2151

Murphy was Dr. Lorenzo Dow Murphy, and he ran the Wells, Fargo & Co. office in his drugstore; one of his assistants was Emma Stanley Cook. He was re-

Dr. Lorenzo D. Murphy, 1913.

Keyston Hall, San Miguel, built 1886.

ferred to as "Old Doc Murphy." The kindness of the gentleman was evident when, after his death, preceded by illness, all of his outstanding bills were found marked "paid."

Dr. L. D. Murphy had arrived in San Miguel in 1886; after his own well was dug, and windmill constructed, he added a 10,000-gallon tank to his own water supply and laid pipe down Mission Street for the first public water system. He was the chairman of a committee of three men who contacted the San Luis Obispo County Board of Supervisors, and got the first bridge across the Salinas River at San Miguel.

One can wonder whether the lack of a listing of an agent for the years 1884 through 1886 was due to the fact that there was no Wells, Fargo & Co. agent with a permit to operate in San Miguel; however, the stages would still use the facilities at the Caledonia. The same question could be asked for the years 1893 through 1898. However, in 1897, the Wells, Fargo & Co. office was located in the south lower half of Keyston Hall on Mission Street. In later years, Gene Gorham was the agent. We can be sure that the stages would run, whether or not Wells, Fargo & Co. had an agent at a certain location.

Those who travel on Highway 101, between Paso Robles and Atascadero, can picture in their minds the two bridges on Highway 101 south of Templeton. When going south, the first bridge crosses Paso Robles Creek, and the next bridge crosses the smaller Graves Creek. Having this scene in mind will help one to picture the following event, which took place on March 3, 1876; the details are from the March 11, 1876 edition of the *Tribune*.

On a rainy morning, stage driver Hendricks was

heading north from San Luis Obispo; riding with him were Mr. William Buckley, General Superintendent of the Coast Line of Stages, and Mr. W. H. "Shotgun" Taylor, Division Agent. Two passengers, H. Reinhardt and J. H. Mitchell had paid the $17 fare for the 36-hour trip to San Francisco.

About one o'clock in the afternoon, the stage arrived at Graves Creek. In all the time he had been driving this route, Hendricks had never seen the creek so high; it ordinarily contained just a trickle of water, or was completely dry. He forced his reluctant animals into the rising Graves Creek, where they plunged and stumbled their way to the opposite bank.

Later, when they reached Paso Robles Creek, one glance told Hendricks that the raging torrent was clearly impassable. He reversed the stage's direction, and they fought their way back across Graves Creek. The stage returned to Campbell's station, where the travelers waited out the storm. Campbell's station was

Keyston Hall shown partly torn down in January of 1977.

located between the Rancho Atascadero and Rancho Santa Margarita, three miles from Santa Margarita. It was later called Cashin's Station.

When the rain abated, they again attempted to cross the swollen stream. Unfortunately, although the rainfall had decreased, the stream had risen. In the middle of Paso Robles Creek, one of the frightened horses stumbled in a hole, and became entangled in the traces. The horse and its harness-mate were dragged to their death in the roiling water. This caused the stage to upset, throwing the driver, Mr. Buckley and Mr. Taylor into the raging creek. Reinhardt and Mitchell were able to cling to the side of the coach.

Fortunately, someone had witnessed their plight. An Indian, Jose Luis, had been watching the struggle. When he saw the coach overturn, he plunged his horse into the water and threw his rope to Hendricks, who was floundering and on the verge of being swept under the water. The rope caught Hendricks' arm, and Jose Luis was able to pull the man to safety.

In the meantime, Mr. Buckley had managed to reach the precarious safety of the overturned coach. Mr. Taylor was putting up a valiant struggle to save the last horse from the dangerous waters. The third horse had scrambled to the safety of the creek bank.

Time and again, the brave Indian and his horse entered the water; they brought to safety each of the three people who had been clinging to the coach. He then turned to help Mr. Taylor. Together, the men were able to save not only the horse, but the mail, the express box and the baggage.

While this was taking place, the strong current had washed the stagecoach down the creek; it became stuck on a sandbar that had formed between the creeks just before they mingled and flowed into the Salinas River.

The wet and exhausted men shivered with the cold until, after several frustrating attempts, they finally were able to start a fire. The streams on either side of them continued to rise; that evening, Jose Luis swam his valiant steed across Graves Creek again. He rode to a small house where a Mexican family gave him a pot of coffee and some tortillas to take to the people who were stranded.

By 9:00 p.m., the waters began to recede, and Jose Luis took the men, one-by-one, to the shelter of the little house; there, through the kindness of the family, they spent the night. The next morning, a south-bound stage returned the men to San Luis Obispo.

Although Mr. Reinhardt lost his wallet, containing $300 in gold notes, Jose Luis was rewarded for his heroism by the $120 that the grateful Reinhardt carried. All came out wiser, and with great respect for the power of a rushing stream.

In 1878, William Buckley & Co. bought the stage line from Soledad to San Luis Obispo, and retained the "Coast Line Stage Co." name.

In February of 1883, Kester & Cass put on a line of stages running from Cayucos, via Paso de Robles Springs, to San Miguel. This gave people along the route a chance to take the weekly steamer at Cayucos, or make quick connection with the Coast Line of Stages north. Mail was also carried between Cambria and Paso Robles, supplying the office at Adelaida, which also received the mail of a former post office called Josephine.

San Miguel was the hub of a wide area in the Salinas Valley. All roads met there; from the northwest, was the road to Jolon, Mission San Antonio and on to Monterey. There was also a road north to Salinas and San Juan Bautista. To the east, the road went to Estrella and Shandon. To the west, the road went through the San Marcos area to Cayucos and San Simeon.

During the end of the nineteenth century, all roads in southern Monterey County and northern San Luis Obispo County converged at San Miguel. This was natural, because the town was located at a point where many valleys and canyons came down to join the Salinas River.

The easiest way for the route of a road to be selected was to follow a watercourse, rather than going over mountains and hills. Most of our present-day highways are built where they are because they followed old trails that had been made by Native Americans; these people traveled where they did because they were following trails that had been made by deer.

Indian Valley came in from the north. There was a road from Hollister via Bitter Water and Peach Tree. Although this road was rugged and dusty, it was much traveled by horse and wagon by those who did not want to travel up the Salinas.

The road from Parkfield crossed a small range of mountains and came directly down Vineyard Canyon to the Mission town. The residents of the area called this road "Yerba Buena," according to Ella Adams.

The other valleys which were directed toward San Miguel were named Mahoney's, Lowe's (previously named San Jacinto, "St. Hyacinth"), Hog and Ranchita. One of the most noteworthy valleys was that of the Estrella River, with its tributaries; it emptied into the

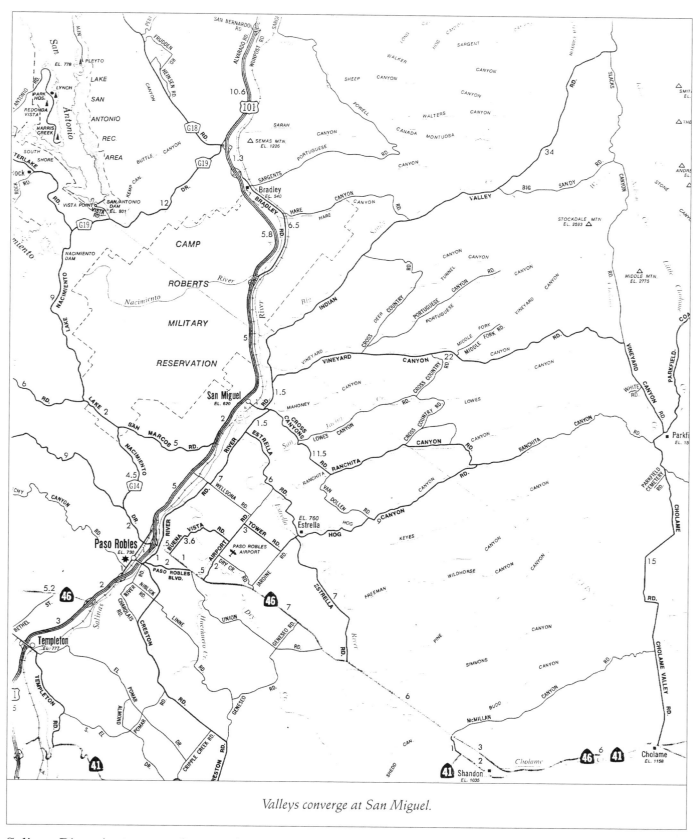

Valleys converge at San Miguel.

Salinas River just across from and south of the Caledonia Adobe. There was a ford across the Salinas River north of that point. A remnant of the old grade remains in 1996. There was another ford downriver, to serve Vineyard Canyon and Indian Valley.

The Inland Messenger, San Miguel's newspaper,

on July 16, 1886, announced that "The stage from San Luis Obispo will arrive in San Miguel at 10 p.m., and from Soledad at 3 a.m., after Tuesday, July 20th." Also in that edition of the paper, "A teamster fell from his wagon, near Low's on the stage road, a few days ago. The wheels passed over his body causing instant death." Although the teamster was not on a stage coach, this item demonstrates the danger they could face.

The July 23, 1886 edition of the newspaper informed its readers that "Last Monday morning, J. Myers, driver of the south-bound stage, had the misfortune to break an axletree about a mile this side of Nacimiento station. A spring wagon was procured at the station, and the mail and part of the passengers were taken through on that vehicle." Readers of this edition of the paper learned that "The stage connected with the railroad at King City, last Tuesday night, and henceforth the hour of departure from San Luis Obispo will be 3 p.m., and from King City 9:15 p.m."

One week later, that paper stated: "J. M. Bennett, manager of the stage line, took the mail on the San Simeon route Wednesday morning, and is making permanent arrangements for the service on that line under the new contract. A double team will be used hereafter, with suitable vehicles for carrying passengers. Business in that direction is increasing, and it is expected that when the railroad is completed to this place the travel will be considerable. We understand that John McGuire will undertake the contract."

A small item, concerning the stage lines, was printed in the August 6, 1886 edition of *The Inland Messenger*. "The family of Mr. Benjamin have gone to Adelaida. Mr. Benjamin has a place and will turn his attention to farming, now he is not driving the Adelaida stage." One week later, the stage-related news was the item that "Several horses belonging to the stage company are sick at Pleyto and Nacimiento."

On August 20, 1886, readers learned that "John Thompson has been carrying the Parkfield mail, of late, under a temporary arrangement with the contractor."

According to the August 27, 1886 edition of *The Inland Messenger*:

Some of the citizens of Indian Valley commenced strawing the ford on the Salinas river, last Wednesday, on the road leading from this place to Indian Valley, preparatory to hauling grain. Now that wheat is being received here for shipment by rail, to be followed in a few months by all kinds of produce that our country can furnish, it behooves our citizens who are interested in business here to see that the main thoroughfares leading to his place are placed in a reasonably good condition.

There is a large amount of wheat south of here that if the roads are kept in good condition will be hauled to this place, which otherwise will go to San Luis Obispo. A large proportion of this grain must come by the Estrella road, and it is a notorious fact that the road is in a condition to be almost impassable for a loaded team.

This is a county road, and the attention of Supervisor Bean has been repeatedly called to the necessity for improvement; yet nothing is done, and some of our people are uncharitable enough to suggest that Mr. Bean finds it to his interest to ignore that part of his official duty. There are points near town which are being improved by subscription raised among our citizens.

The crossing of the river will be covered with straw, and the hill on the east side is being graded so as to make it easy to approach the crossing. But this portion of the county is entitled to a share of the attention of those officials whose duty it is to have general supervision over the roads of the county, and it is hoped that they can be prevailed upon to recognize our claims.

At one time, San Miguel could boast of having four livery stables. But once the railroad arrived, in October of 1886, the Concord stages which came up the valley or over from Jolon were discontinued. However, the outcountry- - -Parkfield, Cholame and Shandon still had to have mail and express service. Service was also needed to Cambria, on the coast. These were based in San Miguel.

Mary Emma Stanley Cook worked at the Express Office in San Miguel when she was a young lady. She writes: "Early in 1900 and late 1890, there were two stage lines that went out of San Miguel carrying passengers, mail and express. One served Estrella, the Fifteen Mile House, Shedd's Springs, Shandon and Cholame. These stages were mostly canopy-topped four-seater spring wagons. Horses were changed at the principal stops; the wagons were drawn by two, four and sometimes six spirited animals.

"The other route was up Vineyard Canyon over to Parkfield, and return by way of Ranchita Canyon. As road conditions improved, the Shandon Route was taken over by Paso Robles interests.

"The stages left San Miguel at seven in the morning. The time of return was determined by the roads and weather." Mrs. Cook goes on to write: "One of the best-known drivers was Gus Kingery. . . .Gus was a kind and obliging man, ever ready to do a chore or to help as he could. Other drivers were Del Hair, Louis Douglas, Ed Ellis and Jim Moore. With the coming of the automobile, their jobs ended."

Augustus "Gus" Kingery was born to Samuel and Cydonah Jane Benefield Kingery on July 8, 1859 in Washington County, Oregon. He married Addie May Bailey on February 14, 1889 at Estrella; she had been born on Santa Rosa Creek on February 1, 1871. Their three children were born on Dry Creek: Ida Hortense, on December 30, 1889, John Wayland, on April 27, 1892 and Margaret Cydonah on October 3, 1895. Addie May took care of Willa May Taylor, born January 25, 1914, in San Francisco, and "she just became Grandma's child." Augustus Kingery's Homestead Certificate #4359 entitled him to 160 acres on June 10, 1892. This land was the SW ¼ of Section 20, Township 26 South, Range 13 East; it was generally in the Jardine area, east of Paso Robles.

A great-granddaughter of Gus Kingery, Shirley Tharaldsen, lives in the San Marcos area today.

The "Fifteen Mile House" that was mentioned stood near what is today, Whitley Gardens, a little south of River Gorge Drive, on the west side of the Estrella River. It was fifteen miles from the railroad in Paso Robles, thus its name. However, Lester Rougeot, who lives in Whitley Gardens, and is from a pioneer family, stated that the place was called the "Twelve Mile House" by residents of San Miguel, because it was twelve miles to the railroad at that place.

The "Shedd Springs" refers to a spring located approximately fifteen miles east of Paso Robles, and a few miles west of present-day Shandon. The area was homesteaded by William T. Sheid in 1868.

On June 18, 1886, a mail run was made from San Miguel to Cambria via Adelaida three times per week. By October 22, 1886, the Ventura *Free Press* reported that the railroad was open for traffic to San Miguel. "It is now possible to reach Paso Robles Springs with only seven miles of staging, and San Luis Obispo with

Augustus "Gus" Kingery, Stage Driver.

thirty-eight." The first passenger trains from San Francisco started running to Paso Robles on October 31, 1886.

The Inland Messenger, on September 17, 1886, informed its readers that "We understand that the stage will continue to connect with the railroad at Kings City till the road is finished to San Miguel. What arrangements will be made for supplying Pleyto, Jolon and San Antonio with mail after the railroad is completed has not been announced."

According to the October 22, 1886 edition of the newspaper, "The postoffices at San Antonio, Jolon and Pleyto are supplied with mail by a daily stage from Kings City to Pleyto. This arrangement will not last long. The stage now connects with the railroad at this place, leaving for the south at the arrival of the train in the evening. It stops over night at Paso Robles and goes through to San Luis in the morning."

On October 29, 1886, Edward Stanley Barry, new Wells, Fargo agent, moved into the Caledonia with his family. *The Inland Messenger* for that date states that "We understand that Mr. E. S. Barry has been appointed agent of Wells, Fargo & Co.'s express office and that the office will be moved to the vicinity of the depot." E. S. Barry had served as the Wells, Fargo & Co. agent at the Rancho Los Coches adobe from 1883 to 1885.

The newspaper on the same date had the following information: "The regular stage now leaves San Luis at 3 p.m. daily, stopping at Paso Robles till about 4 in the morning, and then coming through to connect with the train here at 6:40." On the same date: "A special stage now leaves this place for San Luis at 7 o'clock in the morning every other day, and returns the day following, leaving San Luis at 8 a.m."

Later in the October 29th paper: "The Stage Company are selling off a portion of their horses and harness that have been in use on this line. Parties wishing to purchase should call upon Mr. Bennett, superintendent."

According to the paper, on November 5, 1886, "The express business at this place has been turned over to the new agent, Mr. Barry, and the office is for the present in the S. P. Milling Company's office near the depot."

"Change in the Railroad Time Table," was the title of an article in the November 19, 1886 edition of *The Inland Messenger*.

The train arrives at San Miguel at 4:50 and at Templeton at 5:30 p.m. The stage leaves at once on arrival of the train, and arrives at San Luis at 10:30 p.m. The stage north leaves San Luis at 5:30 a.m., connecting with the train at Templeton at 10:30. The north bound train is due at San Miguel at 11 a.m. and arrives at San Francisco at 7:40 p.m.

Readers of the December 3, 1886 newspaper could learn that "A petition is being circulated in the vicinity of Pleyto, for a public road, starting at Bradley, running thence across the Salinas river and up the San Antonio creek connecting with the stage road near the southwest corner of Sec. 36, T24, S, R 10 East. The proposed road is about four miles long, and crosses the lands of Godfrey, Pinkerton, Porter and the Flint Estate."

On December 24, 1886, the paper had the following news: "A subscription is being liberally signed by citizens of San Miguel and vicinity to build a wagon road across the mountain from the upper Cholame into Vineyard Canyon, from which there is already a road to this place. It looks as though there will be no scarcity of funds to make a good road as soon as it is located with legal formalities."

From the December 31, 1886 edition of the newspaper, we learn that the San Miguel and Parkfield Stage would leave San Miguel for Estrella, Starkey, Cholame and Parkfield on Tuesdays and Fridays of each week at 6:30 a.m. The stage would leave Parkfield, returning on Wednesdays and Saturdays, at 8 a.m. For passage, people were to apply at the Jeffreys' Hotel; P. McAdams was the proprietor.

The Inland Messenger, in the January 14, 1887 issue stated that "A Pleyto correspondent of the *Democrat* reports that on the 2nd instant a highway man stopped the stage near Pleyto and forced the driver to deliver up the express box." This demonstrates that the stage lines were not one hundred percent safe from criminals.

According to *The Inland Messenger*, on February 4, 1887, "Mr. J. J. Bullock, station agent at this place, has been assigned to Menlo Park. He took his leave on Monday. He has made many friends during his short

The San Miguel-Parkfield Stage c. 1906.

sojourn in San Miguel, who regret his departure. C. J. Whisman, of Chualar, has taken the situation vacated by Mr. Bullock."

By April of 1887, the newspaper had changed names. On May 6, 1887, the *San Miguel Messenger* reported that "Mr. N. Fales, of the Cholame Valley, agent of the committee that has charge of building the road across the hill from Parkfield to this place, was in town this week, and collected about $250 from our citizens to aid that enterprise. It is hoped that the work on that road will be prosecuted with energy and that the people of Cholame will soon have the benefit of a good road to San Miguel."

The *San Miguel Messenger*, on May 6, 1887, stated that "It will be seen from a notice appearing elsewhere that the post office department advertise for bids for carrying a tri-weekly mail from this place to Parkfield, via Imusdale. Our Vineyard Canyon and Cholame friends are to be congratulated on the prompt action that has been taken on their petition for mail service on this proposed new route."

The newspaper for the following week, May 13th, carried the following story.

The Board of Supervisors have over-ruled the objections made by residents on the San Marcos road to opening the road on the old line, and having declared the old road a public highway, have ordered all obstructions to be removed. This necessitates the removing of fences, and will cause a temporary inconvenience to a few parties, but the public will be benefited by getting a highway on good ground for a permanent road.

A great improvement has lately been made in the county road commencing at Bridge creek, a mile south of this place, and extending beyond San Marcos creek. The new road

is wholly on the west side of the railroad, doing away with four crossings.

This improvement is the result of Supervisor Baker's negotiations with the Railroad Company, and the expense or the charge is borne by the corporation. Mr. Baker deserves much credit for looking closely after the interests of the county, as well as the public, in matters relating to roads in his district.

By 1887, a stage ran east from San Miguel to Shandon, through Estrella and Bern two days a week. (Bern was the site of the Michael McDonald home. By April 6, 1904, one room of his home was used as a postoffice. At one time, Virgil N. Tognazzini served there as postmaster.)

During 1887, there were five tri-weekly stages, running out of San Miguel, which carried the U.S. mail. One went to Parkfield via Apricot and Imusdale; one to Cholame via Estrella and Starkey Post Office; one to Indian Valley and Valleton Post Office and one went to San Simeon via Adelaida and Cambria. (Apricot was a postoffice in Vineyard Canyon; Valleton was located in Indian Valley. Starkey was a townsite near present-day Shandon.)

The April 29, 1887 edition of the newspaper stated that "We understand that the mail service on the San Miguel and Parkfield route will soon be increased to tri-weekly. The rapid increase of mail matter on this line will fully justify this change."

Three months later, the same news paper stated that "The new stage line to Parkfield is now in full operation under Mr. Ingalls, who is an old hand in the business. Passengers can depend on being taken through in good shape."

Jim McIntosh, driver, and Judge Gould, passenger, on the McIntosh Stage Line from Soledad to Cholame Valley, 1884. Photo taken near Stone Canyon Coal Mine.

The *San Miguel Messenger* for April 29th carried this ad:

The Inland & Coast Stage Co.
W. W. Orr, Proprietor
Lines east and west from San Miguel:
For Estrella, Starkey,
Cholame and Parkfield,
Stage leaves office at 8 AM on Mondays,
Wednesdays and Fridays
For Adelaida, Cambria and San Simeon:
Stage leaves office at 7 AM,
same days as above.
Through tickets to and from
San Francisco at reduced rates.
S. Barry Gen'l Ticket Agent,
Wells, Fargo & Co's office,   San Miguel

Under the lead, "Cholame Valley," the *San Miguel Messenger* for August 5, 1887 provided a lengthy article, which was written from Imusdale by the stringer, "S. G." on July 27, 1887.

The people of this part of the country are highly gratified over the completion of the new road leading over the mountain into Vineyard Canyon, and thence to San Miguel.

Before the road was built to San Miguel, Cholame Valley was quite an isolated place. The nearest railroad station was Soledad, from seventy to eighty miles away, and the nearest town San Luis Obispo, which was also far away, and from lack of roads, difficult of access.

Even after the railroad was built to San Miguel, for a long time many of the farmers preferred to travel over the rough mountain road to Soledad by way of Peach Tree, a distance of seventy-five miles or more, to take their produce to market, and to trade, rather than to climb over the rough mountain trails into Vineyard Canyon, thence to San Miguel. Now, however, all is changed.

The new grade over the mountain, made, it is true, at great outlay of volunteer labor and expense, brings the new and thriving town of San Miguel within easy reach. The ascent on either side of the mountain is gradual, the scenery picturesque, and the mountain breezes, even during the hottest months of summer, delightful.

The old-time stage driver, of Santa Cruz,

familiarly known to everybody as "Dan," awakens the echoes and mountain nymphs, as well as the drowsy settlers along the way: leaving Parkfield at 6 o'clock, Imusdale at 6:30 and making San Miguel before 10 a.m., a distance of 24 miles in less than 4 hours.

The people of the valley now flock to the postoffice three times a week instead of twice as heretofore, to get their mail, and to see the busy young postmistress, whom they think more of now than ever, as they seem to have the impression that their extra letters and papers are owing to her generous and benevolent spirit; whereas they are really due to the new road, the new mail route and the new business interests of the new and booming town of San Miguel.

The road over the mountain was very narrow, with several pull-outs. A team going up would pull out and listen for bells on the freight team coming down the mountain, according to Ella Adams.

Ella Adams also informs us that that Dan Maderia sang on his route, and sometimes played for dances on his over-night stop in Parkfield. The *San Miguel Messenger* for December 23, 1887 carried this ad:

San Miguel, Imusdale and
Parkfield Stage Line
Dan Madeira, Prop.
Leave San Miguel, Monday,
Wednesday and Friday.
Returning leave Parkfield Tuesday,
Thursday and Saturday.
Stage leaves at 8 o'clock a.m.
For passage inquire at E. S. Barry.

On December 2, 1887, the paper informed its readers: "Died: MADERIA - At her husband's residence near this place, December 1st, 1887, Mrs. Dora Maderia, wife of Dan Maderia, aged 47 years. The remains were taken to Santa Cruz by Thursday's train, for interment." [Daniel and Isadora Dennison Maderia lived on a river-bottom ranch for a while; they had ten children, but the children stayed in Santa Cruz because Isadora was dying of cancer.]

In the same newspaper for December 2nd: "Charles W. Johnson is carrying the Parkfield mail in Dan Maderia's absence."

Another ad in the newspaper for December 23, 1887:

The Inland & Coast Stage Company
W. Orr, Proprietor
Lines east and West from San Miguel:
Stage leaves San Miguel for Cholame,
Sundays, Tuesdays & Thursdays,
on arrival of train from
San Francisco at 5 p.m.
Through tickets to & from
San Francisco at reduced rates.
S. Barry Gen'l Ticket Agent
Wells, Fargo & Co's office   San Miguel

The December 9, 1887 edition of the paper informed its readers that "Dan Madeira has purchased the San Miguel and Parkfield Stage line from N. P. Ingalls." The paper added that "A change has been made in the mail schedule on the Cholame route, the mail now leaving San Miguel at 6 a.m. Mondays, Wednesdays and Fridays, returning the same day."

Back on August 12, 1887, a *San Miguel Messenger* article stated that "Our people are inquiring what is the matter with our Supervisor and his Roadmaster that the new road east of the river is not opened for travel. It is an open highway and only a culvert or two required to make it passable, yet the farmers are hauling grain through sand on the old road."

The September 9, 1887 edition of the paper had informed its readers that "A route for a road is talked of from the Cholame by way of Key's Canyon connecting with the Estrella road, making a second easy route from Cholame to San Miguel." One week later, the same newspaper had this to say: "The question is: Why is it that the new road reaching from the Estrella settlement to San Miguel, which has been located and

The bridge over Salinas River at San Miguel.

ordered opened months ago, is still impassable for want of the construction of a small culvert or two. Is Cambria and Paso Robles absorbing not only all the money, but also all the official attention. Our people are getting very impatient over this apparently unnecessary delay in a matter seriously affecting their convenience."

The newspaper on November 4, 1887 printed the following article.

The subject of a bridge at this place is increasing in interest, both among the business men of the town and the hundreds of farmers on the east side of the river. A careful observation has been made of the ground, and it is demonstrated that the length of the bridge at the most convenient and accessible point will be a little less than 700 feet.

On Wednesday, Mr. McCarthy, representative of the Pacific Bridge Company, of San Francisco, (the same company that built the Paso Robles and Templeton bridges) called and made a personal examination of the crossing, and will estimate the expense of the structure. It is expected that the cost of building a bridge that will resist any flood to which the stream is subject, will not exceed $17,000. Considering the importance of the crossing and the large interests demanding the bridge, this is a small sum, and we hope to see steps taken at an early day to assure the structure.

In 1901, August Wolf, Ella Adams' father, drove the horse-drawn stage from San Miguel to Shandon six days a week. This stage served Estrella and Bern. The community of Bern, as has been stated, was located at the Michael McDonald ranch house. From there, he went on to Shandon and Cholame. Ella's father told her that there was a young lady at Estrella who would give him a nickel, and ask him to bring her a spool of crochet thread on his next trip. Sometimes the same lady would give him a nickel and request some liver, with which she could feed her cat.

August Wolf's father, Adalbert Wolf, had been born in Germany; he learned the trade of file-maker, after which he traveled over various parts of Europe working at the trade. During these travels, he learned several languages, which he could speak fluently. After coming to the United States, and working at his trade in Baltimore, Philadelphia and Detroit, he decided to come to the Pacific Coast.

In San Francisco, he established the Union File

Works, and at one time employed fourteen workers in his shop. For years, his factory was the only maker of hand-made files on the west coast. The following is what Ella Adams has to say about her father and grandfather.

When Adalbert Wolf came for his first look at the Paso Robles area, the Southern Pacific Railroad had only been built as far as Soledad. He and his ten-year-old son, August, walked from Soledad to Paso Robles.

He found a small ranch in the Union district, east of Paso Robles. He made a downpayment, not having the full purchase price, and he used the Old World term, "Master," until the debt was paid.

When the rails reached Paso Robles, he moved his family here, built a home on the ranch, where the six children grew up- - -a busy, happy home. Many descendants live in the area today.

Adalbert Wolf was married to Maria Filip, a native of Austria. Their six children were Albert, August, Antonia, Otto, Louis and Mary. He died in 1910, at age 78, at his home in the Union district.

The *Paso Robles Record*, on August 17, 1895, informed its readers that "Parties wishing to travel in the direction of the San Joaquin Valley will find it both cheap and convenient to patronize the stage line from San Miguel to Huron." This line, the "San Miguel & Cholame Stage" ran on Mondays and Fridays. Fare from San Miguel to Huron was $4.00, and H. Nelson was proprietor of the line. [One of the stage coaches is preserved at the Pioneer Museum in Paso Robles.]

The San Miguel Sentinel, on March 31, 1917, brings us more up-to-date on some part of the stage lines. "The Stone Canyon stage line will make a change in its route, commencing Monday. The stage will go as usual up Indian Valley and Big Sandy, but will come back by way of Stone Canyon and then into Slack's Canyon and strike the Indian Valley at Kleggs. This change will accommodate a large number of people that heretofore had to travel eight to ten miles for their mail."

San Miguel has had several bridges, down through the years. The first one was constructed in 1889 with over-head wooden bracing; it served the area until the flood of 1909, which washed away the center span. Repairs were made, only to be swept away during a flood in 1914.

"Mud Wagon"

Drawn by Ernie Morris

In 1919, funds were made available, through a vote of the people, to build a long bridge of cement; it was finished in 1921. After 47 years of use, the cement bridge was washed out on February 24, 1969.

On July 24, 1969, the amount of $1,028,000 was funded by the U. S. Highway and Transportation

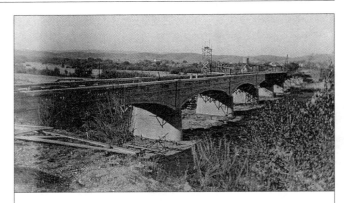

San Miguel Bridge, completed in 1921.

The San Miguel Bridge after the March 1914 flood.

Agency to construct the present bridge, which was opened to traffic on July 30, 1971. [This information has been provided by Ella Adams.]

Our next chapter will examine the mail service more closely, realizing that it is not possible to separate the stage lines and the mail.

MAIL SERVICE FOR THE
LANDS OF MISSION SAN MIGUEL

California's first mail service was during the Spanish regime. The service was performed by ships sailing from San Blas, Mexico, to the ports of California. In addition, an overland route was traveled by couriers from Mexico City; this was supplemented by messengers between the Presidios and the Missions. All mail was delivered to the Presidios for distribution; the paymaster usually acted as postmaster.

The first "post office" in San Miguel would have been located at San Miguel Mission. Military dispatches, and some mail, would have been going to and from Monterey, and also to destinations to the south, down through the years. The mail-carrier was accompanied by an armed soldier.

A book entitled *History of California Post Offices 1849-1976* was published in 1977. That study states that the post office at San Miguel was established on January 4, 1860. Stephen Rios is given as the first postmaster in San Miguel. Records at the National Archives, obtained by Ella Adams, show that "Estevan Rios" was appointed postmaster on that date. This must refer to Estaban Rios, who was a son of Petronilo and Catarina Rios; he was born on December 29, 1839, so he would have been 21 years of age in 1860.

The post office at San Miguel was discontinued on November 9, 1860, then re-established on August 17, 1861, with John C. Lewelling the postmaster. It was discontinued on August 16, 1865, then re-established on January 29, 1869.

On May 2, 1869, "Geo. Butchart," as postmaster, signed a form from the Post Office Department in Washington, D. C. On this form, George Butchart states that the San Marcos Post Office is located 1/8 of a mile from the Salinas River, on the west side of it; the post office was "close" to San Marcos Creek and on the east side of the creek. The nearest post offices were "Warm Springs," 6 ½ miles to the south, and San Antonio 37 miles to the north. George Butchart made the following note on the official form: "This portion of the County is not surveyed, therefore I can not give an accurate description of it."

The post office was moved three miles north, on September 2, 1881, and the name changed to "San Miguel." It might be noted that prior to the arrival of the railroad in 1886, the post office designation was "San Miguel Mission."

The Post Office Department established a post office called "Ascension," on December 9, 1879; it was discontinued January 17, 1881 and moved to Paso Robles. The name was derived from Rancho Asuncion, an 1845 land grant. The anglicized version of the name was used by the Post Office Department, while the Spanish version was used by the Southern Pacific Railroad and the community. This post office was located nine miles south of Paso Robles, and Thomas Cashin was the first postmaster. "Ascension" should not be confused with "Asuncion."

"Mail Service Needed," was the headline on an article in the May 28, 1886 edition of *The Inland Messenger*. "The people of the Indian Valley and Slack's Canyon settlements need a mail route from San Miguel, and are working to get it. A private subscription is being raised for the service by the Government. The population of that region is rapidly increasing, and their request for better mail facilities should be granted without delay."

From the June 25, 1886 issue of the paper, we learn that "Orders have been issued by Postoffice Department to have the new Postoffice, Starkey, supplied by the Parkfield carrier. (Starkey was about three miles south of present-day Shandon.)

The newspaper on July 16, 1886 informed people that "It is stated, upon reliable authority, that after the 20th instant, passengers and mail will meet the stages, for southern points at King's City, 24 miles south of Soledad."

The Inland Messenger for July 23, 1886 carried the information that "We are informed that Postmaster Speyer is soon to have this office supplied with seventy lock boxes. The rapidly increasing business of the office makes such a step almost a necessity."

The same paper for July 30, 1886 carried the item that "Arrangements for mail service on the Parkfield route are not settled. Frank Reed is still carrying the mail temporarily, but he and the contractors have been unable to agree upon a permanent contract. This route will be under the same management as the overland stage line."

Under the date of July 30, 1886, the paper informed readers that "J. M. Bennett, manager of the stage line, took the mail on the San Simeon route Wednesday morning, and is making permanent arrangements for the service on that line under the new contract. A double team will be used hereafter, with suitable vehicles for carrying passengers. Business in that direction is increasing, and it is expected that when the railroad is completed to this place, the travel will be considerable. We understand that John McGuire will undertake the contract."

The Inland Messenger for August 6, 1886 stated that "The new boxes for the Postoffice arrived yesterday and will be placed in position next week. They will be rented to any one wishing to have a lock box in which to have their mail."

The next week's paper had the news that "The family of Postmaster Speyer arrived Sunday, and are comfortable settled in the residence adjoining Goldtree & Co.'s store, which has been elegantly fitted up for their reception."

According to the August 13, 1886 issue of the paper, "The new post office boxes are for rent at 75 cents per quarter, payable in advance. They will prove a great convenience to both postmaster and citizens."

Readers learned from the newspaper of August 20, 1886 that "The Postoffice that has been mentioned as Verna, located about seven miles from here on the Estrella, has been named 'Estrella.' There are blanks in the San Miguel Postoffice for the Estrella postmaster."

The Estrella post office was established on July 8, 1886, and was discontinued on August 15, 1918, when it was moved to San Miguel. Its location was 7 ½ miles southeast of San Miguel, and 18 miles northwest of Cholame.

The "Ten Mile Stage Stop" was located at what is now the eastern intersection of Union Road and Highway 46-East; Union Road was the old route to the San Joaquin Valley. The "Ten Mile" stop was for mail for Estrella plains and the Geneseo area.

On September 17, 1886, the paper stated that "J. C. Croal has taken charge of the Parkfield mail and stage route for P. McAdams the new contractor. Settlers along the line, as well as the general public, will be pleased to learn that it has passed into good hands."

The November 19, 1886 issue of *The Inland Messenger* forwarded the following information: "The San Francisco *Chronicle* announces that Miss Laura Palmer has been nominated Postmistress at this place.

The lady has been strongly recommended and the appointment will doubtless give general satisfaction." Apparently the general satisfaction did not extend to the location of the post office. On December 31, 1886, *The Inland Messenger* informed its readers that "A petition is being circulated to have the post office located in the central part of town."

Back on December 17, 1886, the newspaper had stated that "We understand that the papers necessary to the transfer of the postoffice to new hands have been received and the change will be made in a few days. It will be done under the new management in the Southern California Land and Immigration building."

The new year of 1887 saw changes taking place in the post office. The newspaper stated that "The Postoffice was duly removed on the 1ˢᵗ instant from Goldtree & Co.'s store to the Southern California Land and Immigration Company's building. Miss Palmer, the new postmaster, appears adapted to the situation, bringing to it the careful attention so indispensible to a correct discharge of the duties of that office."

The newspaper for January 21, 1887 stated that "Mr. R. H. Mallory is assisting Miss Palmer in the labors of the postoffice."

"Complaint From Starkey" was the headline on a letter to the editor in the January 24, 1887 edition of *The Inland Messenger*:

> **Editor *Messenger*: On the 11ᵗʰ instant, the Postmaster of Starkey, (Rudolph Mayer) stopped the mail carrier on the route from San Miguel to Parkfield, and demanded the mail bags. The driver, after some hesitation, delivered them over and he proceeded to go through the mail, unlocking and taking out all the mail sacks. This happened three miles from Starkey postoffice on the public highway. 'Jim Cummings' can now take a back seat as this case is unprecedented. Sam M. Dyer Cholame, Jan. 14.**

[Jim Cummings was a member of the Jesse James gang.]

In the next week's newspaper, on January 28, 1887, readers were able to read the following:

> **We cheerfully give place to a communication from Rudolph Mayer, Postmaster at Starkey, explaining the charge made against him by S. M. Dyer, of wrongfully opening the mail bag on the road toward Parkfield. His letter gives the public a full account of what**

was done and the reason for his action. We are pleased to learn that the difficulty with reference to the delivery of the mail at Starkey has been obviated by an arrangement by which the mail carrier drives to that office and delivers the mail.

A Reply From Starkey

Ed. *Messenger*: In reply to a card appearing in your valuable paper I beg to inform you that the Starkey mail has been demanded and delivered ever since I have had this office at the junction of Cholame and Starkey roads, by authority of the Postoffice Department in Washington. On January 5th, the special carrier failed to connect with the stage going to San Miguel; on the 7th, the Starkey mail was sent to Cholame in the mail bag. On the 8th it was sent back to San Miguel.

On the 11th, I drove down myself to the above mentioned place and as there was no separate mail for Starkey I opened the mail bag and looked for the same, where it is supposed to be. As people come for their mail 10 and 15 miles, I have to get the mail the best way I can under the circumstances. The charge of Sam M. Dyer, that I outdone Jim Cummings I will have investigated through the Postoffice Department in Washington.

Yours, Rudolph Mayer, P.M. Starkey, January 22nd 1887.

On February 17, 1887, Laura B. Palmer, as postmaster, completed the Post Office Department's form. From this form, we learn that the San Miguel Post Office was situated in lot 1 of the northeast quarter of Section 20, in Township 25, South Range twelve Mount Diablo Meridian. It is 3/8 of a mile from the Salinas River, and two miles from San Marcos, north of the creek. The nearest post offices are Paso de Robles, nine miles south and Bradley twelve miles north. The nearest office off the route was Estrella, seven miles to the east. The San Miguel Post Office was 500 yards from the San Miguel station of the Southern Pacific Railroad, on the west side of the railroad. The post office was located in Goldtree's Store. [Obviously, this form must have been filled out prior to the move from Goldtree's.]

The *San Miguel Messenger*, on April 29, 1887, informed its readers that "J. C. Croal has taken charge of the mail stage from this place to San Simeon, by Adelaida and Cambria."

The May 6, 1887 edition of the newspaper had some information under the title, "Temporary Mail Service."

Sealed proposals for carrying the United States mails from San Miguel, via Imusdale, to Parkfield, 26 ½ miles, 3 times a week each way, by a schedule of required hours running time each way, from July 1, 1887, until June 30th, 1888, will be received by the Postmaster at San Miguel until Monday, 16th of May, 1887. In all cases the rate per annum to be stated in proposal.

A contract with sureities is required to be executed, and persons bidding must be honest and capable and not less than twenty-one years old. No more will be allowed than a fair and reasonable compensation for the service, to be determined by the Department. Postmasters and assistants cannot bid for such service.

Wm. F. Vllas, Postmaster General

Parties wishing to bid on above will be furnished blanks at the Post Office, San Miguel.

"Important Changes in Mail Routes," was the lead for an item on June 17, 1887, in the *San Miguel Messenger*.

A late dispatch says: Star service has been established as follows. . . San Miguel by Imusdale to Parkfield, 26 ½ miles and back, three times a week, from July 1, 1887 to June 30, 1888. Star service changes have been ordered as follows: Soledad to Imusdale, from July 1, 1887, curtail the 'route' to omit Imusdale'; send at Slack's Canyon, reducing the distance 25 miles.

San Miguel to Parkfield, from July 1, 1887, curtail the 'route' to omit Parkfield; send at Cholame, reducing distance fifteen miles.

The Cholame post office had opened on May 14, 1873, with David Russell the first postmaster.

From the newspaper, on July 8, 1887, readers learned that "The contract for carrying the mail from San Miguel to Parkfield, by way of Vineyard Canyon and Imusdale, has been let to Mr. N. P. Ingalls, formerly of Santa Cruz, and the service has commenced. The schedule is not fully settled, but the mail now leaves this place Tuesday, Thursday and Saturday mornings. Mr. Dan Maderia is driving for the present, and Mr. Ingalls is on business in Santa Cruz."

The July 29, 1887 edition of the *San Miguel Messenger* had this bit of information: "Among postmasters lately appointed is that of Frederick Otts, of Estrella postoffice, and S. G. Parker, of Apricot postoffice in Vineyard Canyon." The newspaper on the same date also informed its readers: "Passengers can now leave Parkfield for San Miguel by Ingall's stage line and connect with the train and reach San Francisco the same evening."

On September 23, 1887, the paper provided this information: "Star mail service has been established from Imusdale to Slack's Canyon twice a week, from October 1st. A change is also made in the route from Kings City to Slack's Canyon, from October 1st, curtailing the route to omit Slack's Canyon, but ending at Peach Tree, reducing the distance twenty-one miles."

One week later, on September 30, 1887, the *San Miguel Messenger* repeated an item which had been published in the Salinas *Index*: "Jesse Brandy has been awarded the contract to carry the mail twice a week from Slack's Canyon to Imusdale. If he does not have much mail, he can at least bring us the news of the day. Under the new schedule for the Cholame mail route, the stage leaves this place Sundays, Tuesdays and Thursdays, after the arrival of mail from the north."

On November 26, 1887, the *San Miguel Messenger* stated: "We understand that D. Sturgis has been appointed postmaster at Bryson, a settlement northwest of Pleyto."

The newspaper carried an interesting article on December 2, 1887, entitled "Mission" San Miguel.

It is a little mortifying to the residents of a large and growing community like that of San Miguel to see the telegraphic communications from this office persistently dated at "Mission" San Miguel. There was a time when San Miguel was known mainly as the location of a mission; when there was nothing visible here except the Mission and a solitary store and hotel on the stage line, in which a small amount of mail and express matter was handled. But a marked change has taken place, of which the telegraph company should take notice. We now have a town of several hundred inhabitants, a railroad station, at which a large amount of freight is handled, and which pays to the railroad company nearly $5,000 per month, and a rapidly developing surrounding country which gives an assurance of permanent growth.

The post office is "San Miguel," in which name is also the railroad station and express office. Why the telegraph company should persist in holding to "Mission" we cannot conceive. The style "Mission San Miguel" is suggestive of a mere station rather than a town, and it is prejudicial to the place to have it represented to the world in that light. Let us appeal to the authorities to do us the justice to give us our true name in telegraphic literature.

The December 23, 1887 edition of the paper informed its readers that "From Mr. Whisman, the obliging operator at this place, we learn that instructions have been issued to drop the "Mission" prefix to San Miguel in telegraph messages. The office will hereafter be simply San Miguel."

Cruessville Post Office was authorized on April 13, 1888 on the mail route from San Miguel to Valleton, 8 miles north of San Miguel and "twenty yards to the east of Big Sandy Creek." According to the *Salinas Valley Index* of August 30, 1888, the post office was not actually established until August 24th. It was discontinued July 16, 1891.

On December 18, 1886, Robert Bousfield applied for a post office to be located in "Glendale, Monterey Co., Calif." It was to be located near Indian Creek 15 miles north of San Miguel and 10 miles south of Slack Canyon. When the post office was approved, on February 7, 1887, it had been named "Valleton." On December 12, 1901, it was moved about one mile to the southwest; in 1917, it was moved a half mile to the north. Valleton Post Office closed June 15, 1918.

It is probably less confusing if we treat the Paso Robles post office in this separate section. The first post office was established, on June 14, 1867, under the name of "Hot Springs," and Edward McCarthy was postmaster. On February 7, 1868, after the post office had been discontinued for two months, Drury W. James was appointed postmaster. Mr. James held the office for two years; on May 2, 1870 the name was changed to Paso Robles, and Charles Knowlton was appointed postmaster. Following Mr. Knowlton, came N. Crocker in 1871, George R. Sanderson in 1874, P. H. Dunn in 1876, E. M. Bennett in 1889, B. C. Farnum in 1892, R. W. Putnam in 1896, A. R. Booth in 1900, and Thomas W. Henry in 1906.

On December 23, 1887, in a section called "Local Brevities," the *San Miguel Messenger* carried the following item: "Mr. L. H. Ward, of Bee Rock, beyond the Nacimiento, has been appointed postmaster of a new office called Nacimiento. It is on the old stage road eight miles from Pleyto, and about the same distance from Bradley."

Concerning post office matters, a few years later, we find that Ruth Cruess was serving as assistant postmaster in San Miguel, in 1917. Ruby Mann also served as postal assistant.

Manuel S. Triguerio served as postmaster for many years. He had been born on October 17, 1879, in Jolon. While working in the sugar factory at Betteravia, in Santa Barbara County, he became crippled by an accident when his foot got caught in some equipment. He walked by using two tall sticks for support. On March 29, 1914, he was appointed postmaster at San Miguel.

In 1940, the post office burned, and in 1941 it was moved into the present building, which had been used as a bakery.

Ella Adams states: "Manuel Triguerio was a member of the Triguerio family out on the Nacimiento River. He told me of the family coming in to see the first train come in. Little Manuel peeked out from his mother's long skirts. He was a good postmaster, and a good friend."

SCHOOLS OF THE SAN MIGUEL AREA

Over the years, the Caledonia adobe has served, two different times as a school-house for the children of the San Miguel vicinity. But it certainly was not the first school in the area; the rooms of Mission San Miguel would have been the first schools. In 1857, when Petronilo Rios spent part of the year as Superintendent of Schools for San Luis Obispo County, part of the Caledonia building was used for school rooms.

The first school building, not counting the Mission itself or the Caledonia adobe, was a high circle of brush, built under a tree at the site of McKay station, on the Salinas River, opposite the mouth of Indian Valley. Since it had no roof, the place could only be used during dry weather. Lucretia Morehouse taught there in 1870 and 1871. Circuit riders also used the brush school for church services.

There was no formal public school between Salinas and San Luis Obispo. In 1871, the San Miguel School District was formed. It came out of a larger Nacimiento District, which had been formed in 1869. This item of information is provided by Ella Adams, "the history lady of San Miguel." Mrs. Adams provided much information concerning the early schools of San Miguel.

James Buckley Mahoney was partly responsible for an early San Miguel school. He came to San Miguel with his family in 1868. The Great Register of San Luis Obispo County in 1871 lists a James B. Mahoney as a native of Ireland. He was naturalized as a citizen in Shasta, in northern California, and registered in San Luis Obispo County on August 4, 1871. His occupation is listed as a laborer, and 53 years is given as his age. He was living in Boston when the "gold fever" seized him, and he came to California in 1850, by way of Panama.

In the spring of 1867, the elder Mahoney had engaged in the hotel business in Whiskey Town, Shasta County; the next year, he went to San Francisco. Soon afterward, he came to San Luis Obispo County, and in the spring he pre-empted land and returned for his family and settled on the place. James Mahoney had married Hannah Wade in Boston in November of 1847. [They had five children, three of whom grew to matu-

rity: Mrs. Mary Murray of Marin County; D. F. Mahoney, San Luis Obispo County Recorder and James J. Mahoney.

The Mahoney family lived in a wing of the San Miguel Mission until buildings were ready on their homestead. He raised grain and had a dairy of thirty cows; he was the first person to make butter, on a large scale, in this section.

In the early 1870s, James B. Mahoney and George Davis built an adobe brick school-house at the north end of present-day San Miguel. Since there was no resident priest at the Mission at that time, they felt free to take used adobe bricks from the ruined walls around the Mission. This school-house was located near where present-day River Road crosses the railroad tracks. It was the only school between San Luis Obispo and Salinas at the time.

By 1882, San Miguel School had thirteen students,

The first San Miguel school in early 1870.

while Paso Robles had twenty-eight students; there were seventy-two attending at Estrella.

Independence School District had been formed in 1879, and included the land from Indian Valley to Hog Canyon. The school was located in upper Ranchita Canyon. The children from upper Vineyard Canyon attended there.

John Fitzgerald and Mr. Wehner met with trustees, and decided to share a teacher. Fitzgerald donated the use of a small adobe on his ranch, and a Mr. Newcum was hired to teach. He taught a half day at Independence School, then rode over the hills and

The site of San Miguel Adobe School, 1997.

taught a half day at the little adobe; he had to travel a distance of about ten miles.

Newcum taught three terms, then left to continue law studies. Miss Leland was the next teacher for all eight grades; she taught four months in Independence School, then four months in Vineyard School, with eight months of vacation at each school. This continued until July 1, 1883; Independence was divided and Vineyard School District was formed.

"The Friends of the Adobes, Inc." has in its archives the Register from Independence School, 1895 to 1898. The names from this period of time include the teacher for the March 1895 term, Clara M. Owsley; girl students listed are: Mary Christopher, Pearl Houghton, Annie Jensen, Anna Lowe, Nellie Houghton, Amelia Jenson, Zoe Lowe, Nellie Shaw and Ida Shaw. Ann Dodd entered after the term had started. Boy students are: Willie Archer, Harry Dittemore, Charles Dittemore, Charles Houghton, Ora M. Houghton, Chester E. Houghton, Clarence Jenson, Charles Jenson, Hamilton Lowe, Guy Lowe and James Work. Willis Dodd and Roy Gruell entered after the beginning of this term. In August of 1895, Ethel Russell attended for a short time.

For the term beginning in March of 1896, Alice Page was the teacher. The same students as above were listed. In August, 1896, additions to the class were Maggie, Irene and Fanny Duncan; also added were Lillie, Stella and Jessie Dover. New names on the list also included Arnold King and Alex Lowe.

The new name in 1897 was Fred Dodd. The August 1898 term saw the addition of Ernest, Wilber, Nolan, Ray and Grace McGuire; Alliance Lowe was also added. [Ella Adams has said that this young lady was named Alliance in celebration of the formation of the Farmers' Alliance, which was formed in San Miguel, to provide competition for the Southern Pa-

cific Milling Company.] A later addition to the roster for August 1898 was Lela Work.

Eagle School was the first school in Indian Valley; the second one was Indian Valley School, for the upper part of the valley. Monroe School was the third institution of learning.

The Eagle School used an adobe building which

Eagle School, Indian Valley

had one large room and no floor; it had been put up by a homesteader who raised sheep. It was located just north of the Gunyeau homestead, which was later known as the Flint place; it was across the road from Firanzi's house. Some of the students who attended this school were: Johnny, Newton and Willie Lasswell; Agnes and Emma Gunyeau; May, Lum, Joe and Nioma Keltner; Mattie, Alice, Frank and Day Reasons. William, Robert, Frank and Thomas Cruess also attended. Many of the students did not go very steady, but others had good attendance records.

The district decided to build a new school, so Miss Marie de Zaldo donated a spot on her homestead around de Zaldo Canyon, in 1887. The school was a

Eagle School, Indian Valley, 1997.

Monroe School, Indian Valley.

box-type building, and the cracks were battened to keep out the wind. Maude Jessup Renoud recalled Miss de Zaldo as being her first teacher; Maude went to school for four days when she was four years old, in order to help "hold the school." She recalled people saying, "Lucky the railroad went through in 1886- - - therefore we could get lumber without hauling from the coast by team." A trip from the coast took one week. The teachers at this school were Miss de Zaldo, Mr. Chauncey Faith, Miss Sullivan, Mr. Minick and Miss Virginia Routeman.

In late 1890 or early 1891, it was decided that the school house would be moved farther up the valley, to an acre which had been donated by Newton Azbell. After this building was outgrown, a new school was constructed, in 1893, and still stands today.

With the increase in homestead families, another school was needed; Mr. T. D. Phelps donated a plot of ground, and the Monroe School was built, in 1893. Among the names of the children attending were Douglas, Firanzi, Garelli, Keltner and Rossi. Mr. Thomas Graves was a long time teacher there, and married Nioma Keltner.

Back in San Miguel, the little adobe school was serving the town when the railroad arrived. *The Inland Messenger*, on September 17, 1886 informed its readers that "Mr. Berry has been lining and papering the school house the past week. It has much improved the appearance of the interior of that structure." The October 29, 1886 edition of that newspaper has an interesting comment: "There is no hall in San Miguel

that is suitable for all public meetings. The schoolhouse might be made to do, but it is too far from the saloons for political purposes."

The *San Miguel Messenger*, on May 6, 1887, presented an editorial article with the heading "Imperative Necessity for Better School Facilities in San Miguel."

The *Messenger* has heretofore called attention to the fact that the school facilities in San Miguel are wholly inadequate to the requirements of the district. Though the subject appears to be one that arouses little interest among our people, we cannot refrain from again mentioning it with a few suggestions to those who have been clothed with authority to control the affairs of the district.

We have a school in progress, and it is well conducted as is possible under the circumstances. But the situation is such as to prejudice, rather than to recommend the town as a place of residence. The schoolhouse is too small to accommodate the pupils now enrolled, and, some are altogether deterred from applying for admission, on account of the crowded condition of the school. The out buildings and the external arrangements are outrageous. The number of children of school age is so rapidly increasing that in a short time it will be impossible to even make a pretense of admitting them to the school. The location of the schoolhouse is not central with reference to the population of the district.

The above briefly outlines the situation, and something will have to be done soon to change it. Why should there be any delay? There will be a great deal of preliminary work to do before a new house can be commenced, and the necessity for prompt action is apparent.

The Pacific Improvement Company would doubtless donate a suitable site for school buildings, if application were made by the proper officers. The old schoolhouse could be easily moved to a new and suitable location, where it could, in connection with a new and larger building, be made to accommodate the primary department. A meeting could be called to vote upon the question of levying a tax to erect a suitable school building. Notices for such a meeting are required to be posted for twenty days; the funds raised by a

tax would not be available before next January, and even if the business were pushed as rapidly as possible the house will be very urgently needed long before it can be made ready for occupancy.

Aside from the arguments mentioned above, the material prosperity of the place depends much upon the educational advantages it can offer. Our neighbors appreciate this fact, and Bradley is completing a new schoolhouse; Paso Robles has levied a tax for $3,000 to build a schoolhouse, and Templeton, though younger and with far fewer inhabitants than San Miguel has a school of advanced grade. Will San Miguel continue this drawback upon its prosperity? The action of the people in the near future will answer.

"Our School Interests," was the headline on an article in the *San Miguel Messenger* of May 20, 1887.

We are glad to observe that a general feeling exists in favor of some early action looking to the erection of suitable school buildings in this district. The only points upon which there is a diversity of opinion are, as to the character and cost of the buildings required, and the mode of raising the funds with which to erect them.

The district is a large one, embracing not only the rapidly growing town of San Miguel, but a considerable extent of surrounding country. It will, in the very near future, require a schoolhouse of not less than three rooms. To construct such an edifice with suitable surroundings will require several thousand dollars, and there are but two methods prescribed by the law of raising money for such a purpose: by a direct present tax, and by issuing bonds running for a number of years.

The use and benefit of such property is to be enjoyed by residents of the district in the future, rather than the present, and there is certainly only justice in carrying the main burden of the expense forward in bonds for five or ten years, when, in the natural order of things, the taxable property of the district will be increased fourfold. The levy of a present tax for the purpose would be felt in some degree as a burden. The payment of bonds at maturity, falling upon more people

at greatly increased property valuation, would be less burdensome. This whole matter rests with the legal voters of the district, and it is a matter that should be intelligently and maturely considered.

The regular annual election for trustees will take place June 4th, and it is probable that if nothing is done toward getting an expression from the people on these questions before that time, it will follow soon after; and it is very desirable that such action be taken as will make it unnecessary to do the work over within the next ten years.

We learn from the May 27, 1887 issue of the paper that "Our public school closes today for the school year. This step is made necessary by the exhaustion of the funds. It is probable that the school will reopen after a reasonable vacation somewhat earlier than usual." On the same date, under "Local Brevities," the paper states that "We are requested to announce that Miss Clara Ganoung will open a private school in the schoolhouse, next Tuesday, at the usual hour."

The *San Miguel Messenger*, on June 10, 1887, published an article entitled, "The School Election."

The result of the school election last Saturday, was the election of O. P. McFadden and F. Winchel for trustees, the former for three years and the latter for two. We understand that both of these gentlemen favor early action looking to the erection of suitable school buildings. The sentiment of our citizens appears to be strongly in favor of putting up a schoolhouse that in size will be sufficient for the accommodation of the district for a series of years, and in style of architecture will do credit to the place.

The do not favor extravagance in this direction; but realizing that the structure is destined to supply the wants of a town that has an assured future, it would be very unwise to build with reference to merely present or immediate future necessities. As the district will be practically without a schoolhouse room on the opening of the new school year, the earlier steps are taken to obtain an expression of the wishes of the people on this important subject the better for all.

According to the paper on June 17, 1887, "Miss Etta Reed, the efficient Census Marshal of the School

District, informs us she reported 124 children between 5 and 17 years of age in the District. This is a very favorable showing, being sufficient to assure the District an allowance for two teachers. The next step is for provision to be made for school rooms, including the construction of a new schoolhouse."

Being aware that people would come to a location where there were good schools and churches, the Pacific Improvement Company (a subsidiary of the Southern Pacific Railroad Company) was generous in donating lots for both institutions. Eight lots in Block 26 on the mesa were donated for a school.

Captain J. C. Currier, of the Board of School Trustees, received the following message from Mr. F. S. Douty, Secretary of the Pacific Improvement Company; this is from the July 1, 1887 edition of the *San Miguel Messenger.*

> **Dear Sir: In regard to donating property for school purposes at San Miguel, I will give six (6) lots in the easterly half of blocks 23, 22, 21, 20, 19 or 18. If you put up a building to cost exceeding $6,000, I will give eight (8) lots in the same location. Please notify me as to which lots you select, so that they can be reserved. Upon completion of the building and the receipt of $3 as cost of conveyance, a deed to the property will be sent. Yours truly, F. S. Douty.**

School was moved from the little adobe to an old wooden building on the mesa, south of the Mission, above the Caledonia. George Hopper used the vacated little adobe as a saloon- - -thus starting the first business in new San Miguel. The following ad appeared in the January 28, 1887 edition of *The Inland Messenger.*

> **First Business Place in New Town.**
> **PIONEER SALOON**
> **opposite Grain Warehouse**
> **Best of liquors,**
> **wines and cigars on hand.**
> **Dutton & Hopper**

Prior to the arrival of the railroad, the town of San Miguel was located between the Caledonia and the Mission. The wooden school was inadequate, and in need of renovation, so the primary grades were moved to a large room in the Caledonia. According to the newspaper on July 15, 1887, "The School Trustees have decided to employ as teachers in this district Mr. E. B.

Caledonia Adobe from the east.

Greenough and Miss Clara Ganoung, selections that will no doubt give full satisfaction. A room will have to be provided for one department until a new school house can be erected."

On July 22, 1887, the *San Miguel Messenger* printed a lengthy article entitled, "The School Bond Election."

> **It will be seen from a notice appearing in this issue that our school officials have moved in the matter of raising the means to build a school-house in San Miguel. The amount proposed is $8,000 on 6 per cent bonds, one-half redeemable in five years, the remainder in ten years from date of issue.**
>
> **As has been before stated in these columns, the necessity for building a school-house in this district is extremely great. Our school will soon open with two teachers, while the district has only one small incommodious room at its disposal. Temporary arrangements will be made for the accommodation of one department. The population of the town as well as the surrounding country within the district is rapidly increasing, and in the near future at least four rooms will probably be required to properly accommodate the school.**
>
> **In view of these facts, it would seem that the amount proposed will be found none too large to erect a suitable building and purchase necessary furniture. It cannot be said that the Board of Trustees have planned on an extravagant scale, or that they are making any allowance for mere show. The building must be made comfortable and commodious, and should be at least respectable in architectural design and finish; and this cannot more than**

be done with $8,000 and leave the amount indispensable for furniture and the arrangement of the surroundings.

The Trustees have acted intelligently and reasonably in the matter and it remains for the legal voters of the district to ratify their action. Should this proposition fail to receive the requisite two-thirds majority, it would doubtless be impracticable to obtain the necessary action of a different proposition to build a house before another year.

If prompt and harmonious action is taken at this time, our young and growing town will soon be able to offer present and prospective residents as good facilities for education as are generally to be found in towns of its size, and a serious drawback will be removed. On the other hand, should minor differences of opinion be permitted to defeat this proposition, the road will be paved to almost endless dissensions, and the town and district will, for an indefinate period in the future, labor under a disadvantage that will suggest to all who have children to educate, to make their homes elsewhere.

The newspaper on July 29, 1887 informed citizens that "School in this district will open next Monday with Mr. E. B. Greenough and Miss Clara Ganoung as teachers. Mr. Greenough's department will embrace pupils in the Fourth Reader and upwards. It is understood that one department will be taught in the Caledonia building, that affording the only available room for the purpose."

On July 29, 1887, the *San Miguel Messenger* printed an article entitled, "Question of the Location of a School House."

As might be expected, in view of definate action looking to the building of a schoolhouse having been taken, a lively interest has developed in the matter of the location of the proposed building.

The Pacific Improvement Company have modified their proposition and now propose to donate eight lots in block 26, a block which is centrally located and in other respects suitable for a schoolhouse location. The location is slightly north of the center of the population of the district, but it is probably as favorable a location as can be had, and we have no doubt that four-fifths of the people in the dis-

trict would be quite satisfied with the selection of that site.

The August 5, 1887 issue of the paper pointed out that "Nipomo voted $6,000 to build a schoolhouse last week. San Miguel will 'go her $2,000 better.'"

"School Trustees," according to the August 12th newspaper, "have decided to accept the site for a schoolhouse tendered in Block 26, being near the new Congregational church. This selection will, we think, meet the general approval of the public. Give us a rousing majority in favor of means to build a good schoolhouse, and San Miguel will be happy."

A bond issue for a new school-house was passed on August 13, 1887. In the days before women's suffrage, 63 men voted yes, and 2 voted no. Four thousand of these bonds were to be paid in five years; the balance was to be paid in 10 years at 6% interest.

The newspaper, on August 26, 1887, informed its readers that "Mr. T. C. Greenough, the efficient principal of our public school, has encountered some rather forcible protests on the part of some of his pupils, against the discipline that is indispensable to a well conducted school; but we are pleased to know that he has the cordial co-operation of the Trustees and the moral support of the community at large."

On September 2, 1887, the *San Miguel Messenger* printed an article entitled "'Visitors.' The school has this week been favored by visitors. Mrs. McFadden and Mrs. Winchell are the first to perform this parental duty. Visitors will not expect to be entertained. They come to encourage the school by their presence, and by frequent visits to note progress. It may not be a pleasure, but it is a duty."

Another item from the same paper was that "Mr. Chandler, who some two weeks since purchased lots in the northern part of town, has erected a dwelling house and has gone after his family. He was influenced in his decision in favor of San Miguel as a place of residence by the prospect of good school facilities."

"Our School Trustees," according to the September 2, 1887 edition of the *San Miguel Messenger*, "are seriously considering whether the interests of the district will not be better subserved by building our schoolhouse of brick than of wood. The high price of lumber at this time gives credit to the statement that the expense of a wooden structure will fully equal one of brick, while it is argued that a house of the latter material will better resist extreme temperatures, and be more permanent."

On September 23, 1887, the newspaper notified its readers of the following information: "Meeting of Citizens of San Miguel School District.' The citizens of San Miguel School District are requested to meet at San Miguel Hall Saturday, October 1st, at 2 o'clock p.m., to give expression to their views relative to the location of the proposed new school building for said district; also whether said building should be constructed of wood or brick. By order of the Board of Trustees."

The *San Miguel Messenger*, on October 14, 1887, announced that "Brickmaking Commenced.

The prospect of a local demand for brick for building purposes in San Miguel has induced Messrs. Sicotte & Hopper, men of experience in that line, to undertake the burning of a brick-kiln. They have found suitable clay near the river bank, a short distance south of the old Caledonia building, and are already preparing the yard, and in a few days will be moulding bricks. They expect to burn a kiln of 200,000 unless heavy rains interrupt the week. They will doubtless furnish brick for the school house, and we understand one or two other brick structures are projected. The price of lumber is so high that there is but little difference between the cost of brick and wood as building material, and there are many other points in favor of the former. We hope to see a number of substantial brick houses in San Miguel before the close of another year.

Wilford Sicotte, of Sicotte & Hopper, was a master mason, and built many brick buildings in San Miguel. Also a trombone player, Wilford contributed his talents to the Paso Robles Concert Band, as demonstrated in a photograph taken in either 1890 or 1891.

While the brick school-house was being constructed, the Caledonia again provided rooms for the children of San Miguel. On July 29, 1887, school opened in the Caledonia; Miss Clara Ganoung taught the primary grades. Laura Reed, a daughter of Emanuel Reed, was a pupil of Miss Ganoung. Mr. E. B. Greenough, the principal, taught the "grammar" grades in a wooden school on the mesa.

Some of the students who attended the "Old Adobe" school were: Mamie Fitzgerald, Walter Thompson and Edith Bayer. Students who went to "Old Town" included: Lena Matthis Clemons, Cecelia Millman Bierer, Percy Bayer and Winifred Jeffreys Allen.

In September of 1887, Superintendent Armstrong, along with some mothers, visited the classes in the Caledonia. The upper-grade students on the mesa reacted: "We poor pupils on the hill are very lonely. The Superintendent thinks us of small importance, our Mammas have forgotten us." A visit to the upper-grades was quickly arranged.

The population of San Miguel was about 500, according the November 11, 1887 issue of the *San Miguel Messenger*. Ninety children were in attendance at the school.

According to the November 18, 1887 edition of the paper, "Sicotte & Hopper have closed their first brick kiln, said to contain over 100,000. The burning is in progress and will be completed next week, after which about a week will be required for cooling."

"The public school at this place has closed and will not, probably, re-open for two or three months. Miss Clara Ganoung will spend the vacation from her labors as teacher, in visiting friends in other localities." This was announced in the *San Miguel Messenger* on November 25, 1887. That paper, on December 2nd informed its readers that "Sicotte & Hopper have brick for sale in quantities to suit the purchaser. They are also prepared to do all kinds of brick work at short notice. Mr. Hopper informs us that the brick burned in the kiln which is now cooling, are of very fine quality. He thinks the clay at the yard is adapted for brick of extra hardness and durability."

A pupil of Miss Ganoung, Lena Matthis Clemons, gives some more information on school days spent at the Caledonia. Lena, a daughter of John and Dora Matthis, was in the group of school children who attended classes in "the long-vacant, semi-haunted 'Caledonia,' while the 'new' San Miguel school-house was being constructed from lumber taken from the old school building." Mrs. Clemons recalled that she and her classmates and teacher occupied a portion of the downstairs section of the Caledonia. Lena Clemons said that one day a band of gypsies came along and the teacher, Miss Clara Ganoung, and the children were so frightened that they locked the doors and the students crawled under the desks.

Dr. A. H. Wilmar remembered that in 1887, a library was located in the room of the Caledonia that is on the first floor, in the center, on the west side of the building. A. H. Wilmar became a physician, and practiced in Paso Robles until his retirement in the 1950s.

According to Lena Clemons, the students "stuck it out for only a few months." She explains, "Then we lost the battle to the fleas. All day in school we scratched, and at night we went home with great red welts on our skins, until our folks all raised 'Ned,' and school was moved to a store building in San Miguel." The students were moved into a vacant store building, and remained there until the new brick school-house was ready for occupancy. [This information about Lena and the fleas is taken from an article written for the *Paso Robles Press* of June 17, 1960, by Joyce Gombos.] This would be the first of two times that the infestation of fleas caused people to move out of the Caledonia. Lena Clemons said that farm animals were kept adjacent to the two-story building, and they were the source of the fleas.

This was the last time that rooms in the Caledonia would be used as school-rooms for the young people of San Miguel. The newly-constructed two-story brick school had four rooms and a bell tower. It served the area for over sixty years.

At the age of eighty-nine, Dr. Leo L. Stanley wrote a paper called "School Days in San Miguel." Dr. Stanley's niece, Rosemary Netto, has graciously allowed us to include his observations of the two-story red brick school-house that had been located next to the hill on Eleventh Street.

There were four large rooms in the school built for the grades from the first to the

eighth. A broad stairway led from the entrance to the second floor. Numerous windows provided ample light, although large glass-shaded kerosene lamps were used at night when the Literary Society and other gatherings convened for the benefit of the children and their parents. Behind the brick school, and close to the hill, were two Out Houses, both of four hole capacity: one for Girls and one for Boys.

And there was a wood-shed in which was stored sufficient fuel for the four pot-bellied stoves which kept the building warm in the winter.

In the four rooms of the school there were about a hundred. There was not one Negro among them, although at Paso Robles, nine miles south, there were many Blacks, brought in to work at the new El Paso de Robles Hotel. There were no Indians. Most of these natives had long been dispersed following the secularization of the Mission.

Class time was usually called by one tap

San Miguel School.

Drawn by Virginia Cassara

of the bell in the tower, at which signal all play came to an abrupt halt. The children remained "frozen" until the second tap sounded, when they formed in lines and, to the beat of a drum, marched to their various rooms. Classes were adjourned at recess, noon and closing by the ringing of the bell. The task of pulling the cord was usually assigned to a Bell Monitor, one of the pupils, who closely observing the big clock on the wall, proudly performed his duty.

There were no buses or other conveyances to bring the pupils in from the surrounding country. District schools were located out in the valleys in close proximity to the farms where the families lived: two in Vineyard, one in Lowe's, another in Ranchita, one in Wellsona, one on the San Marcos and two in Indian Valley. Each of these schools had one teacher who usually boarded at one of the ranches.

The teachers in the San Miguel Grammar School in 1895 were a really remarkable group, well trained, sympathetic, friendly and more than anxious to impart their knowledge to the pupils. The principal was Professor M. R. Trace, a rather portly man of thirty-five... He was strict, but fair in his decisions. His punishments for indiscretions were mild.

Miss Margaret Tungate had charge of the lower classes. She boarded at the brick Makin House, just under the hill. Miss McConnell was smart and pretty. She had been brought up in the Parkfield area, went to Normal School in San Jose, and got her first appointment to teach in San Miguel. And there was Miss Waltenspiel who had come down from San Francisco. Her name was bandied about considerably by the irreverent.

Little attention was given to the grounds, which had sparse vegetation, possibly an umbrella tree or two, and was surrounded by a white picket fence. Girls had the north side and boys the south.

The main playgrounds were just across the street, several unoccupied lots in front of the school. These lots were not entirely vacant. At the beginning of the century there were a number of fruit orchards in the vicinity. To treat and cure the fruit, a drying kiln of small proportions had been built. Into this, wooden tracks had been fashioned so that the prunes, peaches and apricots loaded on trays on small cars could be pushed into the cubicles and subjected to sulphur fumes for preservation.

But there was room for a baseball field of sorts, and a space for the game of "Shinny," which is much like that of hockey. The ball or puck was usually a well-battered tin can and the clubs were made, by the boys, from a well-suited oak branch, with handle and knob on the lower end.

The object of the game was to drive the can into goals at either end of the field. Sides were chosen with the number of players depending on the number available at the time. "Shinny" was an appropriate name, for the shins during the game got many a hard blow from the stout wooden clubs.

A remarkable incident of those early San Miguel school days was that in that short period around the turn of the century, five doctors of medicine should eventuate from that small country school. The Wayland family of eight children lived near that Old Brick School. Among the children were Clyde and Ray. They graduated, went to high school, and then on to medical school where they received their M. D. degrees. They later on established large practices in San Jose and Hollywood.

In nearby Lowe's Canyon, attending the school taught by his mother, Frank Lowe prepared for high school in Paso Robles. He went on to medical school in Los Angeles, graduated, practiced temporarily in Blythe, California, and then on to San Francisco, where he became one of the foremost orthopedists of that northern city.

The Wilmar Family of four boys, Ellery,

View of school house from the south.

Schoolhouse in January 1920.

Earl, Ralph and Alvin Hillis lived within a few blocks of the school. At his mother's bidding, Hillis (as he was then called) went into medicine, and likewise graduated in Southern California. Except for a hitch in the army, Dr. Wilmar spent most of his medical career in the San Miguel area, and established a large practice in Paso Robles, where he continued to minister to the sick and ailing until his retirement.

The fifth Doctor of Medicine to come from San Miguel in that short period of time at the

Mr. Jamison's 5th and 6th Grades
1903-1904 San MiguelSchool

1st Row: Wayland Kingery, Bill Houghton, Harry McFadden, Floyd Cruess, Floyd Gorham, Lucian Perry.
2nd Row: Lill Wickstrom (Murphy), ¿, Pearl Short, Lizzie French, Alta Rucker, Ramona French, Maud Haliburton (Hart), Barbara Wood, Oliver McFadden.
3rd Row: Nell Wickstrom, Lelia Tolleson, Charlie Courier, Mildred Perry (Flentge), Dick Tolleson, Elmer Kitchen, Howard Negley.
4th Row: Goldie Murphy, Steve Sworthout, Nell French, Charlie Houghton, Mr. Jamison, Margaret Stanley (McGowan), Ethel Thralls, Hortense Kingery (Wright), Bertha Mathis (Dittemore).

Mrs. Alabama Williams and her 5th to 8th Grades
1906-1907 San Miguel School

1st Row: Emma Stanley (Cook), Leona Forbes (Stenner), Mary Hoffman (Blechen), Alta Rucker, ¿ Gorham, Fred Hoffman,
Elmer McFadden.
   2nd Row: Zoe Davis, Minnie Sitton (Taylor), Emma Hoffman (Linn), Wayland Kingery, ¿ Swearenger, Earl Negley, Bill
Houghton.
   3rd Row: Harry McFadden, Frank Tornquist, Harry Campbell, Mrs. Williams, Lucian Perry, Bill Braffet.

turn of the century was the writer of this brief resume of memories . . .

The Phillips School got its start on March 5, 1894, when O. A. Perry and Murdock McDonald appeared before the San Luis Obispo County Board of Supervisors; they obtained permission to remove the Folsom school house to a new school district named Phillips. The men paid $45.00 for the permission; O. A. Perry, M. McDonald and Jacob Bump were appointed as trustees.

On March 17, 1895, electors in the district were notified that a vote would be taken, at the residence of O. A. Perry, to decide where the new school house would be. It was decided to erect the school house on the south side of the "Giant's Grave," in Section 10, Township 26 South, Range 13, by the county road. March 21st was the day set for the removal of the Folsom school house to the selected site. On March 21 and 22, the school house was moved by M. McDonald, S. F. Jones, George Murphy, Ronald McDonald and O. A. Perry. Chauncey H. Phillips donated the land, so the school was named for him. The building was placed on skids and pulled down the road by horses. Its location was twelve miles east of San Miguel.

The Census Marshal, Mrs. O. A. Perry, reported that the number of children in the district amounted to 52. At the Phillips school house, an election held on June 1, 1894 produced trustees: Miss L. Gillis, 3 years, Mrs. O. A. Perry, 2 years and Mrs. H. Halter, 1 year.

Bell from the old brick school, now in park, 1990.

On July 7, 1894, Miss Sallie Findley was appointed teacher for 8 months, at $55 per month; the first term was to be July 16 through December 1, and the second term March 4, 1895 to May 29th. The *Paso Robles Record*, on August 17, 1895 reported that the Phillips school, taught by Miss Allie Kelshaw, consisted of 16 pupils, 15 of whom were McDonalds and the other a Perry.

According to September 28, 1895 issue of the *Paso Robles Record*, "Three girls and one boy fainted in the school room at San Miguel yesterday forenoon. This shows the necessity of keeping the rooms well ventilated, especially during the warm weather."

On July 4, 1981, a dedication was held for a ten-foot cupola which was built in the San Miguel park to contain the San Miguel School bell. The bell had been cast in San Francisco in 1890, by the W. T. Garratt & Co. A number 247 is stamped on the bell. Bunn Turnbow designed the gazebo-style bell memorial.

THE NEW TOWN OF SAN MIGUEL —PRIOR TO THE RAILROAD

In this chapter, we will trace the beginning of the town of San Miguel, as it developed, before the arrival of the railroad in October of 1886. Prior to the railroad's arrival, the hotels consisted of rooms in the Caledonia and the McDonald Brothers' accommodations located in rooms of the old Mission. Walter M. Jeffreys opened a hotel in 1874.

George Butchart had a store; the other mercantile establishment was Sittenfeld & Co., a branch of the Goldtree Bros., of San Luis Obispo. This store was on the mesa, near where the present-day cemetery is located. The town also had a school house, stable, at least two saloons, an express office and a post office.

Other businesses that we are aware of were a paint shop, owned and operated by Nathan & Isaac Goldtree, and Croxford's and Woodworth's blacksmith shop and wagon-shop. The town at that time was located between the Caledonia and the Mission.

Shortly before the arrival of the railroad, a disastrous fire leveled the town. The "new" town of San Miguel was rebuilt north of the Mission. According to Ella Adams, a German immigrant donated land for the railroad depot site; the name Kunz came to her mind. The Great Register for San Luis Obispo County lists Gotthard Kunz, a native of Switzerland, who was a merchant in San Miguel.

We will follow the building of the new town of San Miguel by looking at items printed in San Miguel's newspaper, which began on April 30, 1886. Gaius Webster was the founder and publisher. The newspaper began as *The Inland Messenger* and retained that name for its first year; on April 29, 1887, the name was changed to the *San Miguel Messenger*.

On May 7, 1886, the newspaper informed its readers that "In a private letter from Soledad. . .the railroad force at work near there is as follows: about twelve hundred Chinamen, from forty to sixty white men. . . ." Also: "A deed of right of way for a railroad from J. C. Currier to the Southern Pacific Railroad Company was placed on record a few days ago." Other items of interest were: "Frank E. Reed has just opened a shop opposite Jeffreys' Hotel, in this place, and is prepared to do all kinds of harness and saddle repairing at short notice." And: "Brandenstein & Co., of San Francisco, have purchased about 80 head of fat cattle from G. N. Douglas, and 250 from the Flint estate, and the drove started north yesterday."

One week later, readers learned that "Al Almstead is putting up a shed and feed yard near Forsythe & Nichols' blacksmith shop. Deffner and Barlow are doing the work." Also: "Our readers will be pleased to learn that W. C. Parker, a barber, has opened business at this place. He works for the present at Davis Brothers saloon, where he is prepared to do in good shape anything in the line of the tonsorial sort."

On May 14, 1886 the newspaper carried an article entitled "WILL SURVEY."

Goldtree Brothers, who are owners of considerable land here, say they will in a few days have a tract surveyed off into lots and offered for sale. It is a step that might well have been taken earlier. The probable nearness of the time when the depot for San Miguel will be located will now lead many to hold off in proposed investments, but there will doubtless be some demand for these lots wherever the depot may be established.

We are creditably informed that Mr. Charles Maxwell, of San Luis Obispo, will soon open a hotel on the other side of the river near Proctor's shop. The arrangements will be of a temporary character till the depot is located, when permanent buildings will be erected.

[At that time, a railroad had been surveyed to connect Lerdo, in the San Joaquin Valley, and San Miguel. In anticipation, the Maxwell House, and Keleher's blacksmith and carriage shop were operating on the east bank of the Salinas River.]

The Inland Messenger, on May 28, 1886, carried an article entitled, "The Railroad."

There is a dearth of railroad news this week, nothing new having been developed in

the plans or operations of the company. Work is carried on with energy this side of Soledad, the force being estimated at 1,500 men. After passing the San Lorenzo ranch, some eighteen miles out, the route is less difficult and the progress will be more rapid.

We give space to the following paragraph from the *Republic*. Our readers can judge for themselves as to the weight which should be given to the gentleman's conclusions: "A gentleman who came in from Soledad by stage Monday states that while in the hotel at that place, he overheard a conversation among railroad men, from which he learned enough to satisfy him that the railroad shops will be erected on the east side of the river from San Miguel, and that the cars will be running to that point by the 20th day of August next. The railroad is employing every man they can get, and grading is being pushed vigorously.

The newspaper on June 4, 1886 carried an article "TOWN SURVEY."

Surveyor Mennett has been engaged a few days past in laying lots in the town site of San Miguel, from land belonging to Goldtree Brothers. Lots on the west side of Main Street are laid out 50 feet wide by 125 feet deep, which will be the size of the lots on the entire plat, with a few exceptions.

Two wagon loads of furniture were brought here Monday by Almstead's teams for the new Maxwell Hotel on the east side. He is now after another load. Business will be opened in the old Proctor house near the crossing, which is to be fitted up for the purpose.

[The crossing opposite the Mission served the Estrella and Ranchita districts; another crossing, midway between Vineyard Canyon and Indian Valley, served those areas. Before hauling grain, the farmers got together and "strawed" the sandy river crossing to prevent their wagons from sinking into the river bed. Before the railroad arrived, grain was hauled either to the mill in San Luis Obispo, a three-day trip, or to Port Harford to be sent to San Francisco by the Republic Line of coastal steamers. Hogs and turkeys were driven either to Port Harford to be sent by steamer to market, or were driven on foot to Soledad, then the end of the railroad. Live turkeys brought 14

Looking east on the road from Estrella to the ford on the Salinas River, Spring 1996.

to 15-cents per pound, and hogs sold for 2 ¼ to 2 ½ -cents per pound.]

Also in the June 4, 1886 edition of the newspaper: "Among the changes to be made in the assignment of Priests in this Diocese is that of placing Rev. Father Mut, of San Juan Capistrano, in charge of this parish. The new assignment of Father Farley has not been made public. Rev. Father Farley has many friends in this region who will regret his departure." [Father Philip Farrelly served at the Mission from January 1, 1879 to May 20, 1886. Prior to Father Farrelly's arrival, the Mission had gone for 36 years without a resident pastor.]

The Inland Messenger for June 11th contained this information: "Rev. Father Mut arrived Tuesday and has taken charge of this parish. He will celebrate Mass at Mission San Miguel next Sunday; June 20th at San Antonio, and June 27th at Cashin's Station." [Cashin's Station had previously been Campbell's Stage Station;

Looking west on the road from Estrella to the ford on Salinas River, Spring 1996.

it was located on El Camino Real 14 miles north of San Luis Obispo and 3 miles north of Santa Margarita.]

Also in the June 11th newspaper, readers learned that "Gotthard Kunz is preparing to put up a good barn on his place, adjoining town on the north. The size will be 46 by 30 with sheds 12 feet wide running the whole length on both sides." And: "We understand that a number of applicants for lots on the new townsite survey are waiting for the plat to be filed to get the locations and prices, with a view to purchase if terms are satisfactory."

Other items from the June 11th issue: "Terrence McGurk, of San Francisco, has arrived, and will open a boot and shoe shop in this place, as soon as a suitable room can be obtained." And: "J. M. Bennett, superintendent of the stage line, was along the road this week looking after the interests of the company. He stopped over at this place Monday." "Mrs. Maxwell who is to be the hostess of the new hotel, arrived last Sunday from San Luis Obispo, and has already commenced feeding the hungry on the east side of the river."

The newspaper also printed railroad news on June 11, 1886.

The progress of the railroad work south from Soledad has been less rapid than was expected by the public from representations when the work commenced, and from present appearances it can hardly be expected that the cars will be running to San Miguel before September or October. Even the latter date will be early enough to handle the grain crop, if the farmers are assured that it is coming, so that definite plans can be made and contracts entered into for disposing of their produce. Otherwise they will commence early to seek a market through the old channel to the coast.

A gentleman who came up the river a few days ago says construction trains are running about ten miles this side of Soledad.

The June 25th edition of the paper informed its readers that "Dr. Cain will move into the Mission building next week, a part of which has been fitted up for the family." Also: "Considerable lumber is being hauled into this valley from the yard of James Cass & Co., Cayucos." "W. M. Jeffreys has remodeled the shed opposite his hotel, adapting it for the purpose of a wagon house." Also: "Mrs. L. C. Browne has secured the front room of the Almstead Hotel, and has opened a few boxes of notions, fancy dry goods and stationery, that she is selling at very reasonable figures. Persons contemplating purchases in that line should see her goods." [In a letter dated February 19, 1980, Mrs. Dorothy Parker Skold, of Los Gatos, informs us that her grandmother, Letty Hager Browne was a widow with a little boy named Ward. Her grandfather, Wilbur C. Parker, owned and operated a barber shop. Grandmother Parker "stayed at an adobe converted to an inn when she moved to San Miguel."]

The June 25, 1886 edition of the newspaper printed an article entitled "Railroad Progress."

We have nothing new to offer on the subject of the railroad this week. Reliable information from the front reports the grading nearly completed to the San Lorenzo Ranch, some 18 miles from Soledad, and track laid from 12 to 15 miles. There has been talk of the working force being increased, but it is getting old, and the people are settling down to the belief that the road will not reach this point till well into the fall.

The Inland Messenger for July 9, 1886, published items which indicated that Mission San Miguel would be revived. "Father Mut contemplates having some important repairs made on the Mission property." And: "Father Mut expresses himself much encouraged as to the prospect of raising means to build a Catholic church in San Jose Valley." [San Jose Valley is about 20 miles southeast of Santa Margarita, near the community of Pozo. The post office at Pozo was named by G. W. Lingo. The word is Spanish for "well" or "hole." In the 1860s, Bonifacio Manchego had a road built to bring people into the little valley. George W. Lingo was a native of Missouri; he had been born on March 25, 1833, the fifth eldest of twelve children. He came to San Luis Obispo County in 1868, and built the Cambria Hotel, which he managed for 10 years. He sold the hotel, and homesteaded 160 acres near Pozo, then pre-empted 80 additional acres. In 1908, he sold out and retired to Santa Margarita.]

Other items in the July 9th issue included: "The whole number of children in this county under 17 years of age, as shown by the school census, is 4911." "Massey & Carrell are drilling a well for G. Webster, on his homestead about a mile southwest of town." And: "Jas. Kelleher, who was so unfortunate as to have his large wagon shop burned about a year ago, is going to work in conjunction with Ed Proctor, on the east side of the river. Two such thorough artisans ought to command a good business."

Mission San Miguel before repairs.

The Inland Messenger, on July 9, 1886, printed an article entitled "Railroad Survey."

Last Saturday, D. D. Griffiths, a surveyor in the employ of the Southern Pacific Railroad Company, with a force of sixteen men, arrived at a point on the river a few miles below this place, where they are engaged in surveying on the west side of the river. This circumstance would indicate that the location of the road in this vicinity is not yet definitely settled; but the surveys now to be made by Mr. Griffiths will, doubtless be the basis of a final decision as to the course of the road, the location of bridges, if any, and all matters preliminary to the actual construction of the road. We are glad to note this step, as it indicates a disposition on the part of the company to push the work forward as rapidly as practicable.

The July 16th issue had a report on the progress of the railroad construction, as well as other news items. "M. Withers informs us that track is laid twenty miles south of Soledad, and thirty miles of grading completed. The laborers now number 2000 Chinamen and 500 white men."

"In our Fourth of July report we said the supper was given at Jeffreys' Hotel. Such was not the case. It was given in Goldtree Company's warehouse, and under the auspices of the Band. The reason that the mistake occurred is that the 'spot' reporter of this paper was off duty."

"We call special attention to the advertisement of the new firm of Proctor, Keleher and Rader, whose blacksmith shop is located just on the east side of the river. The firm is composed of first-class mechanics and reliable men, and we bespeak for them a liberal share of public patronage."

"Proctor, Keleher & Rader are expecting another mechanic in a few days to assist in their blacksmith and wagon shop on the east side." The following ad was from later in the year.

Ed. Proctor   Jas. Keleher
Blacksmith   Carriage Maker
J. Rader
Blacksmith

Blacksmithing & Carriage Making

San Miguel, Cal.
All kinds of blacksmithing & carriage work done in the neatest and best manner.
Horse Shoeing Warranted to Give Satisfaction
Orders in all branches of the business solicited.
All work guaranteed to give satisfaction.
Agents for all kinds of Farm Wagons and Machinery.
Proctor, Keleher & Rader, Proprietors

"We are pleased to call the attention of our readers to the advertisement of August Scheesslar, who has opened a shoe shop opposite Jeffreys' Hotel. He appears to be a thorough mechanic, in the line of making as well as repairing, and will doubtless find plenty to do."

"Mr. G. N. Douglas is getting together material

for building on his lot immediately south of the blacksmith shop. It is understood that the building will be occupied by Mrs. Browne, as a store. J. J. Deffner will perform the carpenter work."

Readers of the July 16th newspaper were informed that "Last Monday about 10 o'clock, a fire started on the McDonald Brothers' lot, east of the Mission, caused by embers left by a party of campers that morning. Through the prompt action of Miss Amelia Warth, Miss Beatris Corella and Dr. J. H. Cain the flames were held in check until assistance arrived from town, when the fire was put out. Had the fire got a good start much damage would have been the result."

The July 16, 1886 issue of *The Inland Messenger* carried the following item, which today would be considered insensitive, at least. "A Chinese wash-house is the advance guard of an 'opium joint.'" Actually, the wash-house could have been the advance guard for the railroad- - -by July 20th, there were 1,500 Chinese workers laying track near King City.

It seems that the "Chinese wash-house" was not so undesirable that money could not be accepted in order to place the following two ads in the April 29, 1887 edition.

Wing Chung Wo
Near Railroad Turntable, San Miguel
Washing, Ironing, Fluting, etc., done at
cheap rates, and satisfaction guaranteed.
Buttons sewn on.

Yee Wo, Laundry
Located east of the railroad, near the
Jones Bros' Hotel, San Miguel
Washing and Ironing done cheaply and
satisfaction guaranteed.
Chinese Employment Office.

The paper, on July 16, 1886, printed an article entitled "Railroad Building."

For the past two weeks the railroad work has been pushed forward with great rapidity, and the track is now laid about half the distance between Soledad and this place. A private letter written by a gentleman who is watching the progress closely, and whose sources of information are very reliable, says the track will be laid to San Miguel by September 1st. The survey, under the direction of Mr. Griffiths, is being extended upon the west side; it is supposed that it will run up the Pescadero creek and through the Morro Pass.

Of course nothing is definitely known as to the point of crossing the Salinas river, but the prevailing opinion appears now to be that the crossing will be made between the mouth of the Nacimiento and Indian creek. Should this prove true, the location of the depot will become the next point on which the public mind of San Miguel will center. It is gratifying to reflect that all this uncertainty will soon be over.

The paper, on July 23, 1886, informed readers that "Dr. L. D. Murphy, a physician from Tulare City, has been at this place during the week. We understand that he contemplates locating here for the practice of his profession."

The July 23rd issue had this item: "Goldtree & Co. have been doing a rushing business in grain sacks during the past week, having sold about 30,000." Also: "Mrs. E. E. Davis, of San Francisco, a daughter of Mr. G. W. Proctor, arrived in San Miguel Monday, accompanied by her four sons and one daughter. She will probably make her home with us."

"Rev. Father Mut requests a general attendance of his congregation at a meeting to be held immediately after the celebration of Mass, next Sunday morning, to consider the question of raising means to place the Mission property in repair. All persons interested in the project are invited to be present."

"F. Frick, who is an expert in matters pertaining to mortar, adobe, lime, etc., has been experimenting in getting up a brick that will not be affected by water. He has some samples, in the composition of which lime, ashes and sand are the ingredients, that have laid in water for two years without showing any signs of softening."

The newspaper on that date informed its readers that "A party consisting of Chas. Davis, J. Mahoney and Robert Kirk, embarked in a light wagon behind Almstead buckskin colts last Monday, to go to San Luis Obispo. On starting, the animals struck out on quick time, and in making the turn near the blacksmith shop the wheels on one side went into a rut, which threw Davis and Mahoney out wrong end up, the latter tenaciously hanging to the lines. Kirk reached for the lines and went down upon the whiffletrees, and for a minute the situation looked alarming. The horses were soon quieted, however, and the party went on their way covered with dust of the road, but rejoicing that their necks were not broken."

The Inland Messenger, on July 23, 1886 stated that

"The railroad track is laid about twenty-six miles from Soledad, and for a distance from that point the construction will be comparatively easy and the road will probably go on faster than it has for some weeks past." Also: "It is announced that grading for the railroad will be commenced near Porter's place opposite Hames Valley, next week." Other railroad news: "The railroad surveying party moved camp last Tuesday to Paso Robles, in the region of which they are to run several preliminary lines."

One week later, readers learned that "Mr. G. W. Proctor thinks of taking down part of a building that he owns in Cambria, and putting it up at this place as soon as the railroad is located. The building will be about 26 x 60, and two stories high."

Also in the July 30th edition of the paper: "Father Mut went to San Luis Obispo to purchase lumber for repairing the church, last Monday. Father Mut, after celebrating Mass at Cashin's Station, next Sunday, will proceed to San Jose Valley and organize a committee to supervise the erection of a church in that vicinity."

Another item in the July 30th paper: "Last Sunday, after Mass, a meeting was held in the rooms of Rev. Father Mut, at which something over $100 was subscribed, for the purpose of repairing the church and pastoral residence. It was then resolved that, as something over $500 will be necessary to repair the buildings, a concert be given, and that subscription be started in order to procure the same. The entertainment and supper will be given on the evening of August 25th, the place of which will be hereafter announced. It is a commendable cause, and it is hoped that by these methods the desired amount will be raised."

[According to Father Engelhardt, speaking of Father Mut: "To his energy it is due that the row of buildings, comprising the ancient *convento* was preserved. Many of the rafters were decayed and others broken, so that the roof with its heavy tiles threatened to collapse at any time. . . ."]

In the July 30th issue of *The Inland Messenger*, the railroad news was: "There are thirty-five white men and five hundred Chinamen at work at the railroad grade near Porter's place, fifteen miles from here, and though there is a small gap between their work and that of the graders further north, it will soon be closed. The grading is going on rapidly. [Porter's place was at the site where the exit for Mission San Antonio leaves the north-bound freeway 101.]

The August 6th issue brought a little school news: "The new school teacher Miss Macauley will probably be in town to-morrow night." Another item in that issue was that "The rumor is current that the railroad will stop at or near San Miguel until next spring."

"The statement has been made that the reason the Railroad Company decided to build on the west side of the river, was that they deemed it better to build two bridges than to place the road-bed upon the sliding ground on the other side." Also: "Last Tuesday Col. H. D. La Motte, Arthur Brown, J. H. Strobridge and Wm Hood were at this place looking after the railroad interests. Col. La Motte, we are informed, secured the right of way on this side of the river, and it is definitely settled that the road will run on this side of the Salinas."

The August 6th edition of the paper carried this item: "Chas. Thiriet, the genial leader of the San Miguel Brass Band, has 'done gone and taken unto himself a rib'- - -or words to that effect. Last Saturday he took his betrothed, Miss Alma Hillicker, to San Luis Obispo, and on Monday the couple were united in marriage by the Justice of the Peace G. W. Barnes. Their many friends wish the couple a prosperous journey through life, and we in common with the rest of their friends hope it may be years ere they are summoned to 'that undiscovered country from whose bourn

The Mission San Miguel, San Luis Obispo County, California, 1883.

no traveler returns,' and that their bark may never be wrecked upon the shoals of contention. *Bon Voyage.*"

On more mundane matters, that edition of the paper informed readers that "Mrs. L. C. Browne has moved into her new store south of the blacksmith shop." Also: "W. M. Jeffreys, the genial Boniface of Jeffreys' Hotel, treated his guests to juicy venison steak from the carcass of a buck that tipped the beam at 135 pounds."

The Inland Messenger, on August 6, 1886, printed an article entitled, "A Contradiction."

Last week we published the reports concerning the movements of the railroad now being extended south from Soledad. The rumors are so numerous and conflicting that it is a hard matter for one to form a true conclusion regarding the route from San Miguel. That the road will be built to this point there is no doubt; the route from this point, however, is what is agitating the people hereabouts.

The following from the San Francisco *Chronicle* may throw some light upon the subject, and coming as it does from Creed Hamond, the attorney for the road, it may have a significance of more than ordinary weight. Our readers can take it for what it is worth. The statement is a flat denial of those made by the San Francisco papers last week. The *Chronicle* says: "In an interview yesterday (July 30) Creed Hamond of the Southern Pacific Railroad said the published report that the southern extension from San Miguel eastward into Kern county was incorrect. Maps covering such a route were filed some months ago, thus securing the right of way, but that this line will be built for years to come is improbable.

The extension is now building under the Southern Pacific Branch Railroad Co., which is a corporation controlled by the stockholders of the Southern Pacific Railroad, from San Miguel south through Santa Barbara County, touching San Luis Obispo, Santa Barbara and Newhall. The erroneous report arose from the hesitation of the company in deciding whether it would be better to run from Los Angeles to Newhall or directly to San Buenaventura. Maps for the former route have been filed however, and the work will be pushed forward."

The above still leaves the people in doubt as to which side of the river the depot will be located, but it sets at rest the question of the building of the road to Newhall by the coast route.

The following week, on August 13th, readers learned that "The scene on the flat below the Mission was enlivened by a horse-race last Friday. Our reporter was not present." Also: "Mr. Sittinfeld has a force of men at work fencing his land claim, west of this place." The news of progress on the railroad was that "The number of men at work on the railroad north of here is estimated at 2,500."

Under the headline of "Railroad Progress," *The Inland Messenger* for August 13, 1886 presented readers with the following information.

The uncertainty as to the location of the railroad at this point is at an end, it being definitely settled that it will follow the west side, passing near the old Mission and the present site of San Miguel. The location of the depot is not announced, but appearances point to the flat some three-fourths of a mile below the Mission as the point. [The word "below" must refer to the down-river direction; otherwise, it would refer to the location near the old Caledonia adobe.]

It is a fine level tract of several hundred acres, owned by G. Kunz, Davis Bros., the Flint estate and McDonald Bros. It is certain that no better location could be found for a town in this vicinity. Water can be found at a reasonable depth, and good drainage is practicable. The location will probably give as good general satisfaction as any point that could have been selected. As soon as the town site is surveyed and lots offered, we expect to see building open up briskly, to continue till we have a flourishing town in which all branches of trade are represented.

In the same newspaper on August 13, 1886, it was stated that "The Southern Pacific Milling Co.'s scales and etc. are on their way from San Luis Obispo. They will weigh tons at a time, being the largest in the county." And "The firm of Goldtree & Co., at this place who are large buyers of wheat, do not propose to haul any wheat to San Luis Obispo this year. They feel assured that the railroad will be here in time to carry out the entire product of the valley.

The August 13th issue informed people that "A gentleman who has conversed with the chief of the railroad construction force with reference to the bridge across the river below here, says the track will be laid first across the river on a temporary bridge, which will be used till the permanent structure is completed. The bridge will cross the channel by two spans with trestle work to connect with the shore. The structure will be built on spilling that is expected to be driven fifty feet in the ground. The spiles are supposed to be 33 inches in diameter. The engineer seems to anticipate no difficulty in making a bridge stand in this part of the river." (A dictionary defines a "spile" as a heavy stake or timber driven into the ground as a foundation or support.)

The August 20, 1886 edition of the paper informed its readers that "We understand that town lots will soon be laid off on the west side of the river to accommodate those who may want locations for business or residence. Just at what point the survey will be located we are not informed."

Also found in the August 20, 1886 issue: "Capt. Currier announces that he is prepared to purchase or receive wheat on storage, as agent for the Southern Pacific Milling Company and to issue receipts for the same. Loans can be negotiated on wheat placed on storage at the rate of ten per cent, per annum." [In the early 1890s, the Farmers Alliance was started, in opposition to the monopoly of the Southern Pacific Milling Company. Ella Adams provides the interesting note that at the opening celebration for the Farmers Alliance, there was a square-dance on horseback, with Frank Dalton as caller.]

"The Railroad," was the title for an article printed in the August 20, 1886 edition of *The Inland Messenger*.

There is nothing new to report in the movements of the railroad, except that the work

The S. P. Milling Company, 14th and N Streets.

The San Miguel Flouring Mill Company was formerly Farmers' Alliance Co. Flour Mill.

appears to be progressing more rapidly than heretofore. The track is laid to the vicinity of Porter's, some fifteen miles from here. Grade stakes are set past this place, the route being through the Mission property and running close to the Almstead Hotel. The surveyors were busy yesterday forenoon locating the eastern end of the bridge over the Salinas at this place, and it is said they will now proceed southward to Paso Robles.

In the August 27th issue, readers learned that "The guests at the Almstead House were introduced to a new dining room yesterday. It is in the new addition and is well lighted and airy." An item tinged with racism was printed: "A high-toned appearing Chinaman was around Wednesday hunting for a site for a laundry."

Also in the August 27, 1886 edition of the newspaper was the item that "W. F. Dutton and a young man from Hollister are setting the scales for the Milling Company. After that is completed Mr. Dutton will proceed with the erection of an office building for the company, near the site of the future warehouse.

Important railroad news was included in the August 27th issue of *The Inland Messenger*.

Within the past week considerable has been done towards locating the seat of future railway business at this place. Mr. Shackelford of the Southern Pacific Milling Co., in connection with the railroad engineers, selected the site for the warehouse, a short distance below the Mission property. Two side tracks, one on each side of the main line, have been located between Kunz' house and the Mission, making the probable site of the de-

pot much nearer the present San Miguel than was expected two weeks ago. The end of the track is some fifteen miles from here.

The newspaper for September 3, 1886 carried this important item: "A number of men have been inquiring about lots in San Miguel within the past week, and they have been told that the town has not yet been laid off." Also: "It has occurred to us that the proprietors of the town site may be standing in their own light by delaying the survey. Towns are being located both north and south of us, and parties seeking investments or business openings may find what they are looking for elsewhere, when they would have preferred San Miguel if it had been possible to obtain a foothold."

Also in that issue of the newspaper: "There was a free fight somewhere along the line last Monday, and judging from the peculiar marks and brands carried by some of our citizens next day, it must have been a grand success."

The paper, in addition, informed readers: "We call attention to the card of Dr. Neal of Hollister, who will open an office in this place in a few days. He also announces that he will, in connection with a competent druggist, start a drug store. The Doctor has the appearance of an educated gentleman, and we hope the field may prove equal to his reasonable expectations."

"A load of grain belonging to John Curtin, of Vineyard Canyon, was the first weighed on the Southern Pacific Milling Company's new scales," according to the September 3, 1886 edition of *The Inland Messenger*. Also: "The first lumber brought to this place by way of the railroad was hauled from San Ardo this week by John Warth. It was used in repairing the Mission property." [This load of lumber may have come by way of the railroad, but not all the way to San Miguel on the tracks. The railroad was about one month away from San Miguel.]

The newspaper for September 10, 1886 had the following items: "We call attention to the advertisement of the 'New' Saloon of Dutton & Hopper, near the grain warehouse. If there is anything in being early on the ground, these gentlemen have that advantage." And: "W. M. Jeffreys Esq. is building a barn on his homestead, adjoining town." "Almstead's teams went to San Luis Obispo Wednesday for lumber for the new Chinese Laundry." Also: "A new Chinese laundry is to be located south of Goldtree & Co.'s warehouse." Finally, "Dr. Neal is expected to arrive in San Miguel today."

Three items under "Local Brevities" were found in the September 17th issue: "The railroad runs so

The Mission in 1883.

unpleasantly close to the residence of Mr. G. N. Douglas that he will move the house." Also: "The railroad will pass so close to the Almstead house that it will become necessary to move the house back." And: "The railroad will cross the San Marcos creek a few feet above the wagonroad track."

Also found in the September 17, 1886 issue of *The Inland Messenger*: "The railroad engineers moved their camp last Friday to Wells' place some three miles above here. The cars will be in San Miguel in the first week of October, unless some unexpected delay occurs." [Our present-day name of Wellsona comes from the mentioned Wells' place. In 1887, the location was called "Wells' Siding", on the Southern Pacific station list, and "Wellsona" on the 1894 station list.]

The newspaper also informed readers that: "A supply of lumber will be brought here by R. M. Shackelford, to stock a lumber yard as soon as the track is laid." Also: "Mr. Wintemute, the photographer, is making some excellent pictures of the Old Mission. The view of the interior of the Chapel is particularly good. Mr. J. S. Wintemute has come to constitute a part of the city of San Miguel; he has some fine samples of work, and will doubtless give satisfaction to those who desire to preserve their shadows."

Also in the September 17th edition of the newspaper: "We understand that C. H. Reed & Co. will soon open a branch of their hardware and wagon business at this place." And: "A temporary railroad crossing of the Salinas river below here will be made by laying ties upon the sand in the dry river bed. Work on the bridge will go on as fast as practicable, and when it is completed the temporary track will be removed."

"San Miguel is beginning to show signs of increased vitality," according to the September 17th issue. "The hotels are crowded, and men and teams are numerous on the street. A week or two will bring the main railroad force up to this vicinity, when the lonesome San Miguel of former times will be a thing forever in the past."

One week later, the newspaper on September 24th informed its readers that "The railroad track is laid to the river crossing about five miles below here, and next week the whistle of the locomotive will greet the ears of the residents of San Miguel." Also: "The Southern Pacific Milling Company announce that they have decided to go ahead with both the mill and warehouse at this place as soon as lumber and material can be brought through on construction trains. They will not wait for the completion of the mill at King City as heretofore stated; having decided to put in the Morse bolting system which is considered the best in the world. Two or three weeks ought to see the business underway."

Other items in the September 24th paper: "Mr. G. D. Wilson has opened a restaurant near the depot grounds." And: "The Pioneer Saloon in the railroad addition to San Miguel has a new sign of excellent workmanship." Also: "We call attention to the new advertisement of Mr. W. O. Howard, who has opened a fruit and vegetable stand near the depot grounds. This will certainly fill a long-felt want."

"There is to be a literary entertainment at the Mission next Wednesday evening," according to the September 24th newspaper. "It will embrace a varied program that will please the audience, and the proceeds are to be applied in repairing the Mission Property. So worthy a cause ought certainly to bring out a full house."

According to the October 1, 1886 edition of *The Inland Messenger*, "The first train crossed the river below here last Sunday. The track is laid to within about two miles of this place, and we expect it to reach the vicinity of the depot grounds by Saturday night." And: "We understand there is to be a side track on Wells' place, three or four miles above here. One camp of the railroad grading force has moved above town to the vicinity of the San Marcos." Also: "We understand that as the Almstead House will be moved, arrangements have been made to remove the telegraph office to a building near the depot grounds."

Other news in the October 1st paper: "Dr. L. D. Murphy arrived in town yesterday, and will locate here for business." And: "Mr. Wm. Pinkerton and C. W. Jackson arrived Wednesday and are perfecting arrangements for their butchering business and stock yards at this place. They have purchased an acre of land from McDonald Bros. adjoining town, and will commence building as soon as the lumber arrives, which will be early in the coming week. The business will include buying and shipping stock, as well as butchering. We are pleased to note this addition to the business prospects of San Miguel." Also: "Surveyor Mennet will commence next Monday to survey off lots

George Millman, W. A. Wilmar, and Dr. L. D. Murphy.

north of Jeffreys' Hotel on land belonging to Jeffreys and McDonald Bros. This survey will probably connect with that to be made by the Railroad Company still further north." [Dr. Lorenzo Dow Murphy was a native of Kentucky; he came to California in 1854, and first settled in Yolo County. In 1884, he came to San Luis Obispo County, and two years later took up residence in San Miguel. For fourteen years he was the Tulare division surgeon for the Southern Pacific; he was first Master of the Tulare Masonic Lodge and the San Miguel Lodge. Dr. Murphy passed away at Atascadero Hospital on October 1, 1925.]

The October 1, 1886 newspaper carried this church news item: "Rev. Father Mut desires through the columns of the *Messenger* to express thanks to the ladies and gentlemen who took part in the entertainment which was given on the 29th instant for the benefit of the Church. He also would announce that he has over one hundred fine photographs of the Church and Mission of San Miguel, from different views, to be sold, to increase the fund for the repair of the Church and Mission property."

October 8, 1886 was an historic date. The newspaper for that date carried the information that "Monday noon the locomotive blew the first whistle at the San Miguel depot, and the long and thrilling blast was like a cheerful prophecy of the coming success and progress of the natural center of farming and trade." [Perhaps the locomotive made it as far as San Miguel's blossoming "new" town; however, the train would not make it completely through the town until ten days later.]

"There was a temporary interruption of the railroad grading at the Mission property, on account of a difference of opinion between Father Mut, pastor in charge, and the railroad engineers, as to where the tracks should cross the Mission land. The difficulty was settled the next day, and the work moved on." [Father Mut wanted the railroad tracks curved in back of the Mission; the railroad officials wanted the tracks laid in a straight line. After much discussion, the Southern Pacific paid the church $400 to allow the tracks to cross in front of the Mission.]

Also in the October 8th issue of the newspaper was and article entitled, "Town Site Surveys."

Surveyor D. L. Norton, in the employ of the Railroad Company, is engaged in surveying and platting that part of the town site falling upon the land of Gothard Kunz, in the vicinity of the depot. The survey will all be on the west side of the railroad. There will be a reservation for railroad purposes of a strip 75 feet wide next to the track; then comes a street 80 feet wide. A tier of blocks follows, of 400 feet in length, fronting the railroad, by 320 feet in depth. There is an alley 20 feet wide running lengthwise through the center of the blocks, leaving 150 feet on each side, which is the length of the lots. The lots are 25 feet front, making 32 lots to each block. The lots and blocks will be uniform in size on the entire plat, and no special reservations will be made for any purpose.

The tract to be included in this plat, it is understood, will embrace 160 acres, all of which will be on the flat traversed by the railroad and on the first bench above. The latter is well sheltered and yet commands a fine view, and is in all respects adapted for residence purposes. The lower level is well located

The train arrives in San Miguel.

Drawn by Virginia Cassara

View of the Mission's irregularly-shaped arches.

for business houses. Taken all together, it is a fine site for the future city of San Miguel, and in a week or two the work of improvement will be inaugurated to the music of the saw and hammer.

"Business Openings in San Miguel," was the lead on another article in *The Inland Messenger* on October 8, 1886.

We have heretofore had something to say upon the probable growth of San Miguel, and we have yet to see the intelligent man, who is well-acquainted with the extensive region of productive country that finds its natural business center here, who does not concur in our conclusion that the permanent and healthy growth of the place is assured.

The demands of business will call for an immediate boom in building; a movement that will continue till the various branches of business usually maintained in town of one thousand inhabitants are established here. Aside from those branches of business already established or about to open, the place presents an inviting field for the following industries: Planing mill, bank, boot and shoe maker, dentist, tin-shop, livery stable, saddle & harness maker, furniture store & shop, millinery, tailor, watch-maker and jeweler, baker, cannery for fruit & vegetables.

The October 8th issue also informed readers that "Lots will be laid off in a few days on the lands of McDonald Bros. between the Mission and the depot." Also: "Surveyor Mennett has been engaged for several days in surveying lots on the east side of the street on Jeffreys' land in front of Jeffreys' hotel. The plat will embrace the tract between the street and the rail-

road, extending south as far as the Almstead Hotel. The Almstead Hotel will be moved as soon as Mr. Douglas, the owner, can secure an eligible lot on which to place it." And: "Mr. Jeffreys has enlarged his dining room, and rejuvenated and beautified the hotel generally. It is whispered that he has secured a larger safe, but of this the deponent saith not."

The same issue of the paper stated that "Mr. Courter, from Aptos, arrived on last Monday, to act as agent for the Loma Prieta Lumber Co. at this place. He has established his office temporarily in that of the Southern Pacific Milling Company."

"Dr. Murphy has decided to settle in San Miguel," according to the October 8, 1886 issue, "and will proceed as soon as lumber can be had, to put up a drugstore. He informs us that he has a first-class stock already purchased and awaiting shipment. This is a branch of business with the science and details of which the Doctor is thoroughly familiar, and we bespeak for him a liberal patronage."

Readers of the October 8th issue of the newspaper also learned that "Mr. G. W. Proctor, who has rented out his Cambria property, came over last Monday, and says he will remain this side of the mountain for a year at least. He brought over considerable lumber from a building he took down in Cambria, and thinks he may put up a building in San Miguel." Also: "Mrs. Browne is making large additions to her stock of boots and shoes; also completing her assortment of fancy dry goods. Call at the little store before purchasing elsewhere." Additionally: "Mr. Phinney, from San Luis Obispo, has been putting shelving into Jeffreys' Hall this week, to receive the hardware stock of C. H. Reed & Co." "Mr. G. S. Davis, who has been in the hotel business in Santa Barbara, Cambria and elsewhere, is preparing to build a house in this place, and will open for business as soon as possible."

"Town Site Conveyance," was the lead for the October 15, 1886 edition of the newspaper. "Last Tuesday, G. Kunz conveyed to the Southern Pacific Railroad Company a tract of 200 acres, including the grounds for depot, side-tracts and other buildings required by the company. This tract is being laid off and platted, and in a few days the sale of lots will commence. It is probable that from twenty to forty acres will be required for railroad purposes, leaving 160 or upwards for lots."

"The Question of a New County," was the headline on an article in *The Inland Messenger* on October 15, 1886.

There is probably no part of California which has undergone a more complete transformation within two years past than the northern part of San Luis Obispo and the southern part of Monterey Counties. From a pastoral region, occupied in large tracts for grazing, it is being rapidly converted into small farms, on which the whole range of farm products are successfully raised. From unclaimed public domain, with here and there a large ranch as the nucleus of a much larger range, it is passing into the possession and ownership of individual settlers in tracts of 160 acres or less, and all the usual preparations for permanent homes are being made.

One result of this radical change in the occupancy of the country is the creation of a necessity for a change in the political subdivisions into which it is divided. The present county boundaries were fixed many years ago, when very few could have been made to believe in the possibility of what they now see. Here is a tract of productive country seventy-eight miles east and west, by about sixty north and south, over 4,000 square miles, settled by an industrious population, which is rapidly increasing.

It is a country of peculiar topography, differing in its general characteristics from that lying either north or south; it is a region naturally laid out for a distinct county. Yet this region is cut squarely in two by a county line, and many of the people are compelled to travel over one hundred miles to reach their county-seat.

It was some time since intimated that the *Messenger* was not in favor of immediate action on this issue; but it is a question with which the people the two counties must become familiar in the near future. The counties will be divided, and a new county created, of which San Miguel will be the geographical and commercial center.

The proposition may meet with some opposition from other portions of the counties affected. But it is simply an incident of the development of the country. It is one of the inevitable results of progress. It is a thing that will be an accomplished fact in less than five years from this date.

THE NEW TOWN OF SAN MIGUEL —AFTER THE ARRIVAL OF THE RAILROAD

The Inland Messenger published its October 15, 1886 paper as usual on Friday. This was three days prior to the train actually rolling through the town of San Miguel. Readers of the October 15th edition learned: "Five carloads of lumber arrived for the Southern Pacific Milling Company last Tuesday, and other installments will follow as fast as required. The lumber is being sorted preparatory to making the foundation of the warehouse, which will be pushed forward as fast as possible."

Another lumber item: "There are very many of the farmers waiting for lumber to arrive by rail, to build barns, sheds, etc., and it is unfortunate that there has been so much delay in placing a stock upon this market. One farmer told us this week that he had been waiting to get lumber from San Miguel, but feared that he would yet be compelled to go to San Luis or get his hay wet."

Also: "Some people still believe in the old saying: 'Where there's a will there's a way.' One of our intending settlers, being short both of lumber and money, has secured a large lot of the empty powder-boxes the railroad blasters threw away, and as each one makes about four square feet of clear, sound lumber, he'll have enough for a snug little house."

"The Railroad Company have sunk a well at the depot grounds 42 feet in depth, in which they have 16 feet of water. A tank of 60,000 gallons capacity is being placed." This item, and the following one, were in the October 15, 1886 issue of *The Inland Messenger*, as the railroad construction approached the newly-forming town of San Miguel.

As one, putting his ear to the rail, may hear the hum of the coming train, so in San Miguel may be noted the signs of the coming boom. There are many new faces to be seen every day- - -railroad men, business men- - -some seeking lots for definite location, and some only 'looking around'- - -travelers for pleasure, curious to see the future city while still in embryo. Even the city of San Luis is waking from its sleep of years, rubbing the moss from its eyes, and, with long stretch and yawn,

asking what the growing brightness may betoken. Actually, incredible as it may seem, two of the San Luis papers have sent out agents to this region. Heretofore, a man wishing to subscribe had to go to the office, put his own name on the books, and then be on hand each week to get his paper. Well, 'we have changed all that.'

The paper, on October 15, 1886, informed its readers that "Dr. Neal arrived here Friday, to remain permanently. He has opened an office temporarily in his rooms at Jeffreys' Hotel. Dr. Neal's first professional call in town was to attend Mr. John K. Kester, of Ranchita Canyon, who had a severe attack of cholera morbus on Saturday."

Also in the October 15th paper: "Mr. Lee Abernethy has opened a feed-yard at the depot, where animals will be well fed and cared for. A job-wagon is also on hand, and will be a great public convenience." Another item was entitled "More Business at the Depot. Mr. James Walsh has opened the Brewery Saloon, will only keep the best liquors, and has introduced the fashion of big schooner glasses. Interview him if you get a sunstroke or a snake-bite."

The first train rolled into San Miguel on October 18, 1886, according to Loren Nicholson in his book, *Rails Across the Ranchos*. "The stage now connects with the railroad at this place, leaving for the south at the arrival of the train in the evening. It stops over night at Paso Robles and goes through to San Luis in the morning," according to the October 22nd edition of *The Inland Messenger*. The same paper, on that date, gave the information that "The price of a passenger ticket between San Francisco and this place is $7.40."

Other items in the October 22nd edition of the newspaper included the following: "Mr. John Kerns, who has been in the Railroad Company's employ at Kings City, has taken the position of freight agent at San Miguel." "Mr. Harris has opened house for refreshments of all kinds- - -edible and bibible- - -at the depot. He has a large lodging-house, sixty feet long, will cater mainly for the railroad travel, and his place will be first-class in every respect." Church news for the readers was that "Rev. J. H. Warren, Superintendent of the Home Missions of the Congregational Church, arrived Wednesday evening. The S. P. Railroad Company generously propose to donate lots for a Church to be erected by this society, and a site will probably be selected this week."

The following week, there was an item about the railroad progress, and two items concerning the Chinese. "The railroad track is laid some three or four miles south of this place." "Chinamen becoming numerous here." And then: "Our Chinese residents are beginning to go with the tide. The pioneer laundry of the town has an advertisement in this issue. He has always done good work, and on time."

The following letter appeared in the October 29th issue:

Ed. *Messenger*: Your article, last week, on the new county, was the first move towards what must sooner or later become an accomplished fact. And now let us consider the name of the bantling. It seems to me that no better name can be found than 'San Miguel.' It is distinctive, and it is purely local, having been the name of this region of country for more than one hundred years, on account of the Mission. It is easily pronounced at sight, being better in this respect than San Jose, Vallejo and some others. It carries its meaning on its face; it has not to be hunted up in a dictionary, like Ventura and many others. And it preserves the memory of the faithful old Spanish Catholic missionaries, who battled so bravely and endured so much to bring the knowledge of religious truths to the ignorant savages then here. Let it be, then, as always, San Miguel.

The October 29, 1886 issue carried this article: "A gentleman inquired of a businessman at the depot the whereabouts of old San Miguel. 'San Miguel,' replied Mr. Hopper, musingly, 'Oh! Yes, there used to be a town of that name years ago; well, go on a piece, and you'll find an old road; follow it about half a mile, and you find some ruins, that's old San Miguel.'" (The most prominent building comprising the 'ruins' of old San Miguel would have been the old Caledonia adobe.)

The Inland Messenger, on October 29, 1886, carried the item: "The New Church. A very promising beginning has been made for the establishment of a Congregational Church in this place. The Rev. J. H.

Warren of San Francisco, Supt. Home Missions, preached to a large congregation, as many in fact as could be accommodated in the schoolhouse. The good will of our Episcopal friends was expressed by adjourning their own services and worshipping with the Congregationalists. . . .Steps were taken for the immediate formation of a Congregational Church, and reports of progress will be made next Sunday. It is expected that Rev. E. B. Tuthill, recently from Colorado, will take charge of the new Church next Sunday. He will also be minister at Paso Robles."

Additional items in the October 29th edition included: "One of the first shipments of produce from this station by rail is 90 bales of wool, 40,000 pounds, from the Estrella Ranch by G. W. Brewster. The price of wool is now fair, being about 16 cents per pound."

"G. N. Douglas will soon commence a good two-story building in the railroad plat to be occupied by *The Inland Messenger*, the Central Land Agency, and perhaps other offices." Also: "We understand that Mr. & Mrs. G. N. Douglas contemplate making provision for a public reading room in this town. Such an institution will be a great favor to the public."

"Mr. Harris, who has a lodging-house of twenty beds at the depot, reports that he has had his house full every night since he opened." And: "It is to be hoped that new hotels will be erected here, as the present accommodations are wholly inadequate to the wants of the public."

"C. H. Reed & Co. have opened the best assortment of hardware, tin ware and queensware to be found in the county. Their store is opposite Jeffreys' Hotel." Also: "The Railroad Company have appointed Dr. Neal surgeon for the line from Soledad south."

Church news included the following: "Rev. Dr. Warren and others have selected as the site for the proposed Church, lots. . .on the corner of L and 14th streets in the railroad survey. A subscription has been started to raise funds, and there will be $550 from the Congregational Union available only when that sum will finish paying for the property complete."

"Old and Good," was the headline on this October 29th article: "The firm Goldtree & Co. is the most widely-known business house in San Luis county. Many years in trade, strict integrity, and all the liberality consistent with good business policy, have combined to give them a high place in commercial and financial circles. The store in San Miguel is simply the hub around which the business of the region has revolved. A question is often asked: 'Will Goldtree move down to the depot?' Because where Goldtree & Co. is, there is San Miguel. Look out for a new advertisement soon."

Readers of the October 29th edition learned the following:

> **'Railroad Accident.'** The first serious accident that has occurred on the extension this year took place last Friday at the temporary bridge across the Salinas below this place. Several cars became derailed when going at the usual speed, and one of two capsized. M. Mitchell, of Soledad, who has been for years in the employ of the Stage Company as agent, was standing on the rear portion of the smoking car, and was thrown off with great violence and very narrowly escaped being killed by the truck. His arm was broken, and he was otherwise bruised, but is reported to be doing well. Other passengers were considerably shaken up but escaped uninjured.

An item from this issue of the newspaper allows us to put into perspective the county's population. "Through the politeness of County Clerk Dana, we are in possession of a copy of the Great Register for San Luis Obispo County for the year 1886. . . .Taking the usual ratio of 5 persons to one voter, this would indicate a present population of 18,210 in the county." [It is interesting that the year's figures would be available in October. At the present time, it seems that statistics such as these are not available until a couple of years after the numbers are compiled.]

"The map of Jeffreys' addition to San Miguel has been completed, and may be seen in Capt. Currier's Office. It embraces a good many eligible lots, which are offered at a very reasonable figure. The Central Land Agency are selling these lots."

Also found in the October 29, 1886 issue of the newspaper: "Mr. J. P. Nash, formerly of Modesto, has purchased lots, and announces his intention to engage in general merchandising at this place, as soon as a suitable building can be erected. Mr. Nash is a man of means and experience in business, who will be welcomed to the rapidly growing circle of the business men of San Miguel."

The Inland Messenger for November 5, 1886: "About twenty new buildings are in process of construction in this town and more coming." "Mr. Douglas has let a contract to A. T. Barlow to build his new house in the new town. It is to be completed within thirty days from the time the lumber is on the ground. It will be commenced next week. The building is to be two stories high, and 18 x 53 feet in size." Also: "Al Almstead is making preparations to put up a hotel building in the new part of town."

"The Congregational Church," was the headline on an article in the November 5th edition of the paper. "Last Sabbath was an eventful day in the religious history of San Miguel, being the occasion of the organization of a Congregational society and a Sunday School. Dr. Warren preached an able and appropriate sermon to a good congregation in the schoolhouse at 11 o'clock, after which the organization of the Sunday School, commenced a week before, was completed by the appointment of Rev. E. B. Tuthill as Superintendent, Miss M. Macauley Secretary, Mrs. Browne, Mrs. Barry and Mrs. Webster teachers. Mr. T. D. Wells takes charge of the Bible class."

"The Jeffreys Hotel runs a coach to the depot on arrival of all passenger trains." And: "The Southern Pacific Milling Company shipped the first wheat from this region by rail last Monday, five car-loads; and from five to eight car-loads have been shipped daily since." Also: "Charles Ballard, constable for this township, is in very poor health, and has appointed W. C. Parker his deputy."

"John Warth, of this place, has leased 1200 acres of the south-east end of the Porter ranch, seven miles below this place." And: "Samuel Nott, a fruit man of Los Gatos, was here during the present week, looking at the country; and being favorably impressed will probably purchase property in this vicinity."

Additional items of interest that readers could find in the November 5th edition were: "A. Halveson, who purchased a lot on Mission St., at the first sale, is putting up a building for a bakery and lunch stand." "Forsyth & Nichols have bought lots 1, 2 and 3, Block 77, McDonald's Addition, and will put up a blacksmith and wheelwright shop soon." "Payne & Hennessey have put up a good-sized blacksmith-shop west of the railroad, and will be ready for anything in that line of work in a week."

Readers also learned: "We have been shown the plans and specifications of Almstead's new two-story hotel, to be elected near the depot. It promises to be a creditable addition to the town." "A. Lowinger, from San Francisco, has a store-building well under way, on Mission street, which will in a few days be filled with a stock of general merchandise." "W. F. Dutton is putting up Dr. Murphy's drug-store, near the depot. The building is good size, will have a glass front, and judging from the plan, will present a neat appearance." Also: "Geo. Hopper has erected a house west of the depot."

"Considerable uneasiness is felt for W. F. Dutton, who was building Dr. Murphy's drug store. He left his tools at the building as usual last Tuesday night, since which time he has not been seen. There was nothing in his circumstances or business relations that suggests a reason for an unannounced departure. His family reside near the depot."

On November 5, 1886, readers could learn that: "W. M. Jeffreys is re-elected Justice of the Peace, and W. C. Parker Constable." Also: "Mr. A. Sittenfeld has been appointed agent for several good insurance companies, including the old reliable Hartford, and the Connecticut. Parties contemplating insuring property should call on him for a policy, as these are among the best companies doing business on the coast."

"Mr. Nott, a practical tin-smith, has purchased a lot in the McDonald Bros. Addition and has gone to San Francisco to make arrangements to lay in a stock of stoves, house-furniture, crockery, glass and tin ware. He will also have a general jobbing shop in plumbing, gas-fitting and tin-smithing."

"The yard of the Loma Prieta Lumber Co. is crowded with purchasers of building material. The company are making a great effort to meet the demands of the public. From two to four carloads are arriving at the yard daily, and is sold before it can be piled in the yard. Four car-loads of doors, sash, etc. just arrived."

On November 12, 1886, the newspaper informed its readers: "Gothard Kunz, the town-site proprietor, is putting lumber on the ground for a lodging house, on Mission Street, south of the depot." Also: "Mr. Deffner, the carpenter, has been busy this week enlarging the main room of Goldtree & Co.'s Store and putting in new shelving. This move is necessary to accommodate the large stock of new goods now on the way consigned to this house."

"The Estrella Land & Loan Co., C. F. Smith, resident agent, have nearly completed an office building on the McDonald Bros. addition." Also: "Pinkerton & Jackson have completed their slaughter yards &c, and are getting the business fairly under way."

Readers of the November 12 edition could also learn that "Mr. O. P. McFadden, from Cambria, has purchased four residence lots on the high bench west of the depot, and will soon commence the construction of a dwelling house on the same. It will probably be the first residence in that part of the town site. The location is a fine one." Also: "N. G. Millman, a practical painter and paper-hanger, arrived in town Wednesday night from San Francisco. He will open business here at once, and will put in a good stock of paints, wall-paper, building-paper &c, as soon as store rooms can be obtained." Another item in this issue of the newspaper: "Mr. Nash is commencing a store build-ing in Block 57 on the corner of L and 13 street. It will be pushed to completion as soon as possible, and immediately occupied for general merchandise."

One week later: "The Jones Bros. have a two-story frame building well under way, on the east side of the railroad track. It is intending for a boarding house." "Lee Abernethy has completed a large stable adjoining his feed yard. The establishment is styled the 'Mission Feed Yard.' He has horses and buggies to let."

"Messrs. Coy & Spencer, from Salinas, are putting up a building for saloon purposes, west of the depot. The structure is 24 x 50, and will present a neat appearance."

Readers of the paper on November 12, 1886 learned that "The Bank Exchange is a new high-toned place for liquid refreshment just opened in the new town, west of the depot, by Willis & Co. It promises to be a pleasant and lively resort for the long evenings." Also: "The foundation of Mrs. Maxwell's hotel is already laid on the plateau west of the depot."

Additional building information included the following: "There is brick at the station for the foundation of a depot building, which, we understand, will soon be commenced." And: "The Loma Prieta Lumber Company have completed an office building, near the lumber yard, in the north end of town." Also: "The Southern Pacific Milling Company's office, with the express and telegraph, has been moved to the vicinity of the new warehouse." In addition: "We call attention to the new advertisement of Goldtree & Co., appearing on another page. The firm are now receiving the largest and most complete stock of general merchandise ever brought to San Miguel. It looks as though the old firm intend to hold their place in the lead, notwithstanding the multitude of new business houses opening here."

The Inland Messenger for November 26, 1886: "Attend the Church entertainment this (Thursday) night, in Douglas' new building. Douglas' new building, to be occupied by the *Messenger*, is nearly completed, and we hope to be soon in new quarters."

"San Miguel needs a shoemaker. There is plenty of work for a mechanic in that line." "A. Lazar, from Tulare, was in town this week. He expects to open business near the depot soon. Dr. Murphy will erect a building for his use on one of his choice lots."

The Inland Messenger for November 26th informed its readers that "Material for Barry's new concrete building is being placed on the ground. F. W. Dutton is the contractor." (It will be remembered that the November 5th edition of the newspaper had reported that F. W. Dutton had made "an unannounced departure.")

"Messrs. Millman & Courter have laid in a stock of paints, oils, wall-paper and material for furnishing and decorating interiors." "Mr. J. P. Nash has his store on 14th street nearly completed, and a fine stock of merchandise may be looked for there any day."

Also in the November 26th newspaper: "A large force of men have been at work this week on the railroad depot, under the direction of Master Mechanic McKinney. The structure is to be 178 x 25 feet. The passenger department will be 46 x 25 and the freight department 132 x 25. It is the same size and substantially the same style as the depot at Kings City."

More building news: "Messrs. G. T. Darby & G. W. Thompson are putting up a building for a meat market on their lot east of the railroad depot. They expect to get under way next week."

The newspaper on November 26th also carried church news: "There will be a jubilee celebration in the Mission Church this week lasting for three days, Friday, Saturday and Sunday. Mass with an English sermon will be had on each of these days at 10:30 a.m. The pastor, Rev. Father J. Mut has engaged the Rev. Father Victor, O.S.F. to preach the Jubilee, granted by the Pope. Father Victor is a Franciscan, belonging to the same religious order as the early Fathers who established Christianity and founded the different missions on the Pacific coast. All are cordially invited to attend."

The December 3, 1886 edition of the newspaper stated that "There are upwards of forty new houses in San Miguel, including those in process of building." Also: "The frame for the railroad depot is completed, and the passenger department is enclosed. It will soon be ready to accommodate the business of the road at this point."

"The railroad depot was finished last Friday, and the mechanics moved on to Paso Robles. It is a very neat and commodious structure, belonging to the best class of buildings of the kind along the line. The paint-

ing is now in progress." [On February 13, 1979, the Southern Pacific Railroad Company demolished the depot, even though a committee of citizens had been formed to preserve the historic building.]

"J. P. Nash displays an attractive stock of staple and fancy dry goods in his new store on Thirteenth St. Parties making purchases should not fail to look in there." Also: "R. Littlefield & Co., from Santa Rosa, are putting up a good building on Mission Street to be occupied as a grocery store. It will be 22 feet front by 50 feet in length, ceiled and well finished."

"The firm Pinkerton & Jackson have completed their packing house, and expect next week to have their building for smoking and curing meat completed, when they will open that branch of the business."

"Messers. Ellis and Shackelford, directors of the Southern Pacific Milling Company, were in town last Monday, and selected a site for the flouring mill which that company will build here as soon as the season is far enough advanced so that the work can be carried on to the best advantage. The point selected is 600 feet north of the warehouse." In addition: "The store of Mrs. L. C. Browne will be moved into the new part of the town in a few days."

According to the December 3, 1886 edition of *The Inland Messenger*, "McKinney and Co. have purchased the entire stock of drugs brought down by Dr. Murphy, and have opened for business in the new store erected by the latter. This house offers to purchasers the advantage of a fresh, well-selected stock, in the hands of a skillful physician." Also: "F. S. Rogers, the dentist, arrived Monday, and is prepared to do work in the line of his profession. He is at the Jeffreys' Hotel."

Other items of news included the following: "Over 700 barrels of flour have been sold to consumers in San Miguel, in the few weeks that have elapsed since the railroad arrived." And: "E. S. Barry, the express agent, is putting up a windmill of the Althouse patent on his lot east of the depot, preparatory to the erection of his concrete office and residence."

This issue of the newspaper contained some church news: "Rev. Father Mut is repairing the enclosure to the Mission property. He is also making extensive improvement on the buildings." Additional church news in this issue: "A subscription is being circulated for funds to build a Congregational Church at this place, with very fair success." Also: "The Episcopal Society desire through the columns of the *Messenger* to express their thanks to the Misses Davis, Mrs. Ward and Miss Proctor, for their efficient services in dispensing the refreshments at the entertainment of the 25th

Stewart Clemons at depot.

Looking westward toward town of San Miguel c. 1910.

ultimo. Also to many others who rendered assistance in various ways on that occasion." And: "Messers. Reed and Phinney have fitted up and placed in operation here a machine for the manufacture of wire & picket fence."

Readers of the December 3rd edition could learn: "A side track has been laid this week to the warehouse of the Southern Pacific Milling Company, it is expected that 3,000 or 4,000 sacks of grain will be shipped next week. A considerable amount has been shipped the week past." And: "A movement is on foot to put up a building for public purposes in town. A good sized two-story structure is projected, the upper part to be used for society meetings and the first floor for public gatherings. The idea is to incorporate a company to hold and control the property, and we understand there is already stock subscription pledged sufficient to put up the building. We hope soon to be able to report the building an accomplished fact."

The December 10th edition of the paper informed its readers that "A permanent railroad bridge is being constructed over San Marcos Creek." Also: "Millman & Co., are painting the Douglas building. The front will be finished in two colors and will present a very neat appearance." And: "Samuel Nott is making a large addition to his furniture store. It will consist of a 32 foot extension on the west end, and will be roofed with corrugated iron."

Additional items in the December 10th issue: "J. M. Walsh, of the Brewery Saloon will move into his new place about Jan. 1st, 1887. In the meantime he will sell Santa Cruz Beer at wholesale and retail at the old stand." Also: "Fred'k Knights, proprietor of the San Miguel Meat Market, is putting up a building on Mission street to accommodate his business. He will probably have it ready for occupancy within a week." And: "John Hanson, engineer at the railroad pump, is

putting up a nice cottage on the plateau west of the depot."

The newspaper issued on December 17, 1886 informed its readers that "The *Messenger* moved last Friday into a new office in Douglas building, in the new part of San Miguel. In taking leave of the former place of business, we desire to express our gratitude to Goldtree & Co., who kindly made room for the *Messenger* when there was no other building in San Miguel that could be obtained as shelter for printing material. The paper has prospered while under their roof, and we are glad to know that the obliging firm retain room to carry on an immense trade, and that their prosperity is likely to long continue."

The newspaper on December 17, 1886 carried an article entitled "The Growth of San Miguel."

The rapidity with which San Miguel has been building up since the railroad commenced bringing in building material is remarkable, and still the work shows no signs of flagging. The number of business houses that three months ago was six, is now not less than thirty and all seem encouraged with the business outlook.

This growth has not been stimulated by fictitious or extravagant representations by subsidized newspapers or parties interested in the sale of town lots or farms; but on the contrary it is a legitimate, permanent growth, based upon the demands of business and the confidence which the public feel in the location and the resources of the adjacent and surrounding country from which it must derive support. There is, certainly, no town in this portion of the State that can make so favorable a showing; nor is there any that has a better prospect for the future.

"Messers. Mead, Seamans & Co., who are this week opening their store on Mission Street are young men of experience. For several years they have been with Averrett & Stephen, of Soledad, and have thus become acquainted with most of the leading men in the southern part of Monterey County and many in the northern part of San Luis Obispo county. They come highly recommended as honest business men, and we trust success will meet their efforts." Additional informational items from the December 17th edition of the newspaper: "R. R. Kirkpatrick has qualified as one of the Justices of the Peace for this Township." Also: "F. S. Rogers, the dentist, returned to his home at Gilroy, Wednesday. He will probably be here again in about two months."

Also on December 17th, readers could learn that: "G. N. Douglas is putting up a hotel building immediately south of his two-story building which was completed last week. It will be occupied as a hotel by A. G. Almstead, and the new portion of the present Almstead house will be moved and attached to the building now going up, giving ample room for the business contemplated." Also: "The Jones boarding house, on the east side of the railroad is nearly completed and is opened for meals."

Additional items in the paper on December 17, 1886: "The name of the new firm of the 'Pioneer Meat Market' was, in last issue, printed as Thompson and Rucker, whereas it should have been Thompson & Darby. Mr. Darby gives personal attention to the business." And: "Dr. Neal is erecting an office on his lot on Mission Street."

"Only a block from the depot to Meads, Seaman & Co.'s where you can buy your groceries and provisions at lowest living prices." "One of the most substantial and best finished structures in town is the building of G. Kunz, on Mission street. It is hardfinished, and in all respects a well-built house two stories in height. Mr. S. W. Smith will occupy it as a first-class restau-

Looking west on 13th Street, Methodist Church on right.

ber 17, 1886 issue of *The Inland Messenger*: "E. S. Barry has his new windmill in operation in connection with a 4,000 gallon tank and an elegant tankhouse." Also: "Mr. James Armstrong, a practical cordwainer, will open a shop in a few days adjoining the San Miguel Market." [A 'cordwainer' was a leatherworker who made things of cordovan, especially shoes.] "We are pleased to notice that members of the Grand Army of the Republic in this place and vicinity are moving in reference to the establishment of a Post here. We expect soon to see not only this but the various other fraternal societies with flourishing organizations at San Miguel."

"Attention Squad," was the lead over the following article in the December 17th newspaper.

Comrades C. E. Smith, Currier, Nott and others have been active the past few days in finding the names of the 'Boys' who wore the blue during our 'little unpleasantness,' who reside in San Miguel and vicinity.

Twenty-three have thus far been counted and many more are known to exist. A meeting will soon be called to take into consideration the advisability of establishing a Post of the Grand Army of the Republic here. Parties belonging to or qualified to become members of said society are requested to communicate with one of the parties above named.

Former city park and the Park Hotel.

rant with a few bedrooms up stairs. It will probably be opened by the last of next week."

"Dr. Murphy is erecting three new buildings on his block near the depot. We understand two of these are already engaged for business." And: "Mr. J. A. Richards, a mechanic from Gilroy, is putting up a blacksmith shop on Mr. Blake's lot west of the depot. It will probably be completed next week." Also: "Charles Maxwell's new hotel, the St. Michael, is opened to the public. It is in a sightless and pleasant location and the management is so well and favorably known as to need no recommendation."

Other items that readers could see in the Decem-

"Call for Meeting of Citizens," was the lead for a December 17th notice.

The undersigned request the citizens of San Miguel and vicinity to meet at Douglas' new building in San Miguel at 2 o'clock p.m.,

Saturday, December 18th, . . .to consider the best means of improving the streets, roads and bridges in San Miguel and vicinity.

Walter M. Jeffreys
Goldtree & Co.
Mut
Davis Bros.
Chas. E. Smith

The newspaper on December 17th also carried these items: "Rev. S. G. Blanchard, Presiding Elder of the M. E. Church for this (Santa Barbara) district, was in town last Saturday, in company with Mr. Gordenier, of Estrella." And: "The Congregational Society are making arrangements for a Christmas tree for the Sabbath School. The exercises will be held in the schoolhouse, and the public are invited."

"Roads and Bridges," was the heading for an article in the December 24, 1886 edition of *The Inland Messenger*.

Though the attendance at last Saturday's meeting on the subject of roads, bridges, etc., was too small to justify the taking of any action, it is quite evident that there is an awakening of our citizens on this subject, and we hope to see the matter agitated till a better condition of things is reached. In view of the probability of rain at an early day some work ought to be done on the streets of our young city.

Mission street is so level that unless some work is done, both the road and side walk will, in case of rain, become very wet. There is business to be done with reference to the roads. For example, the main thoroughfare leading into town from the north is not a County road this side of the county line. Last Summer there were two or three gates, or bars, to open and shut between the present town and the river crossing, and unless some action is taken to have said road officially laid out, the same state of affairs is liable to exist next Spring.

The subject of bridging the Salinas river at this point is one that may well come in for a share of attention, as there is, and will continue to be, an urgent and growing demand for that improvement till it is consummated. San Miguel is, and must always remain, by far the most considerable town to which the people of Estrella and other valleys lying eastward have access. It is here they will make

their purchases and dispose of the various products of their farms. The necessity for a bridge is too apparent to require argument, and its construction will be urged till it is accomplished.

There are many other matters bearing on this subject that could be profitably discussed by our people, and ways and means of improvement suggested. There is nothing like free discussion and interchange of thought to facilitate such improvement.

The December 24th edition of the newspaper carried several interesting items. "Mrs. L. C. Browne's store was this week moved up to the new town, and is now located in Douglas' block, on Mission street." And: "Dr. Neal has completed his new office at the corner of 11th and Mission streets, where he will hereafter be pleased to meet those who need his services." Also: "The San Miguel Meat Market, Fred Knights proprietor, was moved Tuesday to a new building on Mission St., where the public will find first class provisions and polite attention."

Readers of the December 24th newspaper learned that "The new part of town now contains six wells the average depth of which, being only 46 feet. There is an abundance of water in each well and the quality is unsurpassed. New contracts for additional wells are being made."

Also: "The sound of saw and hammer is still the prevailing music in San Miguel." And: "Mr. M. H. Lawson is putting up a building on his lot west of the depot; it is already leased by Keeler & Bullock and will be occupied as a saloon. M. H. Lawson, assistant agent for the Railroad Company at this place, has been called to Kings City to take charge of that office during the temporary absence of the agent at that place." And: "The firm of Meads, Seaman & Co. have, within the past week, opened out a superior stock of groceries and general merchandise in their new store on Mission street. Go and make their acquaintance and you will not regret it."

Other December 24th items included the following: "Now that the business houses of our town are well underway, we shall soon see that splendid plateau, in the western part of town, covered with residences. For convenience of access, view, drainage and everything that makes a location desirable, it is unsurpassed." Railroad news was that "A force of mechanics have been at work this week constructing a railroad bridge across Bridge creek one-half mile above town." Church news, printed on December 24th: "There will be Christ-

San Miguel from the hill, 1889.

mas services in the Episcopal church in this place, by Rev. J. S. Magowan, to-morrow, Saturday, at eleven o'clock a.m. All are invited."

On December 31, 1886, *The Inland Messenger*, printed an article entitled, "The Bridge Question."

No one will deny that there exists an urgent necessity for a bridge across the Salinas river at this point. It is not a vital matter in the growth of San Miguel, or in the development of the resources of the country adjacent, but is a matter greatly affecting the convenience of the residents of a wide scope of country lying to the eastward. Nature has by irrevocable decree designated San Miguel as the business center of these farmers; their homes are established there, and intercommunication between the town and country will become more necessary and frequent as time passes.

It is the duty of citizens to co-operate with the public officers in improvising the thoroughfares, establishing brides and opening roads. Nothing has thus far been done to call attention to the wants of the public in this particular. No examination has been made of
the river with reference to the construction of a bridge; no man is prepared to give an intelligent answer as to the practicability of erecting a bridge at any particular crossing, or as to the probable cost of one if found practicable. While it is conceded that there are no engineering difficulties in the way of a bridge, steps should be taken to have an estimate made of the minimum cost of such a structure, preliminary to more definite action.

Would it not be well for our people to hold a meeting, and appoint a committee to get an estimate from competent engineers of the probable cost of this improvement.

The December 31, 1886 issue of the paper stated that "San Miguel is attracting trade from all parts of the upper Salinas Valley. Purchasers prefer coming here to buy on account of the number of our business houses and the variety and excellence of the stocks of goods carried by our merchants."

"During the Christmas tree exercises last Friday evening, Mr. Wells informed the audience that Dr. McLane's church in Oakland (the First Congregational) have purchased and presented to the First Congregational Church of San Miguel an organ. It would have been here last week, but it was shipped by mistake to San Luis, and will probably be brought over this week by Mr. Nelson."

"Three new buildings in Murphy's block are nearing completing. Richard's new blacksmith shop on Mission street is open for business. The furniture shop of Binley & McElroy, in the southern part of town, has opened for business." And: "Mr. O. P. McFadden's new residence is completed, and it ranks, for the present, as the best private dwelling in San Miguel."

Oliver Perry McFaddin was born in Marion County, Alabama, in 1827. His parents were William H. McFaddin and Catherine B. Holloway. In the early 1800s the McFaddins moved their family of eight children and numerous slaves to Itawamba County, Mississippi, where they prospered raising cotton.

In 1849, after a stint in the U. S. Army during the Mexican War, Oliver Perry left his home in Mississippi, and set out for the gold fields of California. He prospected in Mariposa County, near Yosemite. After a time he either became disenchanted with mining, or ran out of money; he enlisted in the army again, to fight Indians in Mariposa and Shasta Counties. The McFaddin relatives in Mississippi say that O. P. only sent home one postcard to reassure his mother of his well-being. The card said, "O. P. O. K." Court records in Itawamba County show that they did hear from him again, at least once. In 1872, he filed a protest against the manner in which his brothers settled his father's estate. The McFaddins in Mississippi had suffered greatly during the Civil War. They probably felt that O. P. had not earned the right to share in the family property.

In 1858, Oliver P. McFaddin, who was then about 31 years old, married Victoria Jane Bland, a lass of sixteen; they lived near "Hot Springs," in the area of Paso Robles. Her father, John Bland, was another southerner who came to California looking for gold; he brought his family across the plains in 1849. Victoria Jane was then seven years old. After spending some time in the mines, John turned his attention to agriculture, and settled in the Paso Robles area. A family tradition says that when the Blands arrived in San Miguel, they had to stay within the confines of the Mission for a period of time; a group of white settlers had recently been killed by some Indians. Victoria Jane told her grandchildren this story many times in her later years.

Oliver P. McFaddin, in the 1860 census, was enumerated as working as a mason. In 1865, the family moved to Cambria, where they farmed a section of land, raising apples and dairy cattle. They also raised hogs, which were fed with huge Pismo clams dug with a plow on the nearby beaches.

As noted above, O. P. McFaddin built a home in San Miguel in 1886; they extended their farming to the Estrella area. O. P. was very active in public affairs. During the years 1860 through 1862, he served a supervisor of San Luis Obispo County. A dedicated member of the Masonic order, he was a charter member of the San Simeon Lodge No. 148, and later a member of the San Miguel Lodge No. 285. He was elected to the school board in San Miguel; he served as vice-president of the Agricultural Society.

The children of O. P. and Victoria Jane McFaddin were Hadden, Yancy, Higgins, Edwin, Lewis and Mary Elizabeth (Mollie).

O. P. McFaddin died in 1892, and is buried in the San Miguel Cemetery. All of the McFaddin boys eventually married and settled in the San Miguel area. The terrible drought of 1898 must have taken its toll on the McFaddins. In the 1900 census, Victoria Jane and her 17-year-old daughter, Mollie, are recorded as living alone; Victoria lists farming as her occupation. Higgins lived nearby; Hadden moved to Arizona, and ran a stock ranch in Pima County, and Edwin worked in the copper mines near Bisby, Arizona. Lewis died at an early age; the details are not known. Yancy McFaddin would become sheriff of San Luis Obispo County in 1906.

Other items from the December 31, 1886 edition of the paper: "Pipe has been laid from the railroad tank to Mr. Barry's lot, to furnish the water required in the construction of the concrete building which he is erecting." "G. Kunz' new building is so far completed as to be opened by S. W. Smith. The house is a very substantial structure and well finished. The carpenter work was superintended by W. F. Baron, and Millman & Co., did the painting, paperhanging and decorating."

The Inland Messenger of January 7, 1887 carried this item: "It was Smith & Daves who did the painting on Kunz' new building, not Millman & Co., as stated in our last issue. We are glad to make this correction and give credit to parties to whom it belongs." Also: "Mr. G. W. Miles, of San Luis, has leased Kunz' new building and has opened it as a hotel and restaurant. We are glad to welcome such men as Mr. Miles to San Miguel, and hope his business venture may prove entirely satisfactory."

"A large addition is being made to the rear portion of Mrs. Browne's store. The store room will be enlarged and rooms added for household purposes." Also: "Payne & Hennesey, at the new blacksmith shop, east of the depot have opened for business and are doing a great deal of work. They are thorough mechanics & guarantee satisfaction to their patrons." The first issue for 1887 also had this item: "We call attention to the advertisement of the German Restaurant appearing in another column. It will be found a good place to get a 'square meal.'

GERMAN RESTAURANT
M. Pfau, Prop.
Mission Street, near the Depot.
Meals at all hours.
Tables always supplied with the best the market affords.
A share of patronage solicited.

"A dance was given New Years' Eve by the San Miguel String Band, which was well attended and passed off very pleasantly, as all occasions do under their management. The dancing took place in Douglas' new hall, and a splendid supper was served at the Jeffreys' Hotel."

Items in the newspaper for January 14, 1887 included: "Victor H. Woods, the surveyor, has opened an office in a room in Dr. Murphy's block, where he may be found when not engaged in field work." Also: "Mr. H. W. Jones, from Santa Maria, has opened business as watchmaker & jeweler at the store of Phelps & Stephens, on Mission street." Also: "Dr. Neal is fencing his office lot on Mission street, an example that would be well for others of our townsmen to follow." And: "Binkley & McElroy, of this place, are manufacturing mattresses and other articles of furniture & shipping to other points along the line."

"Jacob Deffner has received the appointment to the office of Constable in this township, and will immediately enter upon the duties." And: "A. G. Almstead & A. R. Brooks have the contract for moving the new part of the Almstead House down to Douglas' block in the new town where it will form a part of a hotel building that is in process of construction."

The January 14th issue printed several interesting items of information. "Last Monday morning a difficulty occurred between the Chinese cook and a waiter at the Jones hotel, in which John was somewhat worsted. Afterward the Chinaman armed himself with a large knife and attacked the waiter and but for the interference of a bystander might have inflicted serious injuries. The proprietor, W. H. Jones, at once discharged the Chinaman and will hereafter employ white help only."

Another item of interest in that issue: "A resident of San Miguel has a thoroughbred bird dog that will eagerly devour tarantulas. He appears to consider the creatures a great delicacy, as he hunts for them, and when found gulps them down with apparent avidity, and the diet appears to agree with him." [Later, in the October 28, 1887 edition of the *San Miguel Messenger*, readers would learn about a "Cure for Tarantula Bite." That edition of the paper stated, "The Gilroy *Advocate* says: A son of Neal O'Brien, of Sargent's dairy, was nipped on the arm in four places by a large tarantula on Sunday morning last. A turkey was at once killed and ripped open and the boy's wounded arm placed into its warm body. The boy was dosed with whisky and brought to town for medical treatment. Another application of raw flesh followed and the venom of the poison extracted. The boy is now well. The prompt action of his father doubtless saved his life."]

"Mr. Hildebrand, formerly of Hollister, has purchased two lots in the northern part of town and is putting up buildings for soda water business. He has a complete outfit and will probably be ready for business within a week. The locality is undoubtedly a good point from which to furnish other places both north

McCutchens and Gorhams in front of San Miguel store.

and south, and we have no doubt Mr. Hildebrand will be able to make the business successful."

"W. F. Dutton is putting up a substantial building on his lot in the northern part of town." Also: "A well is being sunk on the edge of Mission street at the corner of M. H. Lawson's lot, occupied by Keeler & Bullock." And: "James Walsh moved into his new place of business in Dr. Murphy's block last Friday." In addition: "Messrs. Massey & Carrell will immediately commence drilling a well for G. N. Douglas in the rear of the new building occupied by *The Inland Messenger*."

The January 21, 1887 edition of the newspaper informed its readers that "McKinney & Co., of the 'City Drug Store,' have hoisted a nice new sign on their front." And: "To Willis & Co., of the Bank Exchange, belong the honor of putting up the first public watering trough in San Miguel." Also: "Mr. Harris has closed his hotel and is removing his buildings from the railroad reservation to his lots on the hill in the western part of town, where he will rebuild for a residence."

The people in the "new" town of San Miguel also had professional entertainment. The January 21, 1887 issue of the paper announced that "The Boulon & McGinley Musical Specialty and Comedy Co., the California favorites, will appear for one night only at Douglas' Hall, Mission street, on Monday evenings."

The readers on January 28th learned that "Almstead & Brooks last week fulfilled their contract for the removal of a part of the Almstead hotel to Douglas' block in the new town. A. G. Almstead has commenced the construction of a livery, feed and sale stable on Mission street, west of the warehouse. The structure will be fifty feet square and the central part two stories high." And: "A number of members of the Masonic fraternity, residents of San Miguel and vicinity, have taken the preliminary steps for the organization of a lodge of that society. The new organization will probably be able to open with between twenty and thirty members."

"Mr. J. O. Johnson, of Pacific Grove, whose presence in our city was mentioned in the last issue of the *Messenger*, was so favorably impressed with the place that he purchased three lots east of the depot, and will immediately put up a building which will be occupied by another party for a bakery." And: "We understand that the lumber for the building to be erected by Mr. J. O. Johnson, east of the railroad track, will be gotten out in San Francisco and shipped here ready to be put up."

The newspaper on January 28, 1887 also informed readers that "Steps are being taken looking to the organization of a post of the Grand Army of the Republic here. Persons qualified to become charter members are requested to call at Nott's store in San Miguel." Also: "Some enterprising capitalist should establish the banking business in San Miguel. The town presents a good opening for a permanent and growing business in that line." And: "Mr. John P. Courter, of this place, has accepted the agency for the Pajaro nursery, and is prepared to furnish fruit and ornamental trees of the first quality. Our people who are planting orchards or beautifying their homes may find it to their advantage to see him."

"We call attention to the advertisement of Meads, Seaman & Co., whose store is located on Mission street near the center of town. These young men propose dealing only in first class goods and selling on the most favorable terms that the market will justify, to establish a business that will be permanent, and mutually satisfactory to them and their customers." Also: "The advertisement of Mr. J. A. Richards the blacksmith, appears in this issue. Mr. Richards is a young man, a thorough mechanic, and a worthy citizen. We bespeak for him a fair share of the current business."

January 28th readers also learned that "Mr. C. H. Reed, who has been figuring on a lot for a store building, has purchased two lots in the fractional block lying between Mission street and the railroad track. They are located nearly in front of the Douglas block. Mr. Reed expects to put up a substantial building and he has chosen a good location."

The Inland Messenger for February 4, 1887 presented its readers with the following news: "Within another week Mr. Golden will open a bakery and restaurant in his new building next door to Ayers' store. He will serve customers at their homes." Also: "Almstead's new livery and feed stable is opened for business."

Three other items recording the progress of the town's development were: "Mr. Wm. Clark, of San Jose, is having a dwelling house and feed stable erected on his lots in the northern part of town. It is understood that the business will be in the charge of the sons of Mr. Clark." And: "Joseph Cramer, an old resident of Monterey, a saddle & harness maker by trade, and said to be a first class workman, has purchased a lot east of the railroad, and in about two weeks expects to put up a building for a shop and open business." Also: "E. J. Munsch, formerly of Monterey, a house, sign and carriage painter, has purchased a lot on the east side of the depot near Abernethy's feed yard, and will soon build a shop to accommodate his business."

"The price of town lots in San Miguel," according

to the February 11, 1887 edition of the newspaper, "now range about 100 percent above the figures at which they opened last October." Also: "The 'Gem Saloon,' kept by James Walsh, is represented among our new advertisements to-day. The proprietor professes to keep an orderly and first class place in this line."

The February 11, 1887 edition of *The Inland Messenger* also informed its readers that "The condition of our streets during the past week has forcibly suggested the necessity of sidewalks and of a better system of drainage for the streets. There is very little doubt that if we should chance to be visited by a protracted and heavy rain the streets in their present condition would become temporarily impassable for either teams or pedestrians."

"FORWARD, GUIDE CENTER! A business meeting G. A. R. will be held at the office of Capt. Currier, on Wednesday, 16th, with reference to the election of officers and acceptance of charter. Comrades will please present discharge papers. Samuel Nott, Mustering Officer, San Miguel, Feb. 10th 1887."

"The Masonic Fraternity have leased Douglas' Hall for lodge purposes, and it will be finished and fitted up with express reference to society uses. The floor is to be deadened, the stairs extended to near the rear of the building and other changes made." February 11th readers also learned that "A. G. Almstead will take charge of the hotel building in Douglas' block, and open it to the public next week. It will be styled the 'Arlington Hotel,' and will be kept in good style." Also: "Meads, Seaman & Co. have become the agents for Grover & Co., of Santa Cruz, for the sale of lumber, and are stocking a yard east of the track with a general assortment of sawed and split lumber." And: "Mr. G. N. Douglas will soon commence a large blacksmith shop, in the southern part of town, to be occupied by Forsyth & Nichols. This enterprising firm are determined to keep up with the times."

"*San Miguel Messenger* Vol. 2, No. 1, April 29, 1887 'Our New Volume.' With this issue the *Messenger* enters upon its second volume, and we celebrate the anniversary by an increase in the size of the paper. We now furnish our readers with a larger amount of reading matter than is customary with country newspapers, and hope to make the quality of its contents acceptable to all who feel an interest in the progress of improvement in San Miguel and the upper Salinas Valley."

"The *Messenger* was started one year ago without a town, relying upon the certain development of a wide extent of productive country. . . ." That certain development was taking place in the 'new' town of San Miguel is evident by the following items in the April 29th edition of the newspaper: "C. J. Jacobs, agent for the Singer Sewing machine has established himself here and has an office in McElroy's Furniture store, next to the Postoffice." Also: "L. B. Gardener, a watch maker and jeweler from Santa Rosa, arrived Tuesday and has made arrangements to open a shop for business in Barry's concrete building." In addition: "We notice that R. Littlefield & Co., keep the best assortment of Tobacco and the finest Cigars in San Miguel, fact." And: "Ladies should go to E. V. Methever for May-day Slippers and Shoes."

The April 29th edition also had the following information: "A. Halverson has moved his restaurant building back and is putting up a good building 24 by 40 feet in size, to be used as a hall, and when necessary as an addition to his dining room. A hall of this kind is a thing much needed in town at present." And: "Mr. G. N. Douglas is making an addition to the rear portion of the Arlington Hotel." Also: "Goldtree & Co.'s store was placed in its new location Monday, and the force of clerks are busy re-arranging the stock & opening new goods . . ." In addition: "Residents and property own-

Early street scene in San Miguel.

ers on L Street are doing a good work in grading the street from Mission to the bench."

Readers of the April 29th newspapers learned that "A party of laborers constructing a fence each side of the railroad have reached this point, working southward. The fence is quite substantial, consisting of three barbed wires and one board, will be supported by redwood posts." On a different subject: "If you want good soda water, call at the San Miguel Soda Works." And: "For first class Sarsaparilla, call at the San Miguel Soda Works."

According to the April 29th paper: "The Loma Prieta lumber yard and stock at this place has been transferred to the Southern Pacific Milling Company. Messers. S. P. Ellis and R. M. Shackelford have been engaged some days this week in ascertaining the stock on hand and perfecting transfer. The new proprietors of the business propose to keep a very complete stock of lumber and to make many improvements in the yard."

In the April 29, 1887 issue of the *San Miguel Messenger:*

E. S. Barry General News Depot,
Dealer in cigars, tobacco,
smoker's articles, stationery,
school books, cutlery, etc.
Agent for Wells, Fargo & Co.'s Express,
and Parkfield Stage.
General Insurance Agent.
The Latest Newspapers and Novels
always on hand.
Money loaned on Growing Crops and
Grain in Warehouse.

Items of interest from the May 6, 1887 issue of the paper: "George S. Davis sold his lot adjoining McElroy's furniture store to the latter named gentleman." Also: "Meads, Seaman & Co. are putting up a shed in the rear of their store to shelter their stock of plows, mowers, rakes and other farm machinery." Readers also learned that "The Southern Pacific Milling Company is making an extension of 50 feet on the north end of their large warehouse. This addition is required to store agricultural machinery, a large stock of which the company will soon introduce."

The May 6th paper also announced that "The regular meeting of Gen. Buford Post G. A. R. will take place next Saturday, the 7th inst., at 3 o'clock p.m." [G.A.R. refers to the Grand Army of the Republic, and was an organization of veterans of the Union army.] "Halverson's hall will be free for the use of private social parties."

Readers of the May 6th edition also learned that "A carload of the machinery formerly in use in the Los Gatos flouring mill, which has been dismantled by the Central Milling Company, arrived here this week and will be stored till the mill is erected here, when it will be utilized." Also: "Mr. Jeffreys is having two cellars dug on the new site for his hotel. The buildings will be entirely remodeled and while corresponding with the general plan of the old ones, will be greatly improved in both capacity and convenience." In addition: "C. H. Reed & Co. have completed the transfer of their stock of hardware from their old place and the arrangement of their goods in the new store on Mission street. A better stock of hardware, or more neatly displayed cannot be found in the county."

The *San Miguel Messenger* on May 13, 1887 stated that "The most noticeable feature of improvement in the town during the past week is the moving of Jeffreys' hotel buildings, which was well and expeditiously accomplished under the direction of carpenter A. T. Barlow. The establishment gives the southern part of town an increased air of business."

More signs of progress were mentioned in the May 13th edition. "The Western Union Telegraph Co. are taking down the old line of poles between Soledad and this place, and the old poles will be sold. Parties desiring further information on the subject should apply to Mr. J. L. Morrison, who is in charge of the work." Two more signs of progress: "Mr. W. B. Overton has opened a barber shop in Murphy's block, Mission street." And: "A stable has been put up on the rear portion of the Murphy block during the week." Also: "George S. Davis is erecting a dwelling house on L Street."

Other news items from the May 13th paper included: "Mr. A. R. Brooks has moved 225 cubic yards of earth in the improvement of 13th street, near the postoffice." Also: "Mr. R. R. Durham has taken sole charge of the Mission Feed and Livery Stable and is prepared to accommodate the public in that line."

Residents of the area who were interested in having a bank in San Miguel could get encouragement from the followings item in the May 13th edition. "J. D. Carr and A. B. Jackson, of Salinas and Thos. Rea and J. W. Wood, of Gilroy, all men of means, were in town this week looking over the country with C. E. Smith with the view of starting a bank in San Miguel, if they thought the country would justify them in doing so. They expressed themselves as well pleased and said they found a better country and better crops then they expected. A banking house established by such men would command the full confidence of the public, which is necessary to success. We hope to be able to report a favorable decision on the question at an early day."

Fraternal news, on May 13th: "The first regular communication of San Miguel Lodge of American Free and Accepted Masons was held at the hall of the society last Sat., at which the organization of the lodge was perfected. . . .The regular meetings will be held each Sat. evening on and after the full moon. The lodge has opened with a fine prospect of growing into a strong and prosperous organization." Church news, for May 13th was that "The Rev. Mr. Tubb, of Martinez, Cal., it is expected, will be in San Miguel next week, and will hold a series of meetings in the new Congregational Church. Services will begin Wednesday eve., the 18th, and preaching every evening following for a week and more. . . .E. B. Tuthill, Pastor."

Another item in the May 13, 1887 issue of the newspaper: "A Paso Robles dispatch says; J. C. Roberts, a colored gentleman from North Carolina, is here looking at the country with a view to bringing a colony of colored people to this county to locate. He says he is much pleased with the looks of this section." Also: "It will be observed that the Davis Bros. have christened their new saloon the "Palace.""

On May 20th, the *Messenger* informed its readers that "Mr. G. N. Douglas has decided to erect a neat cottage on his lots near C. E. Smith's, in Mc Donald's addition, to be occupied by F. Winchel, of C. H. Reed & Co. The work will commence as soon as practicable, under the direction of J. M. Phinney." Also: "The family of Mr. John P. Courter arrived the latter part of last week, and are duly installed in their new residence in the northern part of town, which has been tastefully furnished for their reception."

As an indication that educational entertainment for the general population was available, the May 20th paper announced that "Prof. Owens lectures on phrenology and mesmerism, at Linck's Hall, Thursday and Friday evenings of this week. First evening free." Readers of the paper on May 20th were able to learn that "The hotel property known as Miles House on Mission street has changed hands. Mr. Geo. S. Davis, a gentleman who has had years of experience in the hotel business, has taken charge. We have no doubt that it will be a well-kept and popular house under Mr. Davis' management."

The paper, on May 20, 1887, printed an article entitled, "Narrow Escape."

What came near being a serious accident occurred on our streets last Monday. Mrs. G. W. Proctor, accompanied by her grandson, Johnnie Davis, was driving along Mission street in a cart, when the horse took fright at a paper carried near him by the wind and ran away.

On turning in to 13th street, one wheel of the cart collapsed, and the occupants were thrown to the ground with great violence, and the lady narrowly escaped being kicked and trampled upon by the excited animal. She was picked up in an unconscious condition and taken to the residence of Geo. Davis, where Dr. Cain, who was at hand furnished such medical assistance as the case required.

It was ascertained that though stunned and much bruised, no bones were broken, and it is hoped that nothing more serious than the prostration caused by the nervous shock has resulted. The boy escaped with comparatively slight bruises.

The horse returned to Mission street, and ran as far a the fence of Davis Bros., below town, and the cart was badly wrecked.

The May 27, 1887 issue noted that "W. C. Parker has disposed of his barber shop and business to Oscar Sittenfeld, who is an accomplished artist in that line." Also: "The hotel formerly known as the Miles House has assumed the name of 'Commercial' and a large sign bearing that name is displayed in the fore rigging." And: "F. G. Brunskill has taken the position vacated by Mr. Black, of bookkeeper at the Southern Pacific Milling Co.'s lumber yard."

The *San Miguel Messenger* of June 3, 1887 related more signs of progress. "Mr. C. W. Jones has purchased a lot adjoining McElroy's furniture store on 13th street, and will proceed to erect a large building thereon. The dimensions of the structure will be about 28 feet front by 90 deep. The front will be partitioned for two stores and the rear 70 feet will be furnished and used as a hall, which will have an entrance from the front." In addition: "E. V. Methever is moving his shoe store to his lot between Phelps and Stephens' store and Richards' blacksmith shop. The location is a very eligible one for business."

An item which could be considered scientific appeared in the June 3rd edition: "F. L. Mennett, the surveyor, brought into town recently two petrifactions found in the McClure, or Cottonwood valley, in the extreme north-western part of Kern county. They appear to be two sections of the vertebra of a small size whale."

The paper on June 10, 1887 informed its readers that "Some of our business men have signed an agreement to pay a sum monthly toward employing a night-watchman and it is probable that, with the co-operation of the S. P. Milling company and the Railroad company a sufficient amount will be assured to justify a reliable man in undertaking the business. Mr. J. M. Smith, who has had considerable experience in that line, is the party now in view for the situation."

Other items in the June 10th edition of the newspaper: "First class board for $1.00 per day, at the Commercial Hotel." "Meals equal to any in San Miguel at the Commercial Hotel for 25 cents. The Commercial Hotel is being improved by the addition of a broad porch." And: "The best meals in town for 25 cents, at Golden's Bakery & Restaurant, east of the railroad track."

Also from the June 10th newspaper: "Millman & Co. are doing some excellent work on the interior of the Jeffreys' Hotel." And: "C. W. Jones has gone to Santa Cruz to purchase lumber for his new hall adjoining McElroy's furniture store. It is expected that the building will be ready for occupancy by the Fourth of July."

"The people of San Miguel are shipping wheat to San Francisco and importing flour from Portland, Oregon. Why is this thus?"

The following week, on June 17, 1887, the *San Miguel Messenger* had this church news: "A new pastor is expected for the Episcopal Church here. Rev. Macgowan's time will hereafter be employed in his work at Jolon, Kings City and San Lucas."

Other items: "E. V. Methever is making an addition to his store building." "For a good hand-made saddle, or set of harness, go to Cramer's shop, east of the depot." And: "The Palace Saloon has been painted in first class style, and now presents a very neat front to Mission street."

There were two items concerning a growing business: "C. H. Reed & Co. are raising the street in front of their store to a level conforming to adjacent improvements." "C. H. Reed & Co. have enclosed and added a square front to their large wareroom, giving their house a 50 foot frontage on Mission street."

Also in the June 17th edition of the paper: "We call attention to the advertisement of J. Cramer, dealer in, and manufacturer of harness, saddles etc. Mr. Cramer is an experienced and first-class workman, having been in the business twenty-five years. He is from Monterey, where his old customers speak well of his work. When in need of anything in that line, call at his place of business east of the depot."

From the June 24, 1887 edition of the newspaper, one could learn that "One of the large windows in the front of McKinney's Drug Store was mashed in by some evil disposed person last Saturday night. The proprietor has not been able to find out who did the mischief, but he found a man who was so sorry to learn that it had been broken that he paid for the repairs."

Also: "The office of the Southern Pacific Milling Company has been moved to a point north of the warehouse, and is being enlarged." And: "A. Halverson, of the Linck Hall and restaurant, gives notice that there will be a dance in the Linck Hall on the night of the Fourth of July. The best of music has been engaged for the occasion." And: "Chas. W. Jones returned from the north Tuesday, and has commenced work in earnest on his large hall building on 13th street."

The June 24th issue carried the following story.

Officer Frank Grady, of San Luis Obispo, appeared here last Monday in search of Chinaman Jim, charged with having entered a room and stealing goods therefrom. He was found in a Chinahouse east of the railroad track, but as Mr. Grady entered the front door Mr. Jim skipped out in the rear and ran. The officer ordered him to stop, which he failed to do, and two or three shots from Grady's revolver only added to his speed. The fleeing fugitive directed his course toward the river, hotly pursued by the officers and one or two assistants. The day was warm and the Chinaman wilted and surrendered before they had gone 100 rods. He was handcuffed and taken south in a carriage. He will doubtless get justice in Judge Gregory's court.

The *San Miguel Messenger*, on July 1, 1887, carried a story with a simple title: "The Jeffreys Hotel."

The work of moving and rebuilding, painting and decorating the Jeffreys Hotel was completed last week, and the house is now one of the leading features of our town. It presents a frontage of 100 feet with a broad veranda extending the whole length, giving it an attractive and home like appearance. The interior has been remodeled, increasing the capacity and adding greatly to the convenience of the house. The dining room is well ventilated, has a high ceiling, and in the matter of finish and decoration is notably not surpassed by anything in San Luis Obispo county. From the dining room and office all the rooms are accessible by a broad, well lighted and tastefully furnished hall, which also communicates with the bath. There is also a large and commodious sample room for the use of commercial travelers. The house has been to a great extent refurnished, and it is not too much to say that the public will find it one of the best locations on this division of the Southern Pacific Railroad.

Other items in the July 1st issue of the newspaper: "J. P. Nash is preparing to put a building 24 x 40 feet in size, on the northeast corner of 'L' and 13th streets, next to his dry goods store. The building will be occupied as a grocery store."

"A body of mechanics in the employ of the Railroad Company arrived here the latter part of last week, and immediately commenced the construction of an ice house for the railroad. It is located near the depot, and appears to be a very substantial structure. It will doubtless be depended upon to store the ice required for the Lerdo branch as well as the main coast line. The nearest house of the kind north is at the Castroville junction."

The following week, items in the paper included the following: "Mr. Nash's buildings are now supplied with water piped from Dr. Murphy's tank." And: "Nash's new building, corner 'L' and 13th streets, is under way. It will be occupied by a Mr. Reed as a grocery store." Also: "The Davis brothers' saloon, Goldtree & Co.'s and Reed and Co.'s stores are supplied with water piped from Jeffreys' tank." Finally: "Mr. Felton Taylor, from Oakland, has taken charge of the books of the Southern Pacific Milling Company, at this place."

Also found in the newspaper for July 8, 1887: "Miss Jessie Kirk, whose advertisement as teacher of drawing and painting appears in this issue, has secured a pleasant room in the Douglas block on Mission street, and will organize her class next Thursday at 10 o'clock a.m." And: "Next Monday, the 11th instant, at 11 o'clock, Constable Deffner will sell at public auction, in front of the City Drug Store, one barrel of wine, formerly the property of George Hopper." Also: "Dr. Neal has material on the ground for a large addition to his office building on Mission street." And: "C. W. Jones has decided to add ten feet to the north end of his new hall building, to be devoted to a stage." Finally: "Mr. John Reed, who is to occupy Nash's new building, has been in San Francisco purchasing a stock of goods. The store will probably be ready for occupancy next week."

The July 8th edition of the newspaper reported an article that had been published in another paper.

The San Luis *Mirror* gives San Miguel the following notice in its special descriptive edition of the 30th ultimo: 'The first town in the northern part of the county on the railroad is San Miguel, named after the old Mission by that name situated in the town; with the railroad came enterprise and business; new houses sprang up, settlers arrived, and San Miguel is now an active place of some three hundred inhabitants; it receives support from a fine agricultural district, and will be the center of a large farming community.'
According to the July 8th edition of the *San Miguel*

Messenger, "One lamentable want of San Miguel is a first class picnic ground, near the town."

Readers of the July 15, 1887 issue were able to receive information concerning their doctors: "Dr. Neal has material on the ground for a large addition to his office building on Mission street." And: "Dr. J. H. Cain, who has been located in this place for more than a year and a half, will leave next Saturday to take charge of a drug store and practice his profession in Tustin City, Los Angeles county; his family will remain for the present." Other items of news in the July 15th paper were: "Mr. E. S. Barry has decided to introduce a stock of first-class groceries, which will be sold for cash and at the lowest possible figures. His concrete building is well adapted by location and otherwise for the business." And: "The ladies of San Miguel have determined upon and are preparing for a social and entertainment to be given in Jones' Hall (to be known hereafter as Central Hall) on or about the 29th instant, for the benefit of the Congregational Church. The program will appear in the next issue of the *Messenger*, with definite announcement as to time."

The *San Miguel Messenger* for July 22, 1887 published an exciting article.

H. R. Mallory, our gentlemanly deputy postmaster, had a rather narrow escape last Sunday. Having hitched up his team for a drive, with Mr. J. Reed as a passenger, started up the hill toward the Maxwell House, when the horses becoming frightened, or being naturally headstrong, turned and partly capsized the buggy. Both gentlemen reached the ground safely, and the team started off at a rapid gait. Mr. Mallory, in his efforts to stop the horse, became entangled in the gearing and was dragged some distance, but fortunately escaped without serious injury. The team ran down to the river and stopped, and though the buggy was dragged bottom up part of the way, it was but little damaged.

Readers of the paper for that date also learned that "Mr. J. M. Smith has secured a sum that he thinks will justify him in acting as night-watchman in San Miguel, and has already entered upon the duties of the position. Mr. Smith has the reputation and appearance of a trustworthy and reliable man, and his presence on our streets at night adds much to the security of property in town." Also: "Mr. Thiriet, who is a thorough watchmaker and jeweler by trade, will open a shop for that branch of business, in about two weeks, in Goldtree & Co.'s store."

Occidental Hotel on north side of 13th Street, with most of the town's citizens.

"Bridging the Salinas River" was the title of a lengthy article in the July 29th newspaper.

C. H. Phillips, manager of the West Coast Land Company, the center of whose operations land interests is the town of Templeton, was the first man in San Luis Obispo county to conspicuously urge the immediate building of a bridge across the Salinas river.

He advanced the idea as being not only a public convenience, but also an assistance in promoting sales of the lands of the West Coast Land Company lying in that vicinity and lots in the town of Templeton. Blackburn Brothers and James, owners of valuable Paso Robles property, not to be outdone in enterprise by a rival locality, came forward with a similar demand for Paso Robles, and the combined influence of the two points succeeded in prevailing upon the Board of Supervisors to submit the question of raising the necessary funds for two bridges by a tax upon the property of the road district. The proposition was voted down by a large majority.

Having failed to secure the desired object, the same business foresight that was instrumental in bringing the project before the public, dictated the building of said bridges as a private enterprise.

Contracts were let, and today the people of the Upper Salinas valley have two good bridges across the stream that separates the large areas of farming land of the Estrella country from the railroad depots at which the products of that region must seek a market.

The primary result of these enterprises has been extensive sales of property at both Paso Robles and Templeton, at figures that in the absence of said improvements, could not have been realized; and the land proprietors at both localities, who paid for the bridges, are financially benefited.

A secondary result is a material advance in the value of taxable real estate in that general region, by which San Luis Obispo county has been financially benefited. The bridges are a success, and would have been had the expense of their construction been paid by the county.

Now, there is a greater public necessity for a bridge at San Miguel than ever existed at Paso Robles or Templeton, or indeed at both of those points combined. But San Miguel has no large tracts of land that are seeking purchasers; no real estate owners who can afford to pay for building a bridge and expect adequate resulting benefits. If a bridge is built here it must be a public measure.

It is undoubtedly the duty of the county authorities to provide such roads and bridges as the convenience of its citizens requires, even when no other benefits are to result. But the construction of a bridge at San Miguel would be the means, not only of promoting the convenience and prosperity of the residents of the northern part of the county, but also of making a large addition to the assessable property of the County.

It is stated that about $2,000,000 have been added to the taxable property of the county in the past year, and it cannot be doubted that the greater part of that increase is the result of the settlement and development of that part of the county lying north and east of the mountains. The county is becoming wealthy and its wealth is being, in a large degree, created by residents in the northerly and northeasterly portions.

The work of development has but just commenced, and it is the part of duty as well as expediency on the part of our Board of Supervisors to make provision for a bridge at San Miguel.

Another lengthy article appeared in the July 29, 1887 edition of the *San Miguel Messenger*; this one was called "Change in Business."

The firm of Goldtree & Company that has done business in San Miguel for the past sixteen years, has been dissolved and a new co-partnership has been formed under the same name that will continue the business.

The new firm consists of Marcus Goldtree, one of the Goldtree Brothers of San Luis Obispo, and A. Sittenfeld, who has been for years connected with the business at this place. The new firm is a strong one, combining ample capital and extensive acquaintance with both the business and people of the upper Salinas valley. Mr. Sittenfeld will give his personal attention to the business, and proposes to carry a large stock of goods and to sell at figures that will make it to the interest of the residents of this region to do business with the firm.

Mr. David Speyer, who has retired from the firm will take into whatever business he may decide to embark, the best wishes of those who have known him during the years of his con-

nection with the mercantile business of San Miguel.

A related item in the July 29th newspaper: "All parties having unsettled business relations with the house of Goldtree & Co. in San Miguel, are requested to call on D. Speyer at the store of Goldtree & Co., and settle the same without delay. This action becomes necessary in closing up the business of the late firm."

"Call for a Fire Organization," was the lead for another article in the July 29th paper: "We are requested to announce that there will be a meeting of the citizens of San Miguel at the Central Hall Friday evening, July 29, at 8 o'clock, to take into consideration the organization of a Fire Department. It requires no argument to convince citizens of the necessity of some organization with reference to protection against fire and it is to be hoped that subject will be given that serious attention that its importance demands."

Two items of church news, on July 29th, included: "Rev. Mr. King, Pastor of the Presbyterian church in Pleasant Valley, will exchange with Rev. Mr. Tuttle and preach at the Congregational church, next Sabbath morning and evening." And: "Rev. M. A. Miller, the new pastor of the Episcopal Church at this place, went to Oakland Monday, expecting to return before the Sabbath. Arrangements will probably be made to enable Mr. Miller to preach at Paso Robles every Sunday evening."

Other items of news, in the *San Miguel Messenger* on July 29th included: "The dwelling house on the McDonald addition, to be occupied by Mr. F. T. Winchell, is nearly completed." And: "A. Halverson, of this place, has leased the Linck Hall to Mrs. Starkey, and left for Lewis, Nevada, last Wednesday." Finally: "B. Carrell has sold his interest in the well-drilling machinery to his partner, A. C. Massey, and the latter has gone to Bradley to sink a well for W. J. Ellis."

The August 5, 1887 edition of the paper informed its readers that "The church entertainment, mentioned in our last issue as being projected by the ladies of the Episcopal Church, should have read: 'for the benefit of the Congregational Church.' The entertainment has been postponed, and the announcement will be renewed next week."

Other items in the August 5th newspaper: "Mr. J. G. Ramsay, whose place is just out of town at the river crossing, has raised a nice patch of sweet potatoes this year. In the light of an experiment, it is encouraging, the prospect at present being favorable as to both quantity and quality of the product." Also: "We call the attention of our readers to a new advertisement by Mr. John Reid, who has opened a grocery store adjoining the Postoffice corner of 'L' and 13th streets. Mr. Reid has a stock of first class goods, and hopes by fairness and attention to business to secure a share of the public patronage. We bespeak success for his business."

The newspaper also printed an article, on August 5th, entitled, "A Rejoinder From the *Messenger.*"

Some of the good people from San Miguel seem to think the *Messenger* has too much to say in favor of Paso Robles and vicinity, much more at least than the *Leader* does for San Miguel. Such local jealousies should be discarded and all work for the good of our common county, or section. However, if those who do so much growling about their local paper would get down into their pockets for three or four yearly subscriptions to be sent to Eastern friends there is no doubt but the *Messenger* would feel more like talking louder for San Miguel. A little of "the root of all evil" goes a long way, sometimes, towards making the machinery of a printing office slip smoothly. Paso Robles *Leader.*

The above paragraph, though kindly intended, does the *Messenger* an injustice. It carries the implication that this paper, being dissatisfied with the people of San Miguel for not subscribing liberally, neglects to represent the place favorably; that greater liberality toward the paper would work a change in the management in that regard, and make it "talk louder for San Miguel," or any less about other locations.

The proposition is quite erroneous. The *Messenger* is satisfied with the patronage extended by the people of San Miguel, and if the course of the paper fails to conform to the ideas of the "good people" referred to, it may be attributed to the fact that said "good people" know better how a paper should be conducted than the editor of the *Messenger.*

The *Messenger* has always endeavored to faithfully represent San Miguel, and the surrounding country within the range of its general circulation, including Paso Robles, at which office it has a good list of paying subscribers. The paper has never received one cent from San Miguel, Paso Robles, or any other locality to pay for special representation; and we will say that no degree of liberality on the part of our local patrons would become an inducement to adopt that extravagant, false and disgusting system of laudation that appears to be desired by a few of the "good people."

San Miguel is a good town; it is a town that, as we fully believe, has a permanently prosperous future. It is the center of an extensive country that is rapidly undergoing the process of development. All this and much more has been represented in the columns of the *Messenger* on every suitable occasion. There may have been facts, and these may have been points of excellence, that have escaped our notice, that have come to the knowledge of some of those "good people;" if so, we should esteem it a favor if they would call our attention to the omission.

The *Messenger* has a good and rapidly increasing subscription patronage extending in all directions from the place of publication, and not a week passes that does not bring spontaneous expressions of appreciation from its readers. This state of affairs implies a measure of success that brings

N Street between 12th and 14th.

some degree of gratification, not withstanding the anonymous complaint that finds expression in the columns of our esteemed contemporary.

News which readers could find in the August 12, 1887 edition of the *San Miguel Messenger* included: "Mr. H. Prentki has opened a store for the sale of cigars, tobacco, candies, notions etc., in one of the front rooms of the new Hall, adjoining McElroy's furniture store. Make your purchase at this place, and give a young man a chance." Also: "Mr. T. C. Slusser, of Vineyard Canyon, is putting up a livery and feed stable on his lot on 12th street. The main structure is 30 x 60 feet, 20 feet to the eaves. A shed will be extended westward 100 feet, and when completed, the establishment will be well adapted in both location and construction for the business intended."

Another item in that paper: "The performance styled the 'Mirror of Ireland' will be given this (Thursday) evening at the San Miguel Hall. The company embraces talent in the line of Irish character, is well equipped and will doubtless furnish an entertainment worthy of a good house."

The August 19, 1887 edition of the newspaper carried two items related to business in the new town: "Charles W. Johnson has purchased the Mission Livery and Feed Stable." And: "Chas. Thiriet will open his watch-making and jewelry establishment in town as soon as the new front to Goldtree & Co.'s store is completed. Work will probably commence on the store next week."

A real estate item from that paper: "A. Mr. Cotton, an attorney from San Francisco, has been in San Miguel some days, with a view to investing in lands."

The August 26, 1887 edition had another lengthy article concerning bridges. The lead on the article was "The Bridges Across the Salinas River."

The Templeton *Times* that took the initiative in advocating the immediate construction of the necessary bridges to accommodate the residents of the northern part of the county, follows up the subject in an article in last week's issue, urging, as a matter of justice as well as expediency, that the county pay for the bridges already built by private enterprise, and provide for the building of another at San Miguel. It says:

At San Miguel, for instance, the crossing of the Salinas river, in the absence of a bridge, is a constant menace to human life. It is con-

ceded on all hands that there will be a largely increased revenue at the disposal of the Board of Supervisors this year and that the increase is mainly the result of the increased values brought into this part of the county as a result of private exertions and private expenditures. At least that portion of the increased revenue which is clearly traceable to the enhanced values hereabouts should be devoted to public improvements.

Public necessity requires the immediate building of another bridge at San Miguel, and public justice dictates that the actual cost of building the two bridges recently constructed should be refunded to the private persons who had the nerve and enterprise to demonstrate the necessity and profitableness of such investments. More than this, the new roads that have been constructed should be declared public highways, and should receive at public cost whatever improvements they may need.

Other roads should be surveyed and to the extent of our contributions to the county treasury every dollar should be spent in opening the country and making it accessible. . . The best and wisest course the Supervisors can pursue in making the tax levy is to provide for a bridge at San Miguel, for the ownership by the country of the two bridges already built, and for a comprehensive and thorough system of improved means of transportation all over this rapidly appreciating section of valuable fruit and agricultural land.

Another item in the August 26th edition of the newspaper: "The young pupils of the drawing class, established by Miss Jessie Kirk, a few weeks since in the Douglas building, are giving much encouragement to their parents and teacher by their rapid progress and interest in the art. Miss Kirk is not only a young artist of much talent, but a faithful teacher."

The September 2, 1887 issue of the *San Miguel Messenger* published this church news: "Rev. M. A. Miller has received the appointment as pastor for the Episcopal church at this place, and will preach at the usual hour next Sunday morning. He will preach at Paso Robles in the evening."

Business news in the September 2nd newspaper included: "Chas. W. Johnson has made an addition to the Mission Livery and Feed Stable, 34 x 50 feet in size." And: "The Southern Pacific Milling Company have purchased the lumber in Meads, Seaman & Co.'s lumber yard, and the latter firm will drop that branch of their business."

The paper on September 9, 1887 informed its readers that "Mr. J. P. Hessel, recently from Wisconsin, a harness maker by trade, has purchased the Dutton building in the northern part of town, and has opened a stock of Millinery goods on Mission street, north of Wells, Fargo & Co.'s Express office. Also agent for the New Home Sewing Machine. Satisfaction guaranteed."

In the September 9th edition, it was stated that "There is, we believe, not a vacant dwelling house in San Miguel, and parties wanting to rent experience difficulty in obtaining suitable places. Would it not be a good move for some of our men of means to put up a few cottages for rent?" Readers were informed that "The question of boring for artesian water in San Miguel is being agitated by some of our enterprising citizens, and from appearances it will not be long before the project assumes a practical form. No one appears to doubt the possibility of obtaining a flowing well within less than 1,000 feet."

According to the September 9th paper: "Nash & McElroy's skating rink will be open next Saturday evening, there will be plenty of skates and 'lots of fun.'"

The *San Miguel Messenger*, on September 9, 1887, printed an article entitled, "Resources & Prospects of San Miguel."

While there have been a considerable number of real estate transactions within the past two weeks in the vicinity of San Miguel, we do not feel warranted in claiming that a boom has yet reached us. There is undoubtedly an increasing demand for lands and town property, but there is but little property in the market, and the showing of actual sales must be small while that state of facts exists.

Booms may be created on premises to an extent fictitious; and an apparent boom exists sometimes, where the genuine article is wholly wanting. In this line of business San Miguel has not sought to compete. There is no combination of interests favoring the forcing of sales or the inflation of real estate values.

But San Miguel has an assured future, and her people have only to be moderately patient to realize any reasonable expectations. Less than one year ago, the first building was erected where there is now presented a busi-

ness street that will compare favorably with many towns of much greater age and more extravagant pretensions.

The town is laid out, and has grown thus far on its merit as the center of extensive tract of agricultural land, and notwithstanding an unfavorable season, the value of surrounding property has steadily advanced- - -an appreciation based solely upon its merit for agriculture. The farmers are better than ever assured that they can maintain prosperous homes in this vicinity.

The development in this region gives increasing assurance that in the near future a new county will be organized here, and that San Miguel will become its county seat.

In addition to all that entered into the prospects of the town one year ago, the disclosure of a large vein of coal in Slack's canyon, steps for the development of which are being taken by the Pacific Improvement Company, will in all probability contribute much to the business of the town in the near future.

Deposits of bituminous rock, lying a few miles west, are passing into the hands of parties that will probably take steps to utilize them, and the growing demand for this favorite paving material justifies the expectation of some increase in surrounding business from that source.

The late coal oil development at Parkfield, a point directly tributary to San Miguel, is of much importance in the estimate of its probable future growth and business. This discovery has been tested to an extent that may be said to almost assure an extraordinary activity in that direction at an early day.

The junction of the Lerdo branch of the Southern Pacific Railroad at this point, a matter that is only a question of time, cannot fail to contribute much to the business and importance of San Miguel.

With all this diversified points in our favor, in addition to the incomparable healthfulness of our climate, the residents of San Miguel can rest assured that their town will maintain its place among the foremost of the young towns of central California.

Church news was included in the September 16, 1887 edition of the *San Miguel Messenger*. "The Pacific Improvement Company have given two lots to the

Episcopal Church, of this place, and the society has purchased one, and the church building will soon be moved to the new location. The new site is both sightly and convenient, being on the plateau westerly from the McFaddin residence."

The *San Miguel Messenger* on September 23, 1887, carried an article with the headline: "Sudden Death. James Johnson, a Painter, Found Dead in His Bed, at the Golden House."

Last Friday evening, James Johnson, a foreman of the painters working on the railroad bridge near this place, came to his boarding place, the Golden restaurant, about 7 o'clock in the evening, apparently in good health. He retired as usual, occupying a room with his brother, who is somewhat deaf. About 10 o'clock he was taken with violent spasms and Dr. Murphy was sent for, and soon appeared, and administered the usual remedy and the patient became easier. Mr. Johnson and his brother occupied separate beds, and supposing that all danger was over, the latter went to sleep and slept soundly till morning, when speaking to his brother he obtained no answer.

He could not be aroused. The doctor was sent for, but the unfortunate patient had passed beyond the assistance of medical skill. He was dead; apparently had been dead for a considerable time.

The Episcopal Church about 1900, near where motel is in 1984.

Photo belonged to Mary Jane Evans who died in 1910.

Mr. Johnson was a young man of good habits, who, we understand, was a resident of Santa Cruz, where his father and other relatives reside. He had recently sold a piece of property in Santa Cruz county, and was going the next day to close the business relating to the sale, instead of which his lifeless body was taken to his former home, where it was consigned to its last rest by sorrowing friends.

An entertainment item in the September 23rd newspaper: "Skating every Saturday evening at San Miguel Hall. Spectators free. Ladies furnished skates free. Gentlemen on skates 25 cents. J. W. McElroy, Manager." Readers of the September 23rd paper learned that "Mr. S. D. Gates has purchased a half interest in Massey's well-drilling machinery and outfit. Mr. Gates will hire a man to represent him in the work. A. C. Massey went to San Ardo Wednesday to drill wells for Brandenstein & Co. He will probably be employed there for a considerable length of time." Other items included: "Dr. Neal's drugs have arrived and will be accessible to the public as soon as shelving can be added to his new building." And: "Goldtree & Co.'s store building now presents the most ornate front in town. The painting, which is of highly artistic character, was done by Maynard & Holmes." Also: "Maynard & Holmes have taken the contract for painting and papering the Congregational Church."

The September 30, 1887 edition of the *San Miguel Messenger* carried a lengthy article with the title "Let Us Bridge the Salinas River."

It is universally admitted that the bridging of the Salinas river at this place is a necessity that must be undertaken in the near future. The convenience of an immense region of country demands it and every day it is postponed is an unnecessary tax upon time and muscle of the yeomanry of the country, who seek a market and shipping point for their products at San Miguel.

Why should the building of the bridge be delayed? The County is abundantly able, and it is a duty to its citizens to provide roads and bridges; and though the providing of these conveniences causes a heavy drain on the funds for the time being, when once provided, they constitute a permanent addition to the revenue-producing resources of the County.

While we contend that it is the duty of the County to construct this bridge, it is the

duty of the citizens to make their wants known to the authorities in a most forciable manner. If the county cannot be prevailed upon to incur the whole expenses of the bridge a large amount could doubtless be raised by private subscription to supplement such funds as might be appropriated. It would even be good financial policy to bond the road district for the purposes. It has been said 'where there is a will there is a way,' and if our people take hold of the matter in earnest, it can be accomplished. But there is preliminary work to be done before intelligent action can be taken toward raising means for this work.

It is necessary to know what point would be the most central and convenient location for a bridge, and it is also indispensable to have a scientific estimate of the cost of constructing a bridge at the designated point.

A fund should be raised forthwith to defray the expense of the plan and estimate for the structure. Let some of our leading citizens set the ball rolling and there will be found means to help keep it moving till success is achieved.

On September 30, 1887, the paper informed its readers that "A gentleman named Rice, from Nebraska, representing an association of capitalists, was in town Tuesday looking at our town with a view to the establishment of a bank. He returned south to report to his associates, and we shall probably hear from him again." Also: "Dr. Neal's new business house has been christened the Mission Drug Store." And: "The work of painting and paper-hanging being in progress in the Congregational Church, no services will be held next Sabbath."

Other news in the September 30th paper: "C. W. Johnson, the new proprietor of the Mission Stable, has been making extensive improvements, including a large addition to the stable, a new front, well, pump, hose, etc., besides painting. It now presents a neat and commodious appearances."

Another item in the September 30th paper: "Messers. Armstrong, King and Champlin, of the San Miguel Gold & Silver Mining Company, returned from Los Burros district Wednesday. The have located a lead which has been christened the Confidence Lead, near the Goodrich Mine. The vein is said to be 10 feet thick and very well defined. They brought out some fine looking samples which have been forwarded for assay."

The newspaper on September 30, 1887 also informed people that "Mr. James Keleher will in a short time put up a carriage shop in 12th street, opposite Slusser's new livery stable. Mr. Keleher is a thorough mechanic and has a reputation for substantial work which will assure him plenty of business."

The October 7, 1887 issue of the *San Miguel Messenger* published the informative fact that "There are upwards of forty license-paying business houses in San Miguel." Also in that edition of the newspaper: "A. Lowinger has lately added a neat and substantial front to his store, besides a lot of new goods adapted to the season. We are pleased to note this sign of prosperity in the affairs of one of San Miguel's most substantial business men."

Other items in the October 7th newspaper: "The contract for moving the Episcopal church to its new site has been awarded to a Mr. Taylor, of Salinas. Work will probably commence next week." Also: "Thos. Reed and Harry Collamore are painting a drop curtain for the San Miguel Hall, which will be a fine piece of work in its line. It will represent in artistically displayed notices many of the leading lines of business in the town, and will form an interesting study for the audience between the acts."

According to the October 7th paper: "A number of our active young men assembled Wednesday night and took the preliminary steps toward the organization of The San Miguel Social and Athletic Club. The object is social recreation and athletic amusements. A regular meeting will be held at the hall next Tuesday evening, at which time officers will be elected. The organization now embraces the names of W. T. Maynard, T. A. Holmes, R. O. Worley, C. Forbes, H. Collamore, Thos. R. Reed, C. J. Jacobs, H. Taylor and H. Walbridge. Parties desiring to join should be present at the next meeting."

Readers of the *San Miguel Messenger* on October 14, 1887 would learn that "Mr. G. N. Douglas, when returning home on horseback from his place one dark night this week, got into a barbed wire fence, and his horse, a very good one, was shockingly cut by the barbs." Other items in the October 14th paper included: "James Keleher is going ahead immediately with the building of his wagon shop on 12th street." And: "R. Dunham has leased the Kunz feed stable in the rear of the Commercial Hotel, and will open it to the public.

"Petition for a Bridge," was the heading for an article in the October 21, 1887 edition of the *San Miguel Messenger*.

The people of the northern part of the county are preparing to urge upon the authorities their just claim for some action looking to the construction of a bridge across the Salinas river at this place. A petition reciting the urgent necessity for such action is being circulated, and will in due time be presented to the Board of Supervisors. Steps will also be taken to ascertain the probable cost of a bridge at a point that will best accommodate the various routes that center in San Miguel from the east side of the river. Not a week passes that does not mark the establishment of new homes on that side, and they must labor at a great inconvenience until a bridge is built to enable them to reach a near railroad depot without wading through sand in the summer and water in the winter. Let the good work go on.

Other items in the October 21st edition: "The front of the new Mission drug store is embellished by a well-executed picture of the old San Miguel Mission, by Thos. R. Reed. Thos. R. Reed has taken charge of the restaurant opposite the depot, and we have no doubt it will be found an excellent boarding place." Also: "Just opened several cases of Dry Goods and Ladies' Notions at Allen's."

"Sicotte & Hopper," according to the newspaper on October 21, 1887, "are rapidly molding bricks at their yard above town." [This brick yard was located to the southeast of the Caledonia adobe.]

The October 28, 1887 issue of the paper informed readers that "The Railroad Restaurant, under Mr. Thos. Reed, has been refurnished and otherwise improved. A first class cook has been installed and the house is prepared to furnish meals at all hours. We bespeak for the business venture a favorable reception by the public. A social hop will take place at the Railroad Restaurant this Thursday evening." Other items in this paper: "C. Whisman resumed his duties as agent at the depot Monday morning." Also: "Carrol & True have their steam well-drilling machine in operation at J. P. Courter's place, in town." And: "Mr. Samuel Nott has purchased from Wm. Pinkerton Lots 9 and 10 in Block 59, adjoining Spencer's saloon, and will move one of his buildings and his business to that location."

Concerning the moving of buildings, "The party who contracted to move the Episcopal church has been delayed at Salinas, but expects to be here at work next week."

"More About the Bridge," was the heading on an article in the November 4, 1887 edition of the *San Miguel Messenger*.

The subject of a bridge at this place is increasing in interest, both among the business men of the town and the hundreds of farmers on the east side of the river. A careful observation has been made of the ground, and it is demonstrated that the length of the bridge at the most convenient and accessible point will be a little less than 700 feet. On Wednesday, Mr. McCarthy, representative of the Pacific Bridge Company, of San Francisco, (the same company that built the Paso Robles and Templeton bridges) called and made a personal examination of the crossing, and will estimate the expense of the structure. It is expected that the cost of building a bridge that will resist any flood to which the stream is subject, will not exceed $17,000. Considering the importance of the crossing and the large interests demanding the bridge, this is a small sum, and we hope to see steps taken at an early day to assure the structure.

The November 4th edition of the newspaper carried an article entitled "'Business Change.' The hardware firm of C. H. Reed & Co. underwent a change on the 1st instant. John P. Courter, formerly connected with the business of the Southern Pacific Milling Company, comes in as full partner. The new member brings into the firm an energetic businessman and plenty of capital, and the stock will be increased and the business pushed to the utmost. This change involves the necessity of the settlement of the accounts of the business prior to November 1st, and parties who have accounts there are requested to call and settle without delay."

Also in the November 4th paper: "J. A. Richards, the blacksmith, has purchased two lots on Mission street, nearly opposite the depot and adjoining the Bank Exchange saloon, and will put up a shop forthwith." And: "The San Miguel Athletic Club will give a ball at the hall on the evening of the 11th instant, for the purpose of raising funds for the apparatus for their gymnasium. A good time may be expected."

The November 4th edition of the *San Miguel Messenger* informed readers that "The installation of the officers of San Miguel Lodge A. F. & A. M., took place at their hall last Saturday evening under the direction of Deputies Grand Master T. Sherman and C. A. Farnham, of Paso Robles. The officers are: Worship-

Mule team at work.

ful Master Dr. L. D. Murphy, Senior Warden W. M. Jeffreys, Junior Warden O. P. McFaddin, Secretary J. C. Currier, Treasurer G. N. Douglas, Senior Deacon Jas. Keleher, Stewards John Thompson and F. Minchell, Tyler, George S. Davis. Thirteen visiting bretheren from Paso Robles assisted in the ceremonies."

"The Bridge," was the heading of an article in the *San Miguel Messenger* on November 11, 1887.

> **A meeting of the citizens of San Miguel and vicinity was held at San Miguel Hall, last Saturday afternoon, to discuss the bridge question, and to select delegates to go to San Luis Obispo to present the petition to the Board of Supervisors.**
>
> **Dr. Murphy was elected chairman, and Capt. Currier secretary. After discussion of the subject, Captain Currier, Dr. Murphy and L. McDonald were chosen delegates to proceed to San Luis Obispo with said petition. The delegates were instructed to use their best endeavors to secure favorable action on the part of the Board. The petition has been generally signed by citizens to whom it was submitted.**

Another lengthy article in the November 11, 1887 edition of the newspaper was entitled "The Movement for a Flouring Mill."

> **The subject of the building of a flouring mill by an association of farmers and business men of San Miguel and vicinity, which was discussed to some extent months since, is being again revived, and we are pleased to see that the idea is received with favor.**
>
> **The plan suggested is to fix the amount of**

> **the stock of the company at $20,000, which, it is supposed, will be sufficient to put in operation in a mill of capacity to meet the present wants of this community. The stock will be represented in shares of $25 each, and all members of the company will be on equal footing in the business, only one vote being allowed to a member, no matter how many shares he owns.**
>
> **The business will be controlled by a board of directors, who will be empowered to appoint such subordinates as may be found necessary. It is thought a company of this kind, properly managed, can afford to buy the farmer's grain at San Francisco prices and sell flour by the same rule, thus saving to the farmers of the upper Salinas valley the sum paid in freight on the grain they raise and the flour they consume, which amounts to many thousand dollars annually. We may add to this the consideration that every consumer of flour, aside from the farming population, will be largely benefited by the reduction in the price of this staple commodity.**
>
> **After deducting these substantial benefits, there will be left the same ration of the milling company that the Central Milling Company realizes, which no doubt is ample to afford liberal dividends to its stockholders.**
>
> **With even ordinarily good management, there is no reason why such an institution should not be made not only a success in itself, but of incalcuable benefit to the large community that has its business center in San Miguel. We are sending abroad raw material and importing a staple article manufactured therefrom, paying not only heavy freights both ways, but large profits to manufacturers and dealers. Intelligent farmers can readily see that such a course is ruinous, when the profits on farming are at all times uncertain, and at best very small. The remedy is in the hands of the people.**

Also in the November 11, 1887 edition of the newspaper: "The Episcopal church will be on its new site by the close of the week." And: "Samuel Nott has sold the buildings and lot formerly occupied by Brinkley and McElroy to Brainard & Holmes, the painters, for consideration of $500. The purchasers will occupy the building as a shop, for which it is well adapted."

The *San Miguel Messenger*, on November 11, 1887,

also carried an article entitled, "A Report from the County Seat."

Capt. Currier, L. McDonald and Dr. Murphy returned from San Luis Thursday, where they had been to lay before the Board of Supervisors the bridge petition that has been very numerously signed in this end of the county. They report having been very courteously treated by the Board, and though no definite action was taken on the petition, the Board expressed a willingness to submit the proposition of issuing bonds for the purpose to the voters of this road district of the people desire.

There was a movement on foot to bond the County in the sum of $200,000, for improvements in the way of roads, bridges, &c., giving to each section its just proportion. Should this measure be adopted a bridge at San Miguel will doubtless be one of the first improvements to which the amount to be expended in the northern part of the county will be applied. This measure will be considered in a mass meeting of citizens in San Luis Saturday, after which it must be submitted to the people. We believe that such a step will meet with a cordial endorsement by the voters of the county, and that properly expended, it will be a very profitable investment.

The newspaper, on the same date, informed people that "H. B. Jones, the carpenter, has taken the contract to rebuild Douglas' building, formerly the Almstead hotel, after it is moved. It will be moved to the rear end of the lot on which the *Messenger* office is located, and will be finished in good style."

One week later, readers learned that "The old Almstead hotel building was moved this week to Douglas' block, and is being rapidly transformed into a neat looking building."

On November 18, 1887, there was printed the following: "A typographical error in our last issue made us say that Brainard & Holmes had purchased one of Nott's buildings. W. T. Maynard and G. A. Holmes are the purchasers, and that they mean business may be seen from their advertisement appearing in this issue." On a different topic, "Father Mut has completed the work of relaying the tiles on the roof of the Mission church and adjoining buildings. The work has been very thoroughly done, new timbers being insti-

tuted for those that were decayed, and the structures are now good for another half century. A few years ago, some $3,000 were spent for repairs to the Old Mission Church."

Readers of the newspaper on November 18th learned that "Mr. Hugh McLeod has purchased two lots between Cramer's harness shop and Matthis' livery stable." Also: A. J. Richards, the blacksmith, and C. W. Stewart, a young wagon maker, have formed a co-partnership for business, and, having purchased a lot on the east side of the railroad track, have commenced a shop in which both trades will be carried on. The building will be 18 by 40 feet in size."

Also in the November 18th edition of the San Miguel newspaper: "Mr. J. F. Cook, who started in this place a year ago with a small stock of goods, had been gradually extending his business, and now carries a fine assortment of stoves, tin-ware, and other lines of hardware, as well as notions. He makes a special announcement to the public in another column of this paper." The following week, his ad stated:

J. F. COOK
Here We Are, Right on Deck
and Kicking!
Kicking out goods at very low prices.
Stoves, tinware, Furniture and a General
Assortment of Yankee Notions.
See my 5c, 10c, 15 and 25c
counters. A thousand and one useful
things are to be found on them.
Christmas is Coming!
And there will be lots of nice things
to please the little ones.
Remember it costs
you nothing to look at them.
A Fine Stock of Feed on hand.
Ground Barley,
Bran, Middlings and Chicken Feed.
Opposite the Depot.   San Miguel, Cal.
J. F. Cook

"The Flouring Mill Movement" was the heading on a November 25, 1887 article.

There are many things indicating that the farmers of this vicinity are becoming very much in earnest in the matter of organizing a company to build a flouring mill. A plan has been arranged upon which it is proposed to organize a company, if the required amount can be raised.

It would seem that neither farmers nor

George Sonnenberg, Jr. and Elizabeth Gorham in Gorham & Sonnenberg General Merchandise, San Miguel.

From the newspaper on November 25, 1887, readers learned that "Goldtree & Co. are moving their large warehouse from the old town. It is to be placed by the side of their store, where it is much needed in the business of the firm."

Readers of the newspaper on November 25, 1887 learned that "The San Miguel Social and Athletic Club have rented Jeffreys' Hall for purposes of its meetings. It is a very convenient place for the purpose." Also: "Samuel Nott is being well fixed up at his new business location. He will have two sales rooms fronting Mission street, in one of which hardware will be kept, while the other will hold a stock of furniture." And: "T. C. Slusser will, next week, commence a dwelling house a short distance west of his new stable, and will occupy it with his family during the winter. The stable will soon be opened for business."

"Water Works for San Miguel," was the heading for an article in the *San Miguel Messenger*, on November 25, 1887.

Dr. Murphy is making permanent arrangements to furnish the town with water. He has received a large invoice of pipe and a 10,000 gallon tank, which will be placed as soon as practicable, and in connection with the large tank that he already has, will be sufficient for present requirements. His main pipe will be laid along the west side of Mission street, extending as far as may be needed. These facilities will be increased as the growth of the town may demand. The Doctor says he expects to keep the supply fully up to the necessities of the town.

"Further on the Flouring Mill Question" was the heading on an article in the December 2, 1887 issue of the *San Miguel Messenger*.

We are pleased to state that the gristmill stock is being liberally subscribed to by the farmers to whom the measure has been presented. The more it is discussed, the plainer can be seen the injustice under which the

business men should hesitate to give the movement their substantial support. One should not wait for another; it is a measure from which no bad results can come. Under the plan proposed, if the required amount is not raised, no one who has subscribed to the stock can be called upon for anything, and the project must fall through.

If the required amount is subscribed, a meeting will be called and measures taken to proceed with business; and at such meeting the articles of agreement can be made to conform to the view of the majority of the members of the company.

The enterprise, under reasonably good management, cannot fail to be a great success—a success not only directly in paying good dividends to the members, but indirectly to the entire producing and consuming classes of the upper Salinas valley. The price of flour, bran, etc., can be placed at a figure below that of the same commodity manufactured elsewhere, and yet leave a profit to the mill as large as other mills receive that are building fortunes for their owners. We have soil that produces the finest grade of wheat known to the markets; why send it away to be manufactured into flour and bring the flour back, paying not only the cost of manufacture and profits to the mill, but freights on shipment both ways and profits to several middle men?

farmers are laboring, and the certainty that the measure proposed is the only way in which they can be assured of receiving the reasonable value of their leading product.

The loss sustained by the farmers on 100,000 centals of wheat, that can be saved if they will work together in the matter of manufacturing their flour at home, is more than $25,000, an amount which would do much toward advancing the prosperity of our farming community.

Under the laws of Oregon and of most of the other States the compensation for manufacturing flour from wheat is fixed at one-eighth, while the farmers in the vicinity of San Miguel are paying more than one-half.

The farmer receives $1.10 per cental, 400 pounds of wheat for $4.40; while for 200 pounds of flour he pays $4.60, and the bran is worth more, pound for pound, than the farmer receives for his first quality wheat.

Suppose the existence of a mill enables the farmer to receive 200 pounds of flour, for 300 pounds of wheat (which is said to be a rule that the mills admit to be just) it would give the farmer $4.60 worth of flour, and $1.00 worth of bran, making $5.60 for 300 pounds, or $1.86 per cental. From this deduct one-eighth, the legal and customary compensation for grinding, and the farmer has $1.62 for his grain.

The running expenses of a mill of a capacity of 100 barrels per day will not, probably, exceed $7,000 per annum. In 300 days it will turn our 30,000 barrels of flour, which at $4.60 per cental would amount to $138,000 and, approximately, 1,500 tons of bran etc., worth $30,000, making a grand total of $168,000.

In manufacturing this the mill has used 90,000 centals of wheat, which at $1.10 was worth $99,000; the running expenses added make the gross expenses of the mill $106,000. Deduct this from $138,000, and we have as the profits of the mill (not including interest or insurance), the sum of $32,000. This amount would be saved.

It would not all be in the profits of the mill, for higher prices would be paid for grain and lower prices received for flour, but it would all come, directly or indirectly, to this community, while the use of the bran would be a far reaching benefit to our industrious hus-

bandmen. There is, evidently, something in this problem, and we hope that our people will not only study it over but bring it to a speedy and successful conclusion.

"The Prospects Brightening" was he heading on a lengthy article in the December 2, 1887 edition of the *San Miguel Messenger*.

Within the past few weeks the prospects for a bridge across the Salinas at this point have materially improved. It is now almost certain that the desired improvements can be secured, and that the accomplishment of the necessary preliminaries is only the matter of a few months time. Some assistance will certainly be rendered by the County; the Board of Supervisors have shown a disposition to favor the measure to the extent that may be deemed consistent with the legal restraints under which they are acting, and it is not to be expected that they will be so derelict in an important duty as to grant an insignificant sum.

Private parties who are interested in the general development of this region of the country and in the growth and business of San Miguel, give voluntary assurance of contributions that will make a fund large enough to place the matter almost beyond question. Only this week a prominent man, the probability of whose assistance has not heretofore been mentioned, came forward with a positive promise of $1,000, with the probability of considerable other indirect assistance.

There are several parties, who are largely interested in the project, who have not been heard from, and who will certainly add a large sum to the list. With our knowledge of the situation, we feel confident that the coming spring will witness the accomplishment of this important work, with great resulting benefits to both town and surrounding country.

According to the December 2nd issue, "We are informed that McDonald Brothers generously propose to give an eligible site for a flouring mill and warehouse at San Miguel, if the means can be raised to erect the buildings and start the business." And: "If you are, or expect to be, either a producer of grain or a consumer of bread in the upper Salinas valley, you are interested in the project of a farmer's flouring mill at

San Miguel. Take a few shares of stock and stand by your own interest and that of your neighbors."

Another item in that issue of the paper: "A gentleman who is in a situation to speak, authoritatively, states that the sale of flour at San Miguel surpass those of Templeton, Paso Robles and Bradley combined. Of course it is not because this staple commodity can be purchased cheaper at San Miguel, but because of a greater number of consumers find it convenient to make purchases here."

Other items in the December 2nd newspaper: "The Davis brothers, having sold their saloon property and closed the business, take this mode of requesting all persons having unsettled accounts with them to call and adjust the same without delay." And: "Davis Bros. have sold their saloon property on Mission street to G. Kunz." Also: "Charles Thiriet has taken charge of the Palace saloon and will occupy a room on the north side with his jeweler business."

Readers learned, from the December 2nd paper, that "G. W. Proctor has commenced the erection of a hotel adjoining the San Miguel Hall on 13th street. A cellar is being dug and a substantial brick foundation laid for the building, which is to be 26 x 60 feet and 22 feet to the eaves. A house now standing on the rear portion of the lot will be used in connection with the new structure. George S. Davis is superintending the work and will take charge of the house when completed. A well conducted house may be looked for."

The December 2nd issue contained the following news: "Sicotte & Hopper have brick for sale in quantities to suit the purchaser. They are also prepared to do all kinds of brick work at short notice." Also: "Mr. Hopper informs us that the brick burned in the kiln which is now cooling, are of very fine quality. He thinks the clay at the yard is adapted for brick of extra hardness and durability." And: "In addition to the appliances for furnishing the town with water, mentioned in our last issue, Dr. Murphy has a steam engine and pump of capacity adapted to the work. It is understood that the tanks will be placed at an elevation of about 100 feet, giving as much pressure as is desirable."

Other December 2, 1887 news included: "Among the deeds lately recorded is that of C. H. Reed to John P. Courter, an undivided half of lots 1 and 2, block 63, San Miguel; $1,150." And: "Still another best place in town to buy groceries, save money, etc., at Littlefields's." Also: "S. W. Fergusson announces that he will soon re-open an office for business in this town." Finally: "John Warth will open a boot and shoe shop in San Miguel next week. Mr. Warth is said to be a thorough mechanic in his line, and we wish him success."

The December 9th edition included information concerning sports.

Base Ball
San Miguel vs Templeton
A match game of base ball was played here last Sunday between the San Miguel and Templeton clubs. The day was fine and there were a good many spectators. Play was called at 1:30 p.m.

The Templeton club appeared in their neat uniforms, consisting of blue shirts and pants, red caps and stockings.

The following comprised the San Miguel nine and the positions: Worley, pitcher; Taylor, catcher and captain; Whisman, first base; Jenks, second base; Oxeneder, short stop; Holmes, right field; Richard, center field; G. Jenks, left field.

Templeton Club
Biers, pitcher; Steele, catcher; Whitney, 1st base; Bennett, 2d base; Lundbeck, 3d base; Stewart, short stop; Reed, right field; Austin, center field; Matthis, left field; L. Tynan, umpire; Mr. Lepsit, scorer. The Templetons came up with only six men and added three from San Miguel.

The score stood, San Miguel 17, Templeton 7, and San Miguel with one inning to spare. The playing, considering the limited opportunities for practice was good. The clubs were evidently on their mettle and acquitted themselves well, in this, their first match game. Taylor, their captain, handled his men with discretion.

The visitors presented a neat appearance in their jaunty uniforms, behaved them in a gentlemanly manner, and took their defeat philosophically. They returned home on the 4:20 p.m. train. These friendly contests between neighboring towns are calculated to promote pleasant relations and should be encouraged. San Miguel may now expect to measure strength with other clubs on the diamond and we believe that they will acquit themselves with credit.

The December 16, 1887 edition of the *San Miguel Messenger* printed some items concerning dentistry. "A short sleep and a pleasant dream about the girl you left behind you and then woke up with your old teeth

The San Miguel baseball team, 1909. Top row, left to right: Eli Wright, Johnny Jones, Jack Robinson, Hank Delaney. Middle row: unidentified, Charles Dittemore, Harry Dittemore. Bottom row: Charlie Houghton, Ed Wickstrom, unidentified.

part of town." And: "Goldtree & Co. have completed the rebuilding of their warehouse, adjacent to their store." Also: "Mr. Maxwell, of the Maxwell House, has been improving his hotel by changes in the kitchen, pantries and dining room, the latter being now 32 feet in length."

Readers of the December 16th newspaper also learned that "Various improvements have been recently made in the Arlington Hotel, including the fitting up of new rooms and a showy sign, executed by Maynard & Holmes. This house appears to be enjoying a liberal share of the public favor." And: "Mr. G. W. Spencer is setting a good example by laying a broad and substantial sidewalk in front of some of his lots on Mission street. The owners of unimproved lots should bear in mind that such action not only improves the appearance of the town, but materially adds to the value of their property. It is money well invested."

The paper on December 23, 1887, informed its readers that "Mrs. J. P. Hessel has a full line of millinery, and will offer great bargains in hats, bonnets, wings, tips, ribbons, velvets and satins; also agent for the New Home Sewing Machine. Will sell at the lowest living prices." An announcement in that paper: "Skating at the San Miguel Hall, Saturday evenings, from 7:30 to 10. . . . Gentlemen on their own skates, 15 cents; gentlemen furnished with skates, 25 cents. Ladies on their own skates, free; ladies furnished with skates, 15 cents. No reduction for children. J. W. McElroy, Manager."

Social news in that issue of the paper: "The Social and Athletic club are making elaborate preparations for their grand New Year's ball that is to take place in one week, the evening of the 30th instant. They expect to make it the leading feature of the holiday amusements in San Miguel. The favorable management and eminent success of the former party given by the Club is a practical guaranty for this, and the attendance will doubtless be as large as they could desire."

out without pain; Dr. Richey and the laughing gas can do it. San Miguel, Dec. 19th to 23rd, 1887. If you once saw those beautiful celluloid plates put up by Dr. Richey, the Chicago dentist, you can never again be induced to wear the filthy rubber which causes such bad breath and taste and often sore mouth."

There was the following church news in the December 16th paper. "Father Mut is having the interior of the Mission improved. The statue of St. Joseph, made in Portugal probably a century ago, is in the hands of Maynard & Holmes and T. R. Reed, to be repainted. It is quite possible that Joseph's second coat will outshine the first."

Progress of the business sector was itemized in the December 16th newspaper. "A. C. Swift, Esq., has moved his law office to his residence in the western

Mission Street copied from a postcard mailed March 13, 1909.

Other items in the paper: "J. Keleher is going to mark his street, 12ᵗʰ, at the junction of Mission. This example should be followed by other citizens." Also: "The new Proctor hotel is about enclosed, and when completed will present a very substantial and commodious appearance." And: "Chas. Thiriet had a side entrance made to his watch-maker and jeweler shop, and customers can call there without passing through the saloon."

The *San Miguel Messenger*, on December 23, 1887, printed an article entitled, "Masonic Installation and Banquet."

The ceremony of installing the officers of San Miguel Lodge No. 285 F. & A. M. was performed last Saturday evening in the lodge rooms. There was a full attendance of members, and a large delegation from Paso Robles, who kindly came to assist their sister lodge.

The installing officer was Bro. C. A. Farnum, Past Master of King Solomon's Lodge. After the completion of the ceremonies the brothers were invited to repair to the house of O. P. McFadden. Upon entering they were met by a delegation of the wives of members and ushered into the brilliantly lighted dining room, where a grand surprise awaited them. Two long tables loaded with delicacies. Everything that could be thought of to tickle the palate was there. Such turkey, pies, cakes

and sweetmeats would have made a gourmand smile. After they had done full justice to the good things, waited on by the ladies, the latter were seated and their turn waited on by the gentlemen

The usual speech making and jokes followed, and after the "Doxology" and "Home, Sweet Home" the party broke up. It was the unanimous verdict that the entertainment was a most successful one, and reflected great credit on the ladies, who planned and carried out the surprise entirely without assistance from the other sex.

To Mrs. O. P. McFadden, Mrs. Murphy, Mrs. Currier, Mrs. Millman, Mrs. Winchell, Mrs. Maxwell, Mrs. Speyer and Mrs. Jeffreys, it is but just to add is due the credit for its success and that the presence of the ladies added greatly to the charms of the banquet.

The following is the list of officers installed for the ensuing year: L. D. Murphy, Master; O. P. McFadden, Senior Warden; W. M. Jeffreys, Junior Warden; J. C. Currier, Secretary; G. N. Douglas, Treasurer; L. H. Meads, Senior Deacon; F. T. Winchell, Junior Deacon; N. G. Millman and F. Knights, Stewards; G. S. Davis, Tyler; J. Keleher, Marshall.

The Lodge starts out on the new year with much promise.

The December 30, 1887 issue of the *San Miguel Messenger* informed its readers that "Father Mut, of the Catholic Church, presents in this issue a statement of the receipts and disbursements of the church at this place, which makes a very creditable showing. Persons who are acquainted with the work accomplished will concede that the funds have been very wisely and judiciously expended. The Mission has been much improved, and the management is highly creditable to the pastor in charge." (It might be noted that the Reverend Jose Mut y Rosello died at Mission San Miguel on October 1, 1889. He is the only priest buried in the mission cemetery.)

The newspaper, on December 30th, informed readers that "Dr. Murphy's system of water works for the town seems to be almost complete. The pipes have been laid to all points where there is a probability of water being required for the present, and they will be extended as the demand increases."

The Masonic Lodge was not the only fraternal organization in San Miguel. The "Hall of Nacimiento Lodge, No. 340 I.O.O.F." held its First Term, First Session on March 13, 1888. The Nacimiento Lodge was instituted by District Deputy Grand Master E. C. Ivins of Hesperian Lodge, No 181. The officers elected and installed were:

Noble Grand	B. G. Allen
Vice Grand	F. T. Winchell
Rec. Secretary	F. D. Miller
Per. Secretary	T. F. McKinney
Treasurer	N. G. Millman

We will bring this chapter on the history of San Miguel to a close by including an article that appeared in the *San Miguel Messenger* on November 11, 1887. It was entitled "A Friendly Notice of San Miguel."

The *Overland Monthly* for November is at hand with its usual variety of choice literature of special interest to residents of the Pacific coast. The business department embraces sketches of several prominent places in the State, including a very friendly notice of San Miguel, from which we reprint the following extract.

One of the most prosperous of the new towns of the coast valleys of California is San Miguel, San Luis Obispo county. It is a brisk and ambitious railroad town, present popu-

Emma Hoffman, Joe Stanley, Dr. Murphy, and Mr. Oaks stand in front of the Wells Fargo Building. Dr. L. D. Murphy was the agent from 1903-1912.

lation about five hundred, and increasing rapidly. The back country is extensive, and full of resources, both mineral and agricultural.

From a recent copy of the *San Miguel Messenger*, edited by G. Webster, we learn that the subdivision of large estates into small fruit farms is going on with unusual energy. The local items show that San Miguel is progressing, new buildings being erected, roads and streets laid out, and general growth manifested in every direction.

The famous old Mission town of San Miguel, founded in 1797, is described by all the early travelers in the southern counties. It is of historical importance, second to no other in the State, and the mission buildings and ruins should be preserved with jealous care. In the official acts of the military governors of California, the name of San Miguel, of the alcalde there, or the old mission, occur frequently.

The new town with its lively American air, its brisk activity, its modern life, forms a strange contrast to the gray adobe walls, towers and gables of the Spanish portions. Stores, shops, hotels, stables, lumber yards, etc., crowd the main street of the new town. The large new warehouse by the railroad track is filled with grain. The depot and freight buildings are new and well built.

For twenty miles or more, to the east and west, a broad reach of excellent farming land extends tributary to San Miguel, and aiding is assured prosperity. The town is situated on a beautiful plateau, near the bank of the Salinas river. A gentle breeze follows the broad valley from the ocean, and tempers the climate.

A tax of $8,000 has just been levied to build a new school-house. There are two teachers employed, and ninety children are in attendance. The town has an Episcopal and a Congregational church. A few years ago some $3,000 were spent for repairs to the old Mission church.

Neighbors of San Miguel

INDIAN VALLEY AND SLACK'S CANYON

In this section, we will follow the progress of the development of the Indian Valley region by citing items that were published in the San Miguel newspaper. It was called *The Inland Messenger* for its first year of publication. Beginning on April 29, 1887, the name was changed to the *San Miguel Messenger*. Indian Valley and Slack's Canyon are both located in Monterey County, but have always had a direct connection with the town of San Miguel.

[In 1854, John W. Slack, then 21 years old, left Kentucky; in San Jose he married Miss Ellen Kamp. He bought cattle, drove them south and took up range in the area now known as Slack's Canyon, about 30 miles northeast of San Miguel. In 1862, Slack sold his holdings and moved to San Luis Obispo. J. W. Slack settled on 200 acres just north of that town. This eventually became Slack's Addition, with a street named after him. After his first wife died in 1869, John W. Slack married Mary J. Downing in 1882.]

On June 4, 1886, the newspaper informed its readers that "The citizens of Indian Valley and adjoining vicinity, will be pleased to learn that a new sawmill began operations on the Big Sandy last week. The distance to this mill is about twenty miles. The timber available for sawing is oak and pine." In the paper on that same date appeared this notice:

$20 Reward. Whereas on or about May 25th some evil-intentioned person shot on my ranch a roan and white Durham bull, the above reward will be paid any one giving positive information of the perpetrator.
Gerard Noel Douglas.

The Inland Messenger, for July 30, 1886, stated that "J. Egan, of Indian Valley, is running a tunnel into the hill for water, and has a good prospect of plenty of water for stock."

In the August 27th edition of the newspaper, it was announced that "Some of the citizens of Indian Valley commenced strawing the ford on the Salinas River, last Wednesday, on the road leading from this place to Indian Valley, preparatory to hauling grain."

The newspaper on September 10, 1886, reported that "T. J. Keltner, J. F. Reason and R. Cruess of Indian Valley started to Cayucos, last Tuesday, with about 240 head of hogs."

One week later, on September 17th, the newspaper provided the following information.

It seems the adobe business is not to be permitted to relapse into a state of total neglect and desuetude after all. At any rate if the efforts of certain residents of Indian Valley to revive the art are significant, this whilom, flourishing industry stands a fair chance of being galvanized into fresh life.

During the past week or two the Messrs. Cruess have erected on their property two substantial adobe buildings, which are meant to subserve the purposes of milk-house and chicken corral respectively.

Mr. Chappell has also laid the foundation and something more of what promises to be a most substantial and commodious edifice for storing milk. Away in the hills to the westward of the Cruess place is the pre-emption of E. W. Platt, who has just added to his dwelling house a commanding chimney, constructed entirely of adobe bricks turned out by his own hands.

Readers of the newspaper on October 1, 1886 learned that "A Sunday School was organized in Indian Valley last Saturday with about twenty scholars; W. Withrow is superintendent." Also: "We are informed that a nice spring of water was lately discovered by John Daves and A. S. Wolf, back of Asbel's and Rose's places, near Indian Valley. It is a locality where no water was supposed to exist."

The following item, from the October 1, 1886 edition of the paper is included here because of its value in recording the origin of a geographical place name. "Mr. James Egan, an old gentleman who has settled

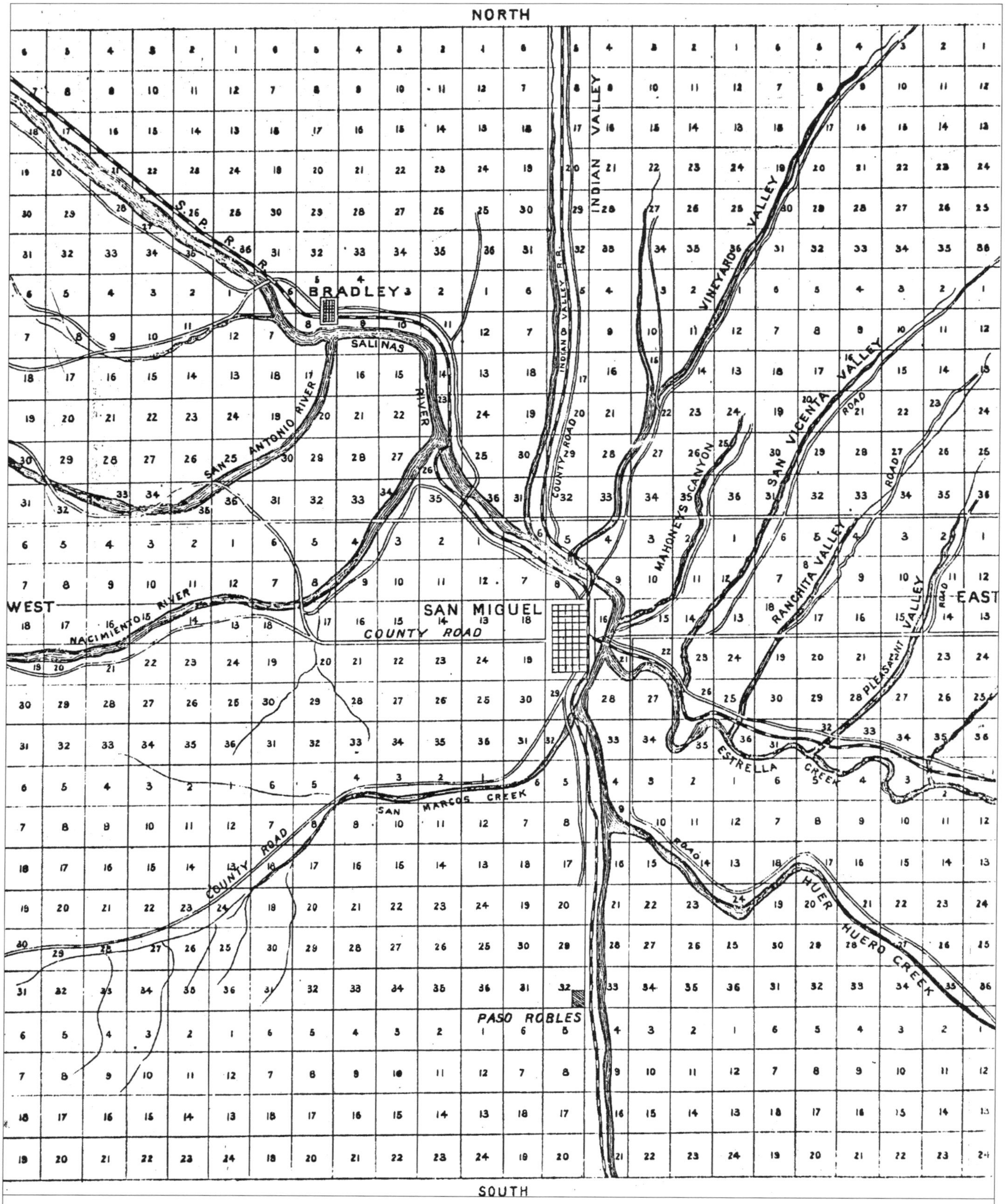

Country surrounding San Miguel.

at a place formerly known as the 'Seep' but now called 'Egan Springs,' west of Indian Valley, was considerably bruised by the falling of his horse last week, but is getting along well." [This must be the same Egan who was mentioned in an item on July 30, 1886.]

The Inland Messenger, October 1st edition, carried an article called, "An Indian Valley Farm."

Within the past few months we have had many opportunities to notice instances of successful fruit and general farming in almost every direction from this place. We take a special pleasure in speaking of these cases, as many of our readers who have lately established homes in localities where the practicability of successful fruit culture has been doubted by the stock-raisers by whom the country was in former years occupied, are deeply interested in the question whether it will be safe to invest money and labor in orchards and vineyards.

Indian Valley has not heretofore been noticed in this line, but having seen numerous samples of fine fruit from the farm of Mr. H. C. Paden, we have compiled the following facts, from which some of our ambitious orchardists may derive a degree of satisfaction.

Mr. Paden last February purchased the Robert Reed place, which, with additions since made by Mr. Paden, embraces 879 acres of land. The greater portion is creek bottom, and the balance rolling land. It is well watered by a living stream. When Mr. Paden took the place it embraced a vineyard of one acre and an orchard of six acres, which he decided to put under good cultivation in order to draw a correct conclusion as to the possibilities of the farm in that direction.

He expresses himself as agreeably disappointed in the result. He has apples, peaches, pears, plums, prunes, apricots, almonds, cherries, figs and nectarines, of standard varieties, and the size and quality of the fruit is simply excellent. The vigorous growth of the trees and character of the fruit completely demonstrate the adaptation of both soil and climate.

Mr. Paden is so well pleased with the growth and products of his orchard and vineyard that he will this winter set out ten acres to vines and probably double the size of his orchard.

[The editor of the *San Miguel Messenger*, almost a year later, on September 23, 1887, stated that "Mr. H. C. Paden, of Valleton, placed this office under obligations the first of the week for a lot of as fine pears as any country can boast of. Thanks!"]

In the October 22, 1886 edition of the paper, readers learned that "Mr. Coan, of Indian Valley, is erecting a new house on his place, west and across the creek from the old one. He expects to have it completed within two weeks." The next week's newspaper informed its readers that "Quails are said to be quite plentiful in the upper part of Indian Valley; a party of two hunters succeeded in killing dozens, one day last week."

Readers of the November 5, 1886 edition of *The Inland Messenger* learned that "A new store is being erected at the junction of Indian Valley and the Big Sandy, near Mr. Coan's place." The November 12th edition announced that "J. C. Elliot, from Santa Maria, has settled in the Indian Valley and has already commenced sowing grain."

The newspaper on November 12, 1886, stated that "C. R. Montgomery, of Indian Valley, advertises for a lost mare colt two years old. See notice in another column."

$10 Reward. On or about the first of September, strayed from my farm in Indian Valley, one brown filly, two years old, branded G. The above reward will be paid for the return of the animal.

C. R. Montgomery

Construction was the news topic for December 3, 1886: "Material is being placed on the ground, in the Indian Valley District, for a new school-house." And: "T. T. Mathieson, of Indian Valley, has erected a barn and is making an addition to his house."

"Proposed New School District in Indian Valley" was the headline on an article in the December 17, 1886 issue of the newspaper.

The citizens of the lower portion of Indian Valley have perfected a petition for their new school district and will immediately forward it for official action.

It takes a strip four miles wide from the south side of Eagle District. A meeting was held last Saturday at the residence of J. B. Tyus, at which A. Parlier was chosen chairman and W. Chappell secretary, to transact the business relating to a new organization. It was resolved that the new district be named

Monroe District; that the school-house be located as near the center of the district as possible, and that J. H. Cain, A. Parlier and J. Lasswell be recommended for Trustees.

Two additional items of news in the same issue of the paper were: "Mrs. Sonnicksen, Mrs. Desaldo, Miss Desaldo, Mr. Sumner and Mr. Sharon, all of San Jose, have taken up land in Indian Valley in the week past, and are building houses. All of the parties have been more or less connected with the fruit industry, and expect to engage in that business here." And: "Dr. Cain is putting up a good house on his Indian Valley farm."

The December 24, 1886 edition of *The Inland Messenger* announced that "J. E. Gaunyaw, of Indian Valley, is putting an addition to his house." The January 14, 1887 issue of the newspaper informed its readers that "John Lasswell, whose place is located at the mouth of Indian Valley, expects to set about 4,000 grape vines this winter- - -providing it rains."

On January 28, 1887, the paper stated that "J. E. Gaunyaw, of Indian Valley, this week perfected his purchase of 163 45/100 acres of land on which he lives, under the Act of January 13, 1881, for the relief of certain settlers, on restored railroad lands. This, we believe, is the first entry of the kind perfected in this region. The business was attended to by the Central Land Agency."

The May 13, 1887 issue of the newspaper reported that "The election held last Saturday in the Monroe school district, in Indian Valley, resulted in a unanimous vote, eleven in number, in favor of a tax to raise $200 to build a school house." The same edition of *The Inland Messenger* stated: "The people of the lower part of Indian Valley are doing good work in the line of improving the road, under the supervision of deputy road master, T. D. Phelps."

"Slack's Canyon Coal," was the headline for an article in the May 20th edition of the newspaper. "We are informed that there are about half a dozen miners at work in the tunnels of the Slack's Canyon coal mine, and that fourteen feet of coal, in the thickness of the vein, is already disclosed, though the limit is not reached. The prospect of a permanent and valuable mine is said to be first class."

George R. McIntosh gave the following description of Slack's Canyon.

Slack's Canyon, the next major stage stop after Peach Tree, was what is now the Walti

Ranch. Slack's Canyon post office, hotel and saloon was started about 1875 as a stage stop and run by George Powell. It was nick-named "Little Cheyenne," because it was considered a rather rough place.

The newspaper for May 27th also informed its readers that "There is considerable excitement in Indian Valley . . . over the proposed new railroad to the Southern Pacific coal mine. Lately a force of men have been put to work on the mine to test the quality of the coal. It has been found to be first-class. The seam is said to be fourteen feet wide, the largest in California. The mine is twenty-five or thirty miles from San Miguel. A railroad will probably be built soon. Most of the settlers along the proposed route are rejoicing in the hope of it."

On May 27, 1887, "Progress in the Slack's Canyon Coal Mine" was the headline on an article. "A party who visited Slack's Canyon last Sunday, reports about ten men employed in the coal mines at that place. Three tunnels are being run, about a quarter of a mile apart. Two of these are the old tunnels commenced years ago, in which it disclosed a fine body of fine coal. In the new tunnel a large body of ashes and coal cinders were struck. . . . Track has been laid in one of the tunnels and coal is being conveyed in a car to the surface where it is dumped. The indications are exceedingly favorable for the deployment of a valuable property."

On June 10, 1887, the newspaper carried these items: "The first annual school election was held in Monroe School District, in Indian Valley, last Saturday, and the following are the names of the trustees chosen: A. Parlier, to serve three years; T. D. Phelps, two years and John Lasswell, one year." And: "The work of building the school-house in Monroe District has commenced and the building is expected to be ready to begin school in by the 5th of July."

Slack's Canyon news, for June 10, 1887, was that "We are informed that the force of workmen at the Slack's Canyon coal mine has been increased to fifteen."

Readers of the June 24th edition of the newspaper learned that "The Indian Valley school, taught by Miss Lottie J. Matthis, will close on the 24th instant. There will be some very pleasant exercises in the afternoon of that day. The patrons are expected to be present." On July 8, 1887, the newspaper reported that "School in the new Monroe school district in Indian Valley opened this week under the tuition of Mrs. Smith."

On August 5, 1887, the newspaper informed readers that "Frank D. and Robert S. Cruess, of Indian Valley, who have been doing business in the name of Cruess Brothers, have dissolved partnership, as will appear from a notice appearing in another column."

There were two Cruess families in the San Miguel area: William Cruess on the Nacimiento, and his brother Robert, farming in Indian Valley. [William V. Cruess grew up on a wheat farm midway between the Nacimiento Ranch house and San Miguel. He went on to become an Emeritus professor of pomology at the University of California, and had one of its buildings named in his honor. Cruess worked in the Department of Nutritional Sciences in the College of Agriculture, becoming an expert on the growing of apples. His writings on the subject became a textbook.]

The Cruessville Post Office was established on April 13, 1888, then discontinued on July 31, 1891, when it was moved to San Miguel. It was located eight miles north of San Miguel, and named for Frank D. Cruess, the first postmaster.

The September 2nd edition of the newspaper informed people that "There was no school in Monroe district, in Indian Valley, the fore part of the week, owing to the illness of the teacher, Mrs. Smith, but we are pleased to learn that she is again able to be at her post of duty."

Illness of the teacher was not the only health problem readers learned about in the September 2, 1887 issue of the *San Miguel Messenger*. "We are informed that a number of cattle have lately died in the upper part of Indian Valley, of a disease resembling Texas fever. Mr. C. R. Montgomery is the heaviest loser so far as reported, he having lost 16 head within the season. Tyus lost one cow last week and J. F. Reasons a bull a few days since. An effort is being made to prevent the spread of the disease by the application of medicine by sub-cutaneous injection."

The newspaper for the same date stated that "B. G. Allen is again at his post in his store, selling goods. He opened a real estate office in Los Gatos last Saturday morning and ran the business successfully for a few hours, reporting sales by telegraph. He decided to quit while the business was good." Two weeks later, on September 16th, the paper said that "B. G. Allen has been putting up a dwelling house on his Indian Valley farm during the present week."

The paper, on September 9, 1887, provided the information that "The land contest of Spaw, claiming adversely to Mrs. and Miss De Zaldo, a tract lying in Indian Valley, has been decided by the San Francisco office in favor of the De Zaldos, with the recommendation that Spaw's pre-emption be cancelled."

On September 9th, the newspaper informed people that "Mr. C. R. Montgomery, of the upper part of Indian Valley, brought into this office last Tuesday some sample of the fruit grown on his farm. They include some fine large clusters of grapes from vines of the third year from cuttings, and peaches from trees two years in the orchard, that for size and color were quite extraordinary. One cannot but think favorably of a locality that produces such a quality of fruit."

The September 16, 1887 issue of the paper printed this ad:

Store & Stock of Goods
For Sale at Valleton, Monterey County
A Central Location at the intersection of
Slack's Canyon and Indian Valley Coal
Mines roads
Special Inducements will be given to a
suitable purchaser.
Team and Wagon also for sale cheap.
Call upon or address   R. Bousfield

The Valleton Post Office was located at the forks of Indian Valley and Big Sandy. It was established on February 7, 1887, then moved four miles southwest on December 12, 1901. It was discontinued on June 15, 1918, when it was moved to San Miguel. Valleton was located twelve miles north of San Miguel, and the first postmaster was Robert Bousfield.

Another item from the September 16, 1887 issue

The Indian Valley Baseball Team. Front row (l to r): Claude Azbell, Charles Carter, Will Rose. Back row (l to r): Delbert Hair, Van Rose, Bill Abernathy, George Azbell, Jim Douglas.

of the *San Miguel Messenger*: "B. G. Allen has been putting up a dwelling house on his Indian Valley farm during the present week." Readers also learned that "A steam engine and fixtures for hoisting and pumping were forwarded from [San Miguel] to Slack's Canyon coal mines this week." The following week, readers were told that "Another invoice of rail arrived this week for the Slack's Canyon coal mine. The San Luis Obispo papers speak of the coal mines in the north-eastern part of the county. The coal mines referred to are in the Slack's canyon region, some fifteen miles north of the county line."

"Attempted Murder: A Citizen Finds Strichnine in his Pot of Bacon and Beans" was the headline on an article in the *San Miguel Messenger* on September 23, 1887.

The Bonnifield, Firanzi and Garelli children, Indian Valley, 1918.

A turn-of-the-century postcard.

On the morning of the 15th instant, Mr. J. H. Dunlap, whose place is located some 15 miles up Indian Valley, left home and attended an auction sale in Valleton.

Returning about 5 o'clock, and being invited to take supper at Mr. Witherow's, he did so and then proceeded home, arriving about 9:30 p.m.

He had a kettle of bacon and beans cooked, from which he took a small quantity and fed his cat and two dogs, and then retired. Arising early, he looked out and saw both dogs and the cat lying dead near the door step. Not being able to account for this otherwise than upon the theory of poison in the food he gave them the night before, he took the bacon and beans and brought them to San Miguel and turned them over to Dr. Murphy for analysis.

An examination disclosed the presence of large quantities of strichnine mixed through the contents of the kettle, a single spoonful of which, in the opinion of the Dr., would have been sufficient to kill an adult person. Mr. Dunlap's escape from a deadly dose of poison may be attributed to his neighbor's friendly invitation to supper.

Dunlap is somewhat at a loss to discover a motive for this attempt on his life, having no difficulty with anyone. But the party who doctored that pot of beans must have meant business.

Another item in the September 23ʳᵈ issue of the newspaper: "Noah N. Daves has sold his Indian Valley land to John F. Cahill; consideration, $1,000."

The paper, on September 30, 1887, carried a lengthy article entitled "Double Murder in Indian Valley : Newton Azbill Settles a Land Contest by Shooting Two Men In Their Beds." [The name should be Azbell.]

Last Friday night, John McArdle and John C. Reardon were camped near Newton Azbill's place in Indian Valley, and the former had put up a notice claiming the land on which they were camped as a pre-emption, it being also claimed by Azbill under the Act for the Relief of Settlers on Restored Railroad Lands. It appears that Azbill had forbidden McArdle to settle there.

Saturday morning, just about sunrise, Mr. & Mrs. Fairington, who live in sight of the camp were aroused by the report of fire arms, two shots being fired in very quick succession and a third after an interval of two or three seconds.

Mrs. Fairington looked out in the direction of the camp and saw Azbill with his gun in his hand standing a short distance from the camp, the smoke still settling over the beds of the unfortunate sleepers. Mr. Fairington was called by his wife and the two saw Azbill walking away, stopping once and taking a step or two toward the camp.

Seeing no signs of life at the camp, and knowing that the men had been sleeping there, Mrs. Fairington hastened to the residence of John Daves, a half a mile distant, and told him what they had seen. Mr. Daves, who had also heard the shooting, accompanied by Mr. D. C. Howell, walked to the camp. There a blood-curdling scene met their gaze. The two men were dead!

Reardon was shot in the brain and McArdle in the heart. They lay in a position as though they had moved but slightly after receiving the fatal shots. There were about six buck shot in McArdle's breast in the region of the heart, while some of the charge appeared to have passed, cutting the vest and carrying portions of the vest to the ground a few feet away.

A pistol lay a few feet away, with one empty chamber. What part this weapon took in the tragedy may never be known, though from the position of the bodies, it would seem to be hardly possible that it had been in the hands of either of the murdered men. They had, apparently, passed 'without a struggle from the repose of sleep to the repose of death.'

A jury of twelve men were summoned by Justice Bousfield and an inquest was held upon the bodies as they lay. A verdict was rendered charging Newton Azbill with the murder.

In the meantime, a warrant had been issued and placed in the hands of Wayne Wayland, constable, who soon found that Azbill had left in a westerly direction, and it was ascertained in the evening that he had gone to San Lucas and surrendered to an officer there.

He was taken to Salinas Sunday, where he will await the action of the machinery provided by law for the punishment of crime. As the case will be made the subject of judicial action, we desire to avoid any expression that may be prejudicial to the prisoner; but the facts disclosed appear to brand the transaction as a murder, deliberate and diabolical, cold-blooded and cowardly. [It would be interesting to read the adjectives the editor would use, had he not desired to avoid being prejudicial.]

The bodies of the murdered men were taken to San Jose, by Sunday's train, to be met by the loved ones from whom they parted but a short time before full of life and hope.

The newspaper, on the same date, carried a story entitled "Young Reardon."

The San Francisco _Chronicle_ contains the following mention of young Reardon, who was killed by Azbill in Indian Valley, last Saturday.

Reardon's body arrived in this city on Sunday night, and will be buried today from St. Joseph's Church, when a solemn requiem high mass will be sung.

Mr. Reardon, the murdered boy's father, is nearly heart-broken over the terrible affair. He expresses his firm determination of going to Monterey as soon as his boy is buried and leaving no stone unturned to bring his murderer to justice.

Young Reardon was only a little over 20

years old, and his friends express the utmost horror and indignation at his murder. He was born in this city and raised here, graduating at St. Ignatius College.

He was a young man of high principles, and, while of an inoffensive disposition, he was fully able to take care of himself and was leader in athletic sports. In personal appearance he was one of the handsomest young men in this city, and was very popular among his large circle of acquaintants.

The September 30, 1887 edition of the newspaper also informed its readers that "Newton Azbill waived examination, admitted the killing of McArdle and Reardon, and was committed for murder, to wait the action of the Superior Court."

"The Azbill Case," was the heading on a lengthy article which appeared in the *San Miguel Messenger*, October 1, 1887.

The statements in our last issue, taken from dispatches to the San Francisco dailies, that Azbill had waived examination, under the charge for killing McArdle and Reardon, prove to have been erroneous.

His examination took place before Justice Roadhouse, in Salinas last Monday. Several witnesses were subpoenaed from the vicinity of the tragedy. The District Attorney was assisted by Robert Farrall, of San Francisco, and Geil & Morehouse appeared for defense. The testimony showed in the main the facts heretofore published; the defense offered no testimony and the prisoner was committed for murder, without bail. John C. Reardon, of San Francisco, father of the murdered young Reardon, and Mrs. McArdle, wife of the other man slain, were present at the examination.

Newton Azbell had been born in Missouri on January 1, 1844; he was brought west by his parents in 1851. In 1868, he married Eliza Davis, the daughter of George and Alecia Davis who had crossed the plains to Oregon in 1841. After his marriage, Newton Azbell moved to Hog Canyon, and engaged in the stock business for ten years; he subsequently went to Indian Valley and obtained 160 acres. His holdings were later increased by homesteading 160 acres more, and by the purchase of 40 acres, all of which he used to pasture sheep. He passed away on July 24, 1903 leaving his wife and five children.

The October 14, 1887 *San Miguel Messenger* publicized the fact that "There is to be a dance at the Monroe District School, Indian Valley, next Friday, the 21st

instant, for the benefit of the building fund of the district. Good music will be provided for the occasion, and an enjoyable time may be expected. Tickets, supper included, $1.50 per couple."

The newspaper on October 21, 1887 informed readers that "There is to be a dance at the Monroe Schoolhouse, Indian Valley, this Friday evening. It is for the benefit of the school.

The newspaper on October 28th stated that "Parties who attended the social dance last Friday evening at the Monroe schoolhouse in Indian Valley, speak of it as a very pleasant gathering, and in all respects a marked success. The net receipts were $71.90, which will materially assist the building fund of the District."

Readers of the November 4, 1887 issue of the *San Miguel Messenger* learned that "Newton Azbill has been arraigned under two informations for murder, to which he pleads not guilty. The case for the murder of Reardon is set for December 12th, and that for the murder of McArdle December 14th."

The newspaper of the following week carried the lead: "'Note from Slack's Canyon.' Among the noticeable improvements in this region is a neat new dwelling house by Mr. Wayland. He announces that he now has 'a cage, but not bird,' but he lives in hope that King Fortune may smile on him and that the bird will be found one of these days.

"He is encouraged by the experience of his neighbor, Mr. A. who recently built a new house under similar circumstances, and the bird was soon found in the presence of a charming young widow, who took charge of the cage and is apparently more than satisfied."

Also in the November 11, 1887 issue of the newspaper was the item: "The steam machinery for pumping is in operation in the Slack's Canyon coal mine, and we understand the mine gives increasing assurance of the existence of an extensive deposit of coal of a good quality."

The *San Miguel Messenger*, on November 18, 1887, informed its readers that "A concert and entertainment will be given at the Indian Valley schoolhouse, (upper district) Saturday evening, the 26th instant. An attractive program will be presented, and those who attend may feel assured of passing an evening very pleasantly. The proceeds will be applied toward paying Rev. S. B King for his service as minister in that neighborhood. We hope the enterprise may be entirely successful."

The November 18, 1887 issue of the *San Miguel Messenger* also carried the item that "R. Bousfield, postmaster at Valleton, has appointed M. Geo. Paden, his deputy, and the duties of the office are discharged by said deputy."

Readers of the newspaper on November 25th learned that "J. H. Rucker, of upper Indian Valley, has sold his farm of 160 acres of patented land, and the possessory right to 160 more to a Mr. Lee, of Delavan, Wisconsin, and the purchaser has gone east for his family. The consideration was $4,500.

"T. B. Royse, with his steam machinery, is engaged in drilling a well for John Cahill on his ranch, nine miles up Indian Valley," according to the newspaper on December 2, 1887.

On December 9th, newspaper readers learned that "The trial of Newton Azbill has been re-set for Monday, January 30th at 10 o'clock."

"Good Report from the Slack's Canyon Coal Mines," was the lead on an article in the December 16th issue of the newspaper.

A Cholame correspondent writes to the Salinas *Index* as follows: 'In conversation with the foreman of the Slack's Canyon coal mines today, he gave it as his opinion that, in less than a year from now, there will be over two hundred men working there. A thriving town will then surely grow up around the mine. The main working tunnel is 700 feet, showing a 14-foot vein of coal as good as any in the State. As they go down, the vein increases in size. The mine will, in all probability, be purchased by the Southern Pacific Improvement Company, and then Cholame will have a railroad.'

The newspaper on the same date stated that "A correspondent says that there are about thirty men employed in the Slack's Canyon Coal Mine. A new shaft is being sunk on account of the trouble from water in the old one."

An article in the December 30, 1887 issue of the *San Miguel Messenger* informed readers that "Rev. E. B. Tuthill will preach in Indian Valley, at the upper school-house at 11 a.m., and at the lower school-house, Monroe district, at 3 p.m. In consequence of this appointment there will be no service next Sabbath in the forenoon, but the usual meeting in the evening in San Miguel." [One value of reading this item, over one hundred years later, is to be able to approximate the locations of Indian Valley schools.]

"Persevering Work at the Coal Mine," was the lead on a December 30, 1887 article in the *San Miguel Messenger.*

It is said that there is about 1,000 tons of good coal on the dump of the Slack's Canyon coal mine, and the work still goes on. The expense of hauling this coal to San Miguel, the nearest shipping point, would be so great that the value of the commodity would not warrant it.

But from the manner in which the railroad authorities persevere in the expensive work of developing the property it would seem probable that they expect as soon as it is ascertained from what point it can be opened and worked to the best advantage to connect the mine with the main line by rail. Such a plan is evidently within the scope of the plans of the company. They have already demonstrated the fact of the existence of a large deposit of good coal, and yet they are spending thousands of dollars in running tunnels and sinking shafts. There is a boom slumbering in that Slack's Canyon coal mine.

This is an appropriate place to consider Stone Canyon, and its coal mines, as they relate to the Stone Canyon Railroad. The *San Luis Obispo Tribune*, on December 4, 1875, published the following article.

Coal Mine.- Last spring we made mention of the discovery of a valuable coal mine in Cholamie Valley. From the Hollister *Advance* of November 27th, we learn that the mine is in the upper end of the valley, in Peach Tree township, Monterey county, just across the line of San Luis Obispo. A company has been organized in Hollister, to develop the mine. F. M. Stone was elected president of the company, F. W. Blake, secretary, and C. L. Weller, of San Francisco, general agent. The *Advance* says the vein is from eight to twenty feet thick, and is open to view at different points for over a mile. The coal is bituminous and not at all pitchy. It yields considerable gas, and burns to a white ash, leaving no cinder. Good judges pronounce it the best coal yet discovered on the Pacific Coast.

The coal, on the San Andreas Fault, was discovered, in 1875, by Francis M. Stone of Hollister. This gentleman must have had some sort of speech problem, because his nickname was "Stutter-buck." On November 13, 1876, he "did enter and pay for" 160 acres in Section 14, Township 22 South, Range 13 East,

Stone Canyon to Bradley Stage.

Drawn by Steve Kalar

"the same being Coal Entry No. 9." A year and a half later, on May 25, 1878, the United States government granted the tract to Stone.

The coal did not out-crop, but was reported to have been discovered from a squirrel digging. A company was formed and mining begun; lack of transportation, however, caused the project to be abandoned. For the next eleven years, the mine was idle. Then, in April of

Railroad trestle to McKay Station from Stone Canyon.

1887, the Southern Pacific Railway Company obtained the property, along with 320 additional acres.

It was determined, in December of 1887, that shipment of the coal could not be done without a railroad; the distance was 25 miles. Again the mines were closed; they opened again in 1889.

While the mine was in operation, a community existed. In addition to the miners' individual homes, there was a cook-house, ice-house, and bunkhouses of one and two story. The community also had a post office, store and saloon. Aside from the mine buildings, there was the superintendent's house; during the years of 1921-1923, a small hospital was on the site.

A stage, operated by the mine company, ran for a few years; it carried both passengers and mail from Bradley to Stone Canyon. The driver made three trips a week, staying alternately at the mine and at Bradley, serving Valleton Post Office at the forks of Indian Valley, Big Sandy Creek and Slacks Canyon en route.

The mine was opened for commercial purposes in 1908, by Joseph A. Chanslor, the Vice-President of Stone Canyon Consolidated Coal Company. This coal

Amos Fraser at the controls of Engine 102 of Stone Canyon Railroad.

was originally hauled down Hare Canyon to Bradley to the Southern Pacific by steam tractor.

After the mine was worked for about one year, it was sold to the Stone Canyon Consolidated Coal Company. In 1911, the company reverted back to the original owner.

What we know as McKay station, three miles north of San Miguel, was first named Chanslor, after the above-named gentleman. The name was changed to McKay, when the line went into receivership; Hood McKay, of New York, was the receiver. According to a letter, written by R. M. Magraw, General Superintendent of the United States Fuel Company, of Hiawatha, Utah, dated October 3, 1920, McKay was formally called Watkins, after T. H. Watkins, president of the Stone Canyon Consolidated Coal Company.

The railroad had been built in 1907 by this company; the line ran up Indian Valley, with the last few miles up a valley called Big Sandy. The Stone Canyon

Stone Canyon R.R., Coal Fields Railway #2288 at McKay on September 12, 1933.
From the collection of the Rail Photo Service

Railroad was sometimes called the Coal Fields Railway. It ran 21 ½ miles from the Southern Pacific siding at McKay to the mines. The elevation at McKay was 500 feet above sea-level, and 1,800 feet above sea-level at the "tipple." (The tipple was the apparatus for tipping the coal from the mine cars.) The elevation at the mine was over 2,700 feet. Two hundred horses, in teams, were used by the Sandercock Construction Company to build the road bed.

A broad-gauge railroad went to the bunker, then a narrow-gauge continued on a double-incline track. The cars came down loaded; to return, the engine would run backwards, pushing the empty cars ahead of it. There were only two level spots on the line: one at the Salinas River crossing, and the other at a siding, about ten miles east of McKay.

The railway, which was built in 1907, crossed the Salinas River on a 1320-foot trestle, 30 feet above the river bottom. At McKay, the river was 15 feet deep. The bridge was washed out in 1909, and again in January of 1914, when the wooden bridge at San Miguel was washed out and then took out part of the trestle.

Over the years, seven men were killed in accidents, including Gregor Kirkham. This 27-year old person, killed in 1902, is buried in a lonely grave up Dead Man's Canyon.

The *San Miguel Sentinel*, on March 30, 1918 printed an article entitled "Fall Off Bridge At McKay."

J. R. Walsh, who has been working for W. P. Gregory tearing down the old Stone Canon railroad trestle over the Salinas river at McKay, fell from the top of the trestle, Friday, to the sand below, a distance of 27 feet, landing on his face and chest. He was brought to his home here and Dr. Murphy was called to attend him.

The lone train wreck of the railroad took place in 1924, when the train flattened a fender on Bob Easton's Overland. Amos Fraser, the engineer, lived at McKay Station for 21 years.

In 1937, both engine and rails were sold for scrap to the Japanese government.

[Most of this information comes from an article written by Ella Adams, and published in the 1976 Pioneer Edition of *The Daily Press*.]

The *San Miguel Sentinel*, on February 23, 1918, carried an item of information which demonstrated the progress of people in Indian Valley.

Charles [Lester] Montgomery of Indian Valley is having a number of wells put down

on his ranch for irrigation. He is also having a large pump and engine fixed up on a portable truck so it can be moved to each well. Charlie says safety first from now on.

VINEYARD, RANCHITA AND LOWE'S CANYONS

In this section, we will follow the progress of the people of Vineyard, Ranchita and Lowe's Canyons, as they develop their region, and as the development is reported in San Miguel's newspaper, *The Inland Messenger*. The paper began on April 30, 1886; its name was changed to the *San Miguel Messenger* on April 29, 1887. Portions of these areas are situated in southern Monterey County, but have always been an important part of the area around San Miguel.

The Inland Messenger, on May 14, 1886, informed its readers that "Miss Lattie Matthis, teacher at the Ranchita Canyon school, was in town last week. She has an excellent school of some twenty-four scholars."

In the same paper, for the same date, readers learned that "B. F. Welker, an enterprising mechanic, is about to open a blacksmith shop at Wallace Low's place, Low's canyon; it is said to be quite a central locality." [Wherever the editor refers to "Low," it should be "Lowe."]

We can gain much information about the Lowe family by referring to an address that Dr. Franklin A. Lowe gave at the Estrella Adobe Church on May 18, 1975. Dr. Lowe spent over 50 years in medical practice in San Francisco and Marin County.

William Wallace Lowe married Elizabeth McMurray in Indiana in 1846. This couple migrated west, missing being members of the original Donner Party by one day. They first settled in Hangtown, now called Placerville; later they moved to Oroville, where William Wallace Lowe was associated with John Bidwell. Next, they spent fourteen years in Healdsburg, in Sonoma County.

In 1868, members of the Lowe family took a buckboard and two saddle horses to the "Lower Country," and en route visited the Fathers at San Antonio Mission. The Lowes continued on horseback, and discovered that in the San Jacinto Canyon, east of San Miguel, wild oats were so tall that they could be tied over the saddle horses' backs.

Believing that they had found a Bonanza, the Lowes returned to Healdsburg to relate their experiences. Deciding to move south, they left Healdsburg on October 22, 1868; it took thirteen days to travel the 357 miles. They arrived at the Nacimiento Ranch on November 3, 1868.

In 1874, William and Elizabeth Lowe homesteaded land, seven miles northeast of San Miguel, in San Jacinto Canyon, which later became "Lowe's Canyon." There they raised their seven children, all of whom had been born north of Healdsburg, at Lyton on the Russian River. The children, and the year of birth for each were: Wallace (1849), Frank Edward (1854), Mark (1856), Martin (1858), Elizabeth Emily (1860), Nancy Ellen (1861) and Harriet Ann (1869).

On a trip to Missouri with his mother, in 1885, Frank Edward Lowe met and married Carrie Belle Jones; he brought his bride west, and they made their home in Lowe's Canyon. Eventually, William and Elizabeth Lowe moved to Arroyo Grande, so Frank and Carrie Belle Lowe took over the homestead.

It was on the original homestead that their seven children were born: Guy (1886), Anna (1888), Franklin Alexander (1890), Alliance (1892), Beatrice (1894), William Jennings Bryan (1896), and Georgia (1899). All of these children were delivered by a mid-wife; "Old Doc" Murphy would come out to the ranch to see if all was well.

Dr. Frank A. Lowe relates the following information from his youth.

> **Harvest life was strenuous, going six miles round trip, twice a day, with a horse-drawn wagon fitted out with water barrels to get enough water for the work horses. It took a six-horse team to plow a 24-inch strip of land. We seeded, using a two-wheel cart with a chain to the sowing machine, feeding the grain out of a hopper, sowing 30 to 40 pounds to the acre.**
>
> **In order to space the rows, a boy rode a horse with a guide line to one of the cart's horses, spacing the rows using the last row seeded as a guide. The seed was covered by harrow or cultivator.**

According to Don McMillan, Frank's uncle, Martin Lowe, used to ferry people across the Salinas River in a row boat, prior to the bridge being built. Dr. Frank Lowe said that Martin spent his summers at Lake Tahoe; he would dive into the lake and catch a trout with his teeth. What observers of this feat did not know was that he had captured a number of fish in advance, and confined them under the pier. While on his way to his annual summer visit to Lake Tahoe, Martin Lowe died of a heart attack on the train near Roseville; his death took place in 1925, when he was 68 years of age.

Frank Edward Lowe passed away from a heart

attack in 1913. Carrie Belle Lowe retained possession of the original homestead; she taught school in the San Miguel and Parkfield areas, mainly at the Vineyard Canyon School, until her retirement. She passed away in 1945 at the age of 83. Upon her death, the property was sold by her heirs.

On May 28, 1886, the newspaper reported that "C. H. Reed, the San Luis Obispo hardware dealer, has taken a land claim near the mouth of Vineyard canyon, and has his house already erected."

The July 30, 1886 edition had an unusual feature. "We have reliable information that Patrick O'Holloran, of Vineyard Canyon, is the possessor of a natural curiosity in the form of a chicken, now some two weeks old, that has four well-developed and perfectly-formed legs and feet. The two used for walking are of natural form and located in the usual portion of the body, while the extra pair are immediately forward of these, of about normal size, with toes turned to the rear. The four limbs are very nearly of a size, and when the chick is not walking it would be difficult to tell which are the supernumerary. The chicken moves about without difficulty, and appears quite hearty."

In the following week's newspaper, readers learned that "The four-legged chicken, mentioned in our last issue, will be on exhibition at this office one week from next Monday, provided nothing happens; it, the chick, having been presented to a reporter of this paper by Mrs. O'Holloran, of Vineyard Canyon." [The O'Hollorans donated land as a site for the Vineyard School.]

The August 6th edition of the newspaper stated that "Mr. Charles Maxwell, of the San Luis *Republic*, has a homestead filing upon 160 acres of land at the head of Vineyard Canyon."

On August 20, 1886, *The Inland Messenger*, informed readers that "Mr. & Mrs. R. R. Kirkpatrick, of the Ranchita country, left yesterday in their own carriage for Oakland. They go to look after property interests there, and will be absent about six weeks."

R. R. Kirkpatrick, a veteran of the Mexican War and our Civil War, had been born in Armstrong County, Pennsylvania, on December 9, 1826. In 1849, he married Libby Lloyd; they were the parents of six children. After fifteen years of marriage, Mrs. Kirkpatrick died; in 1874, he married Mrs. Annie Walker, widow of Frank Walker. The Kirkpatricks arrived in San Luis Obispo County in 1882; they filed a claim on 320 acres, three miles due east of San Miguel.

Readers of the September 10th newspaper were

made aware of the following: "Mr. W. W. Low, of Low's Canyon, relates his success in hog raising. Three years ago he bought one sow, and from the product of this one animal he has sold $250 worth, and now has 300 head left." Also in the September 10th newspaper: "J. V. Houghton, of Ranchita Canyon, has been appointed Deputy County Clerk to register voters in that part of Monterey county. A citizen of Independence precinct thinks there will be 50 or 60 votes cast there the coming election."

The Inland Messenger, on September 17, 1886, announced that "Mr. J. B. Mahoney gives the public notice in another column to cease making roads through his lands in Sections 14 and 15 of this township."

Readers of the newspaper for September 24th were told that "We understand that F. O'Hare of Vineyard Canyon, whose place is located in a region where water has been supposed to be scarce, came across a fine spring on his hillside a few days since. It is only necessary to lay a pipe to have an abundance of water at his house."

The October 8, 1886 edition of the paper printed a letter entitled "A Protest."

Ed. *Messenger*: **The settlers of Vineyard, Ranchita and Lowe's canyons are being introduced to a new form of "Surprise Party." This is done by spreading the report that on a certain night there will be a dance at a friend's house. When that time arrives, the one to be surprised is astonished to find himself, without a moment's notice being given, hemmed in on all sides by eager friends who wish to shake their feet at his floor. This practice should be stopped, as it is very disagreeable. It only causes ill-feeling, and places both parties in an uncomfortable position, especially when the would-be surprisers forget their lunch baskets, and furnish no fiddler.**
A subscriber.

The newspaper on October 15, 1886 publicized the information that "Mr. Thomas Trainor, of the Santa Clara Valley, was in this region last week, and selected a tract of land between Indian Valley and Vineyard Canyon, where he proposes to make a large fruit-farm. He is a practical orchardist, and thinks this climate well adapted for both the raising and curing of fruit. The best varieties for this country, he thinks, are French prunes and apricots."

Readers were also informed, in the October 15th

issue of the paper that "N. V. Ingram has sold his place in Low's Canyon to Mr. J. B. Nelson, who is moving to his new home."

The October 22, 1886 issue of the newspaper reported that "Last Friday, Wm. Forsyth, who purchased a quantity of hay at a Constable's sale on the premises of Wm. M. Davis of Vineyard Canyon, went there to remove it, when Davis came out and threatened to kill any man who should attempt to open the fence or handle any of the hay. Of course pitchforks were no match for the Winchester rifle that Davis said he possessed and the party retreated. But Mr. Davis has been arrested for threatening to commit a crime, and been taken before Justice Stone, of Parkfield, for examination." An additional item in the same issue of the paper stated that "Wm. M. Davis, whose threat to kill Wm. Forsyth is mentioned elsewhere, was placed under $500 bonds by Justice Stone of Parkfield. Whether the required security has been given we are unable to say."

Readers on October 29, 1886 were informed that "W. W. Low, of Low's Canyon, took another drove of hogs to San Luis last Friday." The November 26th paper passed on the information that "W. W. Low, of Low's Canyon, has been much annoyed of late by a small band of coyotes, who were making havoc among his pigs and turkeys. He purchased some traps last week, and has already succeeded in catching three large ones. These animals are said to be more troublesome than usual, probably on account of the absence of their prey of former years- - -the sheep."

The Inland Messenger, on January 7, 1887, announced: "A church social and supper for the benefit of the Ranchita M. E. Church fund, was advertised to

Methodist Episcopal Church, Estrella, California, E. Guy Talbott, Pastor.

take place at Mr. Gordenier's place on Estrella, last (Thursday) evening." By summertime, funds were still being raised for the church. [Gordenier's place was near the intersection of today's Estrella Road and Airport Road.]

The March 4, 1887 edition of the paper carried this item: "G. N. Douglas this week sold 160 acres in Vineyard Canyon to T. C. Slusser, for $1,700. The sale was negotiated by the Central Land Agency."

Readers on May 6, 1887 learned that "Mr. Fales, from near Parkfield, passed through Vineyard Canyon last week. His mission was to ascertain who would give the right of way for the contemplated county road. He only found four persons who wanted compensation."

The newspaper for the following week stated that "Jesse D. Carr, the purchaser of the Adams place a few miles east of here, is having the orchard pruned and the place otherwise improved." The news on June 10th was that "A Vineyard Canyon farmer reports that the squirrels have made great havoc among his young turkeys this year. In a single day when left alone forty-six of the chicks were killed."

The same issue of the paper informed people that "A dime festival at J. E. McCord's residence in Ranchita Canyon, last Friday evening, was well attended and all present had a good time. It was for the benefit of the library of the Ranchita M. E. Church."

On June 17, 1887, the *San Miguel Messenger* carried this story: "A petition is being circulated for a road from the northern end of the San Miguel town site to the County line in Vineyard Canyon, by a nearly direct course. The proposed road touches the lands of Kunz, Davis, Mahoney, Currier, Toolson and Phinney, nearly all of whom propose to give the right of way. Mr. J. B. Mahoney is called upon to make a greater sacrifice for the public welfare in that connection than any other citizen, but manifests a spirit of liberality that is very commendable."

Another item in the June 17th edition of the paper: "On the 28th ult. there was a picnic at the residence of Mr. J. A. Grout, in Vineyard Canyon; about fifty people from the neighborhood being present. There is a beautiful grove at the place where dinner was taken and amusements indulged in till near evening, when the company went to the residence of Mr. H. Lawson and danced till midnight. The occasion was highly enjoyed by all present."

The June 24, 1887 edition of the *San Miguel Messenger* reported that "A friend has furnished us the following list of land owners on the line of the new road from Parkfield to the County line in Vineyard Canyon, who were magnanimous enough to give the necessary right of way to Monterey county without charge: G. W. Clark, Geo. S. Gould, F. O'Hare, W. C. Watson, W. M. Davis, Samuel G. Parker, Peter Mullen, R. M. Hilliker and F. M. Morgan."

On July 1, 1887, the newspaper educated readers that "We are informed that the land contest between Wm. H. Wheeler and S. Houghton, involving the right of entry to 160 acres in Ranchita, has been decided in favor of contestant Wheeler. Mr. Houghton's entry was under the Timber Culture Law, while Wheeler relied upon the land as not being subject to the Timber Culture entry."

The paper on July 1, 1887, carried a lengthy article entitled "The Sequel of a Tragedy."

The death of John C. Croall, which occurred in Vineyard Canyon last Tuesday, was the direct result of a bloody tragedy that occurred in San Miguel two years ago.

Croall had formed an attachment for Miss Elsie Cotter, a girl about 16 years of age, who resided with her parents in Vineyard Canyon, and a contract of marriage was formed between them.

The marriage was violently opposed by the Cotter family, and especially by the sons, William and Lewis. Croall procured a license and it was arranged that the girl should meet him, and that they should go away and have the marriage solemnized. Croall proceeded at night with his wagon to a point where the girl was expected to appear, and not seeing her, he left the wagon with a friend and went in search of the object of his affection.

During his absence, the Cotter brothers came and took Croall's team away from the party who had it in charge and concealed it. In the meantime the girl had been taken by a friend as far as Jolon, on the stage road.

The next morning, the Cotter boys and Croall met on the road and high words passed between them. Croall came on to San Miguel and tried to get out a warrant for their arrest for taking his wagon, but failing in that he met the Cotter brothers again near Goldtree & Co.'s store, and another altercation ensued in which abusive epithets were mutually passed.

William Cotter ran to his wagon which was standing in front of Jeffreys Hotel, seized his gun and stepping to the porch of Goldtree & Co.'s store, took aim at Croall and fired. His

victim, who was two or three rods away, fell with a bullet in his hip; another shot was fired as the wounded man lay upon the ground.

Croall was taken up and properly cared for, and after many months was able to move about and drive a team. Slowly but surely, the process of dissolution has been going forward for two years, and John C. Croall breathed his last in the arms of his brother last Tuesday evening, from the effect- - -as the doctors say- - -of the wound received at the hands of William Cotter.

The case has never been made the subject of a judicial investigation.

The following article appeared later in the July 1, 1887 edition of the *San Miguel Messenger*: "DIED. CROALL - At the residence of F. McMannus, in Vineyard Canyon, June 28, 1887, John C. Croall, aged 36 years. The subject of the above notice was a native of Jamaica, of English parentage, who had no relatives in this country except a brother, Charles D. Croall, of Mountain View, who was at his bedside at the time of his death. He was a quiet, well-disposed man who communicated the esteem of those with whom he associated. The body was taken to Mountain View by Wednesday's train, for interment."

The July 1, 1887 issue also informed readers that "We are informed that Mr. J. B. Mahoney has sold two sections of his land, numbers 14 and 15, lying east of town, to a company of capitalists with the Southern Pacific Railroad Company. The price is reported to be about $12 per acre."

One week later, the newspaper reported that "Patrick O'Holloran, of Vineyard Canyon, has lately sold 800 head of sheep to Mr. Dagnery, of McClure Valley." The July 15, 1887 issue also informed readers that "Mr. I. C. Jones, of the upper Cholame, roadmaster of the district embracing the new road over the mountain by the way of Vineyard Canyon, was in town Wednesday. The road is nearly completed." [Ella Adams said that the people referred to this road as "Yerba Buena."]

Another item in the July 15th newspaper was that "Carrell & Massey have been drilling a well for James Knight, in Ranchita Valley, the past week, and have struck water at 204 feet."

The August 12, 1887 edition of the *San Miguel Messenger* printed a lengthy article entitled "A Direct Road to Ranchita Canyon."

A movement is on foot to open up a new road from this place direct to Kirkpatrick's

place, accommodating the settlers of Ranchita and Low's canyons and two or three smaller valleys, all of whom are now compelled to reach this place by way of the Estrella creek, some two or three miles further than the distance by the route proposed. Mr. G. W. Proctor, who has carefully studied the country over which the road should pass, reports an excellent route, being nearly level.

A small amount of labor would suffice to put the road in good condition, if once established. There is no doubt that this is one of the natural highways of the country, that will soon be opened up. It will traverse the tract recently sold by J. B. Mahoney to some San Francisco parties and another large tract owned by non-residents. It is probable that the owners of these lands will see that the opening of a good road will make the lands more available for sale in small tracts, and will readily grant the necessary rights of way to the county. It is to be hoped that the large population to be accommodated by their road will follow up the matter till the highway is an established fact.

The August 19th edition of the newspaper provided some real estate information: "Mr. Chas. Thiriet has sold his ranch in Vineyard Canyon to A. R. Cotton, Esq., for the sum of $2,000." And: "Nicholas Molenus, of Vineyard Canyon, has sold his farm, of 160 acres, together with the possessory right to a homestead, for $1,950. The purchaser is Mr. Judson Rice, of San Jose."

Readers of the August 26th issue of the paper had a report that: "A big fire has been burning in the upper part of Vineyard Canyon during the latter part of last week and the first of this week, doing a good deal of damage to feed. Robert Kirk's barn and four or five tons of hay were destroyed."

On September 2nd, readers of the newspaper learned that "We are informed that Mr. C. H. Shultze, of Vineyard Canyon, narrowly escaped being burned out by the fire of last week. He attributes the saving of his property to the timely aid of neighbors from the Cholame valley, who came over and fought the fire heroically."

The September 2, 1887 newspaper also announced that "R. R. Kirkpatrick, Esq., is putting up windmill, tank, house and barn on his ranch, at the foot of Ranchita valley. These improvements will be of a substantial character, and when they are completed the farm will be one of the best equipped places in the section."

The following week, newspaper readers on September 9th learned that "The people of Ellis school district propose to have a ball at an early day for the benefit of the school building fund."

The *San Miguel Messenger* for September 16, 1887 informed readers that: "Mr. M. Withers has purchased the Spencer Childers place, in Ranchita, for $1,500." The following week, on September 23rd, readers learned that "Our friend W. W. Low, took his departure Wednesday for his new home in Arizona. He has taken an interest in a large band of cattle in that territory, belonging to E. J. Stone of Parkfield, and expects to remain at least three years. We wish him abundant success."

On October 7, 1887, readers of the newspaper could learn that "Mr. T. C. Slusser is painting his dwelling house and other buildings on his farm in Vineyard Canyon. He is also walling up his well with hard brick. All his improvements are of a very substantial character." Two other items of news were: "W. W. Orr, of the Inland & Coach Stage Company, has located a nice tract of public land near Vineyard Canyon." And: "Patrick O'Holloran, one of the substantial farmers of Vineyard Canyon, is fencing his tract of land adjoining John Fitzgerald's farm." Ranchita Canyon news, in the October 7th newspaper, was that "J. A. Grout and Wm. Rouan have traded lands in Ranchita Canyon for property in Pacific Grove. The purchaser is J. O. Johnson, of Pacific Grove."

Readers of the *San Miguel Messenger* on October 14, 1887, learned that "The dance at the school in Ellis District last Friday night is said to have been a very pleasant affair. There was a large attendance and the occasion was fully enjoyed by all present."

"That Ranchita Road," was the lead on an article in the October 21, 1887 issue of the paper.

Some weeks since, the subject of a new road eastward from this place, reaching the Ranchita settlement by a much shorter and better route than the one now traveled, was agitated.

Land owners along the proposed road were consulted, and expressions favorable to the road were everywhere met. Mr. A. I. Burbank, of Los Angeles, the owner of a large tract on the line of the road, came promptly forward and proposed to grant a right of way. H. R. Judah, of the Southern Pacific Company and others are owners of two sections of land on the line of which, we understand, this road will run.

Ralph Von Dollen, Kenneth Sinclair, Clarence Sinclair, Fred Von Dollen, Mabel Sinclair, Margaret Von Dollen, Maybelle Kinny-Teacher, and Marie Von Dollen standing in the yard of Ranchita Canyon School, 1929-1930. (The school faced west.)

If a right of way can be obtained from these parties, what is to prevent a petition being sent to the Board of Supervisors immediately for the establishment of a public highway on this route? The proposed road is destined to become one of the leading avenues into San Miguel. It will accommodate a large population in Ranchita and Hog Canyons, and will intersect the new road from the Cholame. Will not some of our enterprising citizens take the preliminary steps to have the road established?

The October 28, 1887 issue of the paper informed readers that "The Ranchita District School taught by Miss E. Mackey, of San Francisco, is progressing finely. There are at present eighteen scholars in attendance." The same issue of the paper stated that "Mr. Ernest Wehner, brother of the purchaser of the Parker and Muller places in Vineyard Canyon, arrived Wednesday. We understand that he will improve the property."

Also on October 28th, readers learned that "Mr. C. P. Faulkner, who has a nice tract of land in Ranchita Valley, on which he is making a home, came down from San Francisco on the 14th. He already has a thrifty young orchard, among other improvements, which is making such rapid growth that he is encouraged to plan for setting out 10,000 vines the coming spring."

On November 4, 1887, the newspaper carried an article entitled "Death of John A. Grout." Readers learned that "John A. Grout was killed Wednesday of last week. He was engaged in hauling a load of iron pipe from Monterey to the ranch for repairs on the pipe line, and let his four-horse team stand while he went down to the river to get a drink. While gone, the horses started to run away, and he, in trying to stop them, was thrown under the wagon, and the wheel, passing over his head, crushed out his life almost instantly.

"He held a $3,000 policy in the Chosen Friends. He was a widower, and leaves surviving him a daughter somewhere in the Eastern States. He was well known here, having lived for about a year in Ranchita Canyon, where he perfected a title to a tract of land. A few months since he accepted a situation as teamster for the Pacific Improvement Company. He bore the characteristics of a good citizen."

The *San Miguel Messenger*, on November 25, 1887, informed readers that "Dr. Neal has put up a house on his place in Oak Canyon and is running a tunnel for water." [Oak Canyon was also called Mahoney Canyon; it is situated between Vineyard and Lowe's Canyons.] The same issue of the newspaper announced that "W. H. Wheeler, of Ranchita, arrived with his bride from Sacramento County, last Friday. He is putting up a new house and otherwise fitting up for a home."

"Serious Accident" was the headline on an article in the December 2, 1887 issue of the paper.

Last Saturday, as Mrs. Dickenson, of Vineyard Canyon, was driving into town accompanied by Mrs. Brooks, her elder sister, recently from Colorado, the horse took fright at a passing train and sheering out of the road brought the wagon against the bank. The wagon was overturned, throwing the occupants out with great violence. Mrs. Brooks suffered the fracture of her leg at the thigh, and Mrs. Dickenson was somewhat bruised.

Dr. Murphy was called and set the fractured limb of Mrs. Brooks, who is a lady over sixty years of age. She is at the residence of Charles Thiriet, and is doing as well as could be expected.

The next week, readers were told that "The Ranchita M. E. Church society desire to tender a hearty vote of thanks to the merchants of San Miguel and others who so kindly contributed to the parsonage fund."

The same newspaper, on December 9th, stated that "A deed has been sent to Captain Currier, prepared by the Board of Supervisors of Monterey County, for the right of way for the road from Parkfield down Vineyard Canyon to the county line, and parties whose land is crossed by said road as located are requested to call and sign the document."

One week later, the December 16, 1887 issue of the *San Miguel Messenger* announced that "One of the most pleasurable events in upper Ranchita for many days was the closing exercises of the Independence school. The program was a pleasing variety and was well rendered. . . .Miss Matthis, the teacher, has well won the esteem of all in her school work and Ranchita society mourns the loss of one of its leaders. On the strength of this sentiment a choice present of a beautiful toilet set was presented."

The same issue of the newspaper announced that "The pupils of Ranchita school, taught by Miss E. Mackey, will give an entertainment and supper at the Ranchita M. E. Church this (Friday) evening, at 6:30 o'clock. An interesting time is expected and all who can do so are cordially invited to attend."

In 1886, Gustav Dauth, and his wife Francisca Streibinger Dauth, arrived in the San Miguel area; they homesteaded in Lowe's Canyon along with Gustav's parents. Gustav and Francisca were the parents of Carl, Otto, Adolph and Emily. Francisca died at a young age, and Gustav did not remarry. After his children were grown, Gustav left Lowe's Canyon and spent the rest of his life in South America.

Otto Dauth, born in 1888, remained in Lowe's Canyon, and was an expert handler of mule teams. For a time, he worked on Tom Rougeot's Hog Canyon ranch. In 1913, Otto married Sarah Rougeot, Tom's oldest daughter. Otto and Sarah raised three children: Velma, Raymond and Lester. In 1928, the family moved to Paso Robles. Shortly thereafter, Sarah passed away; Otto brought up the children by himself. While raising the children, he supervised the farming of the family ranch, and also ran his Paso Robles Laundry.

Raymond was a World War II pilot, lost in the Pacific in 1945.

Velma Dauth married Walter Maxwell "Max" Rhyne in 1933. They were the parents of Maxine, Keith and Glen. Glen and Linda (Marin) Rhyne are the parents of Wade, Sarah and Audrey.

Henry Stuart Foote Rhyne, had been born in Mis-

sissippi in 1852, and came to California in 1869. He met and married Nellie Kitchen in Salinas, and they were the parents of ten children; they homesteaded and pre-empted 320 acres on the Huer Huero River in 1882. Walter married, Isabel Reynolds, the daughter of Dwight and Mary Johnson Reynolds. Dwight came to California in 1860; he traveled by ship, from New York, the trip taking 21 days. In 1874, he settled in San Luis Obispo County, and in 1875 he married Mary. Walter and Isabel Rhyne raised four children: Ruth Juanita, Mildred Isabel, Walter Maxwell and Carol May.

Lester Dauth, the youngest son, married Adella Testerman, and became the parents of Vicki and Raymond. After Adella passed away in 1975, Lester married Marilyn Kester Taylor; he still supervises the farming of land that has been in the family for five generations.

PLEASANT VALLEY, HOG CANYON, KEYES CANYON AND ESTRELLA

The growth and development of the settlements in Pleasant Valley, Hog Canyon, Keyes Canyon and Estrella can be followed by reading the items which mention these areas in *The Inland Messenger*, beginning on April 30, 1886, then reading from the *San Miguel Messenger*, as the paper's name became on April 29, 1887. The first mention of these areas appears in *The Inland Messenger*, on May 7, 1886, when the community of Verna is noted; we know the location today as Estrella Circle. According to the May 7th edition, "Growing. The embryo town of Verna is about to receive its second business establishment in the shape of a blacksmith shop, to be erected immediately by a man named Jackett, formerly of West Virginia. He will also erect a dwelling house near the shop."

"The new blacksmith shop at Verna has opened up for business, and is said to be doing well," according to the paper on May 28th.

Estrella is mentioned in this newspaper on June 11, 1886. "A petition is being circulated for a county road up the San Jacinto canyon, connecting with the Estrella road near Thompson's." Two other items concerning Estrella were found in the June 11, 1886 edition of the newspaper. "From Verna. - A gentleman from Verna says the Postoffice Department has taken favorable action on the petition for a postoffice at that place, and it is expected that the machine will be in running order in a month or so. An Oakland man is talking of going into the furniture business there, and the prospects of the town generally are considered good."

"Place Sold. - Capt. Currier last week negotiated the sale to Thos. F. Faw, of Gonzales, of the Blockman place, 320 acres, about four miles up the Estrella. The price is said to have been about $11 per acre. The purchase is probably for speculation."

An Estrella item from the June 25th edition of the newspaper was entitled "Good Showing. - Many people who have listened to the woeful stories that 'nothing but sheep would grow in this region,' have visited this section within the past three months, and were surprised to find waving fields of grain, orchards, vineyards and vegetable gardens as fine as any in the State.

"Mr. H. W. Rhyne has twelve acres set out to trees and vines, on the Estrella Plain, which were planted three years ago. Mr. Marden, of the adjoining place, also has a fine orchard. The growth of the trees seen upon Mr. Rhyne's farm is simply marvelous, and he informed a reporter of this paper that, although the fruit does not attain so large a growth as in some other portions of the State, the flavor is far superior to that of fruits raised upon irrigated land. Mr. F. Rhyne and Mr. Wm. Penman, as well as other orchardists on the Estrella, believe that the chief reason the fruit does not grow large, arises from the fact that the trees bear too abundantly. . . ."

"Dry Creek Items," was the lead on an article in the June 25, 1886 newspaper. "Wm. Penman has an orchard of 250 trees and 200 well-selected grape vines. He planted trees sixteen months ago, and they will bear fruit this season. A pretty good indication that trees and vines will thrive here, and without irrigation, too."

The Inland Messenger on June 25, 1886 also stated that "On Friday, July 2d, the school in this district will close. There will be an examination of the pupils during the day, and a concert and exhibition at night. Prof.

This photo, taken in 1936, shows (l to r) Gladys Rougeot, Eileen Wells, Doris Wells, Roween Wells, Mildred Rougeot and Lester Rougeot.

Photo courtesy Thelma Jardine

Sanders has spared no pains to perfect the scholars and no fears are entertained as to the success of the entertainment."

The June 25, 1886 edition informed readers that "Mr. John Dickie has gone to Cayucos for lumber and material for a house that he will soon erect on his ranch in Keyes Canyon." [Keyes Canyon was possibly named for James Keyes, who had $5,150 in assessed property in 1860.] Also in that paper: "The Proctor house on the east side has been vacated by its former owner and now constitutes a part of the Maxwell Hotel property. Mr. Proctor has moved some two miles up the Estrella." Readers of that edition learned that "It is reported that seven threshing crews will be at work on Estrella Plains this season."

The next mention of these areas was on July 23, 1886. "Some fine samples of corn from Hog Canyon were brought to this office last Saturday, by Mrs.

Keyes Canyon School, Spring, 1915.

Shuey. The man that asserted that this is not a corn country would probably take it back if he were to see a field like these samples."

[Josephus Martin Shuey came to Hog Canyon in 1884; his wife was Sarah Newland. They were the parents of three daughters: Luella, Emma and Ida May. Luella Shuey married James Elliott Gorham; Luella Gorham later married George Von Dollen. Ida May is an ancestor of Gladys Craspay. The George Work ranch is located at the former Shuey property. Hog Canyon was previously known as Echo Canyon; it may have received its name for the wild hogs which were numerous in the area.]

Another item in the July 23rd edition of the paper

Pleasant Valley School.

was that "Mr. Gordenier, of the Estrella, is running a fence around his ranch of 488 acres. The fence will consist of 5 and 6 wires, and around the orchard he is using some pickets." The same newspaper informed people that "Almstead & McFadden have threshed about 900 sacks of barley; their wheat crop is not quite finished."

Estrella, 1895 (l to r): Dora, Mrs. Etta, William, Josephine and Byron Lee Fortney.

The Inland Messenger, on July 30, 1886, printed the information that "A petition is being numerously signed in the Estrella region for the establishment of a new voting precinct embracing Pleasant Valley, Estrella and Dry Creek School districts. It is supposed that the precinct will be able to poll about 100 votes. The petition will probably be presented at the next meeting of the Board of Supervisors."

On August 6, 1886, the newspaper reported that "E. B. Greenough, from Humboldt county, has been engaged to teach the Pleasant Valley school." Two weeks later, on August 20th, readers learned that "The Independence District school opens next week, Miss Matthis teacher."

On August 20th, readers learned that "F. Ott has opened a boot and shoe shop at Verna. John Sawyer has built a family residence near his shop, in Verna.

Pleasant Valley School in 1911: Elisabeth Lichti-second from left, Irene Leisy Hege-fourth, Anita Schowalter Neufeld-sixth, John Lichti-eighth.

Mr. T. Sherman, of Cambria, will soon engage in the carriage and wagon manufacturing business at Verna. W. J. Sherman, the postmaster at Verna, has fitted up an office in his store, and assumed the duties of the office."

Other items in that issue of the newspaper included the fact that "J. H. Rader's family moved from Cambria last week to Mr. Rader's land claim near the mouth of the Estrella. He has a nicely located tract of 40 acres, upon which the family will make their home."

The August 20, 1886 issue of the newspaper also included "Notes From Cayucos - The McMillan Bros., and Mr. Cook left here this morning with large loads of lumber and posts for their ranchos on the Estrella." Also: "Parties who have paid $2.50 for Government land, within the restored lands of the Atlantic & Pacific Railroad grant should apply to G. Webster, at his office, and have one-half the amount recovered back."

The paper, on August 27th, told its readers that "School in the newly established district at the head of Hog Canyon, will open September 5th. Strong efforts will be made to erect a schoolhouse by that time. If it is not completed, the school will be held for a time in a private residence." Another item in this issue of the newspaper was that "Mrs. Shuey has the thanks of this office for a fine sample of the melons grown at the family homestead in Hog Canyon."

Readers of *The Inland Messenger* on September 17, 1886 learned that "The people of Hog Canyon are by general consent adopting the name Pleasant Valley for their country- - -a favorable change certainly, in which the public will gladly acquiesce."

Also in the September 17th issue of the newspaper, "Patrick Foley, a young man who commenced improving a new place in Pleasant Valley last winter, raised 833 bushels of wheat, besides doing a large amount of other work on the place."

Estrella did not make it into the pages of *The Inland Messenger* again until October 29, 1886; then the readers learned that "There is a party of railroad surveyors on the lower Estrella, probably locating the Lerdo branch." [This refers to the branch of the railroad which was intended to connect Lerdo, in the San Joaquin Valley, with the Pacific Coast. It was due to this prospect of a railroad that the community of Verna was established.]

The newspaper on November 12, 1886 reported this school-related item: "Mr. E. B. Greenough has resigned his position as teacher in the Pleasant Valley District, and Miss Kittie Jared will complete the term."

One week later, the newspaper had some church-related news. "The new Presbyterian Church edifice in Pleasant Valley neighborhood will be dedicated by Rev. S. B. King next Sunday at 11 o'clock. In consequence of this appointment, the usual morning service by Rev. Tuthill at this place will not be held, but there will be Sunday School at the usual hour." [The Presbyterian Church had been located next to the present-day Pleasant Valley Cemetery.]

"Church Dedication," was the headline on a November 26th article: "Pursuant to announcement, the new Presbyterian church of Pleasant Valley was dedicated last Sunday, Rev. J. McDonald officiating. The attendance was large, and the house was nicely decorated for the occasion. David Jacks, from Monterey, was present and took a leading part especially in the contribution, donating in all $75. There was about $200 raised, placing the Church out of debt and providing for the purchase of an organ."

Pleasant Valley items in the December 24th issue included the following: "Christmas exercises will be held at the house of Rev. S. B. King, in Pleasant Valley, this evening, for the children. A Christmas sermon will be delivered at the church at 11 a.m. Christmas Day by Rev. S. B. King. All are invited." Also: "The new organ for the Pleasant Valley Presbyterian Church arrived last Wednesday. The money for the organ was secured through the efforts of the Pastor, Rev. S. B. King, Mr. Jacks, Rev. J. S. McDonald and others, at the dedication of the new church a few weeks since."

In the December 31, 1886 issue of *The Inland Messenger*, readers found this item: "An intelligent citizen from the Estrella reports a strong sentiment among the voters of that region against the proposed special tax upon Road District No. 12, to build two bridges across the Salinas."

It was not until the May 13, 1887 newspaper that one could read that "Theo. Rougeot and F. Kilby went to the city Sunday, the former to prove upon his preemption and the latter is one of the witnesses."

The "Theo. Rougeot" must refer to Clarence Theodore Rougeot; he was one of seven children of Thomas H. and Ida May Rougeot. His siblings were Sarah May, Frank H., Ada Luella, Wilma Adell and twins, Fay E. and Ray A. Their father, Thomas H. Rougeot, had been born near Rome, Oneida County, New York, on May 2, 1864. His father, Cadet T. Rougeot, had been born in France and Cadet's wife, Sarah Cooley Rougeot, had been born in Ireland. Thomas was the second youngest in a family of six children.

Thomas H. Rougeot arrived in the Estrella area in 1887, and farmed leased land in Keyes Canyon for several years. He married Ida May Shuey on December 14, 1891 in the Hog Canyon home of Josephus and Sarah Shuey, who were among the earliest settlers of the area. Thomas Rougeot assisted in getting a county road put in between San Miguel and the canyons to the east, then he was instrumental in obtaining mail service along the road.

The next week, newspaper readers learned that "The Estrella postoffice, it is supposed, will soon change hands. Mr. Sherman, the present incumbent, has tendered his resignation and Mr. Ott, his present deputy, has been strongly recommended for the appointment by petition of residents within the delivery of the office."

The Estrella postoffice had been established on July 8, 1886; it was discontinued on August 15, 1918, when it was moved to San Miguel. Its location was 7 ½ miles southeast of San Miguel and 18 miles northwest of Cholame.

Rega Dent Freeman, the son of Thomas Francis Freeman and Susan Brown Freeman, had married Melissa Dovie Nicklas in Texas, in 1897. This couple eventually arrived in Ranchita Canyon.

While on their way to California, Rega and Melissa Freeman became the parents of Thelma in Globe, Arizona in 1903. The Freemans first settled in Bradley, and then moved to the Estrella area in 1910. Thelma had two sisters: Margaret and Ona, and five brothers: Thomas Richard, Harold Ralph, Jesse Eugene, Rega Jr. and Ernest. Thelma and Margaret (Kalar) were the only two of the siblings who remained in the area.

In 1922, Thelma married Clarence Rougeot, who had been born in 1901. His maternal grandparents (Josephus and Sarah Shuey) had crossed the plains in 1859. As already mentioned, Ida May Shuey, one of their daughters, married Thomas Rougeot.

The children of Clarence and Thelma Rougeot were: Gladys Fay, Lester, Chester and Mildred. This family lived on the old Shuey homestead until 1928, when they moved to Hog Canyon.

In 1938, they bought the Rougeot ranch in Indian Valley, where Thelma remained until 1972; they then moved to Paso Robles. Clarence had passed away in 1964, and in 1975, Thelma married John H. Jardine, who passed away in 1976.

On May 20, 1887, the *San Miguel Messenger*, as *The Inland Messenger* was renamed on April 29, 1887, reported that "Mr. J. C. Kester has sold his fine 160 acre farm near the Pleasant Valley Church. O. P. McFadden, of this place, was the purchaser, and the price paid was $3,000."

The newspaper, on June 10, 1887, carried the following news from Hog Canyon.

> **Patrick Foley, whose farm is located in Hog Canyon, a region where water is not very plentiful or easy to find, decided to dig a well, and Willie Sinclair, a boy of 14, designated a place where he thought water could be obtained. Other water experts differed; but Mr. Foley commenced digging on the boy's location, and struck water at 84 feet which rose in the shaft 41 feet within 24 hours. The water came in so fast and rose with such rapidity that Mr. Foley was compelled to make lively time in getting out. He is highly pleased with the result of his confidence in the boy's skill as a waterwitch.**

School news was carried in the June 10, 1887 issue of the newspaper. "We are informed that quite a lively interest was manifested in the school election last Saturday in the Estrella Plains district. It will be remembered that last year some litigation was caused by the refusal of the officers to issue certificates of election on the ground of alleged irregularities in the election. The last election resulted in the choice of Mr. Geo. Mills as trustee by a fair majority."

The newspaper on June 24, 1887 informed readers that "Rev. B. F. Rattray will preach a temperance sermon in the Pleasant Valley Presbyterian Church next Sabbath, the 26th, at 10 o'clock a.m. All are cordially invited."

Another water-related item appeared in the August 5, 1887 edition of the paper. "Mr. Thomas, whose homestead is located in a valley between Hog and Ranchita canyons, sometimes called Pleasant canyon, obtained an abundant supply of water at a depth of 55 feet. The experts had failed to locate water in that region, and this is the first water obtained in the upper part of that valley."

"Mr. H. M. Moody has recently refused an offer of $24,000 for a tract of 960 on the Estrella creek," according to the *San Miguel Messenger* of September 16, 1887.

The September 23rd issue carried this church news: "There will be services by Rev. S. B. King in the recently-erected schoolhouse in Pinyon Canyon (known as Hog Canyon) next Sunday the 25th, at 3:30 p.m. Sunday school at 2 p.m."

Also in the September 23, 1887 issue of the newspaper, readers could see an innocent-appearing item, to the effect that "The case of Rios vs Thos. F. Faw in the Superior court, involving a claim to 320 acres of land near this place, was dismissed at the plaintiff's cost, on Tuesday."

We need to pause at this point, and examine the results of Cases 853 and 967, in the San Luis Obispo County Superior Court. In the end, the family members of Petronilo Rios, who were still living, lost the final portion of their property.

These Superior Court cases involved the land surrounding La Estrella Adobe. Catarina Avila Rios sued Ernest Cerf. The facts she alleged were that on June 30, 1884, Stephen M. Rios was the owner of a Certificate of Purchase, and had paid the State for the land in full; on July 28, 1884, the State patent was, in some way unexplained, issued to Ernest Cerf. On November 15, 1884, the defendant sold the land.

Stephen M. Rios was then dead, and Catarina Avila Rios was his "heir at law." The complaint was verified on November 18, 1887 and filed on November 21, 1887.

On April 4, 1870, Stephen M. Rios had been in possession of the land for eight years, and stated that it "has valuable improvements erected thereon to the value of over one thousand dollars for which he agrees to pay to the State of California one dollar and twenty-five cents per acre, in gold or silver coin of the United States, in the following manner: Twenty per cent of the purchase money together with interest on the balance at the rate of ten per cent per annum, in advance, from the date of the approval of the location in the Surveyor General's office." This document was subscribed and sworn before Walter Murray, Notary Public.

On June 24, 1873, Stephen M. Rios paid to the State of California the sum of ninety-nine and 50/100 dollars, being twenty percent of the purchase money and interest on the balance up to January 1, 1884, in advance, for 320 acres of state school land. The balance of the purchase price was $320, with interest computed from May 21, 1873. On July 16, 1873, the Register of the Land Office issued to Stephen M. Rios a Certificate of Purchase No. 5340; this was a State School Land Grant of Sections 16 and 36, at a price of $1.25 per acre.

The Register of the State Land Office stated that afterwards, Rios made payments to the Treasurer of the County of San Luis Obispo; finally, on the 30th day of June 1884, Rios paid $400, which was payment in full of the purchase price, both principal and interest.

The last payment was made through the agency of the defendant, Ernest Cerf, and upon payment thereof, Stephen M. Rios was entitled to receive letters patent for the land from the State of California.

It was claimed in court that Ernest Cerf, on July 23, 1884, "wrongfully, unlawfully, without cause and by falsely pretending that he was the assignee and owner of the said certificate of purchase, and all the privileges accruing therefrom, and the successor in interest to the said Stephen M. Rios, procured and obtained the issuance to him by said State of California, letters patent for the said land."

On November 15, 1884, it was claimed, "the said defendant for a valuable consideration, conveyed the said land to Thomas F. Faw and David K. Edwards." At the time the land was conveyed to them "neither the said Faw nor the said Edwards had any notice whatever of any claim or title to the said land by the plaintiff or by any person whatever other than the said Cerf; but said Edwards and Faw paid to the said Cerf in good faith the purchase money for the said land. . . $32,000."

The law suit brought out the fact that, for some reason, on August 17, 1886, in Superior Court of the City and County of San Francisco, Catarina Avila Rios was adjudged and decreed to be an incompetent person; Petronila Mendoza was appointed guardian "of her person and estate." In the suit against Ernest Cerf, it was claimed that the plaintiff had been damaged in the amount of $15,000, and her costs of the suit.

Petronila Mendoza was a grand-daughter of Petronilo and Catarina Rios. She had been baptized at Mission San Miguel on June 27, 1852, with the name Petronila Maria de Santisssima Trinidad Mendoza. Her mother was Maria Luisa Rios, who married Jose Maria Mendoza.

The file for the case, in Superior Court archives, contains two depositions; one taken in May 16, 1887, was that of David K. Edwards. It shows that he was 35 years of age, and a resident of Los Angeles. He stated that the first time he had any knowledge that Catarina Avila Rios made any claim to the property was "sometime in January, 1887, after this suit was commenced." When asked about any business dealings between himself and Faw, he said "Yes. We were partners in warehouse and grain dealing business; we also bought real estate in partnership. We bought this property in partnership." Faw was the one who negotiated the purchase. When asked if Faw had talked to Edwards about the purchase before he bought, the answer was, "My recollection is he did not. He told me after the purchase."

The second deposition is in a sealed envelope; it has not been opened since September 20, 1887. The person giving the deposition was William J. Byrd.

Ernest Cerf "avers that Francisco Rios paid $102.50 on June 24, 1873; $32.00 on December 24, 1874; $64.00 on February 1st 1878." Cerf claimed that Francisco Rios paid on his own account, and not on account of Stephen M. Rios. Cerf said that "long prior to June 9th 1886: to wit on November 15, 1884 defendant conveyed the land to William Byrd." According to Cerf, on August 24, 1878, he had come into possession of the land "by a deed executed by the Sheriff of San Luis Obispo County at a sale and a decree of foreclosure." A. Blockman and others were plaintiff, and Francisco Rios defendant. On November 15, 1884, Cerf, then holding legal title, delivered to William J. Byrd a deed in return for $32,000 in gold coin.

The legal action taken by Catarina Avila Rios resulted in "The plaintiff and all the defendants herein appearing in open Court. . .mutually consent to dismissal of the action and of the cross-action; each party to pay his or her own costs." The decision was dated September 20, 1887.

The *San Miguel Messenger*, on September 23, 1887, also informed readers that "The new road across the Middagh & Hall places, on the lower Estrella, was opened for travel Wednesday. It could be improved by more work, but it is now a great improvement over the old road."

One week later, on September 30, 1887, the newspaper stated that "We are requested to announce that there will be preaching in the Pleasant Valley Presbyterian Church next Saturday at 3 p.m. Also on the following Sabbath, at 11 a.m., which will be followed by the ordinances of baptism and the Lord's supper. All are cordially invited to attend."

The September 30th edition also stated that "A new bridge has been constructed on the Estrella road, a short distance below Sheid's, at a washout that has always been known as a bad place."

The paper, on September 30, 1887, informed readers that "The party in the Ellis School District, Hog Canyon, mentioned in a former issue of this paper, will take place Friday evening, October 7th. The proceeds are for the benefit of the school, and we hope they may have a good turnout." [Ellis School was probably named for the parents of Wilber and Bella

Ellis. On March 21, 1901, William Ellis deeded 4 2/10 acres to Monterey County; it is assumed that this was a school site. The Ellis school closed about 1937-1938; it was burned down by an arsonist about 1974.]

Readers of the October 17, 1887 issue of the *San Miguel Messenger* learned that "G. W. Brewster is preparing to build a fine brick dwelling house about seven miles from this place, on the Estrella, on land deeded from Mr. Henry Moody. He expects to use about 30,000 bricks in the building, which will be the first brick residence in the upper Salinas basin."

The newspaper on November 4, 1887 stated that "The Adams farm on the Estrella plains, which was purchased a few months since by Hon. J. D. Carr, has been again sold, A. R. Cotton, Esq., being the purchaser, and $3,600 the price paid."

The following week, the paper informed people that "The good people of Estrella have raised funds to bring a parsonage for the pastor of the M. E. Church, Mr. Leach. W. C. Kendrick has donated an eligible site and we are informed that work on the foundation has already commenced."

The newspaper, on November 18, 1887, informed its readers that: "J. H. Barry had a well dug on his homestead near Hog Canyon, and struck a plentiful supply of water, the week before last, at a depth of seventy feet. The well was located on a ridge far above the valley."

One week later, on November 25th, the paper reported that "Mr. Marcus E. Von Dollen, of Hog Canyon, has been experimenting this season in a crop of canary seed, and this week he brought to Goldtree's store samples of the product. It is exceedingly fine, both in the plumpness of the seed and size of straw; in

The Martin Von Dollen Home at the intersection of Von Dollen Road and Ranchita Canyon Road. Photo taken approximately 1920.

fact the little crop is a success. There may be something in this for our farmers."

The Von Dollen family originated in the Schleswig-Holstein area of Germany. Marcus Von Dollen, after spending some years as a sailor, came to San Francisco in 1859; he returned to the sea, and studied for the examination for first mate. However, he decided to locate in California, where he mined for a while and then worked on a ranch in Alameda County.

Marcus Von Dollen had been born on February 25, 1841; he married Annie Wartemborg in San Francisco, on May 25, 1873; she had arrived in that city in 1870. Mrs. Von Dollen had been born near Hamburg, Germany, on December 26, 1844. The children born of this marriage were Henry C., George A. and Annie, Mrs. Arthur Ennis of Contra Costa County. Marcus, whose name became Martin in America, was the eldest child in the family of seven children. His brother Johann H., the youngest, who in America became John, soon joined him. Martin moved to San Miguel in 1885, and homesteaded 160 acres in Hog Canyon, where he began grain and stock-raising. He leased other lands, operating in all 2,600 acres. He quit farming on a large scale in 1910, and sold his place; he purchased 160 acres in Pleasant Valley.

John Von Dollen brought his family to California

Another view of the Martin Von Dollen Home also taken approximately 1920.

in 1886, and to San Miguel in 1888. The two brothers, Martin and John, homesteaded land in the Keyes Canyon-Hog Canyon areas; much of the land remains in the family, although John died on February 5, 1917.

The children of Mr. & Mrs. John Von Dollen were: Max, Henry, Johnnie, Carrie, Elsie and Emma; a girl, Annie, died when five years of age, and Fred was accidentally killed as a result of being thrown from a horse at the age of nineteen.

Max Von Dollen, a son of John H. Von Dollen, had been born in Germany on February 27, 1880. In 1906, he began farming on his own, leasing a ranch in Keyes Canyon; he also purchased a half-section of grazing land in the vicinity. He later leased his uncle Martin E. E. Von Dollen's place for four years and then purchased the property. Max married Bertha Henning. Their children are Doris, Amelia, Ella and Ruth.

In 1888, Johnnie Von Dollen had been born in Keyes Canyon; he married Mary Hodel, who had come to the Estrella area with her family when she was a small child. The children of Johnnie and Mary Hodel Von Dollen included Margaret, Frederick, Ralph, Marie, Esther, Robert, Arthur, Helen, John, Earl, Joann and Leroy.

Fred Von Dollen became a grain farmer, even though he had earned a high school teaching credential at California State, at Fresno.

Arthur, who had been born in 1927, married the former Florence Stephens; they have four children: Lawrence, Karl, Roy and Elaine.

We will end this section with an item which was published in the *San Miguel Messenger* on Friday, December 16, 1887. It concerned a member of a prominent pioneer family with descendants still prominent in the area.

DIED. Huston - At the residence of her daughter, Mrs. F. Smith, 15 miles east of the Estrella postoffice, Dec. 10th, 1887, after an illness of about one month, Mrs. Joanna, wife of James Huston, aged 73 years.

Our Mother,

Deceased, was born in North Carolina, her father having served in the Revolutionary War; she, with her husband, now 76 years of age, migrated to Ohio, thence to Illinois, and in 1863 came to California, settling in Contra Costa county.

Some nine years ago, the family moved to this vicinity where they have since resided. She leaves her aged consort, 5 children, 14 grandchildren and three great-grandchildren, all but three of whom are living in this vicinity.

She has sustained consistent membership in the Methodist and Presbyterian churches, and always bore a character above reproach. As a wife and mother, she was careful and sympathetic; as a neighbor, hospitable and obliging. Her joy, her care, and the objects of her prayers were her children, by whom she will be ever affectionately remembered.

CHOLAME & PARKFIELD

San Miguel's newspaper began on April 30, 1886 and was published every Friday by Gaius Webster. It was called *The Inland Messenger*, until the name was changed to the *San Miguel Messenger* on April 29, 1887. It is informative to follow the development of Parkfield and Cholame by reading what the newspaper's editor had to say about these communities. [Cholame was a Salinan *rancheria* located fourteen leagues from Mission San Miguel. The site is mentioned in mission records as early as January 29, 1804, as *Cholan*.]

On February 7, 1844, the Cholame Rancho was granted to Mauricio Gonzales; it consisted of 26,621.82 acres. Because of its location in the path of the marauding Indians of the Tulares, it was abandoned after a short occupancy. Six or seven years elapsed before Mauricio Gonzales succeeded in maintaining either livestock or men on this property. [Leonard Blomquist obtained this item of information from Land Case No. 71, S. D.]

The claim for the title was filed on March 1, 1852, but was rejected by the United States Land Commission on January 17, 1854. An appeal of this decision was dismissed.

The land was patented on April 1, 1865 by Ellen E. White, a daughter of Mauricio Gonzales. Most of the property was later transferred to William F. Ryland and W. T. Wallace.

In 1867, the Cholame Rancho was acquired by William Wells Hollister (1818-1886). Hollister had been born in Ohio; in 1852, he brought between 200 and 300 head of cattle to California. After selling the cattle, he returned home. In 1853, he, along with his brother, Joseph Hubbard Hollister, drove some 5,000 sheep from St. Louis, Missouri, to San Diego County.

W. W. Hollister developed California's sheep industry at the San Justo Ranch in what is today's San Benito County. John Hubbard Hollister became the owner of El Chorro Rancho, between San Luis Obispo and present-day Morro Bay. He was elected Supervisor of San Luis Obispo County in 1879, even though he was only 23 years old. In 1882, he was elected to the State Assembly; in 1906 and 1910, he was elected County Assessor. John Hubbard Hollister had married Flora May Stocking, of Morro Bay, on April 12, 1880; he died on November 7, 1913.

In 1860, the Hollisters bought the 32,000-acre Cholame Ranch and later put it under the management of Robert Edgar Jack, son of a Maine sea captain. Robert E. Jack had been born in 1841; he had arrived in California in 1864.

Robert E. Jack married Nellie Hollister, a daughter of Joseph Hubbard and Ellen Mossman Hollister. Robert E. Jack bought half of the Cholame Ranch as a wedding gift, in 1869, for $27,500. Jack agreed to pay off the land within a ten-year period; he fulfilled this obligation by 1873.

In 1890, a San Francisco newspaper listed R. E. Jack as the richest man in San Luis Obispo County; he had interests in banks in San Luis Obispo and Paso Robles; later, he was a partner in the West Coast Land Company.

In the spring of 1896, the West Coast Land Company was formed to buy land in San Luis Obispo County. Chauncey H. Phillips was the manager, with Templeton designated as the main office. In the period of three days, they had purchased the Paso Robles Grant, of 23,000 acres, from Blackburn & Godchaux; the Santa Ysabel Grant, of 22,000 acres, from Ephriam Hatch; and the Eureka Ranch, of 18,000 acres, from C. R. Callendar.

Hannah Hollister, the widow of William W. Hollister, sold the remaining one-half interest in the Cholame Ranch to R. E. Jack in 1910; the price was $85,000.

Howard Vail Jack, son of Robert E. and Nellie Hollister Jack, was born in San Luis Obispo County on June 25, 1887. He eventually became the owner of the Circle C brand, which is said to be the oldest continuously-registered brand in California. The Jack family owned and operated the Cholame Ranch until it was sold, for $7 million, to the Hearst Corporation in 1966. Howard Vail Jack passed away, in a San Luis Obispo hospital, on August 14, 1974.

The Inland Messenger, on August 20, 1886, printed its first reference to Parkfield. "Dr. A. Anderson, an old mining camp physician and surgeon, formerly of Bodie and Candelaria, has located a homestead claim four miles south from Parkfield. The gentleman will attend calls, and the people should give him a trial when in need of a physician."

The September 17, 1886 issue of the paper printed another reference to Parkfield. The item had been repeated from another newspaper. "A Parkfield correspondent of the Salinas *Index* says: 'There is being circulated a subscription paper to raise means to open a wagon road to connect with the railroad at San Miguel. This will lessen the distance from Parkfield to San Miguel 23 miles and will be a great convenience to the people in this neighborhood.'"

Readers on October 1, 1886 learned that "A blacksmith shop and dwelling house are being erected by Mr. Russell, at Parkfield, giving the place quite a business air." Also: "John Croal, carrier of the Parkfield mail, informs us that the recent fire in the Cholame Valley burned over about 1000 acres of the Cholame ranch, and extended east as far as Shorts place in the Polonio Pass."

In the October 15th edition, readers could learn that "F. M. Stone, Esq., who has a mountain farm about eight miles from Parkfield, is experimenting with orange trees. There is very little frost in that locality and the indications are very favorable." In addition, readers learned that "The people of the Melville School District, in the Cholame Valley, have lately put up a schoolhouse. Being a little short of means to pay for it, a dance will be given to-night for the benefit of the building fund."

"Parkfield," was the simple headline on an article in the October 22, 1886 edition of *The Inland Messenger*.

This little hamlet is located in the Upper Cholame Valley, 43 miles from San Miguel, and forms the local center of business for the Upper Cholame Valley. It is skirted by low hills on the east, north and west, and presents a beautiful picture, with its fertile valleys alternating with rolling, grass covered hills.

The name is well chosen, for the location is a natural park. Oak trees of all sizes stud the plain, while the rivulet known as the Little Cholame meanders through the valley to its junction with the main creek bearing the same name. It is a place of remarkable natural beauty; and a few years hence, when the direct road to San Miguel is completed, it will be a pleasant half-day's drive to reach its shady valleys.

It cannot be expected that Parkfield will soon become a town of much size, but it will grow with the increase of business in the valley. The upper Cholame, if divided into holdings of moderate size, would support a large population. The soil is excellent, and the facilities for irrigation better than can be found within a circuit of many miles.

The mercantile firm of Hunter & Co. are doing a flourishing business, which, together with good school-house, blacksmith shop &c, form the nucleus of a town. Mr. Redmond supplies the weary traveler with refreshments. D.

Russell, the town-site proprietor, is a man of liberal views who will encourage the development of the place. The region forms a part of the Cholame judicial township, and F. M. Stone, the resident Justice of the Peace, dispenses justice with an impartial hand. Mr. Westofield officiates as Constable. Taken together, Parkfield is an attractive place, and its picturesque scenery and invigorating air add much to the probability of its future growth.

Those persons reading the November 12th edition of the newspaper learned that "We understand that Mr. F. M. Stone, of Parkfield, is re-elected Justice of the Peace for Cholame Township."

The December 17, 1886 edition of the newspaper stated that "W. J. Byrd, Esq., of Cholame, called on Tuesday. He reports the country settling up fast in his locality, but says he has still in view some good tracts for homestead and pre-emption which he will show to bona fide settlers."

On December 24, 1886, the newspaper informed its readers that "Mr. G. S. Gould has opened business as real estate dealer at his home at Imusdale, in the upper Cholame."

A "Personal Mention" item, in the January 28, 1887 issue of the newspaper, although short, is important for the historical purpose of recording a name that might otherwise not be generally preserved- - -"David Russell, postmaster at Cholame, was in town Wednesday."

According to the March 4, 1887 issue of *The Inland Messenger*, "The Still brothers, of the Cholame country, passed through here last Friday with some 2200 head of sheep purchased from James Lynch. They go to the Cholame range." [James Lynch (1826-1909) came to California, at age 20, in 1847 as a soldier with Col. J. D. Stevenson's First New York Volunteers. In 1859, he and his wife, Alice Kennedy Lynch (1833-1911) established themselves at Tierra Redonda; it was at the north edge of San Luis Obispo County, just above present-day Lake Nacimiento.]

The *San Miguel Messenger* for April 29, 1887 informed its readers that "Mr. O. H. Willoughby this week purchased from Cholame owners some 400 head of hogs and shipped them to Watsonville, where they will be converted into bacon."

According to the May 13, 1887 issue of the newspaper, "E. P. Brubaker, of the Cholame region, has purchased a tract of 120 acres at the mouth of the Cholame creek from C. B. Turner, of Santa Clara county; consideration, $2,000." And: "A party who came down from the Cholame hills Wednesday says they are getting an excellent grade over the mountains from Parkfield to this place, and that the road is completed to a point this side of the summit. Within another week the road will be so far completed that a wagon can be driven over it with comfort."

One week later, on May 20th, the newspaper stated that "W. J. Byrd, the land locating agent from Cholame was in town Wednesday. He says the country is rapidly filling up with settlers in his locality, but complains that there is too great a percentage of bachelors. He says there are a few good claims left, on which he would prefer to locate families or female settlers."

The paper on June 3, 1887, informed its readers that "A party of four, including G. S. Gould and James Cochran, both of Imusdale, came over the new road from the upper Cholame Monday. They report the grain of that locality as uninjured by the heat wave. The new road is fast assuming a satisfactory shape. They found no difficulty in driving through." Another item of information: "The sawmill in the Cholame valley is running again on full time, and the demand for lumber has increased to such an extent that the price has raised from $15 to $25 per thousand."

On June 24, 1887, the San Miguel newspaper reported that" Mr. G. S. Gould of Imusdale was in town Wednesday, having come over the new road from the Cholame with the viewers and the surveyor of the road. The distance from Imusdale to the county line is 15 ¼ miles, making the distance to Parkfield 19 ¾ miles. The whole distance from Parkfield to San Miguel, thus reliably estimated, by the proposed direct road across Mahoney's land, is 22 ¾ miles. This is a more favorable showing than the most sanguine friends of the route ever claimed."

Imusdale was named for the first settlers there, the Imus family, who arrived in the Cholame Valley in 1854 or 1855. The brothers Charles, William and Edwin Imus arrived first, and were followed by the Imus sisters, Eliza, Harriet, Melvina, Minerva and Sara A. These people were among the twelve children of Hiram Imus Jr., who crossed the plains from Illinois in 1849.

The post office at Imusdale was established on September 2, 1875 and discontinued on August 15, 1902. George Sullivan Gould was the first postmaster. "Judge" Gould was one of the first settlers in Cholame Valley. He had been born in Wilton, Maine, on July 13, 1831. Eventually arriving in the Cholame Valley, he took up a homestead some 4 ½ miles from Parkfield. He died in Monterey on May 21, 1922.

The newspaper, on August 5, 1887, stated that "Sylvester Gardner, an experienced teacher, as well as a practical bookkeeper, is instructing a class in bookkeeping in the Cholame."

On August 26th, the newspaper reported that "Over 400 head of hogs were brought from the upper Cholame and shipped from that place last Friday. The business of buying and shipping this class of stock is being carried on quite extensively by G. S. Gould, of Imusdale."

The *San Miguel Messenger* for September 2, 1887 carried an article entitled "The Parkfield Experiment."

A dispatch to the *Call*, from Parkfield says: 'The discovery of petroleum on and in the immediate vicinity of the lands owned by G. Q. Russell, M. H. Lawson, J. Taylor, J. E. Redmond, E. Lee and John Fisher in Little Cholame Valley, is causing considerable excitement in this part of the country.

San Francisco coal oil experts have examined the locality and pronounce this the finest petroleum prospect in California. The Slack's Canyon coal mines, which are now being developed by the Southern Pacific Company, are within eight miles of the petroleum district, and work has already been begun on a petroleum well on G. Q. Russell's ranch.

An item in the September 2nd newspaper stated that "Miss Lou Guttridge has secured the Orange school in Cholame Valley and will commence teaching September 10th." And: "Mr. Dan Maderia, the driver of the Parkfield stage, is largely interested in the coal oil locations in the upper Cholame." Also: "Miss Arabella Thompson, of Salinas, stayed over at the Maxwell House Friday night, on her way to Parkfield to take charge of the school at that place. We wish her success."

The paper on September 9, 1887 published an article entitled "Parkfield Petroleum Work of Drilling Wells for Oil Soon to Commence."

Another party of coal oil prospectors visited the Cholame petroleum district last Saturday and returned Monday, with glowing accounts of the probable wealth of that region. This party, in addition to parties mentioned heretofore as figuring in the enterprise, included Mr. Thayer, a man not only of wide range of experience and observation in the various oil regions, but also a practical borer of oil wells. He pronounces the Cholame dis-

trict the best showing he has seen on the coast. He has all the necessary machinery and tools for drilling wells, and will commence operations in this field as soon as practicable.

Parties are taking hold of this matter that have plenty of means, and the field will be thoroughly tested before operations will be suspended.

Another item in the September 9th paper: "A route for a road is talked of from the Cholame by way of Key's canyon connecting with the Estrella road, making a second easy route from Cholame to San Miguel."

The *San Miguel Messenger* for September 23rd published an article entitled "Will Incorporate. A Company with $100,000 Capital Stock to be Formed to Develop the Parkfield Petroleum."

The parties interested in the coal claims of the upper Cholame, are taking steps to consolidate their interests and will incorporate a company with a capital stock of $100,000, and proceed to test the value of their property. They already have shallow excavations, from which the crude petroleum can be dipped up in considerable quantities, and it flows into these excavations, including the existence of a large deposit of oil that may be reached by drill. All parties who have examined the indications speak in the highest terms of the prospect. In comparison with other petroleum fields, the indications are said to be far ahead of any heretofore disclosed on the Pacific Slope.

The September 23, 1887 *San Miguel Messenger* informed its readers that "G. Q. Russell has sold an undivided half of 160 acres of land, at Parkfield, to Mr. E. Parkerson, from Los Angeles, for $2,500." And: "Messers. A. and F. Lang, with their respective families, arrived last Monday from Marshfield, Oregon. They proceeded the day following to the Cholame valley, near Parkfield, where they have purchased property, and will make their future home."

One week later, the newspaper reported that "Mr. Charles H. Royse sold 160 acres of land near Parkfield, last week to G. L. Turner, for $2,500."

On October 7, 1887, the paper informed its readers that "J. M. Gore, civil engineer, has gone to Parkfield to make a survey and plat of that rising town." And: "Mr. E. Parkinson, of Parkfield, was in town Wednesday, making arrangements to have the

town of Parkfield, of which he is now half owner, surveyed and platted, preparatory to placing it on record."

The following issue of the paper, on October 14, 1887, published an article called "The Cholame and Vineyard Road."

Complaint is made that the Roadmaster of Cholame district, in Monterey County, has suspended work on the new county road, via Vineyard Canyon and is working on a road not yet declared a public highway further south.

While people are pleased to see as many roads in the county as will add to the public convenience, they think the first mentioned should be made in reasonably good condition for travel before it is officially abandoned. The mail is carried that way and there is a large amount of general travel. But there is some more work required to make it conveniently passable. It is probable that when the attention of Superintendent Pinkerton is

RAISING THE FLAG AT PARKFIELD SCHOOL
1918, TEACHER: MISS EDA KIRBY   CHOLAME VALLEY, C.A.
© DONALEE THOMASON '95

Parkfield School.
Drawn by Donalee Thomason

called to the condition of the road he will direct it to be improved.

Another item in the October 14, 1887 edition of the paper announced that "It is reported that Mr. G. W. Spencer, of this place, will soon open a saloon in Parkfield." Also in that edition of the newspaper: "The postoffice at Dudley, in the McClure Valley, in Tulare County but near the line, has been opened for business. Miss Julia Hughes is postmaster. The office is served from Cholame."

The *San Miguel Messenger*, on October 21, 1887,

informed readers that "The Eagle School, in the Cholame region, is taught by Miss M. B. Serl."

The newspaper on October 21, 1887, included this letter: "C. E. Tobey, of Cholame, writes . . .in favor of brick, adobe and paper building material in this country, where lumber is so expensive. He recommends patrons to use other material besides lumber when practicable and adds: "I have seen very good, comfortable adobe houses, and lined with the paper made for that purpose. Old adobe Mission homes more than a hundred years old are frequently to be seen, so we need not fear earthquakes.""

In the same issue of the paper, there was an article entitled "Parkfield Townsite."

J. M. Gore, civil engineer, returned last Saturday from Cholame, where he had been for a week engaged in laying out and platting the town of Parkfield. A tract of nine blocks has been platted and will be recorded, and lots are now offered for sale by Parkinson & Russell the proprietors.

The town-site is exceptionally well located, and the surroundings are picturesque and helpful. The prospects of development are good.

The agricultural resources of the surrounding country are considerable, and the

Cholame Hall, Parkfield, 1882
Drawn by Donalee Thomason

claims of Parkfield as the trading center are, we believe, undisputed. The coal oil properties of the region are a very important element in the prospects of the town.

A community has been incorporated to sink wells, and there is a strong probability, so the experts say, of developing a rich petroleum district. Wood and water are handy, and

everything that nature can do toward designing a place for a prosperous future appears to have been done for Parkfield. We know of no town in this vicinity, except San Miguel, that has a better prospect.

The October 28th issue of the newspaper carried an article entitled "Machinery for the Cholame Oil Fields."

A steam engine, boiler, drills, pipes and other machinery for drilling for oil arrived at the depot this week, and have been forwarded to Parkfield.

The work will be carried on by the corporation known as the Cholame Valley Oil Company, and it is expected that they will be able to get the machinery in operation within a week or two. Operations will be commenced on the east side of the valley about a mile and a half from Parkfield.

The newspaper, one week later, reported that "The last installment of supplies and machinery for drilling oil wells in the Cholame were forwarded Thursday. A Mr. Hayne will have immediate charge of the work, while Mr. Raymond will be general manager of the affairs of the company."

The November 11, 1887 *San Miguel Messenger* printed several articles pertaining to Parkfield and Cholame. "G. S. Gould ships 150 fine fat hogs to San Francisco to-day. Some forty of the best of them came from the farms of Dr. Fales in Cholame valley." And: "A citizen reports that when coming from the east side the other day he met eighteen teams from San Miguel for Cholame, loaded with lumber." Also: "Mr. W. B. Gilbert, a practical surveyor, has established himself for business at Parkfield. He is prepared to attend to business in that line at short notice and for reasonable compensation." Finally: "Oil City is what they call the place of operations in the Cholame oil district."

The *San Miguel Messenger*, on November 18, 1887, informed its readers that "In the Monterey county Board of Supervisors last week, John H. Garber, A. J. Gillett and T. J. Ballard were appointed viewers to examine a proposed road in Cholame district over the lands of John Cahill and others. Report to be made Jan. 3rd, 1888. Additionally, John H. Garber, A. Gillett and T. J. Ballard were appointed viewers to examine a proposed road in Cholame road district, over lands of G. McConnell, B. F. Pense, Eli Lee and others. Report to be made Jan. 3rd, 1888."

The same issue of the newspaper stated that "The

G. E. Crane Store in Parkfield
Drawn by Donalee Thomason

work of drilling for oil near Parkfield is supposed to have commenced yesterday. The company have a very complete outfit, and will doubtless make a thorough job of it."

Readers of the November 18th issue learned that "The firm of F. W. Hunter & Co. of Parkfield, dealers in general merchandise, present an advertisement in another column of this paper. This enterprising firm carry a large and well selected stock of goods, and enjoy the business confidence of the people among whom they do business."

The ad was the following:

F. W. HUNTER & CO.,
Dealers in
General Merchandise,
Parkfield, Monterey Co. - - - -California.
(23 ½ miles northeast from San Miguel,
Near Southern Pacific coal mines and
Cholame Valley Coal Oil Wells.)
We keep
A Full Line of General Merchandise on
Hand with Prices to suit the Times.
Country Produce taken in
Exchange for Goods.
- - -
Insurance Agents
A Good Hotel and Feed Yard
in Connection.

The December 2, 1887 issue of the newspaper reported that "George Graves, the Cholame Constable, of whom it was stated that he had been cited by the Board of Supervisors to show cause why his commission should not be cancelled on account of the shooting of Robert Miller, sends us evidence that said cita-

tion was not for the reason stated, but because one of his bondsmen is not now considered responsible. The citation informs him that he must file a new bond if he desires to hold the office."

On December 2nd, the newspaper also published a section entitled "Parkfield Items." Included were: "Mr. Linder has finished a fine building and has started business. Our oil-well-borers will start up in full blast next week." Also: "Mr. Charles Royse has built a hall and livery stable and will soon start up business in that line." And: "Mr. F. W. Hunter will commence a fine building soon, and report says he will take a partner. Mr. N. Kester, the blacksmith, has as much work as he can do and is happy as a king."

The "Parkfield Items" section for the following week's paper included: "Mr. Royse has completed his hotel and livery stable, and will be ready for business in a few days. Mr. S. R. Maynard and Kester will give a turkey-shooting on December 24th. The boys are making preparations for the occasion, cleaning up their guns, etc." And: "Mr. Charles Maynard has bought out the butcher business formerly conducted by F. W. Hunter & S. K. Maynard." Finally: "Col. Smith is building a fine residence near town."

The *San Miguel Messenger*, on December 16, 1887, reported that "Chas. Royse, of Parkfield, was in San Miguel on Monday purchasing furniture for his new hotel." And: "The drill for the Cholame Valley Oil Company has not arrived but is expected." Finally: "Mr. G. K. Truesdale of Cholame, was in town this week on business relating to his pension. He carries a bullet in his shoulder received at the battle of Corinth, in consequence of which he was discharged totally disabled."

"A Voice From Parkfield," was the heading on a letter, published in the newspaper on December 16, 1887.

The Charles Royse Stable, just before being torn down.

Editor *Messenger*: - Having seen an article in the Paso Robles *Moon* saying that the citizens of Paso Robles should take active measures to get the star route mail service now from San Miguel transferred to Paso Robles, now sir, as a citizen of this vicinity, and being directly interested in the matter I desire to say to the people of Paso Robles that I, with many other citizens with whom I have conversed on the subject, do not care how much they boom their town, so long as they do not interfere with our mail service, which is now entirely satisfactory to our people.

When they so interfere they will get a job on their hands that they will not get off soon; for we do not care to stage eighteen or twenty miles further than at present, and furthermore, we think ourselves competent to manage our own business, for the present at least, and would like to be permitted to try it for a short time to come. In conclusion, I would respectfully inform the people of Paso Robles that we know and fully understand that Paso Robles has a bridge across the Salinas river.

Respectfully yours, Parkfield. Dec. 12, 1887

Readers of the *San Miguel Messenger* on December 23, 1887 learned that "Miss Nina F. Williams has closed her school at Cholame, for the winter vacation, and the trustees have shown their appreciation of her labors by re-engaging her for the coming term."

"Parkfield" was the heading on an article in the December 23rd newspaper.

Christ Church - Episcopal
Drawn by Donalee Thomason

The fine prospects for coal and petroleum in the region of the upper Cholame is bringing the hitherto obscure hamlet of Parkfield into notice as a place that gives promise of a brilliant future. A number of new houses have lately been erected in the town, and lots are being purchased as investment by parties who have taken a look at the place and its surroundings. The agricultural resources of that region are considerable, and it is scarcely possible that lots in the town can ever be worth less than they are today, while should the resources surrounding prove anywhere near what experts claim, the town will eclipse all other booms of this part of the State and the profits on money invested there will be enormous. Lots are now for sale at prices and on terms that place them within the reach of all.

The second "white" family to live in the Cholame Valley was that of William Murley; the Imus family having been the first in the valley. William Murley had been born in Pennsylvania in 1813. He was living in the Cholame Valley by 1862, and his ranch was quite close to the site which later became Parkfield. Due to the drought, he went to the area around Hayward, California; the family returned to Parkfield in 1864. William Murley and his wife, Emma Cooley, were the parents of thirteen children: Lucinda and Augusta (who married brothers Almon "Ali" and Jim Gillette); Mary; William; Georgia; James; Robert; Daniel; Josephine; Almon; Sarah; Detta and Allie, the youngest.

Almon Gillette was a blacksmith, and Lucinda Murley Gillette often served the area as a midwife. Mrs. Gillette passed away in 1914 and Almon, or "Ali" not until 1937.

Jim Gillette and his wife, Augusta, figure in a very sad event at the end of the last century. The *Salinas Index*, on June 13, 1899 carried the story.

Tragedy in Parkfield - J. O. Gillett Kills His Brother-in-Law, J. B. Jones
The story of a murder, which occurred at Parkfield, came to light in this city yesterday. From the facts obtained from the scene of the tragedy as well as from persons here who profess to be acquainted with the situation, it seems that for a long time past trouble has been brewing between the families of James Gillett and John B. Jones, both families live near Parkfield in the southern end of Monterey County.

Gillett and Jones married sisters, two Murley girls, daughters of a prominent family in that section. Jones has four daughters and Gillett has several children. The two men have never agreed and numerous quarrels have taken place between them. Several years ago, Jones moved to this part of the county and farmed the Arthur place near Santa Rita. He also at one time was ranching on the Stone place near Parkfield, and had a falling out with Stone, whom he sued for a considerable amount of money in December 1897.

In March following, judgement was reached in favor of the defendant. Gillett and his family moved to Tuolumne county last year and returned to Parkfield only about three weeks ago, settling on a ranch just across from his brother-in-law's place. The old feud was renewed and came to a climax Sunday afternoon when Gillett killed Jones with a Winchester rifle, killing him instantly, it is supposed.

Gillett gave himself up to Constable Stone, stating that he had killed Jones in self-defence and informing him just where the body could be found. The body was found at the spot indicated, and taken to Parkfield. It is said that no weapon was found upon the dead man.

District Attorney Andersen left yesterday afternoon for the scene of the tragedy and particulars will undoubtedly be indicated at the preliminary examination of Gillett.

On September 29, 1899, the *Salinas Index* printed the headline and story, "J. O. Gillette Sentenced to seven years in State Prison at San Quentin."

James O. Gillette who shot and killed J. B. Jones at Parkfield on June 11ᵗʰ and who was tried for the crime of murder and convicted of manslaughter, was yesterday sentenced to seven years at State Prison at San Quentin. Gillette was brought into the courtroom yesterday morning, accompanied by his wife. Since his incarceration has failed physically and aged perceptibly.

Gillette was ordered to stand up when the Judge Dorn read from the information and indictment, after which he asked the prisoner if there was any reason why the sentence should not be pronounced.

At this juncture, Attorney S. F. Gill who defended Gillett, arose and moved for a new trial, giving reasons wherein he thought the court had erred and citing numerous authorities in support of his notice.

Judge Dorn briefly but clearly disposed of the points made by the attorney and then denied a new trial. Mr. Gill then dwelt on the good qualities, character and reputation of the prisoner at the bar, saying that he was now past fifty years of age and in poor health, and concluded with an eloquent ploy for leniency on behalf of his client.

Judge Dorn, in pronouncing sentence, said that there was far too much in use of deadly weapons, that the example that would be made of the defendant would serve as a warning to others to refrain from use of deadly weapons. His honor then sentenced the prisoner to seven years in State Prison at San Quentin.

During all proceedings, Gillette seemed totally oblivious to all of his surroundings, but anguish of his wife manifested itself in sobs which she could not control. In leaving the courtroom, however, Gillette broke down and was visibly affected. Judge Dorn granted a stay of execution of the sentence for five days.

George R. McIntosh, in his book *Mc's Stage Line*, provides some background information and some particulars. His father had taken a homestead in the upper end of Lang's Canyon, which branched off from the main Cholame Valley several miles west of Parkfield. The road went through the upper end of the C. P. Gould and Ali Gillette ranches; it crossed the Imusdale Creek and went up through the Jim Gillette ranch to the Lang, Bandy and McIntosh ranches. George stated that soon after they moved to that part of the country, his father and Mrs. Jim Gillette took a mutual dislike to each other. Mrs. Gillette was friendly one day and unfriendly the next.

When they moved to the area, there was a gate going into the Gillette property, another one between the Gillette-Lang property, and a gate between the Lang-McIntosh-Bandy properties. The distance was at least two miles. However, after Mr. McIntosh and Mrs. Gillette decided not to be good neighbors, there were gates and fences installed on the Gillette property every few months.

The Gillettes had re-routed the road up the side of a steep hill, and there were gates about one quarter of a mile apart. While going up the hill, Mr. McIntosh's buggy tipped over. He took an axe, which he always carried in the buggy, and chopped down both gates; he went to the Gillette ranch, and informed Mrs. Gillette what he had done, and dared her, or anyone else, to put the gates up again. If they did so, he would tear down every fence in the whole area. George McIntosh stated that his father said, "You were the cause of one good man having to go to San Quentin for a sense-less killing when the other man had no gun; you did everything but pull the trigger. Now maybe you would like to start with me. And I am going to have a road up through this valley with no gates on it and no side-hill roads and I will give you a week to make up your mind to have the road where it originally was, with a cattle-guard at each end of your property, or I will see what can be done!"

At the end of the week, the gates were back up. Mr. McIntosh got his axe and went to work on the gates. Then he went to San Miguel and boarded a train for Salinas. Within a week, a Monterey County surveyor and crew were looking at the situation. After speaking with C. P. Gould, Ali Gillette, Sloss King (who owned the ranch which adjoined that of Gillette), it was decided the new county road would eliminate all gates.

The county surveyor notified the Jim Gillettes of the decision, and Mrs. Gillette put up a heated argument. The surveyor informed her that there were nine gates within a distance of about 1 ½ miles; in addition, the original road had been in place for forty years, and she had no right to change the original route. Although the original road went through the center of their property, he was going to locate it along one side of the property. They could fence the property or leave it open, but if the McIntoshes, or anyone else, ran over their stock in the road, it was the Gillettes' problem.

Later on, in a year when Jim Gillette was working on a threshing rig, some of the crew members were doing some target practice during their lunch break; they invited Jim to take his turn with a few shots. His answer was, "No thanks boys. I made a shot once for which I have been sorry ever since and I'll never shoot again."

Years later, Constable Albert Parker received an urgent call from the Gillette ranch; he was told that Jim Gillette had lost his mind. When he arrived, Constable Parker learned that Jim's wife had been nagging him for so long that he got tired of it. He had picked her up and sat her on the hot, wood-burning cook stove- - -not once, but several times. Mrs. Gillette never gave her husband or her neighbors any more trouble.

There was also good news for the Cholame Valley, at the turn of the century. The *Paso Robles Record*, on March 3, 1900, stated that "Cholame Valley has fine schools, Parkfield, Melville, Redmond, Woll, Imusdale, and they are turning out some excellent scholars."

THE EASTERN PART OF THE COUNTY

The three major sections of the eastern part of the county, that we will consider, will be divided into the regions of the area around Shandon, the : area to its south and La Panza.

When the first survey at Shandon was made in 1855, a spring of good water is mentioned. The area around this spring, a few miles west of the future town of Shandon and about 15 miles east of Paso Robles, had been homesteaded by William T. Sheid; he was an early sheepman. The spring was located on the north side of what became the "old, old Highway 41."

Sheid built a residence and planted an orchard in the winter of 1868. Mr. Sheid was said to have had a "magnificent fountain," and the site was a stopping place for over 40 years. William T. Sheid, a native of Tennessee, passed away on March 9, 1896, aged 75 years, near Shandon. [Coburn and Brewster bought the Sheid Ranch from a Mr. Green in 1918, and sold it in 1957. The property then became known as the Allen Hereford Ranch.]

The county tax records for the year 1864 list the following: "Cox & Clarke" with a holding of 880 acres, known as the Sacramento Ranch, $440; improvements on same $200; also 500 stock cattle, 10 tame horses. Total value: $1,655; tax $53.79, marked "paid." There

Clarke Adobe, built before 1865, on Sacramento Ranch near Shandon. (View from the south.)

is a two-story adobe house on the Sacramento Ranch, two miles west of present-day Shandon. It has been estimated that the adobe was built before 1865. The reason for choosing this year is that tax was paid on "improvements" in 1864, as listed above.

The last people to occupy the old adobe were Clarke Hall, his wife and eight children. Clarke Hall was the great-grandson of the original owner. This family lived there for over 20 years, and ran cattle until the ranch was sold in 1966. Prior to the occupancy by the Clarke Hall family, Roy and Emma Kester lived in the adobe; Alta McMillan, a sister of Roy Kester, stated that the adobe had been covered by wood, inside and out.

Around 1867, Greenberg B. Taylor obtained some of the lands near Shandon. He sold out to Crawford W. Clarke and Frederick Cox. As noted above, Cox & Clarke were paying taxes on some land in 1864. (Clarke incorporated the company in 1909; he had completed acquisition of the big cattle and grain ranch in 1880.)

In 1883, George K. Truesdale filed the first homestead, of 160 acres, on Shandon flat. He had served in Company G, 81st Ohio Volunteer Infantry, during the Civil War; in 1875, he came to Ventura. In addition to his homestead, George K. Truesdale had an 80-acre timber claim. To these 240 acres, he added 30 more. His wife, Martha E. Smith, had been born at Poland, Ohio.

In 1884, homesteads then were established by the D. B. Shaw, Baxter Grainger and George Pfost families. A school district was established in 1884; the district took in four townships, and was called the Spring Valley District.

The first school house was built on the northeast corner of the George Pfost land, and was as near the center of the flat as possible. A small store was built near the school by C. J. Shaw.

Twin boys had been born into the George K. Truesdale family in Lima, Ohio, in 1873. Two years later, twin girls were born to C. Baxter Grainger and Jennie Gardner Grainger, of Perry, Kansas. The Truesdales named their twins Hillis and Willis; the Graingers named their daughters Nora and Zora. These two families found their individual ways to Shandon. C. Baxter Grainger, a native of Missouri, had come to California in 1876; in 1884, he homesteaded two miles south of what is now Shandon, and was one of the early merchants of that town.

Of the five pupils in the school at one time, two

Hillis and Nora with Willis and Zora Truesdale, Wedding Photo, October 24, 1895.

were Nora and Zora Grainger. Later, Hillis and Willis enrolled in the schoolhouse.

The social event of the year was the wedding which took place on October 24, 1895; exchanging their wedding vows were Hillis and Nora, and Willis and Zora.

Both families went into farming; Willis and Zora farmed land about a mile west of Shandon on what is Highway 41, at the present time. They began their raising of grain and stock by leasing 320 acres, and afterwards leased other lands until they farmed a thousand acres.

In 1897, they leased 880 acres two miles south of Shandon; after operating it for ten years, they purchased it. Later, the brothers took over the Baxter Grainger ranch, of 160 acres, and worked there for 48 years. They had 1,040 acres in one body on San Juan Creek. In addition, they leased about 900 acres of stock land, and raised cattle and horses. One year, they raised grain amounting to 6,000 sacks, which had required 15 days to harvest. Using two eight-horse teams, it took six weeks to haul the crop to Paso Robles.

In November of 1914, the brothers bought the store at Shandon from Shimmin & Stevens, and also the stage line between Shandon and Paso Robles. The stage made a daily round trip of 42 miles.

In 1914, Willis brought his family to Paso Robles. A child Edwin had died in infancy; the other children were Bertha, Berniece, Thomas, Orville, Clarence, George and Ruth.

Hillis and Nora were the parents of five children: Edna, Ralph, Hugh, Kyle and Everett.

The Inland Messenger, on August 20, 1886, informed readers that "Mr. R. Mayer, the postmaster at Starkey, has made arrangements to meet the Parkfield mail-carrier at Sheid's and receive the Starkey mail sack, until the misunderstanding can be settled." [Starkey was a few miles southeast of present-day Shandon. Nicholas Mayer had established the post office at Starkey on December 14, 1885. It would be moved to the new settlement of Shandon on June 30, 1891.]

On October 8, 1886, the newspaper provided the information that "A school-house has been lately built in the Spring Valley District, at a cost of $1,000." [Spring Valley was located near the mouth of Cholame Creek.]

By November 5th, the newspaper had a more accurate cost for the new school-house in Spring Valley. "The people of the Spring Valley school district, near the mouth of Cholame creek, have just completed a $1,200 schoolhouse. It is said to be an excellent building, having a bell and belfry and all the other modern conveniences. The construction of such a building by a new district speaks well for the enterprise and intelligence of the people."

According to the December 17, 1886 edition of *The Inland Messenger*, "It is stated that there are thirty-eight bachelors settled in a neighborhood east of the mouth of Cholame Creek. That neighborhood would be a good place to colonize some of the surplus women of our sister states east."

The December 31, 1886 issue of the newspaper informed its readers that "Surveyor Mennet returned Wednesday from an extended surveying tour in McClure, Antelope and Palo Prieta valleys, in the employ of the Southern California Land & Immigration Co."

On January 7, 1887, one could read "Notes From Starkey."

This locality, at the junction of the Cholame and San Juan creeks, presents an air of thrift and prosperity. During the sojourn of your correspondent among the intelligent settlers this week, he noticed the gang plows on every side turning up the mellow soil, **evincing the faith of the farmers in the promise that seed time and harvest shall not fail, appearances to the contrary notwithstanding.**

The merry ring of the anvil mingled with the tones of the school-bell suggest the co-operation of intelligence and labor in this community. The school-house is a beauty; a model of good taste and durability, it has no equal this side of the mountains.

In April of 1887, the newspaper's name was changed to the *San Miguel Messenger*. The April 29th edition of the paper carried the following story.

Last Saturday afternoon, about 30 settlers met at the house of Mr. Wm. Carter, in Palo Prieta Canyon, pursuant to a call made two weeks previous, the object being to petition for a postoffice and select a postmaster. Mr. J. W. Truesdale received a majority of the votes cast, and the petition signed by about fifty names, has been forwarded to Washington. This settlement has already a large population and they stand much in need of the mail facilities they petition for.

The following item, from the May 13th issue of the newspaper, concerned a region that is farther southeast of San Miguel than either Parkfield or Cholame: "Several citizens, among whom are Messers. Hughes and E. E. Mann, have lately located good tracts of Government land in the San Juan valley, some thirty miles south-east of here." [The people of this region would go on to form a school district in 1895, which became a part of the Park Hill district in 1901.]

On May 20, 1887, the newspaper informed its readers that "A pleasant social dance took place at the new schoolhouse near Starkey, last Friday night. It was well attended and passed off with the most perfect harmony and good feeling."

The same newspaper, on the same date, stated that "The Sacramento ranch house is being repaired and improved. Mr. R. B. Still, manager of the property, keeps everything about it in good order. Though the ranch is devoted to stock raising, there is a nice young orchard around the house that is heavily loaded with fruit.

Another item in the May 20, 1887 issue of the *San Miguel Messenger*, said that "C. J. Shaw has just opened a store at Starkey, near the mouth of Cholame Creek. Mr. Shaw was formerly in business in Los Alamos in Santa Barbara county where he held the position of Justice of the Peace. His new location is quite central and he appears to have a fair prospect of success."

Readers on June 3, 1887 learned that "The people of Choice Valley school district, in the Palo Prieta region, are to hold an election next Saturday to determine whether they will levy a tax on the property of the district to raise $800 to build a school house."

One week later, the newspaper printed the following article. "From Choice Valley - The election in the Choice Valley School District last Saturday, resulted in the defeat of the tax for a new schoolhouse, only one vote being cast for the tax. The trustees elected are G. I. White, W. R. Wells and M. B. Gillis."

An article in the July 8th issue of the newspaper stated that "The Antelope Valley *News* is credited with a new receipt [sic] for curing the bite of a rattlesnake as follows: Pour on the wound a small quantity of gunpowder - a thimblefull - then touch the powder off. The operation is not especially painful and the wound will soon heal."

Another item in the July 8th issue was that "J. Dagney, of the McClure Valley, drove 4,000 head of sheep north this week. They go to the stubble pastures of the lower Salinas."

The July 15, 1887 edition of the *San Miguel Messenger* had three news items concerning the far eastern section of the county. "A number of new settlers are moving upon a tract of unsurveyed land in the Palo Prieta canyon, that has been fenced and used by the stock ranchers." And: "Mr. Truesdale, the newly appointed postmaster at Mineola, in the Palo Prieta canyon, has filed his bond and will probably soon enter upon the duties of the office." Also: "We are informed that Mrs. Hughes, of the McClure (Cottonwood) Valley, has received the appointment of Postmaster at the new office of Dudley, lately established in that settlement."

The newspaper on August, 19, 1887, stated that "The roads known as Palo Prieta, Cholame valley, Ortega canyon and La Panza roads have been formally declared public highways by the Board of Supervisors, on the ground that they have been used and traveled as public highways for a period of more than five years, and have thereby become dedicated to public use."

The *San Miguel Messenger*, on November 4, 1887, published an article entitled "Shooting in Palo Prieta Canyon."

Thursday of last week Mr. Robert Miller, of Palo Prieta Canyon, was shot by George Graves. The bullet struck a watch in Miller's pocket, battering the case considerably and passing into his side. He was brought to the

Jeffreys Hotel. The bullet was extracted by Dr. Murphy, and the patient is in a fair way to soon be about as usual. It was a very close call and both parties may be thankful that the result of the shot was no more serious. We understand that the shooting was a hasty and uncalled for act, which Mr. Graves deeply regretted as soon as it was done.

The newspaper on November 18, 1887 carried an item entitled, "Put Up or Shut Up."

Last Friday, the following letter was received at the *Messenger* office. It needs no explanation.

Parkfield, Cal. Nov. 7, 1887
Editor *Messenger*: - An article in your last issue regarding the Palo Prieta shooting states that a San Miguel surgeon extracted the bullet. I was called to see Mr. Miller the night he was shot, and examined the case critically and pronounced it impossible to find the ball, and from symptoms did not consider the patient in danger. Now I will wager $20 that the ball is still in Mr. Miller's body. Put up or shut up.
Respectfully, A. Anderson, M.D.

Referring to the above letter, I will say that I accept the wager offered by Dr. Anderson, and herewith deposit $20 in gold coin with G. Webster, editor of the *Messenger*. The Doctor is hereby informed that I will go him as much better as he dares to venture on his proposition. The Doctor will please follow his own advice and "put up or shut up."
San Miguel, Nov. 12, 1887 L. D. Murphy, M.D.

We would say that Dr. Murphy has left $20 in the *Messenger* office to be deposited with such party as may be agreed upon to hold the "stake."

On December 16, 1887, the newspaper stated that "Mr. Jasper Kolb, of Dudley, in the McClure or Sunflower Valley, has invested in a half section of land in the artesian belt in Kern County."

Another item in the same paper informed its readers that "Capt. Jasper Kolb, of the Sunflower Valley, was in town Saturday. He reports considerable rain in that region and everything prosperous. A great many new settlers are locating in the valley, some fourteen new houses being erected recently within two weeks."

In November 1888, Starkey consisted of a post office, Shaw's store, a drug store owned by Dr. Hughes, the new school house and William Rockwell's blacksmith shop.

The Shandon town site was surveyed and the map filed in the County Recorder's Office in July of 1890. "Sunset" was the name Charles E. Tobey selected for the new town. However, postal authorities rejected this name, because a post office with that name already existed.

The name "Shandon" was selected at the instigation of Dr. John Hughes. *Harper's* magazine, in 1882, had published a story Hughes enjoyed, entitled "Shandon Bells." This provided the inspiration for a new name, and it was officially accepted by the postal authorities in 1891.

Early settlers got their mail from the Cholame post office, with men taking turns bringing the mail for their neighborhood. Later, a post office was located in a saloon operated by Rudolf Mayer, and situated about ¾ mile southwest of Shandon. The post office was moved to the Shandon townsite in 1891, as noted earlier. The first building in the town of Shandon was the Shandon Hotel, constructed by a Mr. Worden.

According to the writings of Don McMillan, the old Shandon school house was originally built in 1885 on the Starkey Flats, two miles south of the present Shandon School. Before any of the schools in the area were built, a shack had been erected on the original site of Starkey Flats, and five students attended.

In 1898, the school was moved, by placing pine trees underneath it, like a sled; it was drawn through the fields closer to the blacksmith shop, post office and church. The church had been moved in 1891.

The original school was sold to Tom Jones, who used it as a warehouse. It was then moved again, two blocks down from its former site, in 1914; it eventually burned to the ground.

The *Paso Robles Leader*, on May 27, 1891, printed two items concerning Sunset. The first was that "The members of the M. E. Church are trying to raise means to build a church at this place. The West Coast Land Co. have donated two lots for the building." The second item was that "Post Master Shaw says that while he has moved his store to Sunset yet the Post Office still remains in Starkey, the Government not having ordered a change."

According to Laura Grainger, the first trustee meeting of the Sunset Methodist Episcopal Church was held in the school house in Starkey, on the evening of June 13, 1891. Members present included A. N. Fields, pastor and chairman, along with Richard Tiffin, James Jones and Henry Hammond. The church had been organized, and trustees elected, on May 21, 1891.

A record book for the church contains information written by Pastor Fields.

On the 11th of August, 1891, the members and friends of the M. E. Church of Shandon hauled the lumber for the M. E. Church in four days. They were hauling off their wheat to Paso Robles where they purchased the lumber for the church.

Mr. Hillis Truesdale brought the first load of lumber and Tommy Jones the last. The older members and friends filled in between and did work well and cheerfully, without money or price.

A number came to haul lumber, when to their surprise it was too late, for the lumber had all been hauled.

A meeting of trustees was held on September 1, 1891; in addition to the pastor, people present included Charles Wickstrom, Mrs. M. E. Howell, Richard Tiffin, treasurer, and Phillip H. Hammond, secretary. The building committee consisted of Isaac Newton Truesdale, George Pfost and C. B. Grainger.

The first sermon was preached in the Shandon M. E. Church on Sunday, September 13, 1891, by the Rev. A. N. Fields. The collection amounted to $12.50.

Many who helped erect the church building, both with money and labor, were members of the Presbyterian Church; on the list were George White, the three McMillan brothers, D. C., James and Peter. Also included were Harry Truesdale and Ira Tiffin, whose names appear on the subscription list for children.

The Presbyterians did not have a building of their own, so for many years both groups used the Methodist building, with the ministers preaching on alternate Sundays. Since both pastors were on a "circuit," they were kept busy at either Creston or Estrella when not preaching at Shandon. Later, the Methodist minister lived at Estrella until Shandon built a parsonage; then, Shandon became the headquarters for the pastor. San Miguel was later added to the circuit, and the ministers lived there. A church had been established at San Miguel in 1887; the first pastor was the Rev. Adam Bland, and the last the Rev. J. F. Redinger. A Mrs.

Nora Pendery wrote that "We had a very good church until so many went into other denominations, as it is so close to Paso Robles."

One of the largest real estate sales in San Luis Obispo County history was the 1966 transfer of the 38,000 acres of the C. W. Clarke Company ranch to Peck Lands Company of Los Angeles. The price was around $4 million. The sale of the ranch was announced by Clarke Hall of Shandon, president of the company, and one of the three owners who made the sale. The others were his cousin, Mrs. W. H. Hansen of Santa Barbara and Dr. Cameron Hall of Los Angeles. Hall is the great-grandson of C. W. Clarke. The land for Shandon's park was deeded by Clarke's daughter.

Greenberg B. Taylor had obtained the original grant; he sold to C. W. Clarke in the 1890s. Clarke incorporated in 1909, and the land became known as the Sacramento Ranch.

The principal owner of Peck Lands Company was Mrs. Dorothy Thayer Peck Flynn of Santa Barbara and her daughter, Carolyn Rowan. Dorothy Peck Flynn had a new roof placed on the adobe, and had the siding, which had been placed on the adobe walls, removed. Alta McMillan had told Maurice Coates that the adobe had been covered by wood, inside and out. Jess Nickerson did the work on the roof about 1976.

The adobe walls were patched with mud from the Estrella River, where the original adobe had come from. Paso Robles Judge Dean McNutt lived at the adobe, with his parents, when he was a small boy.

Just north of the adobe, toward the Estrella River, Walter Knott worked on 7 ½ acres of rich bottom land which was watered by a huge artesian well. He moved south in 1921, and went on to develop Knott's Berry Farm.

The ranchos which were the nearest to the gold fields were La Panza, the Carrisa, the Cammatti and the San Juan. There were also a couple of trapper's camps and a camp where men stayed who were out to capture wild horses in that region.

The Franciscan padres were said to have brought some Indian neophytes to this area to hunt for gold in the early 1800s. The operations were closed down when the Mexican government took over the missions in the 1830s.

The name *La Panza*, given to a region in the eastern part of San Luis Obispo County, was first mentioned in 1828, by Sebastian Rodriguez, when it was referred to as *Paraje La Panza*, or "place of the paunch." The word refers to the paunch of a beef that the local Indians made use of in order to kill bears. The paunch would be poisoned and then hung in a tree; a bear that ate the paunch would be slowed enough by the action of the poison that the Indians could more easily kill it.

The paunch was also used by *vaqueros*, without the poison, as simply bait to lure bears within reach of their traps or their ropes. At other times, *vaqueros* would use *La Paleta* (the shoulder blade) and *El Carnaso* (the loin) as bait; these terms joined *La Panza* as local place names.

While on the topic of gold in eastern San Luis Obispo County, we have an opportunity to examine the "rush" for gold in this region. The person who is given credit for launching this "gold rush" was named Epifanio Trujillo. He was a *vaquero* who had gone deer-hunting in 1878; while eating lunch near what is now called Placer Creek, he spotted some gold nuggets in the water. One of the nuggets was said to have been worth $21.00. Since gold was worth $20 per ounce at the time, most authorities doubt this alleged size of the gold nugget.

Between 500 and 600 people came to sift the sand and gravels of Placer Canyon and Bear-Trap Creek. Four-fifths of these miners were Mexicans or Californians of Mexican descent. Frank and Jesse James came to this area later to visit the brother of their father, Robert James. [In 1882, Thomas Porter, an Idaho miner, located at the head of Placer Creek, and called it Cleveland Basin. Porter was the first person in this part of the country to use the hydraulic method of mining. In 1900, Henry Chester took mining claims in Cleveland Basin and renamed it the "Queen Bee."]

There were several *Californio* families living in the flats along the San Juan River. This river rises in the southeastern part of the county, and flows almost

Clarke Adobe viewed from the west.

the entire length of the county, and enters the Salinas River under the name of Estrella.

The San Juan branch of the Estrella River owes its name to an old grant that was eventually disallowed by the U. S. government. Part of this land was bought up by Robert G. Flint, and his partners, to become the San Juan Ranch.

In 1846, ten leagues of land, called San Juan Capistrano del Camate, or Camote, were granted to Trineo Herrera and Geronimo Quintana. They were unsuccessful in receiving a patent for this land. The name Camate comes from an Indian village in the area, and is shown on San Miguel Mission records. According to Don McMillan, around 1847 Herrera and Quintana built two adobe houses in the approximate center of the San Juan Capistrano del Camate. Four years prior to this construction, these two men brought several thousand sheep from Taos, New Mexico, to the San Juan Ranch. The San Juan Ranch, at its peak, reached from some five miles southeast of present-day Shandon up the San Juan River to within a quarter mile of Highway 58, and out across the Carrisa Plains to the Temblor Range.

From 1878 to 1879, $50,000 in gold was sold from the areas of La Panza, but this included mines extending along the Navajo Creek and other creeks and canyons of the surrounding areas. Navajo Creek acquired its name because a local miner named Briggs had a Navajo woman for a wife and another miner, Slaven, had a Navajo man as a companion.

The noted Ah Louis is said to have had as many as 400 men working and sifting sands, especially of Navajo Creek. He also operated a food store at the La Panza mining operations prior to setting up a large general store in San Luis Obispo.

Ah Louis (1838-1936) had been born in Canton, China; he came to California in 1856, and arrived in San Luis Obispo County sometime after 1860. For a while, he was a cook at Mission San Miguel. Captain John Harford is responsible for his name; when he was hired, as "Wong On," by Harford, he was renamed "Ah Luis," a name which was later changed to the form of "Louis." He took the job of supplying laborers for construction projects; these included the Pacific Coast Railway from San Luis Obispo to Port Harford, and at the beginning of this century, the crews to work at the Klau Quicksilver Mine.

Early settlers on Rancho San Juan Capistrano del Camate were M. Jose Borel and Bartolo Baratie, who came from Oakland, and located at what was called French Camp. Ten days later, these men, who were French sheepherders, were murdered on May 12, 1858 by the Pio Linares/Jack Powers gang. Jack Gilkey, who was located on the Camate, was also murdered the same evening.

Other settlers of this eastern region of San Luis Obispo County, by the 1860s, were (according to Myron Angel) Phillip Biddle, James Mitchell, Drury W. James, John D. Thompson, Joseph Zumwalt and Robert G. Flint.

Jim Jones and Jacob Schoenfeld bought the La Panza and Carrisa ranches from Drury James and John Thompson in 1869. Frank Fotheringham's older sister, Ida, had married Jim Jones. Frank, one of a family of ten brothers and sisters, had been born on March 11, 1861 at Sutter Creek, Amador County, California; when Frank took a permanent job on the Carrisa ranch, he was given the foreman's position on the combined ranches.

On January 3, 1877 Frank Fotheringham was married to Maud Meredith of San Francisco and brought his bride to the Carrisa Ranch. Frank remained as foreman on the La Panza-Carrisa Ranches until the death of Jim Jones in 1903, and for several years longer.

The final settlement of Jones' estate forced a division of the ranch property; the Jones heirs took La Panza. In 1916, Henry Cowell bought La Panza, and Frank and his wife moved to Santa Margarita.

There were at least two men by the name of Robert G. Flint in San Luis Obispo County, and this fact makes it difficult to give definite details of the San Juan Ranch, as well as the Nacimiento Ranch. [Lura Rawson, a county historian, stated that the two Robert G. Flints were first cousins.]

J. M. Guinn, in his 1903 history, informs us that Robert G. Flint's father was named Pirney. Lura Rawson, writing in 1989, states that "The exact date is not known, but he is believed to have come from the Mother Lode country with only a pack mule." He became a naturalized citizen while in Sacramento County; he arrived at the San Juan Ranch about 1852. In 1860, a Robert G. Flint was at San Juan Capistrano Ranch, because his tax assessment amounted to $5,675. On January 20, 1869, Robert G. Flint bought land from Wm. F. Donnelley and his wife.

Lura Rawson must have been referring to a person who came to be known as "Old Man" Flint, presumably Pirney. He married Ann Elson, a native of Canada. Guinn states that Robert G. Flint had been born in London, Ontario, Canada on February 27, 1862.

"Old Man" Flint was a stone mason, and he would have been the person who engineered and constructed the famous stock-watering place on the Pinole portion of the San Juan Ranch, known as Pinole Springs.

According to Don McMillan, writing in 1975, Robert G. Flint bought the San Juan Ranch headquarters and extensive acreage, along the San Juan River, from the U. S. Government on January 28, 1874. The transfer of title also included the names of Lena, Ella, Ida R. and Hannah Flint. There is a problem here, because if Robert G. Flint had been born in 1862, he would have been only 12 years old when the San Juan Ranch was purchased. The San Juan Ranch must have been bought by "Old Man" Flint. He built a large log and adobe house with space for his home and room for a store, where other settlers and travelers could buy supplies. This structure was demolished in 1940, and some of the adobe bricks were used in another structure nearby.

Don McMillan, "the Sage of Shandon," was reading a magazine called *The Western Horseman*; he saw a letter from Lloyd W. Blinn, of London, Ontario, Canada. There was a photo of an old-time pair of spurs, a rawhide riata, and a horsehair cinch; the writer stated that they had come from a great-great uncle's ranch in San Luis Obispo County many, many years previously. The name of the relative was Robert G. Flint. In 1980, Don McMillan and Lloyd W. Blinn exchanged letters. Blinn sent him a copy of a letter Robert G. Flint had written to his mother in Canada. McMillan gave a copy of the letter to Ella M. Adams, and she has made it available for our use. It was written during the middle of the worst drought that ever hit California - - -1862 to 1864.

San Juan Capistrano
Dec. 6, 1863

My Dear Mother

I received your kind letter today and will answer it imediately to avoid the charge of nelegct, which I in part diserve, for delaying to answer the last so long after it was received, but the reason was I had just started with a drove of cattle, and hoped to realise anoughf to come and see you. . . .

You wish to hear what kind of country I live in. I am not good at description but will do the best I can. In the first place California belonged to old Spain. The people revolted, as did the United States, at that time the Spaniards had mixed with Indians and the country was possesed by a mongrel race, who were to lazy to work at anything but herding and taking care of cattle. I may state that the country is good for little else, but grazing sheep and cattle, excepting for mining intrest. The face of California present but a series of mountains covered, some with bush others with dwarfed oaks, others north with large ceader the most stateliest trees I ever saw. Then there is a range of mountains called the Serria Navada range they run parallel with the ocian, for five hundred miles covered with a forest of pine trees. The largest that ever growed out of the earth, in some places a hundred miles across this forest of trees, the entire length of the State is about nine hundred miles long and from three to four wide, and take it all in all the poorest body of land I ever saw. There are a few valleys and bottom lands along side some of the rivers that is good, but for one good acre, there is a hundred that will yeald but a poor crop of grass. That is if it rains in the winter or it will not yeald that.

Such being the country it was giving to different persons to settle, in this wise, when there was a valley or low hills surrounded by high mountains, with suffcient grass to sustain, say from three to ten thousand cattle, it was given to different individuals, for that purpose, each place called by a different name. The place I occupy is called by the name I {?} this from, it was a eleven square legues of land, granted by the Mexican Goverment, to Thomas Arravor, but the American Government never confirmed it to Arravor, consequently it came into market as public lands and I bought what I could of the best of it, when I came here for the first year my nearest neighbor was thirty miles from me. Now they are within ten miles, and that is closer than I want them we require a wide range for cattle.

You enquire if I attend church regular. I should be glad to answer in the affirmitive. The fact is this county of San Luis Obispo is one hundred miles square and at the county seat there is a Romain Catholic church and that is the only religious house I know of this side San Jose which is two hundred and fifty miles from here but the peopl of a new country think themselves good enough without churches for myself I am a pretty fair kind of a man barran I'm old.

You enquired how I get along cooking and

messing by myself (and should you ever feel an inclination to approach that subject again do it in the most feeling and polite way language will admit of.) I mean my housekeeping, doing let me say for myself, that should not say it, but for fear it will not be said I'll say it. There's few that are my equals, the misfortune is I am seldom or never alone consequently I have to eat whatever is cooked and you are right in calling them messes for they are scarecely indurable only in cases of starvation.

You wonder if I ever think of an other world you may rest easy about that. The last time I was going to San Francisco with a heard of fat cattle, I was on guard with the cattle and they stampeaded. That is they take fright and jump to there feet, and the first you know they are running over one another, and anything that's in their way; well this time it was very dark and rainy and in the mountains. I was on a good horse but he fell and spilt me, and the cattle went on the next morning we found the horse, he fell the second time and this time over a bank twenty feet high, and broke his neck. Well I thought the door to kingdom come was pretty wide open for me, but I passed that time and others. I get my memory goged pretty often about that kind of thing; why only the other day a confounded mule that I got on got mad about it, and commenced jumping up and down, well the reins broak and I fell, and he kept jumping up and down and that on the top of me, in a very careless manner. I though he wanted to ram me into the earth, but it was a very hard place, although if he did not succeed one way he came near it in an other, but I am pretty well except an ocational pain in the side.

I try to escape as many of these kind of things as possible, and I hope I've passed them all, as I've no wish to go overboard yet although life this far has been a pretty rugged road, one thing is certain I shall come home and soon.

I am pleased to hear Mary and family are well; remember me kindly to them all, also to Pirney and his family, I wish very much to see them all. Should you see Mrs. and Mr. Thomas give them my best respects also to Mrs. Hall I am sorry to hear of her loss.

My dear Mother for yourself accept my sincere thank for you, kind and believe me you affectionate son,
       Robt. G. Flint

The manner in which Robert G. Flint refers to "Pirney & his family" does not sound as if he were referring to his own father. So this interesting letter does not solve the question concerning the several Robert G. Flints.

The *Paso Robles Record*, on January 18, 1896, printed the following article.

> It is reported that John H. Wise has sold all of his cattle in this county to C. W. Clark, who has rented the San Juan cattle ranch of Robt. Flint. This ranch consists of about 66,000 acres and it is likely that all the Wise cattle will be transferred to this ranch.

"Old Man" Flint married Ann Elson, who had been born in Canada; her sister, Elizabeth, married another early-day settler of the San Juan-Camate area, Walter Lewis. Elizabeth had been born, in London, Ontario, Canada on April 4, 1852.

Elizabeth Lewis was the grandmother of Henry Wreden III, Bob, Don and Nick Lewis, and Amy (Jardine) Sinclair, as well as numerous others.

Henry Charles Wreden had been born in San Francisco on October 14, 1877; he was a son of Henry and Margarite (Wrobioff) Wreden. His father had been born at Lintig, Germany, on July 16, 1844, and came to the United States in 1863. The following year, he journeyed to San Francisco and joined his brother in the brewery business. It was in San Francisco that he married Margarite; she had been born at Bramhoffer, Germany, on October 28, 1854. Her parents brought her to San Francisco when she was sixteen years old.

On March 15, 1898, Henry Wreden came to San Luis Obispo County, and immediately engaged in the cattle business. He had completed grade school and high school in San Francisco, and spent two years at the University of San Francisco and two years at the Berkeley Seminary. On December 8, 1908, Henry Wreden married Jane Lewis at the Navajo Ranch. She had been born at the Cammatti Ranch on December 6, 1883.

Her father, Walter Lewis, had arrived in San Luis Obispo County in 1869. Born on March 11, 1847 at Worchestershire, England, Walter Lewis was married to Elizabeth Elson, a native of London, Canada, as mentioned above. Elizabeth had been born on April 4, 1852.

In the June 4, 1886 issue of *The Inland Messenger*, it was stated that "The Flint estate is selling a large number of cattle to Godchaux & Brandstein, of San Francisco. A band of three hundred were driven north from the San Juan ranch last week."

The calamitous "dry year" of 1897-1898 afforded Henry Wreden I the opportunity to acquire the entire San Juan Ranch, of 57,175 acres, which had been owned by the Flints. The drought had caused financial difficulties for many, including the Flint heirs. Wreden bought the ranch, and with the aid of his sons, Henry II and Charles, operated it for many years.

After Henry Wreden's death in 1931, the 57,175-acre cattle ranch remained an undivided estate among his heirs. In 1942, it was divided into six equal-in-value portions. William Wreden would have inherited the Pinole portion of the ranch, but he preceded his father in death. The Pinole was left to Will P. Wreden, Jr., Will's son. He had operated the Pinole Ranch since

(Above) Indian paintings, inside La Piedra Pintada, from early 1890's.
(Right) Inside "The Painted Rock."

The Painted Rock

Photo by Bill Dellard

1937, and leased his portion of the estate until 1942, when the estate was officially divided.

PLEYTO AND JOLON

Beginning on April 30, 1886, it is possible to trace the progress of San Miguel's neighbors, by reading items about those communities in San Miguel's newspaper, *The Inland Messenger*. The name of the newspaper was changed to the *San Miguel Messenger* on April 29, 1887.

In this section, we will take a look at two communities which were located on the route of El Camino Real, when that road went from Mission San Miguel to Mission San Antonio de Padua. It was not until years later that the highway followed the Salinas River between San Miguel and King City. El Camino Real went from Mission San Miguel, in almost a straight line, to the Nacimiento River; after crossing the river, El Camino Real went to Pleyto, on the San Antonio River. Pleyto is now covered by San Antonio Lake; the site of Pleyto is very near the base of the present-day San Antonio Dam, which impounds the water of the lake.

Pleyto was located at the junction of Pleyto Road and the road to Bradley, along the south side of the San Antonio River. The town was planned by William Pinkerton, who bought a large portion of Rancho Pleyto in 1868. In 1894, Pleyto had one store, one hotel, one blacksmith shop and a post office. But by the 1960s, the town had largely disappeared; this was even before the creation of San Antonio Lake.

The post office was originally approved, with Edward Wobken as the first postmaster, on December 14, 1870, under the name "Pleito." Then, service was discontinued on August 26, 1872, but the office was reopened on November 6, 1874, only to be closed again on August 12, 1876.

On October 6, 1884, the post office was opened again, still under the name "Pleito," but the name was changed to "Pleyto" on December 8, 1884. This post office closed for the last time on February 4, 1925.

The area around Pleyto was the location where the lands of Mission San Miguel met the lands of Mission San Antonio de Padua. The area was called Rancho San Bartolome. The word "pleito" is a Spanish term, meaning "litigation" or "dispute." It is possible that there may have been some dispute between Missions San Miguel and San Antonio de Padua concerning rights to the property at Rancho San Bartolome.

After Pleyto, the next stop north was the Dutton Hotel at Jolon. The name "Jolon" is a Salinan Indian word which is said to mean "valley of dead trees." There was an Indian village called *Holomna* near this location when the Portola expedition came through the region in 1769.

We will take a closer look at Jolon. This was outside the area of Mission San Miguel, but always had a direct link with San Miguel, due to being on the stage coach route between San Miguel and Monterey.

A man named Antonio Ramirez came to the area from Monterey, around 1849, and constructed a one-story adobe "with all doors opening onto the porch, California style." This adobe became the nucleus of a settlement on the site of the Indian village. He used it as a store; it was designated the "Ramiriz house" on the May 1866 map of Rancho Milpitas. The town would grow up around this adobe.

Antonio Ramirez sold to a Mr. Bowen, who in turn sold to John Lee in 1871. About 1870, the lands had been opened to settlers. Heaty C. Dodge purchased the building, which, by that time, was being used as a hotel. Dodge sold the building to a pair of old army friends, Lieutenant George Dutton and Captain

Dutton Hotel at Jolon.

Tidball, who had fought Indians together in Arizona. Lt. George Dutton married the former Deborah Winslow Dodge; she had met Dutton, a native of Wallingford, Connecticut, in San Francisco. He had

been raised in Canada, and had been in Australia before he came to California during the gold rush. The Duttons were the parents of six children.

Dutton ultimately became the sole owner of the hotel in 1876, and finally purchased the building and 100 acres for $1,000. Dutton furnished supplies for neighboring homes until a road was built through King City in 1886. That road proved to be the near death of Jolon. The village never boasted of more than eight residences, one saloon, two blacksmith shops and three stores.

Dutton remodeled, added on and operated a spacious, comfortable two-storied hotel and store; he and his wife, Deborah, maintained the place until their respective deaths, hers in 1896 and his in 1905.

The May 14, 1886 issue of *The Inland Messenger* informed its readers that "Mr. Geo. Dutton, postmaster and express agent at Jolon has lately been making extensive improvements in and about his hotel and store. The place now presents a very attractive appearance." In the July 16th issue, it was reported that: "One grape vine at the Hotel of Geo. Dutton, in Jolon,

Asphaltum outcrop on San Antonio River.

will produce about a ton of grapes this season. This vine bears heavily every year."

The newspaper on May 21, 1886, informed readers that "The people from Jolon and vicinity are moving with commendable promptness in the matter of locating roads by which to reach the railroad at the nearest and most convenient point. They are elated with the idea of being able to reach the railroad in one day instead of five."

Readers of the September 10, 1886 newspaper learned that "There is a bed of asphaltum some twelve miles northwest of here, on the stage-road, that has attracted the attention of observing travelers for many years past. The great distance from transportation lines has hitherto stood in the way of any attempt to even prospect it satisfactorily, but the approach of the railroad in this vicinity will probably lead to its development. It is a substance rapidly growing in favor for walks and pavements, and such a deposit may come handy for such purposes in the towns now being started along the railroad."

On November 12, 1886, *The Inland Messenger* reported that: "The Pleyto school closed last Friday. Miss Kelly, the teacher, has returned to San Francisco."

Information concerning Jolon was given in the November 26th edition of the newspaper. "The building up of new towns along the railroad does not appear to have injured the business of Jolon, as Mr. Tidball who runs a hotel and store finds it necessary to make an addition to his buildings to accommodate increasing business." Also: "The old stand owned and kept by George Dutton, at Jolon, has been much improved during the past summer."

In the December 10, 1886 issue, it was reported that "Capt. R. A. Williams, of the U. S. Navy has purchased property from Mr. James Lynch, west of Pleyto, and has erected a nice house."

Reported in the December 24, 1886 edition of *The Inland Messenger* was the fact that "A Pleyto correspondent has taken the pains to enumerate the tramps that have passed there since last March, and gives the number as 522." Also in the December 24th issue, in a section entitled "Pleyto Items," was the information that "Much needed repairs are being made on the old San Antonio Mission."

The readers of the *San Miguel Messenger* on April 29, 1887 learned that "Information has been received by Supervisor Pinkerton of the recent death of his brother-in-law, Claude H. Smith, who was manager of a mine in Sinaloa, Mexico. Mr. Smith was for a number of years foreman of the Milpitas ranch, near Jolon, and was well known by the old residents of that region."

The paper printed an item in the May 13, 1887 edition that is of interest, because of its relationship to the family of Petronilo Rios: "'Road Viewers in Monterey County.' The Board of Supervisors for Monterey County have appointed viewers on each of the following roads . . .new road in the Pleyto Road District over lands of A. Rios and others."

On May 27, 1887, the paper informed its readers that "A correspondent of the [Salinas] *Index* describes the condition of the Old Mission at Jolon as follows:

Everything has gone to ruin there. The flowers are dead, the trees broken down and left to the mercy of the cattle, there having been no keepers since Padre Ambris died. Occasionally Father Mut, of San Miguel, comes over and holds Mass in the old building. The fences have fallen down, the tiles have slidden off the walls, the old mill and the wine vat are in ruins, the bricks having been taken for other purposes.

On May 27, 1887 was printed "Report From the Excursionists."

A party consisting of R. G. Kirk, Chas. W. Currier, J. J. Mahoney, John Gillis and E. W. Platt, returned last Saturday from a two week's sojourn in the mountains west of Jolon. . .In their journeyings they passed an Indian reservation, where exist about 30 of the 'native sons' and daughters of the wilderness. They also found, way back in the hills, a number of Mexican families that live in a very primitive manner, keeping a few head of sheep, of the old Mexican breed, a few goats, plowing their little patches of ground with oxen and in other respects as much behind this progressive age.

The paper on June 10, 1887 stated: "The patriotic people of Pleyto and vicinity are preparing to have a grand barbecue, picnic and dance on the coming Fourth, at the Pleyto grove. They will doubtless make it a success."

On June 17, 1887, the newspaper printed the following letter:

Jolon, June 4, 1887

G. N. Douglas, Esq.
Dear Sir: Your letter with a check for fifty dollars from members of my mission field at San Miguel was a pleasant surprise.

Sapaque Area, Boone Ford Cabin in Copperhead Canyon.

Such a token of kind feeling and appreciation of my work in founding the Church there, is received by me as a token of your love and zeal in the good work of Church extension.

Allow me, through you, to thank the kind donors for this token of their love to me, and I trust they all reap the rich reward of Him who said: 'It is more blessed to give than receive.'

I remain, with much respect, your servant in the Ministry,

J. S. McGowan

On July 22, 1887, the newspaper informed its readers that "Crops on the Godfrey ranch, west of this place, owned by W. Burnett, are said to be very good. They finished heading last week."

In a section of the newspaper called "Pleyto Items," readers of the September 30, 1887 edition were presented with this story: "Snakes and tarantulas are numerous in this vicinity; they are even so bold as to enter the parlors and kitchens."

The paper, on October 14, 1887, stated that "Mr. L. D. Smith is engaged in opening up the asphaltum deposit claimed by Douglas and Godfrey, some twelve miles west of here. Several tons have already been taken out."

Another item in the October 14th paper: "Rev. D.

G. Wright announces his regular appointments to preach as follows: First Sunday in each month, at Dry creek schoolhouse; second Sunday, at Hesperia schoolhouse, and evening of the same day at Sapaque schoolhouse; third Sunday at Bradley schoolhouse, and fourth Sunday, at Pleasant View schoolhouse, near Jolon." [Sapaque, said to mean "battleground," is pronounced Sep-pay-wee.]

The *San Miguel Messenger*, on November 4, 1887, stated that "The San Antonio postoffice has been discontinued, and all mail for that place now stops at Kings City."

According to the newspaper on November 18, 1887: "A correspondent says, the commodious new store in course of erection at Pleyto, will, it is rumored, be the occasion for a Thanksgiving dance." The same edition of the newspaper stated that "A grand Thanksgiving

Dutton Hotel, 1889.

ball will be given at Pleyto on the evening of the 24th inst. in the new hall. Posters are out announcing it to be free."

The next week's paper, on November 25th informed readers: "On the evening of the 12th instant, a social dance was given on the Nacimiento, at the residence of Mrs. Ann Forbes, in honor of her son John's arrival from Salt Lake." The same newspaper also stated that "We understand that D. Sturgis has been appointed postmaster at Bryson, a settlement northwest of Pleyto." [Bryson was originally called Sapaque, which is said to mean "battleground." Olive Wollesen has said that some old timers called the region "War Valley." It is located 5 miles west of Harris Valley, and just north of the Monterey-San Luis Obispo County line.]

"The Thanksgiving Ball at Pleyto," was the lead for an article in the December 2, 1887 edition of the *San Miguel Messenger.*

Mr. Henry Gimbal's wedding was celebrated by a grand ball, Thanksgiving at Pleyto. If the Pleytonians were permitted to state the most pleasant dance of the season the chosen one would be the ball here mentioned, as it was, most decidedly, the best ever given at Pleyto.

The old store now being used as a dancing hall was lighted about 7 o'clock in the evening, and the room was soon filled with 'fair women and brave men,' moving to the inspiring strains of music furnished by Cox's String Band.

After an elegant supper which was served about midnight, dancing was resumed and **kept up till day-break, when the tired revelers dispersed, all wishing Mr. and Mrs. Gimbal as much pleasure through life as they had experienced at their wedding ball.**

Another item included: "An interesting problem to the farmers is what to do with the squirrels and coyotes."

According to the December 9th newspaper: "Miss A. B. Cox, of Watsonville, has been re-engaged to teach the Pinkerton school." A somber article informed readers that: "James Haskell Lawn was found dead in the bottom of his well, near Jolon, Thursday Nov. 24th. A coroner's inquest was held the next day by Justice Whitlock, the jury finding that the deceased was a native of Illinois, about 47 years of age, and that he is supposed to have fallen in the well while in the act of drawing water, on or about the 9th of November, breaking his neck."

It was found necessary to destroy the town of Pleyto in order to construct San Antonio Dam. The community of Jolon declined after the railroad was built between Soledad and San Miguel, and further declined after the highway was constructed between San Miguel and King City.

SAN ARDO, SAN LUCAS AND BRADLEY: SAN MIGUEL'S NEIGHBORS TO THE NORTH

The towns of San Ardo, San Lucas and Bradley are located in southern Monterey County; unlike San Miguel, they largely came into being as the railroad passed through their area. It is of interest to trace their birth and growth by following mention of them in the newspaper published in San Miguel. The paper began as *The Inland Messenger* on April 30, 1886; on April 29, 1887, it was renamed the *San Miguel Messenger*.

On June 11, 1886, *The Inland Messenger* printed a story entitled, "Hames Valley."

There are very few localities of so much importance as Hames Valley about which so little is known. Like many other portions of the southern part of Monterey county it has hitherto been so isolated that it required a special effort to obtain information as to its location, character or extent, but the extension of the railroad and the impetus that it has given to the settlement of the country is bringing these places to notice.

The "valley" as it is termed, is near the southern boundary of Monterey, lying west of the Salinas river and east of the San Lucia range of mountains and embraces a plateau of about 10,000 acres. The soil is fertile, and the climate genial, both being adapted to general farming or fruit raising.

It was originally settled by John Hames, who three or four years ago sold his land, embracing the best portion of the valley, to Mr. Ed Porter, who still holds it. Mr. Porter keeps a good many sheep and does some general farming.

The settlement now includes about forty-five families, and the number is increasing. They hope that in the future Mr. Porter may find it more profitable to subdivide his land and sell it in moderate sized farms. The ultimate outlet to this settlement will be at a point on the railroad some fifteen miles northwest of San Miguel, where it is expected a depot will be established and a town built.

A number of changes have lately taken place in the ownership of land claims, and it is supposed that the "late unpleasantness" there will be the indirect cause of a good many others. A few years will doubtless revolutionize the settlement, both in its personal and material characteristics.

"Another Town," was the headline on an article in the June 25, 1886 issue of the newspaper. "Another railroad town has been located north of here, on Godchaux & Brandenstein's ranch. The location is said to be quite central, being the natural depot for the Jolon and Pleyto country. It has been christened San Bernardo, and will doubtless commence to improve as soon as the railroad reaches that point."

The June 25, 1886 newspaper also stated that "Hundreds of tons of hay will be hauled to the new railroad town, San Lorenzo, for shipment, from the Bitterwater region."

On July 16, 1886, the readers learned that "The place here-to-fore known as San Lorenzo, 20 miles from Soledad, has been finally christened King's City."

Also reported in the July 16, 1886 issue of the newspaper: "M. Withers informs us that track is laid twenty miles south of Soledad, and thirty miles of grading completed. The laborers now number 2000 Chinamen and 500 white men." The following week's paper announced that "There are thirty-five white men and five hundred Chinamen at work at the railroad grade near Porter's place, fifteen miles from here, and though there is a small gap between their work and that of the graders further north, it will soon be closed. The grading is going on rapidly." Present-day readers need to know that "Porter's Place" was located where the north-bound freeway exit to Mission San Antonio exists today.

The San Miguel newspaper on July 30, 1886 announced that "The French residents of Paris Valley celebrated the 'Fall of the Bastile' with much enthusiasm on the 13th instant."

Readers of the August 27th edition of the newspaper learned that "The name of the new town of San Bernardo has been changed to San Ardo."

San Ardo, between San Lucas and Bradley, was established in 1886 by Meyer Brandenstein and Edmond Godchaux, in the middle of their San Bernardo Ranch. Phil T. Hanna has the following to say in his *Dictionary of California Land Names.*

> **This locality has the distinction of being the only point in California bearing the name of a saint canoninzed by the Post Office Department. When confusion began to exist between San Bernardino and San Bernardo . . .postal authorities arbitrarily clipped the first syllable off this saint's name and created a new one.**

On July 28, 1886, John Wilburn Martin applied for a new post office to be located in the newly-surveyed town of San Bernardo. It was approved on November 13, 1886; the name changed to San Ardo on May 13, 1887, with Conrad Seideman as post master. So, for half a year, the town's post office actually bore the name San Bernardo.

The Inland Messenger, on August 27, 1886, printed an article entitled, "The Town of San Bernardo."

> **The new town of San Bernardo at Godchaux & Brandenstein's ranch, appears to be making a fine start. A plat has been filed by the proprietors, and the railroad is opened for traffic to that point. The [Salinas] *Index* says a lumber yard has been started there, and a hotel is being erected.**
>
> **Other enterprises are mentioned as follows: A. M. Dutra is coming over from Jolon to start a saddle & harness shop, and W. R. Smith, of Slack's Canyon, will run a livery stable and feed yard. Thos. S. Soberanes is arranging for a butcher shop, and Berges & Garrissere will keep a liquor store. C. P. Nance, of Salinas, is going to open a general merchandise store. It is also understood that J. M. Soto, of Santa Rita, will embark in business here. A large grain warehouse will also be constructed and perhaps a flour mill.**
>
> **Messrs. Brandenstein & Co. have generously donated two blocks in town for school purposes; also a lot for a church and grounds for a park.**

The September 3, 1886 issue of the newspaper informed readers that "Seideman, Bromberger & Co., business men of enterprise and capital, are preparing to open a large general merchandising house at the new town of San Ardo.

Progress on the railroad construction was reported on September 10, 1886.

> **There are numerous rumors in circulation about the railroad work being stopped by the executors of the Flint estate; but the state of affairs appears to be that the executors of said estate, to protect the interests of the heirs, have given notice to the railroad force not to construct the road across the lands of the estate where no right of way has been granted. It is probable that proceedings in court will be instituted to condemn a right of way and that the work will go ahead without delay.**

Another railroad item in the newspaper on that date:

> **Work on the railroad has reached the point where it is to cross the Salinas, five-and-a-half miles below this place, though it is some eight miles further to the end of the track. At the proposed crossing they have already sunk several caissons and performed other work preliminary to the construction of the bridge.**

The September 10th paper also reported that "The Southern Pacific Milling Company will proceed at once to put up a corral and to make other arrangements to receive grain at Hames Valley (Porter's). They will build a warehouse there as soon as the one at San Ardo is completed."

Also in the September 10th edition, readers could learn that "The road between Jolon and San Lucas will be in a condition to be traveled within a week or so, when the hauling of grain to that point will begin immediately." Also: "Supervisor Pinkerton of the Pleyto ranch has opened a butcher shop at Porter's station."

"The Town of Bradley," was the lead on an article in the September 24, 1886 edition of *The Inland Messenger*. "The town and station at Porter's have received the name Bradley. Mr. Sargent, the proprietor of the site, has been on the ground this week laying off town lots. The place is a central point for Hames Valley and Sargent's Canyon, and, when the roads are constructed, a portion of Indian Valley. It will doubtless develop into a place of considerable business."

Also in the September 24th edition: "Wm.

Pinkerton proprietor of the Pleyto ranch was at this place in the early part of the week making preliminary arrangements to open a wholesale butchering establishment. He expects to establish his yards and slaughter-house near the river below the Mission. Mr. Pinkerton has already opened a retail shop in the same line at Bradley, and has a contract for supplying the railroad force." [William J. Pinkerton had married Mollie Earl of Rancho Milpitas in the 1870s, and purchased one-half of the 13,299-acre Rancho Pleyto, which is now under water behind San Antonio Dam. During the 1880's, Pinkerton would serve as a supervisor for Monterey County.]

Another item in the September issue of *The Inland Messenger* was that "The proprietors of the San Ardo town site are opening up a road to Jolon. San Lucas and San Ardo will be competitors for the Jolon trade. The distance is nearly the same."

"The store of Seideman & Bromberger at San Ardo is completed and has opened business with good prospects," according to the October 1, 1886 issue of the paper.

The same issue of the paper informed its readers of the following: "The Salinas *Index* says: Mountains of gypsum exist within five miles of San Lucas. It can be used as a fertilizer and will some day become a great industry, as it is apparently inexhaustible."

On October 8, 1886, readers learned that "By the politeness of Mr. J. Berry, we hear from the new town of Bradley, of which he proudly claims to be a resident: Dick Sargent has sold a lot for a hotel to Mr. Gunn, of Hames Valley; also several other lots to parties in the vicinity. He also sold to parties in Salinas City eight lots . . . ." Another October 8th item concerning Bradley: "The warehouse will be ready for grain in a week." Also: "Work on the Bradley warehouse has been delayed for want of lumber, the road being occupied in carrying construction material."

The same issue of the newspaper had an article, "From San Ardo."

The new town of San Ardo is booming. . .The store of Seideman, Bromberger & Co. is doing an immense business on account of their low prices. . .The lumber-yard is selling lumber cheaper than at any of the new towns on the line. . .The hotel is crowded to its full extent. . .The road to the Jolon valley is open for light wagons to San Ardo, and will be finished to cross with all vehicles in a few days. . .Dr. K. Urban has his office and drug-store established also, which is a great convenience

to the people of this vicinity. . .There will be a grand ball, free to all, at San Ardo, on Tuesday, October 12th. Every effort will be made to make the occasion a most enjoyable success. Mr. John A. Jackson Craig is one of the Committee-at-Large. . .For the above items we are indebted to the politeness of Mr. Seideman, of the new firm, which has the *Messenger's* best wishes for its full measure of success.

One week later, on October 15, 1886, *The Inland Messenger* reported that "The new town of Bradley is putting on metropolitan airs- - -a new saloon is opened there. It's called the Pioneer." Also: "Parties named Gunn and Clique, of Hames Valley, have opened the hotel business in a tent at the new town of Bradley, and are doing well."

"Party at Bradley," was the headline for an article in the October 29th edition of the newspaper. "A barbecue and dance was given by B. Sargent at the new town of Bradley, last Tuesday. There was a public dinner during the day, which was well attended. The crowd was much larger in the evening, and Gimbal's new store building was the scene of life and pleasure till the approach of morning suggested the homeward march. Mr. Sargent is proprietor of the town site, and the station bears his name - - -Bradley."

An item in the November 19th issue of *The Inland Messenger*: "Bradley expects a postoffice soon, and we understand that Mr. W. Ellis, a son of M. C. Ellis, of the Southern Pacific Milling Company, will be postmaster."

The Inland Messenger on November 26, 1886 passed on some information to its readers: "The Salinas *Index* has this to say of Bradley: 'The greatest ornaments are Mr. Ellis' fine new store and Mr. Sargent's unfinished residence. The principal streets are Pleyto, San Miguel and Railroad. Also there is a small land excitement in the surrounding country that keeps the surveyor busy surveying and locating. Altogether times are very lively." Another item in that issue of the newspaper: "Wm. Jeter, a former resident of Los Gatos, is in business at San Lucas. He keeps a popular resort for thirsty travelers. Many of his former friends of Santa Clara and Santa Cruz have 'found him out' there."

According to the newspaper on December 3, 1886: "Some eighteen or twenty new claims have been settled upon lately, on the East side of the railroad, between the mouth of Pine Valley and San Ardo."

"The firm of H. Gimbal & Sons, of Bradley, some twelve miles north from this place, is doing a flourishing business. This house keeps a full line of goods usually found in country stores, among which are fresh groceries, hats, caps, boots, shoes, dry goods, blankets, quilts, etc. . . . ."

The December 17, 1886 issue of the newspaper printed two items concerning the new town of Bradley: "Joe Crumb is doing some good work in the line of painting, paper-hanging, decorating, etc. in Bradley." Also: "It is announced that A. F. Gimbal has been appointed postmaster at Bradley, and Simon Goldwater to the same office at San Lucas."

On December 24, 1886, the newspaper stated that "G. S. Gould effected a sale last week of one hundred sixty acres of land belonging to Miss Johnson, near San Lucas, the purchaser being Mr. P. Hanson. It sold at $10 per acre."

The Inland Messenger ran this ad on December 24, 1886:

BRADLEY SALOON
Jose Boronda, Prop.
Choice Wines, Liquors and Cigars.
Rooms for private card parties.
Courteous treatment guaranteed to
all my customers.

Dr. Leo L. Stanley has written that the most popular of the several saloons was that of Chino Boronda, a "tall, well-groomed, amiable and business-like proprietor. He had a waxed mustache, slick-combed hair, a white shirt and plaid vest in addition to his white apron which he wore behind the bar. Chino was a horse-lover and he kept the best of saddle animals. One of his

Bradley Saloon (riders unidentified).

mares he kept tied near the saloon so that if business lulled, he could mount and ride down to the river or over to the eastern hills."

The paper, on January 14, 1887, informed its readers that "A family arrived at Bradley a short time since, all the way from Kansas in a wagon." Another item in that issue of the newspaper was that "We understand that Godchaux & Brandenstein are shipping off cattle from the San Bernardo ranch, and will lease the ranch in small tracts for farming. This step is favorable for the future business of San Ardo."

"Railroad Rumors of Interest," was the headline for a May 6, 1887 article:

Among the railroad rumors of the day, of interest to our readers, is the statement that the Southern Pacific Company have in contemplation a branch line from Bradley to Jolon, by way of Pleyto. It is said that the surveyors of the Atchison, Topeka and Santa Fe Railroad were through this region some time since, ascertaining its practicability as a railroad route, and that it has been bound to possess no serious engineering obstacles. It is conjectured that it is the possibility of the latter company taking in that region in their course to San Francisco, that has led the Southern Pacific to select it as a field to be tapped by their system of 'feeders.' Should our neighbors of the Nacimiento and San Antonio be favored as this report would indicate, the land owners of that region will experience a substantial benefit and an important addition will be made to the business of the southern part of Monterey county.

The May 27, 1887 edition of the *San Miguel Messenger* made an announcement entitled "Soledad." It stated that "The young men of this place feel hard at San Miguel, San Lucas and San Ardo, as nearly all of the young ladies have gone there, we tried to be gallant, well we have a hope that next season will bring us plenty of rain, plenty of girls and that the good old days will again return to Soledad."

The July 1, 1887 issue of the paper printed three items about the new town of Bradley. "J. Hackett has lately put up a large livery and feed stable in Bradley." Also: "Hon. B. V. Sargent has agreed to donate a 400-pound bell for the new schoolhouse in Bradley." And finally: "Miss Maggie Matthis, of Indian Valley, has been engaged to teach in the new schoolhouse at Bradley."

On July 22, 1887, the newspaper informed its readers that "The Monterey county Board of Supervisors paid A. Trescony $500 for the right of way and construction of the new road from Jolon to San Lucas." On September 2, 1887, the newspaper stated that "A Bradley correspondent says: 'Dr. Neal, of San Miguel, makes professional visits twice a week to Bradley for the benefit of those who require his services.'"

The paper, on August 12, 1887 provided the information that "Some 2,200 head of sheep belonging to Mr. Cook, of San Lucas, were driven south Monday. They are being taken to the vicinity of San Luis for pasture."

One week later, readers could learn that "The new table for the mail between Bradley and Pleyto is as follows: Leaves Pleyto every day except Sunday at 7 a.m., arriving in Bradley at 10 a.m., and leaves Bradley at 4:30 p.m., arriving at Pleyto at 7:30 p.m."

The *San Miguel Messenger*, on October 21, 1887, featured an article entitled, "The San Ardo Ranch to be Subdivided."

Mr. John Martin, agent in charge of the large tract of land belonging to M. Brandenstein & Co., on which the town of San Ardo is located, was in town Wednesday on business. He states that the owners of this valuable property have decided to survey the land off into farms of convenient size and place it on the market. This move is of great importance in reference to the development of that part of Monterey county. It is to be hoped that other large land owners of Southern Monterey will follow the wise example of Mr. Brandenstein.

According to the October 21, 1887 issue of the *San Miguel Messenger*, "Lenora," a racy correspondent of the [Salinas] *Index*, says: "As the new county agitation has been inaugurated, Bradley will take timely opportunity by presenting her claims for becoming the County Seat. This town is the center of the proposed district and outlet of the vast agricultural region, including Hames Valley, the Sapaque and Highlands of Bradley."

The same issue of the newspaper stated that "The Watsonville *Transcript*, always practical in its conclusions, says: "A move is on foot to form a new county out of the northern portion of San Luis Obispo county and the southern part of Monterey county. It is bound to come at no distant day."

The October 28th newspaper stated that "Rev. E. B. Tuthill preached at Bradley last Sunday; his next appointment there is the fourth Sunday in next month,

November 27th." Readers of the November 4, 1887 issue of the *San Miguel Messenger* were informed that "John Kerns, for some time agent for the Southern Pacific Company, at this place, and later of Santa Cruz, has been transferred to San Lucas." In the same issue of the newspaper on that date, readers could find a section entitled "Bradley Gleanings." Items included the following: "Though our embryo town has not been heard from, directly, for some time, it still thrives, and gradually, but surely gains in population and resources. Main Street has a bright appearance of late, owing to the painter's brush, and it also boasts a new building, intended, we understand, for a grocery and fruit store." And: "The four hundred pound bell, donated by Mr. Sargent for the schoolhouse, is hither bound, and it is rumored that the hanging of it will be the occasion of another 'hop.'" Also: "The school is prospering under the management of Miss Matthis. There is an attendance of twenty-two pupils at present." Another "gleaning" from that edition of the newspaper included: "A very enjoyable party was had last Friday evening, the 28th inst., at the schoolhouse, for the purpose of raising funds to be used in purchasing apparatus for the school."

The October 28, 1887 *San Miguel Messenger* reported that "It is stated that C. Hagan, of Hames Valley, has already sown 200 acres in grain."

The November 11th edition of the newspaper announced that "A new saloon was opened in Bradley a short time since by one Alonzo Mead, from Contra Costa county." And: "A petition to the Board of Supervisors of Monterey county has been numerously signed in Bradley and vicinity for the appointment of Capt. J. A. Gilmore as Justice of the Peace in the new Township, which includes that town. The selection is said to be a good one."

An item in the November 11, 1887 issue of the paper informed its readers that "A new Catholic church has been completed at San Ardo, and Rev. Father Mut has fixed upon Sunday, the 20th instant, as the date when the first Grand Mass will be celebrated therein, at 11:30 a.m. Bishop Mora, of Los Angeles, is expected to be present to pronounce the usual benediction."

"Catholic Church Affairs," was the lead on an article in the December 2, 1887 issue of the newspaper. "We are informed from a reliable source that the first and second Grand Mass was celebrated in the new Catholic Church at San Ardo, last Sunday and the Sunday before, by Rev. Father Mut of San Miguel. This church has been mainly built from contributions by the pious people of Paris Valley, and the opening of the religious ceremonies therein was an important event.

The choir was composed of the ladies and gentlemen from the Quinardo, and Mrs. Julia Tresconi. Miss L. Brown presided at the organ. Miss Madero, Mrs. Narvaez and Mrs. S. Garcia sang the Mass, which was admirably executed."

"Father Mut expects the same ladies and gentlemen next Sunday, December 4th, at San Miguel, when the Right Rev. Bishop Mora, Bishop of Monterey and Los Angeles will be present for the purpose of administering the Sacrament of Confirmation and attending to other affairs of the church at this place and at San Ardo.

"On Thursday, December 8th, being the feast of the Immaculate Conception, with the assistance of Rev. Father Mut, he will bless the new bell of the church at San Ardo, and attend to other important business at that place."

Another item in the December 2, 1887 issue of the newspaper was that "Henry Gimbal has been appointed a Notary Public at Bradley." The following week, the newspaper printed an item that "It is stated that M. Brandenstein & Company, of San Bernardo ranch at San Ardo, have received 22 car loads of cattle from their ranch in Nevada."

"Decisions for the Defendants," was the lead on an article in the December 9, 1887 issue of the *San Miguel Messenger.*

The case of the State vs Brandenstein & Godchaux, for wrongfully and unlawfully enclosing Government land in connection with their large ranch at San Ardo, in Monterey county, which has been pending in the U. S. District Court in San Francisco for some

Elmer Bollinger at Bradley Crossing of Salinas River.

months past, has been decided in favor of the defendants. It appears that the fences were run on land of which the defendants were owners or in lawful possession, and that the Government land within the enclosure was in small tracts; also that the gates were provided enabling those who might desire to settle to pass through without interruption. No attempt appeared to have been made to prevent the occupancy of the public land within the enclosure, and Judge Hoffman holds that the case does not present facts to warrant an order for the removal of the fences.

The same edition of the newspaper informed readers that "Milton Smith will continue to carry the mail between Bradley and Pleyto till his father recovers from injuries sustained from a horse kicking him and breaking two or three of his ribs."

On December 9, 1887, the newspaper printed what it called "Hames Valley Items." "On the 23rd ult., Miss Jones, teacher of the Hames Valley school, gave an entertainment that was a perfect success. There were 73 citizens in attendance; the exercises were opened by prayer by Rev. D. G. Wright. The exercises were interesting, and the enterprising teacher in charge has the best wishes of many friends, the old maids and bachelors included. Mrs. Jacobson elicited much applause with her German songs."

A final item from the December 9, 1887 newspaper: "Rev. D. G. Wright preached an able sermon in the Hames Valley school-house, Thanksgiving day, to a crowded house. A bountiful dinner was served to which ample justice was done by those present."

E. B. Kelly, Editor, and E. G. Goldwater, Publisher, produced *The San Lucas Herald*. Their motto: "Here

Wreck at Bradley on May 29, 1907.

the press the peoples rights maintain. Unawed by influence and unbribed by gain."

On April 4, 1889, advertisements were printed for "M. Goldwater, proprietor of the Crystal Palace, Billiard and Club Rooms. The finest."

"Newloves Livery Stable and Feed Yard. Good turnouts, both single and double. Also Saddle horses. Hay and grain." The Pleasant View Hotel, Frank Williams, proprietor, was located directly opposite the railroad depot. J. P. Basham had a blacksmith shop; Joe Dosh did professional well-drilling. S. Wilderspin made boots and shoes to order. Sing Wah had a Chinese Laundry. A French Liquor Store was provided by Berges and Garrissere.

The final advertisement in that issue was for "C. W. Sawyer, Surveyor. Locating Settlers a Specialty. Correspondence Solicited. Jolon, Monterey Co., Cal."

NEIGHBORS TO THE SOUTH AND TEMPLETON

San Miguel's newspaper, *The Inland Messenger*, was first published on April 30, 1886. Gaius Webster, the editor, published the paper each Friday. Beginning on April 29, 1887, the newspaper was named the *San Miguel Messenger*. It is instructive to follow the development of San Miguel's neighboring areas by looking at the mention of them in the *Messenger*.

On May 21, 1886, readers saw an article entitled "Land Sale. - The Beattie place on the Salinas river, a short distance below this place, was sold Thursday of last week to Thomas F. Faw, of Gonzales; terms private. The sale was negotiated through Capt. Currier's agency." One week earlier, the newspaper had announced that "Hon. T. F. Faw, ex-Assemblyman from Monterey county, was in town Wednesday. He reports an abundant harvest in and around Gonzales." We are not necessarily interested in the Gonzales harvests, but this item is helpful in giving some of the background of Thomas F. Faw.

An article in the June 11, 1886 edition also had an item entitled "Land Sale. The sale of 800 acres of land by Jacob Winterol to James Liddle and Robt. Briggs was perfected last week. The consideration was $9,600. The tract is located about six miles southwest of this place on San Marcos Creek and Oak Flat. The sale was effected through Mr. Fergusson's agency. The purchasers have returned to their home in Hamilton, White Pine County, Nevada."

Readers of the July 16, 1886 edition of *The Inland Messenger* learned that "Professor Kelshaw opened school in the San Marcos District, last Monday."

The August 27th issue announced that "Miss E. M. Woods, a lady who is engaged to teach school in the vicinity of Adelaida, arrived here last Friday in time to take the Cambria stage to her destination." Also: "Mr. Gilbert Middagh, who resides about two miles from here on the Salinas bottom, brought to this office some fine samples of almonds of the paper-shell variety, which were grown on three-year-old seedling trees. The trees bore some nuts last year. This shows something of what may be done in that line."

Readers of the newspaper on October 1, 1886 learned that "Mr. T. D. Wells, we understand, proposes to lay off a town on his place three or four miles above here. It is a fine location."

The newspaper on December 10, 1886 informed its readers that "Mr. F. Frick has just opened a new lime kiln on Oak Flat, and expects to supply this place, Paso Robles and Templeton." One week later, the newspaper related that "The Southern California Land and Immigration Company report the sale of 320 acres of land about two-and-a-half miles from town- - -the Hanlon tract- - -to Faw and Edwards, of Gonzales at $20 per acre." Also: "The Adams & Latourette tract some four miles up the river, price and name of purchaser not stated."

Two items which appeared in the December 24th edition of the newspaper were: "Massey & Carrel have just finished drilling a well for S. D. Gates near the mouth of San Marcos. The location is high, and water in sufficient quantity was struck at a depth of 110 feet." And: "L. A. Opetz is building a good house on his farm on the San Marcos."

The issue of December 31, 1886 carried the article: "FATAL ACCIDENT :

A. A. GRISMORE FALLS UPON THE TRACK AND IS KILLED."

About 1 o'clock p.m. Wednesday, A. A. Grismore, a foreman of carpenters in the employ of the railroad, who had been to this place after material to be used on the turn-table at Templeton, boarded a spile driver train that was going up above the San Marcos, thinking to ride as far as the train went and walk on to Paso Robles and there wait for the evening train.

A short distance south of town, on passing from one flat-car to another he stepped on a chip, slipped and fell on the track and was caught by the truck and one truck passed over his left leg and arm.... He was taken to the Almstead House and Drs. Neal and Murphy immediately summoned, but medical aid was of no avail. The patient gradually

sunk from the first and died from the shock at about 8 o'clock. . . .Mr. Grismore was a native of the United States, and a very bright young man of about 22 years of age. . .

The May 13, 1887 issue of the newspaper stated that "A great improvement has lately been made in the county road commencing at Bridge creek, a mile south of this place, and extending beyond San Marcos creek. The new road is wholly on the west side of the railroad, doing away with four crossings. The improvement is the result of Supervisor Baker's negotiations with the Railroad Company, and the expense or the charge is borne by the corporation. Mr. Baker deserves much credit for looking closely after the interests of the county, as well as the public, in matters relating to roads in his district."

The *San Miguel Messenger* for May 27, 1887 stated that "T. F. Faw, of Gonzales, has purchased from Spencer, through C. E. Smith's agency, 320 acres of land lying immediately east of the Beattie tract, purchased by the same party nearly a year ago."

On August 5, 1887, the paper informed its readers that "J. F. Dixon, the milkman, has leased the Wells property about three miles south of this town, and will move his dairy to that place." [It is probable that Mr. Wells contributed his name to the area later called "Wellsona." The Wellsona Post Office was established on February 7, 1898, then discontinued on August 22, 1898 when it was moved to San Miguel. James C. Westerfield was appointed the first postmaster but he declined; on April 18, 1898, E.Y.P. Miller took the position.]

Two weeks later, on August 19th, the newspaper related that "Thomas F. Faw, of Gonzales, has been in town this week, looking after his interests in the vicinity. Thomas F. Faw, owner of the Beatty tract, about 2 ½ miles southeast of this place, 525 acres, is preparing to surround the tract with a substantial fence." (It is noted that in this item, there is a different spelling of the tract.)

In the September 2, 1887 newspaper, it was stated that "Mr. J. B. Nelson has sold his farm of 160 acres, about four miles south of this place on the county road, to A. R. Cotton, Esq., for $4,300. The purchaser will take possession this fall."

The newspaper on September 23, 1887 informed its readers that "Mr. T. D. Wells, having rented his place near here, has become a resident of Paso Robles and has purchased property there."

The *San Miguel Messenger*, on October 7, 1887, printed an article with the heading, "Will Subdivide and Improve Land."

We are glad to be able to state that A. R. Cotton, Esq., the purchaser of several places in this vicinity, is making arrangements to divide his purchases into tracts of forty or fifty acres and set out four or five acres on each to fruit. These orchards will be cared for and the property will be offered for sale to those seeking cheap and productive tracts for homes. This is the practice that will build up our country and soon place the upper Salinas valley on an equality with the most favored portions of the State.

On October 14, 1887, readers learned that "Mr. August Loose, the purchaser of the Marcus Wright place on San Marcos Creek, has arrived with his family and is hauling lumber for new buildings on the place." [August Loose was a native of Germany who came to California, and shipped railroad ties from Cuffeys Cove, Mendocino County, until 1886. He was married to Louise Hess, also a native of Germany; she had been previously married to Charles Blechen, who died in Mendocino County. There were three children by her first marriage and two by her union with August Loose. Young August Loose, Jr. had been born in Cuffeys Cove on February 4, 1882; he was reared in San Luis Obispo County from the age of four. After he became of age, he and his half-brother, George Blechen, rented 640 acres and raised grain and horses. In 1912 he quit ranching, leased the land to his brother, and started a draying business in San Miguel; two years later he sold this and started a garage, which he ran until 1916.]

Readers, on October 21, 1887, were informed that "We understand that Mr. A. R. Cotton contemplates setting 100 acres of the Nelson farm, a short distance south of this place to fruit." More details were given: "Mr. H. C. Dunn, formerly of Vacaville, has taken charge of the Nelson farm near this place, for the owner, Mr. Cotton, and will proceed to improve the place by setting out fruit trees, including apricots, peaches, prunes and pears."

On November 18, 1887, it was reported that "The railroad surveyors are said to be at work about six miles from Templeton, and are supposed to be setting grade stakes."

One week later, on November 25, 1887, the newspaper reported that "Mr. E. B. Greenough, who set out quite an orchard last spring on his place south of town, reports that his trees have made an excellent growth. He will make some additions to his orchard the coming season."

In the December 30th edition of the newspaper, readers learned that "Isaac C. Hall, who last week sold his land near here, purchased of the West Coast Land Co. 42 acres between Paso Robles and Templeton, paying $35 per acre."

The present-day community of Templeton is situated on land which was the southeastern part of El Paso de Robles Rancho. The town is approximately one mile north of the site where the ranch house of El Paso de Robles had been built, under the supervision of the San Miguel Mission Fathers, in 1813.

The West Coast Land Company was incorporated on March 27, 1886; its immediate purpose was to purchase and develop for sale the 64,000 acres of land which made up the ranchos of El Paso de Robles, Santa Ysabel and the unsold portion of Huer Huero. The manager of this company was Chauncey Hatch Phillips; he, along with H. M. Warden, had started a bank in San Luis Obispo in the fall of 1871.

On August 27, 1886, San Miguel's newspaper, *The Inland Messenger*, stated that "A new town called Crocker is proposed on the Paso Robles ranch six miles south of the Paso Robles Springs." The same paper, on September 3, 1886, had the following article, under the title, "The New Town of Crocker."

The San Luis Obispo *Tribune*, speaking of the location prospect of the town of Crocker, lately laid out near Blackburn's, by the West Coast Land Company, says: "The plans for the town will embrace most approved results of modern thought. A fine public square is to be provided; arrangements are well advanced for a church of beautiful design; lots are set apart for school and municipal purposes. A wealthy citizen of San Luis Obispo has secured privileges for the construction of large brick warehouses which are to be put up at once upon the approach of the railroad, and locations are already secured for a livery stable, handsome store, blacksmith shop and hotel. The site is 17 miles from San Miguel and 22 from San Luis Obispo and few of our people appreciate the fact that about 500 square miles of fine agricultural country will be tributary to it."

On September 13, 1886, Phillips instructed surveyor R. R. Harris to lay out a town of business and residential lots on 160 acres of the former El Paso de Robles Rancho. The lots were 100 by 150 feet, with larger "villa lots" on the outskirts of town.

"We acknowledge the receipt of a map of the Paso Robles ranch, including the town sites of Crocker and Roblar, together with a descriptive catalogue of the subdivision of 64,000 acres of land held for sale by the West Coast Land Company." This is from the October 15, 1886 edition of *The Inland Messenger*. "These lands and towns have merit to recommend them, and twelve months will witness a great revolution in affairs in that part of the country." [Roblar was to be located four miles west on the Las Tablas Road (now Vineyard Drive) near the intersection with Willow Creek Road.]

The San Luis Obispo *Daily Republic*, on September 30, 1886, printed the following article.

The town of Roblar, platted by the West Coast Land Company on the Paso Robles Ranch, six miles west of Crocker, is located on a fine plateau at the junction of the Cayucos and Las Tablas roads. Roblar, surrounded as it is with white and live oak timber, presents to the eye one of those rare pictures of beauty that can only be found in California, and we predict in the future many happy homes will be established in the town and vicinity.

On October 29, 1886, the same newspaper carried the following article: "W. E. Lawton, the enterprising druggist of San Luis Obispo, is putting a building in the town of Crocker and will put in a stock of goods in his line as soon as the house is ready to receive it."

Chauncey H. Phillips intended to name the new town "Crocker," in honor of the Vice-President of the Southern Pacific Railroad. It was learned that the rural community was displeased with the Southern Pacific; the name was soon changed to "Templeton," for Templeton Crocker.

"A large amount of lumber has been hauled from Cayucos to Crocker within the past few weeks," noted the November 5, 1886 issue of *The Inland Messenger*. That newspaper the following week, on November 12th, informed readers that "The name of the present railroad terminus has been changed from Crocker to Templeton, and it is understood that W. E. Lawton will be postmaster."

On November 12, 1886, the San Miguel newspaper printed an article called, "Improvements at Templeton."

The new town of Templeton, formerly Crocker, presents a lively appearance. Among the new buildings noticeable are a large boarding house, two stone buildings, a stable

C. M. Steinbeck, depot agent, standing in front of the Templeton Depot c. 1897

and several other houses, the intended occupancy of which we have not learned. A blacksmith shop is to be moved from San Luis, we understand, and various other structures are projected. The fact that it is to be the terminus of the railroad till next summer will give it quite an impetus, and its central locality and pleasant surroundings strongly recommend it as a place with a good prospect.

The November 12th issue of the newspaper also informed its readers: "It is stated that A. E. Averett, of Soledad, will open an agricultural implement establishment at Templeton, in connection with the lumber business."

A. J. Hudson, who owned a ranch in the Oakdale district, had settled there in 1865. He became a real estate agent, and for a month ran the first Templeton hotel. The hotel was a two-story building on the corner of Main and Fourth Streets, facing east. It had a number of different managers, but a Mr. Cook was in charge during the "boom" of 1887.

In 1845, A. J. Hudson came to California; his wagon train of 100 men was said to be the first emigrant train that crossed the Sierra Nevada to California. He was part of the Bear Flag Party that captured Sonoma and took General Vallejo to Sutter's Fort. In 1863, he married Sarah Burnett; they were the parents of nine children.

Some young, present-day descendants of A. J.

Hudson, are Dominic, Juliane, Danielle, Jeffery and Lauren Mora; they are the children of Lawrence and Linda Mora. The children's' great-grandmother, Elinore Hudson Woone, was the daughter of William and Eva Hudson of Templeton. William's father, A. J. Hudson, had been born in Missouri on March 3, 1837.

On the paternal side of the family, the children of Lawrence and Linda Mora are descended from Francisca, one of the daughters of Jose Ynocente Garcia. A widow with nine children, Francisca married Rafael A. Mora, Sr., who had homesteaded the Keystone Mine in the San Simeon area, arriving about 1827. Francisca bore Rafael one child, Rafael A. Mora, Jr., the Mora children's' great-grandfather.

The first newspaper was the Templeton *Times*, financed by the West Coast Lumber Company, and edited by Captain Haley. Later, Ben Bierer owned and edited the *Advance*, while a man named Osgood owned the *Times*.

The Inland Messenger, on November 19, 1886, informed readers that "The Southern Pacific Milling Company are arranging for lumber yards and warehouses at Paso Robles and Templeton. Mr. F. Earle is their agent at Paso Robles, and Mr. McWilliams at Templeton."

According to the November 19th issue of *The Inland Messenger*, a San Luis Obispo newspaper; the *Republic*, had this to say:

Prof. Summers will proceed immediately with the Institute at Templeton, and will open school January 17th, 1887, with accommodations for 60 pupils. The San Luis *Tribune* informs the public that J. A. E. Summers, recently from the east, has received considerable encouragement for the establishment of an educational institution, to be located at Templeton. Mr. Summers has the reputation of being an educator of ability and experience and the surroundings of Templeton are such as to strongly recommend it as the seat of such an institution as is contemplated

College Hill was the site for the institute, proposed by Professor A. E. Summers. He built a small building and taught a private school for a short time, at the intersection of Old County Road and Sixth Street. Today, the hill between Templeton and Highway 101 is still known as College Hill.

On November 26th, readers of *The Inland Messenger* were able to learn that "The hotel at Templeton has changed hands, a Mr. Cook being the new host."

The San Luis Obispo *Tribune*, on November 26, 1886, informed readers that "The Southern Pacific Milling Co. in charge of Mr. McWilliams has opened a lumber yard here. Five cars of lumber reached the yard on the 18th and were sold at once without being unloaded.

"Mr. Charles Knapp, of San Jose, is our pioneer

learn that "The Templeton Institute will be opened by Prof. Summers, January 18, 1887."

The San Miguel newspaper, on December 3, 1886, printed a story entitled, "That Highway Robbery."

We have been able to obtain from Mr. Beavers full particulars of his being "stood up" and robbed near Templeton, on the night of the 18th ult. The evening was quite dark and at about 8 o'clock Mr. Beavers was riding homeward on horseback. On reaching a point about two miles from Templeton, two men hailed him. He halted, and being sociably inclined, remarked that it was a cold evening.

One of the party said it had to be d—d cold if it interfered with their business. He then ordered Beavers to dismount while his comrade cocked a pistol. Mr. Beavers dismounted and the silent man, with a handkerchief around the lower part of his face, searched his pockets for valuables.

Finding nothing but tobacco he appropriated that, and ordered Beavers to remount and ride away, which he cheerfully did. Mr. Beavers is of the opinion that they were not professionals, but he is forced to admit that their want of skill did not stand in the way of their success.

Mrs. C. E. Gamble, Prop., and daughter, Gladys Gamble Ford, Templeton, 1919.

grocer. His store is to be located on his lot at 11th and Main Streets. B. N. Beebee and C. W. Wheeler of Napa start the first hardware store. It is to be located on their lots directly opposite Knapp's place. H. C. Whitney has opened a meat market and is now in full swing of successful business."

A Civil War veteran, H. C. Whitney built his meat market at Fourth and Main Streets, with living quarters in the rear. Part of the building became the post office, with Whitney the first postmaster.

On December 3rd, readers of the San Miguel newspaper saw this article: "Frank Hanson, of Soledad, is putting up a hotel in Templeton- - -so says the *Mirror*." Also from the same newspaper on that date, we

One week later, readers of the December 10th issue were presented an article entitled, "The Templeton Institute."

We present in this issue an advertisement of the Templeton Institute, a high school that is being established in the new town of Templeton, under the management of Professor Summers.

The building up of a school of the character indicated by this announcement is a great work, and one that requires time to accomplish. It rises above the character of a local institution and should meet with encourage-

ment from all sources. San Luis Obispo county cannot claim distinction for her educational institutions, and it is to be hoped that this school will become a permanent institution that will supply the demand for tuition in the higher branches of the sciences. The location is healthful, central and beautiful. The reputation of Professor Summers is such as to warrant the utmost confidence in the management. We bespeak for the Institution such support and encouragement as may be within the power of our citizens to extend.

According to *The Inland Messenger* of December 10, 1886: "The Templeton *Times* will be out on Saturday the 18th instant." The same newspaper on that date informed people that "The stage company now runs two coaches each way from Templeton to San Luis Obispo daily. This step has become necessary to accommodate the rapidly increasing travel." Also in that issue of the paper: "There are said to be responsible parties who are willing to wager $1,000 that at the next general election Templeton will have 300 voters."

Another item from the December 10th paper: "Among the schemes on foot to add to the attractions of the embryo city of Templeton is the bringing in of the waters of a large sulphur spring from the Santa Ysabel ranch, on the east side of the river. This spring is on the lands of the West Coast Land Company, and surveys that have lately been made give assurance of fall sufficient to make such a step quite practicable. The temperature of these waters is said to be about 100 degrees and the quantity of water discharged is immense."

"S. Jacobowitz and Julian Golliber will soon open a general store at Templeton, in a good two-story building that is being erected by A. Crum. The upper story will be fitted up for offices." This was according to the December 10th issue of the San Miguel newspaper.

Albert Crum was the first man to arrive and then stay throughout the boom, and then the down time of the community. On October 16, 1886, he had purchased a lot on the southeast corner of Main and Sixth Streets. Crum built a two-story building and rented the lower floor to Jacobowitz & Golliber for a store. The upper floor was used for a hall until 1888; then Crum married Eunice Wright, and converted the upper floor into living quarters for his new family. They wanted a one-story home, so they took off the top story and planted it on Crocker Street and Sixth. Later, the bottom part of the building was moved uptown from its original location to 416 Main Street.

Jacobowitz & Golliber's store failed. Crum then established a General Store. The railroad station was a boxcar, with Lyman Brewer as agent; he remained the agent until 1892, when he left to become assistant cashier for the newly-opened Citizens Bank in Paso Robles.

Frank Hansen, the hotel-builder, also installed a livery stable; Harry Scheele was a painter and decorator. G. H. Fisher and Eben Ward were blacksmiths; H. B. Morrison handled farm machinery.

The Inland Messenger, on December 10, 1886, carried the following story.

The new hotel in Templeton is being enlarged, and when completed will be the largest building of the kind in this part of the State. The length is 164 feet; breadth, 26 feet; and height, two full stories. There will be a veranda twelve feet wide along the front, giving the exterior a decidedly neat appearance. The rooms will be large, airy and well-finished. It is quite evident that if Templeton does not attract a fair share of the transient public, it will not be for want of hotel facilities.

A person by the name of Pendleton was the first physician; Dr. Sigrid Helgesen, a Norwegian medical missionary, was the town's first woman doctor. She began practice at Templeton about 1896. Dr. Helgesen died on August 12, 1915, when her auto plunged off the unpaved grade at the Cuesta; she had swerved to avoid a young man on horseback.

William Horstman built the first brick building in town. He and his wife, Amelia Petersen Horstman, had been born in Germany. When he was 22, he came to America and settled in Iowa. In 1886, he had decided to live near Templeton, where he bought about 800 acres. In 1887, he moved his family to a substantial home he had built for them on the north end of the community. The Horstmans were the parents of twelve children, two of whom died while young children.

The first bank in the North County was established by William Horstman; his oldest son, Adolph, was placed in charge. His son Charles was in charge of a mercantile business, located in the building which has since been used as "The Iron Horse" restaurant, and later as "The Beef Palace."

Horstman's father-in-law, Hans Petersen, started out in the hardware business, buying the Lawton

Building. Petersen was forced to rebuild, after a fire started in a saloon next to Whitney's, and swept the whole block. Petersen added groceries to his business and then turned the whole thing over to his sons, and moved to Pismo Beach in 1908.

The Eddy brothers were cattlemen who established first-class meat markets in Templeton and in Paso Robles. Gus Frederickson operated a harness and shoe shop. Dupont operated a charcoal powder works at Templeton for some years.

At one time, the Templeton park site had been sold

Petersen Hardware Store.

for taxes; William Cherry, the successor to C. H. Phillips as agent for the West Coast Land Company, out-bid all others, and returned the park to the community. [At the present time, Templeton has an expanding residential development called "Cherry Meadows."]

On December 10, 1886, *The Inland Messenger* had the following article, entitled "An Important Work."

There is probably no private enterprise in San Luis Obispo County from which the public are deriving greater benefits than that of the West Coast Land Company. This corporation have undertaken the subdivision and sale of the lands embraced in three large land grants, viz. The San Ysabel, Eureka and Paso Robles, and though only the latter has been platted in small tracts and placed on the market, $126,479.12 worth of small farms and lots had been sold from it up to last Saturday.

These sales include $12,025 from town lots in Templeton. . .

"Another change has occurred in the Templeton Hotel," according to an item in the December 24, 1886 edition of *The Inland Messenger*, "Mr. Stull retiring."

According to the San Miguel newspaper on January 7, 1887: "The railroad turn-table at Templeton is completed and the trains going north are not now delayed to turn the engines at this place, as heretofore."

On January 14, 1887, the paper reported that "The people of Templeton are petitioning the Board of Supervisors for the appointment of a Justice of the Peace and Constable; but there appears to be a legal point in the way of this request. There are already two Justices in this Township, which is all that the law allows. The creation of a new judicial township would, perhaps, help them out of the dilemma."

The same newspaper, on the same date, informed its readers that "W. E. Lawson, the druggist, has been appointed postmaster at Templeton." Also in that paper: "In a former issue, the *Messenger* copied from a Hollister paper the statement that R. M. Shackelford, of the Southern Pacific Milling Company would make his home in Templeton. It appears to have been an error, as he is building a fine residence at Paso Robles, where he will reside."

The Inland Messenger, on January 14, 1887, published an item which had appeared in the *San Luis Obispo Republic*. "Wednesday evening as Mr. King Stoker was on his way from Templeton to this city, he was met near Gen. Murphy's residence on the Santa Margarita by two men who presented pistols and ordered him to throw up his hands, in regular highwayman's style. Complying with their unceremonious request the robbers proceeded to examine his person and relieve him of what valuables and money he possessed, and then told him to proceed on his journey."

Much information about the educational prospects in Templeton can be learned from the advertisement which was printed in the January 21, 1887 issue of *The Inland Messenger*.

TEMPLETON INSTITUTE

The first session of this institution will open on Tuesday, January 18, 1887. We have come to make this our future home, and to build up

A School of High Order

in this beautiful country. We invite the attention of all good people in town, county and State. We intend to have a School to which the young of both sexes may come and find a home, as well as a place of thought and instruction.

Instruction to be of such a nature as to prepare both male and female

For Society and Practical Life

care shall be taken that our pupils shall not be slaves to text-books, but that their lessons be eminently natural and practical. The experience of the Principal covers twenty years, and his success testifies to his eminence as a well-known scholar and educator. The Institution will be chartered at the earliest possible time, thus allowing those who complete the course to graduate from a Home Institution. The classes to be carefully graded, from which promotions will be made each Semester. We have determined upon four departments, so that we may meet all demands.

Scholastic Year to be divided into Semesters of five months each. Terms of Tuition for Five Months:

Primary $12.50   Academic $20.00

High School $15.00   Collegiate $25.00

Provision will be made, under the direct supervision of the Principal, for all pupils desiring board.

For further information, please apply to the Principal, J. A. E. Summers, PH.D. in Templeton, or to C. H. Phillips, Esq., San Luis Obispo, Cal.

Respectfully, J. A. E. Summers, PH. D.

On February 11, 1887, *The Inland Messenger* informed its readers that "A round house for locomotives is being erected by the Railroad company at Templeton, which leads the sanguine people of that burg to expect their town to become a permanent division station. San Miguel, on account of being the junction of the Lerdo branch, will probably get away with that prize." [The Lerdo branch of the railroad, which was proposed to run between the San Joaquin Valley and the coast, was never constructed.]

On April 29, 1887, *The Inland Messenger* became the *San Miguel Messenger*. On May 13, 1887, that newspaper printed the information that "Rumor at points south says work is extending the railroad from Templeton will be commenced in a week or two."

The *San Miguel Messenger*, on May 20, 1887, informed its readers that "W. D. Haley, of the Templeton *Times*, will deliver the address on the occasion of the exercises on Memorial Day, May 30th, at San Luis Obispo."

The following week, the San Miguel newspaper said that "It is stated that the Southern Pacific Milling Company will soon erect a grain warehouse at Templeton." The same newspaper carried the item: "Main street in Templeton is sprinkled daily, the expense being borne by a subscription by the business men of the place." [Templeton's present grain elevator, said to be the largest one west of the Mississippi, was built in 1951.]

The paper, on June 3, 1887, printed the following article:

The temporary structure on the East shore of the Salinas river at Templeton was completed several days ago and the work of driving piles began on Monday. When the first pile had been driven twenty-one feet firm holding ground was reached and others were driven twenty-two feet.

All of the piers were completed last Wednesday evening and the bridge will be nearly if not finished by a week from to-day and will be opened for travel within two weeks. Enough has been done to show that it will be a very substantial structure and will fulfill the expectations of its projectors.

"New Roads," was the lead for an article in the June 10, 1887 edition of the *San Miguel Messenger*.

The new roads between Creston and Templeton are spoken of by the Templeton *Times* as follows: "One of these, called the lower road, is now finished and in good order and brings Creston travel over an easy grade of about ten miles into Templeton...A second road, which will place Creston within eight miles and a half of this place requires only one week's work to finish it. The road to the Iron Springs District is finished from this end as far as the point at which the people of that district are expected to do the work, that is to say about three and a half miles from the Iron Springs District.

With the expenditures of a very little energy and labor on the part of the people who are most to be benefited by it, the last road can be completed so that teams can travel over it with loads on the day when the bridge will be open for public use." [The

Templeton-Linne Road is now called Neal Springs Road.]

The same issue of the newspaper added: "The new bridge at Templeton is nearly completed."

The following week, the paper informed its readers that "Bids are wanted for excavating and filling at the ends of the new Templeton bridge. They should be handed to C. H. Phillips before next Monday."

Another item of interest, in the June 17th issue, was: "A new school district has been created at Templeton, out of the territory before belonging to the Paso Robles district." The June 17th newspaper also carried the following story:

> A drummer named John Howard did two foolish things on Thursday. He carried a self-cocking revolver and like many other foolish people pulled it out to shoot at every squirrel he saw between San Luis Obispo and this place.
>
> He finished by shooting himself in the leg and was brought to Templeton in a badly frightened condition. His injury proved to be only a flesh wound but will be painful and will keep him off the road for some time.
>
> He was conveyed to Paso Robles for medical care. Unfortunately there is no means of enforcing a separation between fools and pistols, and the only surprising thing is that their frequent connection is not productive of more frequent fatal results. Templeton *Times*.

["Drummer" was a term for a traveling salesman.]

According to the June 24, 1887 edition of the *San Miguel Messenger*, "Wm. Horstman has completed his $2,000 residence on subdivision PP adjoining the town of Templeton. Mr. Horstman is recently from Iowa and is one of our most enterprising citizens." Templeton *Times*.

The July 8, 1887 issue of the San Miguel newspaper stated that "Mail Route No. 46,351 from San Luis Obispo to Creston, is changed to take effect July 11th. From that date, mail for Creston will be transferred at Templeton, and the Creston people will receive their mail from one to three days sooner than they have been getting it."

The *San Miguel Messenger*, on July 8th, also informed its readers that "The stock and fixtures of Schneidk & Christensen's saloon in Templeton were sold at Sheriff's sale last Saturday."

The July 15, 1887 issue of the San Miguel news-

paper stated that "The Templeton *Times* reports that two young men from the back country recently ran their horses through the streets of that town on Sunday and narrowly escaped being shot by Constable Cook. A warrant has been issued for their arrest. If they make another visit, charges of misdemeanor and resisting an officer hang over them." One week later, the same newspaper had the news that "J. W. Cook has resigned as Constable at Templeton, and Col. Seeley is his successor."

The *San Miguel Messenger*, on July 29, 1887, informed people that "The new bridge at Templeton was first crossed Wednesday of last week, by H. S. Misenheimer, and the bridge is now open for public travel." [The first bridge ever built across the Salinas River was this bridge in Templeton. It was destroyed by flood in 1913.]

The July 29, 1887 edition of the paper stated that "The Templeton Hotel has passed into the hands of S. W. Short, long and favorably known as manager of the eating saloon at the Gilroy depot."

On August 5, 1887, the San Miguel newspaper informed its readers that "The ladies of Templeton are raising means by an entertainment to erect a flagstaff to be placed on the public square." Two weeks later,

The first bridge constructed across Salinas River. It was first crossed in July of 1887.

the newspaper stated that "Herman Hendricksen has been appointed Constable in Hot Springs Township, residing at Templeton."

The September 2, 1887 issue of the paper carried an article entitled, "The Railroad Extension."

> **Indications point to an early resumption of work on the railroad at Templeton. A summary of railroad news in Sunday's *Chronicle* states that a portion of the grading force of the California & Oregon line will be transferred to Templeton next month to renew the work of extending the line. It is now believed**

The first bank and first brick building in Templeton. Built by William Horstman on the southeast corner of 5th and Main Streets.

on the same page of the newspaper: "The following important dispatch was sent to the *Republic*: Cambria, Sept. 16. - Not a durned thing has happened for a week."

The *San Miguel Messenger*, on October 7, 1887, printed an article entitled, "Overcome by Gas in a Well."

A sad affair occurred near Templeton last Saturday, the particulars of which, are related in a *Chronicle* dispatch as follows:

Three miles west of this town, on the ranch of Newell Stone, G. A. Peterson, who was digging a well for Stone, forty feet deep, went down into the well this morning, and was overcome by gas. His sister, Miss Annie Peterson, insisted on going down to her brother's relief, and she was also overcome by gas. A third party went down part way and gave a signal to be hoisted out, as the gas was too strong.

A messenger was immediately sent to this town for assistance, which was quickly given. A party was lowered in the well, and Miss Peterson was brought out barely alive. Her brother was brought to the surface immediately after, but life was extinct.

The physicians think that by careful nursing and attention, Miss Peterson may recover. At present, she is very low. Both parties were

that connection will be made with the line from Santa Barbara by the end of March next, if sufficient labor can be secured.

A San Luis dispatch quotes Senator Stanford as saying that the long tunnel through the mountain will delay its reaching San Luis. This may be said to import that the Cuesta route has been decided upon, instead of that via Morro pass. The railroad officials have studiously and successfully concealed their purpose in relation to the choice of routes from Templeton to San Luis, and interested parties will anxiously watch the signs till the question is settled.

The same edition of the newspaper stated that "A Templeton dispatch announces that the trustees of the public school have called an election to issue bonds for $6,000 to build a schoolhouse. The vote will be practically unanimous. The West Coast Land Company gave a block worth $4,000 for a schoolhouse site."

One week later, the San Miguel newspaper stated that "Heavy sales of land in the vicinity of Templeton, by the West Coast Land Company, are reported, yet they have many fine tracts left which are offered on very favorable terms."

On September 23, 1887, the *San Miguel Messenger* stated that "The *Times* says that R. M. Shackelford has undertaken to construct the water system for Templeton, and that it is expected to be completed within thirty days." It is interesting to contrast the activity in Templeton with the following item found

Farmers Produce Exchange in Templeton

well known in this community, highly respected and very popular. This is the first
death that has occurred since the laying out
of this town.

Readers of the San Miguel newspaper, on October
21, 1887, learned that "A water tank holding 35,000
gallons has been placed on top of a framework sixty
feet high, as a reservoir to supply the town of
Templeton."

The *San Miguel Messenger*, on December 8, 1887,
reprinted an item which had appeared in the Templeton
Times: "The work of setting grade stakes for the extension of the railroad is completed about four miles
south of Templeton. The elevation on the divide between the Paso Robles and Atascadero creeks is found
to be 1,000 feet above the sea level. On top of the rails
at the Templeton depot the elevation is 770."

The San Miguel newspaper on the following week
informed readers that "The Templeton *Times* has
closed its first volume, and this week enters upon the
second under favorable auspices. It is a credit to its
editor, and the place; and though it has witnessed a
rapid development in the past year, we predict that
the coming year will far surpass it."

On December 30, 1887, the San Miguel newspaper carried another article, which had been published
in the Templeton *Times*: "Some heavy sales have been
made on the Santa Ysabel this week and a large one
on the Eureka. All have San Francisco parties as purchasers, who are in a position to anticipate important
movements. There is plenty of chance for outsiders to
surmise and for the knowing ones to profit. All the
recent sales of land will be followed by improvements."

The *San Miguel Messenger*, on December 30th also
carried the following item about Templeton: "Isaac
C. Hall, who last week sold his land near here, purchased of the West Coast Land Company 42 acres between Paso Robles and Templeton, paying $35 per
acre."

At one time, there was a proposed town located
about four miles southeast of Templeton, on what became the Heilmann Ranch, near where Highway 41
crosses the Salinas River. The town of Vasa had been
laid out by the Eureka Improvement Company for
Swedish immigrants, and was named after Vasa, Sweden. The idea of this community, on a portion of the
Eureka Ranch, was promoted by Briggs, Ferguson &
Company. It did not materialize as a town, but one of
the early settlers, August Johnson, raised his family
at the spot where the Templeton Road and Highway
41 meet.

The August 13, 1893 edition of *The Moon*, the Paso
Robles newspaper made the following report.

**The road from Templeton to Vasa was
declared a public highway by the Board of
Supervisors at their last meeting in July. *The
Advance* says this opens up a much shorter
road to Santa Margarita than the old stage
road, and will accommodate a large section
of country with a short road to market.**

The religious needs of Templeton were not over-
looked. A large brick church belonged to the Swedish
Lutheran Society. The Presbyterian Church was constructed at Sixth and Main Streets on a lot which had
been given by the West Coast Land Company. The
church was formally organized on May 8, 1887 after
the congregation had met in the drug store, the new
school-house and in vacant buildings. The dedication
service was held November 11, 1888, with the Reverend J. M. Newell, president. [Forty years later, on
November 11, 1928, Rev. Newell presided at the anniversary celebration.]

Pastors of the church, during the early years included: Francis H. Robinson, November 14, 1886 to
1898; W. W. Wells, 1890 to 1891; Isaac Baird, 1892 to
1898; W. S. Lowry 1899 to 1900. John W. Quay served
from 1901 to 1903; T. J. MacMurray 1903 to 1905; John
T. McLennan 1905 to 1909; A. W. Marshall 1909 to 1910;
James Thompson 1911 to 1916, and John R. Willhoit
1916 to 1927. [John R. Willhoit's son, Alfred H.
Willhoit, served as postmaster of Templeton from 1954
until he retired in 1977.]

The Ladies Aid of the Presbyterian Church provided the first staged entertainment for the town;
Annie Morrison was in charge. Annie Morrison would

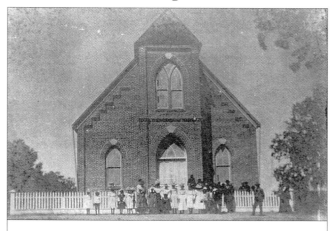

The Swedish Lutheran Church in Templeton.

go on to be the co-author of an important history of San Luis Obispo County.

On January 21, 1893, A. R. Austin wrote an article for the San Luis Obispo *Tribune* entitled "Around The Country." On that date, he wrote about Templeton.

The country for a mile or two west of Paso Robles and a mile south, is better adapted . . . for fruit raising than for gardening. The soil to that extent is what is known as chalk rock gravel and loam—upland.

The distance from Paso Robles to Templeton is six miles and the last five of it through an excellent grade of land with good buildings, fine orchards and a prosperous appearance. The Browning Butler Nursery company have their possessions along the road about midway. Mr. Ole Peterson has a fine orchard of twenty-two acres in prunes, adjoining the last named. This section of land is held at from $50 to $100 per acre.

Templeton as a village is a small town; a sort of twin step sister to Santa Margarita. They have a bank, two saloons, churches, stores enough, a newspaper- - -the *Advance*- - -Mr. Bull, a tip-top man, proprietor; a good hotel, under the management of Mr. James Farren and who deserves patronage to a greater degree than the town affords. They have a $7,000 school house with three rooms and teachers for each. Among the enterprising men I found in the village was Mr. A. J. Hudson, a large landowner, fruit grower and engaged in the real estate business.

He has 530 acres in his home place three miles out, with ten acres in prunes. Fruit growing, generally prunes, is quite extensively engaged in for several miles around and the returns from the industry are eminently satisfactory.

I took two considerable drives for some miles to the west and was much pleased with the prosperous outlook. Five miles out I found in the Oakdale district, a $5,000 school house; about a half mile from the school house I called upon Mr. J. C. Gibson, who has a very fine ranch of 1,700 acres, mainly cultivated to grain, and with first class farm buildings, and a mile south of town Mr. Nelse Johnson has 400 acres of equally good land,

mostly in grain. From Mr. C. N. Steinbach, the gentlemanly manager here of the Southern Pacific Milling company, I learned that the yearly shipments of grain amount to 300 carloads from this point. The large holdings of land in the vicinity were formerly: The Huer Huero ranch, 48,000 acres; the Paso Robles ranch, 22,000 acres; the Santa Ysabel ranch, 22,000 acres, and the Eureka ranch of 11,000 acres, now all subdivided and sold to actual users in comparatively small farms.

Chauncey H. Phillips has left his mark on Templeton in more than simply influencing the Southern Pacific Railroad to make Templeton the southernmost terminus in 1886, where the roundhouse and depot were placed at Third and Main Streets. In 1889, the terminus was moved to Santa Margarita.

Born in Wadsworth, Ohio, on July 5, 1837 of English ancestry, Chauncey Hatch Phillips came to California in 1864. He worked for the Internal Revenue office, and lived in San Francisco until November 30, 1871.

In the fall of that year, he brought his family to the town of San Luis Obispo, where he engaged in banking with Horatio M. Warden, under the name of Warden and Phillips. He directed the organization of the Bank of San Luis Obispo. Beginning in 1878, he devoted his energy to selling real estate, and in March of 1886, he was one of the people who incorporated the West Coast Land Company.

On January 18, 1862, Chauncey Hatch Phillips had married Jane Woods, at Fond du Lac, Wisconsin. They had a residence at Templeton, but their permanent home was in San Luis Obispo.

The *San Luis Obispo Tribune*, on March 4, 1902, printed the following.

DEATH CLAIMS C. H. PHILLIPS

C. H. Phillips is no more among the living. He passed away yesterday at his home at San Jose at 10:30 a.m. Mr. Phillips was apparently in the very best of health. At six o'clock in the morning he suffered a stroke of apoplexy and gradually sank away, death claiming him in four and a half hours after he sustained the shock.

In the death of C. H. Phillips, California loses one of her most progressive and foremost citizens, a man who ten years ago was prominently mentioned as a candidate for Governor of the state.

Filled with energy and inspired by splendid possibilities of the state, Mr. Phillips led an active live. He was ever up and doing. He was a hard worker. He took hold of big enterprises and rushed them through. His work was for the upbuilding of the state.

For a number of years, Mr. Phillips was a resident of San Luis Obispo county, for a time at Templeton and later in this city. He realized that San Luis Obispo had a glorious future and he set actively to work to induce immigration. He subdivided large bodies of land and in a few years sold hundreds of small ranches to homemakers. Among the tracts which he sold were the Oak Park section, San Miguelito ranch, Morro and Cayucos lands, Huer Huero grant and other big tracts. In 1886 he organized the West Coast Land Company. Among other business ventures, Mr. Phillips organized the first banking institution in San Luis Obispo, December 13, 1871. In October 1873, it was merged with the Bank of San Luis Obispo, with H. M. Warden as President and C. H. Phillips as cashier, which position he held four years, then serving one year as president.

San Luis Obispo county owes much of its development to the energetic efforts of Mr. Phillips. He was for years the county's foremost citizen. He was in the front rank of every enterprise. In the early nineties he was the leader in the efforts to induce the Southern Pacific to commence the work of bridging the "gap" on the coast line. Mr. Phillips gave his associates in every enterprise the assurance of success. He was interested in Chino for several years.

In politics, Mr. Phillips was a Republican. He was a Deputy County Clerk in San Francisco and Deputy Internal Revenue Collector. He was a candidate against Stoneman for Railroad Commissioner. He served several terms on the city council here.

Chauncey Hatch Phillips was born in Wadsworth, Medina county, Ohio, July 5, 1837. Mr. Phillips was married at Fond du Lac,

January 18, 1862 to Jane Woods, a native of Vermont. In 1864 he and his wife came to California. His first years in this state were spent in Napa, where he taught school. Deceased leaves a wife and several children.

The home for Phillips, his wife and their seven children had been built in 1886-1887. The family lived in it for five years, then sold it to Mr. H. Wessel. This man, from Iowa, had bought into the Bank of Templeton. During World War II, the Phillips house was divided into apartments. Then, from 1964-1966, it was owned by a family named Pennington. From 1966 to 1972, George Dutra and his wife owned the house, and restored it to its original beauty.

For a year, the house was owned by the Catos; then in 1973, it was sold to Mr. Smoot, a retired postal inspector. Mr. Martin Wolff, an attorney, bought the

An unknown person stands with Chester, Joe, and Lydia Nelson and Chan, the Chinese cook, in front of the Chauncey Hatch Phillips House, 91 Main Street, Templeton. Photo taken in 1887.

house in 1978 and lived there until 1981, when it was sold to Barbara Ford. She and a partner established the Country House Inn. The house, with six bedrooms and two parlors, was purchased by Diane Garth in 1987.

This building is a symbol of the past and the present in Templeton.

SAN MIGUEL AND THE RIOS CALEDONIA PROPERTY

1797 TO 1874

The land upon which the Rios-Caledonia adobe now stands belonged to Mission San Miguel, during the years of 1797 through 1846. [At times, we will refer to the adobe building as the "Caledonia," although it did not receive that name until the late 1860s.]

On July 4, 1846, Mission San Miguel and its property were purchased by Petronilo Rios, William Reed and Miguel Garcia. This purchase, from Governor Pio Pico, was declared illegal, in 1859. Miguel Garcia dropped out of sight almost immediately after the purchase. Bancroft's *California Pioneer Register and Index 1542-1848* lists only that Garcia was a grantee of the San Miguel Rancho in 1846. Reed and Rios grazed sheep and cattle on the former mission lands.

A family gathering perhaps after 1913, the year his wife, Mary Antonia Rios had died. Seated: James Rios and the father, Camilo Rios. Standing, left to right: Charles A. Rios, Victoria (Rios) Mounier, Josie (Rios) Frazzi, Egobilo Rios and Canuto Rios.

Governor Pio Pico, with the approach of the American forces, fled to Mexico, on August 10, 1846; he figures further in California history at a later date. William Reed had lived, with his family, in the buildings of Mission San Miguel as early as 1845. They continued to live there until the entire family, along with friends and workers, was murdered on the night of December 5, 1848. After this tragic event, Petronilo Rios was considered the sole legal owner of the mission buildings and lands; he and his family lived in an adobe home on Rancho La Estrella, six miles southeast of the mission. This adobe had been constructed during early mission days, to be used by the *mayordomo*, or foreman, of Rancho La Estrella.

Most people acknowledged Rios' ownership of the mission's lands until the time that clear title could not be obtained from the United States Land Commission in the early 1850s. Once it was realized that the federal government considered lands which had formerly belonged to Mission San Miguel to be public lands which now belonged to the state, settlers began to cast their eyes on these properties. (These so-called public lands did not include the grants, made from Mission San Miguel property totaling approximately 196,105 acres, which had been made between January 1840 through March of 1846.)

In an earlier chapter, we read a description of the countryside written by Alfred Robinson in 1834. Work on the two-story adobe we now call the Rios-Caledonia, would not begin for another year. The eldest son, and first child, of Petronilo and Catarina Rios was Jose Camilo, born July 19, 1833 in San Miguel.

We are given a description of San Miguel in 1846, by the writings of Edwin Bryant, a 1st Lieutenant in Company H of Fremont's Battalion of Mounted Riflemen. Also serving in this battalion was William Blackburn, 2nd Lieutenant in an Artillery Company. He was an older brother of two of the founders of the community of El Paso de Robles.

In his book, *What I Saw In California*, Bryant relates the following:

We passed the mission of San Miguel about 3 o'clock, and encamped in a grove of large oak timber three or four miles south of it. This mission is situated on the upper waters of the Salinas, in an extensive plain. Under the administration of the *padres* it was a wealthy establishment, and manufactures of various kinds were carried on. They raised immense numbers of sheep, the fleeces of which were manufactured by the Indians into blankets and coarse cloths.

Their granaries were filled with an abundance of maize and frijoles, and their storerooms with other necessaries of life from the ranchos belonging on the mission lands in the vicinity.

Now all the buildings, except the Church and the principal range of houses contiguous, have fallen into ruins, and an Englishman, his wife and one small child, with two or three Indian servants, are the sole inhabitants.

The church is the largest I have seen in the country, and its interior is in good repair, although it has not probably been used for the purpose of worship for many years. The Englishman professes to have purchased the mission and all the lands belonging to it for 300!

Our stock of cattle being exhausted, we feasted on Californian mutton, sheep being more abundant than cattle at this mission. The wool, I noticed, was coarse, but the mutton was of an excellent quality. The country over which we have traveled to-day, shows the marks of long drought previous to the recent rains.

The soil is sandy and gravelly, and the dead vegetation upon it is thin and stunted. About eighty of our horses are reported to have given out and been left behind.

. . .We encamped near the rancho of a friendly Californian,- - -the man who was taken prisoner the other day and set at large.

[The above was written on December 12, 1846; the friendly Californian he referred to was Petronilo Rios. We will have a closer look at this incident in another chapter.]

At the time this incident was taking place, Jose Camilo Rios, the first child of Petronilo and Catarina Rios would have been about 13 years of age.

Jose Camilo Rios, according to his youngest child, attended the seminary at Santa Ynez. Mrs. T. A. Mounier, in a 1930 book, *The Mission of the Passes: Santa Ines*, provides this information. The seminary, one of the oldest educational institutions in California, was established by Bishop Garcia Diego on May 4, 1844, at Mission Santa Ynez. The first seminary in California had been opened in 1842, in several rooms of the old mission buildings at Santa Barbara. This was only a temporary arrangement, and as the number of students increased, the facilities became inadequate. Bishop Garcia Diego decided to erect a new seminary adjacent to Santa Ynez Mission.

The purpose of the institution was to educate native priests- - -ones from the Indian and Mexican population. Up to that time, priests for California had been educated in Mexico. Old mission books at Santa Ynez state that in 1845, there were 33 students at the seminary, but only a few were studying for the priesthood. According to Mrs. T. A. Mounier, her father was among the first 20 or 30 to attend the school; school-mates named by Mrs. Mounier include: Frank Dana and Cressino Covarrubias. Camilo Rios would have been about twelve years of age at that time. Victoria Mounier said that her father was a tenor singer in the Santa Ynez choir.

Educational facilities were so few at the time, the Bishop had decided to open a primary school for boys at Mission Santa Ynez; each parent was supposed to give $150 a year for a boy's education. Nothing was said about education of girls.

The seminary was eventually transferred to the Rancho Refugio, some three miles from the mission. It was called the College of Our Lady of Refuge, and it operated until the year 1881.

Back to the earlier years in San Miguel, J. Ross Browne had arrived in California on August 5, 1849. He had been commissioned as "Inspector of Postal Service" by the Secretary of the U. S. Treasury. Browne was instructed to establish a line of post offices on the inland route from San Francisco to San Luis Obispo. The only post office he was able to institute on his journey was at San Jose. The story of his journey to San Luis Obispo gives a fascinating look at our area of concern in the year 1849.

When Browne was between four or five miles northwest of San Miguel, his mule ran away when he was near a small adobe house. Two mounted men he had met earlier were coming down the trail, so he sought the security of the old adobe. He was able to brace the door closed, but the men attempted to batter it down. Browne shot through the door, and heard a man exclaim that he had been shot through the shoulder; Browne was able to shoot the second man, but only through the wrist. As Browne headed toward a corner of the adobe to sit down to rest, he stumbled over a dead body. He later discovered that there were

An old adobe house in northern San Luis Obispo County.

three other bodies lying in the room: one on a bed—a woman with her throat cut from ear to ear—and two children he guessed to be eight to ten years old.

It was a bright and beautiful morning as I left the house and turned toward San Miguel. . . .In about an hour I saw the red tile roofs and motley collection of ruinous old buildings that comprised the former mission station of San Miguel. A gang of lean wolfish dogs ran out to meet me as I approached, and it was not without difficulty that I could keep them off without resorting to my revolver. . .As I approached the main buildings I was struck with the singularly wild and desolate aspect of the place.

Not a living being was in sight. The carcass of a dead ox lay in front of the door, upon which a voracious brood of buzzards were feeding; and a coyote sat howling on an eminence a little beyond. I walked into a dark, dirty room, and called out, in what little Spanish I knew, for the man of the house.

Browne met a vaquero, who gave him jerked beef and tortillas, in return for a plug of tobacco. After eating, he rambled around the ruins of the mission for about an hour. "A few lazy and thriftless Indians, lying in the sun here and there, were all the inhabitants of the place I could see. This ranch must have been a very desirable residence in former times." Browne goes on to relate that "The country, for many miles after leaving San Miguel was very wild and picturesque. . .It was a very lonesome road all the way to the valley of Santa Margarita, not a house or human being to be seen for twenty miles at a stretch."

We will take the time to look at the background of

Maria Antonia Castillo, wife of Jose Camilo Rios, the first-born child of Petronilo and Catarina Rios. Jose Camilo, about 1856, married Maria Antonia Castillo (1843-1913). She had been raised by the Soberanes family near present-day King City. This was most likely the family of Mariano Soberanes, who was the grantee of Rancho San Bernardino, in 1841.

The land was along the Salinas River, north and south of today's town of San Ardo; the grant consisted of 13,346 acres, and was patented on March 9, 1874. Mariano Soberanes, in 1845, had served as *juez de campo* at San Miguel.

Mariano Soberanes was granted the Rancho Los Ojitos ("The Little Springs") in 1842. This grant consisted of 8,900.17 acres, and extended along the San Antonio River in Monterey County. During the Mexican War, Mariano and his sons were arrested by John Charles Fremont; some of the Soberanes property at Los Ojitos was destroyed. He later filed a claim against the state for this damage. The amount of the claim was $19,930, of which, $423 was paid.

The patent on this grant was issued to Mariano Soberanes on April 18, 1871; the rancho was still owned by the sons of Mariano in 1885.

Having taken a quick look at Maria Castillo's history, we move forward with our story. Camilo and Maria had eleven children between the years 1858 and 1875; all of these children were born in San Miguel. In later years, Camilo and Maria Castillo Rios made their home in Lompoc, at the corner of Cypress and K Streets. There, Maria operated a nursing home, and she made and sold tamales from that house. The old Rios home was destroyed by the Lompoc Fire Department in the 1960s.

The last child of Camilo and Maria Rios was Victoria Evelyn Rios, born about 1875; she may have been the reason that the family delayed the move to Lompoc at its founding in 1874 as a temperance colony. Victoria later became Mrs. T. A. Mounier.

Victoria Rios poses a slight problem concerning the time at which her family moved away from San Miguel. She is included in a report of San Miguel school, in the November 18, 1887 *San Miguel Messenger*: "During the week ending November 11th, the following pupils were neither absent nor tardy: Primary . . . Victoria Rios." She would have been 12 years old during 1887. She could have been residing with another family in San Miguel.

The 1870 census of San Luis Obispo County shows Camilo Rios' assessments of $1,000 in real estate and $10,000 in personal property. Camilo Rios' name appears on the Great Register of San Luis Obispo County

in 1871, as a farmer, at Hot Springs; on the Great Register of 1880, he appears as a laborer at San Miguel. Between 1875 and 1889, the family moved to Lompoc.

Camilo Rios was remembered in Lompoc as a tall, handsome man with a white beard. He drove big teams pulling wagons of grain to town. The big wagons and Camilo made a very impressive sight, rolling into Lompoc up to the time that trucks began being used.

We have in indication that the Rios family was using the adobe, later known as the Caledonia, as their residence in 1854. In that year, Virginia McMahon (Espinosa) made a trip from the Natividad Ranch, near Salinas, to San Luis Obispo, where she spent her childhood, as godchild of Mrs. Rosa Simmler. Virginia had been born in 1842 at Monterey; her parents were Jeremiah McMahon and Ramona Butron. The trip from Natividad to San Luis Obispo took one week; an over-night stop was made at "the famous old Caledonia Inn near the San Miguel Mission," according to her.

La Casa de los Rios c. 1919.

The Caledonia was then the home of the Rios family. In that year, Petronilo and Catarina Rios' oldest child would have been about 21 years old. This information about Virginia McMahon came in an interview given on January 2, 1931, when she was 89 years of age.

During the month of November 1855, Isaac B. Wall, the collector at the Port of Monterey, and Thomas B. Williamson, an officer of Monterey County, were on their way to San Luis Obispo with a pack-train. On the "dark and bloody ground" of the Nacimiento these two men were waylaid and murdered. No direct trace of the murderers was ever found.

There is no connection with the Rios family or the Caledonia adobe; the incident is related to remind us that our region of concern could still be a dangerous place. Walter Murray, newspaper writer and editor, arrived in San Luis Obispo in the fall of 1853. He had written that "at a place near the mouth of the Nacimiento . . . this river and the ground for miles on each side is 'THE DARK AND BLOODY GROUND' of this section of the country."

An artist by the name of Henry Miller was traveling between San Francisco and San Diego, in 1856; he was visiting and sketching the missions. Miller writes of being shown the interior of Mission San Miguel by "Mr. Del Rios," who Miller refers to as "the present proprietor." This statement could refer to either Petronilo or his son, Camilo, but Petronilo would have been about 50 years old, and Camilo would have been about 23 years of age.

The Mission of San Miguel forms a large square, on which a great number of adobe houses remain. However, with the exception of the church and a few buildings next to it, all are unroofed and partly in ruins.

The land formerly belonging to the mission, of which some is very fertile, was of great extent to the amount of 50 or 60 leagues. There are no Indians, except a few in the employ of Mr. Del Rios, the present proprietor.

The above gentleman showed me the interior of the church, which varies in nothing from all the other mission churches, being a long but narrow building, with whitewashed walls daubed with some course fresco painting, an altar stripped of its silver plate, which are replaced with tin. I met eight horsemen here, en route to the Tulare Valley to hunt wild horses.

After having taken a sketch of this mission, I left towards the Mission San Luis Obispo which is 14 leagues from here. . . .My road led alongside the San Miguel River, with a wide sandy bed, but without a drop of water.

The grass of the country over which I traveled today had all burned off, some incautious travellers having left fire behind, which, being blown by the wind, had run on for a number of miles. Finding a pool of fine clear water I camped here for the night.

In the morning early I arrived at a rancho, built of adobe, called El Paso De Robles, which was inhabited by some hunters. I found deer to be very plentiful in the vicinity.

After crossing a small river near the rancho, I struck into a dry and barren tract of 10 or 12 miles, after which the country im-

proved; hills and valleys were covered with wild oats and timber and offered a most refreshing aspect, till I arrived in the vicinity of the Santa Margarita Rancho. . .

The population of San Luis Obispo County, by 1860, had reached a total of 1,782 persons. According to Lura Rawson, the late local historian, the town of San Miguel was destroyed by fire in 1860. At that time, whatever "town" existed at San Miguel was situated between the Caledonia and the Mission. Fred K. Knights had a meat market at the mission in the 1870s, and he sold fish brought over from Cayucos once a week. He also took orders for fresh vegetables for Mark Wright, who had the first commercial garden out on San Marcos Creek. Goldtree's store began business in San Miguel in 1871.

An ad in the December 8, 1886 issue of *The Inland Messenger* shows that Frederick Knights had a continuing business.

San Miguel Meat Market
In the Mission
Fresh meats of all kinds
Bacon and Fish
Orders by mail promptly attended to.
Prices Reasonable, for cash.
Potatoes, onions and all kinds of vegetables.
Cash paid for butter and eggs.

Fredk. Knights

Jose Camilo Rios and his family are said to have lived at the Rios-Caledonia during the entire period of 1858 to 1875. We have seen that Camilo was listed as being in San Luis Obispo County in 1880. The census for Lompoc, also 1880, lists Camilo Rios. It is possible that Camilo Rios may have reached some sort of gentleman's agreement whereby the family was permitted to continue living on the property, although they may not have owned it. As far as the family was concerned, there were probably few, if any, consequences from the change of ownership, except that they paid their rent to a different land-lord.

An indication that the Rios family occupied the Caledonia adobe during the 1860s comes from a person named Robert S. Cruess. Mr. Cruess was born about 1859, and came to San Miguel in 1869. In a newspaper article written on October 8, 1936, Mr. Cruess states that when he came to San Miguel, the Camilo Rios family was living at the Caledonia.

We will see later that at least three sources inform

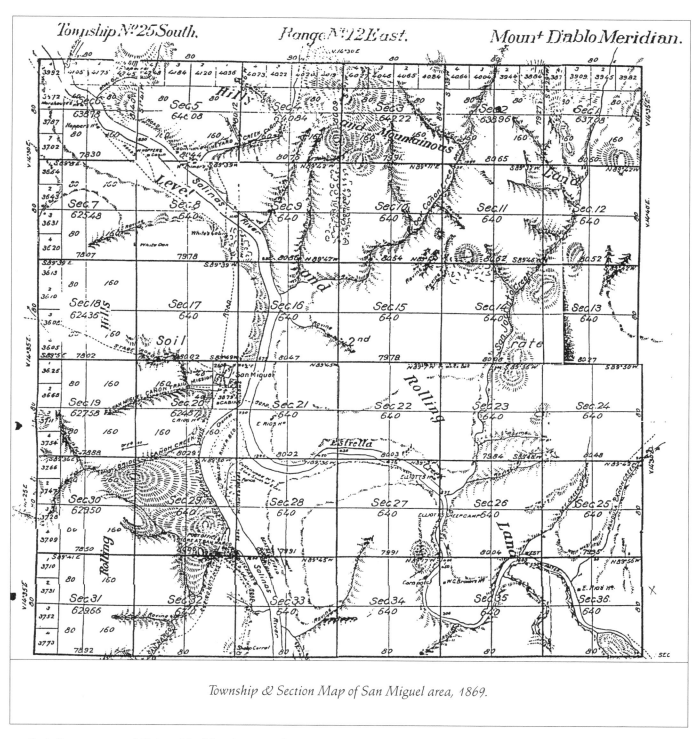

Township & Section Map of San Miguel area, 1869.

us that there were additional habitations on the Rios property, next to the Caledonia, so the family did not have to actually live in the two-story adobe.

The 1870 census shows that the Camilo Rios family lived in San Miguel; of course, the census does not specify where in San Miguel they resided. However, the "C. Rios house" was used as one of the landmarks when the township line survey was done in 1855, and again when the section line survey was done in 1869.

We can assume that the family used the two-story building as their home until at least the year 1869.

Also shown on the survey maps are the Rios home at La Estrella, as well as an "E. Rios house" on the east side of the Salinas River, near where present-day River Road crosses the Estrella River. William Norin, in his book, *The McDonald Clan on the Estrella*, says that Frank Rios, born in 1843 and 27 years old in 1870, "became one of the major sheepmen of San Miguel.

His land was three miles from San Miguel." The "E" on the survey map, could stand for Estaban, son of Petronilo and Catarina Rios, who was born on December 26, 1839. He was a brother of Camilo Rios.

The survey map also shows an "E. Rios" at the location of La Estrella adobe. This is most likely where Petronilo and Catarina Rios and their family lived during the period of approximately 1846, when the mission's property was purchased, and 1851, when they moved into the Caledonia building. In 1981, only a crumbling wall remained of this historic La Estrella adobe.

There is a legend that Egobilo Rios (born 1863) took the deed to the Estrella property with him to Mexico, where he was murdered. A new deed was supposed to have been made out to Camilo Rios, his father. Three problems with the legend are: First, his grandfather (Petronilo Rios) had to move from this property for the specific reason that he could not get a title to the property from the United States Land Commission. Second, Egobilo Rios was alive and filed for a homestead in the southeastern part of the county.

Third, Egobilo died in 1936, which is too late to fit into the title scenario. (Egobilo Rios' homestead was situated to the northeast of Cuyama Number 2, and the patent was approved by President Warren G. Harding on November 17, 1922.)

Let us look back at the location which is designated "C. Rios" home on the survey maps. During 1857, part of the adobe was used to house schoolrooms. The Caledonia has been used two different times as a school building. During the period of 1858-1875, the property was owned by various people, and the building was being used as a stage-stop, hotel and tavern.

There were two large and two smaller rooms upstairs, and two large and two smaller rooms downstairs, plus the kitchen and other out-buildings. All travelers who passed by the door of the Caledonia on El Camino Real were welcomed to stay overnight.

There were several out-buildings to the west of the main adobe structure, so it is reasonable to assume that there was enough room for the family of Camilo Rios to reside there at the same time the adobe was

La Estrella Adobe being allowed to go to ruins.

Drawn by Steve Kalar

being used for other purposes. Steve Buelna told Ella Adams that his birth, in 1885, took place in an adobe building in back of the two-story Caledonia. There were several adobe structures just west of the main adobe building.

The year 1861 is an important date in California; during that year, a tri-weekly stage and mail service began between San Francisco and Los Angeles. In 1862, this service was expanded into a daily four-horse stage. (In another chapter, the stage-coach business in our area of concern is examined in more detail.)

Lt. Col. Vivian N. Scott wrote for *The Dispatch*, a newspaper printed at Camp Roberts. Under the date of January 21, 1944, he related the following story by Mariano Gil, who had been born in 1853; the following would have taken place about the year 1861.

I was about eight years old when my aunt came to San Miguel for several days visit and we stayed at the adobe house of Rios. Guests, due to long distance and slow conveyance, usually stayed a week or two while visiting in the pioneer days.

The parties always conceived in their honor were extremely convivial affairs- - -hilarious, very often. Dancing was the order every evening with it being a common understanding that all of the entire community were invited to attend at will. Dancing continued all night long if it was the pleasure of the party.

On this particular visit, I had a most memorable experience; I found myself an unsolicited job. Music for dancing at this time was provided at the Rios House by an old grind-organ. I was just big enough successfully to wind the crank, which operated the bellows to provide air to make the organ go.

I successfully cranked for what seemed to me interminable hours, but after a while I got tired and dozed off to sleep- - -but not for long, for a resounding thump on my head woke me up.

I was so tired and I presume I didn't even respond to thumps, for I next recall awakening in bed next morning. I also recall how much joking there was over my cranking and thumping.

The years 1862, 1863 and 1864 were not easy ones.

There were torrential floods during the spring of 1862, and they devastated most of California. The rains were followed by an equally devastating drought in 1863 and 1864.

The land about which we will be having the most discussion is located at the SW ¼ of SE ¼ Section 20, Township 25 South, Range 12 East, Mt. Diablo Meridian.

On July 8, 1862, Warren C. Rickard purchased the Rios property, composed of 160 acres, from the state on a possessory claim. ("Possessory claim" sounds like a polite way to say that Rickard was a "squatter" on the property.) It is fairly easy to understand how a "squatter"- - -if he was one- - -could get this claim.

The purchase of the San Miguel Mission and its property had been declared illegal, so the Rios family would have had no title to this property. On December 26, 1862, Warren C. Rickard sold 80 acres to J. B. Ham for $800. This transaction was recorded in Deed Book A, page 503, County of San Luis Obispo Recorder.

On April 20, 1852, the United States Congress had passed legislation entitled, "An Act to Ascertain and Settle Private Land in the State of California." A result of the act had been to prescribe the mode of maintaining possessory actions on public land, and to regulate grazing and cultivation in the new state.

Rickard's new property commenced at a blazed oak tree 800 yards west of the stage road, went southerly 880 yards crossing the San Marcos Creek to an oak tree blazed; thence easterly 880 yards along the line of Jonathan Bixby's claim to a stake in the bed of the Salinas River. Then northerly along the bed of the river to a stake 880 yards; westerly direction crossing the stage road 880 yards to the beginning, containing 160 acres of land. (Deed Book C, page 317, in the office of the San Luis Obispo County Recorder.)

Slightly over one year later, on July 18, 1863, Rickard sold his acquisition to a B. F. Stevens, for $1,500. (Deed Book A, page 549.) June 14, 1865 finds Warren C. Rickard again the owner of the Rios-Caledonia property. This time, Mr. Stevens sold Rickard the former Rios property, a total of 160 acres, for $150. (The deed was recorded on September 18, 1865 in Deed Book A, page 760.)

Warren C. Rickard, and his brother William C. Rickard, jointly owned mining and land claims to the west of the San Marcos Creek area near Adelaida. They took up squatter's rights on the coast at Leffingwell Creek, and opened a store which was called Rickard's Log Store, the first store on the north coast. They had previously opened a store in the Adelaida

*La Casa
de Rios.*

*Drawn by
Keith Tarwater*

area, according to Geneva Hamilton, in her book, *Where the Highway Ends*. William C. Rickard managed most of the coast business, and Warren C. Rickard spent his time on the San Marcos Creek property.

In 1864, the county tax assessment records show that a group called "Rickard & Company" had the following assessments: improvements at San Marcos, $200; house at San Simeon, $150. Also, taxes were levied on 6 tame horses, 4 tame colts, 4 American cows, 3 sets of harness & wagons. The total value of $1,856 called for a tax of $60.32.

The drought during the years 1862 to 1864, is seen as marking the end of rancho days along the central coast of California. As many as 300,000 head of cattle and 100,000 sheep died during these years of no rain.

According to Myrtle Reese Bridge, in her book *Early History of San Luis Obispo County*, the population of San Miguel in 1868 was 150 persons.

In the unpublished writings of Edith Buckland Webb, she includes information she received from Eva Carpenter Iversen, a local historian who was a teacher at the Union School, east of Paso Robles, in 1901. Mrs. Iversen made the statement that "The Morgans came in 1868. Before their coming, the stage station had been changed to the adobe south of the mission. This house was then known by its Spanish title, *la Casa de los Rios*. In 1871, Peter Cheney went to work for Morgan, and was told that a short time before Morgan's arrival a band of bandits had ridden up just as the stage was leaving the mission, shot the driver, ..." She goes on to say that "Morgan said that the station was changed to the Rios House at this time as it was deemed safer."

To further quote Mrs. Iversen, "As soon as Morgan was well established in the mission, he opened a

Old Caledonia Adobe from the south. Note attached kitchen structure on the west side of the building.

store in one of the rooms of the *convento*. . . .A short time later, he opened a saloon in another of the *convento* rooms."

"Settlers began coming in and taking up homesteads and there was a demand for a place of amusement other than a saloon. Morgan supplied the need by removing the inner wall between the two rooms that joined the church at the north end of the *convento*, and turned them into a dance hall. . . .At present, there is a driveway where these rooms once were.

"Just when the outer walls were removed to make way for traffic Peter did not remember. Many of the old residents contend that this driveway was always there, but markings on the adjoining walls and foundations would seem to prove that Peter was right."

In 1868, George Butchart entered the scene. He had a store and post office at San Marcos Creek, three miles south of the Rios-Caledonia. He bought the Rios property on May 7, 1868, for $2,600, and built a large wooden barn to house horses; this barn was across the creek which ran just south of the adobe.

According to the 1870 census, George Butchart was a retired merchant, 60 years of age; wife, Sarah, born in Ireland, was the same age. Their two sons, Norval and James Bruce, were born in Canada. George Butchart had been born in Scotland. George Butchart was the person who named the adobe "Caledonia"- - - the Scottish word for "Scotland." Somehow, the idea that Caledonia means "welcome" has gained acceptance. This "welcome" meaning has mistakenly been connected with the adobe for about a hundred years. It is true that people were always welcome at the Caledonia, but that is *not* the literal meaning of the word.

Butchart did some remodeling, in order to convert the place into a stage-stop, hotel, saloon and store, as well as the post office for San Miguel. Virginia Peterson was told by Grace Pate Heaton (1872-1963) that Grace's father installed windows and doors in the Caledonia about 1876. Grace's parents, David L. and Susan M. Pate, were formerly of Tennessee; they made the long voyage around Cape Horn in 1859. The Pates settled in the Jack Creek region, west of Paso Robles. After working in San Miguel, David Pate went to Oregon, where he was killed by Indians, leaving Susan Mary Lassiter Pate to raise the family.

George Butchart built a one-story room, to use as a saloon, on one end of the adobe; there is a question as to whether this addition was on the southern or the northern end of the building. Anecdotal records say that the addition was on the south; photographic evidence shows a one-story annex on the north end of the adobe.

The 1870 San Luis Obispo County census gave the total residents at 4,700 people. The Salinas Township contained 679 persons. The Harris Map of 1874, of San Luis Obispo County, shows a post office and the name Butchart.

The land Butchart purchased was in the Salinas Township at the junction of San Marcos Creek with the Salinas River. The purchase consisted of 260 acres; 100 acres of this property were on the east side of the Salinas River, and were fenced. The remaining 160 acres were on the west side of the river near where the San Marcos store was located. (The deed was recorded, Book B, page 319, on July 25, 1868.)

There is a hand-drawn map, dated July 23, 1868, which shows the location of some property located in part of SW ¼ of NE ¼ of Section 20, along the stage road to Monterey. On the north side of the road, three lots, each 66 feet wide along the road and 132 feet deep, are indicated. The southern-most lot shows: "George Butchart to Charles B. Douglass." The middle lot shows: "Asa Croxford to C. B. Douglass." The two lots appear to be used for Blacksmith and Wagon Shops. The northernmost lot of the three shows: "Nathan and Isaac Goldtree to James Kelley."

Across the stage road, and in line with the middle and northern lot, are two lots of the same size. Lot 1 on the north, and Lot 2 on the south show: "Asa Croxford to C. B. Douglass." Across the two lots is written: "Dwelling House."

Charles Blomfield Douglas (1843-1899) and Gerard Noel Douglas (1843-1922) were twins. Since the Douglases at one time owned part of the Caledonia property, and the fact that they were prominent early pioneers of the San Miguel area, we will take the time to examine their lives.

The Douglas twins were born on April 6, 1843 at Ottery St. Mary, Devonshire, England. When they were about seventeen years old, they left England for New Zealand; there, they raised sheep near Dunedin in the southern part of the South Island. Their brother, John Ambrose Douglas (1837-1890), was six years their senior and had preceded them to New Zealand.

When it came time to return to England, the Douglas twins planned to sail to San Francisco, travel by railroad to New York, and from there to set sail for England. The reason for the stop in San Francisco was to visit their sister, who was the wife of the British Consul General there.

William Pinkerton, a person they had met in New Zealand, asked them to visit him in California.

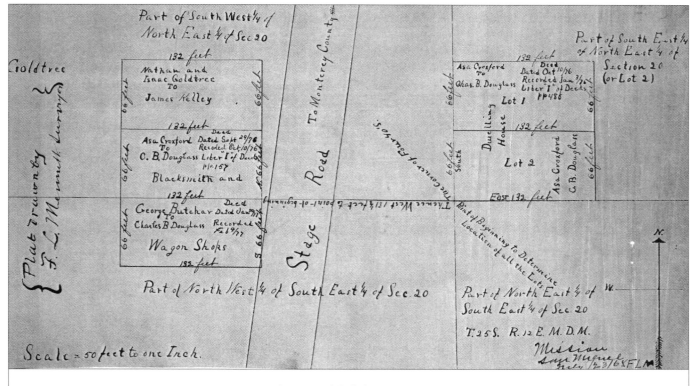

1868 Map of Caledonia Property

Pinkerton had settled near Pleyto, up the San Antonio River near the southern Salinas Valley. He helped convince the twins to cancel their trip home. The Douglas twins began buying parcels of land in southern Monterey County lying on the east side of the Salinas River. This land was generally south of Bradley and north of San Miguel.

The first recorded land purchase of the Douglas twins was 640 acres, bought on April 6, 1874. This irregularly-shaped tract of land was called Las Juntas ("the joining"), because of its proximity to the juncture of the San Antonio and Nacimiento Rivers with the Salinas River. The Douglases bought parcels of land until Las Juntas comprised about 7,000 acres. About half of the old Las Juntas ranch is now inside the boundary of Camp Roberts.

Bruce McVey, a descendant of the Douglases, has given a description of the boundaries of Las Juntas, at its largest extent, proceeding in a counter-clockwise direction. Go six miles north up Indian Valley from the San Luis Obispo/Monterey County line, then due west to Portuguese Canyon along a line parallel to the county line, but six miles north of it. Turn southwest down Portuguese Canyon to the Salinas River, almost to Bradley, then southeast along the river back to the county line. Proceed along the county line between the Salinas River and the mouth of Indian Canyon.

Land records show that on November 6, 1874, the Douglases bought an isolated 160-acre parcel in Vineyard Canyon, a couple of miles from the closest part of their ranch. By January 1875, they owned 7,320 acres- - -more than eleven square miles.

The R. R. Harris Map of the County of San Luis Obispo, published in September of 1874, gives the estimated population of the county as 8,000; of these people, 1,843 were children between 5 and 17 years of age. There were 2,369 enrolled voters.

The estimated area of San Luis Obispo County was given as 3,160 square miles. Mexican grants covered 481,237 acres, while public lands accounted for 1,541,163 acres. The number of horses, of all kinds, amounted to 5,936. There were 37,768 cattle and 256,223 sheep.

In the next section, we will look at further Douglas acquisitions of some of the Caledonia property, as we follow the history of the region during the period of 1875 through 1885.

1875-1885

1875 is a fairly significant year in the history of the Caledonia, because during that year, the Camilo Rios family is said to have moved from San Miguel to Lompoc. This would be the first time since 1854 that someone from the Rios family did not live at what is today called the Rios-Caledonia adobe. The 1880 census for Lompoc shows the Camilo Rios family living in the Lompoc area. As far as can be determined, few of the Camilo Rios children remained in San Miguel when they reached maturity, or returned to live in San Miguel.

"Frank" Rios, a younger brother of Camilo Rios, was the only member of that generation of the Rios family who did remain in the San Miguel area for an extended period of time. He is listed on the San Luis Obispo County census in 1870, as a sheep-raiser. The Great Register of San Luis Obispo County in 1871 lists him as a farmer, 24 years old, in the Hot Springs district. In 1880, the Great Register shows him to be a stock-raiser in the Hot Springs district.

Jose Francisco Rios had been born on July 6, 1843, and was also called Jose Juan Franquilino. Most of the following information, about Jose Francisco and his family, comes from Tony Rios, a great-grandson of Petronilo and Catarina Rios. Tony learned most of this information from his grandmother, who was the wife of Jose Francisco Rios. Some recent vital information has been supplied by Patrick Orozco.

On November 12, 1873, Jose Francisco Rios married Mariana Ynez Castanos, who had been born in 1854. She said that her favorite brother had been baptized on the counter of her father's store, which she said was located in "the gold fields of San Jose." The San Jose, to which she refers, is most likely the San Jose Valley in the Pozo area of eastern San Luis Obispo County.

It was in this region of San Luis Obispo County that Mariana Ynez Castanos was born; her father, Jose Maria Castanos, had married a Spanish lady, Ynez Buelna, in 1848; they would become the parents of eight children. Mariana said that her father later purchased a store in San Luis Obispo.

The meeting between Francisco Rios and Mariana Ynez Castanos took place at a *fandango* at Mission San Luis Obispo when she was fifteen years old- - -about 1870. At that time, she was returning from Spain, where she had been sent to be educated. She had come by ship to Mexico, and then was traveling overland by stage-coach to San Luis Obispo.

Francisco and Mariana Rios had eight children; two were born while they were living on the San Miguel Rancho. By this time, the "San Miguel Rancho" probably refers to the area near where the Estrella River is crossed by River Road today. It would have been near the high ground north of the Estrella River, and would include the site where the "E. Rios house" is shown on the township and section maps.

Their first child was a daughter they named Porfira, born on September 15, 1874, in San Luis Obispo; the god-parents were John Morgan and Josefa Rios. Their second child was a son, born in San Luis Obispo on October 24, 1875; they named him Petronilo Eduardo. The third child, Magdelina, was born in 1876; she died in Santa Barbara in 1951. Their fourth child died at birth, and Mariana buried the baby's body "under the altar at the Mission." From the year 1842 until 1878, Mission San Miguel had no resident priest; it was attended to, on occasion, by priests from Mission San Luis Obispo. Therefore, it is not difficult to believe that Mariana Ynez Castanos Rios would feel free to bury her baby inside Mission San Miguel. (In 1878, the Bishop of Monterey-Los Angeles, Right Reverend Francis Mora, decided to send Father Philip Farrelly to Mission San Miguel as pastor.)

The rest of the children of Francisco and Mariana Rios, with birthplaces are: Manuel Bonaventura Rios (1878-1897), Carpinteria; Manuel J. Rios (1879-1929), Carpinteria; Katherina L. Rios (1880-1969), Montecito; and Agatha Y. Rios (1882-1967), Santa Barbara. These records are from Our Lady of Sorrows Church and Calvary Cemetery in Santa Barbara.

During the drought of the late 1870s, Francisco and his wife and small child headed south to the Casitas Pass area. The reason for that location as a destination was that Mariana had relatives there, and they would be able to provide help to this small family. Francisco died in Santa Barbara on March 14, 1883, at the age of 40.

After Mariana lost the San Miguel ranch, by a default of some kind, she bought a plot of land at Arlington and Anacapa Streets in Santa Barbara.

A family legend that Tony Rios learned from his grandmother had Petronilo Rios leaving Spain to escape the wrath of his father. According to this story, Petronilo had hit his schoolmaster with a rock, and thought that he had killed him. To help insure that his father would not be able to find him, Petronilo changed his last name from De Los Rios to simply Rios. Since we are speculating on legends- - -could the rock-throwing person have been Petronilo's father? Various records state that Petronilo had been born in Mexico, and not in Spain, as this legend would have it.

Virginia Culbert, while serving as the President of "The Friends of the Adobes, Inc.," had a February 1980 interview with Myrtle Rios. Myrtle was the widow of Herbert Rios (1875-1971); Herbert was a great-grandson of Petronilo. Herbert's father was Charles Osbando Rios (1867-1934), a son of Camilo Rios. According to Myrtle Rios, Petronilo's father came from Spain with a group of monks, but was not himself a monk. Could there be some accurate information mixed up in these two stories? Could Petronilo's father have been the one who shipped out for Mexico, in order to escape *his father's* wrath?

Mariana said that her husband had resumed the use of the name "De Los Rios."

Since 1981, researchers in "The Friends of the Adobes, Inc." have believed that Petronilo Rios died in Santa Barbara in 1895, and was buried there. While doing research in Santa Barbara in the spring of 1996, it was learned that the person named Petronilo Rios, who died in 1895, was *not* the patriarch of the Rios family.

The record at Our Lady of Sorrows Church in Santa Barbara states:

1895 Dia 20 de Agosto di sepultura eclesiastica al cadavir de Petronilo Fr. Rios, de 18 y 8 meses di edad, hijo de Francisco ye de Mariana.

The Morning Press: Santa Barbara for Tuesday morning, August 20, 1895, carried the following item:

DIED. RIOS - Sunday morning at Chatsworth, Los Angeles County, Frank Rios, aged 18 years and eight months. (Funeral this morning in Santa Barbara at 8 o'clock from the Parochial church. Friends invited.)

We return to the Rios property and the Caledonia in the year 1875- - -the year often given as the one in which Camilo Rios and his family moved to Lompoc.

In 1875, De Guy Cooper published *Resources of San Luis Obispo County-Its Geography, Climate, Location, Soil, Productions and Institutions*. This book mentions that a portion of the mission buildings are occupied as a hotel and saloon by the McDonald Brothers. He states that "There are but two stores in the place- - -one kept by Mr. Geo. Butchart, who also keeps a neat hotel, which presents a most inviting appearance to the weary traveler; the other mercantile establishment is that of Sittenfeld & Co., a branch of the Goldtree Bros., of San Luis Obispo." Cooper also states that "Croxford & Woodworth have the only blacksmith and wagon-shop in the place. . ."

Lauchlin McDonald and Mary "Molly" Mc Adams, June 16, 1878, wedding photo.

L. L. Paulson, in 1875, published a *Hand-Book & Directory*. From this publication, we can learn the names of the businessmen of San Miguel. N. P. Duncan is listed as a physician; we have not seen his name, other than in Paulson's handbook. The names of the merchants are: Abraham Blumenthal, James Bruce Butchart, George Butchart, Norval Butchart, J. C. Currier and Hugh D. Menton. Listed under "General Merchandise" are: Arnold Sittenfeld, and Sittenfeld & Co. People listed as clerks are: J. Carter, J. S. Farbish, E. F. Sautter, and E. R. Spaulding.

Paulson lists one blacksmith, a J. M. Black; James Keleher is the only wagonmaker on the list. The only carpenter in town was T. F. Burt. Paulson's publication states that "The town comprises two hotels, two stores, two saloons, one blacksmith shop and wagon shop, with a population of about fifty persons. . ." He also states that George Butchart & Sons, San Marcos had "a hotel containing every convenience for guests; also ten cottages for the use of families, in connection with the hotel."

The only bar-keeper on Paulson's list is Frank

Camp. Persons with the occupation of "laborer" were: J. Gillespy, H. M. Jones, H. Martin, W. Mitchell, Daniel E. Orr, J. A. Rivera, S. Shelton and D. White.

Stock-raisers in the area were: A. C. Beattie, George Davis, W. M. Jeffreys, J. A. Patchell, Patterson & Purcell, A. J. Patterson, J. W. Pliant, A. E. Purcell, Francisco Rios, Camilo Rios, J. B. Simmons, J. Thompson, M. N. Warren and A. Wells.

The longest list was made up of the names of the area farmers: J. T. Black, H. H. Borden, R. D. Cofer, J. B. Davis, P. Devine, R. Elliott, Jesus Green, J. D. Griffin, J. Guhlstorff, William Hopper, T. Kirkendall, P. Klippel, P. Lahey, P. McAdam, R. P. Merril, W. H. Menton, G. Middagh, N. B. Morehouse, William Jackson Oaks, J. A. Palmer, G. W. Parrish, J. D. Peters, J. Ramage, G. Ray, H. W. Rhyne, Estaban Rios, C. C. Sankey, W. I. Scales, J. Sheehan, J. Thompson, J. Waier, A. M. Wallace, W. Webb, N. Weir and D. C. Wright.

According to the book, *Early History of San Luis Obispo County*, written by Myrtle Reese Bridge in 1961, in 1877 there were fifteen buildings in the town of San Miguel.

In 1875, Charles E. Woodworth and Asa Croxford became the owners of some of the Rios property- - -a lot measuring 66 feet by 132 feet; Asa Croxford owned a paint shop north of the adobe. The Great Register of San Luis Obispo County of 1880 lists Croxford as a native of Maine; the date of registration was given as August 9, 1870. Charles E. Woodworth is listed in the Great Register of 1871, with the occupation of butcher; the date of registration was October 1, 1868.

On March 12, 1875, Charles E. Woodworth sold to Asa Croxford, for $800, the "dwelling house" which he and Asa occupied on land that had belonged to George Butchart. During the same month, on March 30th, George Butchart and his wife, Sara Jane, sold to Asa Croxford, for $50, the 66 by 132 foot Lot #2 of SE ¼ NE ¼ of Section 20, Township 25 South, Range 12 of East Meridian of Mount Diablo. It amounted to a total of 1/5 of an acre.

About one month later, Asa Croxford mortgaged his new purchase to Charles Blomfield Douglas, in order to secure repayment of $1,500 within one year. The property mortgaged was the "dwelling house" and Lot #2; the lot was 66 feet by 132 feet. Power of sale was given, in case of default. (Book "D" of Mortgages, page 162.)

On May 19, 1876, there was a court action concerning the Butcharts. People by the name of A. Blochman, M. Cerf, E. Cerf, and L. M. Kaiser, partners under the firm name of A. Blochman & Co., were the plaintiffs.

Geo. Butchart, Norval Butchart and James Bruce Butchart, partners under the name of Geo. Butchart & Sons, were the defendants. The plaintiffs recovered $1,000 with interest.

We will digress for a moment, and take the time for a closer look at the people who became the plaintiffs. Three years earlier than the court action against the Butcharts, in February of 1873, Blochman & Cerf had purchased the People's Wharf near San Luis Obispo. In May of that year, they extended the wharf to deep water so that vessels could lie along side it. The Cerf name is associated with the following grants in the southern part of the county: Bolsa de Chamisal, in the 1860s'; Arroyo Grande in 1869; Corral de Piedra, in the 1860s and 1870s; and El Pismo in 1871.

A. Blochman is noted for having erected a brick store in San Luis Obispo in 1870. A. Blochman & Co. were also owners of the San Jose mines, which were discovered in the La Panza region in 1872. By 1877, Blochman & Co., of San Luis Obispo owned 640 acres in the San Jose Valley in the eastern part of the county.

Not every item of news concerning A. Blochman & Co. was good news. On September 8, 1878 at the Paletta Rancho, belonging to A. Blochman & Co., an Indian herder and his wife were murdered. The location of this rancho was most likely in the La Panza region.

The San Luis Obispo *Tribune* on February 23, 1883 announced: "On Monday last we were shown by Mr. Cerf of Blochman & Co., a fine lot of several hundred dollars' worth of gold-dust from the mines of La Panza, in this county." So, when Geo. Butchart & Sons got entangled with Blochman & Co., they were not dealing with amateurs.

The name E. Cerf also has an association with La Estrella property. Tax records for 1874 show that "Steven M. Rios" and Francisco Rios were paying taxes on the La Estrella property. F. Rios got the property from his brother, Stephen M Rios, on September 11, 1875. E. Cerf obtained the property from Francisco Rios on August 29, 1878; Cerf held the title until he sold the property to William Byrd on November 14, 1884. On July 1, 1886, William Byrd sold the property to Thomas Faw.

Sittenfeld & Co. appears in 1874 on the county tax records with personal property, liquor and goods in store listed. The Great Register of San Luis Obispo County in 1880 lists Arnold Sittenfeld as a native of Germany, 22 years of age. He was naturalized on May 20, 1876 in San Luis Obispo, and is listed as a mer-

chant in San Miguel. The Great Register of 1882 shows him as a saloon-keeper in Cambria. Arnold Sittenfeld was the first postmaster at Parkfield. That post office was established on January 29, 1884 and discontinued on February 28, 1954, when it was moved to San Miguel.

In 1876, Asa Croxford purchased from George and Sara Jane Butchart all of Lot #2 for $100; this was a total of 2 2/5 acres. Also in 1876, George Butchart & Sons, plaintiffs, filed a "Writ of Attachment" against Asa Croxford, defendant. This action was in demand for $247.77, plus interest of 1 ½ % per month from March 31, 1875.

March 17, 1876 finds that Asa Croxford had given two promissory notes to a J. B. Douglas to secure payment of $2,500. One note was dated February 22, 1875 and the other July 25, 1875. These notes were recorded on March 17, 1876, in Book ""D" of Mortgages, page 336. [Who "J. B." Douglas may have been is not known at this time. Charles B. and Gerard Noel Douglas were twins, who had been born in 1843. It is possible that "J. B." could be a penmanship error.]

In September and October of 1876, Asa Croxford sold Lot #2 and the wagon shop to Charles B. Douglas for $2,850. October 10, 1876 finds the owners of this part of the Caledonia property to be Charles Blomfield Douglas and J. B. Douglas. Charles B. Douglas owned a blacksmith and wagon shop by the year 1877.

The purchase, by the Douglases, of the house and wagon shop for a total of $5,350, would have been an investment of about $50,000 in 1990 dollars. Around the time of these purchases, Gerard Noel Douglas returned to England and married Charlotte Louisa Elton; Gerard brought his new bride back to California immediately.

In late 1879, Charles Douglas sold his entire interest in Las Juntas to his brother for $100; he then returned to New Zealand. By 1883, Gerard had to sell 6,856 acres in order to avoid foreclosure on the mortgage on Las Juntas. More misfortune befell Gerard Douglas, and eventually by the time of his death in 1922, Gerard's holdings had been reduced to the 160-acre parcel in Indian Valley.

On October 9, 1888, Gerard Noel Douglas received $300 in gold coin, from the County of Monterey, for land to be used for purposes of a county highway. The land was a strip 45 feet wide and 9 75/100 miles long, from Bradley to Indian Valley.

In 1899, Charles Douglas, who had married

Gerard's wife's sister, Katherine Elton, died in New Zealand. His widow returned to California with her four children and joined her sister and brother-in-law in Indian Valley. She had a separate home built there.

It is important to know that prior to the arrival of the railroad in 1886, what became known as "old town" San Miguel was located between the mission and the Rios-Caledonia adobe.

George Butchart operated the local post office, and was the distributor for the San Luis Obispo newspaper. August 2, 1875 found Norval Butchart serving as the judge for the state election in San Miguel. Norval Butchart appears on the county tax records in 1874 as owning acreage in Section 33, Township 25 South, Range 12. This was south of San Marcos, with the property divided in half by the Salinas River.

The *San Luis Obispo Tribune*, on January 8, 1876, printed the following note.

> **From San Marcos.- An "Eye Witness" writes us that Mr. J. Bruce Butchart, in attempting to cross the Salinas river, on Monday last, came near being drowned. The current was so strong that his horse washed over, falling on top of Mr. Butchart, who extricated himself with difficulty. He was so exhausted by the effort that he could not swim, but regained his feet, and remained there for over two hours, until his brother and some friends came to his rescue. His horse drifted down the stream on his back for some distance, but finally recovered himself, and swam ashore.**

In 1876, W. H. Menton ran a hotel in a wing of Mission San Miguel; Jacob Althans rented one of the rooms for his shoe shop. According to Myron Angel's *History of San Luis Obispo County*, in 1877 the population of San Miguel was reckoned at thirty; the town was composed of fifteen buildings. These included a school house, store, stable, two saloons, blacksmith shop, carriage shop, express office and a post office. The store was a branch of Goldtree & Co., of San Luis Obispo. It was managed by David Speyer and Isador Schwartz. Schwartz later became postmaster. In 1877, this store was robbed of about $400 in money and valuables, "by parties unknown."

On January 22, 1877, William Jackson Oaks, Constable, gave a "Certificate of Sale" to George Butchart & Sons, plaintiffs vs Asa Croxford, defendant, for the $247.77, plus damages of $69.20 interest and costs. Oaks sold, at public auction, all rights, title and inter-

est of said defendant's property. Two pieces of property were sold for only a total of $40 in gold coin. (W. J. Oaks had been born in Missouri, and came to California in 1850; he arrived in San Luis Obispo County in 1869. Oaks was elected Sheriff in 1877 and re-elected in 1879.)

Other actions on the Caledonia property during 1877 included the following: George Butchart sold the wagon shop to Charles B. Douglas for $100, on January 30th, (Book "I" of Deeds, page 452.); he sold the adobe and Lot #2 to his son, James B. Butchart, for $3,000 on April 25, 1877.

A newspaper article from the mid-1870s states that "The shearing season has commenced and flocks of Flint, Butchart, Trimble and others, such as Rios, an old-time settler, are undergoing the shears."

James B. Butchart filed a "Declaration of Homestead," which was recorded on September 19, 1877. The legal description of the property, on which he and his wife lived at the time, was: NW ¼ of SE ¼ and Lot #2 of Section 20, Township 25 South, Range 12, East Mount Diablo Meridian. The property value was given as $3,000. On September 21, 1877 we find Nathan Goldtree, plaintiff, vs George B. Butchart. Goldtree filed an attachment for the above-described property, plus $385.97 and the cost of the suit.

A newspaper article stated that "The roads are much improved, having been repaired under supervision of Mr. Norval Butchart. The travel is heavy and the daily stage coaches are well filled and running on time."

The year 1878 saw the Caledonia property in the hands of three different owners: Morgan Brians, James B. Butchart and Nathan Goldtree. Part of the reason for this fact may be found in the writings of Myron Angel. He informs us that "The dry years of 1877 and 1879 were so destructive to sheep and cattle that two-thirds of all of them died or had to be driven to other regions to save them." During the 1878-1879 year, there were only 8 inches of rainfall in the San Miguel area. Edith Buckland Webb, in her book *Indian Life at the Old Missions*, said that the last of the mission stock was taken to Lompoc about this time.

The drought may have had something to do with the property changing hands three times in 1878. Even without the drought, it is possible that these people learned that the amount of land that could be successfully farmed which was included in the Caledonia property was not in sufficient quantity for them to make a living on it.

On April 19, 1878, James B. Butchart and his wife, Lulu J. Butchart, mortgaged their property to secure payment of $756; then they also put up the property to cover a loan of $320 made by Morgan Brians. Meanwhile, George Butchart, Norval Butchart and James Bruce Butchart were defendants in a suit brought by Schwartz, Harford & Company.

James B. Butchart and Lulu Butchart found themselves in the First Judicial District Court, concerning

Old Caledonia with roof tiles removed.

their property transactions. Nathan Goldtree took action to foreclose on the mortgage. The action was filed on October 24, 1879 and the decree of foreclosure was filed on April 9, 1880.

On January 1, 1881, Nathan Goldtree bought the Caledonia property at a sheriff's sale; on November 8th of that year, Goldtree sold his recently-acquired property to Walter M. Jeffreys for $1,000. This sale was for all land situated and described as NW ¼ of SE ¼ and Lot #2 of Sec. 20, T. 25 S., R. 12 E. M. D. M., and containing 78-79 acres, "the said premise being known as the Butchart property adjoining that of Goldtree Brothers in the town of San Miguel on the east and south." This was recorded on November 1, 1881.

May 2, 1882 was the date on which William J. Oaks, Sheriff of San Luis Obispo County gave to Nathan Goldtree the "Certificate of Sale" of NW ¼ of SE ¼ Section 20, Township 25 South, Range 12 East Mount Diablo Meridian, and Lot #2. The high bid was $1,155.05.

Also in 1882, the Superior Court for the County of San Luis Obispo found the University of California, plaintiff, vs George Butchart and Falkner Bell & Co., defendants, to pay $120 as balance due on certificate of purchase of NW ¼ of SE ¼ and Lot #2, as described above. In case of failure to pay said sum, the certificate would be canceled and the plaintiff would have possession of said lands- - -the adobe and Lot #2. This action was filed on April 18, 1882. The plaintiff's attorney filed an order of dismissal on May 22, 1882.

Year 1883 seemed to be a quiet one for legal transactions on the Caledonia and its property.

Under the date of January 1, 1884, Walter Morgan Jeffreys gave three acres of property to the Protestant Episcopal Diocese of California, in trust, for a Protestant Episcopal Church at San Miguel. This was recorded on October 30, 1885, in Book "U" of Deeds, page 89. This property is used for part of the cemetery on the hill west of the Caledonia.

Walter M. Jeffreys, who was Justice of the Peace for Salinas Township, also served as school trustee for several terms. A closer look at this person is in order.

According to Yda Addis Storke, in her history book published in 1891, Walter M. Jeffreys had been born in Liverpool, England, on January 15, 1848. In 1868, he married Margaret Wilson; they lived in San Luis Obispo County in the latter part of that year. Jeffreys was successful in the sheep-raising business. They then purchased a valuable tract of land, 500 acres in extent, adjoining the town of San Miguel, near the old mission building. (Could part of this have been land on the Caledonia Ranch?)

In 1874, the judge had the Jeffreys Hotel built- - - said to be the pioneer hotel of the town. "It is said- - - though it may not be true- - -that the Jeffreys Hotel is so crowded that the rule of 'standing room only' is enforced. They say a lot of guests are put to bed and when sound asleep are stood up against the wall, making room for another batch, and so on. In the morning the standing sleepers, in regular order, are put to bed, waked up and sent out for an 'eye opener'- - -whatever that may be." This whimsical passage was published in the October 22, 1886 edition of the *San Miguel Messenger*. [Some may consider the renowned Occidental Hotel the pioneer hotel in San Miguel; however, it was not opened until February 22, 1888. Unfortunately, on Sunday, April 7th in 1901, flames would sweep San Miguel from a fire that would start in the rear of the Occidental Hotel about 1:30 a.m.]

Walter M. Jeffreys had his name in the *San Miguel Messenger* many times, during 1886. Some examples are: "The Jeffreys Hotel is receiving a new coat of paint; J. Jenks is the artist," (June 4, 1886). "W. M. Jeffreys has remodeled the shed opposite his hotel, adapting it for the purpose of a wagon house." (June 25, 1886). "W. M. Jeffreys, Esq., is building a barn on his homestead adjoining town." And "Walter M. Jeffreys made proof and payment on his homestead, south of town, last Saturday." These last two comments, from the September 10th issue, must refer to the Caledonia property.

The May 14, 1886 issue of *The Inland Messenger* carried a story entitled, "Audacious and Hungry."

A party who passes by the name of Tom McGovern, who had been around here for some days, walked into John Warth's rooms at the Mission, last Saturday and frightened the children out, helped himself liberally to what provisions he found handy, and went away. About suppertime he put in an appearance again, when the men folks were at home, and Mr. Warth gave him a forcible invitation to retire, which he prudently did without delay.

It might we well to remember that after the railroad arrived in October of 1886, the town of San Miguel moved from the area between the Caledonia and the Mission, to north of the Mission; this was mainly so that business places would be near the depot.

On September 22, 1886, the State of California issued Patent Certificate No. 467 to Walter M. Jeffreys. The grant was for Lot #2 and the NW ¼ SE ¼ of Sec. 20, T.25 S., R. 12, E. M. D. M., containing 68.79 acres, taken in lieu of 80 acres.

The *San Miguel Messenger*, on November 5, 1886, announced that "W. M. Jeffreys is re-elected Justice of the Peace, and W. C. Parker Constable." On November 19, 1886, the same paper stated that "A deed was recently recorded from Walter M. Jeffreys to Margaret J. Jeffreys for the Jeffreys Hotel property in San Miguel; consideration, $1." The title to the property passed to Margaret Jeffreys, on November 8, 1886, as recorded in Book "U", page 270 in the San Luis Obispo Recorder's office. The property consisted of 78.78 acres.

On December 31, 1886, the *San Miguel Messenger* provided the following information: "The title to the Almstead Hotel property appears likely to become the subject of litigation. It is claimed by Mrs. Margaret Jeffreys by virtue of asserted ownership of the legal subdivision on which it is located, Mr. Douglas claiming under another chain of title."

W. M. Jeffreys and Margaret Jeffreys gave to the Southern Pacific Railroad Company for consideration of "benefits derived from the construction of the Southern Pacific Railroad and $1.00, a strip of land 50 feet wide on each side of said center line to the southerly line of their land; containing an area of 11.15 acres, more or less."

The next year, on May 6, 1887, the *San Miguel Messenger* informed its readers that "Mr. Jeffreys is having two cellars dug on the new site for his hotel.

The buildings will be entirely remodeled and while corresponding with the general plan of the old one will be greatly improved in both capacity and convenience."

The *San Miguel Messenger* for June 10, 1887 announced that "W. M. Jeffreys is putting up a cyclone windmill and a 5,000 gallon tank at his well in the rear of the hotel. This arrangement will assure first class facilities for water." Two weeks later, the same newspaper stated that "W. M. Jeffreys, Esq., is putting up a very substantial fence along the country road on his land adjoining town on the south." Again, this would refer to the Caledonia property.

Before we leave Judge Jeffreys and his wife, we will go forward in time, and look at an article from September 22, 1917- - -by that time, the newspaper was the *San Miguel Sentinel*.

The estate of Walter Jeffreys who died at San Miguel in 1890 is now in the public administrator's hands, there being no administrator living; Walter Thompson and Jasper Turner who were appointed administrators have both been dead for some years. Mr. Jeffreys owned a hotel in San Miguel and was well known throughout this end of the county in early years.

Mrs. Anna Baker, Pioneer Day Queen in Paso Robles in 1935, said that in 1885 she and her husband had moved to Adelaida. According to Mrs. Baker, Paso Robles at that time was just a post office, and a stage-stop- - -which was not often used. She and her neighbors obtained their provisions at either Cambria or Cayucos. According to her, "San Miguel had just the Mission and the Caledonia Inn. The priest stayed there." This is the only reference we have found that a priest lived at the Caledonia.

On January 1, 1885, Estaban Ramon Buelna, better known as Steve, was born on the Caledonia property. He was the son of Geronimo and his second wife, Josefa Moreno Buelna. Steve was born in another adobe building, near the Caledonia. There were huge adobe ovens also located there; the ovens were large enough for Steve to play in as a child. This information was given by Steve to Ella Adams, who is widely noted as "the history lady of San Miguel."

As a *vaquero* on the Atascadero Ranch of J. H. Henry, from 1903 to 1905, Steve remembered the ranch being used for vast U. S. Army encampments during the years 1903 to 1910.

Geronimo Buelna, Steve's father, worked as a

cattle-boss on the Nacimiento Ranch, and at one time owned the Las Tablas Rancho, which was later known as the 7-X Ranch. Steve Buelna told a story that Tiburcio Vasquez, noted Mexican bandit, once visited his father's stable; Vasquez left his own horse, a pistol and a five-sided $50 gold coin, in exchange for a Buelna horse.

Steve remembers an adobe wall running from the "Caledonia House" all the way to the mission. He and his playmates walked barefoot on the wall. While we are on the subject of adobe walls, some information can be learned from the booklet written by John P. Courter, Jr. in 1905; it was named *The History of San Miguel Mission*. Rosemary Netto of San Miguel has graciously loaned her copy of the booklet to "The Friends of the Adobes, Inc.," for research. On page 11 of Courter's book, he states that "It is estimated that at one time 22 miles of wall surrounded the Church and other buildings, but now little of it remains. The wall averages eight feet high and 2 ½ feet thick, and is built of large, flat adobe bricks." [Twenty-two miles of adobe walls seems like an excessive number. It is doubtful that children would walk on a wall eight feet high.]

Steve Buelna died on November 7, 1968.

Two events of note took place in 1885. First, Antonio Smith and Leonarda Contreras were married at Mission San Miguel, and the reception was held at the Caledonia. Second, Henry Huston, on July 7, 1885, suffering wounds from the "shoot-out" on Estrella Plains, was taken to a doctor whose office was in the Caledonia. A newspaper column, written by Dr. Leo Stanley in July of 1967, quotes from a *Tribune* article, which gives us some information on this "shoot-out."

July 17, 1885 - A shooting affray occurred on the Estrella near the old adobe church built in 1878. A young man named Sanders was teaching school, and said a heading gang of men insulted him. The header men had shotguns with them, and had been shooting rabbits which were very plentiful in the grain fields.

As Sanders and his friends carried guns, shots were soon fired. Two men were killed outright, and one left crippled for life. Long trials cost the county large sums of money. Two men were sent to prison but eventually pardoned, one from each side. The shooting resulted not only in needless death but caused a feud on the Estrella which lasted for years.

Estrella School, located across the road from the Adobe Church.

The doctor to whom Henry Huston was taken had his office in the Caledonia adobe. It is probable that the name of the physician was George Washington Jenks.

William Zimmerman, in his book, *A Short & Complete History of San Miguel Mission*, published in 1890, relates an interesting story.

Adolf Pfister, a young Alsacian, was in 1847, in Reed's employ. Afterwards he settled in San Jose where he became one of the representative men, having been mayor of that burg in the seventies.

In May, 1888, Mr. Pfister related some San Miguel recollections. One Sunday morning the boys around the mission resolved to have some grapes, and about a half a dozen of them saddled their ponies and rode up the neighboring Vineyard valley. When arriving near the vineyard, they found already other visitors on the spot, who had evidently come for a similar purpose.

There were numerous grizzly bears in the vineyard. At the approach of the cavalcade *ursus horribilis* trotted leisurely off, and Pfister could count eighteen bears. However, the young men suddenly lost their appetites for grapes and hastily returned without taking any of the sweet fruit along.

1886-1900s

The name Gaius Webster is one which should be somewhat famous, in the annals of San Miguel history. He established and published the first newspaper in northern San Luis Obispo County.

Before railroad construction reached San Miguel, Gaius Webster had arrived. Gaius Webster, and his wife Anna West Webster, moved to San Miguel from Soquel, California. Upon arrival in San Miguel, they stayed in the "Old Caledonia Adobe Inn" with three other families, and remained in the Caledonia until June of 1886.

Aside from the newspaper, Gaius Webster had a 30-acre fruit farm near the town of San Miguel. The Andrew "Bud" Schmitz family is now on that property, and their one-story home is what is left of the two-story Webster home, as it had been modified by the Franklin family. A closer look at Gaius Webster is in order.

Webster had been born in New York on November 22, 1842. Twenty years later, in August of 1862, he enlisted in Co. A 144 Regiment of the New York Volunteers, and served in the infantry until July of 1865. Gaius Webster was admitted to the bar in the state of Oregon in September of 1867. He married Anna West in 1870. After working for newspapers in various places, they moved to Santa Cruz County in the winter of 1882, and later to San Miguel. He and his wife were the parents of two sons and two daughters.

Their son, Alexander Webster, married Lois Trace, daughter of M. R. Trace. The *Paso Robles Record*,

Webster Home while still a two-story building.

for August 17, 1895, informed its readers that "A Mr. Jones, a Berkeley graduate, has accepted the principalship of the union high school in Cambria in the place of M. R. Trace, who has accepted the principalship of the San Miguel School." After their time in San Miguel, M. R. Trace moved to San Jose, and taught for many years; the M. R. Trace Elementary School there is named in his memory.

In February of 1886, Gaius Webster had established *The Inland Messenger*. This newspaper was

published weekly, and a subscription was $2.50 per year. The paper stated that if one did not have the $2.50 for a subscription, to bring in "anything edible for man or beast" and it would be accepted in payment.

Later, Webster changed the name of his paper to the *San Miguel Messenger*. This was the first newspaper published north of San Luis Obispo, and began publication in Goldtree's store. Goldtree had started this store in San Miguel in 1871, in "old" San Miguel. The store was up on the mesa where the cemetery is now located, and was the first known office of Wells, Fargo & Co. in San Miguel, as shown on an 1874 stage route map.

Gaius Webster, with his sons Alex and J. C. Webster, edited *The Paso Robles Record* for a time; he established the law firm of G. & A. Webster, his son Alex being the junior partner. The Alexander Websters moved to Paso Robles, where Alexander practiced law, as city attorney, for twenty-five years.

After the railroad built the depot north of the Mission, businesses moved north. The Goldtree store dissolved the old partnership, and re-opened with Marcus Goldtree and Arnold Sittenfeld as partners, still retaining the Goldtree name.

(Gaius Webster would die on January 12, 1904 after several years of declining health, due to a head injury sustained upon falling out of a horse-drawn cart. He was buried in San Miguel cemetery and was later moved to the Paso Robles cemetery.)

We now return our attention to San Miguel to see how the Caledonia adobe is surviving changes to that town. *The Inland Messenger* for May 28, 1886 printed this ad:

W. B. Reed upholsterer & Mattress
Maker San Miguel
Spring mattresses made to order.
Old Mattresses, Lounges & Sofa uphol-
stered and repaired.
Satisfaction guaranteed.
Shop in Caledonia Building.

The above ad would indicate that W. B. Reed was most likely Walter Reed, a son of E. L. Reed, whose connection with the Caledonia is covered later in this chapter.

On August 27, 1886 we read in *The Inland Messenger* that "The first business opened on the supposed new town site is that of a saloon kept by George Hopper in the old adobe school house." The old adobe school had been built at the north end of town, near where River Road crosses the railroad tracks today.

According to a "Local Brevities" section of the newspaper, an item dated October 1, 1886 states that "Mr. David Jeffreys is fitting up the upper portion of the Caledonia building for a residence." David Jeffreys was a brother of Walter M. Jeffreys. Mr. Jeffreys had his name in the newspaper, again, on November 26, 1886. "David Jeffreys was tried in Justice Wyss' court, last Monday for disturbing the peace, and was adjudged guilty and fined thirty dollars."

Going forward in time, the *San Miguel Messenger* of May 27, 1887 had these items: "Died. Jeffreys - At the Asylum for the Insane in Stockton, May 21st, 1887, David Jeffreys, aged 45 years. Deceased was a native of Liverpool, England, and came to this country in 1867. He filled the office of County Clerk of Mono County two terms; was engaged in business in Santa Ynez, Santa Barbara County, from which he retired about a year ago, when he came to this place. Some six months since he developed symptoms of mental derangement, which soon became so marked and serious a character that he was sent to the Asylum at Stockton, where he died. He was a man of excellent business qualifications, and up to the time of development of his unfortunate mental malady, bore the character of a good citizen. He was a brother of Walter M. Jeffreys, Esq., of this place, and leaves a widow and two children."

Another item in the same newspaper stated that "Walter M. Jeffreys, Esq., was called to Stockton Monday by the death of his brother in the asylum at that place. He was compelled to stop at Salinas as a witness on his return, but he is expected home daily."

A letter, written by Alfred Edwin Reed in September of 1974, informs us that his father told him that the boys of the family slept in out-buildings, which were located west of the Caledonia. This is one of several references that relate information that there were other buildings in a group to the west of the two-story adobe. E. L. Reed had operated the Caledonia as a hotel and stage-stop for his father-in-law, Morgan Brians.

Al Reed said that his grandmother, Mary Jane Brians Reed, told him a story about discovering a demented man in the downstairs living room of the Caledonia; the man was siting there, reading a book, while drying his clothes. Mrs. Reed told the man that she was going to go pick up something, but instead notified the younger boys of the man's presence; the boys went by horseback for help. They learned that the man had escaped, past his keeper, from an upstairs

barred room in San Miguel. This story came to mind while this writer read two items from the newspaper; the first, that David Jeffreys had been tried and found guilty of disturbing the peace; the second that David Jeffreys died in an insane asylum. Not intending to impugn Mr. Jeffreys' character or mental state, it is wondered whether the "deranged man" who was found drying his clothing in the Caledonia might not have been David Jeffreys. We do not know what date the clothes-drying incident took place, but it is possible that it could have been after the time Mr. Jeffreys lived there; in his mind, perhaps he felt at home.

The Inland Messenger tells us that on October 18, 1886 the train crew had arrived. "The old town of San Miguel was between the Mission and the old Caledonia, and when the depot was finally located and a new townsite surveyed, stores, hotels, post office, telegraph and express offices were moved to the newly surveyed townsite laid out by the Pacific Improvement Company, a subsidiary of the Southern Pacific Company." Although it was quite a long sentence, it chronicles an event of major importance to the San Miguel area.

The newspaper on October 15, 1886 stated the following.

It is remarked that where the railroad company has had occasion to alter the course of the county road, it has always made the new part better than the old. One incident will show the thoroughness of the work. Near the Caledonian, a bridge had been moved, and made better than it was before. A few days after, a horse put his foot through a defective plank, and left a bad hole. Word was sent to Mr. Stanton, in charge of construction, and the bridge was at once put into 'merchantable' order.

On October 29, 1886, *The Inland Messenger* informed readers that "Mr. E. S. Barry, the new agent of Wells, Fargo & Co. here, has moved with his family into the Caledonia Building." Edward Stanley Barry was the Wells, Fargo agent in San Miguel during the years 1887 through 1892. From 1883 to 1885, Edward Stanley Barry had been the Wells, Fargo agent at Rancho Los Coches adobe, near Soledad.

Prior to Barry's arrival, Goldtree & Co. had been the agent, from 1874 to 1886. This information was obtained by Ella Adams from the Wells, Fargo headquarters. By 1897, the Wells, Fargo & Co. office was

Caledonia Adobe from the south.

located in the south lower half of Keyston Hall on Mission Street.

E. S. Barry had been born February 22, 1845, in Galena, Illinois; he came to California in 1869. Barry became employed by the North Pacific Transportation Co., Holladay & Brenham, agents, in San Francisco. Afterward, he worked with the Southern Pacific Railroad Company; he later went into mining. In 1874, he married Ella M. Little of Hollister.

From the November 26, 1886 edition of the paper we learn that "S. D. Gates, recently from Iowa, has purchased E. L. Reed's homestead on the high land north-west of the San Marcos ranch, and will make his home there at once."

The December 31, 1886 issue of *The Inland Messenger* printed this ad:

Dressmaking!
Cutting and Fitting by Tailor System.
Stamping done to order.   Mrs. L. Moore
Caledonian House   San Miguel

Although businesses were moving from "old town" San Miguel, to up near the newly-constructed railroad depot, some business was still conducted in the Caledonia adobe.

A list of unclaimed letters was displayed at the San Miguel post office, on July 1, 1887, and published in the newspaper. A letter written in Spanish was addressed to Don Camilo Rios. This demonstrates that

the Camilo Rios family had moved away before this date.

A news item on July 15, 1887 states that about 200 head of wild steers were bound for Santa Maria, from the Piojo Ranch, which is in the San Antonio Valley toward Mission San Antonio. This herd passed the town, and then stampeded near the Caledonia. The cattle tore through the fences, and a number of them fell into a deep ditch; one was killed and another had its leg broken in the fall. ["El Piojo" means "the louse."]

Sara A. Cooper was living in the Caledonia on May 5, 1888, according to a note written in a guest register kept by Mr. Charles F. Dorries when he later owned the property. In 1888, Charles B. Douglas and Gerard Noel Douglas became owners of part of the Caledonia property, but did not take up residence there.

On May 15, 1888, G. N. Douglas sold to Walter M. Jeffreys, property described as Lot #2 of Section 20, Township 25 south, Range 12 East Mount Diablo Meridian. The cost for the deed was $25.

On September 5, 1888, Chester Allen Jenks, the first child of Joseph McEwen Jenks and his wife, Etta May Reed Jenks, was born in the Caledonia.

Charles J. Cooper, on May 14, 1892, sold some land to Gaius Webster for use as a cemetery. Charles J. Cooper is listed in the Great Register of San Luis Obispo County 1890 as a druggist, who had been born in Ohio. When Cooper registered, in August of 1887, his age was given as 35 years. C. J. Cooper had purchased two pieces of property: one of 78.78 acres and one of 40 acres, from the estate of Margaret Jeffreys; on June 9, 1892, the transaction is recorded in Book 16, page 272, in the County Recorder's office. Property, in the amount of 108.79 acres, was bought at public auction from the estate of W. M. Jeffreys and wife Margaret Jeffreys, both deceased. The buyers were Robert Balfour, Robert Brodie Erman and Alexander Guthrie. They paid $1,500 on April 1, 1893.

In 1895, Charles J. Cooper obtained title to 60 acres, "more or less." On October 9, 1895, Hattie L. Cooper is recorded, in Volume 29, page 226, as the owner of the property after the death of her husband.

The *Paso Robles Record*, on January 20, 1895, printed the following item.

The large barn, the end of which intruded
into the road, at the Caledonia house about a

Hattie Louise Davis Cooper and Charles Cooper in front of the Occidental Hotel.

mile this side of San Miguel, has been lately torn down. It was an old landmark . . .having been built over twenty years ago.

On Christmas Eve of 1889, the San Miguel Athletic Club had sponsored the "First Grand Ball." This was held at the San Miguel Hall. There is no claim being made that this hall was in the Caledonia. However, the fact that a Dalton signed a lady's dance card (which is in the San Luis Obispo County Historical Museum), proved that the Daltons really did live in the area. The dance card belonged to Belle Courter, whose father ran the San Miguel Mercantile Company. Aside from the Daltons and others, Belle also danced with Dan Mahoney, whom she later married. Dan Mahoney later became Recorder for San Luis Obispo County.

Belle's brother, John P. Courter, Jr., wrote *The History of San Miguel Mission*, dated May 29, 1905. A copy of this work, published by Charles A. Black of San Luis Obispo, has been graciously loaned to "The Friends of the Adobes, Inc.," by Rosemary Netto of San Miguel.

Mason Dalton, also called Bill, arrived in San Luis Obispo County in 1887, and farmed on the Cotton Ranch, about 10 miles east of San Miguel. This Cotton Ranch was on the Estrella River, near the Clark Bliven Ranch (owned by a man named Barrett). Clark happened to be Bill Dalton's brother-in-law. Littleton Dalton, another brother, owned and operated a saloon

in San Miguel in 1888 and 1889. Brother Bob, Emmett and Grat Dalton, to escape the law in Oklahoma, came to Bill's place on the Cotton Ranch to hide out. They became well-known in the saloons of San Miguel, Paso Robles and San Luis Obispo as heavy drinkers and bar-room brawlers. Otherwise- - -they were said to be law-abiding while in San Luis Obispo County.

In an undated newspaper article, R. C. Heaton of Paso Robles related that people around Paso Robles had such a high opinion of Bill Dalton that they almost backed him for assemblyman one year. About 1889, when Bill Dalton came to this area to farm along the Estrella River, Frank Halter was his closest neighbor.

Halter recounted that "Bill was a good musician and the life of any crowd. At old dances we used to have here, we didn't have any fun at all if he wasn't here." Out of a family of fifteen children, only the three youngest boys, Bob, Grat and Emmett were criminally inclined.

"The first of the Daltons to come here from the family homestead in Oklahoma was Littlefield; he arrived about 1885, and opened a saloon in San Miguel. In 1889, Bob, Grat and Emmett came to visit Brother Bill.

"One day in '91, Bill asked to borrow my saddle. He said the boys were going out to the hill country, west of San Miguel, after milk cows," Halter continued. "Well, this saddle turned out to be just about the most famous one around here a few weeks later, when it was used to identify the Dalton boys in connection with an attempted train robbery near Alila, in Tulare county.

"The tapaderos and stirrups from my saddle were found near where the train was stopped. They were traced to me, and officers paid me for the saddle, which was used for evidence. I was subpoenaed by the grand jury as a witness and taken to Visalia for the trial of Grat, the only one who was caught. Even he later escaped."

It was Bill Dalton who signed Belle Mahoney's dance card.

On March 4, 1891, the *Paso Robles Leader* printed an article with the headline "TRAIN ROBBERS CAPTURED. Three Arrests Made Near Cholame. Sheriff O'Neal Assisted by Railroad Detectives W. Smith and W. E. Hickey Make a Neat Capture."

The gang of men who have been making periodical raids upon the railroad trains in the San Joaquin Valley, and who evidently reside in eastern San Luis Obispo and western Tulare County is about to be broken up.

The attempted robbery at the small station of Alila caused the railroad authorities to offer $5,000 for the capture of the gang. The incentive is so great that there have been a score or more of detectives and officers in this vicinity during the past three weeks.

Last week Grets Dalton was arrested by Sheriff O'Neal, assisted by W. Smith, a railroad detective from Los Angeles. The arrest was made at the ranch of his brother William, who resides some twelve miles north-east of here.

Last Monday Sheriff O'Neal, W. Smith and W. E. Hickey made another trip to the Dalton ranch, and in that neighborhood arrested Cole Dalton and Jack Parker, for complicity in the same robbery. Tuesday these men were taken to San Francisco, where they were turned over to Sheriff Kay of Tulare County. It is reported that the Daltons were cousins of the Younger brothers, the notorious out-laws.

It is not at all improbable that it was one of this gang that held up the San Luis stage sometime since on the Cuesta grade above Borondas.

The officers claim that they have the evidence that will convict the men arrested.

Readers of the *Paso Robles Leader*, on April 29, 1891, could learn more about this matter. That issue of the newspaper printed an article entitled "Mrs. William Dalton in Visalia."

Mrs. William Dalton of Paso Robles, wife of William Dalton who is now in the county jail charged with being implicated in the Alila train robbery arrived in town on Tuesday evening of last week to see her husband. Immediately upon arriving she went to the jail, but was not allowed to see her husband, as it was after visiting hours. She commenced to cry, and begged and pleaded to be allowed to see her imprisoned husband, but Jailer Williams would not grant the request.

Last Wednesday morning she returned to the jail and was allowed to see her husband, and an affecting scene took place when they met. Dalton was removed to the crazy cell up stairs, and there throughout the day Mrs. Dalton remained by the side of her husband. Dalton is a fine singer and plays the guitar nicely. The two spent the greater part of the day in singing pathetic songs, quite out of keeping with the surroundings. Mrs. Dalton sings sweetly, and the two voices blend well, and the sounds of their voices and the music of the guitar penetrated the furthermost recesses of the jail, and had a wonderfully subduing effect on the "hoboes" in the lower part of the county bastile.

Mrs. Dalton is quite a nice looking young lady, and seems much affected by her husband's trouble. Mrs. Dalton is a daughter of a well-to-do rancher of Merced county. She left for home after a few days' visit with her husband.

After Grat and Bob Dalton were killed in Coffeyville, Kansas in 1892, Bill Dalton and his wife left Estrella for the Oklahoma Territory. Bill Dalton was killed in Oklahoma, on the morning of June 8, 1894; he tried to break through a group of U. S. Marshals who had surrounded the cabin where he was staying.

The person who owned the Cotton Ranch, mentioned above, had land in various places in the San Miguel area. We are introduced to Mr. Cotton in the August 19, 1887 edition of the *San Miguel Messenger*. "A Mr. Cotton, an attorney from San Francisco, has been in San Miguel some days, with a view to investing in lands. Mr. Chas. Thiriet has sold his ranch in Vineyard Canyon to A. R. Cotton, Esq., for the sum of $2,000."

The September 9, 1887 edition of the *San Miguel Messenger* informed its readers that "A. R. Cotton, Esq., has made several land purchases since our last issue, including the Detro place in Vineyard Canyon, for $1,680, the Anthony place in the Estrella region and another piece of property, of which we have not been able to learn particulars." The paper also noted that "M. Detro has gone into the saloon business at Fresno Hot Springs, in Fresno County."

We learn a little more concerning the extent of A.

R. Cotton's land-holdings from the writings of Dr. Leo Stanley, who rode his bicycle to Paso Robles to go to high school, around the turn of the century. (After graduating from Paso Robles High School, Leo Stanley attended Stanford University, beginning in 1903. He graduated from Cooper Medical College in 1912; he retired from medical practice in 1951.)

In describing the path he took, Stanley says of the road: "Across the sandy bottom it went east of the Fred Dean ranch, down by the railroad tracks to Wellsona, bordered the Judge Cotton ranch, on by the Hatch and Stockdale farms. Again it dipped into French Joe's Canyon, across a small wooden bridge, up again and followed the steep grade to the mud baths." We notice that by the turn of the century, "A. R. Cotton, Esq." has become "Judge Cotton."

A. R. Cotton is not the only person who became a land-owner near the Caledonia property. One of the people who owned much land in the area was Johnson Marshall Kalar. He had been born near Kearns, Randolph County, West Virginia on September 15, 1864. He attended school, and also worked industriously on a farm until he was about 17 years of age. On July 21, 1881, he "bought his time" from his father, by promising him that if his father would let him go into the world and do for himself, he would send back to his father the sum of one hundred dollars, each year, until he reached the age of 21. Although his father needed his help on the farm, he allowed his son to go.

Eventually, young Johnson M. Kalar found himself in the town of Chualar, in Monterey County, with just five-cents left in his pocket. He used this money to pay the postage with which to write to his mother. He had borrowed $25, so added to the $400 he owed his father ($100 per year from age 17 to 21), Johnson started out with obligations to the extent of $425 staring him in the face.

Three weeks later, having performed hard work on a hay press, he had $40. He applied himself by driving a header, or a plow, or by filling sacks. For a while, he farmed with an uncle; the then sold certain interests and moved to Butte County. There, he both farmed and engaged in mining. Becoming somewhat successful, he came to Soledad with the intention of selling teams he had left there, and returning home to his parents. However, he was unable to dispose of the teams to his advantage, so he decided to remain in California.

Thomas Faw, owner of several northern San Luis Obispo County properties, induced Kalar to rent some land and become involved in agriculture on his own.

Johnson Marshall Kalar.
Born September 15, 1864 in Randolph Co., West Virginia. Married Bertha Ellen Dake, February 3, 1895. Died August 17, 1937, Hanford, California. Buried in the San Miguel Cemetery.

The first year, Kalar lost everything; in order to keep going, he gave a crop mortgage to R. M. Shackelford. From that time on, Johnson M. Kalar began to succeed.

The first two seasons of raising grain and stock enabled him to pay off his obligations; in 1898, he began to buy land. Kalar accumulated land until he had 1,711 acres in the home place, east of the Salinas River, and 440 acres west of the state highway about a mile from San Miguel. These ranches would extend for a distance of five miles, were it not for a break of half a mile, which was owned by another party.

Mr. Kalar became greatly interested in horticulture, making almonds a specialty. On his home ranch, he set out 86 ½ acres in four varieties of almond. The 440 acres west of the river was subdivided into tracts ranging from 6 to 25 acres; 1/5 of this area was set to almonds. Over 100 acres was sown to alfalfa, and 11,000 feet of cement pipe was laid in order to irrigate this land.

The *Paso Robles Record*, on July 14, 1900, printed an article entitled, "Irrigation On An Extensive Scale. A New Enterprise for the Upper Salinas Valley."

Mr. Faw, owner of land between this city and San Miguel, spent several days in town and at his ranch which is farmed by Johnson Kalar. Mr. Faw desires to put his ranch on a better paying basis and as a consequence is considering the plan of putting in an extensive irrigation plant and raising several hundred acres of alfalfa. Upon this green pasture his idea is to start an extensive dairy ranch. Mr. Tracy of the Tracy Engineering Co., who has put in the machinery for several successful irrigation plants, was here this week looking over Mr. Faw's place with a view to putting up the machinery.

The plan of irrigating the river bottoms is a splendid one. Hundreds of acres of fine bottom land along the river might be increased many times its value by irrigation. Mr. Faw's plan deserves the commendation and support of our business men. Should it be carried out, which now seems assured, it will be the starting point of a new enterprise for the Upper Salinas Valley.

Kalar had five different sets of buildings constructed, composed of seven large barns, and a cheese factory 54' by 20' with a 13-foot ceiling. He had wells sunk and he installed pumps, gas, water and, eventually, electrical apparatus to operate the machinery. He rented out the dairy, which included between 60 and 70 cows.

On February 3, 1895, at San Miguel, Johnson M. Kalar married Miss Bertha Dake, who had been born in Oregon, a daughter of John & Harriet (Bixby) Dake. They were natives, respectively, of New York and Wisconsin. After their marriage in Wisconsin, this couple crossed the plains with ox-teams and wagons to Oregon. There, Mr. Dake engaged in lumbering and burning charcoal. In 1880, the family moved to San Jose, thence to Santa Cruz and later to San Miguel, where the father died. The mother passed away in Santa Rosa.

Mrs. Johnson Kalar is the fourth child in a family of nine children; she grew up and was educated in Santa Cruz. Mr. & Mrs. Johnson Kalar had nine children: George, Carl, Marion, Douglas, Woodrow, Hiram, John and Jack; the only girl was Lillian. (George Kalar was the grandfather of David and Steve Kalar, current citizens of northern San Luis Obispo County.)

The *San Miguel Sentinel*, on May 26, 1917 printed an article entitled "Dairy Changes Hands."

Bertha Kalar

J. M. Kalar has leased his dairy, which is located south of San Miguel, to Mr. Rossi who has been working for Clark and Marzorini on their large ranch near there. The lease was given for five years and includes about a hundred acres of alfalfa and all the equipment for the manufacturing of cheese, also farming implements and about fifty head of milk cows.

Mr. Rossi will take possession about June first and expects to start an up to date sanitary cheese factory. Mr. Kalar has been separating the cream and shipping it to the butter factories, but Mr. Rossi, being an expert cheese maker, and the prices higher at this time for cheese, figures there is more to be made making cheese than shipping the cream.

On September 8, 1917, the *San Miguel Sentinel* informed its readers that "J. M. Kalar purchased a carload of registered Holstein cows at Soledad the first of the week to add to his dairy ranch here."

"Kalar Dairy and Cheese Factory Changes Hands," was the headline on an article in the October 27, 1917 issue of the *San Miguel Sentinel*.

George Kalar

Rossi and Salvestrin, who have had the J. M. Kalar dairy leased for some time past, sold out this week. For some time they have been short of milkers and have been unable to hire anyone. Mr. Antoni Del Castillo, the new owner, has four sons and so expects to have no trouble from labor shortage. He will continue to make cheese and ship it to the San Francisco market.

Mr. Rossi and Salvestrin have not as yet decided where they will locate next, although Mr. Rossi says he will try to get some small place in this vicinity that he can handle himself, without hiring help.

The name of Stanley has been of major importance in the area of San Miguel since 1895. Hartwell Barrium Stanley had been born in Indiana on June 23, 1852; he came to California from Indiana to teach in a one-room school in Auburn County; he then taught in Georgetown, El Dorado County. There he met and married one of his pupils, Mary Emma Irish, on De-

cember 23, 1877. She had been born on December 1, 1859 at Rose Springs, El Dorado County, California.

He took his bride to San Francisco so that he would be able to study medicine; later, he went to the University of Oregon, where he earned his medical degree. Mr. & Mrs. Hartwell B. Stanley first moved to Arbuckle, Colusa County, where Joseph Hartwell Stanley, the first of six children, was born on November 12, 1878. Charles Herbert Stanley was born in Greenwood, El Dorado County, on February 23, 1881; William Winfield Stanley was born in Cold Springs, El Dorado County, on February 9, 1883. Leo Leonidas was born at Buena Vista, Polk County, Oregon, on March 8, 1886, and Margaret was born in Buena Vista, on May 18, 1888. Mary Emma Stanley was born on November 4, 1893 at Dallas, Polk County, Oregon.

On October 19, 1909, Margaret Stanley married the Rev. E. A. McGowan, at St. John's Episcopal Church in San Miguel; performing the ceremony was the Rev. J. S. McGowan, father of the groom.

(Charles H. Stanley married Katherine Wright, one of two daughters of Eli Wright; Charley and Katherine were the parents of Shirley Tharaldsen.)

Mary Emma Stanley Cook, the sister of Dr. Leo Leonidas Stanley, who was the author of the book, *San Miguel at the Turn of the Century*, passed away on November 1, 1979.

The *Paso Robles Record*, on May 4, 1895, informed its readers that "Dr. Stanley left San Miguel last week for Oregon, expecting to return soon with his family." This reference was, of course, to Dr. Hartwell B. Stanley; this family arrived in September of 1895.

In 1898, the family went to the Mother Lode country, east of Merced. It was there that Joseph Hartwell Stanley met and married Lena Reeb, whose parents, George and Rosina Hunziker, owned the butcher shop. Joseph Stanley and Lena Reeb were married in 1902, and in that year they moved to San Miguel. Joseph worked for the railroad, and also on several area ranches, doing carpentry work. He also served as San Luis Obispo County Deputy Assessor.

[Dr. Leo Stanley spent 38 years of his career as the Chief Surgeon and Resident at San Quentin, 1913 to 1951. The other books written by Dr. Stanley were: *Men at their Worst*, in 1940, and *My Most Unforgettable Convicts*, in 1967. During World War II, he spent four years in the U.S. Navy. Following his retirement, he served as ship's surgeon for the Matson Navigation Company and the American Presidents Line. He established the Romaine Josephine Stanley Fund at Stanford University; it provides scholarships to medical students, and was named for his first wife. Dr. Stanley later married Bernice Holthouse, "Bunny," at the old home in San Miguel, by the Episcopal minister, Rev. E. A. McGowan, to whom his sister, Margaret, was married. According to a letter written by Emma Stanley Cook, dated January 26, 1966, the "Stanley House" had been built by Ralph Eugene Gorham in the 1890s, and had only been owned by the Gorhams and the Stanleys. The beautiful home was razed in 1960, in order to make way for Highway 101.]

To Mr. & Mrs. Joseph H. Stanley was born Josephine, on September 14, 1904. She graduated from San Miguel Grammar School, and then Paso Robles High School, in 1922. She studied in the nurses' training program at Stanford Hospital in San Francisco

Dr. Leo Leonidas Stanley (left) and Dr. Hartwell B. Stanley (right).

from 1922 to 1924. There, she met and married Roy Wieneke from Albuquerque, New Mexico; he worked for Southern Pacific Railroad Company as a telegrapher.

Roy and Josephine Wieneke were the parents of two children: LeRoy Wieneke and Rosemary Netto. Josephine worked for the Southern Pacific Railroad Company, from 1945 to 1965, as a cashier and ticket clerk. Roy passed away in 1961, after 47 years of marriage.

Josephine met Alfred Bequette, an orchardist, in Watsonville. He had previously married Charlotte Montgomery, daughter of Willow Creek pioneers, Charles and Maude Montgomery. After the death of Roy and of Charlotte, Josephine and Alfred were married in 1963. They moved to San Miguel in 1965, in order for Josephine to be near her family. Josephine said that she now slept in the bed in which she had been born. Alfred had one daughter, Shirley Crum, who taught school in Watsonville.

Josephine Rosalie Bequette passed away on February 27, 1996.

Returning to the subject of the Caledonia, in 1889, the population of San Miguel was given as 500 people. Frank William Rios, a grandson of Petronilo and Catarina Rios, and son of James Rios, was born in the Caledonia in April of 1901. This information comes from another note in Mr. Dorries' guest register. (In 1933, Frank Rios married Irene Albert; they had no children. Frank died on February 6, 1971.)

Between 1889 and 1902, the Alexander Telford family lived at the Caledonia and had a dairy on the property. According to Dr. A. H. Wilmar, a personal friend of Fred Westlake Telford, Alexander was referred to as "Fred," and son Fred Westlake was referred to as "Fred, Jr." Alexander Ruby Telford and Clara Budd Westlake Telford had three sons and one daughter. The boys were named Fred Westlake Telford, William Francis Telford and Hiram Kenneth Telford; the last two boys were twins. The lone girl, Edith Isabelle Telford, was born in the Caledonia adobe on December 1, 1889. (Edith's daughter provided the above information in a letter dated December 12, 1981.)

During the early 1890s, the Given family owned part of what had been the Caledonia property. The administrator of the estate of Walter Jeffreys sold the following property to John Given, on December 14, 1891, for $2,095 in gold coin: Lot #2, Section 20, Town-

Caledonia in 1896

ship 25 S., Range 12; the size was 132 feet square. He also bought Block 60, Lots 13, 14,15 and 16 in San Miguel; also, NE ¼ SE ¼ Section 20, Township 25 S., Range 12.

On January 11, 1892, Arnold Sittenfeld sold to John Given, for $100, Lot #12, Block 60 in San Miguel. Two years later, on January 25, 1894, Mrs. Caroline Given received Lot #12, Block 60 in San Miguel; on March 26, 1895, she received from her husband NE ¼ SE ¼ Section 20; this was 40 acres for $5 in gold.

John Given had been born in Ireland about 1827; he became a U. S. citizen on August 21, 1889. He married Caroline J. Crediford, of Indian Valley, on December 15, 1893; she had been born on July 1, 1870 in Hawaii. She died on June 2, 1957 in Paso Robles, and is buried in San Miguel.

After John Given married Caroline, the last name gained an "s." John Given died July 28, 1902, on his Estrella ranch. The son of John and Caroline was John Ernest Givens, called "Ernie" by many people. A too shortened summary of his life would state that he was born on September 7, 1894 in San Miguel; he was married on September 18, 1918, and died on July 3, 1952.

On January 25, 1893, the San Luis Obispo *Tribune* printed an article, by A. S. Austin, entitled "Around The Country." On this date, the subject of his article was San Miguel. Selections from his column are given in the following.

This is a town of about 800 inhabitants, lying on the west side of the Salinas river, about five miles south of the north boundary line of the county.

At the north extremity of the streets are the Farmer's Alliance Mills, with a capacity of forty barrels per day, now temporarily idle. The railroad company have good station buildings and the Southern Pacific Milling company extensive warehouses here. At the office of the latter I met Mr. W. A. Wilmar, an intelligent, obliging gentleman, who put himself to considerable trouble to present me to the leading men about town and otherwise aid me in my researches.

About 600 car loads of grain are handled here annually. The town is the trading center for a large extent of adjacent country to the east, west and north into Monterey county as far as Parkfield.

All of the town can be seen from the railroad, and, consequently, shows up for what it is worth. The town is well supplied with hotel accommodations. The Occidental, kept by Mr. Geo. R. Davis; the French House, kept by Mr. Maxwell, formerly of the *Tribune*, and the Levinger House, kept by Mr. J. B. Levinger, being all of good repute.

The Makin lodging house is a good two-story brick building, nicely furnished and a good deal patronized by traveling people. There are plenty of stores, among which, the Farmer's Union has an extensive trade.

There is a bank, weekly newspaper, *The Courier*, a $6,000 school district school building of brick- - -and, in that direction, a graded school is much needed. There are also five churches, made up of Methodist, South Meth-

Early San Miguel Street Scene.

odist, Congregational, Episcopal and Catholic denominations.

There are three good livery stables and other necessary industries of various nations, among which about a dozen saloons count their share. There are two or three firms of real estate agents and, from Mr. Whisman, of

Maxwell House on hill had been moved from across the river.

the firm of Clark & Whisman, managers of the Central California Land Co., I receive much assistance. Mr. Whisman is agent for the Wells, Fargo & Co's. express . . . .

He very kindly procured a rig from the livery stable of Mr. S. T. Campbell and, in company with the latter gentleman, I was driven over a considerable portion of the Flint ranch of 40,000 acres to the west of the town. Before reaching the ranch we passed through a valley of limited width, upon each side of which are ridges of good land for fruit and grain raising, and for sale at reasonable prices- - -$10 to $20 per acre. The Flint prop-

Methodist Episcopal Church, San Miguel

erty is altogether devoted to the stock range and extends from a point a little to the east of the Salinas river to and across the Nacimiento, and covers some very fine bot-

toms. The tract is in a way of being subdivided within the next year or two, and placed upon the market for sale.

I met, at the hotel, one of the Flint boys, who is the owner of another ranch of 60,000 acres about thirty miles to the east, that I did not have time to visit. There is some very fine land east of the river, outside of the Flint ranch, that is well cultivated to grain and fruit. Back among the hills, about three miles east of town, is a belt of land, outside the frost line, where oranges are successfully grown.

Dr. Leo L. Stanley, in an article he called, "School Days in San Miguel," described the area at the end of the nineteenth century.

The celebration of the first centennial of the founding of Mission San Miguel, in 1897, was a three-day event with visitors from all over the state coming in by special trains. High Mass was served by Bishop Montgomery. There were horse races, rodeos, band concerts, parades, oratory and all that goes with such occasion. The cattle had grown fat on the western ranges and having brought to market brought high prices. . . .

Unfortunately, the next year 1898 was one of the driest in all the history of the Upper Salinas Valley. San Miguel went into decline and has never fully recovered in spite of the building of two great dams and the formation of Nacimiento and San Antonio Lakes, which assure that the lower valley shall never lack for water.

Dr. Leo L. Stanley, at a meeting of the Paso Robles Senior Citizens, on May 8, 1976, entertained the audience with the following poem.

San Miguel! San Miguel!
Where in Hell is San Miguel?

Go sou'east from Monterey,
or no'east from Morro Bay.

Sun comes up o'er San Joaquin,

Paso Robles in between.

It's deep inland and free from fog,
Sunshine drenched. There is no smog.

From the Mission to the mill,
From the river to the Hill.

San Miguel! San Miguel!
That is where in hell is San Miguel.

Dr. Leo L. Stanley, in an unpublished autobiography he called *A Long and Happy One*, states that when his father arrived in San Miguel in 1895, he found "three, two-storied wooden hotels, two livery stables, three blacksmith shops, four or five mercantile establishments, thirteen saloons and behind a high boarded fence not far from the hotel, an adobe in which we were told lived the 'bad women.'" He informs us that "there were three or four churches beside the Old Mission where Father O'Reilly held services and administered to his Catholic flock."

The San Luis Obispo *Morning Tribune*, on July 18, 1891 informed its readers of the following.

On July 17, 1891, at 4 o'clock in the morning, a disastrous fire started in San Miguel. All the buildings of the Farmers' Union block, a large hardware and grocery firm, were totally destroyed. The loss was $25,000, with insurance about $9,000.

The fire was first discovered by the occupants of the Palace Saloon. The Farmers' Union Building was owned by Reed and Courter. The building of M. Goldtree, also occupied by the Farmers' Union, and A. C. Swift's office and the saloon owned by D. Speyer were the buildings consumed.

There was an imminent danger that the buildings opposite on Mission Street, owned by Gerard Douglass, would be burned. The building adjoining the Arlington Hotel, occupied on the lower floor by Justice Faw's court, was charred by the heat.

On Sunday, April 7, 1901, disaster again struck San Miguel. The April 8, 1901 edition of the *San Luis Obispo Breeze* headlined: "Flames Sweep the Town of San Miguel- - -A Devastating Fire Broke Out Early Sunday Morning Doing Great Damage."

A number of buildings have been burned to the ground, including two hotels, the City Hall and the Methodist Church. The fire started in the rear of the Occidental Hotel about half-past one o'clock Sunday morning, and had made considerable headway before it was discovered. . . .

The fire quickly spread to the City Hall and burned fiercely. An old paint shop was next seized by the flames. . . .The Levinger Hotel fell into the clutches of the fierce, driving flames and it was soon evident that its complete destruction was sure.

The Nash property, occupied by a saloon and a barber shop, was easy prey to the flames and an empty store adjoining also fell a ready victim.

The fire now reached the Barry Building. This building is of concrete and proved to be an effective barrier to the devastating flames. A great and finally successful attempt was made to save Dr. Murphy's house and drug store. For if these had caught fire, it is thought that the greater part of the town would have been burned to the ground. As it is, the loss is much greater than the town can stand and it will be long before it recovers from the blow.

From left to right: Leo Stanley, Johnnie Courter, Bill Stanley, Earl Wilmar, and Ellery Wilmar, about 1896.

Dr. McCarthy, who was manager of the Levinger Hotel, has moved what goods he saved into the Woodmansee Building and will there furnish his guests with the best accommodations possible under the circumstances. The property destroyed as far as known are as follows: Levinger Hotel, I. Levinger of San Francisco; Occidental Hotel, C. E. Davis, Petaluma City; City Hall, J. W. Goodwin, San Francisco; Methodist Church, Methodist Society.

The Nygren family was the last one to live in the Caledonia Adobe. Alfred, or Axel, and Anna Persson Nygren had been married in Sweden. Alfred had been born on November 13, 1856; he came to the United States sometime in the 1880s, and first went to Iowa. Alfred then worked for P. A. Lundblade, in 1888, in Nebraska; there he became a United States citizen on April 30, 1894. He was a carpenter-cabinet maker by trade; he returned to Sweden and brought back his wife in 1902. They came to Idaho Falls, where Alfred's sister, Caroline Lundblade, lived.

The Nygren's first child, Elsa, was born in Idaho Falls, on July 1, 1902; she died in 1934. William A. Wilmar, a first cousin to Alfred Nygren, had written to Alfred that San Miguel was a healthy place to live, and that there were 'good buys' in land. So, Alfred brought his young bride, who knew little English, to the Wilmar's to visit. The Nygrens rented the Woodward place across the Salinas River from the Caledonia. Then, in 1903, they bought the 160-acre Caledonia Ranch.

The Nygren's relationship with the Wilmar family allows us to take a look at another of the most important families in the area. The William A. Wilmar family had its roots in Sweden. William A. Wilmar, from Boone, Iowa, arrived in California in 1889, with his wife, Matilda, and four sons: Ellery, Earl, Alvin Hillis and Ralph. The Wilmar family went to where Matilda's father, Henry Nelson, had settled on a tract of land thirteen miles south of San Miguel, and three miles south of Paso Robles. Henry Nelson, also from Iowa, built his home on a hill on 18 acres south of Paso Robles in 1888.

The Southern Pacific Milling Company hired William A. Wilmar, after observing his work as a bookkeeper in Santa Margarita. He became the manager of the grain and lumber business in San Miguel. The "old town" had recently burned, so every piece of lumber that went into the new houses came under his care. (The three-story milling section of the Southern Pacific Milling Company burned down in 1933.)

The man who ran the warehouse was a big, strong Norwegian by the name of Gunder Gunderson. This man and his brother, Charles, had homesteaded a ranch in the mountains east of San Miguel. When the time came that they wanted to sell, Mr. Wilmar bought their 800 acres. W. A. Wilmar bought more land and leased it to farmers and ranchers. Over the years, he purchased land until he owned 2,000 acres.

Alvin Hillis Wilmar graduated from Paso Robles High School in 1907 and went to the University of Southern California, where he became a physician; he returned to Paso Robles and began his practice in 1912. He worked as a physician until his retirement in the

A young W. A. Wilmar.

1950s, and later acquired Grandpa Nelson's ranch, where he lived. He also had a cattle ranch in Deer Valley, at the head of Vineyard Canyon, not far from San Miguel.

Dr. Wilmar established a scholarship at Paso Robles High School, with a donation of $25,000; the interest from his original gift is used each year to give a

The elder W. A. Wilmar

substantial scholarship to two graduating seniors who plan to concentrate in the field of science or medicine.

William A. Wilmar's oldest son, Ellery, was engaged to be married, but died of pneumonia on May 9, 1910. Earl went to the University of California, Berkeley, and became an engineer. Ralph worked in the steel industry in Torrance, after returning from the service in World War I.

The *San Miguel Sentinel* informed its readers, on April 13, 1918, that Earl V. Wilmar, age 32, was the office manager for the Columbia Steel Company at Pittsburg, California; he resigned his position and enlisted in the Signal Corps of the Army.

The same newspaper, on April 20, 1918 carried a story with the title, "All Three Wilmar Boys Now in the Army."

Dr. A. H. Wilmar, son of Mr. & Mrs. W. A. Wilmar of San Miguel, has received a commission as 1st Lieutenant in the U. S. Medical Corps. He was granted thirty days time to prepare for leaving. He will continue his practice at Paso Robles until called.

Mr. & Mrs. W. A. Wilmar have three sons and no daughters. Their youngest son Ralph enlisted several months ago in the Aerial

Corps, and about two weeks ago their son Earl enlisted in the Signal Corps, and now with the doctor receiving a commission places all the boys in the service.

One week later, on April 27, 1918, the *San Miguel Sentinel* had to bring the news to its readers that "1st S.L.O. County Boy Killed in Action."

The first news of the death of one of the boys of this county killed in action in France, came last Saturday to Mrs. Geo. Blancett at Union. The telegram read "Red Cross reports Private A. Blancett killed in action March 13. A finer truer man never lived." He was 35 years old and had been at the front just four weeks before he answered the last call.

He enlisted in the Canadian Cavalry. He leaves a father and mother, five sisters and three brothers, two of whom are now in the U. S. Army.

At the time of World War I, the *San Miguel Sentinel* printed a story on March 16, 1918 entitled "J. Work Will Furnish Land to Men Not in Business Essential to Winning the War."

Mr. John Work of this place offers from one to six hundred acres of farming land to any business man in San Miguel, who is not engaged in a business that is essential to the winning of the war. The man must work the land himself and raise wheat. All that Mr. Work asks is that he pay the taxes on the land he occupies. This offer is for the period of the war, but the farmer has the privilege of harvesting the crop he has planted, at the end of the war.

As Mr. Work has sold his cattle and has some land that is not rented, he makes this offer and suggests that men in other places who have land that is not being used, should make a like offer to those in their vicinity. This is the time to start summer-fallowing.

John Work had been born at Littleness in Shetland Island, in 1861, the son of Thomas Work who was also born there. John's grandfather, Captain Thomas Work, was the master of a whaler for many years, and died at age 99.

Thomas Work also followed the sea as a fisherman; he was also a farmer. He married Agnes Robertson; she died when son John was fifteen years old. Thomas Work finally came to California, where he died at age 67.

Mr. and Mrs. Thomas Work were the parents of five children: John, Janet (later Mrs. Garrick in San Francisco), Mary (who died in Monterey), Agnes (Mrs. Atkins, who lived near Watsonville) and Thomas A.(who lived in Pacific Grove.)

John R. Work had come to the United States in 1878, when he was seventeen years old. He arrived in California in the spring of 1881. After living in the vicinity of Monterey, he came to the San Miguel area in 1887. He purchased his first 160 acres, by buying a possession right and paying $1,000. He selected the place because it had a good spring; the began buying land and accumulated about 7,000 acres.

The Work Ranch was located in the old Independence precinct in upper Ranchita Canyon, where over thirty families originally made their homes. In 1889, John Work married Mattie Jones, whose father, John T. Jones, was a homesteader in Lowes Canyon; John and Mattie Work were the parents of Agnes, Robert, Belle, Alice and Ardelia.

The grandmother, Matilda C. Jones, and their mother, Mattie Jones Work, spent their first night in the area in the Caledonia; Mattie was 15 years old at the time.

Returning to the Nygren family, we learn that on July 21, 1904, Lillie Ester Helena Nygren was born, in the Caledonia adobe; she died in 1964. Anna F. Nygren, the last child to have been born in the Caledonia, was born on June 7, 1907. Alfred (Axel) Nygren was buying the Caledonia on time payments, so he could not make any structural changes until he owned the place. He did build his family a new house on the property in 1910.

A clearer picture of the transaction by which Hattie Davis Cooper sold the Caledonia Ranch to Alfred Nygren comes from the following in Hattie's diary:

May 23, 1910 - Saw Haley's Comet.
June 2, 1910 - Signed papers selling Caledonia
June 13 - Received remainder of money for Caledonia, about 60 acres sold for $1,000.
Costs - certificate of title $10.00, making our half $490.

Haydn C. Davis was a grandson of George S. Davis, who died in San Miguel on January 13, 1891. Haydn

Anna Nygren and children behind the Caledonia Adobe, 1906-1907.

was also a nephew of Hattie Davis Cooper. Hattie Louise Elvira Davis was born on January 6, 1874 in Cambria; she was a daughter of George Davis, and married Charles Cooper on June 10, 1893. Haydn informs us: "Hattie sold to Alfred Nygren, and the 1910 pay-off was the balance of the mortgage; as we say, 'she was carrying the papers.'"

In 1917, Mr. Nygren sold the roof tile from the Caledonia, in good faith, to be used on Mission San Luis Obispo. According to an October 29, 1930 article in a Santa Barbara newspaper, the tiles were eventually used to roof the home of the Wrigleys, on a hill above Avalon Bay on Catalina Island. William Wrigley had purchased Catalina Island in 1919 from Captain William Banning and his brothers, Joseph and Hancock.

The November 17, 1917 edition of the *San Miguel Messenger* informs us that Mr. Nygren "left Saturday for Idaho Falls, Idaho to visit his sister who is dangerously ill." Illness was no stranger to the Nygren family. Alfred's wife, Anna, contracted T. B. after having suffered from Spanish influenza; she died in a Pasadena hospital in November of 1919. Mrs. Nygren had worked many hours helping neighbors during the flu epidemic. Anna, the youngest child, was 12 years old when her mother died.

Alfred Nygren sold two portions of the Caledonia property in 1920: one, to Mrs. Johnston of Los Angeles, 3 ½ acres of the southern part of the property, bordering on the gulch where Nygren Road is today; the other, to Mr. Matt Poll of Los Angeles, 4 acres which bordered the above-mentioned property on the north.

In 1923, the adobe and six surrounding acres were sold to Pierce Realty. We will examine this in detail in a later chapter. Alfred, who was 24 years older than

Caledonia Adobe with tile roof removed.

Anna, Elsie, and Lillian Nygren (r to l).

his wife, died on May 9, 1927. Alfred and Anna are buried next to each other in the San Miguel Cemetery---located on land that was once part of their property.

Earlier, we saw that Mr. Nygren had built a new home for his family in 1910; in 1931, the house was moved westerly against the hill west of the adobe, to allow the two-lane Highway 101 to go through. Later, in 1954, when the Highway 101 was made into a freeway, the ranch house was moved again; this time, it was moved ¼ mile to the south, to allow room for two lanes of south-bound traffic.

The two older Nygren girls never married; in 1928, Anna Nygren married Arthur R. Hebel. What was left of the Caledonia ranch property remained in the Nygren girls' possession until World War II, when it was sold to a Mr. Tutin, a real estate agent in San Miguel. Otto B. Van Horn, realtor in Paso Robles, sent a check in the amount of $2,348.93 to Anna Nygren Hebel in Carpinteria, on May 4, 1945. This was for "payment in full for your San Miguel home." Anna noted: "With gas rationing so I couldn't take care of our place, we thought it best to sell. The price was poor---the whole deal was poor and we came out poor."

Anna Nygren Hebel died on December 21, 1988,

and is buried in Carpinteria, as were her two older sisters.

Today, there are three acres of land remaining with the Caledonia adobe.

But we are getting ahead of ourselves.

The Nygren family's story of life at the adobe will be learned by our reading, verbatim, the story written by Anna Nygren Hebel in 1970.

THE OLD CALEDONIA ON EL CAMINO REAL: THE HOUSE BY THE SIDE OF THE ROAD

By Anna Nygren Hebel

On a warm June day in 1907, father opened the old paneled door of the Spanish adobe house and partly entering the cool interior, said "Has it come yet?" The attending lady answered, "Oh yes, and it's a girl." A groan was heard and something like, "I needed a boy," was mumbled as he went out, disappointment fairly dripping like his perspiration, for I was his third daughter. When I later learned of this reaction I said, "I'll be your boy, Papa"- - -and I was. I helped him cord wood, chase runaway cows, irrigate, sharpen tools on the foot-operated grinder, climb the windmill tower, bring in hay, and other kinds of farm chores.

The old Caledonia, as the Spanish adobe is called, is on the El Camino Real, near the bank of the Salinas River just south of the mouth of the Estrella River. The railroad runs between the road and the stream. A fourth of a mile to the north is the San Miguel Mission, and the town of San Miguel is just beyond. Here in the dry, hot summer, on former Mission land, in an old Monterey-type house, I was born; and here I grew up and lived until I went away to college.

Ours was the last family to live in the old building and I must have been the last baby born there. Mother was used to lots of lakes and short, clean summers so it was a hard adjustment from the green, beautiful Southern Sweden to the dry, dusty Salinas Valley. The adobe was so cool; and coming in from the heat "one could catch his death of cold"- - -so my mother wanted a board house, and as will be explained later, there was also another reason.

The adobe ranch house was built by Senor Petronelo (Petronillo) Rios some time between 1830 and 1848 with the aid of Indian friends. Its thick adobe walls were covered with a hard white plaster of lime, river sand and animal hair mixture.

The porch and balcony across the front was typical Monterey architecture—a large room with a staircase going up to the second floor had a door to a one-story kitchen to the right of the stairway; and a door through the left wall into a small room that had an outside door in back. The other rooms only had outside entrances from the porch in front and directly from the yard in back, with no windows. The upstairs had two large rooms which went the length of the house, from back to balcony, and two smaller rooms on the south end.

There were niches in the thick walls of the large rooms where statues were placed. The interior of the niches was a beautiful blue and I loved to put bouquets of wild flowers in them. The attic was entered from one of these large bedrooms by a ladder. The rough pole rafters were tied in place with leather thongs. Pigeons had established a colony up there and it was my job to catch the squabs for eating. I had the opportunity then to examine the construction closely and asked by father why they had not used nails.

Governor Pio Pico had sold the Mission lands to Senor Rios and an Englishman, William Reed. Reed

Caledonia Adobe from northwest, about 1910.

and his family lived in the San Miguel Mission where the partners operated a store, and Rios and his wife and three children had this adobe house one-fourth of a mile to the south.

In an account by Rios' grand-daughter (Saunders, Charles F. and Chase, J. S., *The California Padres and Their Missions*, Houghton Mifflin Company, 1914, page 254), Senora Leon Gil, she said that he had moved to Templeton with his family and faithful Indians in 1848 when he heard of the fate of his partner. Two ranchers, Mr. Branch of Arroyo Grande, and Captain Pryce of Los Osos could arouse no one at the Mission. Rios sent them to notify the officers in San Luis Obispo, and when they came, all went back together to the Mission where they found the grisly remains of the Reed family and the servants who had been murdered. This has been called the worst murder in early California.

Rios operated the rancho for the next ten years. In 1859, the United States District Court declared the sale by Pico invalid. The next year, it was sold to a Mr. W. B. Bursherd or a George or W. B. Butchard, who gave it the name, "Caledonia," which means welcome, and established it as an inn and stage stop. The road to Jolon went west just above the Mission, so the Caledonia was right on the stage coach route. Many early residents spent their first night in San Miguel in the Caledonia; and until the Southern Pacific Railroad was finished, it was a busy place. The pools in the Salinas River just in front of the house washed the dust from many of the traveling guests who enjoyed the beautiful view of the stream with its cottonwood tree border from the second story balcony.

Butchard sold the Inn in 1877 or 1878 to Morgan Brians and Sons, who continued to serve the stage coach travelers until 1886 when the first trains rumbled by about sixty feet away from the front door. The trade immediately declined but the railroad brought a flood of homesteaders.

The first town was built near the adobe. Shortly after the trains came, a disastrous fire roared through the settlement. It was rebuilt in its present location north of the Mission as it was no longer necessary for the town to be on the stage road to Jolon. With the influx of families, a larger school was needed. A wooden building on the rise above the adobe house was used. The primary grades moved into the large room in the Caledonia. It was evident that a school building was needed. The Southern Pacific Railroad and its Pacific Improvement Company donated eight lots on the mesa to the north of the Mission. The men of the area decided to build a brick two-story school. A Mr.

Sicotte and Mr. G. Hopper were hired to do the work. They opened a brick yard on the river bank south of the Caledonia and made over a hundred thousand bricks of the first burning. It took a week to burn and a week to cool. The deep holes and broken bricks were there when my father started to farm the land.

He partially filled the holes by scraping the soil down from the sides, but nothing would grow where the kiln had killed the soil. With these bricks they built a school that lasted for over sixty years and we and all our friends were among its graduates.

In the years that passed, the adobe was a store, post office and tavern. According to my father's record, a Mr. Cooper owned the place and sold a portion in 1895 to a Mr. Webster for the San Miguel cemetery. In 1895 and 1896, the Fred Telford family lived in the house; and many years later in the south front room we girls would rummage through boxes of letters and records that the Telfords left.

The building and their surroundings began to decline. The large wooden barn on the other side of the creek that housed the stage and riding horses began to sag. The hills behind the mesa were planted to wheat and barley, and cattle grazed along the river. By the time my parents purchased the 160 acres, in 1903, the buildings were in poor condition. Mother was a particular housekeeper and the impossible job of keeping the worn, wooden floors clean and the broken plastered walls neat discouraged her; but the greatest bother was the vermin that had collected in the cracks during the years of disuse. Lice and fleas she killed with "Buack." For ants and other larger bugs, she used coal oil (kerosene) but the bed bugs were too much. She used everything available, and finally in desperation, she poured boiling water over her large varnished bedstead, saying that she couldn't help it if it ruined the finish. "I can't have bugs," she flatly stated, so Papa built a house across the creek. He had torn down the dilapidated huge barn with its enormous heaps of manure and straw. He scraped and plowed and leveled the ground, for it was the best place for the wooden house. I was three but I remember playing under the partly-finished floor and gathering the hammer for my father.

The day we moved the last things stands out in my memories. There was a ten-foot deep gully between the two houses. Papa had spanned the crevice with two long cottonwood tree trunks and nailed three-foot slats across the poles. This uneven bridge without rails was our passageway. I ran with ease; Mama, calling to be careful, followed cautiously across with armloads of clothes and household goods. I had a homemade rag doll with an oil-painted face that was very important and I saw to it that it came along with the boxes and buckets and tubs of essentials.

The old well behind the adobe house had caved in, so it was filled and a new well was dug by hand above our new house. My father dug and shored up the walls, then dug more, hauling up the soil in buckets. He hired hoboes who came by regularly each Spring and back each Fall. They stayed three or four days and helped do the jobs Papa could not do alone. The well was forty feet deep. He had to augment the supply by pumping water from the river and obtained a water right-of-way under the railroad which we had the rest of our stay there. Father built a reservoir into the slope of the bank at the creek. I remember the frogs that lived under the board cover. They croaked a chorus every evening in unison with the thousands along the river bank. My father had a gasoline engine pump on the river bank that thieves finally took. It was tampered with regularly.

The cemetery was on a high mesa above the Caledonia. Below it where the highway is now was the old bitter almond orchard. No one liked the bitter taste of the nuts but every Spring the gnarled old trees were beautiful with large blossoms. We picked big bouquets as long as the orchard was there.

Along the old road behind the Mission where we walked on our way to school were peaches from the old Mission plantings. Probably they were seedling because the fruit was poor and thin-fleshed; but the beautiful deep pink blossoms were picked and taken to school each Spring. Some of these trees were still alive until the highway took them out. There were two old olive stumps with a little scraggly growth that finally died when I was small.

Anise grew outside the back door. Each year a fresh new growth covered the old stalks. Mrs. Espenosa, our neighbor, told Mama that it was a favorite spice by the Spanish and Indian cooks. An earlier resident had planted seven eucalyptus trees around the Caledonia; they grew very tall. One wet winter during a strong wind, one tree fell across the highway during the night. My father hurried to get it cut before any traffic was impeded. Some years later, it was

Nygren Ranch, June 1915: Mrs. Anna P. Nygren-next to horse, Elsa Nygren-white hat, Lillian Nygren-white bows, Anna Nygren-on horse, Faye Lundblade-in white.

so cold, down to seven degrees above, that two trees froze and died. The old ones close to the house recovered, and one tall one is still there.

The cottonwood trees grew rapidly and would fill the river bottom if the rainfall was light with little run-off. They would then be an obstruction for flood debris and cause a change of course of the stream. My father was kept busy between carpenter jobs and farming, cutting the trees for light firewood. He sold the wood for quick fires in the summer time. Oak was burned for longer heat in the winters. The heavy rains and floods of 1913-1914 scoured out the brush and trees along our banks; but lower, where the trees had not been cut, the raging water took out an acre or two of the neighbor's land.

It was hard making a living on the place. The ground was rich with humus from the old barn yard. At first, our vegetables shot up and then wilted. Papa said they were "burned" by so much manure. We raised some luscious green beans, corn, melons, and root vegetables there; and potatoes, corn and squash on the land strip along the river between the railroad tracks and the bank. The rabbits, coyotes and tramps helped themselves. The ground squirrels and gopher undermined our efforts. A cold freeze could kill as late as April or May, or a searing wind could burn the plants and stunt the ones which survived.

To the west of the mesa, steep hills were lined with gullies. On the top of these knolls, the wheat and barley fields were planted. I remember taking coffee to the harvest crew in a gallon lard pail, with cups on a wire ring. Sugar and cream were put in the hot liquid so the men only needed to pour and drink. Twenty-horse teams pulled the threshing machines. The hard golden grain was sacked and sold to the S. P. Milling Company, which had a flour mill in San Miguel. Mama said the flour was too heavy, so she bought flour at the store for her heavenly-light homemade bread.

When I was about eleven, my father sold most of the hills for almond orchards. Two of these new owners wanted frontage land on which to build. In 1920, four acres were sold to Mr. Matt Poll, and three and one-half acres to a Mrs. Johnston of Los Angeles. At first, they camped in the summer and cleared and planted the orchards. Later, our part-time neighbors built the two houses on the mesa to the south of us.

Soon after we moved from the Caledonia, the tramps moved in. There were three or four every night. As the nights were very cold in the winter, they tore up the worn old wooden floors and built fires in the rooms. The south-east room was the most used; in fact, even before we moved, this unused room was

slept in, and Mama found evidence of unknown guests in three of the lower rooms. After the floor had gone up in smoke, the hoboes started tearing out the window frame in the big room. Papa mended it and put up a sign. He then took out the doors, for he was afraid they would be the next firewood.

It was truly the Inn for these wanderers. Some who worked for us told my father that they had a regular itinerary and the old adobe house was a definite stopover. Our farm was ideal for the hoboes; a house, water for washing, bathing and cooking, plenty of wood along the river, and a planted garden to raid. They came to the door to beg milk and eggs, doing a chore or two in return. This set-up was the death of the old house. The smoke darkened the interior and it smelled very strong. The wooden floors were gone and the dirt was full of debris. The floor in the upper southeast room was dangerous when we were there, so Papa nailed a barrier across the door. Later it gave way and the tramps were quick to tear the wood out and burn it.

With the doors gone, the cattle went into the cool interior during the heat of the day, and this did not improve conditions. Boards nailed across the openings were soon burned, too. My father became discouraged about the trespassing. Nowadays, we would call the building an attractive nuisance. Papa saw no use in keeping it up; no one was interested in it. One day a man came with a request. He would like the tile on the roof. He needed the old Mission-made tile for an improvement to the San Luis Obispo Mission. Why not help renovate a really important building? There was no reason to doubt the intentions of the buyer, so father agreed to sell the roof tile. Much later, we

Caledonia Adobe from the east.

learned that he bought it for resale for a profit, and we were saddened by the deceit. This was about 1917.

The highway was squeezed in between the Caledonia and the railroad right-of-way. When it was to be paved in 1915, they took some more of the front yard. The fence was right up against the porch now, and quite a cut was made, so the bank was steep.

Right after World War I, there was unemployment, and a vivid memory remains of the hundreds of men walking on the road looking for any work that would mean a meal. One day at school, we heard that the town had been notified that a large marching group of I.W.W.s (Wobblies) were going to arrive about lunch time the next day, and the people of the community had better prepare to feed them! The stores furnished large tin wash tubs and wash boilers; men hurried to dig a long pit for a fire; the grocers furnished beans, which were put on to cook in the tubs on the galvanized tin covers over the fire. I remember the excited, apprehensive air about town. A friendly merchant told me that I had better hurry home, as it would not be safe to be on the road. About 10:30 in the morning of the day, we heard a rumbling of voices and saw dust clouds to the south. Soon we could distinguish the hordes of men walking full abreast with no room for any other objects on the road.

Loud and jostling, they came. As we watched from our window, one man crawled under the fence and tried to catch a chicken, which flew for its life. It was a fearsome sight. Afterward, we heard of their rough treatment of their hosts and saw the stacks and stacks of tin plates still colored with beans and scraps of bread. It took quite a while for the storekeepers to recover from the ordeal.

The El Camino Real was very dusty in the summer. The soil was powder-soft from many wheels. It felt soft and velvety on bare feet and I used to walk in the wheel track, letting the warm dust "squish" between my toes. No one else enjoyed the nuisance.

The rains would make mud, and often wagon drivers would ask Papa to help pull them out of a low, muddy hold which was north of the adobe. A Mr. Free-

Caledonia Adobe from the southwest.

man came every Fall with a six-horse team and a large lumber wagon loaded with boxes of apples. He usually arrived late in the afternoon and maneuvered his outfit through our gate with a flourish, drawing close to the house, the dust flying. The smell of apples wafting into the house brought all of us out to greet him. He always stayed overnight, leaving boxes of red and green and golden fruit. One Fall it rained during the night. At breakfast, before sun up, the men discussed how the heavy load could be pulled through the low place. They decided to get some cottonwood poles and lay them across, making a log "floor." These logs were left there and became part of the road. Papa did not have to pull anyone out that winter.

The Pan-Pacific Exposition at San Diego and San Francisco brought lots of travelers. When this was planned, they saw the need for better roads, and a paving program was pushed. We watched as the slow progress of the cement mixers came closer to our place. It seemed so wide and smooth, that ribbon of white miracle that eliminated the clouds of dust and the mud, but in reality it was narrow, and one had to drive slowly when meeting anyone. The pavement was in front of the Caledonia and the Mission. Some of this can be seen there now, with weeds growing in the cracks.

By 1922, the old adobe had reached a sad condition. In the summer, I would go over and climb up to the second floor and, with caution, go out on the decaying veranda. It was fun to imagine who had stood there in the past; but it was depressing to see the deterioration. One day a man approached my father with a request for the old place. Papa did not like the man, and told him it was not for sale. Later in the week, Mr. Pierce, a realtor from Paso Robles, came and offered to buy the land on the other side of the creek that included the adobe. Papa sold six acres to Mr. Pierce in 1923, and he in turn sold it to Mr. Charles Dorries. It was during this transaction that the old Spanish deed was "lost" and Mr. Pierce brought a modern deed in its place.

Mr. Dorries saw the possibility of making the old Caledonia a tourist attraction. To do this, he first built a small shack above the building in which to camp. He scoured the area for all memorabilia. From the pictures that he found, and my father's description, he rebuilt the kitchen. The adobe bricks were made on the place. When they were drying, he went about trying to interest townspeople in his project; but he was not popular and did not receive any help. He wrote to the California Historical Society in San Francisco. They replied they had no money, and were not interested in Southern projects, but just around the Bay area.

THE OLD CALEDONIA ON EL CAMINO REAL: THE HOUSE BY THE SIDE OF THE ROAD

After he laid a stone floor in the main room, he decided to cut a door through the wall to have access to the next room to the south. The stairway was replaced, and he put up a sign that the public was welcome. Not long after, an inspector came and told him it was not safe and he could not charge admission. He felt that some local person was making trouble for him and became bitter.

Lots of hard work was done all alone. He mended the roof, plastered the front, and planted most of the plants and trees- - -only the eucalyptus was there when he came. He built the kitchen entirely, the two small houses, the wishing well, and the garden walls. He had a well dug and developed an irrigation system.

The highway had to be widened. The California Division of Highways threatened all his efforts by surveying right through the place. Dorries fought hard, and aroused enough help to change the state's plans and they routed the road west of the Caledonia. In so doing, they took out our house and filled in our gully.

Nearly all the level land was taken. The house was moved up on the slope of the mesa, but it was never the same. We were all living away by that time. Papa had died in 1927 and the place had been rented.

Mr. Dorries built the second building as a store and gift shop so that he would have a legitimate reason for having the public on the property. He sold almonds and postcards and other souvenirs. He would warn anyone who wanted to see the old adobe that it was not safe, but that they could go in at their own risk. He had a great many guests, but he always regretted that he could not make a paying proposition of his long-cherished dream of making the old Caledonia a landmark.

When he became too ill to stay, he went to a veterans' hospital and there died. The family wanted to hold the property and were not willing to have it made a County landmark; but now that it is in better hands, it is nearly too late to save the old adobe by the King's Highway. A roof has been erected over it and soon it may be a tourist stop and park.

MISSION SAN MIGUEL THE LATER YEARS

After thirty-six years without a resident pastor, a priest was assigned to Mission San Miguel in the person of Father Philip Farrelly; he served from January 1, 1879 to May 20, 1886. "Father Felipe" was transferred to Mission Santa Ynez, and was followed by Father Joseph Mut, whose period of service was June 13, 1886 to October 30, 1889. Father Mut is the only priest to be buried in the cemetery of Mission San Miguel; he rests there with the 2,249 Indians buried at the mission.

Grave site of Father Mut

Father Zephyrin Engelhardt has this to say about Father Jose Mut. "To his energy is due that the row of buildings comprising the ancient *convento* was preserved. Many of the rafters were decayed and others were broken, so that the roof with its heavy tiles threatened to collapse at any time. Father Mut, therefore, undertook to collect the necessary funds. The people, delighted that their beloved landmark should be preserved, gave freely. $3,000 were secured. With this amount the energetic priest replaced the rotten timbers and broken tiles with new material, and thus rendered the rooms habitable and safe."

While Father Mut lived at Mission San Miguel for three years, he also served Mission San Antonio to the north and Cashin's Station and the San Jose Valley to the south. He made the circuit once a month with two horses hitched to a light wagon.

Father Mut was followed by Father Carolus Franchi (1889 to 1894), then Father Henry S. O'Reilly (1894-1889). There is a gap of time from 1889 until Father Philip J. O'Reilly's service from February 12, 1900 to March of 1903. During that gap, Rev. George Montgomery signed the Registers on June 16, 1895 and March 25, 1900.

From August 16, 1903 until August 21, 1905, Father Hugh Curran was pastor at the Mission; he was followed by Father Patrick Murphy, from August of 1905 to May of 1908. Father William Power served from June 7, 1908 until November 13, 1909; he was followed by Father William Nevin, November 1909 to September 1922.

Father Patrick Ryan served the Mission from 1922 until November of 1924. (In 1922, St. Rose of Lima parish was formed in Paso Robles.) Father Ascensio Segarra was pastor from December of 1924 until August of 1928. After 86 years of absence, the Franciscan Fathers again took charge of Mission San Miguel, on August 1, 1928.

We have already seen that the mission had been founded in 1797; the first church burned in 1806. Ten

Mission San Miguel, California — 1923

Church at Mission San Miguel featuring the All-Seeing Eye of God.

years were spent making and storing adobe bricks to be sure that enough were on hand when the construction of the present church was begun. It was completed in 1818-1819. The church portion is 144 feet long, 27 feet wide and 40 feet tall. Most of the walls are 5 feet 10 inches thick.

The mission building had been enclosed by a high adobe wall. At least two people have told of a low adobe wall extending from the Caledonia adobe to the Mission. Steve Buelna, born at the Caledonia on January 1, 1885, and Maude Viola ("Babe") Wright born at Oat Springs, on September 14, 1894, speak about walking on top of this adobe wall.

"Babe," as a young child was carrying a bucket of milk from a dairy herd near the Caledonia to her home in town. The Telfords had a dairy at the Caledonia between 1889 and 1902. On the way, she tripped and the milk was lost; she went home, dreading what the reaction would be. When she arrived, everyone in the household was upset at the news that grandfather had just died; the spilled milk was the least of their worries.

During stage-coach days, the courtyard of the mission was used to hold the stage horses. During the course of repairs in 1930, a crudely-lettered sign was uncovered on the end pillar: "Corral For Stock."

Edith Buckland Webb, who wrote *Indian Life at the Old Missions*, included in some of her unpublished material some information that had been gathered by Eva Carpenter Iversen, a Paso Robles historian. The following concerns a visit made in August of 1931.

> **The church of today was built against the front wall of the old or second church, or the front wall of the second church became part of the rear wall of the third church, which is the church now standing.**
>
> **The inner wall of the third church was on a line with that of the previous church, but the outer wall extends several feet beyond the outer wall of the second church. In other words, the church begun in 1816 to take the place of the church of 1798, was a bigger and better one.**
>
> **This church of 1798 had 22 feet added to it, in length, in 1804. It was apparently merely a continuation of the rooms of the north wing of the quadrangle and suffered damage to its roof at the time of the fire of 1806. Engelhardt stated that "The church was repaired as well as possible, but plans were made for the erection of a more spacious structure."**
>
> **There was one door, near the entrance of the church on the north side which opened into the baptistery. This baptistery was the first room, or building in that long line which extended in a northeast direction from the church and formed one wing of the Indian village.**
>
> **Mrs. Kate Brown, daughter of John Warth, bell-ringer at San Miguel for at least forty years as well as man-of-all-jobs, says that during Father Mut's time. . .she remembers the baptismal font which was of stone and was placed upon an adobe foundation or pedestal, set in the room adjoining the church as before stated.**

In April of 1935, Mrs. Webb received information from Mrs. Kate Brown of "Morro Beach," daughter of John Warth. Among other things she said, was that "in the first little room to the right of the church was a large stone basin or bowl in which she and the other children played "fishing."

Edith Buckland Webb has written that "In the spring of 1932, we took Peter Cheney, now almost eighty years old, to visit the mission. Peter said he remembered when the first serious break was made in the north wall of the Indian village. This was made over in the northeast corner in order to have a longer track for horse-racing. The races were run over a straight-away course which was from 600 to 1200 yards in length and lay in front of the mission."

In her book, *Indian Life at the Old Missions*, Edith Buckland Webb states that Stephen Rios remembered a sort of "basement" which stood at the extreme front end of the front wing of San Miguel's quadrangle. She states that "Early photographs show buildings beyond those now existing at that mission---buildings whose foundations have never been uncovered."

Around the same time period, Brother Benedict was rebuilding the altar. During his work, the long-sought escape tunnel was discovered. The tunnel, since filled in, led away to the river.

During the time of Father Mut's stay at the mission, John Warth and his two daughters were occupying a room in the Father's dwelling. Nearest the church were Father Mut's quarters, then a Doctor's office, a meat market, the Warth's, other people, then continuing along the south wing, Mexicans were living in the rooms.

Anna Nygren Hebel, writing in 1923, stated that there were twenty rooms in the southern wing of the Mission. In the small houses along the walls, the Indians had been taught various trades. Mrs. Hebel had been told by the pastor, in 1923, that as many as 2,000 Indians could gather inside the mission church. The Indians were hard to control, and instead of shaking hands to greet each other, they patted one another on the cheek. This cheek-patting by several hundred Indians made much noise; the Padres placed curtains over the windows, because the darkness frightened the Indians into silence.

In 1905, Alvin Hillis Wilmar wrote the following for the Paso Robles High School yearbook.

SONNET TO SAN MIGUEL MISSION

Methinks I see thee as thou wast of old;
Thy clay-brick walls, that many courts surround,
Rise bleak and mighty from the fruitful ground,
Making thee seem formidable and bold.
Then of thee was the happy story told,
That near thy courts was heard no profane sound,
For every soul was to the Padres bound.
The Padres with a loving hand controlled.

But now thy mighty walls lie low in waste,
Thy inmates driven from the scenes they love;

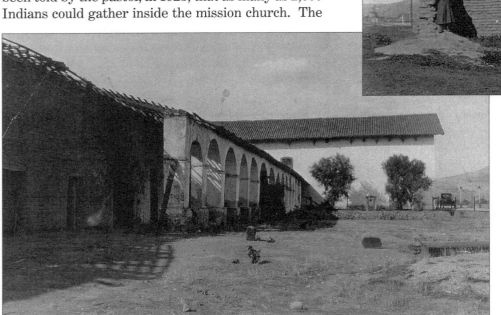

Above, adobe bricks returning "to earth from whence thou'rt come."
Left, Mission San Miguel in the 1920s.

**Thyself decaying, slowly, crumb by crumb.
Till stern old Time by far too much in haste,
Eats thy great timbers till they, helpless, fall,
And thou returnest to earth from whence
thou'rt come.**

In 1934, Father Wand, pastor at Mission San Miguel, invited Jess Crettol and his sons to come to San Miguel and help restore the mission. Jess Crettol had been born in Switzerland on May 5, 1883. He studied for the priesthood, for a period of time, in Spain. While there, he learned the art of making adobe bricks. Crettol left Spain, and eventually arrived in Bakersfield, where he married Blanch L. Crettol, who had been born on December 4, 1879, in England.

Their son, Jesse, was born on October 1, 1913; he became a stone mason. Son Joseph George Crettol was born on February 23, 1925; he was a member of the Coast Guard, and died on August 1, 1943.

Upon being invited to help restore the mission, Jess Crettol and his sons had originally planned to do

Bell tower constructed by Jess Crettol.

only a partial restoration; they later decided to do a complete job on the foundations of the old quadrangle. When they started the job, the mission had almost been reduced to rubble. During one year, 250,000 adobe bricks were made.

Mission San Miguel Arcangel

Drawn by Colleen Conner Cobb

The Crettols made the adobe bricks and restored the quadrangle first; then Jesse built the bell tower at the south end of the mission property. The elder builder, Jess, built the rock and masonry bell tower adjacent to the mission cemetery. Previously, the huge bell had been mounted on a short wooden tower. The wall in front of the mission was constructed in 1937.

In the 1950s, a new wing and a wall around the south end of the mission were added. The Crettols are also credited with aiding the rebuilding of the Estrella Adobe Church, as well as Mission San Antonio. For all of these projects, Jesse designed and had a Paso Robles blacksmith, Fred Cuendet, build an adobe mud-mixer; the machine, built on a 1931 Chevy chassis, looks like a cross between a truck and a tractor.

Bell "S.S. Gabriel A.D. 1800."

Jesse's building was interrupted by World War II. After the war, Jesse returned to San Miguel, and married Lucille Crettol. She had been born on August 16, 1907.

Louise Crettol later related that some of the old adobe bricks that the men found had been made with the bodies of birds inside, used instead of straw. Dan Krieger, history professor at California State Polytechnic University in San Luis Obispo, has stated that San Miguel's adobe bricks ordinarily had ox-blood and horse manure blended with the adobe soil.

[There is a stucco house at 11ᵗʰ and L Streets in San Miguel, which was built by Jess Crettol and his son. It contains a wall which features cement plaques which represent the signs of the zodiac and the four phases of the moon. Also featured is a barbecue pit with a stone chimney in the shape of a dragon; it is designed to release smoke through the dragon's mouth and nostrils when the pit is being used.]

The tennis courts and handball courts were the final projects; they were constructed in the 1960s. Jesse Crettol worked on the mission buildings until 1967; that year, he went to work for San Luis Obispo County Parks and Recreation Department in San Miguel.

Blanch L. Crettol passed away on February 9, 1958; she was followed in death by her husband, Jess, on December 15, 1958. Jesse Crettol died on May 18, 1989; Lucille Crettol passed away on May 25, 1993.

The daughter of Jesse and Lucille is Lynne Schmitz. She and her husband, Andrew "Bud" Schmitz, live and work on the property across from the mission; it was once the mission pear orchard and was later a dairy.

San Miguel never had a large bell tower of adobe construction. Its bells usually hung on wooden standards. The original bell, used at the dedication of the mission, was found to have a crack in it. Mission San Antonio loaned a smaller Mexican bell; it is inscribed "S. S. Gabriel A. D. 1800." This bell is suspended under the eaves of the corridor. There is also a bell that had been cast in Lima, Peru, in 1698.

During the summer of 1886, Jeff Stockdale, using his freight team, took a collection of broken bells to the end of the tracks at San Ardo. A large bell was recast, from the several mission bells, in 1888 at the Glove Bell & Brass Foundry in San Francisco. Its translated inscription reads "Blessed Michael Archangel dedicated the day before October 1888."

In August of 1888, a newspaper article which was printed in the San Luis Obispo *Tribune* and the *Daily Republic* stated that "The new brass bell for San Miguel Mission arrived, and is at the depot. The whole affair weighs 2,800 pounds, and cost, laid down in San Miguel, $653. Father Mut says it will- - -or should- - - be heard as far away as Paso Robles."

In October of 1888, the newspaper reported that "Father Mut furnishes a financial statement of work, from which it seems that there was raised for the purchase of the bell from individual subscriptions $521.15; from the proceeds of the sale of the old bells from San

The Mission with its bell on a low, wooden standard.

The Mission with its bell and standard on the south side of the church.

Ella Adams says "In 1930, parishioner Frank Serpa was ringing the bell, when the clapper fell out, just grazing his hat brim and digging a hole at his feet. Incentive for prayer was good that morning." The clapper weighs 70 pounds.

Luis Mission, about which we gave a detailed account some months since, $87.20; and from the Ladies' Fair $289.25 (for) a total of $898.25. The new bell cost, with incidental expenses, is exactly $700 and the balance left, with such moneys as may be raised later, is to be applied to the erection of a suitable belfry."

The bell was hung in a low wooden tower, directly in front of the mission; later, the tower and bell were moved to the south side of the mission church. When the bell was on the short tower, and situated in front of the church, Ella Adams says "Its mellow tones, echoing against the mission church, could be heard five miles away."

A steel tower was sent out from Chicago, and arrived at the mission in time for Christmas of 1902. The bell hung on this spindly steel tower for many years.

Recent view of Mission San Miguel from remains of wall to the northeast of the Mission.

"CHARLES F. DORRIES: A CHAPTER IN THE HISTORY OF THE CALEDONIA ADOBE"

By Lucille Mason

This brief biography of Charles F. Dorries, as told to this writer by his daughter, Mrs. Grace Dorries Teresi, is herewith offered as an insight into the life of the last man to privately own and occupy the Caledonia Adobe at San Miguel, California.

Charles F. Dorries was born in Hanover, Germany, on August 31, 1876. He was the second of four sons, William, Charles, August and John, born to William and Wilhelmina Dorries. Mr. William Dorries brought his family to America when Charles was a very small boy; they settled somewhere in New Jersey.

Even as a small child, Charles' air of independence and his indomitable spirit marked him as a loner; and by the time he reached his 'teens, he had grown somewhat indifferent to the conventional family ties. When he was just 14 years old, Charles left home to make his own way. He first earned his keep as a carriage-spring maker; but the spirit of wanderlust possessed him, and he moved on, working his way West.

Still a young man and seeking adventure, Charles arrived in California and contemplated his future- - - but not for long. The Spanish-American War broke out and he enlisted in the Army. An old paper, found among his personal effects, reveals this military record:

Spanish-American War - 1898
Charles Dorries, a Private of Battery B of the 1st California Heavy Artillery, U. S. Volunteers
Enlisted in San Francisco, California on the 9th day of May 1898 for a term of two years, unless sooner discharged by muster out of Battery.
Served during Spanish-American War under first call for troops by the President.
Discharged. Remarks:
Character excellent, Service honest and faithful.
Member of the United Spanish-American War Veterans No. 17960 at large.

Charles F. Dorries

Member of National Headquarters Camp, Washington, D. C.

Charles F. Dorries met - courted - and married - Miss Sarah Franklin in 1900. Shortly thereafter, the couple moved to Southern California. Four children, Fred, Harold, Grace and Charles, Jr., blessed this union.

An aura of mystery surrounds most of his personal life, and to those he considered "too inquisitive," he quipped, "Curiosity once killed a cat." That usually ended the interrogation. But once, in a more expansive mood, he mentioned a voyage down the coast in an old sailing schooner. Whether he was accompanied by his bride, or not, cannot now be verified.

Sometime after the turn of the century, Mr. Dorries visited the city of Long Beach, California. He envisioned greater development there and in the surrounding areas; so he became a Real Estate Broker. Associating himself with a Mr. Bixby (the leading land developer in Long Beach at that time), Mr. Dorries handled the sale of properties in Long Beach, San Pedro, Lomita and Signal Hill.

Then, in 1921, he shifted his interest to the (then) small city of Santa Monica, a beach town about 40 or 50 miles to the north of Long Beach. He opened an office, bought and sold real estate and became active in community life. But business was slow and his interest soon palled, so he made his next move.

San Fernando Valley was opening up and excur-

Caledonia from the east, about 1920.

sions to the Valley (box lunch included) were being offered by land developers in the Bay Area. Bright colored flags marked subdivisions, lending a carnival-like atmosphere to the scene. Property was cheap - people were buying - and Mr. Dorries was selling.

Just when, or under what circumstances, Mr. Dorries first saw the old Caledonia Adobe in the sleepy little town of San Miguel is not known. But whatever - it was love at first sight.

The old Adobe exercised a strong hold on him and he was being drawn - as if by a magnetic force - North. His office in Santa Monica was practically deserted as time and again, he drove north to San Miguel; and neither distance nor the long, monotonous hours on the road could cool his ardor for the old Caledonia Adobe.

As he drove the weary miles, Mr. Dorries had plenty of time to scan the countryside; and he noticed

Left, Charles F. Dorries (1876-1962). Above, an auto on west side of Caledonia.

that historical plaques dotted El Camino Real (The King's Highway), but a precious few old buildings of historical significance were to be seen. It appeared that soon all traces of California's past would be obliterated, either by the hand of man - or by the elements; and an integral part of the history of the State lost forever.

The old Adobe was showing signs of neglect and deterioration. Plaster and adobe bricks were crumbling, wood was decaying - and weeds had taken over the garden. The grounds and the road were choked with dust in the summer and buried in mud in the winter.

Like a shady lady with a dubious past - and an uncertain future, the Caledonia sat in lonely solitude - away from the crowd - awaiting her next benefactor. She had quite a story to tell; but she needed a sympathetic ear and an understanding (and affluent) friend who was willing to listen.

Just as Mr. Dorries' life was shrouded with mystery, so was the old Adobe's. But according to the stories of the townspeople, it had been built by the Indians as a home for Don Petronilo Rios, a Spanish-Californian, and his wife Dona Catarina Avila.

Don Rios had a partner, William Reed, said by some to be a Scotsman - and by others, an Englishman, married to an Indian. There were varying versions of Reed's exploits in the gold fields, of his incurable braggadocia - and of the bloody massacre at the Mission San Miguel in which he was murdered.

It was told that Reed's ghost haunted Don Rios, so he sold the old Adobe to a Mr. Buchard (or W. B. Busherd), who converted it into a Tavern and Stage Coach stop. He named the old Adobe "Caledonia," meaning "welcome." The next owners were Morgan Brians and Sons, and Judge Jeffries, a Justice of the Peace.

The old Adobe had been the scene of grand balls and lively fiestas. Prominent personalities had been lavishly entertained at Caledonia - but then again - the doors had been opened to the most notorious bandits of that era. Bullet holes in the ceiling attested to that story. Gossips whispered that "Ladies of the Evening" had - - - well, no matter; you could believe what you liked. It was used as a school house, then abandoned; and some said that ghosts walked in the night - it was haunted! During the depression years, it became a temporary haven for itinerant families; then it was deserted and left to fall into ruins.

In the many articles written by historians, no mention can be found to bear out the claim that the old Adobe was taken over by the Army and used as a Mili-

Caledonia about the time of World War I.

tary Headquarters during the Spanish-American War. But such a story did persist and may one day be clarified.

Mr. Dorries listened to the many accounts with keen interest; and what he heard - whether fact or fancy - intrigued him. He decided to buy this old place - (God and the owner willing) - not for speculation nor monetary gain, but so that he might preserve it as an historical monument for the generations to come.

And so - as he traversed the narrow, twisting, bumpy roads, he made his plans - and he dreamed along the way. He would restore the faded beauty of this once-lovely hacienda and recapture the old-world enchantment and romance.

Finally, in 1923, Mr. Dorries successfully negotiated the purchase of the old Caledonia Adobe and its surrounding acreage from Mr. Jim Pierce, a Realtor in Paso Robles. Restoration work on the old Adobe began almost immediately; and for the next 31 years, he was to devote his life to the herculean task before him. He labored long hours - driven by a will too strong to admit defeat.

The bare dirt floors were covered with flagstone; and adobe brick walls were plastered inside and out. Door and window casings and frames - badly weathered by the ravages of time - were repaired, and broken glass replaced. Old Colonial doors, hand-made and put together with wooden pegs, were rescued from atop the chicken coop; mended with loving and meticulous care and hung in their rightful place. Sagging, hand-hewn ceiling beams and poled rafters were shored up to support the upstairs rooms and the balcony. Roof sheathings were reinforced, and the roof was stripped of its heavy tile and shake shingles were laid in their place.

Caledonia in the early 1930s; highway now located on the west side.

A kitchen was added; then shrubs, bushes, flowers, and fruit and ornamental trees were planted (excluding the big eucalyptus tree just north of the kitchen). In due time, stone planters and walls were built upon the grounds; and a new water pump was installed to draw water from the well.

Next came a Wishing Well and a Sun Dial. And to add to this picturesque setting, old wagon wheels leaned wearily against the fence, and an old Ox-cart rested by the front gate - reminiscent of the days when Indians inhabited the land and a proud Spanish Don owned the sprawling Rancho. And in an upstairs bedroom of the hacienda, a large Crucifix hung in a recess in the thick wall, and a kneeling-bench sat upon the planked floor just beneath. Here, in years past, the Dona had knelt to tell her Rosary and offer her prayers.

German Roller Canary birds were housed in an aviary just a few steps away from the Wishing Well; and their bright golden plumage was a joy to behold, and their heavenly choir offerings - a Benediction.

The almond trees in the orchard (the oldest orchard in the County) yielded lush crops - more fruit than Mr. Dorries and his friends could consume - so an Almond Stand was put up and the nuts were sold to the tourists. Gasoline Service Stations were sparsely situated in that part of the country and "road service" almost unheard of. To relieve this problem, a gasoline pump was installed for the convenience of visitors to Caledonia.

Another addition in the 1930s was a second adobe building, consisting of two large rooms and an overhanging portico across the front of the house. Mr. Dorries made the adobe bricks himself - using the same formula for the bricks as had been used on the original Adobe. This was later opened as a Gift Shop.

No history of the old Caledonia Adobe would be complete without further mention of the Mission San Miguel. It was the sixteenth in a chain of California Missions founded by Padre Junipero Serra, a missionary of the Franciscan Order of Monks. Mission San Miguel, founded in 1797, was built of adobe bricks, painted white, and covered with a red tile roof. The Mission and the old Caledonia Adobe - just a stone's throw apart - complimented each other; and their close proximity made a tourist's stop-over doubly enjoyable. For those who chose to heed the call to worship, the doors were open - as, no doubt they had been during California's Pastoral Era.

Mr. Dorries had gathered relics, petrified rocks, fossilized shells, Indian artifacts, priceless antique music boxes and furniture - and all sorts of interesting memorabilia from around the countryside, and he proudly put them on display. The transformation he had brought about made it seem as if history had come alive, and visitors to Caledonia could almost feel the presence of generations past.

And now - or so it seemed - he could reap the harvest of his unremitting toil and enjoy the fruits of his labors. He could pause to admire his handiwork, or he could sit in quiet meditation under the lovely shade trees - or just doze. It was a good life. There was time now to set aside his chores and go into the town to visit with his cronies, or - if the mood was upon him - drive over to Monterey Bay for delicious seafood.

When visitors stopped by, he entertained them with

The Adobe about 1925, with Dorries Addition on the north.

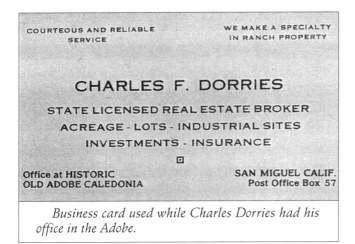

Business card used while Charles Dorries had his office in the Adobe.

stories about the old Adobe. There was the proud Spaniard who once owned the Rancho - the vaqueros who rode the range - the impoverished Indians - and the Monks who tried to convert them to Christianity. He could mesmerize his audience with awesome tales of raiding bandits and hard-riding posses, and sometimes he regaled his guests with choice tid-bits of gossip about Caledonia's naughty past - *sotto voce* of course. And as they toured the grounds, he would point (with pardonable pride) to the improvements he had made in the old place. He instinctively recognized undesirables and made short-shrift of their stop-over; but a welcome guest was gifted with sacks of almonds and succulent fruit from the pear and apple trees. And to a very special friend, he gave a beautiful canary bird, complete with cage.

Then, in 1930, the old Caledonia Adobe appeared to be doomed. The California State Division of Highways planned a two-lane 101 highway to run straight through "El Adobe."

A long, hard and bitter battle between Mr. Dorries and the State ensued. He fought to prevent the demolition of his cherished old landmark, and he appealed to the citizens of San Miguel and local organizations to assist him in his contest against the State. And he carried on his relentless battle - clinging to his convictions with the tenacity of a bulldog - until finally, in 1931, the State Division of Highways conceded.

Ref: State Division of Highways Office District #5 San Luis Obispo, Cal. 1931 line change to miss "El Adobe" on contract from Paso Robles to Monterey County Line.

This controversial two-lane highway is still in use as the two north-bound freeway lanes on Highway 101. The fight for the survival of this historical old landmark was over. The State had served the people, and

the old Caledonia Adobe was safe - or so he thought. But Fate had yet another chapter to add.

Newcomers poured into the State, and the highways became increasingly congested. It was up to the State Highway Division to relieve traffic problems and so, for the second time within a few short years, Caledonia was threatened. Once again, progress was making its demands upon the land. More footage was needed to widen the highway.

Consequently, in 1954, the State requested - and acquired - more Caledonia acreage. This time, it was the almond orchard. The fruit trees were uprooted, and wide ribbons of asphalt were poured in their place. And today, two south-bound freeway lanes stretch across this once-fertile ground, and high-speed cars zoom past the old Rancho - their occupants oblivious to the sacrifice that had to be made for their convenience.

The year 1954 was indeed a troublesome time for Mr. Dorries. Shortly after his second encounter with

Charles F. Dorries - Preserved and Restored the Adobe.

the State was settled, he was seriously injured in an automobile accident and was hospitalized (as it turned out) for the remainder of his life. The ailing old soldier did try to return to Caledonia, but each attempt weakened him more - and had to be stopped. He was never to see Caledonia again.

The old building was boarded up and left unattended. Then the vandals took over. They ripped out heavy doors and the shattered windows to gain entrance. Once inside, they destroyed treasured old relics; and they burned (or otherwise mutilated) irreplaceable historical documents. Ancient photographs of early pioneers - some dating back to the original owners of the Rancho - were grotesquely disfigured and left to lie in heaps upon the floor.

Furniture was broken to pieces and used as firewood in the pot-bellied stoves, and the floors were strewn with the contents of chests and showcases - and shattered glass and china added to the debris. There was shocking evidence that drunken vagrants had wallowed in their own filth; and they left their filth throughout the buildings to stagnate and attract vermin. Then they left their "calling cards" - empty cheap wine bottles - in defiance of the laws of common decency.

Souvenir collectors stripped the buildings and grounds of everything that could be carried away; while treasure-hunters, equipped with metal detectors, knocked holes in the thick walls in search of a secret cache. It was heart-breaking to see, but impossible to stop. Repeated efforts by Mr. Dorries' family to shield old Caledonia against encroachment by the curious and the greedy proved futile.

Charles F. Dorries, the last man to privately own and occupy the old Caledonia Adobe, is credited with

Charles F. Dorries toward the end of his life.

the restoration and preservation of this old landmark. His dedication to the improvement and maintenance of the buildings and grounds, and his unshakable resolve to prevent the highway from forever eradicating this part of California's rich historical heritage is a matter of record.

As its Defender - and as much as one lone man could make it so - he left the old Caledonia Adobe intact and as a lasting monument to the old families of California - the real pioneers of this great State.

And that was as it should be.

On Good Friday, April 20, 1962, Charles Dorries, Spanish-American War Veteran No. 17960, passed away in the hospital at the Veteran's Center in West Los Angeles, California (once referred to as "The Old Soldier's Home in Sawtelle"). He was buried in the Veterans Administration Cemetery, Section 1 - Row Y - Grave 22 - with military honors.

Vaya con Dios, Mr. Dorries.

In 1964, M. Roland Gates, Chairman of the San Luis Obispo County Board of Supervisors, completed negotiations to purchase the old Caledonia Adobe by the County from Mr. Dorries' heirs, Charles Dorries, Jr., and Mrs. Grace Dorries Teresi. The County had long been interested in acquiring the property for expansion of the present County Park, and as an historical monument.

Restoration of the buildings and grounds is now rapidly going forward, and efforts are being made to recover lost articles of historic value. Park Ranger II, Arthur T. Robinson, is in residence there now, and is working with the same dedication as did his predecessor.

And this, too, is as it should be.

BIBLIOGRAPHY

Angel, Myron
History of San Luis Obispo County, Valley Publishers,
Fresno, 1979

Archibald, Robert
The Economic Aspects of the California Missions,
Academy of American Franciscan History, Washing-
ton, D. C., 1978

Avina, Rose Hollenbaugh
Spanish and Mexican Land Grants in California,
University of California, Thesis, Berkeley, 1932

Bancroft, Hubert Howe
California Pioneer Register & Index 1542-1848,
Regional Publishing, Baltimore, 1964

Bancroft, Hubert Howe
History of California, Volumes I-IV, Wallace Hebberd,
Santa Barbara, 1963

Bean, Walton
California: An Interpretive History, McGraw-Hill,
New York, 1968

Berger, John A.
The Franciscan Missions of California, Doubleday &
Co., Garden City, N.Y., 1941

Biggs, Donald C.
*Conquer & Colonize: Stevenson's Regiment and
California*, Presidio Press, San Rafael, 1977

Blomquist, Leonard R.
*A Regional Study of the Changes in Life and Institu-
tions in the San Luis Obispo District 1830-1850*,
University of California, Thesis, Berkeley, 1943

Bridge, Myrtle Reese
Early History of San Luis Obispo County, Los Padres
Chapter, Daughters of the American Revolution,
Cambria, 1961

Browne, J. Ross
A Dangerous Journey, California 1849, Arthur Lites
Press Palo Alto, 1950

Bryant, Edwin
*What I Saw in California:. . .Being a Journal of a Tour. .
.Across the Continent of North America. . .in the Years
1846, 1847*, Ross and Haines, Inc., Minneapolis, 1849;
1967

Busch, Briton Cooper
*Alta California 1840-1841: The Journal & Observa-
tions of William Dane Phelps, Master of Ship Alert*,
Arthur H. Clark Co., Glendale, 1983

Casey, Beatrice
Padres & People of Old Mission San Antonio, Casey
Newspapers, King City, 1976

Caughey, John Walton
California, Prentice-Hall, Englewood Cliffs, N.J., 1953

Clark, Donald Thomas
*Monterey County Place Names: A Geographical
Dictionary*
Kestrel Press, Carmel Valley, CA, 1991

Cleland, Robert Glass
*Cattle on a Thousand Hills: Southern California 1850-
1880*, Ward Ritchie Press, Los Angeles, 1951

Cleland, Robert Glass
From Wilderness to Empire, Alfred A. Knopf, New
York, 1966

Cole, Martin, Editor
Don Pio Pico's Historical Narrative, Arthur H. Clarke
Co., Glendale, 1973

Cooper, De Guy
*Resources of San Luis Obispo County-Its Geography,
Climate, Location, Soil, Productions and Institutions*,
Bacon & Company, San Francisco, 1875

Courter, John P., Jr.
A History of San Miguel Mission, Charles A. Black,
San Luis Obispo, 1905

Cowan, Robert G.
*Ranchos of California: A List of Spanish Concessions
(1775-1822) and Mexican Grants (1822-1846)*,
Academy Library Guild, Fresno, 1956

Crump, Spencer
California's Spanish Missions Yesterday and Today
Trans-Anglo Books, Los Angeles, 1964

Dakin, Susanna B.
The Lives of William Hartnell, Stanford University
Press, Stanford, 1949

Dart, Marguerite M.
The History of the Lompoc Valley, California, University of California, Thesis, Berkeley, 1937

Davis, William Heath
Seventy-Five Years in California, John Howell Books, San Francisco, 1967

Dellard, Bill and Barbara, Editors
Centennial Family Memories, "The Daily Press," Paso Robles, 1989

Eddy, Dale Rae
The History of the Upper Salinas Valley, University of Southern California, Thesis, Los Angeles, 1938

Engelhardt, Zephyrin, O.F.M
San Miguel, Arcangel: The Mission on the Highway, Acoma Books, Ramona, 1929; 1971

Engenhoff, Elisabeth L.
Fabricas: A Collection of Pictures & Statements on the Mineral Materials Used in Building in California Prior to 1850, California Journal of Mines & Geology, Sacramento, April 1952

Fink, Augusta
Adobes in the Sun: Portraits of a Tranquil Era, Chronicle Books, San Francisco, 1972

Fink, Augusta
Monterey County: The Dramatic Story of its Past, Valley Publishers, Fresno, 1971

Fisher, Anne B.
The Salinas - Upside Down River, Valley Publishers, Fresno, 1945; 1971

Garcia, Inocente
Garcia Hechos & Other Garcia Papers, University of California, Berkeley, 1974

Garner, William Robert
Letters From California 1846-1847, University of California Press, Berkeley, 1970

Garrison, Myrtle
Romance and History of California Ranchos, Harr Wagner Publishing Co., San Francisco, 1935

Geiger, Maynard
Franciscan Missionaries in Hispanic California 1769-1848, Huntington Library, San Marino, 1969

Gidney, C. M.
History of Santa Barbara, San Luis Obispo and Ventura Counties California, The Lewis Publishing Company, Chicago, 1917

Giffen, Helen S.
Casas & Courtyards: Historic Adobe Houses of California, Biobooks, Oakland, 1955

Gillett, Rachel
Memories of the San Antonio Valley, San Antonio Valley Historical Association, King City, 1990

Gudde, Erwin G.
California Place Names: The Origin & Etymology of Current Geographical Names, University of California Press, Berkeley, 1974

Gwinn, J. M.
History of the State of California & Biographical Records of Santa Cruz, San Benito, Monterey and San Luis Obispo Counties, Chapman Publishing, Chicago, 1904

Hague, Harlan and Langrum, David J.
Thomas O. Larkin: A Life of Patriotism & Profit in Old California, University of Oklahoma Press, Norman, 1990

Hall-Patton, Mark P.
Memories of the Land: Place Names of San Luis Obispo County, E-Z Nature Books, San Luis Obispo, 1994

Hamilton, Geneva
Where The Highway Ends-Cambria, San Simeon and the Ranchos, Padre Productions, San Luis Obispo, 1974

Hammond, George Peter
Larkin Papers, Volumes I-IV, University of California Press, Berkeley, 1953

Hannah, Shirley H.
The Early Development of the Salinas Valley, University of California, Los Angeles Thesis, 1934

Hart, James D.
A Companion to California, Oxford University Press, New York, 1978

Harth, Stan and Liz Krieger, Dan Krieger, Editors *War Comes to the Middle Kingdom, Vol. 1, 1939-1942*, E-Z Nature Books, San Luis Obispo, 1991

Hawgood, John A., Editor
First & Last Consul: Thomas Oliver Larkin & The Americanization of California - A Selection of Letters, Pacific Books, Palo Alto, 1970

Hawthorne, Hildegarde
California's Missions: Their Romance and Beauty, D. Appleton-Century Company, Inc., New York & London, 1942

Hittell, Theodore H.
History of California, Volume II, Pacific Press Publishing House & Occidental Publishing Co., San Francisco, 1885

Howard, Donald M.
Adobes & Indian Middens, Volume II, Monterey County Archaeological Society, Monterey, 1980

Howard, Donald M.
California's Lost Fortress: The Royal Presidio of Monterey, Angel Press, Monterey, 1976

Howard, Donald M.
Ranchos of Monterey County, Angel Press, Monterey, 1978

Hussey, John Adam
The Wolfskill Party in California, University of California, Berkeley, Thesis, Berkeley, 1935

Hutchinson, C. Allen
Frontier Settlement in Mexican California: The Hijar-Padres Colony & Its Origins, 1769-1835, Yale Union Press, New Haven & London, 1969

Hutchinson, W. H.
California: The Golden Shore By the Sundown Sea, Star Publishing, Palo Alto, 1980

Hutchinson, W. H.
California: Two Centuries of Man, Land & Growth in the Golden State, American West Publishing, Palo Alto, 1969

Iversen, Eva C.
Mission San Miguel Archangel, Old Mission San Miguel, no date.

Jesperson, Christian N. and Audrey V. Kell, et al.
History of San Luis Obispo County, State of California, H. M. Meier, 1939

Jackson, W. Turrine
Stages, Mails & Express in Southern California: The Role of Wells, Fargo & Co. in the Pre-Railroad Period, Historical Society of Southern California, Fall 1974

Johnson, Paul
The Golden Era of the Missions: 1769-1834, Chronicle Books, San Francisco, 1974

Kocher, Paul H.
Mission San Luis Obispo de Tolosa: A Historical Sketch, Blake Printing & Publishing, Inc. San Luis Obispo, 1972

Kenneally, Finbar O.F.M, Editor and Translator
Writings of Fermin de Lasuen, Vol. I and II, Academy of American Franciscan History, Washington, D. C., 1965

Krieger, Daniel E.
San Luis Obispo: Looking Backward Into the Middle Kingdom, Windsor Publishing, Inc., Northridge, 1988

Langrum, Daniel J.
Law & Community on the Mexican California Frontier: Anglo-American Expatriates & The Clash of Legal Traditions 1821-1846, University of Oklahoma Press, Norman, 1987

Larios, Rodolfo
Alta California, Estados Unidos Mexicanos: A Cultural Interpretive History & Geography, Privately printed, 1983

Latta, Frank
Dalton Gang Days, Bear State Books, Santa Cruz, 1976

Lavender, David
California: Land of New Beginnings, Harper & Row, New York, 1972

Leonard, Ralph J.
The San Miguel Mission Murders, "La Vista," Vol. 4, No. 1, San Luis Obispo County Historical Society, San Luis Obispo, June 1980

MacGillivray, J. Fraser
The Story of Adelaida, Privately printed, 1992

McIntosh, George R.
Mac's Stage Line, Privately printed, 1972

McDonald, Donald
Among the Oaks at Paso Robles Hot Springs Where Sunshine, Blue Skies, Pure Air and Beautiful Surroundings Make the Sick Well and the Well Better, reprinted from "Sunset Magazine, September 1902

McKittrick, Myrtle M.
Vallejo- Son of California, Binfords & Mort, Portland, 1944

Miossi, Harold
Historic Trails of Cuesta Canyon, "La Vista," Special Edition, San Luis Obispo County Historical Society, San Luis Obispo, January 1975

Morefield, Richard Henry
The Mexican Adaptation in American California 1846-1875, R & E Associates, San Francisco, 1971

Morrison, Annie L. and John H. Haydon
History of San Luis Obispo County and Environs, Historic Record Company, Los Angeles, 1917

Morse, Malcolm
A Treatise on the Hot Sulphur Springs . . . Paso Robles, California,
Eaton & Edwards, San Francisco, 1874

Mutnick, Dorothy Gittinger
Some Alta California Pioneers & Descendants, Past Time Publications, Lafayette, CA, 1982

Nicholson, Loren
Rails Across the Ranchos, Valley Publishers, Fresno, 1980

Nicholson, Loren
Romualdo Pacheco's California! The Mexican-American Who Won,
California Heritage Printing Associates, San Jose & San Luis Obispo, 1990

Norin, William W.
McDonald Clan on Estrella, Privately printed, 1980

Ord, Angustia De la Guerra
Occurrences in Hispanic California, Academy of American Franciscan History,
Washington, D. C., 1956

Osio, Antonio Maria
The History of Alta California: A Memoir of Mexican California, translated by Rose Marie Beebe and Robert M. Senkewicz, The University of Wisconsin Press, Madison, 1996

Outland, Charles
Stagecoaching on El Camino Real: Los Angeles to San Francisco 1861-1901, The Arthur H. Clark Co., Glendale, 1973

Perez, Crisostomo N.
Land Grants in Alta California, Landmark Enterprises, Rancho Cordova, CA, 1996

Pico, Jose de Jesus
Acontecimientos en California: Don Jose de Jesus Pico, 1807-1892,
Los Californianos, San Francisco, 1986

Reese, Robert W.
A Brief History of Old Monterey, Colonial Press, Monterey, 1969

Robinson, Alfred
Life in California, During a Residence of Several Years in That Territory, Peregrine Press, Santa Barbara, 1970

Robinson, William W.
Land in California: The Story of Mission Lands, Ranchos, Squatters, Mining Claims, Railroad Grants, Land Scrip, Homesteads, University of California Press, Berkeley, 1948

Robinson, William W.
The Story of San Luis Obispo County, Title Insurance & Trust Company,
Los Angeles, 1957

Roche, John D.
Rancho la Cienega o Paso de la Tijera, John D. Roche Studios, Los Angeles, 1970

Romney, Joseph B.
A Research Guide to the History of San Luis Obispo County California, Millhollow Publishers, Rexburg, Idaho, 1983

Ross, Ivy Belle
Confirmation of Spanish & Mexican Land Grants, University of California, Thesis, Berkeley, 1928

Rowland, Leon
Santa Cruz: The Early Years, Paper Vision Press, Santa Cruz, 1980

Salley, H. E.
History of California Post Offices: 1849-1976, La Mesa, 1977

Saunders, Charles F. and J. Smeaton Chase
The California Padres and Their Missions, Houghton-Mifflin Company, Boston, 1915

Sawyer, Frank W.
Paso Robles Hot Springs, Sunset Publishing House, San Francisco, No date

Shinn, Charles Howard
A Study of San Luis Obispo County California, Reprinted from "Sunset Magazine," September 1901

Staniford, Edward
The Pattern of California History, Harper & Row, New York, 1975

Steglich, William
Salt of the Earth, "The Rustler-Herald," King City, 1951

Storke, Yda Annis
History of Ventura, Santa Barbara and San Luis Obispo Counties, Lewis Publishing Co., Chicago, 1890

Sullivan, Colleen and Mary Ann Finocchi
Viejo Monterey, Angel Publishing, Monterey, 1969

Teggart, Frederick J., Editor
The Anza Expedition of 1775-1776: Diary of Pedro Font, University of California, Berekeley, 1913

Thomason, Donalee Ludeke
Cholama the Beautiful One: Cholame Valley History and Its Pioneer People, Tabula Rasa Press, San Luis Obispo, 1988

Vallejo, Platon M. G.
Memories of Vallejo, James D. Stevenson Publisher, Fairfield, 1994

Van Harreveld, Constance
Adobe Diary, "La Vista," Special Conference Edition, San Luis Obispo County Historical Society, San Luis Obispo, February 1975

Verardo, Jennie Dennis and Denzil
The Salinas Valley: An Illustrated History, Windsor Publications Chatsworth, 1989

Walsh, Marie T.
Mission of the Passes: Santa Ines, Times-Mirror Press, Los Angeles, 1930
Watkins, Rolin C., Editor

History of Monterey and Santa Cruz Counties, S. J. Clark Publishing Company, Chicago, 1925

Webb, Edith Buckland
Indian Life At the Old Missions, University of Nebraska Press, Lincoln & London, 1952; 1982

Weber, Francis J.
Century of Fulfillment: The Roman Catholic Church in Southern California 1840-1947, Libra Press, Ltd., Hong Kong, 1990

Weber, Francis J.
Mission on the Highway: A Documentary History of San Miguel, Arcangel, Libra Press, Ltd., Hong Kong, 1981

Weeks, George F.
The Santa Ysabel Hot Springs, H. S. Crocker & Co., San Francisco, 1889

Wilson, Florence Slocum
Windows on Early California, The National Society of the Colonial Dames, Los Angeles-Pasadena, 1971

Zimmerman, William
A Short & Complete History of the San Miguel Mission, No publisher, 1890

In Loving Memory

Charles Richard Montgomery (1841-1928)
Delia Matthis Montgomery (1849-1935)

John Benjamin Jones (1864-1899)
Josephine Murley Jones (1868-1905)

Charles Lester Montgomery (1878-1944)
Frances Jones Montgomery (1888-1972)

Lester Charles Montgomery (1906-1954)
Charlotte Walteretta Montgomery (1909-1989)
Florence Montgomery Strohl (1905-1989)

From the 5th generation in Indian Valley

Lester Charles Montgomery, Jr.
Shirley Lynn Montgomery

In Memory of
Verner G. Modin
(1912-1997)

In Loving Memory of

Joyce & Harold Guiver

Ernie & Barbara E. Robinson

Joan & Andy Patarak
Andy Patarak, Jr.
Ken Patarak

In Loving Memory of

Constance & Elbert Brooks

Vine Coates

In Loving Memory of
Amy Jessup Curtis
(1887-1966)
A lifetime resident of Indian Valley

To the Memory of
Cecil Boatman
(1917-1995)

To the Memory of

Rex & Dolly Awalt

Dean Burton

Ruth Cruess

Charles F. Dorries

Mildred Finley

Rollie Gates

Gil & Marilyn Hanson

Anna Nygren Hebel

Hans Heilmann

Paul Jones

Thomas and Margurite Lannigan

Ruby Mann

Don and Alta McMillan

Al Reed

Frank William Rios

Ernest V. Rossi

Peggy Wolf

Margaret Work

A Memorial to

Charles Bloomfield Douglas (1843-1899)
and his wife
Katharine Pauline Elton (1847-1936)

Gerard Noel Douglas (1843-1922)
and his wife
Charlotte Louisa Elton (1848-1928)

To the Memory of

Mary M. and William O. Dresser

Agnes Mobley and Thomas A. Luttrell

Birdie L. and William Rollo Dresser

Ralph O. Dresser, M.D.

In Loving Memory of
Thelma Freeman Rougeot Jardine
(1903-1996)

In Memory of
Mildred Rhyne Finley
who loved the folded hills of
San Miguel

In Memory of
John P. and Laura Evans Crother

In Memory of
Josephine Rosalie Bequette
(1904-1996)

In Memory of
Alfred Juhl Bequette
(1901-1990)

To the Memory of
Elwain "Buck" Culbert
(1912-1984)

In Memory of
LeRoy Wieneke
(1924-1997)

We are grateful to the following benefactors who made the printing of this book possible:

Ella M. Adams
Myrtle Boatman
Jon Cagliero
Mr. & Mrs. Maurice Coates
Mr. & Mrs. John Craspay
Virginia Culbert
Mr. & Mrs. Dave Foltz
Dorothy Ferrin
Mr. & Mrs. Alpheus Garrissere
Donna Helt
Huer Huero Golf Course
Rose Gil Rios Jones
Bruce D. McVey
Paso Robles Glass Shop
Virginia Peterson
Betty Curtis Renard
Art and Barbara Robinson
San Miguel Lions Club
Specialty Silicone Fabrications

Tom Baron
Tom Bordonaro, Jr.
Dr. Alexander Castellanos
Betty Cousins
Mr. & Mrs. John Crother
Vicki Dauth
Ennis Business Forms
Mr. & Mrs. Robert Freeman
Mike and Carolyn Hawk
Ben Holsted
Hunter Ranch Golf Course
Patrick McMahon
Mr. & Mrs. Charlie Montgomery
Paso Robles Insurance
Ranchita Canyon Vineyard
Velma Rhyne
Mike Ronan
Mr. & Mrs. Robert Schafer
Valliwide Bank

ENNIS BUSINESS FORMS

A Great Place To Work

P.O. BOX 7004
PASO ROBLES, CA 93447

DR. ALEXANDER CASTELLANOS

RANCHITA CANYON VINEYARD

DAVE FOLTZ AUTOMOTIVE

PASO ROBLES GLASS

PASO ROBLES INSURANCE

HUNTER RANCH GOLF COURSE

THE FUTURE HUER HUERO GOLF COURSE

SPECIALTY SILICONE FABRICATORS, INC.

3077 ROLLIE GATES DRIVE
PASO ROBLES, CA 93446

INDEX

About The Author

Wallace V. Ohles, a resident of San Luis Obispo County since 1967, became interested in local history during his twenty-five years as a high school teacher in Paso Robles. A history major at the University of Portland, in Oregon, Ohles found little written on the history of the northern part of the county and decided to correct this oversight. Ohles has served "The Friends of the Adobes, Inc." in many capacities over the years. This is his first book-length work.